JAMES BOND 007

007

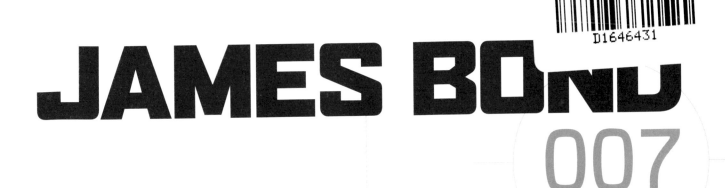

THE PHOENIX PROJECT

JAMES BOND 007: THE PHOENIX PROJECT

ISBN 1 84576 312 2
ISBN-13: 9781845763121

Published by Titan Books,
a division of Titan Publishing Group Ltd.
144 Southwark St
London SE1 0UP

A CIP catalogue record for this title is available from the British Library.

First edition: February 2007.
1 3 5 7 9 10 8 6 4 2

Printed in Italy.

Also available from Titan Books:
James Bond: Casino Royale (ISBN: 1 84023 843 7)
James Bond: Dr No (ISBN: 1 84576 089 1)
James Bond: Goldfinger (ISBN: 1 84023 908 5)
James Bond: On Her Majesty's Secret Service (ISBN: 1 84023 674 4)
James Bond: The Man with the Golden Gun (ISBN: 1 84023 690 6)
James Bond: Octopussy (ISBN: 1 84023 743 0)
James Bond: The Spy Who Loved Me (ISBN: 1 84576 174 X)
James Bond: Colonel Sun (ISBN: 1 84576 175 8)
James Bond: The Golden Ghost (ISBN: 1 84576 261 4)
James Bond: Trouble Spot (ISBN: 1 84576 269 X)

Huge thanks to Vicky Reed at the Daily Express, everyone at http://www.mi6.co.uk, Peter Knight at Knight Features, Vipul Patel, Zoe Watkins and Fleur Gooch, without whom this book would never have happened.

Introduction © Tania Mallett 2006.

"Fatal Beauties" feature © James Wheatley, Matthias Garretway & James Page 2006.

What did you think of this book? We love to hear from our readers. Please email us at: readerfeedback@titanemail.com, or write to us at the above address. You can also visit us at www.titanbooks.com

To subscribe to our regular newsletter for up-to-the-minute news, great offers and competitions, email: booksezine@titanemail.com

Much of the comic strip material used by Titan in this edition is exceedingly rare. As such, we hope that readers appreciate that the quality of the materials can be variable.

JAMES BOND
007

THE PHOENIX PROJECT

IAN FLEMING
JIM LAWRENCE  YAROSLAV HORAK

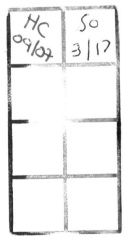
TITAN BOOKS

MIDAS TOUCH

Introduction by
TANIA MALLETT

In 1962, *Dr No* exploded onto the scene, followed by *From Russia With Love*. *Goldfinger* was the third *James Bond* film, and to many, the best. I think, at the time, everyone was fed up with the all-conquering American hero, who single-handedly beat every Indian in the West or who, with a couple of buddies, flattened Hitler's army and liberated Europe. At last, here was James Bond — our very own British hero — and we were ready to worship.

I remember drawing up to the red carpet in Leicester Square and being completely overwhelmed by the sheer number of fans. I don't believe anything like it had been seen there before; certainly, the police were quite unprepared, and just as I began to move towards the foyer, the cordon broke and there was a stampede. I heard the plate glass windows shatter so I picked up my skirts and ran for the stairs. Luckily, no-one was seriously hurt and order was soon restored — but it was a pretty scary moment.

The other vivid memory I have of *Goldfinger* is when we were filming in Switzerland. It was decided to strap a cameraman onto the bonnet of my Mustang to film the close-ups. All went well until we rounded an S-bend — and coming towards us was a tiny car containing a Swiss family out for a Sunday spin. I just had time to see their horrified faces as we flashed past. The last I saw of them was in my mirrors as they ploughed headlong into the cliff face, no doubt thinking they were witness to an horrific accident!

If you have never read a *James Bond* novel, the comic strip version is a great introduction; I hope it will open up for you the wonderful and exciting world created by Ian Fleming.

Tania Mallett
October 2006

Tania Mallett has had several small movie roles, but is overwhelmingly known to moviegoers for her role as Tilly Masterson in Goldfinger. After the movie was released, she returned to her modelling career.

FATAL BEAUTIES: THE *BOND* GIRLS IN COMICS

[Editor's note: *Thunderball* is omitted from this article, due to the strip being aborted partway through. The other *Bond* girls are covered in the collection *James Bond: Trouble Spot*.]

LISL BAUM
Risico

This Austrian beauty has clear loyalties to her smuggler boss, Enrico Colombo, and first appears in strip #862. We learn her name is Lisl Baum four strips later, when she is sent to bait Bond with her feminine charms. Lisl leads Bond into a trap which enables him to learn the truth about the man he has been hunting.

Appearing only fourteen times in total, artist John McLusky reinvents the character's appearance with a light-coloured, side-parted bob cut and slim figure, compared to Fleming's description of a plump blonde.

The adventure concludes with Bond heading to Venice and Colombo providing Bond with a hotel key, at Baum's request. This plot point can be traced back to Fleming's original novel, in which Lisl is a Viennese call-girl who invites Bond to spend time with her upon the completion of the mission.

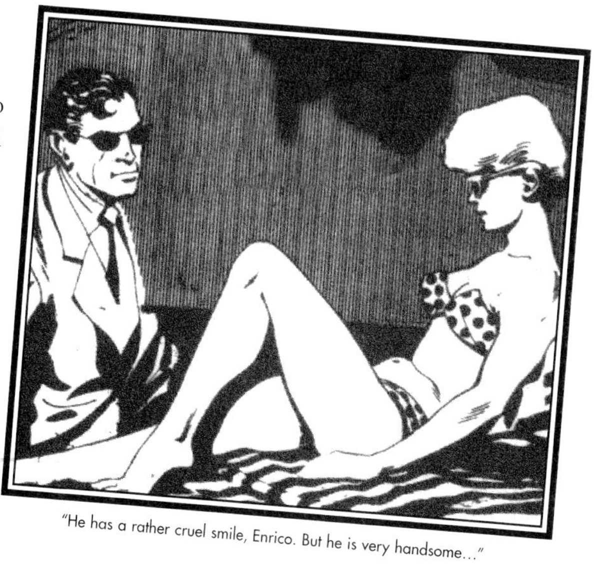

"He has a rather cruel smile, Enrico. But he is very handsome..."

MARY ANN RUSSELL (Agent 765)
A View To A Kill

Mary Ann Russell appears in Fleming's collection of short stories issued in 1960 under the title *For Your Eyes Only*, with the strip adaptation following a year later.

Appearing early on in the adventure, Russell is 007's duty officer whilst he is on assignment. Working at Station F Headquarters in Paris, she has become an adept driver who can handle the Parisian traffic.

Her illustrated appearance is simpler compared to other interpretations of *Bond* girls, with her most notable feature being her tall bun of hair. Appearing in only twelve strips over the course of the story, she nonetheless saves 007's life with a crack shot from her pistol, and finishes the strip adventure in a rather indecorous manner, as Bond summons her to "look for a bird's nest" in some bushes — as opposed to Fleming's ending, which had them make a date for dinner and pink champagne in "some place like Armenonville."

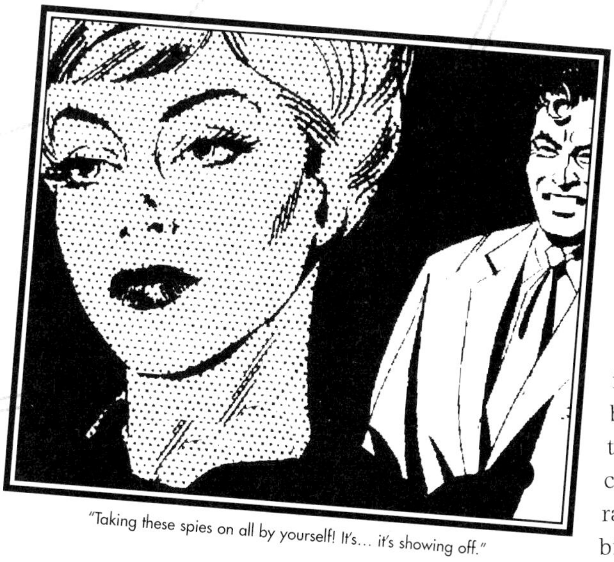

"Taking these spies on all by yourself! It's... it's showing off."

JUDY HAVELOCK
For Your Eyes Only

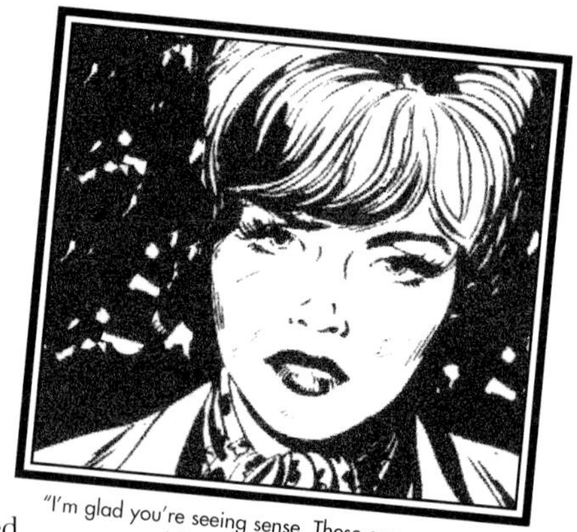

"I'm glad you're seeing sense. These arrows are difficult to pull out..."

Judy Havelock is a character almost perfectly suited to Bond, in a romantic sense. After her parents are both murdered for their property in Jamaica, she is emotionally needy but still strong-willed enough to kill for revenge. At virtually any point in the strip, Judy shows deep-rooted decisiveness and independence, aptly demonstrated by her opening line, "Move an inch and I'll kill you!" It is only a few strips later that we see her ordering Bond about, telling him what he's going to do and not do. Thankfully, however, Bond's reasoning and charm wins her around and help soften — or at least modify — her plans for revenge. Her strident personality is well captured by artist John McLusky: her hair neatly set, her clothing neat and form-fitting, and her poses often stiff, with hands on hips — however, McClusky offsets this stiffness with the softness he imparts to her eyes.

Add to the mix that she is foolhardy enough to attempt to take out both the villain and his henchmen armed with only a bow, and it is obvious to see that she and Bond — according to Fleming's recipe — are almost perfect for one another. It should come as no surprise that at the end of the very short strip, the two are well enough acquainted to head for the motel Ko-Zee over the Canadian border.

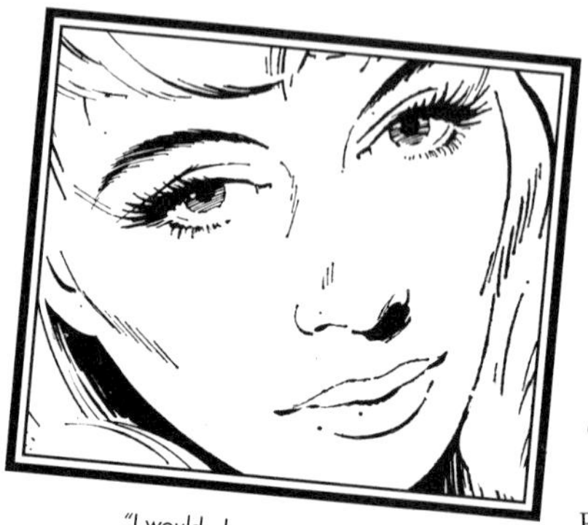

"I would always outdrive you. You want to stay alive, and I — no!"

COMTESSE TERESA ('TRACY') DI VICENZO
On Her Majesty's Secret Service

Tracy is perhaps the only girl who can give Bond a genuine run for his money. At the start of *On Her Majesty's Secret Service*, we see her racing past Bond at breakneck speed — something that really gets under 007's skin. How could he be overtaken by a woman? The incident causes as much rage as it does curiosity and admiration, and even at this stage it is clear that Bond may be falling in love. Slightly shorter than Bond, with light, shoulder-length hair, Tracy shares one trait with the other *Bond* girls depicted in the strips: she's stunning.

Following the plot of Fleming's novel, Bond does not have to wait to the end of the story to get his way romantically; neither does he get it on his own terms. Tracy is very forward with him and is his match on many levels. But no girl can be a perfect equal to 007, and must have some weaknesses. As in the novel, the strip version of Tracy is depressed — to the point of suicidal — and is emotionally needy, something artist McLusky conveys masterfully via close-ups and depictions of Tracy's anguished face, with a particularly fine example in the second panel of strip #34.

Bond's love for Tracy takes him time and a certain amount of persuasion from her father to fully realise. Staying almost identical to the original Fleming text, Tracy is the first (but not last) girl to marry Bond in the strip series, only for their happy honeymoon to be cut short by an assassin's bullet. A true love turns into tragedy.

Though Tracy (like all of the *Bond* girls) is beautiful, she really does break the mould of the stereotypical *Bond* girl plot sequence.

RUBY WINDSOR
On Her Majesty's Secret Service

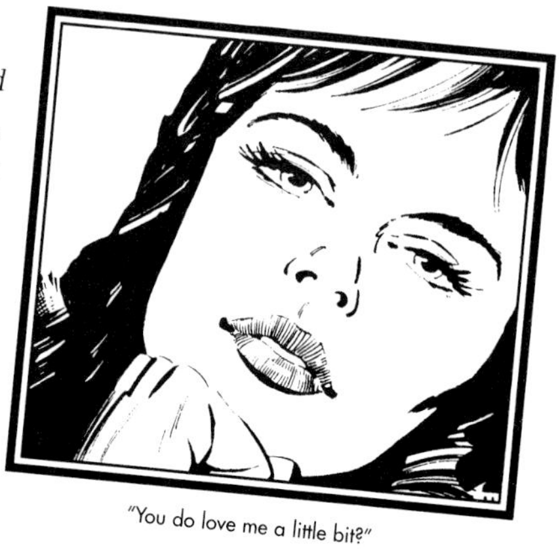

"You do love me a little bit?"

Ruby's smooth curves and short black hair give her a great physical appearance for a *Bond* girl. Having to stay at Piz Gloria means that she only has a few male figures around her, giving her an emotional need for Bond's companionship. It is partly because of this that she falls into Bond's arms so easily, not requiring the full length of the story to make the leap.

Sticking close to Fleming's original work, Ruby is naïve, although breaking the house rules in order to be with 007 obviously gives her the independence required for a *Bond* girl. It does not take Bond long to spot that she is more his match than most of the other girls at Piz Gloria... but then again, she's no Tracy.

KISSY SUZUKI
You Only Live Twice

Kissy Suzuki is a movie starlet who returns to Japan for a quiet life after being exploited by Hollywood moguls. Kissy is now a diver, or "Ama girl", who collects Awabi shells which are then sold in the West. She spends much of her time with her ailing father, who does not appear by name in the strip. One of her most useful abilities is to hold her breath underwater for a minute.

"I would help him to go, even to his death, if he wanted to — I love him."

A non-traditionalist, Kissy spends much of her time naked or wearing very little. She is also religious and prays to the Jizo Guardians and believes in local legends and folk law. Shorter than Bond, this 'Japanese Greta Garbo' has long, flowing black hair, and is beautiful in every way. Over the course of the story's 200 strips, Kissy appears eighty-seven times, making her one of the most heavily-featured *Bond* girls in the strip adaptations.

Kissy and Bond become lovers, and later husband and wife. "Mrs Bond" truly loves him and lets him leave to unravel his lost memory. Kissy reveals later that she is with child, but never admits it to James. She is the second lady to marry Bond, but the only character known to become pregnant with his child. In Fleming's novel we learn that Bond has a son, whereas in the strip we never learn any further details.

CHITRA "TAJ" MAHAL
The Man With The Golden Gun

"Do I have to spell it out?"

Chitra Mahal is an original creation by strip writer Jim Lawrence and artist Yaroslav Horak. "Taj" serves as a nurse to Mr Margesson. She has a slight Oriental look, set off by her bobbed dark hair and high cheekbones.

This femme fatale proves big trouble for Bond, and she packs a pistol in a thigh holster. We learn her name and backstory a few strips after her introduction: she joined the Communist Party at 16 and was assigned by the KGB's Dutch branch to spy on Margesson. When 007 catches her eavesdropping on his conversation, she bites his hand and manages to kill Margesson. She later commits suicide... but manages to give Bond a vital clue with her dying breath.

MARY GOODNIGHT
The Man With The Golden Gun

Mary Goodnight makes a debut supporting appearance in *You Only Live Twice*. Appearing only eight times, she is seen cleaning out James Bond's desk when he is presumed dead. Drawn in the first instance by John McLusky, she appears very businesslike, sporting glasses. We learn that she is being reassigned to Jamaica to work for Commander Ross.

She is tall with long legs and long blonde hair, and is fashionably dressed for her posting in Jamaica. A central character in her second appearance, she appears forty-nine times in total (including a cameo in the following story, *Octopussy*.) As Horak's artwork shows, Mary can handle herself in a fight — with a well placed kick from those long pins. Horak's depiction could be likened to Tanya Roberts — who played Stacy Sutton in *A View To A Kill* some years later — rather than the character's eventual onscreen representative, Britt Ekland.

"I'll enjoy... this!"

Mary comes through for 007, both saving his life and enabling him to kill "Pistols" Scaramanga. Goodnight finally gets some quiet time with Bond while he recuperates after being wounded by Scaramanga.

In her third appearance in the strip series, Goodnight is again very quick-thinking and always willing to help. Following her ealier romantic involvement with 007, Goodnight is still hungry for Bond in this story. Unlike many of the other girls in the strips, Mary is rather cheeky, and this adds to her charm as she sparks with Bond. Evidence of this can be seen as early as her first line, "Oh yes Mr. Hazard... and that's not all I have for you!"

"TRIGGER"
The Living Daylights

The last set of short stories that Fleming wrote contained *The Living Daylights*. With no traditional *Bond* girl featured in the story, the closely-adapted strip sees Bond pining for a blonde cellist from a distance. Codenamed "Trigger" in both Fleming's story and the strip adaptation, the stunningly beautiful top Russian sniper is charged with assassinating a British spy. Appearing in the strip before 007 does, Trigger remains a faceless figure until strip #238, when Bond lays eyes on her for the first time. The world-champion markswoman has long, flowing hair to the small of her back and a pert, feminine body, courtesy of artist Horak.

"Tune-up for murder, eh?"

Set over three days, the anxiety of the killer is not shown in Horak's feminine rendition of "Trigger". She is offered sleeping pills, whereas a haggard Bond chooses drink. Her beauty ultimately means that 007 is unable to kill her, thus sparing her for her masters' wrath. In the concluding panels of the strip we learn of her death from a newspaper headline — a clarification added by the adaptation's writer, Jim Lawrence.

"Mein gott! Is there nothing we can — "

TRUDI OBERHAUSER
Octopussy

With the plot of Fleming's short story lacking in girls, writer Jim Lawrence added Trudi to the plot. Despite the lack of literary heritage, her traits still follow the Fleming recipe for a successful female companion.

She is a friend of Bond's, due to the close relationship between him and her father. This factor means that love does not blossom according to the standard *Bond* formula... which, given the connection between Bond and her father, would have risked Bond appearing to be taking advantage of young Trudi.

Compassion is something that Trudi certainly has and shows in the strip, as even when Dexter Smythe is dying she is willing to help him. It is obvious that Bond sees this as a redeeming feature. With her light-coloured hair and model-like complexion she is aesthetically pleasing, though more importantly, very capable compared to most of Bond's female companions. Whereas many girls ultimately hinder Bond when trying to help, Trudi's efforts really hit the spot.

LIZ KREST
The Hildebrand Rarity

Liz Krest has a slim, beautifully shaped figure along with long blonde hair down to her mid-back, an appearance that would instantly attract Bond — or any other red-blooded man. However, unlike virtually all of the other *Bond* girls, she lacks independence and a sense of adventure, to the point where she provides little appeal for Bond. Living on a luxury yacht and spending most of her days sunbathing is her idea of the good life.

"All this luxury... like living in a fairy tale!"

The price she pays for this luxury is abuse from her husband who whips her with his stingray-tail "corrector", when he deems her to have acted inappropriately. To Krest, his wife is more a trophy than a companion. Bond finds these beatings unacceptable, and he wants to lash out at Krest for the abuse. In Fleming's opinion, women like the whip — as long as it is followed by the kiss — and it is in the beating scenes that we see Fleming's own ideas showing through, with Bond disapproving of such one-sided brutality... but unwilling to get involved between a man and his wife.

Liz may have enjoyed the ultimate revenge, though, when Krest is found murdered. However, the addition of another female character to the story leaves a cliff-hanger as to the identity of the culprit.

NYLA LARSEN
The Hildebrand Rarity

An original character added to Fleming's short story by strip writer Jim Lawrence, Nyla Larsen's allegiances are ever-shifting during the story. She is initially working for Mr Krest, and is first seen spying on Bond. But she is more than happy to switch sides after she gets to know 007 a little better, and witnesses how Krest treats his wife. It is easy to see similarities between Nyla and the cinematic character Domino from *Thunderball*, released in cinemas a year before this strip's publication.

When it comes to work, Nyla is not scared of doing what is necessary to get a job done. She certainly knows how to charm people in order to get closer to them, a trait often seen in the women of Fleming's novels. She has many aspects about her which would have cemented her role as a *Bond* girl, but her willingness to change allegiance seems to keep him at arm's length. This is something of a shame for Bond, as her slender figure, dark black hair and pithy candor would certainly appeal to his desires.

"Suddenly I get the feeling this assignment could be fun!"

"Rather yummy-looking, actually — in a sinister way!"

RONA VAIL
The Spy Who Loved Me

This story reintroduces SPECTRE through Rona Vail and confirms MI6's worst fears. SPECTRE are back! A new creation of writer Lawrence and illustrator Horak, Rona serves as an undercover SPECTRE agent. She is sent to spy on test pilot Mike Farrar, in an original prelude to Fleming's material.

Posing as Mike's attractive neighbour, this high-cheekboned looker is the complete opposite to the story's main character Vivienne Michel. The tough vixen only breaks down after 007 shows Vail her dead colleagues. She is last seen being hauled away in handcuffs by Special Branch.

VIVIENNE MICHEL
The Spy Who Loved Me

True to the original novel by Ian Fleming, Vivienne Michel is one of the most detailed female characters created in the James Bond canon. With such rich source material, Lawrence and Horak are able to make perhaps the truest translation of a *Bond* girl from prose to strip, and they feature her heavily in the story, in a total of 94 strips.

A naïve but strong-willed woman, Vivienne (or "Viv" to her friends) meets James Bond during a time of need, as 007 gets more then he bargains for when he stops off for the night on his way to Washington DC.

We first meet Viv in strip #708 and learn a lot about this short, dark-haired, well-spoken girl. She is originally French-Canadian, but picked up English whilst studying in London. She is a dab hand around the kitchen and enjoys the odd cigarette. Most importantly, she is shown keeping her diary. After one of the worst nights of her life, just as in Fleming's novel, she plans to drive down south to the warmer waters of Florida on her scooter.

"Are you sure we sh-shouldn't stay together?"

**James Wheatley, Matthias Garretway
& James Page**

THE PHOENIX PROJECT

*T*he Phoenix Project follows in the fine tradition of Lawrence-penned, sci-fi-influenced stories, with a suit of indestructible armour as the titular item which Bond must recover.

Bond himself is presented in two very different lights within the story: he is clearly seen as being uncomfortable with the notion of blackmail, even going so far as to question M, although he is ruthless once tasked with his mission. However, Bond's breezier persona in the latter half of the story reveals a lighter side to his character, somewhat reminiscent of Roger Moore in the film role. It is perhaps not coincidental, as Moore took his first bow as 007 in *Live and Let Die* around nine months before this story appeared in the *Daily Express*.

The *Bond* girls in this story are also of interest; while Jenny Starbuck recalls the vengeful Jill Masterson of *Goldfinger*, the MI6 agent 007 ends up with at the end, Hafford, is more like *From A View To A Kill*'s Mary Ann Russell, replete with risqué jokes. The free use of nudity at the end of the strip, as well as semi-nudity almost throughout the second half, again indicate that the earlier *The League Of Vampires* may have opened the floodgates for such material, and the next stories would seem to support the theory....

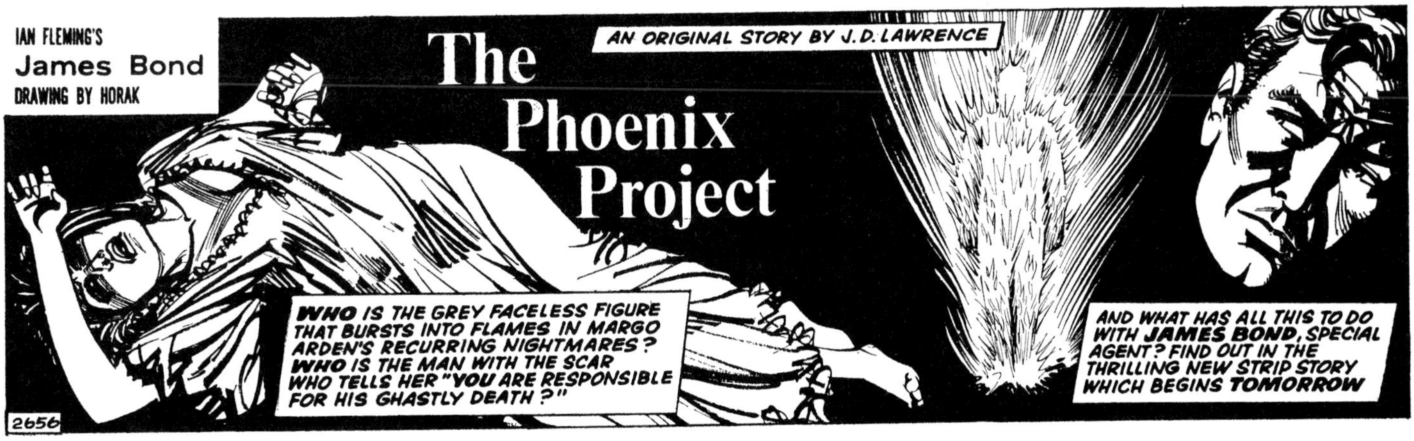
IAN FLEMING'S
James Bond
DRAWING BY HORAK
The Phoenix Project
AN ORIGINAL STORY BY J.D. LAWRENCE
WHO IS THE GREY FACELESS FIGURE THAT BURSTS INTO FLAMES IN MARGO ARDEN'S RECURRING NIGHTMARES? WHO IS THE MAN WITH THE SCAR WHO TELLS HER "YOU ARE RESPONSIBLE FOR HIS GHASTLY DEATH?"
AND WHAT HAS ALL THIS TO DO WITH JAMES BOND, SPECIAL AGENT? FIND OUT IN THE THRILLING NEW STRIP STORY WHICH BEGINS TOMORROW
2656

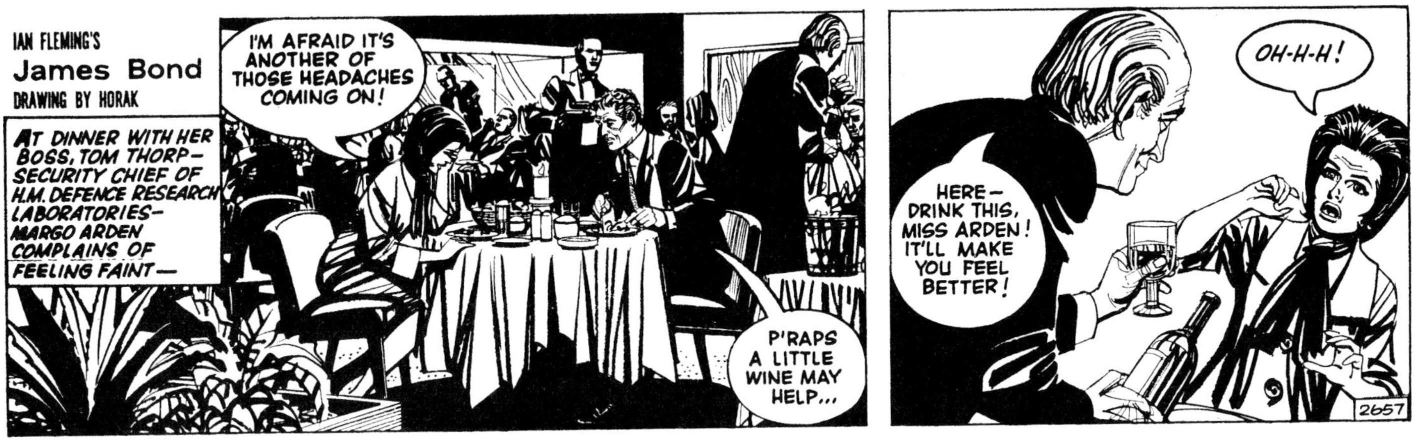
IAN FLEMING'S
James Bond
DRAWING BY HORAK
AT DINNER WITH HER BOSS, TOM THORP – SECURITY CHIEF OF H.M. DEFENCE RESEARCH LABORATORIES – MARGO ARDEN COMPLAINS OF FEELING FAINT –
I'M AFRAID IT'S ANOTHER OF THOSE HEADACHES COMING ON!
P'RAPS A LITTLE WINE MAY HELP...
OH-H-H!
HERE – DRINK THIS, MISS ARDEN! IT'LL MAKE YOU FEEL BETTER!
2657

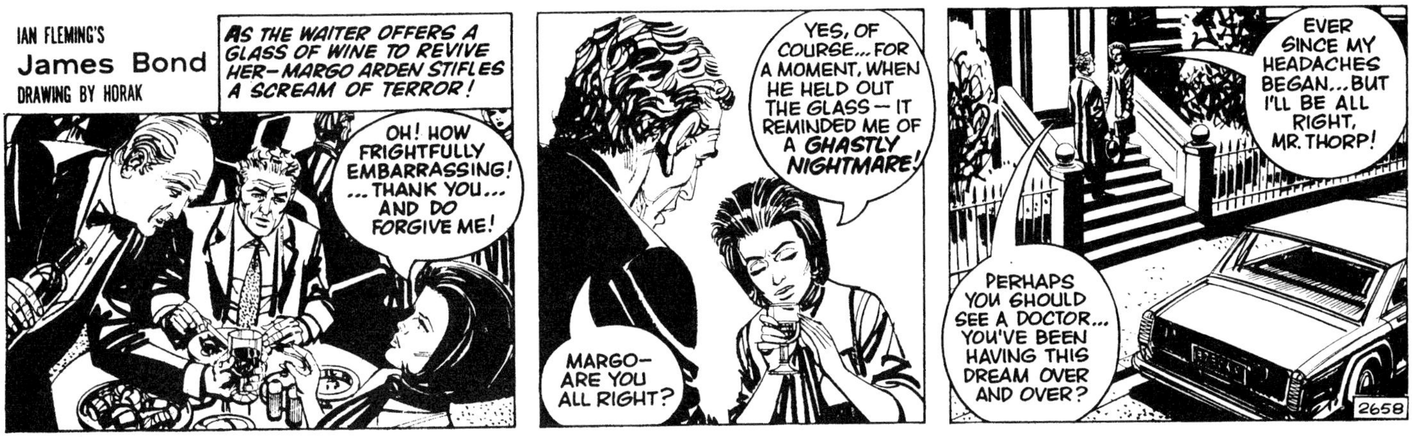
IAN FLEMING'S
James Bond
DRAWING BY HORAK
AS THE WAITER OFFERS A GLASS OF WINE TO REVIVE HER – MARGO ARDEN STIFLES A SCREAM OF TERROR!
OH! HOW FRIGHTFULLY EMBARRASSING! ... THANK YOU... AND DO FORGIVE ME!
MARGO – ARE YOU ALL RIGHT?
YES, OF COURSE... FOR A MOMENT, WHEN HE HELD OUT THE GLASS – IT REMINDED ME OF A GHASTLY NIGHTMARE!
PERHAPS YOU SHOULD SEE A DOCTOR... YOU'VE BEEN HAVING THIS DREAM OVER AND OVER?
EVER SINCE MY HEADACHES BEGAN... BUT I'LL BE ALL RIGHT, MR. THORP!
2658

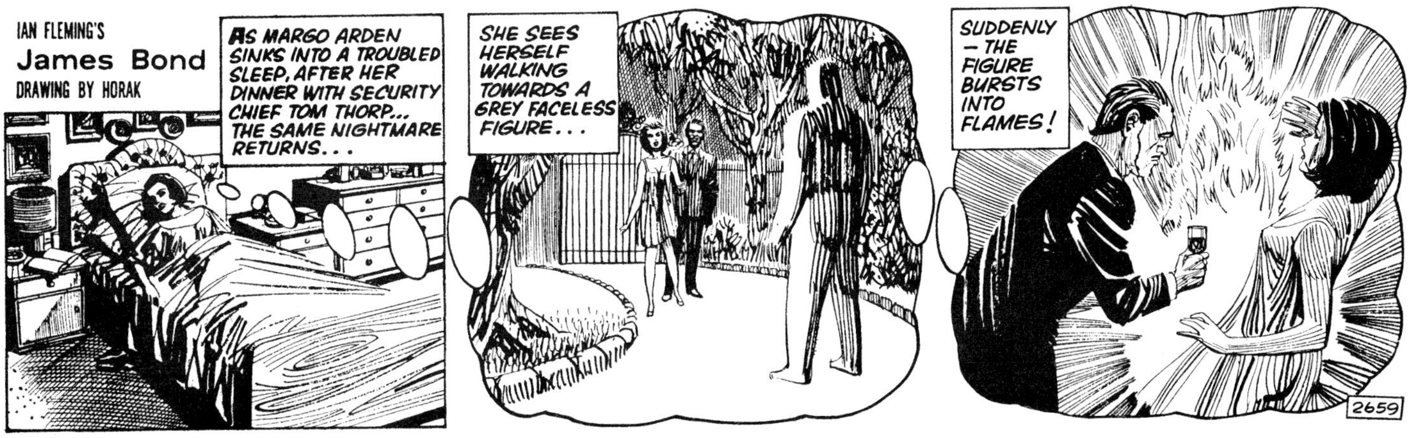
IAN FLEMING'S
James Bond
DRAWING BY HORAK
AS MARGO ARDEN SINKS INTO A TROUBLED SLEEP, AFTER HER DINNER WITH SECURITY CHIEF TOM THORP... THE SAME NIGHTMARE RETURNS...
SHE SEES HERSELF WALKING TOWARDS A GREY FACELESS FIGURE...
SUDDENLY – THE FIGURE BURSTS INTO FLAMES!
2659

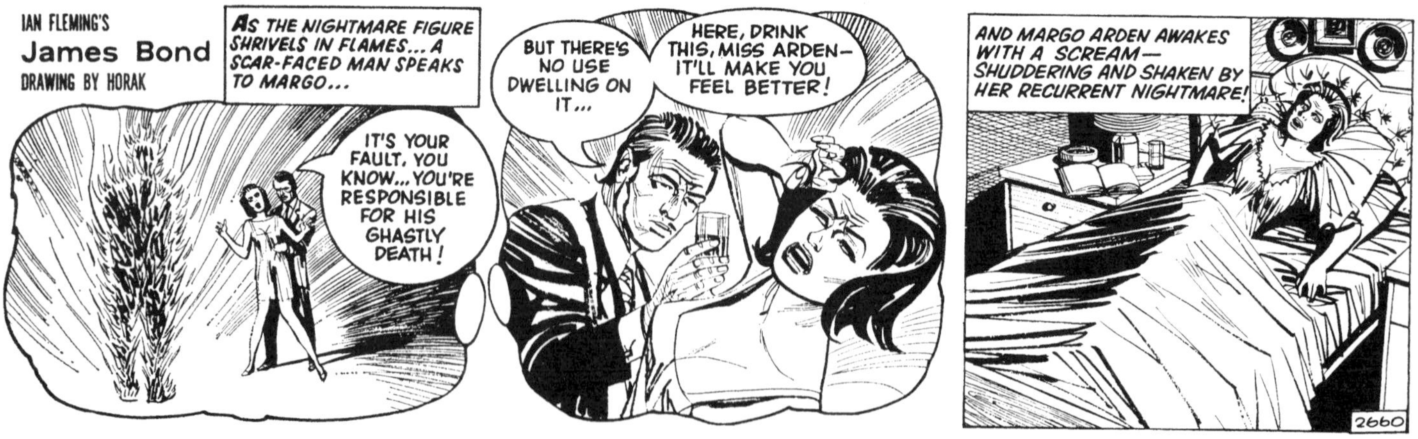
IAN FLEMING'S
James Bond
DRAWING BY HORAK
AS THE NIGHTMARE FIGURE SHRIVELS IN FLAMES... A SCAR-FACED MAN SPEAKS TO MARGO...
IT'S YOUR FAULT, YOU KNOW... YOU'RE RESPONSIBLE FOR HIS GHASTLY DEATH!
BUT THERE'S NO USE DWELLING ON IT...
HERE, DRINK THIS, MISS ARDEN— IT'LL MAKE YOU FEEL BETTER!
AND MARGO ARDEN AWAKES WITH A SCREAM— SHUDDERING AND SHAKEN BY HER RECURRENT NIGHTMARE!
2660

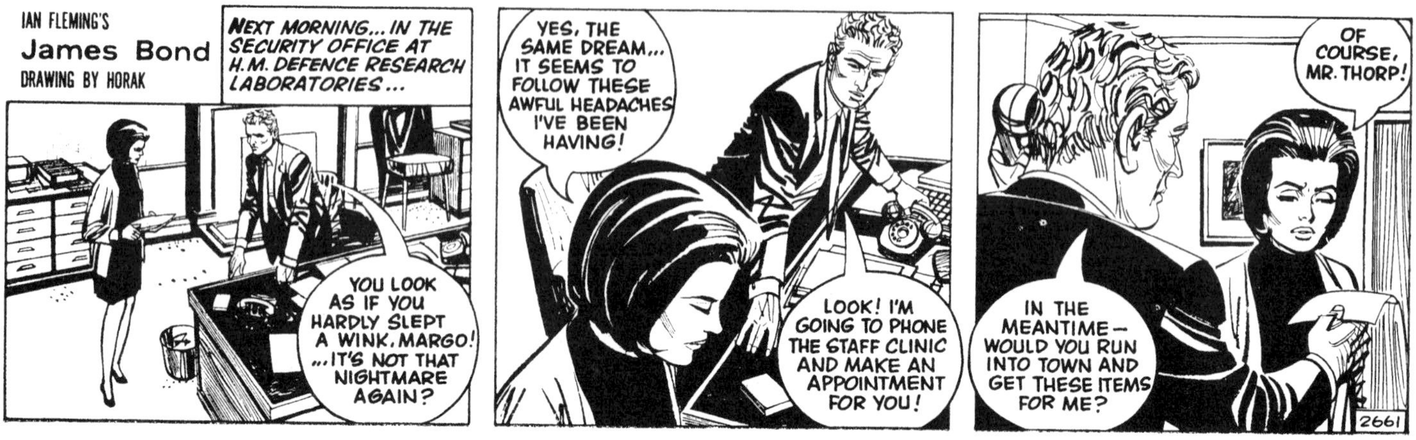
IAN FLEMING'S
James Bond
DRAWING BY HORAK
NEXT MORNING... IN THE SECURITY OFFICE AT H.M. DEFENCE RESEARCH LABORATORIES...
YOU LOOK AS IF YOU HARDLY SLEPT A WINK, MARGO! ...IT'S NOT THAT NIGHTMARE AGAIN?
YES, THE SAME DREAM... IT SEEMS TO FOLLOW THESE AWFUL HEADACHES I'VE BEEN HAVING!
LOOK! I'M GOING TO PHONE THE STAFF CLINIC AND MAKE AN APPOINTMENT FOR YOU!
OF COURSE, MR. THORP!
IN THE MEANTIME— WOULD YOU RUN INTO TOWN AND GET THESE ITEMS FOR ME?
2661

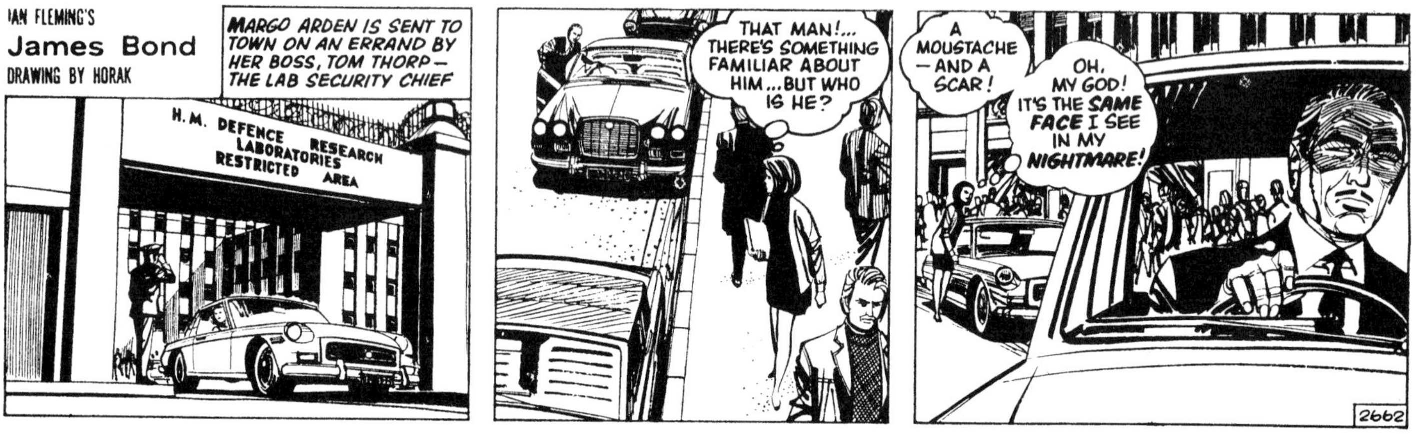
IAN FLEMING'S
James Bond
DRAWING BY HORAK
MARGO ARDEN IS SENT TO TOWN ON AN ERRAND BY HER BOSS, TOM THORP— THE LAB SECURITY CHIEF
H. M. DEFENCE RESEARCH LABORATORIES RESTRICTED AREA
THAT MAN!... THERE'S SOMETHING FAMILIAR ABOUT HIM... BUT WHO IS HE?
A MOUSTACHE —AND A SCAR!
OH, MY GOD! IT'S THE SAME FACE I SEE IN MY NIGHTMARE!
2662

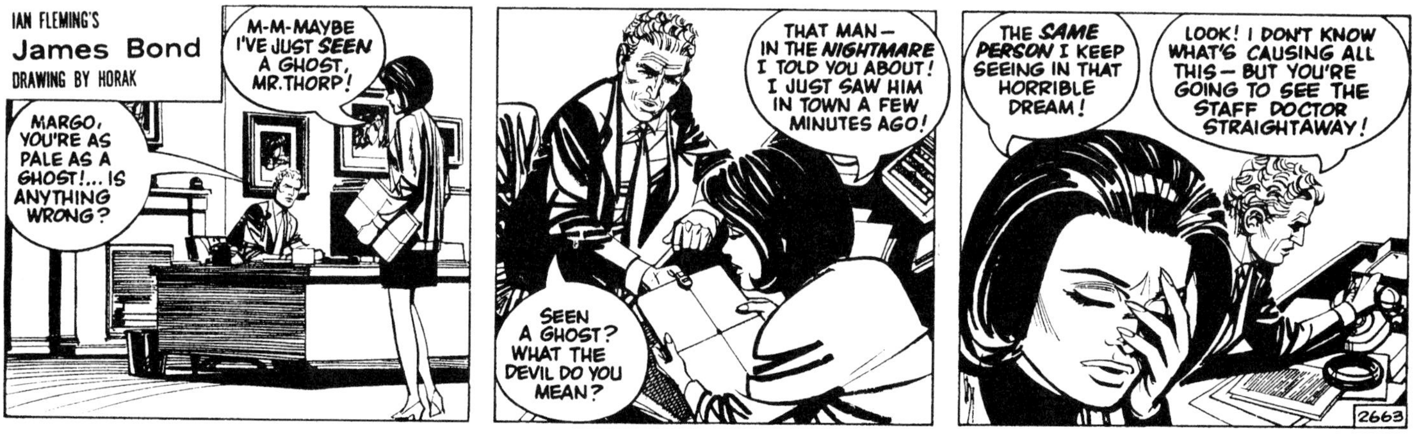
IAN FLEMING'S
James Bond
DRAWING BY HORAK
MARGO, YOU'RE AS PALE AS A GHOST!... IS ANYTHING WRONG?
M-M-MAYBE I'VE JUST SEEN A GHOST, MR. THORP!
SEEN A GHOST? WHAT THE DEVIL DO YOU MEAN?
THAT MAN— IN THE NIGHTMARE I TOLD YOU ABOUT! I JUST SAW HIM IN TOWN A FEW MINUTES AGO!
THE SAME PERSON I KEEP SEEING IN THAT HORRIBLE DREAM!
LOOK! I DON'T KNOW WHAT'S CAUSING ALL THIS— BUT YOU'RE GOING TO SEE THE STAFF DOCTOR STRAIGHTAWAY!
2663

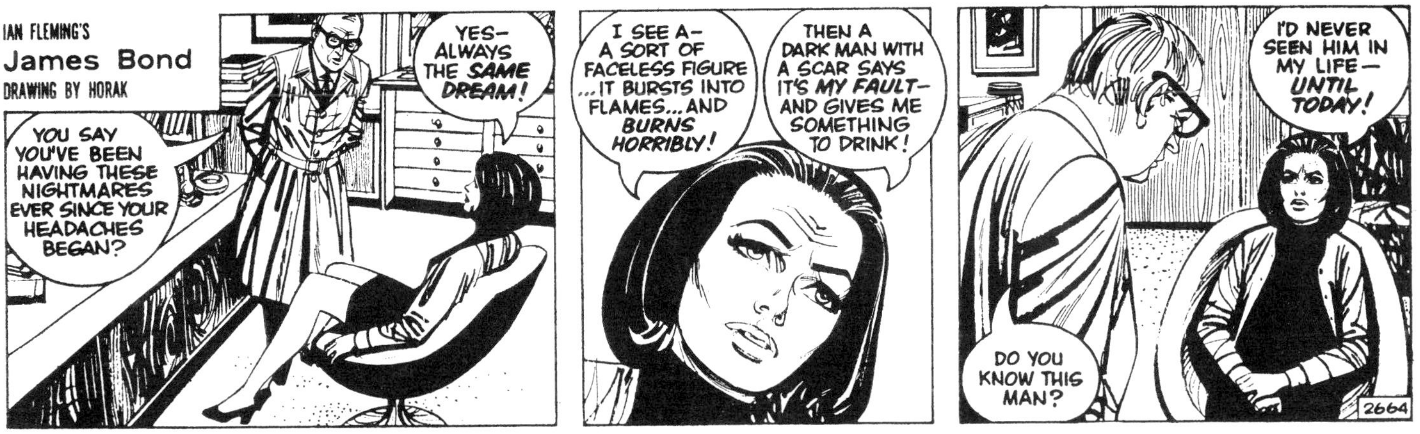
IAN FLEMING'S
James Bond
DRAWING BY HORAK
YOU SAY YOU'VE BEEN HAVING THESE NIGHTMARES EVER SINCE YOUR HEADACHES BEGAN?
YES— ALWAYS THE SAME DREAM!
I SEE A— A SORT OF FACELESS FIGURE ...IT BURSTS INTO FLAMES... AND BURNS HORRIBLY!
THEN A DARK MAN WITH A SCAR SAYS IT'S MY FAULT— AND GIVES ME SOMETHING TO DRINK!
DO YOU KNOW THIS MAN?
I'D NEVER SEEN HIM IN MY LIFE— UNTIL TODAY!
2664

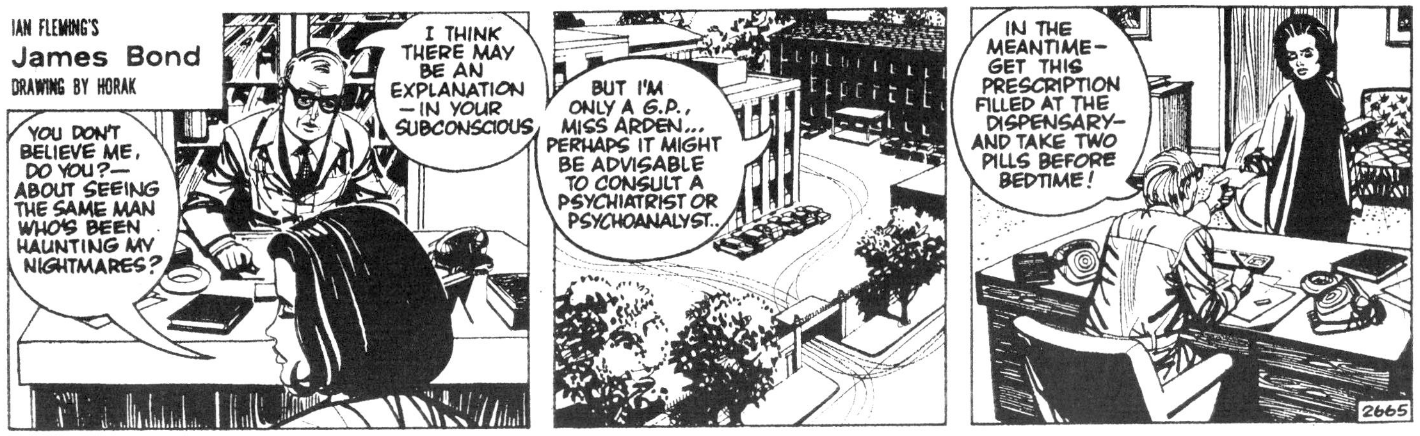
IAN FLEMING'S
James Bond
DRAWING BY HORAK
YOU DON'T BELIEVE ME, DO YOU?— ABOUT SEEING THE SAME MAN WHO'S BEEN HAUNTING MY NIGHTMARES?
I THINK THERE MAY BE AN EXPLANATION —IN YOUR SUBCONSCIOUS
BUT I'M ONLY A G.P., MISS ARDEN... PERHAPS IT MIGHT BE ADVISABLE TO CONSULT A PSYCHIATRIST OR PSYCHOANALYST...
IN THE MEANTIME— GET THIS PRESCRIPTION FILLED AT THE DISPENSARY— AND TAKE TWO PILLS BEFORE BEDTIME!
2665

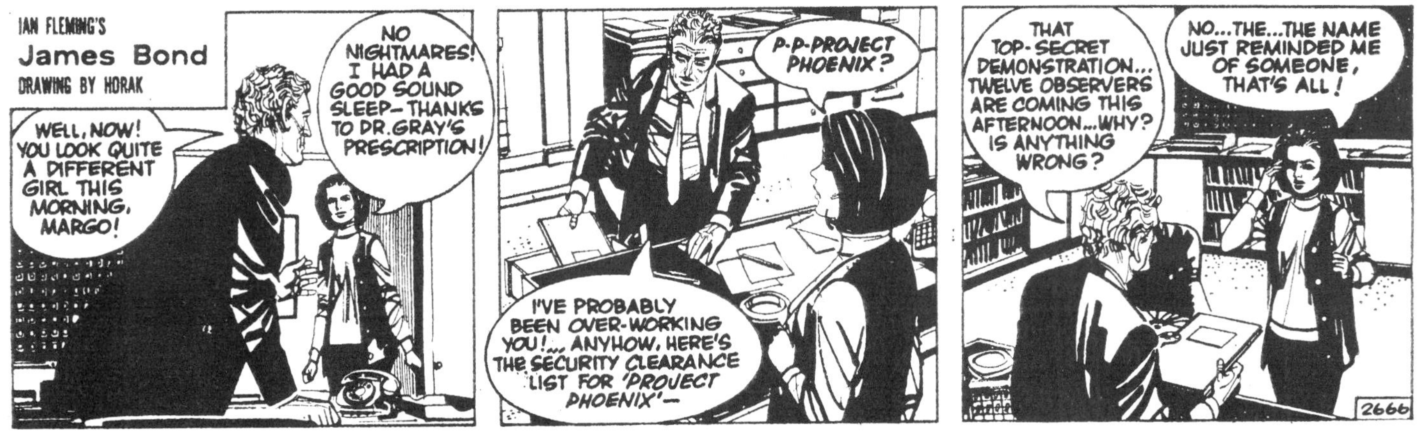
IAN FLEMING'S
James Bond
DRAWING BY HORAK
WELL, NOW! YOU LOOK QUITE A DIFFERENT GIRL THIS MORNING, MARGO!
NO NIGHTMARES! I HAD A GOOD SOUND SLEEP— THANKS TO DR. GRAY'S PRESCRIPTION!
I'VE PROBABLY BEEN OVER-WORKING YOU!... ANYHOW, HERE'S THE SECURITY CLEARANCE LIST FOR 'PROJECT PHOENIX'—
P-P-PROJECT PHOENIX?
THAT TOP-SECRET DEMONSTRATION... TWELVE OBSERVERS ARE COMING THIS AFTERNOON...WHY? IS ANYTHING WRONG?
NO...THE...THE NAME JUST REMINDED ME OF SOMEONE, THAT'S ALL!
2666

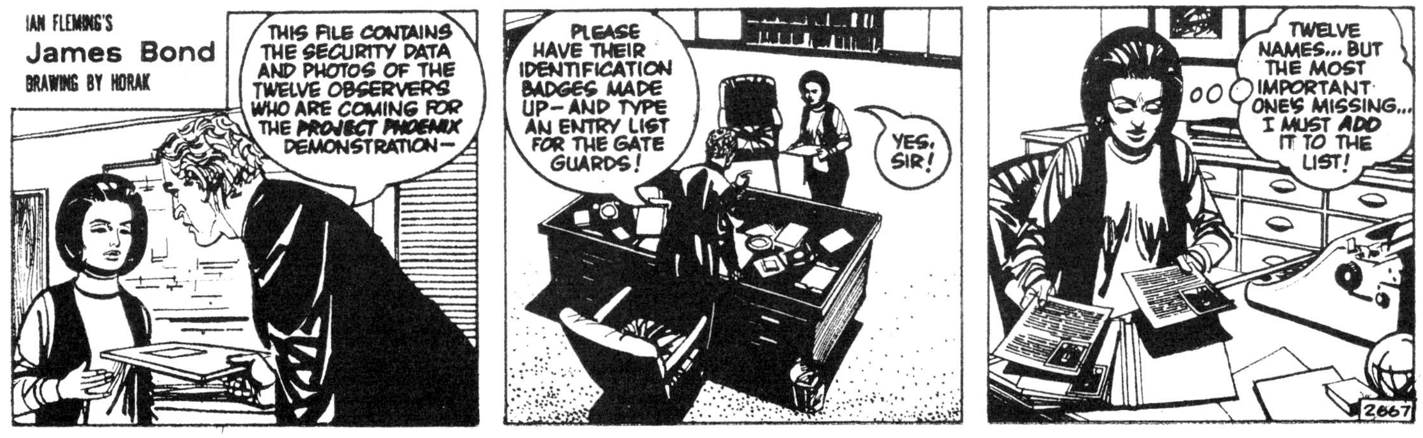
IAN FLEMING'S
James Bond
DRAWING BY HORAK
THIS FILE CONTAINS THE SECURITY DATA AND PHOTOS OF THE TWELVE OBSERVERS WHO ARE COMING FOR THE PROJECT PHOENIX DEMONSTRATION—
PLEASE HAVE THEIR IDENTIFICATION BADGES MADE UP— AND TYPE AN ENTRY LIST FOR THE GATE GUARDS!
YES, SIR!
TWELVE NAMES... BUT THE MOST IMPORTANT ONE'S MISSING... I MUST ADD IT TO THE LIST!
2667

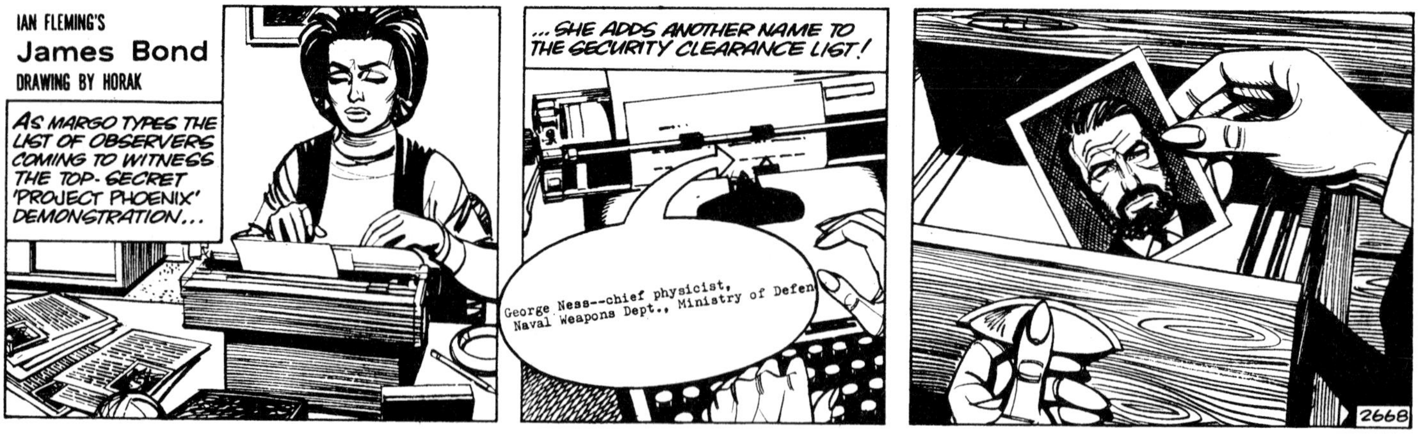
IAN FLEMING'S
James Bond
DRAWING BY HORAK
AS MARGO TYPES THE LIST OF OBSERVERS COMING TO WITNESS THE TOP-SECRET 'PROJECT PHOENIX' DEMONSTRATION...
...SHE ADDS ANOTHER NAME TO THE SECURITY CLEARANCE LIST!
George Ness--chief physicist, Naval Weapons Dept., Ministry of Defen
2668

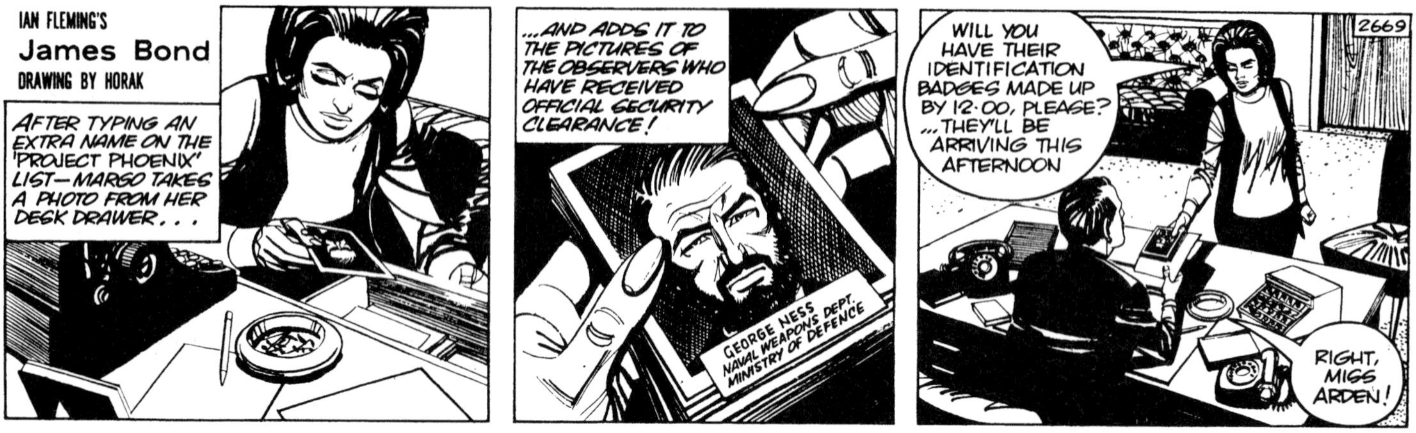
IAN FLEMING'S
James Bond
DRAWING BY HORAK
AFTER TYPING AN EXTRA NAME ON THE 'PROJECT PHOENIX' LIST—MARGO TAKES A PHOTO FROM HER DESK DRAWER...
...AND ADDS IT TO THE PICTURES OF THE OBSERVERS WHO HAVE RECEIVED OFFICIAL SECURITY CLEARANCE!
GEORGE NESS NAVAL WEAPONS DEPT. MINISTRY OF DEFENCE
2669
WILL YOU HAVE THEIR IDENTIFICATION BADGES MADE UP BY 12·00, PLEASE? ...THEY'LL BE ARRIVING THIS AFTERNOON
RIGHT, MISS ARDEN!

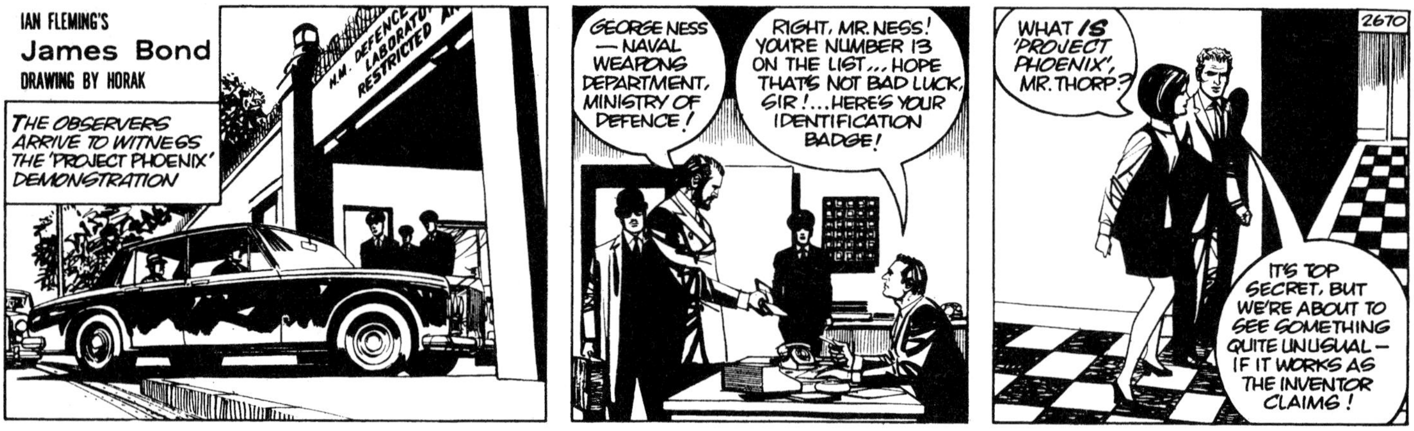
IAN FLEMING'S
James Bond
DRAWING BY HORAK
THE OBSERVERS ARRIVE TO WITNESS THE 'PROJECT PHOENIX' DEMONSTRATION
H.M. DEFENCE LABORATO RESTRICTED
GEORGE NESS —NAVAL WEAPONS DEPARTMENT, MINISTRY OF DEFENCE!
RIGHT, MR. NESS! YOU'RE NUMBER 13 ON THE LIST... HOPE THAT'S NOT BAD LUCK, SIR!... HERE'S YOUR IDENTIFICATION BADGE!
2670
WHAT IS 'PROJECT PHOENIX', MR. THORP?
IT'S TOP SECRET, BUT WE'RE ABOUT TO SEE SOMETHING QUITE UNUSUAL—IF IT WORKS AS THE INVENTOR CLAIMS!

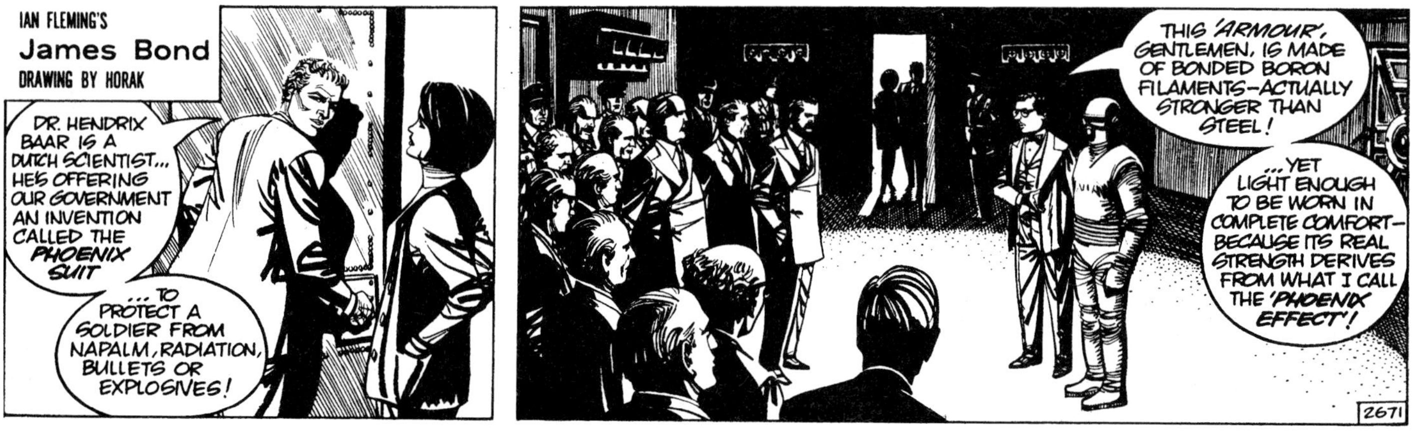
IAN FLEMING'S
James Bond
DRAWING BY HORAK
DR. HENDRIX BAAR IS A DUTCH SCIENTIST... HE'S OFFERING OUR GOVERNMENT AN INVENTION CALLED THE PHOENIX SUIT
...TO PROTECT A SOLDIER FROM NAPALM, RADIATION, BULLETS OR EXPLOSIVES!
THIS 'ARMOUR', GENTLEMEN, IS MADE OF BONDED BORON FILAMENTS—ACTUALLY STRONGER THAN STEEL!
...YET LIGHT ENOUGH TO BE WORN IN COMPLETE COMFORT—BECAUSE ITS REAL STRENGTH DERIVES FROM WHAT I CALL THE 'PHOENIX EFFECT'!
2671

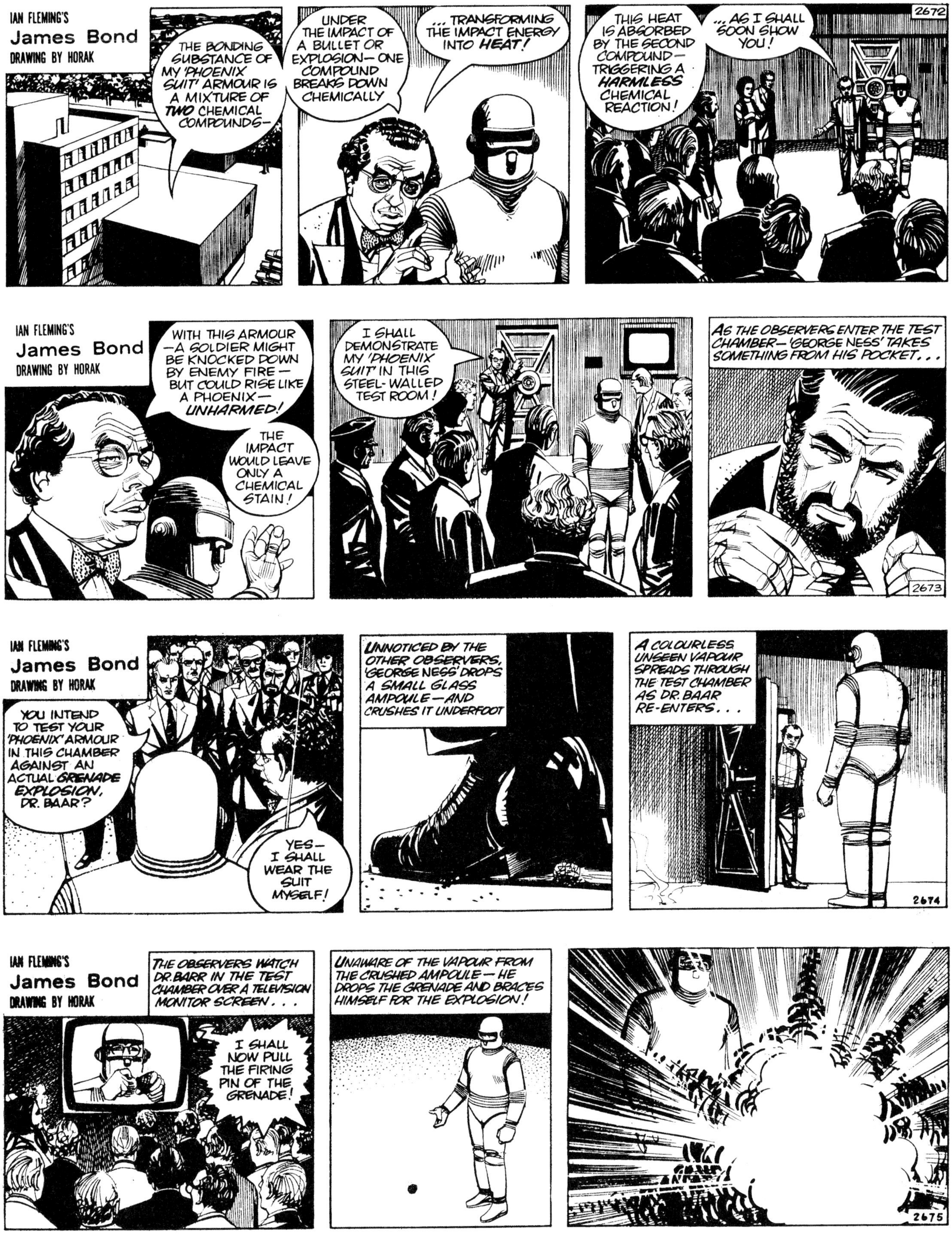
IAN FLEMING'S
James Bond
DRAWING BY HORAK
THE BONDING SUBSTANCE OF MY 'PHOENIX SUIT' ARMOUR IS A MIXTURE OF TWO CHEMICAL COMPOUNDS–
UNDER THE IMPACT OF A BULLET OR EXPLOSION– ONE COMPOUND BREAKS DOWN CHEMICALLY
... TRANSFORMING THE IMPACT ENERGY INTO HEAT!
2672
THIS HEAT IS ABSORBED BY THE SECOND COMPOUND– TRIGGERING A HARMLESS CHEMICAL REACTION!
... AS I SHALL SOON SHOW YOU!
IAN FLEMING'S
James Bond
DRAWING BY HORAK
WITH THIS ARMOUR –A SOLDIER MIGHT BE KNOCKED DOWN BY ENEMY FIRE– BUT COULD RISE LIKE A PHOENIX– UNHARMED!
THE IMPACT WOULD LEAVE ONLY A CHEMICAL STAIN!
I SHALL DEMONSTRATE MY 'PHOENIX SUIT' IN THIS STEEL-WALLED TEST ROOM!
AS THE OBSERVERS ENTER THE TEST CHAMBER– 'GEORGE NESS' TAKES SOMETHING FROM HIS POCKET...
2673
IAN FLEMING'S
James Bond
DRAWING BY HORAK
YOU INTEND TO TEST YOUR 'PHOENIX' ARMOUR IN THIS CHAMBER AGAINST AN ACTUAL GRENADE EXPLOSION, DR. BAAR?
YES– I SHALL WEAR THE SUIT MYSELF!
UNNOTICED BY THE OTHER OBSERVERS, 'GEORGE NESS' DROPS A SMALL GLASS AMPOULE– AND CRUSHES IT UNDERFOOT
A COLOURLESS UNSEEN VAPOUR SPREADS THROUGH THE TEST CHAMBER AS DR. BAAR RE-ENTERS...
2674
IAN FLEMING'S
James Bond
DRAWING BY HORAK
THE OBSERVERS WATCH DR. BARR IN THE TEST CHAMBER OVER A TELEVISION MONITOR SCREEN...
I SHALL NOW PULL THE FIRING PIN OF THE GRENADE!
UNAWARE OF THE VAPOUR FROM THE CRUSHED AMPOULE– HE DROPS THE GRENADE AND BRACES HIMSELF FOR THE EXPLOSION!
2675

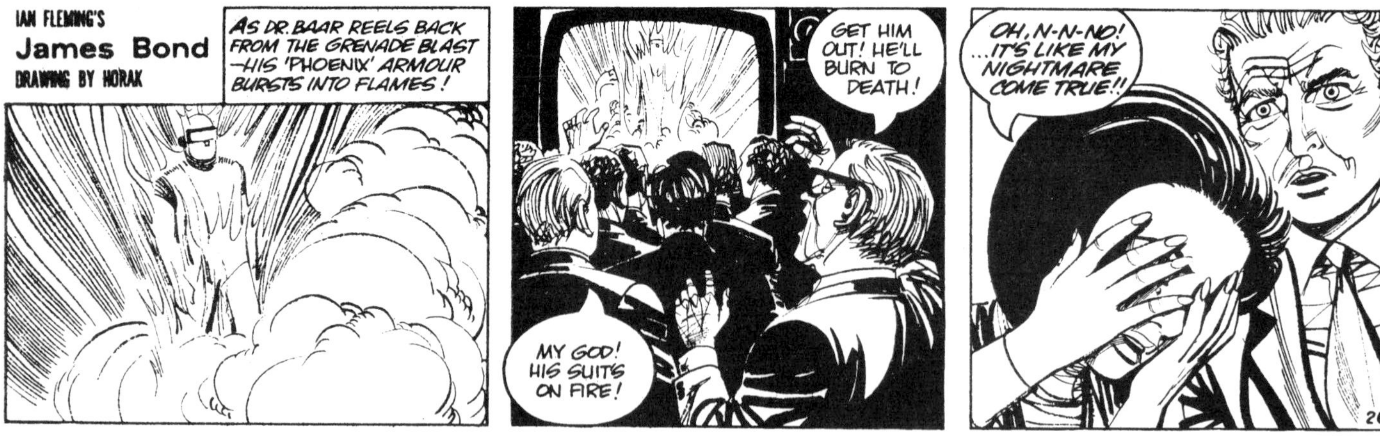
IAN FLEMING'S
James Bond
DRAWING BY HORAK
AS DR. BAAR REELS BACK FROM THE GRENADE BLAST —HIS 'PHOENIX' ARMOUR BURSTS INTO FLAMES!
GET HIM OUT! HE'LL BURN TO DEATH!
MY GOD! HIS SUIT'S ON FIRE!
OH, N-N-NO! ...IT'S LIKE MY NIGHTMARE COME TRUE!!
2676

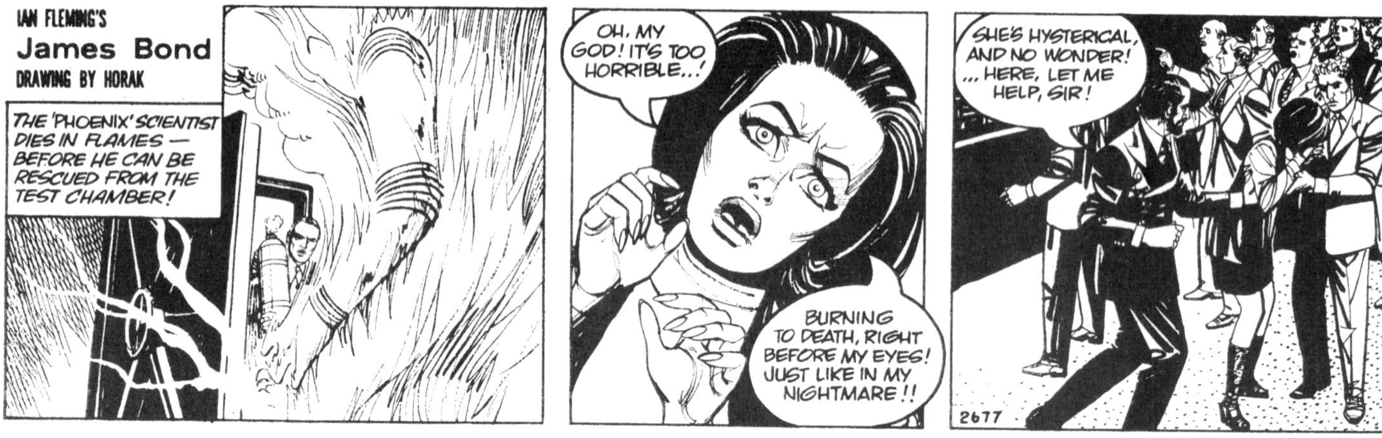
IAN FLEMING'S
James Bond
DRAWING BY HORAK
THE 'PHOENIX' SCIENTIST DIES IN FLAMES — BEFORE HE CAN BE RESCUED FROM THE TEST CHAMBER!
OH, MY GOD! IT'S TOO HORRIBLE...!
BURNING TO DEATH, RIGHT BEFORE MY EYES! JUST LIKE IN MY NIGHTMARE!!
SHE'S HYSTERICAL, AND NO WONDER! ... HERE, LET ME HELP, SIR!
2677

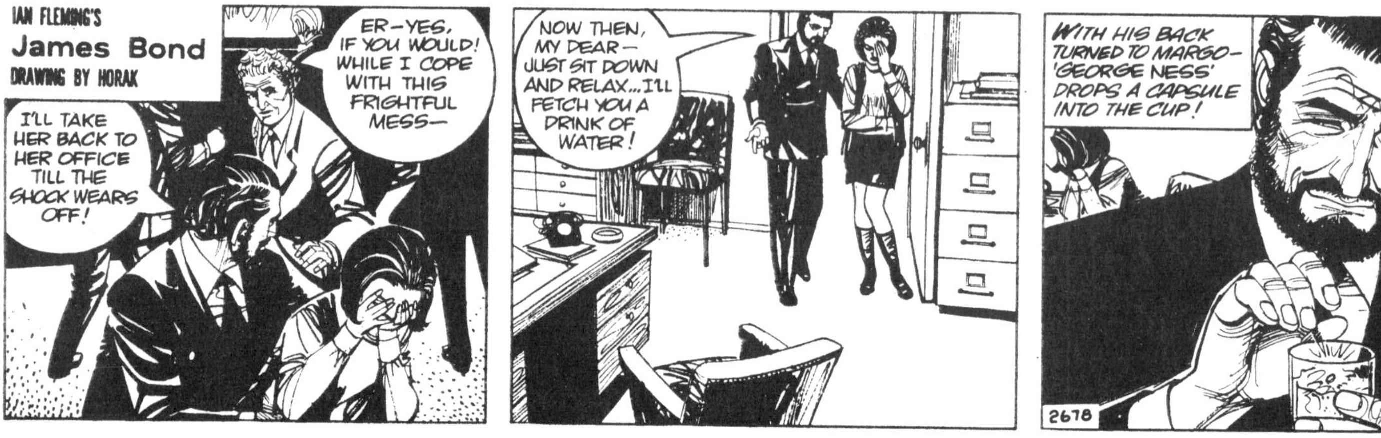
IAN FLEMING'S
James Bond
DRAWING BY HORAK
I'LL TAKE HER BACK TO HER OFFICE TILL THE SHOCK WEARS OFF!
ER—YES, IF YOU WOULD! WHILE I COPE WITH THIS FRIGHTFUL MESS—
NOW THEN, MY DEAR— JUST SIT DOWN AND RELAX...I'LL FETCH YOU A DRINK OF WATER!
WITH HIS BACK TURNED TO MARGO— 'GEORGE NESS' DROPS A CAPSULE INTO THE CUP!
2678

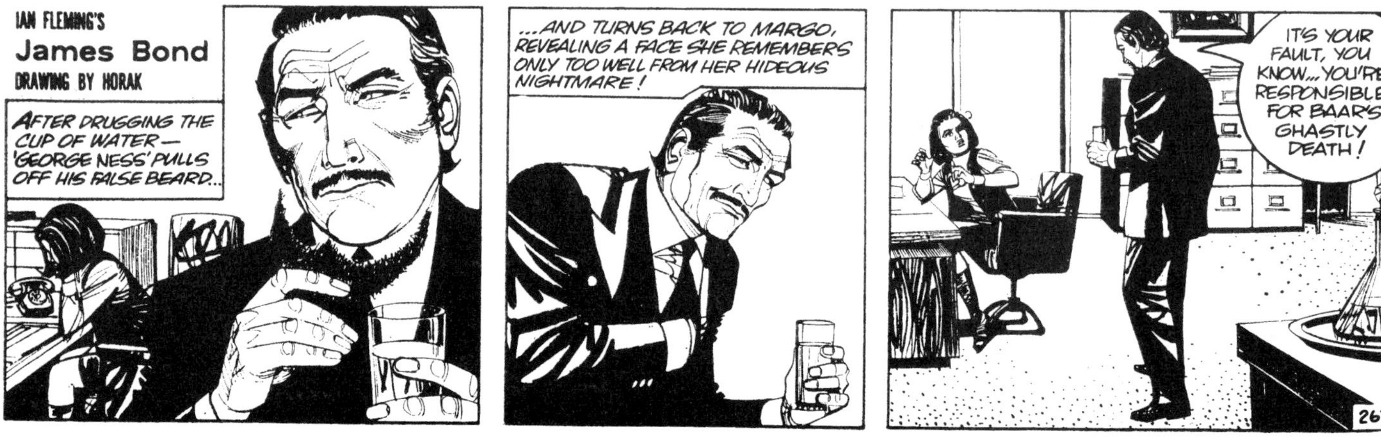
IAN FLEMING'S
James Bond
DRAWING BY HORAK
AFTER DRUGGING THE CUP OF WATER— 'GEORGE NESS' PULLS OFF HIS FALSE BEARD...
...AND TURNS BACK TO MARGO, REVEALING A FACE SHE REMEMBERS ONLY TOO WELL FROM HER HIDEOUS NIGHTMARE!
IT'S YOUR FAULT, YOU KNOW... YOU'RE RESPONSIBLE FOR BAAR'S GHASTLY DEATH!
2679

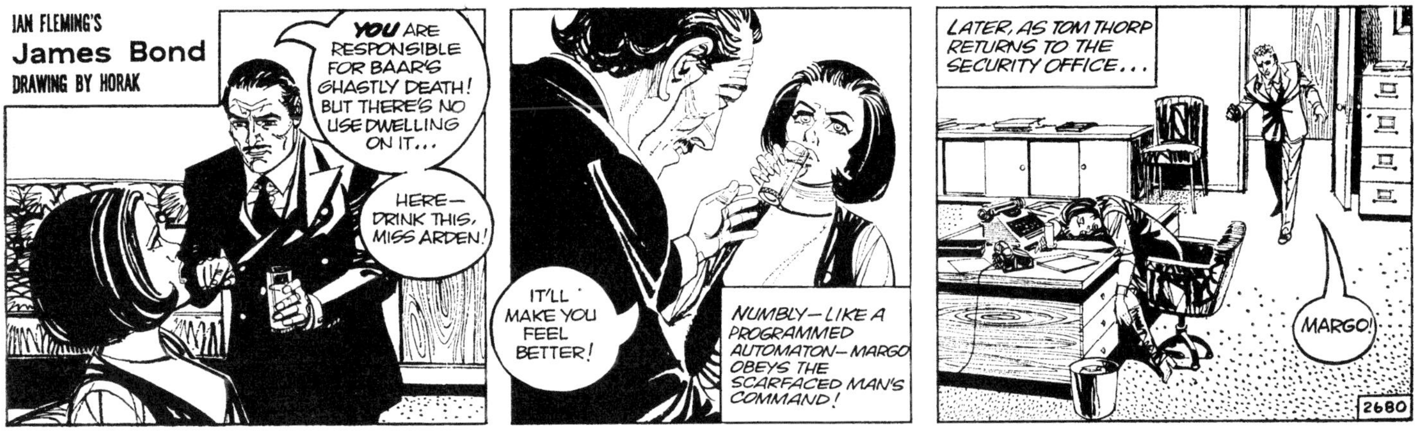
IAN FLEMING'S
James Bond
DRAWING BY HORAK
YOU ARE RESPONSIBLE FOR BAAR'S GHASTLY DEATH! BUT THERE'S NO USE DWELLING ON IT...
HERE— DRINK THIS, MISS ARDEN!
IT'LL MAKE YOU FEEL BETTER!
NUMBLY—LIKE A PROGRAMMED AUTOMATON—MARGO OBEYS THE SCARFACED MAN'S COMMAND!
LATER, AS TOM THORP RETURNS TO THE SECURITY OFFICE...
MARGO!
2680

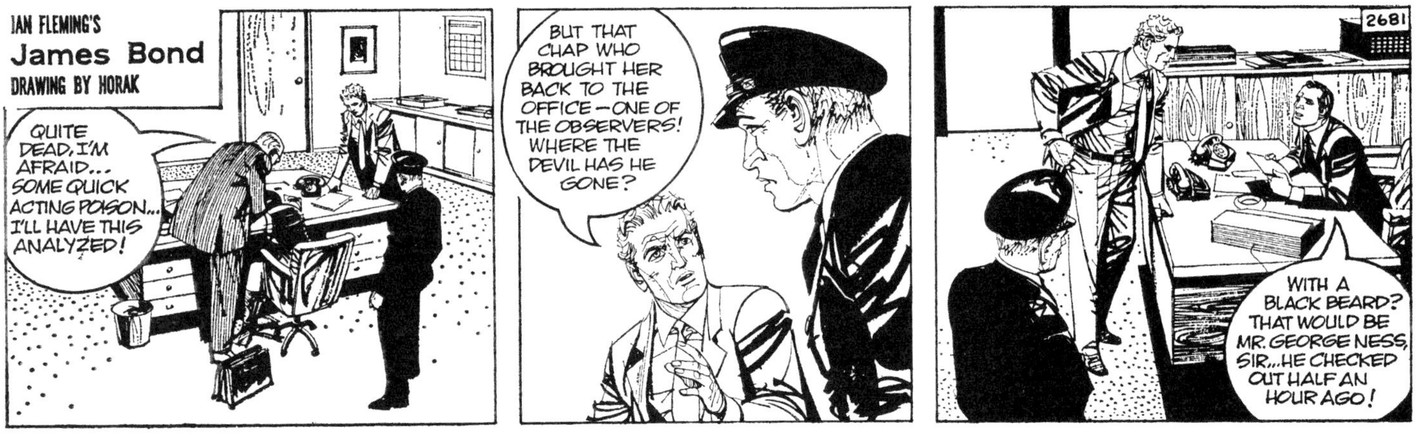
IAN FLEMING'S
James Bond
DRAWING BY HORAK
QUITE DEAD, I'M AFRAID... SOME QUICK ACTING POISON... I'LL HAVE THIS ANALYZED!
BUT THAT CHAP WHO BROUGHT HER BACK TO THE OFFICE—ONE OF THE OBSERVERS! WHERE THE DEVIL HAS HE GONE?
2681
WITH A BLACK BEARD? THAT WOULD BE MR. GEORGE NESS, SIR... HE CHECKED OUT HALF AN HOUR AGO!

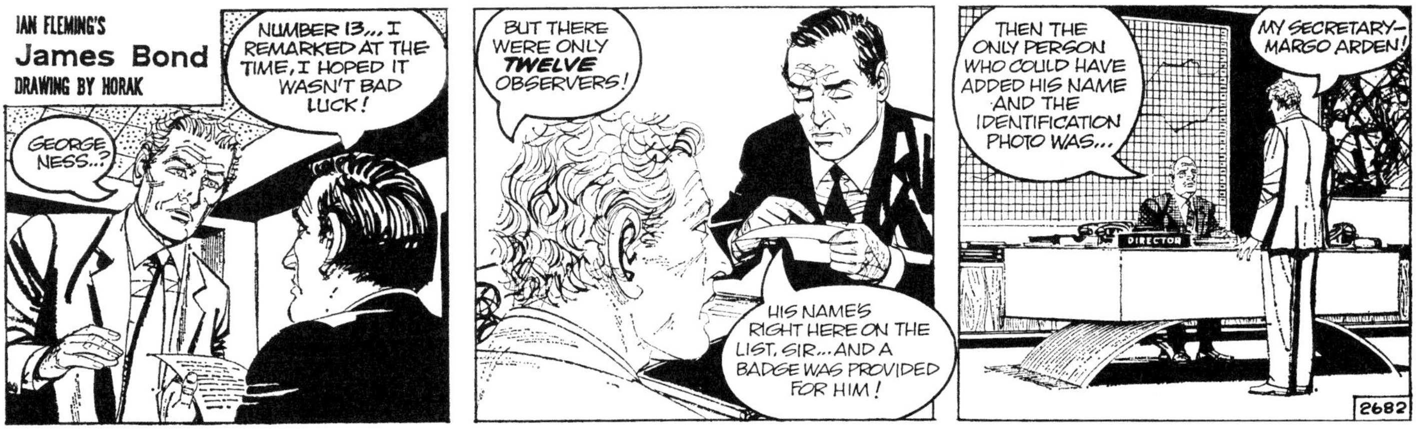
IAN FLEMING'S
James Bond
DRAWING BY HORAK
GEORGE NESS...?
NUMBER 13... I REMARKED AT THE TIME, I HOPED IT WASN'T BAD LUCK!
BUT THERE WERE ONLY TWELVE OBSERVERS!
HIS NAME'S RIGHT HERE ON THE LIST, SIR... AND A BADGE WAS PROVIDED FOR HIM!
THEN THE ONLY PERSON WHO COULD HAVE ADDED HIS NAME AND THE IDENTIFICATION PHOTO WAS...
MY SECRETARY— MARGO ARDEN!
DIRECTOR
2682

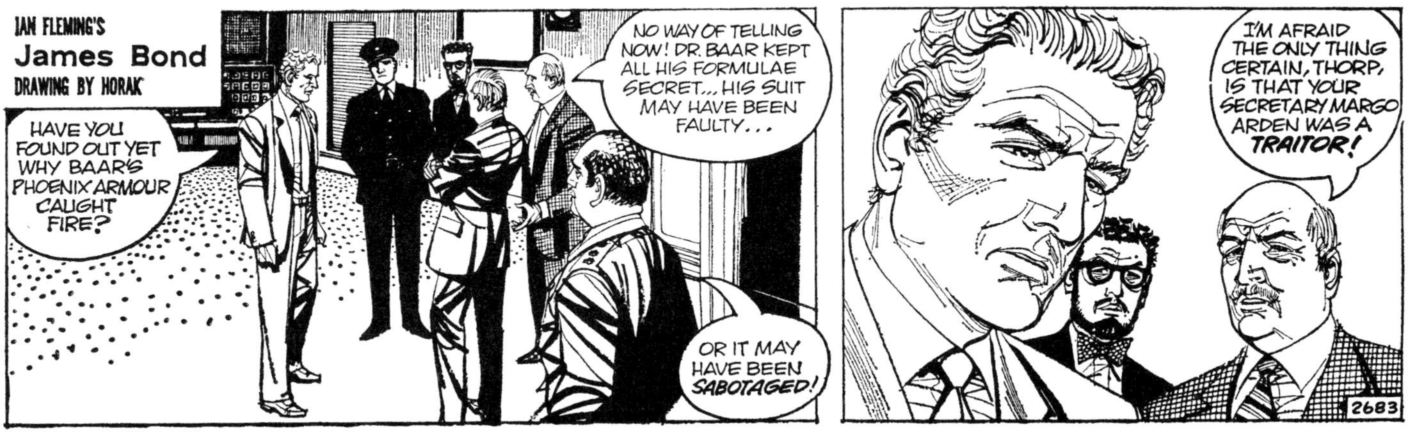
IAN FLEMING'S
James Bond
DRAWING BY HORAK
HAVE YOU FOUND OUT YET WHY BAAR'S PHOENIX ARMOUR CAUGHT FIRE?
NO WAY OF TELLING NOW! DR. BAAR KEPT ALL HIS FORMULAE SECRET... HIS SUIT MAY HAVE BEEN FAULTY...
OR IT MAY HAVE BEEN SABOTAGED!
I'M AFRAID THE ONLY THING CERTAIN, THORP, IS THAT YOUR SECRETARY MARGO ARDEN WAS A TRAITOR!
2683

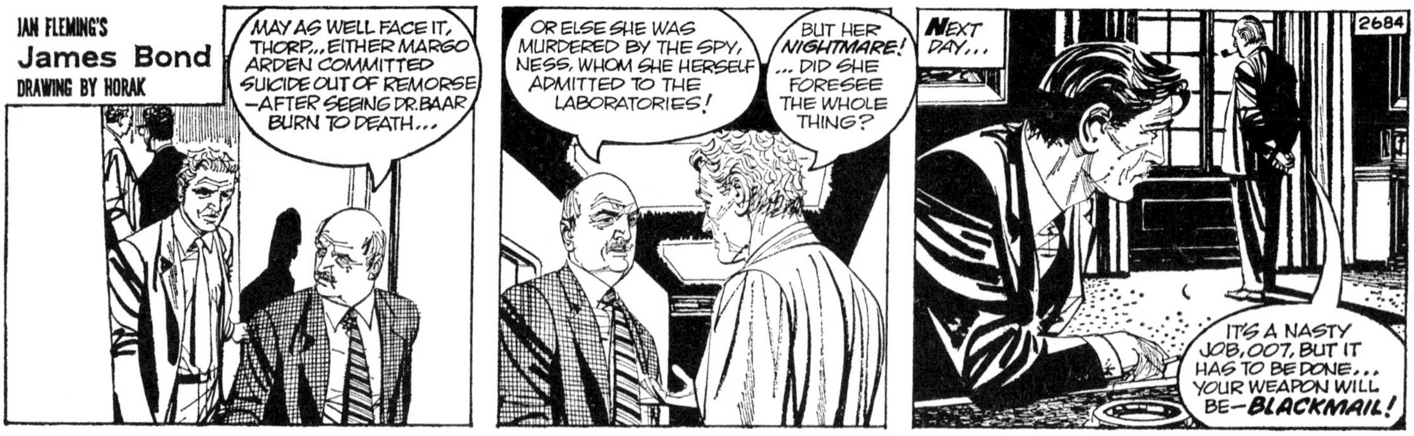
IAN FLEMING'S
James Bond
DRAWING BY HORAK
MAY AS WELL FACE IT, THORP... EITHER MARGO ARDEN COMMITTED SUICIDE OUT OF REMORSE —AFTER SEEING DR. BAAR BURN TO DEATH...
OR ELSE SHE WAS MURDERED BY THE SPY, NESS, WHOM SHE HERSELF ADMITTED TO THE LABORATORIES!
BUT HER NIGHTMARE! ... DID SHE FORESEE THE WHOLE THING?
NEXT DAY...
2684
IT'S A NASTY JOB, 007, BUT IT HAS TO BE DONE... YOUR WEAPON WILL BE—BLACKMAIL!

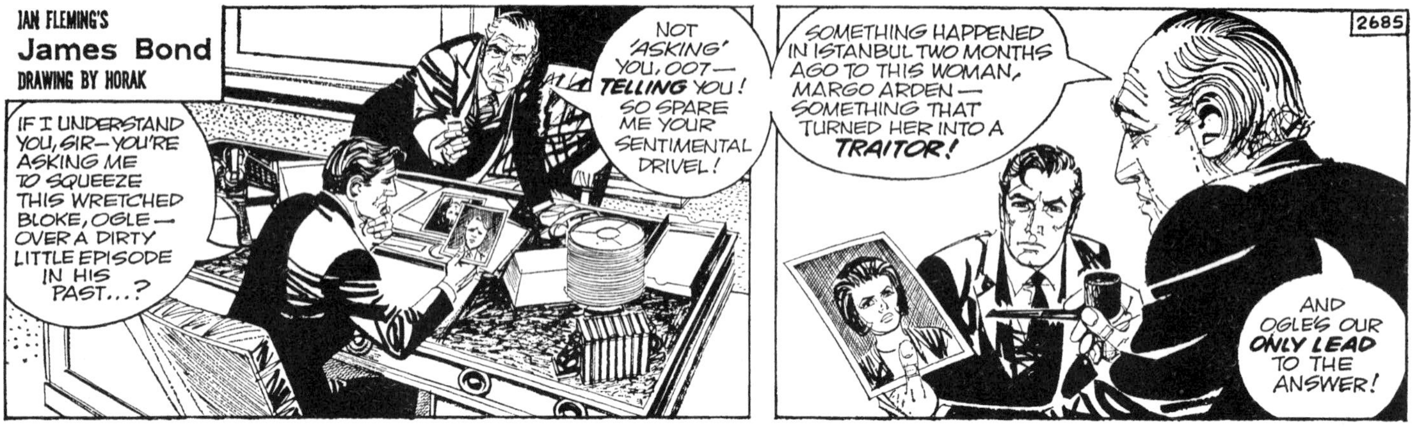
IAN FLEMING'S
James Bond
DRAWING BY HORAK
IF I UNDERSTAND YOU, SIR—YOU'RE ASKING ME TO SQUEEZE THIS WRETCHED BLOKE, OGLE— OVER A DIRTY LITTLE EPISODE IN HIS PAST...?
NOT 'ASKING' YOU, 007— TELLING YOU! SO SPARE ME YOUR SENTIMENTAL DRIVEL!
SOMETHING HAPPENED IN ISTANBUL TWO MONTHS AGO TO THIS WOMAN, MARGO ARDEN — SOMETHING THAT TURNED HER INTO A TRAITOR!
2685
AND OGLE'S OUR ONLY LEAD TO THE ANSWER!

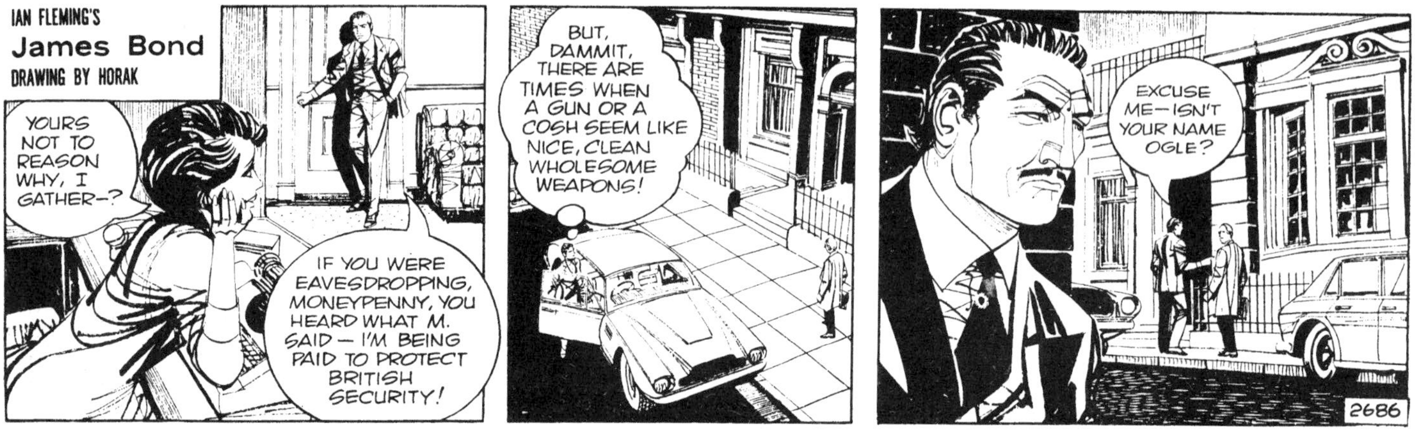
IAN FLEMING'S
James Bond
DRAWING BY HORAK
YOURS NOT TO REASON WHY, I GATHER—?
IF YOU WERE EAVESDROPPING, MONEYPENNY, YOU HEARD WHAT M. SAID — I'M BEING PAID TO PROTECT BRITISH SECURITY!
BUT, DAMMIT, THERE ARE TIMES WHEN A GUN OR A COSH SEEM LIKE NICE, CLEAN WHOLESOME WEAPONS!
EXCUSE ME—ISN'T YOUR NAME OGLE?
2686

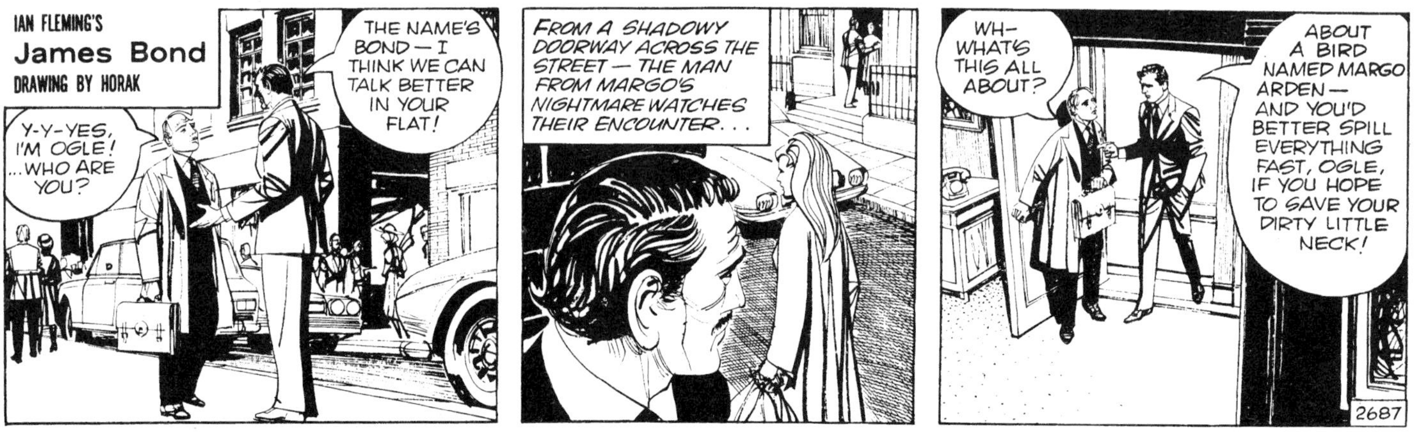
IAN FLEMING'S
James Bond
DRAWING BY HORAK
Y-Y-YES, I'M OGLE! ...WHO ARE YOU?
THE NAME'S BOND — I THINK WE CAN TALK BETTER IN YOUR FLAT!
FROM A SHADOWY DOORWAY ACROSS THE STREET — THE MAN FROM MARGO'S NIGHTMARE WATCHES THEIR ENCOUNTER...
WH-WHAT'S THIS ALL ABOUT?
ABOUT A BIRD NAMED MARGO ARDEN— AND YOU'D BETTER SPILL EVERYTHING FAST, OGLE, IF YOU HOPE TO SAVE YOUR DIRTY LITTLE NECK!
2687

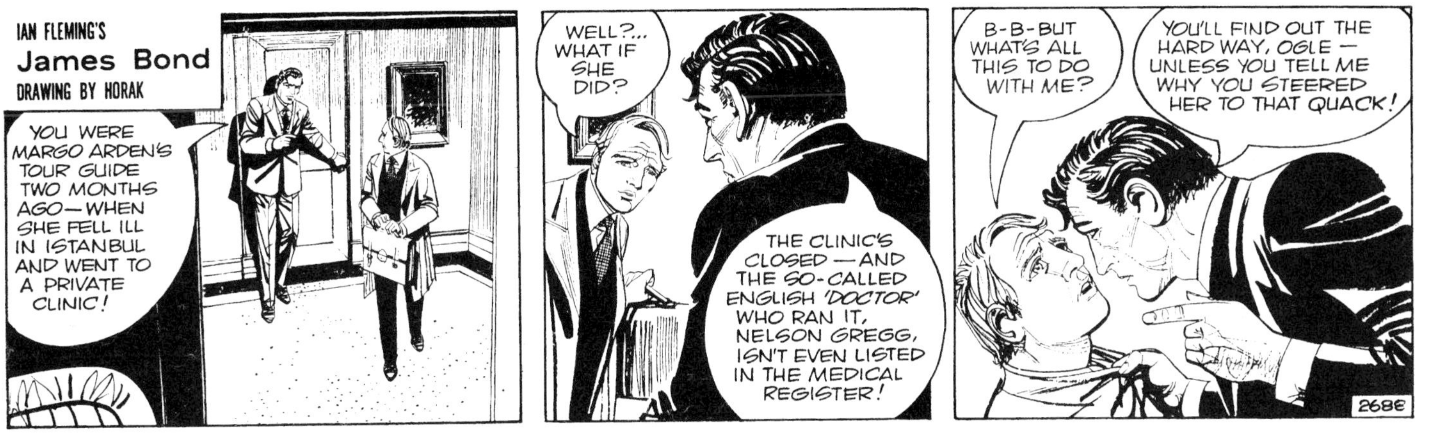
IAN FLEMING'S
James Bond
DRAWING BY HORAK
YOU WERE MARGO ARDEN'S TOUR GUIDE TWO MONTHS AGO—WHEN SHE FELL ILL IN ISTANBUL AND WENT TO A PRIVATE CLINIC!
WELL?... WHAT IF SHE DID?
THE CLINIC'S CLOSED—AND THE SO-CALLED ENGLISH *'DOCTOR'* WHO RAN IT, NELSON GREGG, ISN'T EVEN LISTED IN THE MEDICAL REGISTER!
B-B-BUT WHAT'S ALL THIS TO DO WITH ME?
YOU'LL FIND OUT THE HARD WAY, OGLE—UNLESS YOU TELL ME WHY YOU STEERED HER TO THAT *QUACK*!
2688

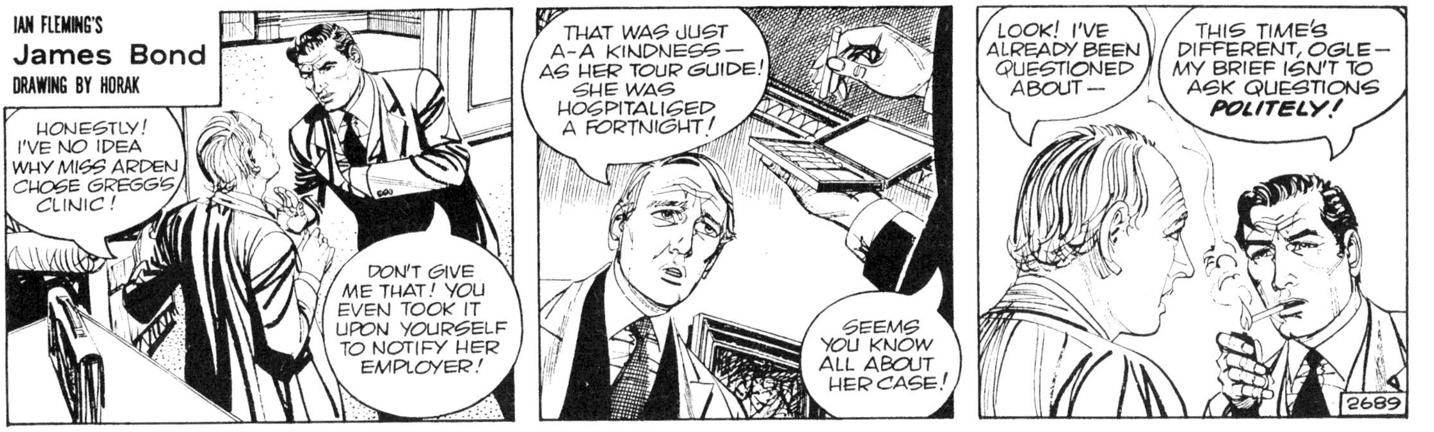
IAN FLEMING'S
James Bond
DRAWING BY HORAK
HONESTLY! I'VE NO IDEA WHY MISS ARDEN CHOSE GREGG'S CLINIC!
DON'T GIVE ME THAT! YOU EVEN TOOK IT UPON YOURSELF TO NOTIFY HER EMPLOYER!
THAT WAS JUST A-A KINDNESS—AS HER TOUR GUIDE! SHE WAS HOSPITALISED A FORTNIGHT!
SEEMS YOU KNOW ALL ABOUT HER CASE!
LOOK! I'VE ALREADY BEEN QUESTIONED ABOUT—
THIS TIME'S DIFFERENT, OGLE—MY BRIEF ISN'T TO ASK QUESTIONS ***POLITELY!***
2689

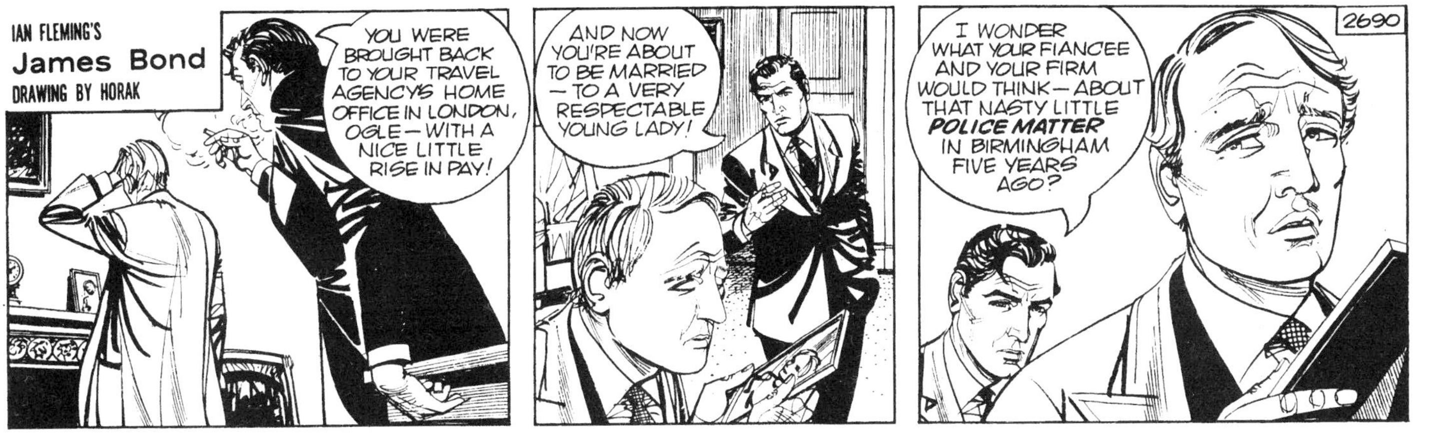
IAN FLEMING'S
James Bond
DRAWING BY HORAK
YOU WERE BROUGHT BACK TO YOUR TRAVEL AGENCY'S HOME OFFICE IN LONDON, OGLE—WITH A NICE LITTLE RISE IN PAY!
AND NOW YOU'RE ABOUT TO BE MARRIED—TO A VERY RESPECTABLE YOUNG LADY!
2690
I WONDER WHAT YOUR FIANCEE AND YOUR FIRM WOULD THINK—ABOUT THAT NASTY LITTLE ***POLICE MATTER*** IN BIRMINGHAM FIVE YEARS AGO?

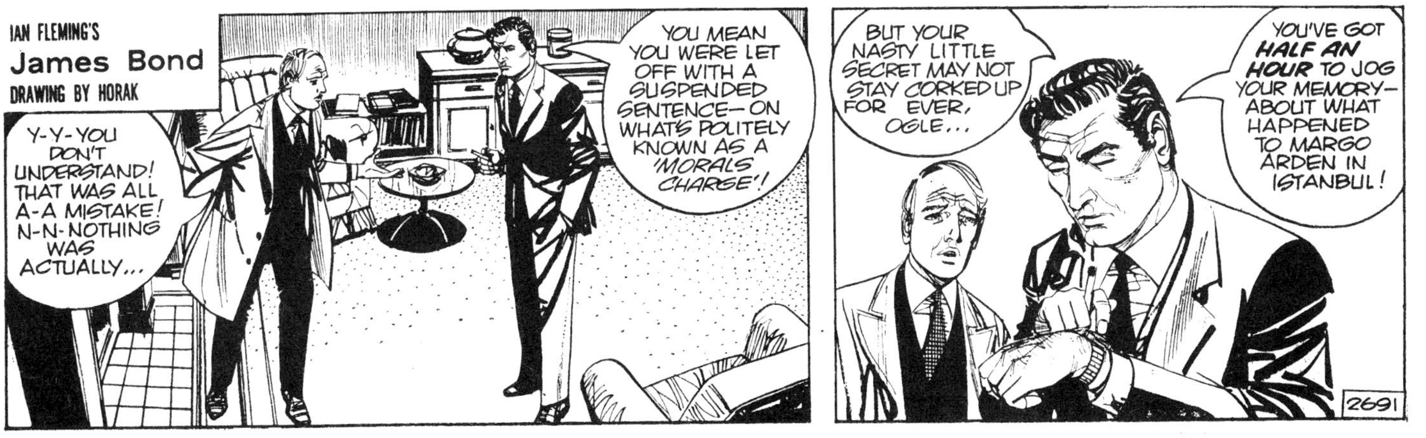
IAN FLEMING'S
James Bond
DRAWING BY HORAK
Y-Y-YOU DON'T UNDERSTAND! THAT WAS ALL A-A MISTAKE! N-N-NOTHING WAS ACTUALLY...
YOU MEAN YOU WERE LET OFF WITH A SUSPENDED SENTENCE—ON WHAT'S POLITELY KNOWN AS A *'MORALS CHARGE'*!
BUT YOUR NASTY LITTLE SECRET MAY NOT STAY CORKED UP FOR EVER, OGLE...
YOU'VE GOT ***HALF AN HOUR*** TO JOG YOUR MEMORY—ABOUT WHAT HAPPENED TO MARGO ARDEN IN ISTANBUL!
2691

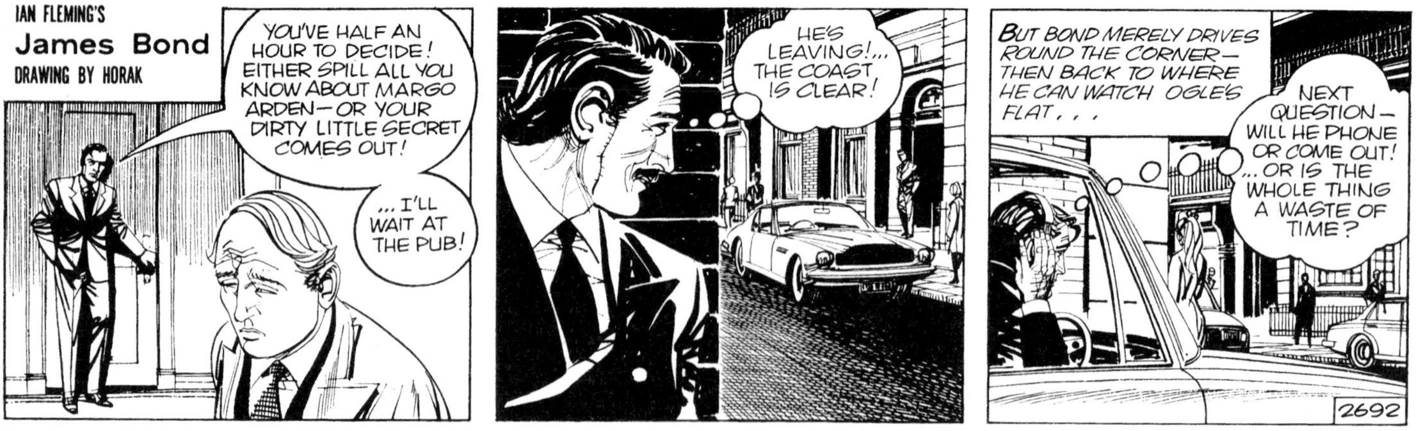
IAN FLEMING'S
James Bond
DRAWING BY HORAK
YOU'VE HALF AN HOUR TO DECIDE! EITHER SPILL ALL YOU KNOW ABOUT MARGO ARDEN—OR YOUR DIRTY LITTLE SECRET COMES OUT!
... I'LL WAIT AT THE PUB!
HE'S LEAVING!... THE COAST IS CLEAR!
BUT BOND MERELY DRIVES ROUND THE CORNER—THEN BACK TO WHERE HE CAN WATCH OGLE'S FLAT . . .
NEXT QUESTION—WILL HE PHONE OR COME OUT! ... OR IS THE WHOLE THING A WASTE OF TIME?
2692

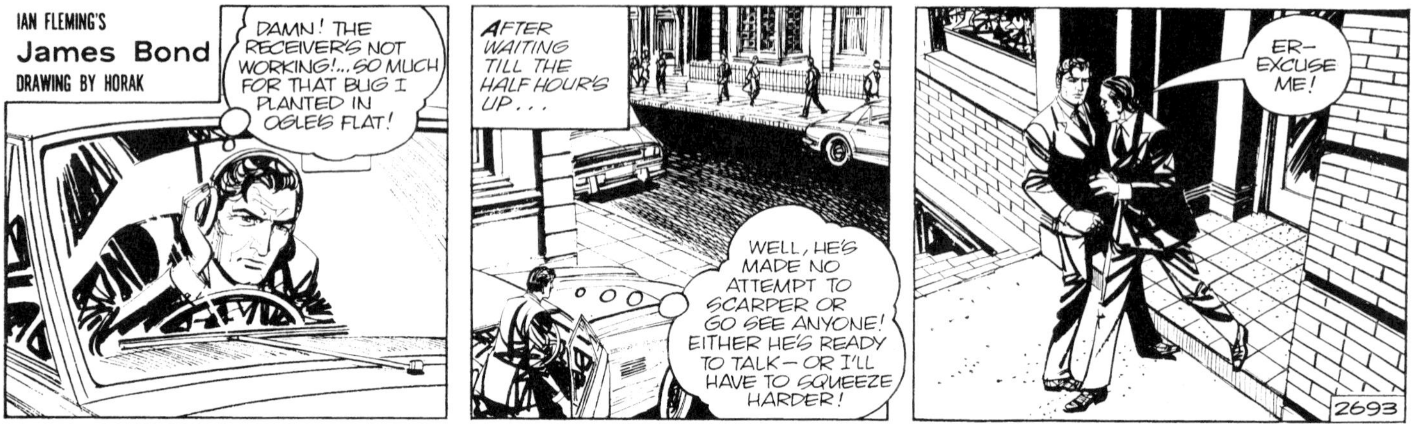
IAN FLEMING'S
James Bond
DRAWING BY HORAK
DAMN! THE RECEIVER'S NOT WORKING!... SO MUCH FOR THAT BUG I PLANTED IN OGLE'S FLAT!
AFTER WAITING TILL THE HALF HOUR'S UP . . .
WELL, HE'S MADE NO ATTEMPT TO SCARPER OR GO SEE ANYONE! EITHER HE'S READY TO TALK—OR I'LL HAVE TO SQUEEZE HARDER!
ER—EXCUSE ME!
2693

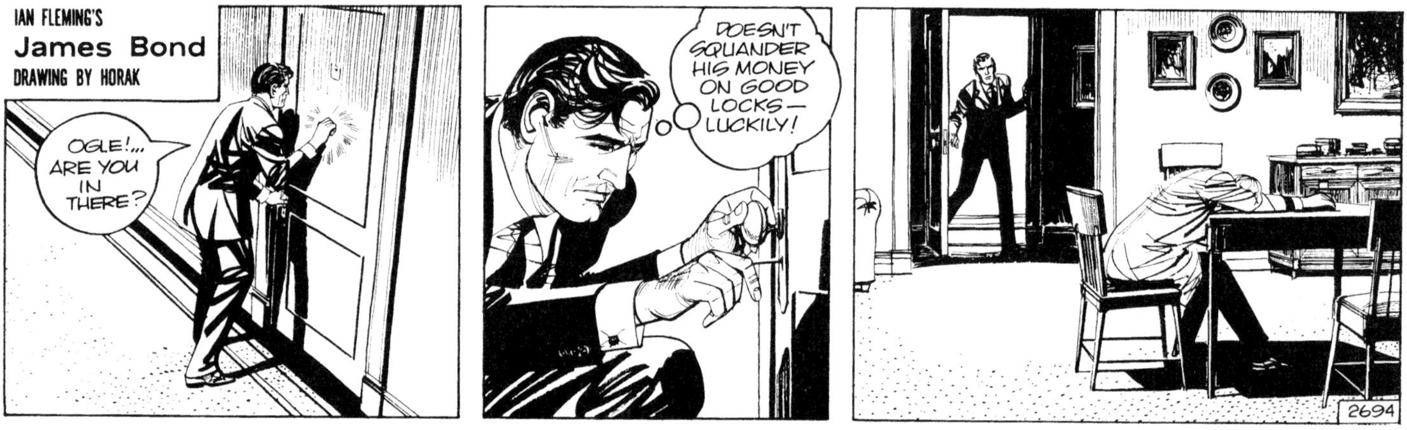
IAN FLEMING'S
James Bond
DRAWING BY HORAK
OGLE!... ARE YOU IN THERE?
DOESN'T SQUANDER HIS MONEY ON GOOD LOCKS—LUCKILY!
2694

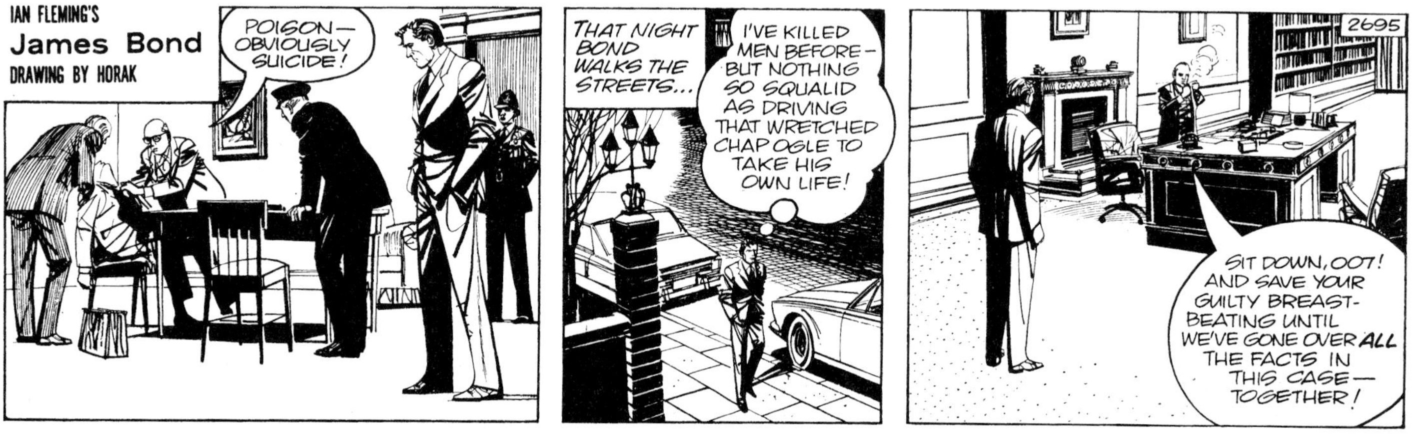
IAN FLEMING'S
James Bond
DRAWING BY HORAK
POISON—OBVIOUSLY SUICIDE!
THAT NIGHT BOND WALKS THE STREETS...
I'VE KILLED MEN BEFORE—BUT NOTHING SO SQUALID AS DRIVING THAT WRETCHED CHAP OGLE TO TAKE HIS OWN LIFE!
2695
SIT DOWN, 007! AND SAVE YOUR GUILTY BREAST-BEATING UNTIL WE'VE GONE OVER ALL THE FACTS IN THIS CASE—TOGETHER!

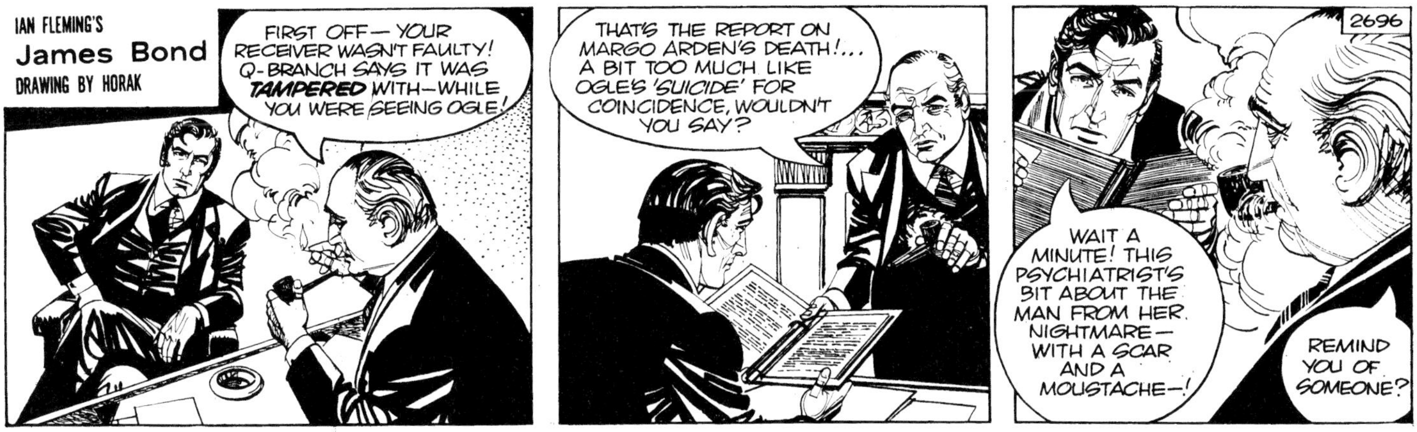
IAN FLEMING'S
James Bond
DRAWING BY HORAK
FIRST OFF—YOUR RECEIVER WASN'T FAULTY! Q-BRANCH SAYS IT WAS TAMPERED WITH—WHILE YOU WERE SEEING OGLE!
THAT'S THE REPORT ON MARGO ARDEN'S DEATH!... A BIT TOO MUCH LIKE OGLE'S 'SUICIDE' FOR COINCIDENCE, WOULDN'T YOU SAY?
2696
WAIT A MINUTE! THIS PSYCHIATRIST'S BIT ABOUT THE MAN FROM HER NIGHTMARE—WITH A SCAR AND A MOUSTACHE—!
REMIND YOU OF SOMEONE?

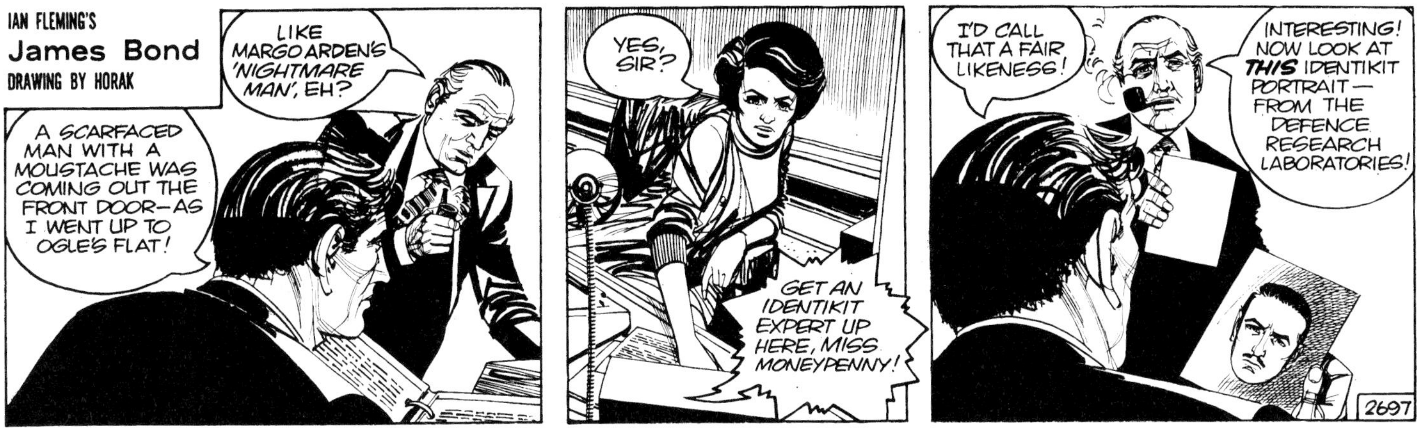
IAN FLEMING'S
James Bond
DRAWING BY HORAK
LIKE MARGO ARDEN'S 'NIGHTMARE MAN', EH?
A SCARFACED MAN WITH A MOUSTACHE WAS COMING OUT THE FRONT DOOR—AS I WENT UP TO OGLE'S FLAT!
YES, SIR?
GET AN IDENTIKIT EXPERT UP HERE, MISS MONEYPENNY!
I'D CALL THAT A FAIR LIKENESS!
INTERESTING! NOW LOOK AT THIS IDENTIKIT PORTRAIT—FROM THE DEFENCE RESEARCH LABORATORIES!
2697

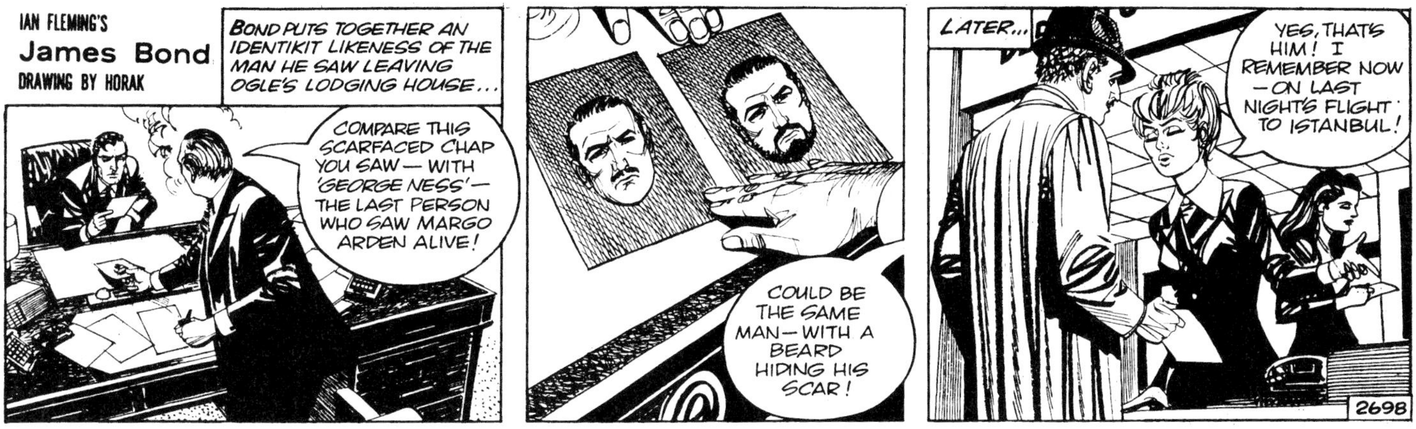
IAN FLEMING'S
James Bond
DRAWING BY HORAK
BOND PUTS TOGETHER AN IDENTIKIT LIKENESS OF THE MAN HE SAW LEAVING OGLE'S LODGING HOUSE...
COMPARE THIS SCARFACED CHAP YOU SAW—WITH 'GEORGE NESS'—THE LAST PERSON WHO SAW MARGO ARDEN ALIVE!
COULD BE THE SAME MAN—WITH A BEARD HIDING HIS SCAR!
LATER...
YES, THAT'S HIM! I REMEMBER NOW—ON LAST NIGHT'S FLIGHT TO ISTANBUL!
2698

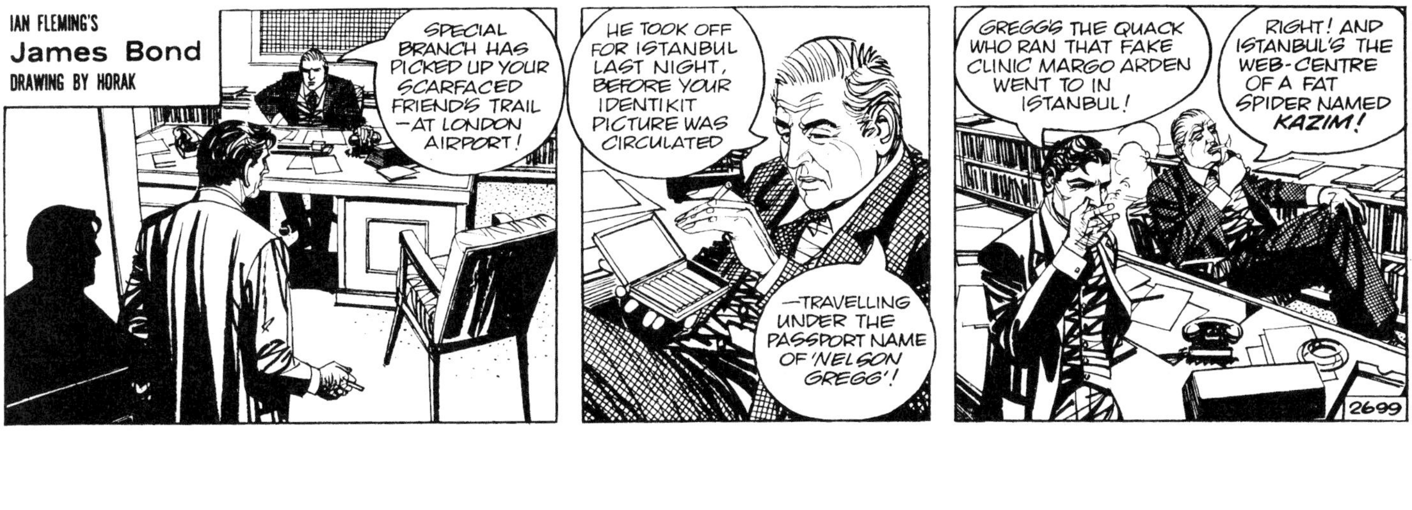
IAN FLEMING'S
James Bond
DRAWING BY HORAK
SPECIAL BRANCH HAS PICKED UP YOUR SCARFACED FRIEND'S TRAIL—AT LONDON AIRPORT!
HE TOOK OFF FOR ISTANBUL LAST NIGHT, BEFORE YOUR IDENTIKIT PICTURE WAS CIRCULATED
—TRAVELLING UNDER THE PASSPORT NAME OF 'NELSON GREGG'!
GREGG'S THE QUACK WHO RAN THAT FAKE CLINIC MARGO ARDEN WENT TO IN ISTANBUL!
RIGHT! AND ISTANBUL'S THE WEB-CENTRE OF A FAT SPIDER NAMED KAZIM!
2699

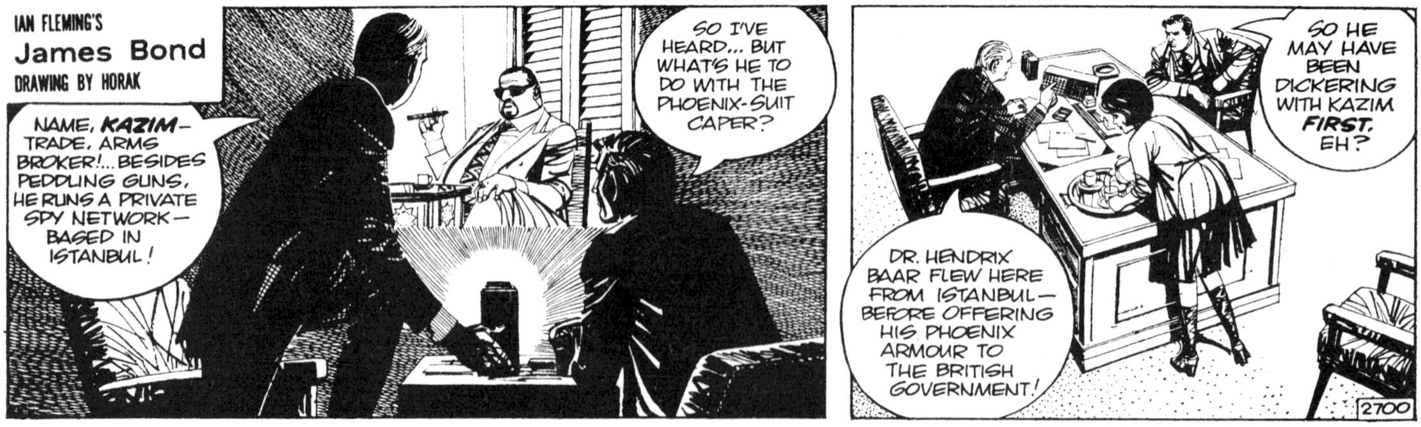
IAN FLEMING'S
James Bond
DRAWING BY HORAK
NAME, KAZIM—TRADE, ARMS BROKER!... BESIDES PEDDLING GUNS, HE RUNS A PRIVATE SPY NETWORK—BASED IN ISTANBUL!
SO I'VE HEARD... BUT WHAT'S HE TO DO WITH THE PHOENIX-SUIT CAPER?
DR. HENDRIX BAAR FLEW HERE FROM ISTANBUL—BEFORE OFFERING HIS PHOENIX ARMOUR TO THE BRITISH GOVERNMENT!
SO HE MAY HAVE BEEN DICKERING WITH KAZIM FIRST, EH?
2700

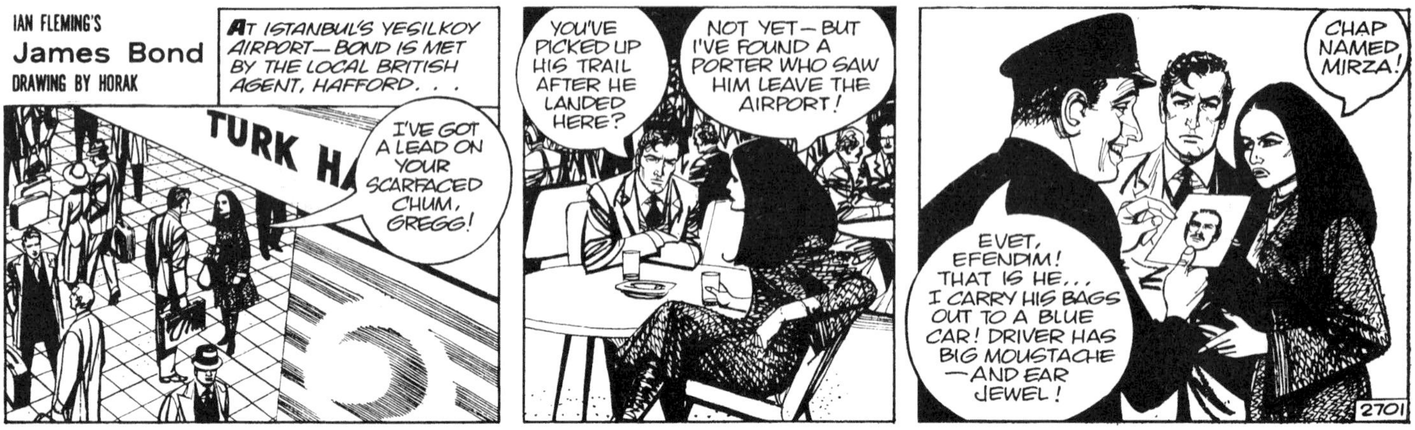
IAN FLEMING'S
James Bond
DRAWING BY HORAK
AT ISTANBUL'S YESILKOY AIRPORT—BOND IS MET BY THE LOCAL BRITISH AGENT, HAFFORD . . .
TURK HA
I'VE GOT A LEAD ON YOUR SCARFACED CHUM, GREGG!
YOU'VE PICKED UP HIS TRAIL AFTER HE LANDED HERE?
NOT YET—BUT I'VE FOUND A PORTER WHO SAW HIM LEAVE THE AIRPORT!
CHAP NAMED, MIRZA!
EVET, EFENDIM! THAT IS HE... I CARRY HIS BAGS OUT TO A BLUE CAR! DRIVER HAS BIG MOUSTACHE —AND EAR JEWEL!
2701

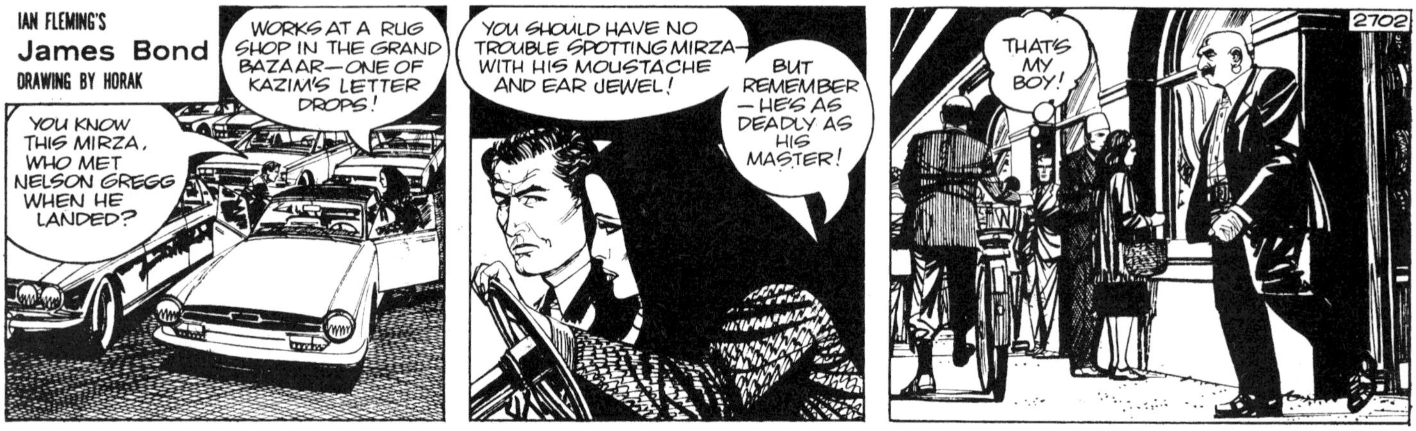
IAN FLEMING'S
James Bond
DRAWING BY HORAK
YOU KNOW THIS MIRZA, WHO MET NELSON GREGG WHEN HE LANDED?
WORKS AT A RUG SHOP IN THE GRAND BAZAAR—ONE OF KAZIM'S LETTER DROPS!
YOU SHOULD HAVE NO TROUBLE SPOTTING MIRZA—WITH HIS MOUSTACHE AND EAR JEWEL!
BUT REMEMBER —HE'S AS DEADLY AS HIS MASTER!
2702
THAT'S MY BOY!

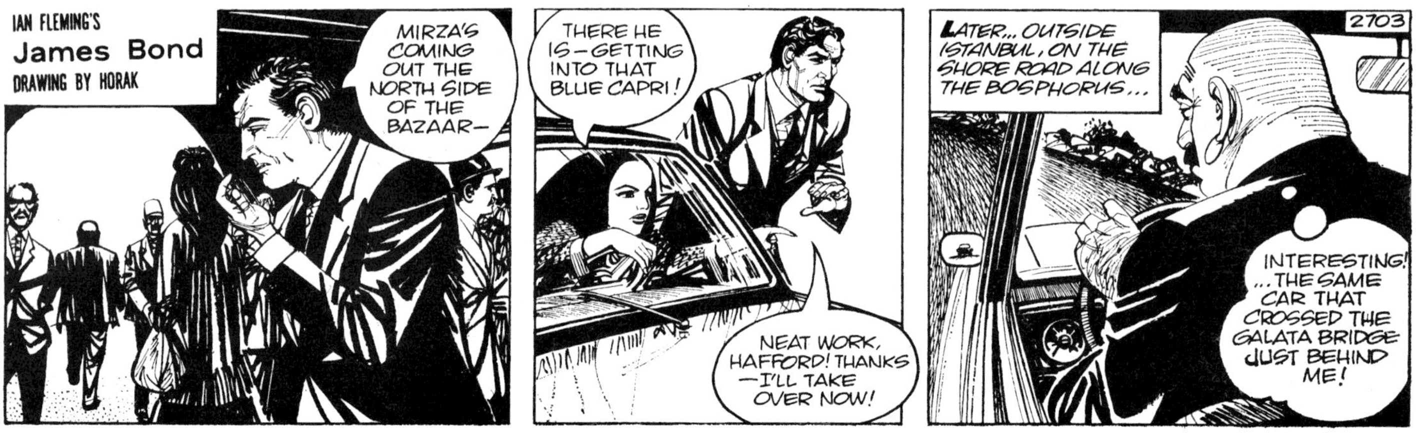
IAN FLEMING'S
James Bond
DRAWING BY HORAK
MIRZA'S COMING OUT THE NORTH SIDE OF THE BAZAAR—
THERE HE IS—GETTING INTO THAT BLUE CAPRI!
NEAT WORK, HAFFORD! THANKS —I'LL TAKE OVER NOW!
2703
LATER... OUTSIDE ISTANBUL, ON THE SHORE ROAD ALONG THE BOSPHORUS...
INTERESTING! ...THE SAME CAR THAT CROSSED THE GALATA BRIDGE JUST BEHIND ME!

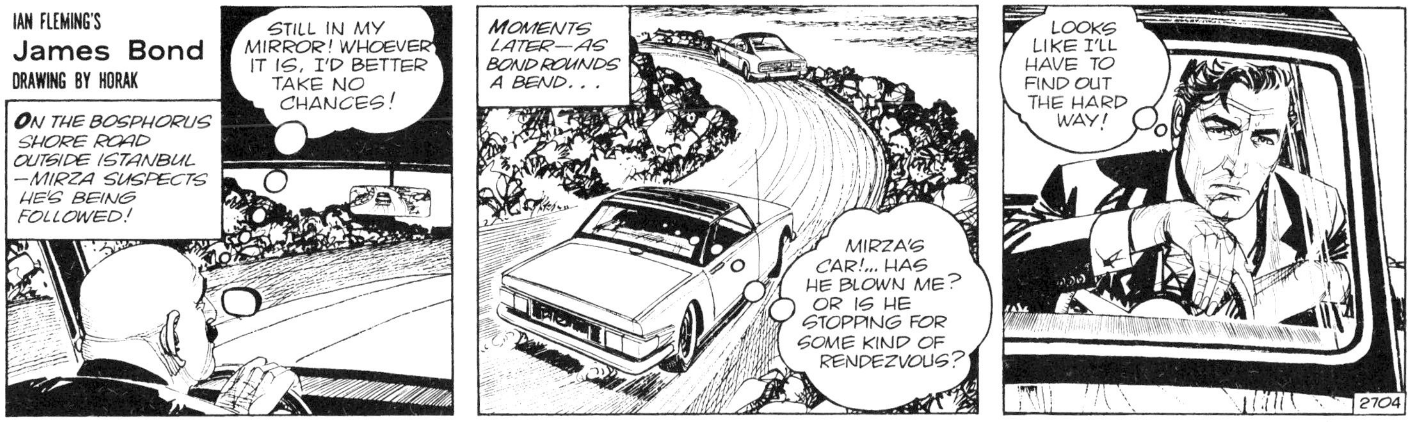
IAN FLEMING'S
James Bond
DRAWING BY HORAK
ON THE BOSPHORUS SHORE ROAD OUTSIDE ISTANBUL —MIRZA SUSPECTS HE'S BEING FOLLOWED!
STILL IN MY MIRROR! WHOEVER IT IS, I'D BETTER TAKE NO CHANCES!
MOMENTS LATER—AS BOND ROUNDS A BEND...
MIRZA'S CAR!... HAS HE BLOWN ME? OR IS HE STOPPING FOR SOME KIND OF RENDEZVOUS?
LOOKS LIKE I'LL HAVE TO FIND OUT THE HARD WAY!
2704

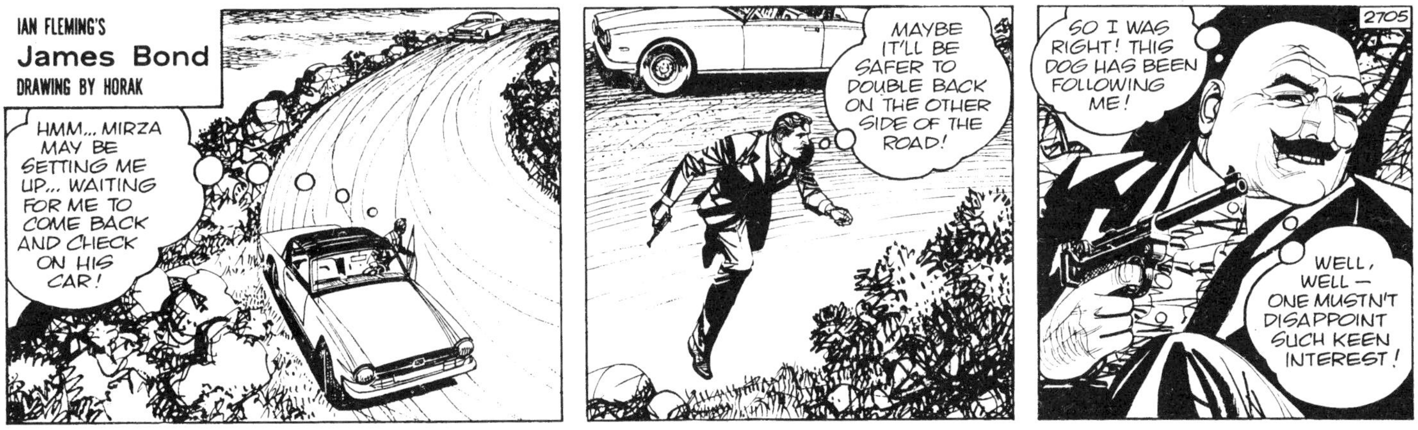
IAN FLEMING'S
James Bond
DRAWING BY HORAK
HMM... MIRZA MAY BE SETTING ME UP... WAITING FOR ME TO COME BACK AND CHECK ON HIS CAR!
MAYBE IT'LL BE SAFER TO DOUBLE BACK ON THE OTHER SIDE OF THE ROAD!
2705
SO I WAS RIGHT! THIS DOG HAS BEEN FOLLOWING ME!
WELL, WELL — ONE MUSTN'T DISAPPOINT SUCH KEEN INTEREST!

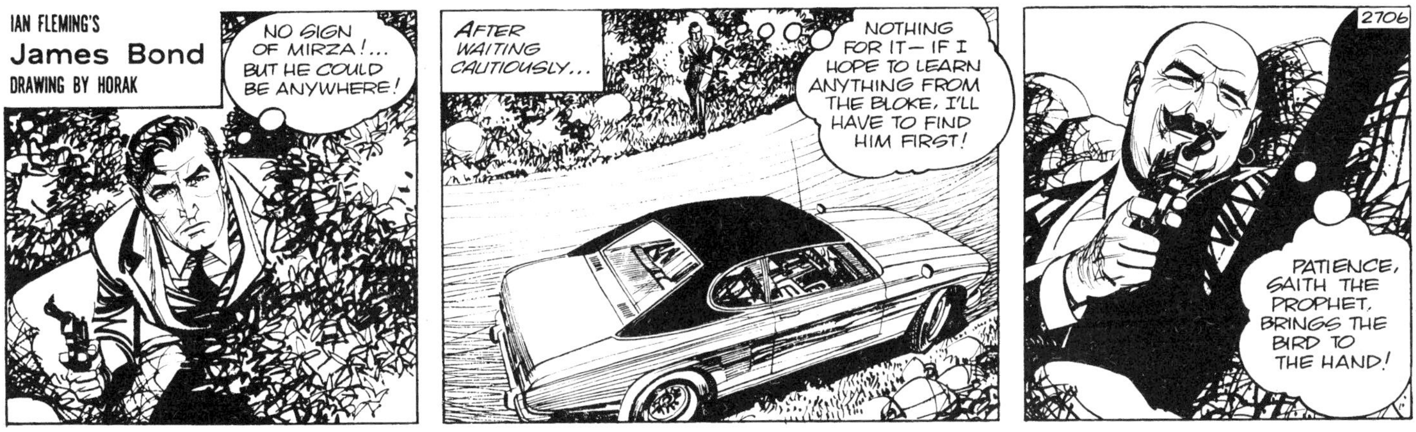
IAN FLEMING'S
James Bond
DRAWING BY HORAK
NO SIGN OF MIRZA!... BUT HE COULD BE ANYWHERE!
AFTER WAITING CAUTIOUSLY...
NOTHING FOR IT— IF I HOPE TO LEARN ANYTHING FROM THE BLOKE, I'LL HAVE TO FIND HIM FIRST!
2706
PATIENCE, SAITH THE PROPHET, BRINGS THE BIRD TO THE HAND!

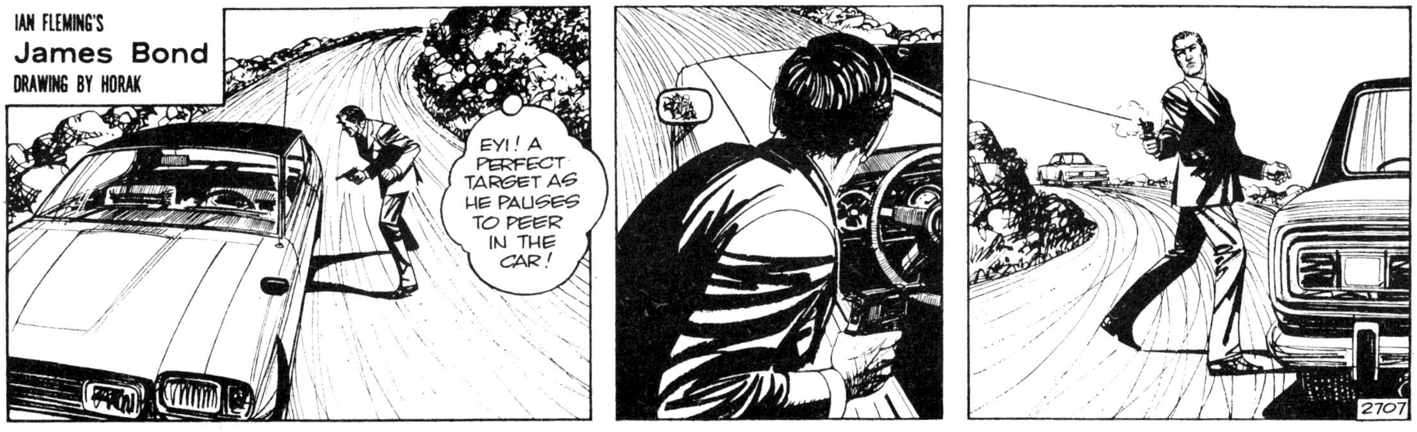
IAN FLEMING'S
James Bond
DRAWING BY HORAK
EYI! A PERFECT TARGET AS HE PAUSES TO PEER IN THE CAR!
2707

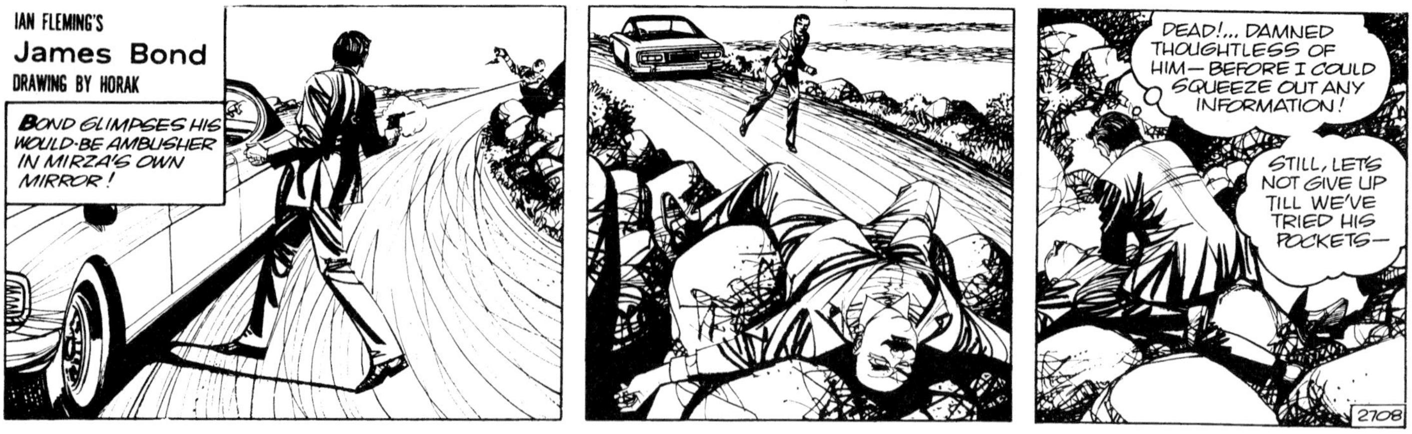
IAN FLEMING'S
James Bond
DRAWING BY HORAK
BOND GLIMPSES HIS WOULD-BE AMBUSHER IN MIRZA'S OWN MIRROR!
DEAD!... DAMNED THOUGHTLESS OF HIM—BEFORE I COULD SQUEEZE OUT ANY INFORMATION!
STILL, LET'S NOT GIVE UP TILL WE'VE TRIED HIS POCKETS—
2708

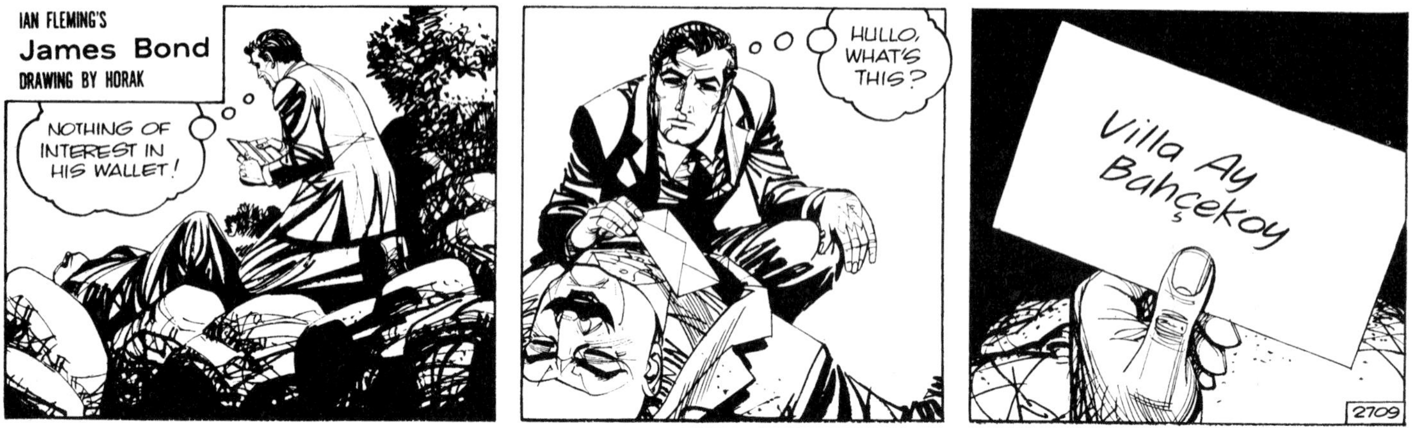
IAN FLEMING'S
James Bond
DRAWING BY HORAK
NOTHING OF INTEREST IN HIS WALLET!
HULLO, WHAT'S THIS?
Villa Ay Bahçekoy
2709

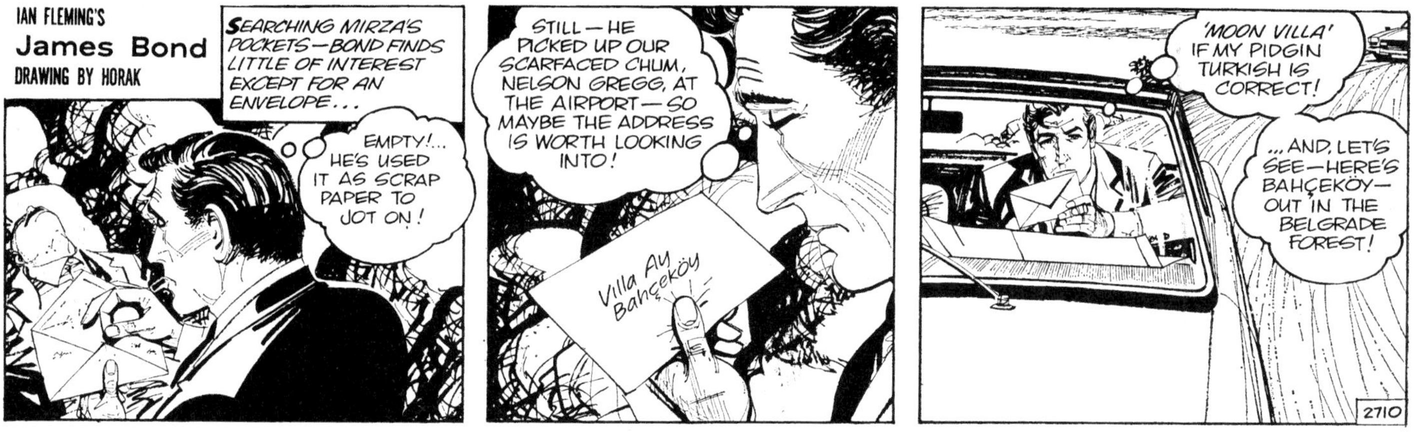
IAN FLEMING'S
James Bond
DRAWING BY HORAK
SEARCHING MIRZA'S POCKETS—BOND FINDS LITTLE OF INTEREST EXCEPT FOR AN ENVELOPE...
EMPTY!... HE'S USED IT AS SCRAP PAPER TO JOT ON!
STILL—HE PICKED UP OUR SCARFACED CHUM, NELSON GREGG, AT THE AIRPORT—SO MAYBE THE ADDRESS IS WORTH LOOKING INTO!
Villa Ay Bahçeköy
'MOON VILLA' IF MY PIDGIN TURKISH IS CORRECT!
...AND, LET'S SEE—HERE'S BAHÇEKÖY—OUT IN THE BELGRADE FOREST!
2710

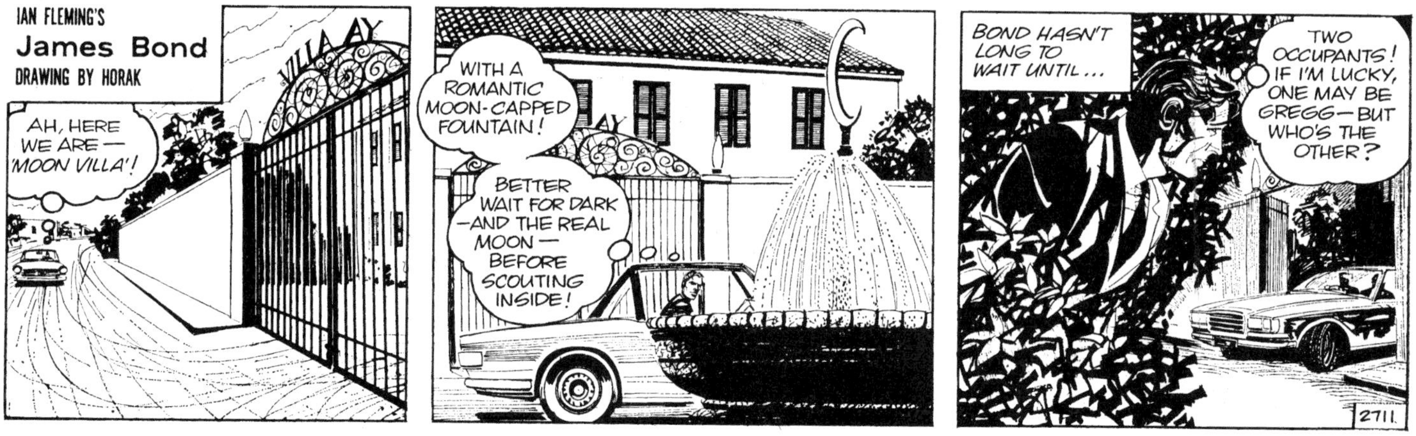
IAN FLEMING'S
James Bond
DRAWING BY HORAK
VILLA AY
AH, HERE WE ARE—'MOON VILLA'!
WITH A ROMANTIC MOON-CAPPED FOUNTAIN!
BETTER WAIT FOR DARK—AND THE REAL MOON—BEFORE SCOUTING INSIDE!
BOND HASN'T LONG TO WAIT UNTIL...
TWO OCCUPANTS! IF I'M LUCKY, ONE MAY BE GREGG—BUT WHO'S THE OTHER?
2711

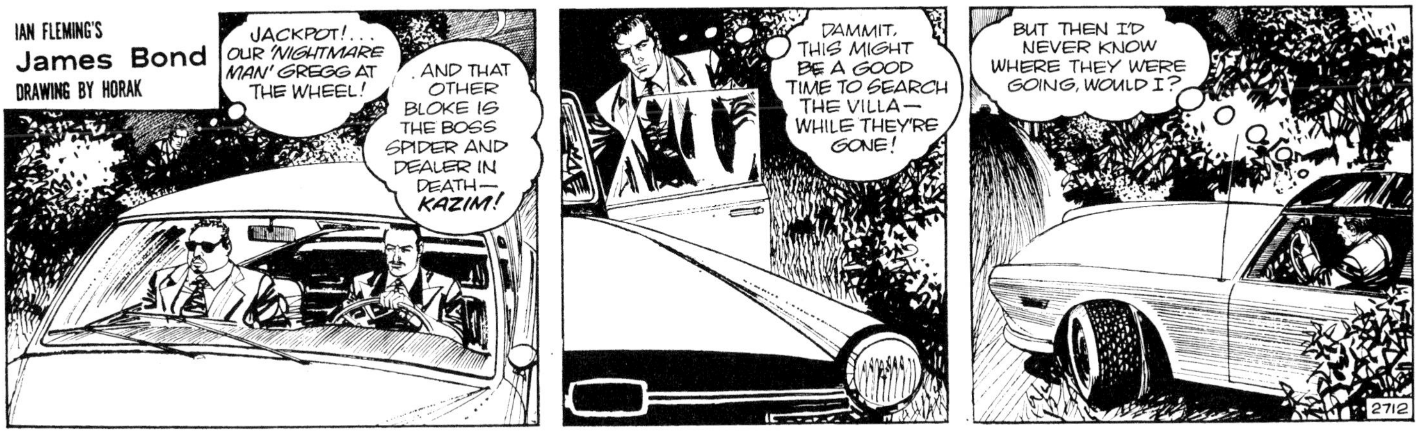
IAN FLEMING'S
James Bond
DRAWING BY HORAK
JACKPOT!... OUR 'NIGHTMARE MAN' GREGG AT THE WHEEL!
...AND THAT OTHER BLOKE IS THE BOSS SPIDER AND DEALER IN DEATH— KAZIM!
DAMMIT, THIS MIGHT BE A GOOD TIME TO SEARCH THE VILLA— WHILE THEY'RE GONE!
BUT THEN I'D NEVER KNOW WHERE THEY WERE GOING, WOULD I?
2712

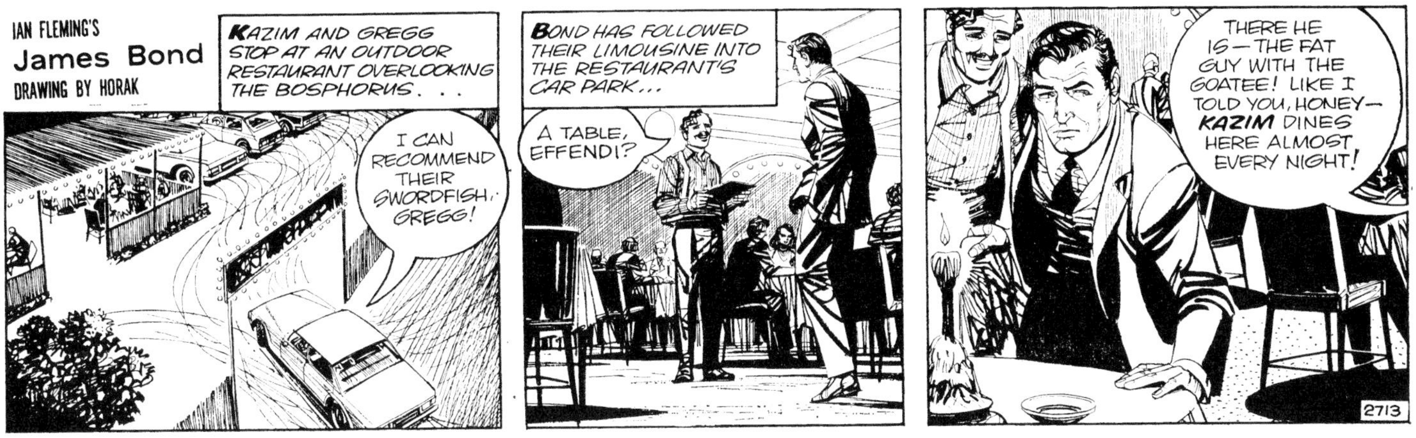
IAN FLEMING'S
James Bond
DRAWING BY HORAK
KAZIM AND GREGG STOP AT AN OUTDOOR RESTAURANT OVERLOOKING THE BOSPHORUS . . .
I CAN RECOMMEND THEIR SWORDFISH, GREGG!
BOND HAS FOLLOWED THEIR LIMOUSINE INTO THE RESTAURANT'S CAR PARK...
A TABLE, EFFENDI?
THERE HE IS—THE FAT GUY WITH THE GOATEE! LIKE I TOLD YOU, HONEY— KAZIM DINES HERE ALMOST EVERY NIGHT!
2713

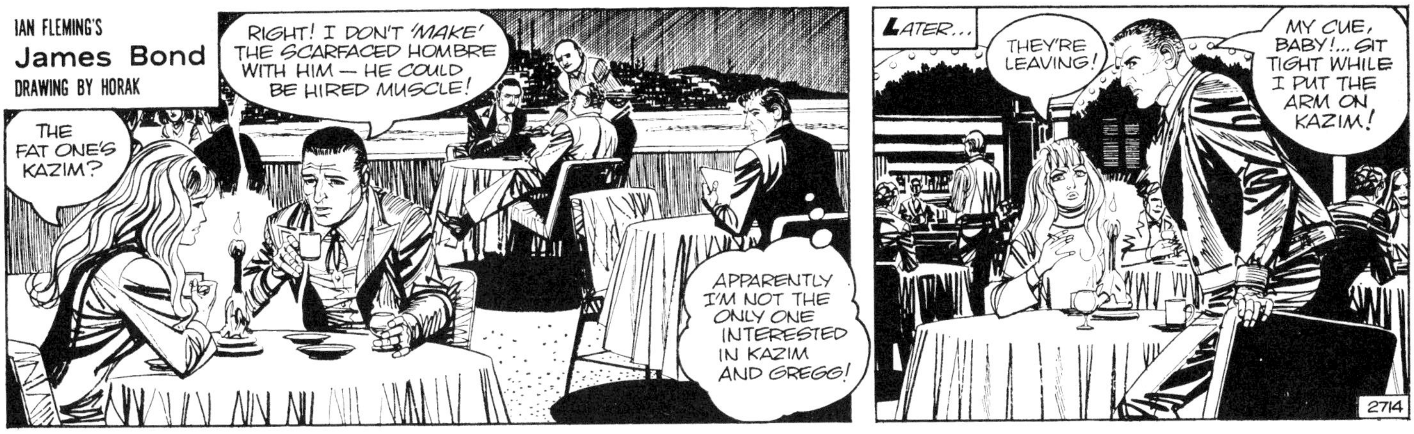
IAN FLEMING'S
James Bond
DRAWING BY HORAK
THE FAT ONE'S KAZIM?
RIGHT! I DON'T 'MAKE' THE SCARFACED HOMBRE WITH HIM — HE COULD BE HIRED MUSCLE!
APPARENTLY I'M NOT THE ONLY ONE INTERESTED IN KAZIM AND GREGG!
LATER...
THEY'RE LEAVING!
MY CUE, BABY!... SIT TIGHT WHILE I PUT THE ARM ON KAZIM!
2714

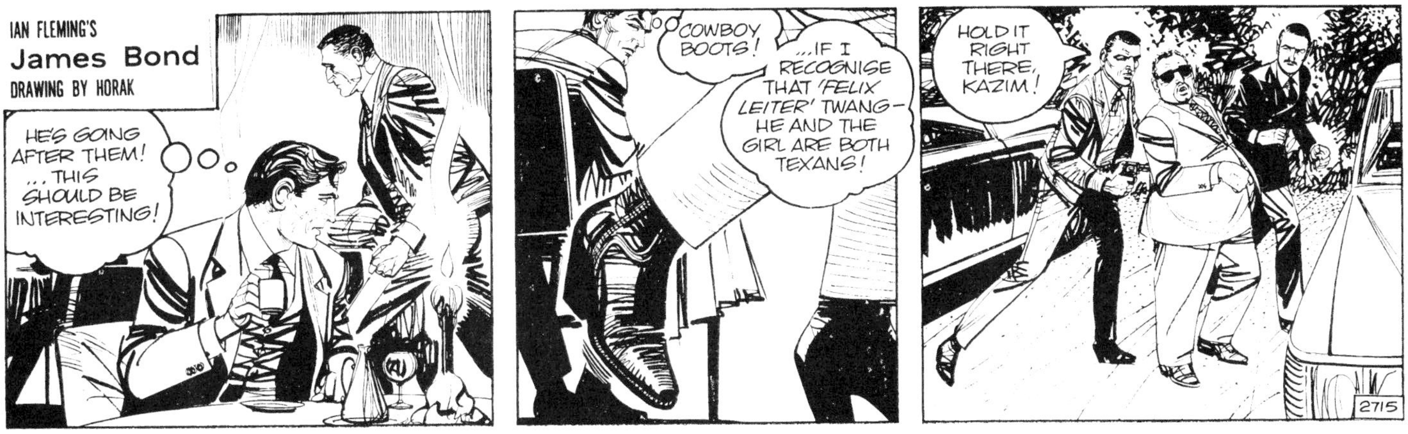
IAN FLEMING'S
James Bond
DRAWING BY HORAK
HE'S GOING AFTER THEM! ...THIS SHOULD BE INTERESTING!
COWBOY BOOTS!
...IF I RECOGNISE THAT 'FELIX LEITER' TWANG— HE AND THE GIRL ARE BOTH TEXANS!
HOLD IT RIGHT THERE, KAZIM!
2715

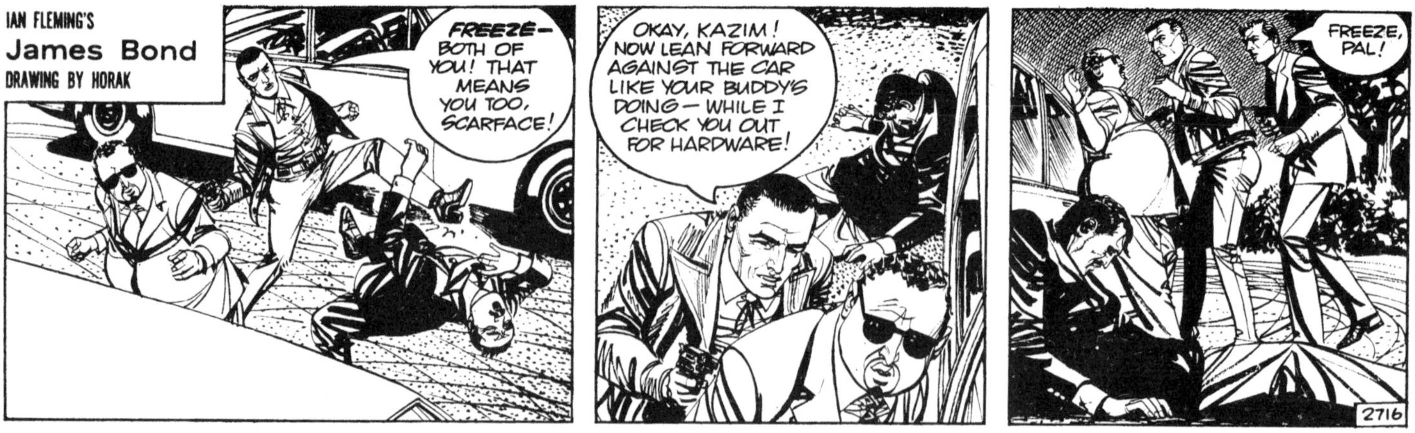
IAN FLEMING'S
James Bond
DRAWING BY HORAK
FREEZE— BOTH OF YOU! THAT MEANS YOU TOO, SCARFACE!
OKAY, KAZIM! NOW LEAN FORWARD AGAINST THE CAR LIKE YOUR BUDDY'S DOING— WHILE I CHECK YOU OUT FOR HARDWARE!
FREEZE, PAL!
2716

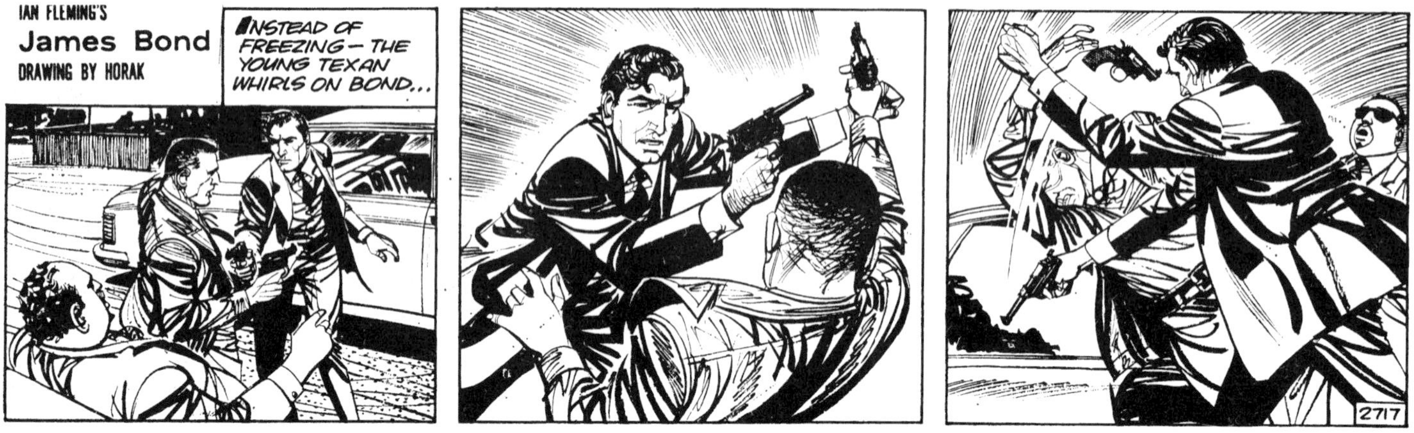
IAN FLEMING'S
James Bond
DRAWING BY HORAK
INSTEAD OF FREEZING— THE YOUNG TEXAN WHIRLS ON BOND...
2717

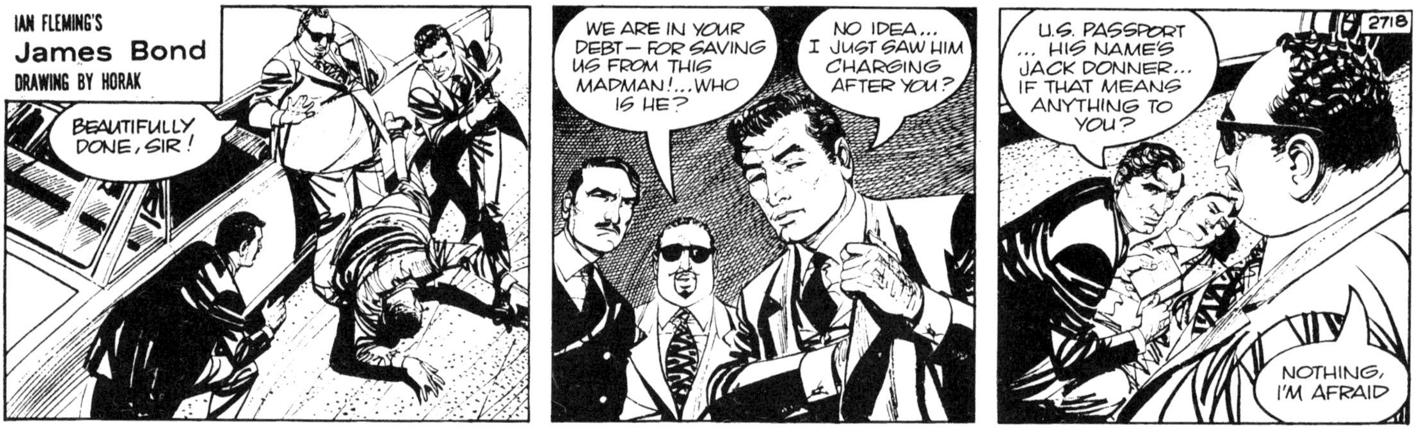
IAN FLEMING'S
James Bond
DRAWING BY HORAK
BEAUTIFULLY DONE, SIR!
WE ARE IN YOUR DEBT— FOR SAVING US FROM THIS MADMAN!... WHO IS HE?
NO IDEA... I JUST SAW HIM CHARGING AFTER YOU?
2718
U.S. PASSPORT ... HIS NAME'S JACK DONNER... IF THAT MEANS ANYTHING TO YOU?
NOTHING, I'M AFRAID

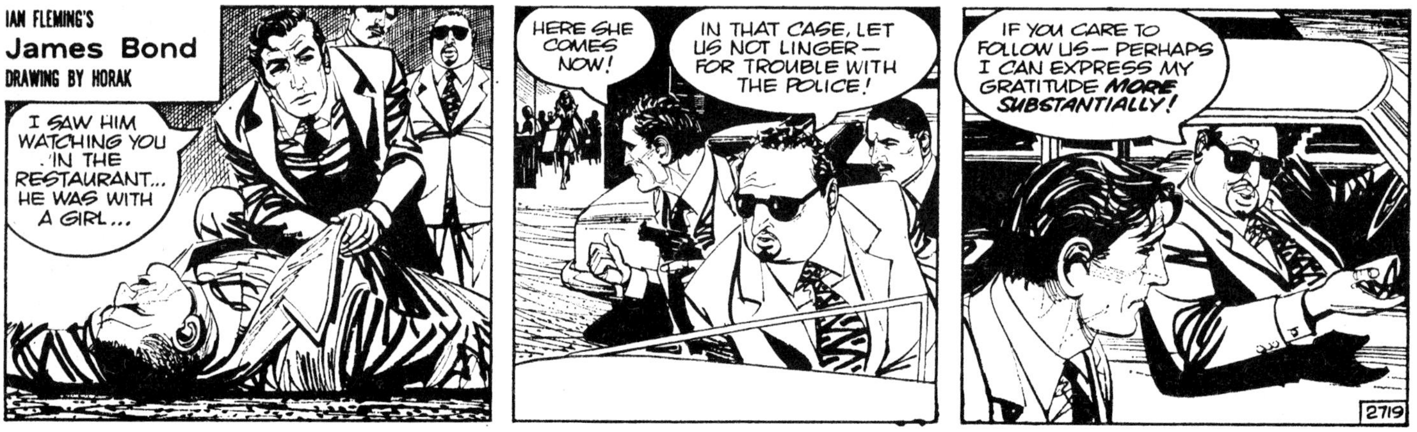
IAN FLEMING'S
James Bond
DRAWING BY HORAK
I SAW HIM WATCHING YOU IN THE RESTAURANT... HE WAS WITH A GIRL...
HERE SHE COMES NOW!
IN THAT CASE, LET US NOT LINGER— FOR TROUBLE WITH THE POLICE!
IF YOU CARE TO FOLLOW US— PERHAPS I CAN EXPRESS MY GRATITUDE MORE SUBSTANTIALLY!
2719

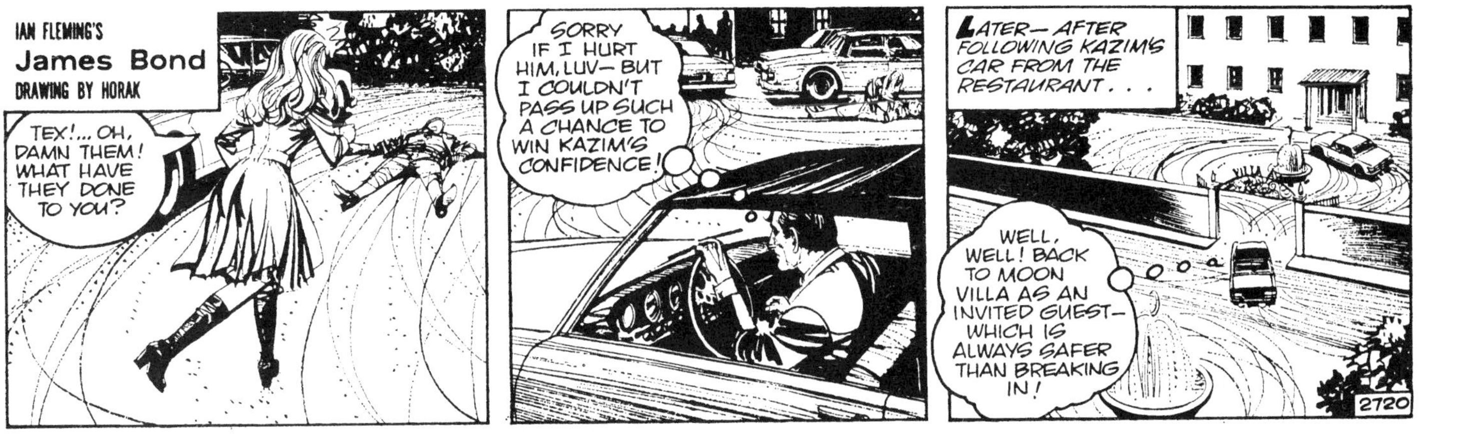
IAN FLEMING'S
James Bond
DRAWING BY HORAK
TEX!... OH, DAMN THEM! WHAT HAVE THEY DONE TO YOU?
SORRY IF I HURT HIM, LUV— BUT I COULDN'T PASS UP SUCH A CHANCE TO WIN KAZIM'S CONFIDENCE!
LATER— AFTER FOLLOWING KAZIM'S CAR FROM THE RESTAURANT . . .
WELL, WELL! BACK TO MOON VILLA AS AN INVITED GUEST— WHICH IS ALWAYS SAFER THAN BREAKING IN!
2720

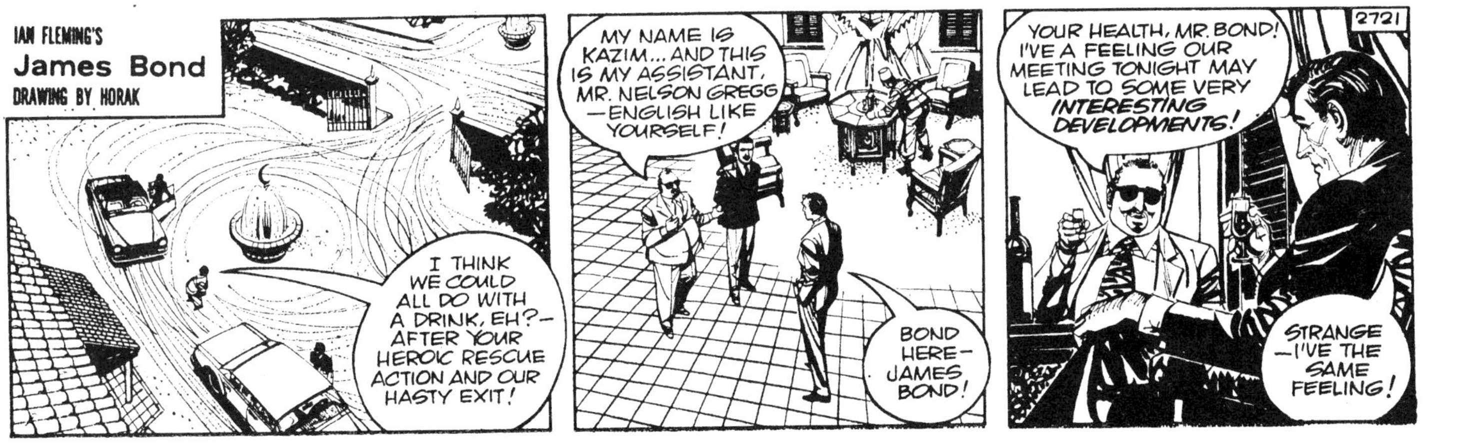
IAN FLEMING'S
James Bond
DRAWING BY HORAK
I THINK WE COULD ALL DO WITH A DRINK, EH?— AFTER YOUR HEROIC RESCUE ACTION AND OUR HASTY EXIT!
MY NAME IS KAZIM... AND THIS IS MY ASSISTANT, MR. NELSON GREGG —ENGLISH LIKE YOURSELF!
BOND HERE— JAMES BOND!
2721
YOUR HEALTH, MR. BOND! I'VE A FEELING OUR MEETING TONIGHT MAY LEAD TO SOME VERY INTERESTING DEVELOPMENTS!
STRANGE —I'VE THE SAME FEELING!

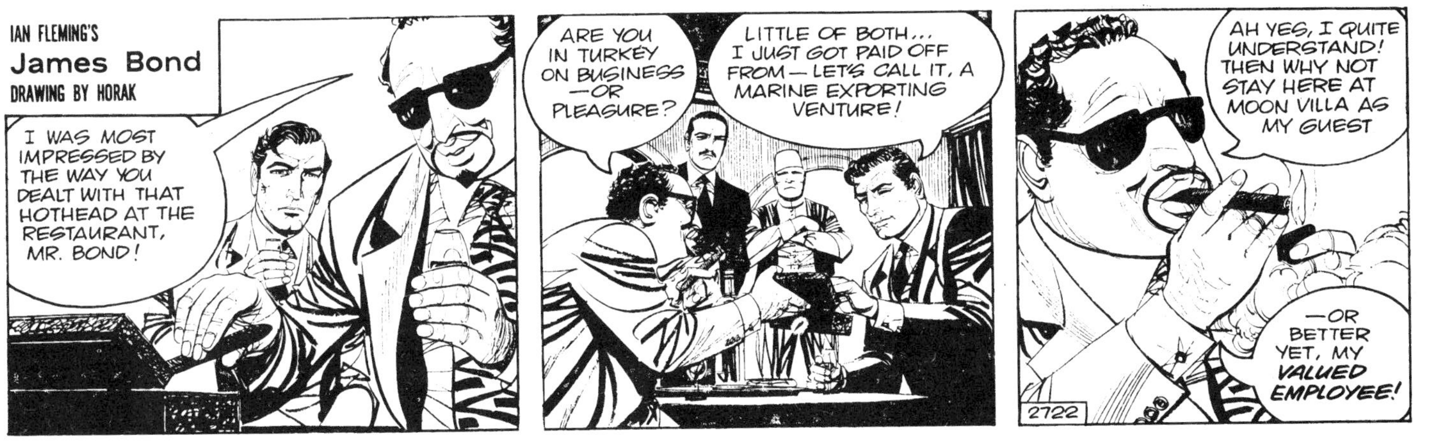
IAN FLEMING'S
James Bond
DRAWING BY HORAK
I WAS MOST IMPRESSED BY THE WAY YOU DEALT WITH THAT HOTHEAD AT THE RESTAURANT, MR. BOND!
ARE YOU IN TURKEY ON BUSINESS —OR PLEASURE?
LITTLE OF BOTH... I JUST GOT PAID OFF FROM— LET'S CALL IT, A MARINE EXPORTING VENTURE!
AH YES, I QUITE UNDERSTAND! THEN WHY NOT STAY HERE AT MOON VILLA AS MY GUEST
—OR BETTER YET, MY VALUED EMPLOYEE!
2722

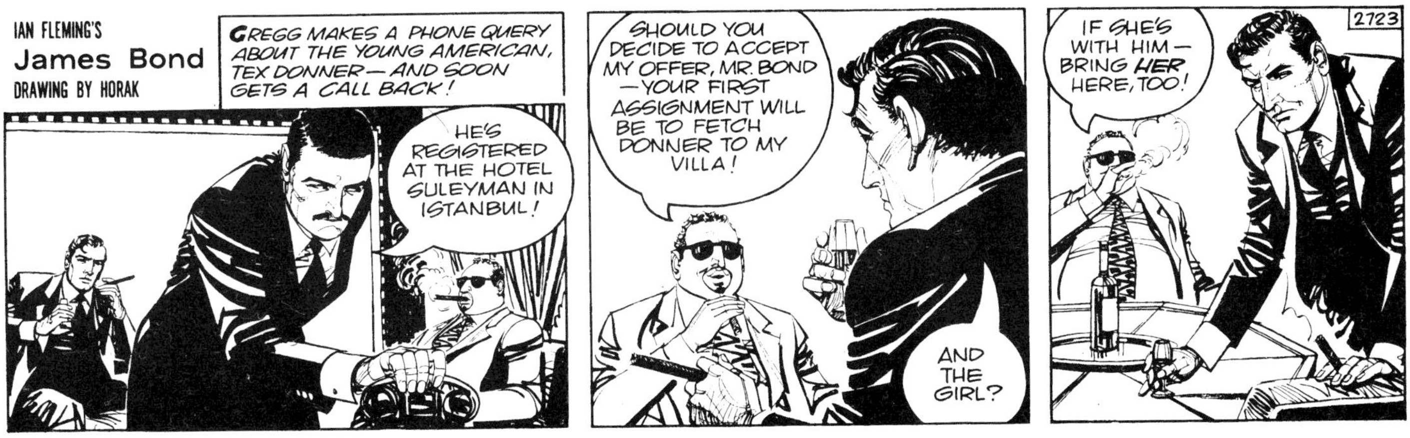
IAN FLEMING'S
James Bond
DRAWING BY HORAK
GREGG MAKES A PHONE QUERY ABOUT THE YOUNG AMERICAN, TEX DONNER— AND SOON GETS A CALL BACK!
HE'S REGISTERED AT THE HOTEL SULEYMAN IN ISTANBUL!
SHOULD YOU DECIDE TO ACCEPT MY OFFER, MR. BOND —YOUR FIRST ASSIGNMENT WILL BE TO FETCH DONNER TO MY VILLA!
AND THE GIRL?
2723
IF SHE'S WITH HIM— BRING HER HERE, TOO!

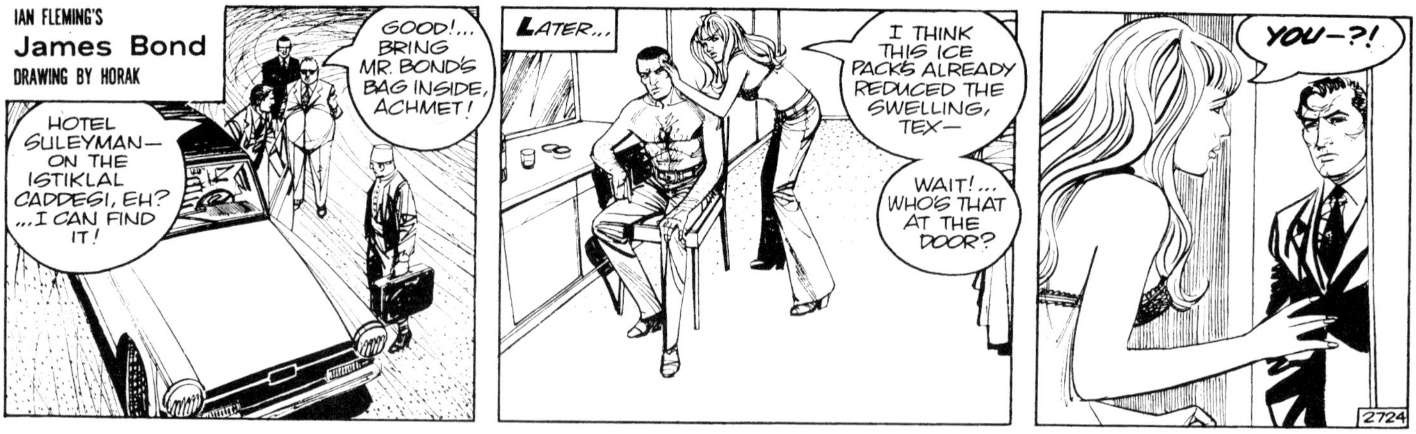
IAN FLEMING'S
James Bond
DRAWING BY HORAK
HOTEL SULEYMAN— ON THE ISTIKLAL CADDESI, EH? ...I CAN FIND IT!
GOOD!... BRING MR. BOND'S BAG INSIDE, ACHMET!
LATER...
I THINK THIS ICE PACK'S ALREADY REDUCED THE SWELLING, TEX—
WAIT!... WHO'S THAT AT THE DOOR?
YOU—?!
2724

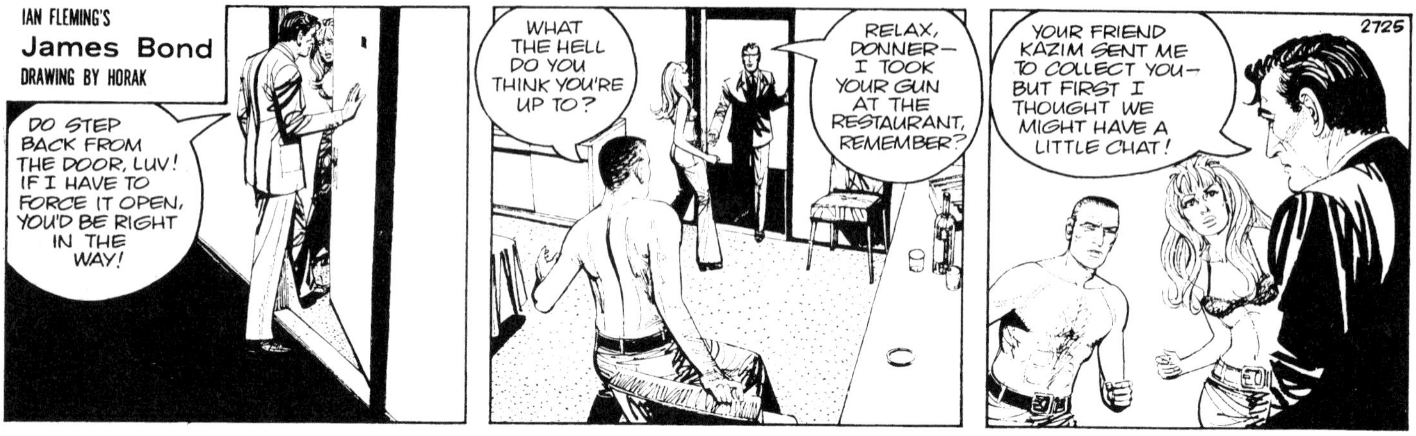
IAN FLEMING'S
James Bond
DRAWING BY HORAK
DO STEP BACK FROM THE DOOR, LUV! IF I HAVE TO FORCE IT OPEN, YOU'D BE RIGHT IN THE WAY!
WHAT THE HELL DO YOU THINK YOU'RE UP TO?
RELAX, DONNER— I TOOK YOUR GUN AT THE RESTAURANT, REMEMBER?
2725
YOUR FRIEND KAZIM SENT ME TO COLLECT YOU— BUT FIRST I THOUGHT WE MIGHT HAVE A LITTLE CHAT!

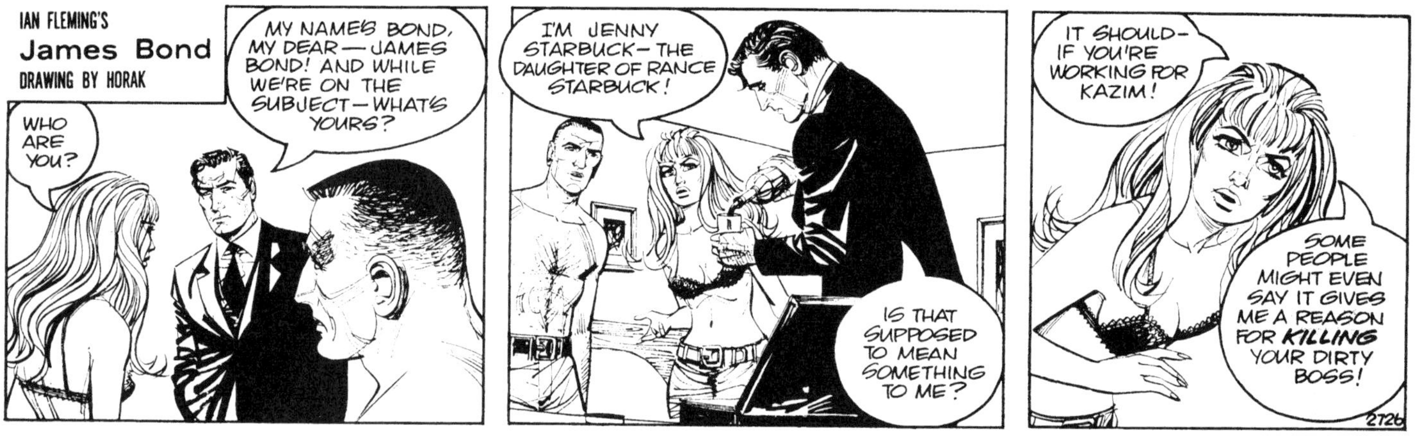
IAN FLEMING'S
James Bond
DRAWING BY HORAK
WHO ARE YOU?
MY NAME'S BOND, MY DEAR — JAMES BOND! AND WHILE WE'RE ON THE SUBJECT— WHAT'S YOURS?
I'M JENNY STARBUCK— THE DAUGHTER OF RANCE STARBUCK!
IS THAT SUPPOSED TO MEAN SOMETHING TO ME?
IT SHOULD— IF YOU'RE WORKING FOR KAZIM!
SOME PEOPLE MIGHT EVEN SAY IT GIVES ME A REASON FOR KILLING YOUR DIRTY BOSS!
2726

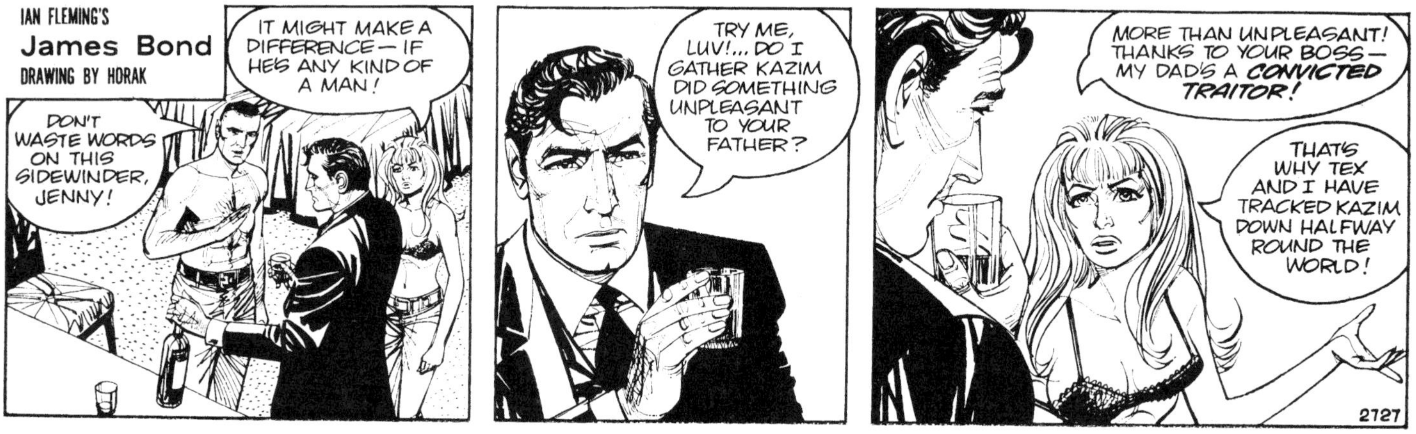
IAN FLEMING'S
James Bond
DRAWING BY HORAK
DON'T WASTE WORDS ON THIS SIDEWINDER, JENNY!
IT MIGHT MAKE A DIFFERENCE— IF HE'S ANY KIND OF A MAN!
TRY ME, LUV!... DO I GATHER KAZIM DID SOMETHING UNPLEASANT TO YOUR FATHER?
MORE THAN UNPLEASANT! THANKS TO YOUR BOSS— MY DAD'S A CONVICTED TRAITOR!
THAT'S WHY TEX AND I HAVE TRACKED KAZIM DOWN HALFWAY ROUND THE WORLD!
2727

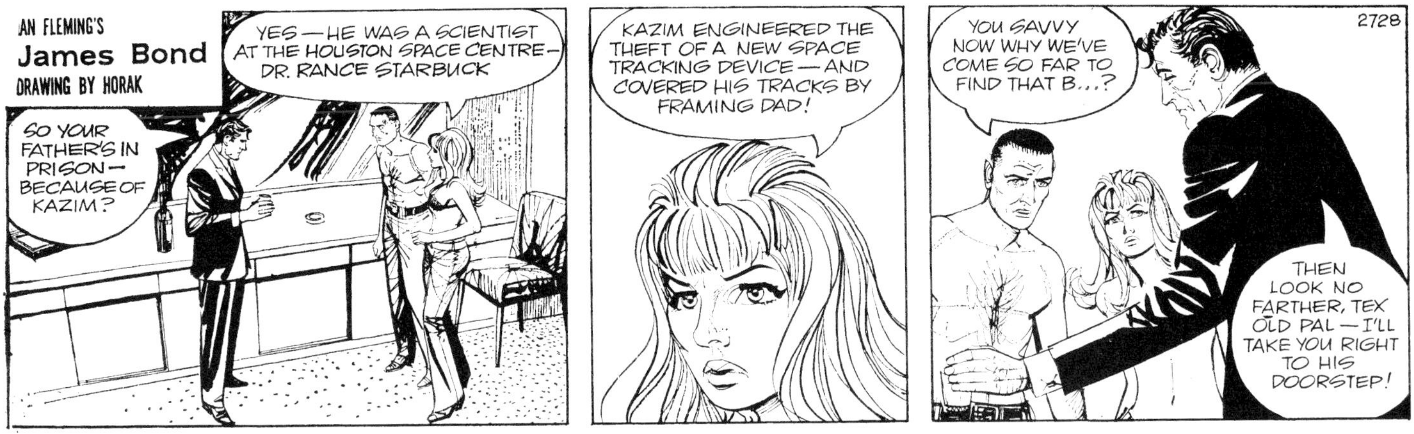
IAN FLEMING'S
James Bond
DRAWING BY HORAK
SO YOUR FATHER'S IN PRISON — BECAUSE OF KAZIM?
YES — HE WAS A SCIENTIST AT THE HOUSTON SPACE CENTRE — DR. RANCE STARBUCK
KAZIM ENGINEERED THE THEFT OF A NEW SPACE TRACKING DEVICE — AND COVERED HIS TRACKS BY FRAMING DAD!
2728
YOU SAVVY NOW WHY WE'VE COME SO FAR TO FIND THAT B...?
THEN LOOK NO FARTHER, TEX OLD PAL — I'LL TAKE YOU RIGHT TO HIS DOORSTEP!

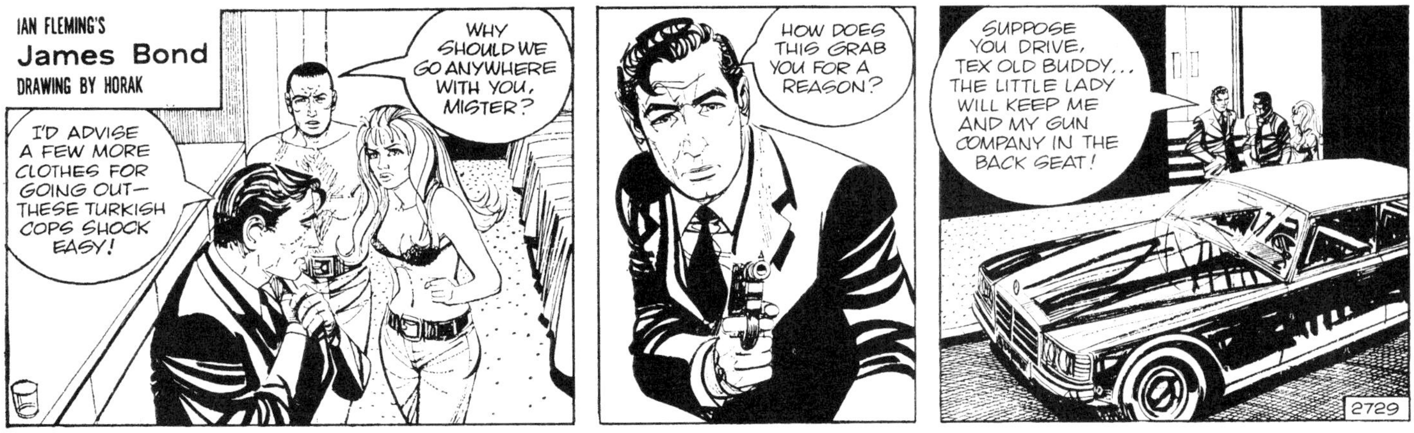
IAN FLEMING'S
James Bond
DRAWING BY HORAK
I'D ADVISE A FEW MORE CLOTHES FOR GOING OUT — THESE TURKISH COPS SHOCK EASY!
WHY SHOULD WE GO ANYWHERE WITH YOU, MISTER?
HOW DOES THIS GRAB YOU FOR A REASON?
SUPPOSE YOU DRIVE, TEX OLD BUDDY... THE LITTLE LADY WILL KEEP ME AND MY GUN COMPANY IN THE BACK SEAT!
2729

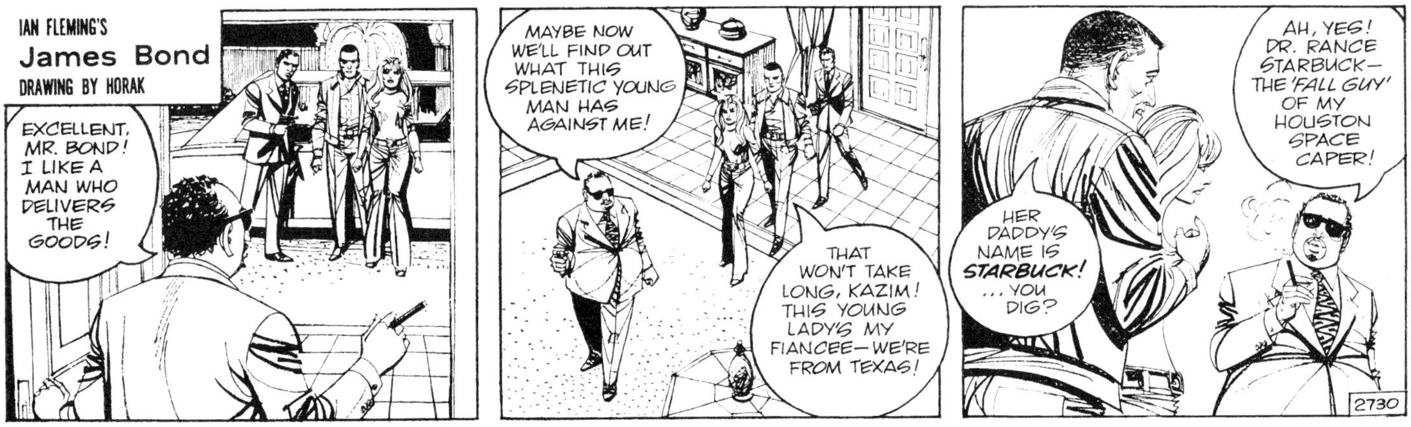
IAN FLEMING'S
James Bond
DRAWING BY HORAK
EXCELLENT, MR. BOND! I LIKE A MAN WHO DELIVERS THE GOODS!
MAYBE NOW WE'LL FIND OUT WHAT THIS SPLENETIC YOUNG MAN HAS AGAINST ME!
THAT WON'T TAKE LONG, KAZIM! THIS YOUNG LADY'S MY FIANCEE — WE'RE FROM TEXAS!
HER DADDY'S NAME IS STARBUCK! ... YOU DIG?
AH, YES! DR. RANCE STARBUCK — THE 'FALL GUY' OF MY HOUSTON SPACE CAPER!
2730

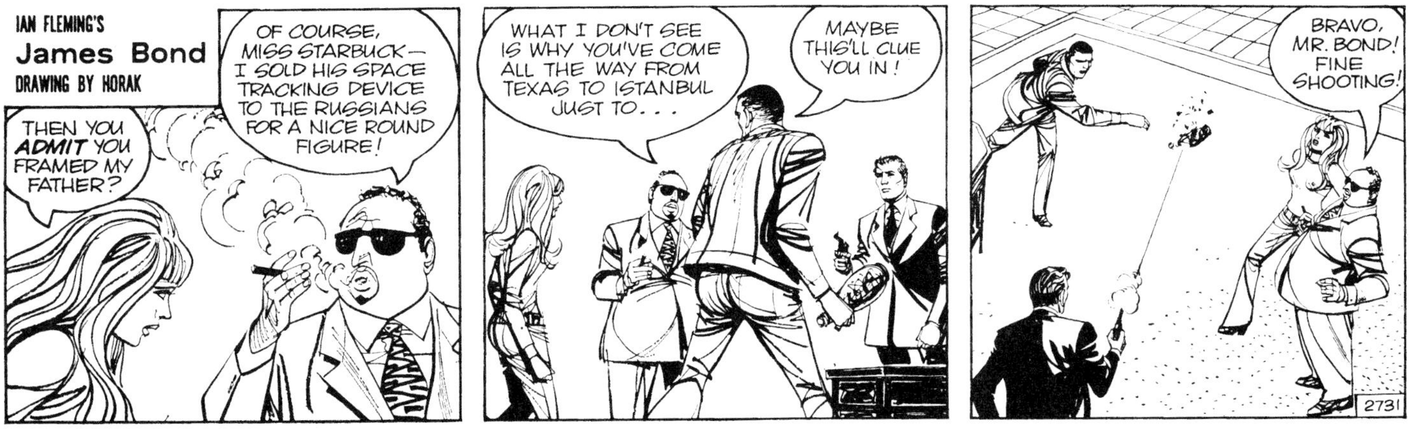
IAN FLEMING'S
James Bond
DRAWING BY HORAK
THEN YOU ADMIT YOU FRAMED MY FATHER?
OF COURSE, MISS STARBUCK — I SOLD HIS SPACE TRACKING DEVICE TO THE RUSSIANS FOR A NICE ROUND FIGURE!
WHAT I DON'T SEE IS WHY YOU'VE COME ALL THE WAY FROM TEXAS TO ISTANBUL JUST TO...
MAYBE THIS'LL CLUE YOU IN!
BRAVO, MR. BOND! FINE SHOOTING!
2731

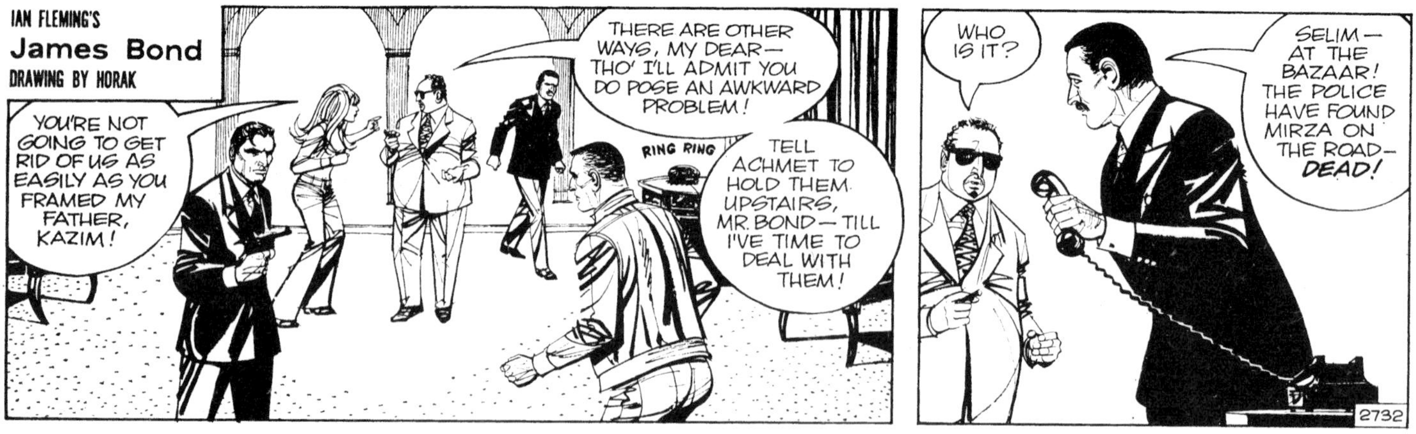
IAN FLEMING'S
James Bond
DRAWING BY HORAK
YOU'RE NOT GOING TO GET RID OF US AS EASILY AS YOU FRAMED MY FATHER, KAZIM!
THERE ARE OTHER WAYS, MY DEAR— THO' I'LL ADMIT YOU DO POSE AN AWKWARD PROBLEM!
RING RING
TELL ACHMET TO HOLD THEM UPSTAIRS, MR. BOND— TILL I'VE TIME TO DEAL WITH THEM!
WHO IS IT?
SELIM— AT THE BAZAAR! THE POLICE HAVE FOUND MIRZA ON THE ROAD— DEAD!
2732

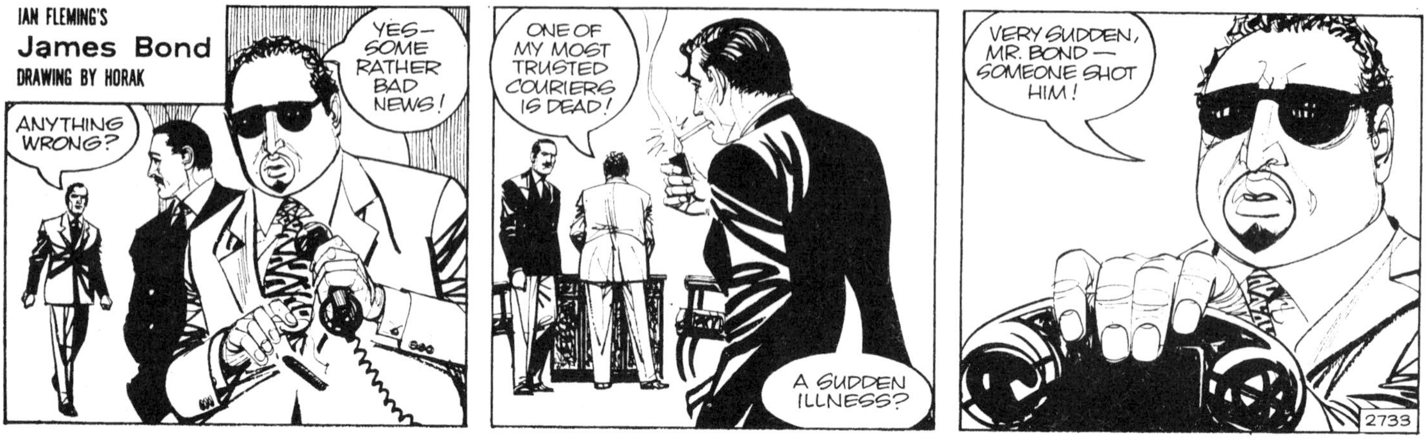
IAN FLEMING'S
James Bond
DRAWING BY HORAK
ANYTHING WRONG?
YES— SOME RATHER BAD NEWS!
ONE OF MY MOST TRUSTED COURIERS IS DEAD!
A SUDDEN ILLNESS?
VERY SUDDEN, MR. BOND— SOMEONE SHOT HIM!
2733

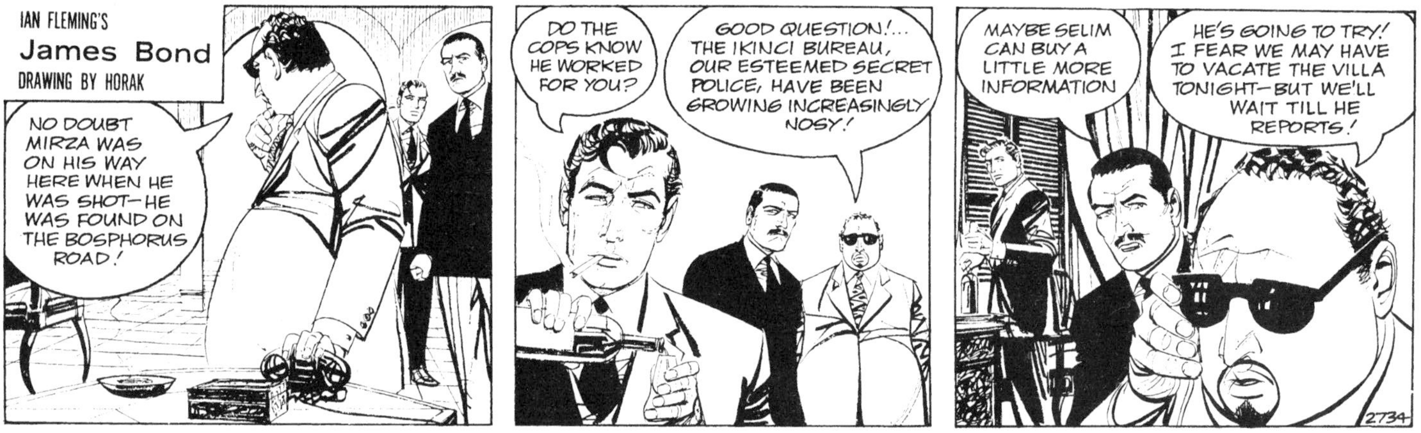
IAN FLEMING'S
James Bond
DRAWING BY HORAK
NO DOUBT MIRZA WAS ON HIS WAY HERE WHEN HE WAS SHOT— HE WAS FOUND ON THE BOSPHORUS ROAD!
DO THE COPS KNOW HE WORKED FOR YOU?
GOOD QUESTION!... THE IKINCI BUREAU, OUR ESTEEMED SECRET POLICE, HAVE BEEN GROWING INCREASINGLY NOSY!
MAYBE SELIM CAN BUY A LITTLE MORE INFORMATION
HE'S GOING TO TRY! I FEAR WE MAY HAVE TO VACATE THE VILLA TONIGHT— BUT WE'LL WAIT TILL HE REPORTS!
2734

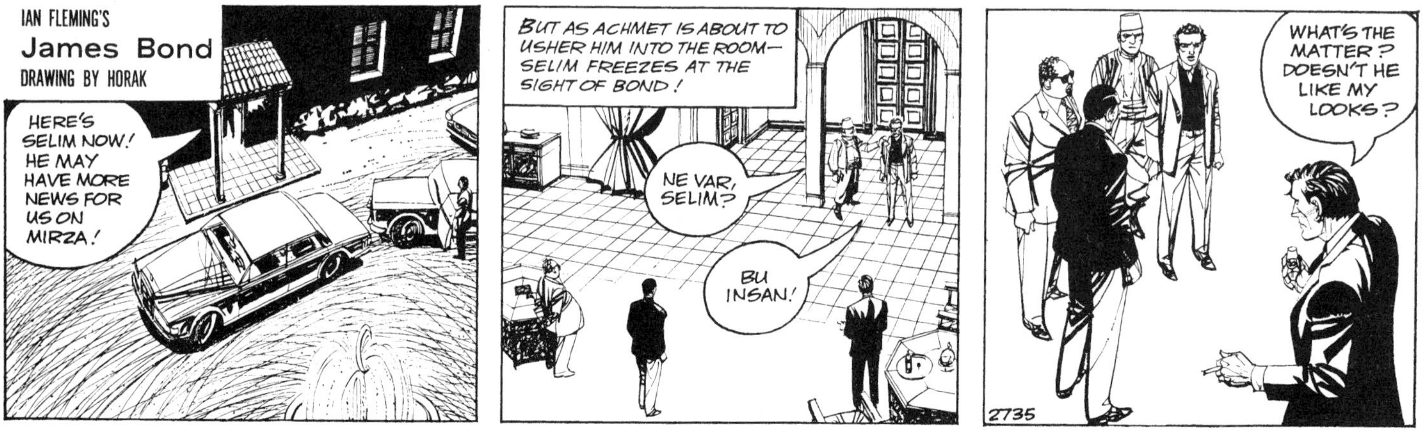
IAN FLEMING'S
James Bond
DRAWING BY HORAK
HERE'S SELIM NOW! HE MAY HAVE MORE NEWS FOR US ON MIRZA!
BUT AS ACHMET IS ABOUT TO USHER HIM INTO THE ROOM— SELIM FREEZES AT THE SIGHT OF BOND!
NE VAR, SELIM?
BU INSAN!
WHAT'S THE MATTER? DOESN'T HE LIKE MY LOOKS?
2735

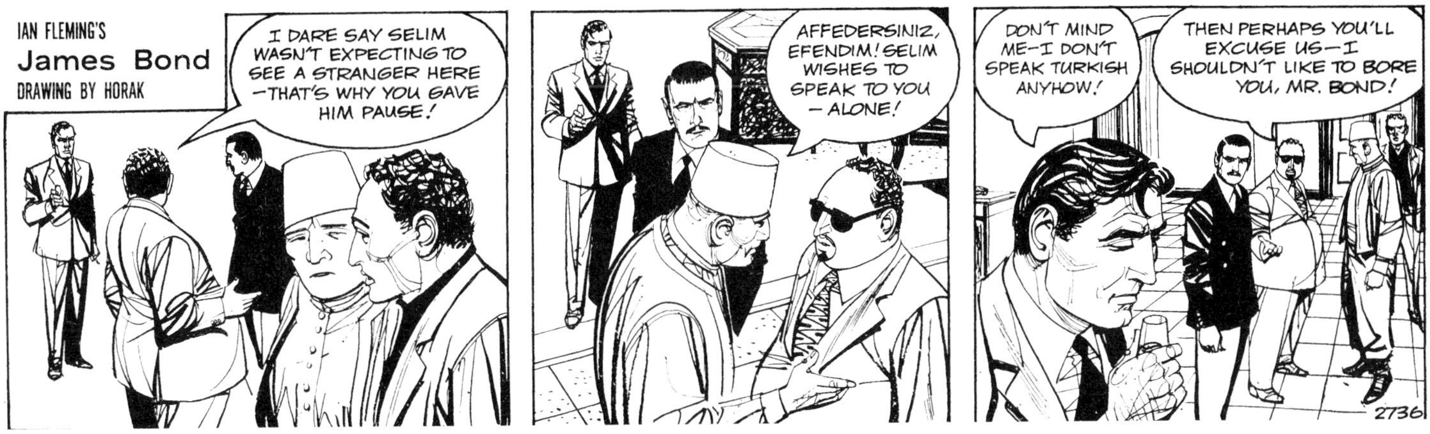
IAN FLEMING'S
James Bond
DRAWING BY HORAK
I DARE SAY SELIM WASN'T EXPECTING TO SEE A STRANGER HERE —THAT'S WHY YOU GAVE HIM PAUSE!
AFFEDERSINIZ, EFENDIM! SELIM WISHES TO SPEAK TO YOU —ALONE!
DON'T MIND ME—I DON'T SPEAK TURKISH ANYHOW!
THEN PERHAPS YOU'LL EXCUSE US—I SHOULDN'T LIKE TO BORE YOU, MR. BOND!
2736

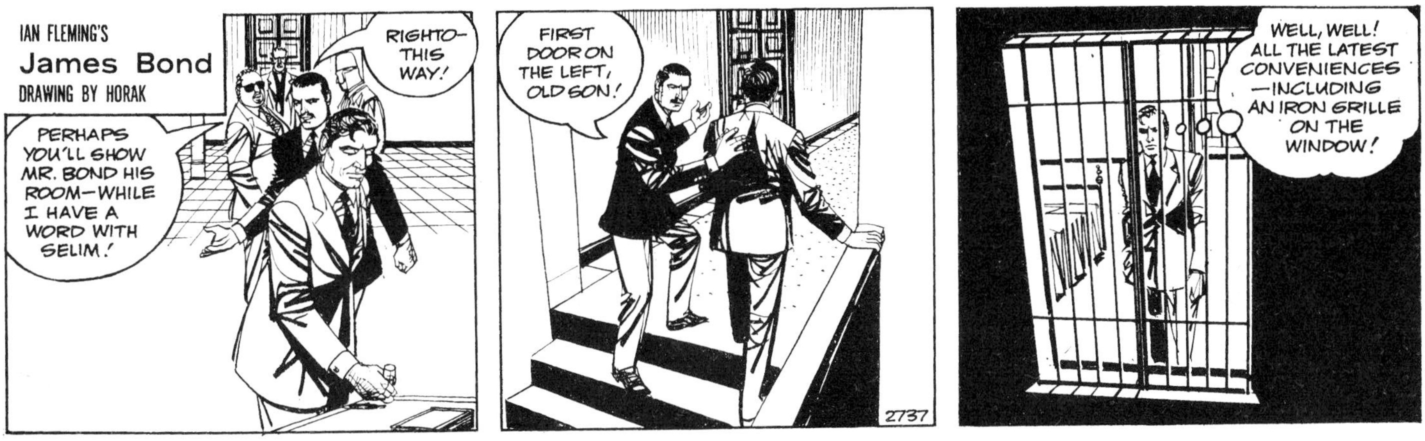
IAN FLEMING'S
James Bond
DRAWING BY HORAK
PERHAPS YOU'LL SHOW MR. BOND HIS ROOM—WHILE I HAVE A WORD WITH SELIM!
RIGHTO—THIS WAY!
FIRST DOOR ON THE LEFT, OLD SON!
2737
WELL, WELL! ALL THE LATEST CONVENIENCES —INCLUDING AN IRON GRILLE ON THE WINDOW!

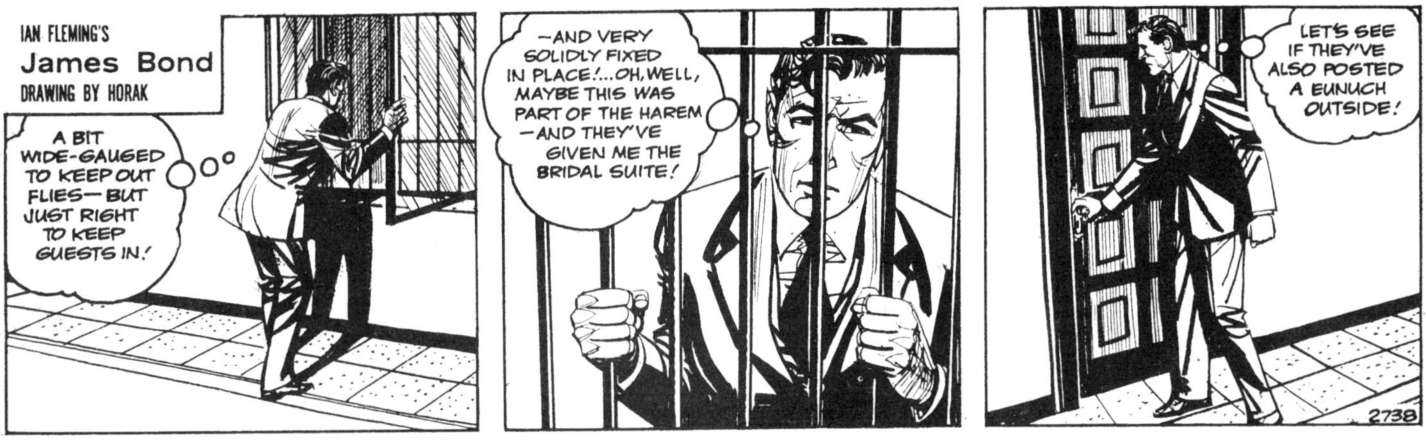
IAN FLEMING'S
James Bond
DRAWING BY HORAK
A BIT WIDE-GAUGED TO KEEP OUT FLIES—BUT JUST RIGHT TO KEEP GUESTS IN!
—AND VERY SOLIDLY FIXED IN PLACE!...OH, WELL, MAYBE THIS WAS PART OF THE HAREM —AND THEY'VE GIVEN ME THE BRIDAL SUITE!
LET'S SEE IF THEY'VE ALSO POSTED A EUNUCH OUTSIDE!
2738

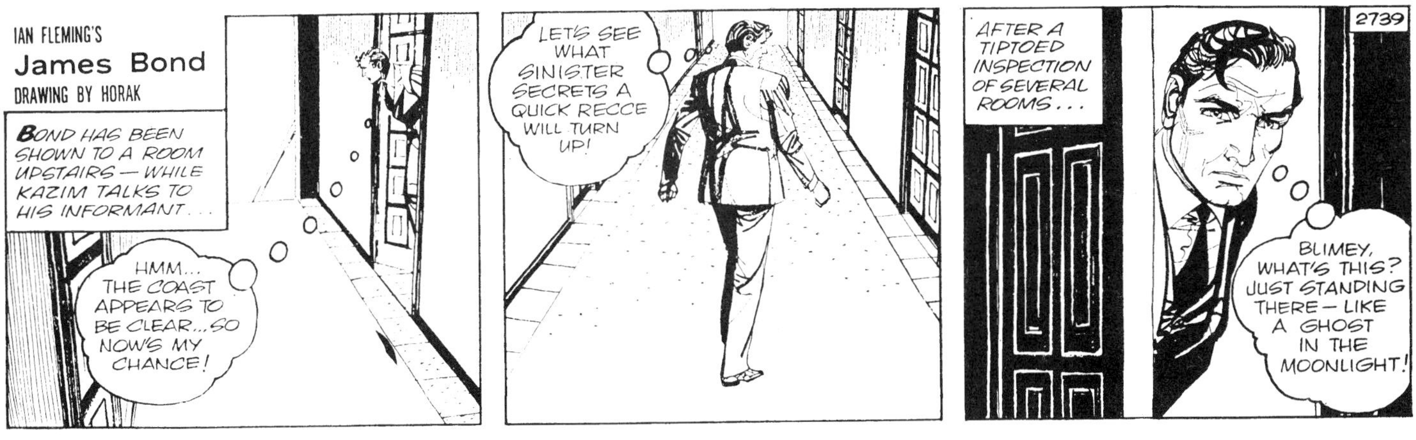
IAN FLEMING'S
James Bond
DRAWING BY HORAK
BOND HAS BEEN SHOWN TO A ROOM UPSTAIRS — WHILE KAZIM TALKS TO HIS INFORMANT . . .
HMM... THE COAST APPEARS TO BE CLEAR...SO NOW'S MY CHANCE!
LET'S SEE WHAT SINISTER SECRETS A QUICK RECCE WILL TURN UP!
AFTER A TIPTOED INSPECTION OF SEVERAL ROOMS . . .
2739
BLIMEY, WHAT'S THIS? JUST STANDING THERE— LIKE A GHOST IN THE MOONLIGHT!

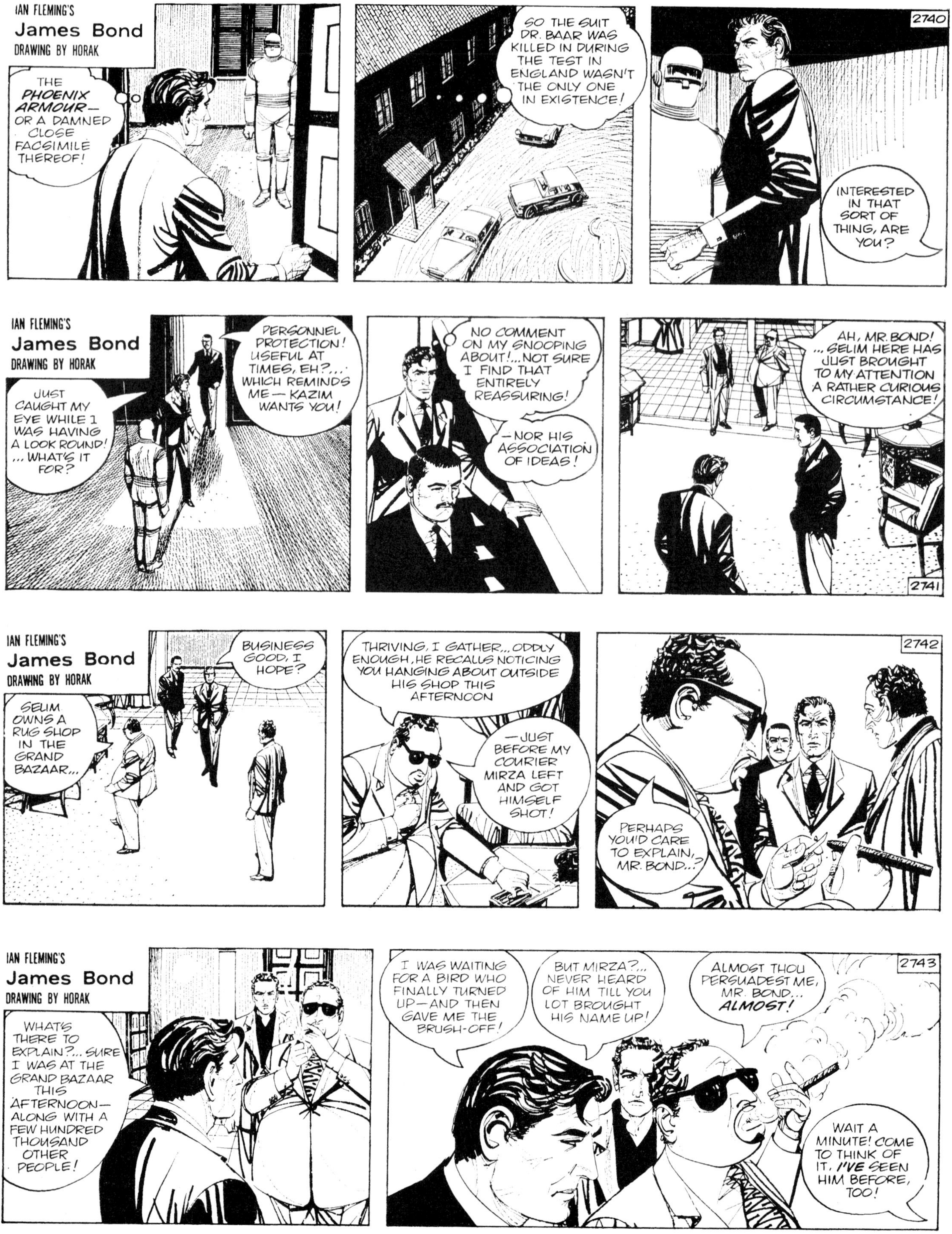
IAN FLEMING'S
James Bond
DRAWING BY HORAK
THE PHOENIX ARMOUR— OR A DAMNED CLOSE FACSIMILE THEREOF!
SO THE SUIT DR. BAAR WAS KILLED IN DURING THE TEST IN ENGLAND WASN'T THE ONLY ONE IN EXISTENCE!
2740
INTERESTED IN THAT SORT OF THING, ARE YOU?
IAN FLEMING'S
James Bond
DRAWING BY HORAK
JUST CAUGHT MY EYE WHILE I WAS HAVING A LOOK ROUND! ... WHAT'S IT FOR?
PERSONNEL PROTECTION! USEFUL AT TIMES, EH?... WHICH REMINDS ME — KAZIM WANTS YOU!
NO COMMENT ON MY SNOOPING ABOUT!... NOT SURE I FIND THAT ENTIRELY REASSURING!
—NOR HIS ASSOCIATION OF IDEAS!
AH, MR. BOND! ... SELIM HERE HAS JUST BROUGHT TO MY ATTENTION A RATHER CURIOUS CIRCUMSTANCE!
2741
IAN FLEMING'S
James Bond
DRAWING BY HORAK
SELIM OWNS A RUG SHOP IN THE GRAND BAZAAR...
BUSINESS GOOD, I HOPE?
THRIVING, I GATHER... ODDLY ENOUGH, HE RECALLS NOTICING YOU HANGING ABOUT OUTSIDE HIS SHOP THIS AFTERNOON
—JUST BEFORE MY COURIER MIRZA LEFT AND GOT HIMSELF SHOT!
2742
PERHAPS YOU'D CARE TO EXPLAIN, MR. BOND...?
IAN FLEMING'S
James Bond
DRAWING BY HORAK
WHAT'S THERE TO EXPLAIN?... SURE I WAS AT THE GRAND BAZAAR THIS AFTERNOON— ALONG WITH A FEW HUNDRED THOUSAND OTHER PEOPLE!
I WAS WAITING FOR A BIRD WHO FINALLY TURNED UP—AND THEN GAVE ME THE BRUSH-OFF!
BUT MIRZA?... NEVER HEARD OF HIM TILL YOU LOT BROUGHT HIS NAME UP!
ALMOST THOU PERSUADEST ME, MR. BOND... ALMOST!
2743
WAIT A MINUTE! COME TO THINK OF IT, I'VE SEEN HIM BEFORE, TOO!

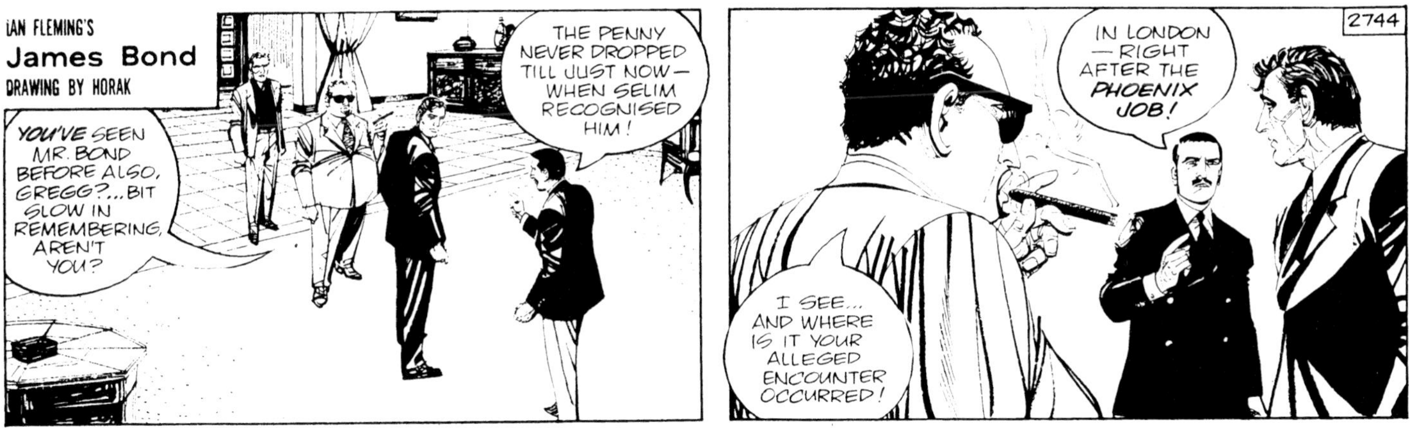
IAN FLEMING'S
James Bond
DRAWING BY HORAK
YOU'VE SEEN MR. BOND BEFORE ALSO, GREGG?... BIT SLOW IN REMEMBERING, AREN'T YOU?
THE PENNY NEVER DROPPED TILL JUST NOW— WHEN SELIM RECOGNISED HIM!
2744
I SEE... AND WHERE IS IT YOUR ALLEGED ENCOUNTER OCCURRED!
IN LONDON —RIGHT AFTER THE PHOENIX JOB!

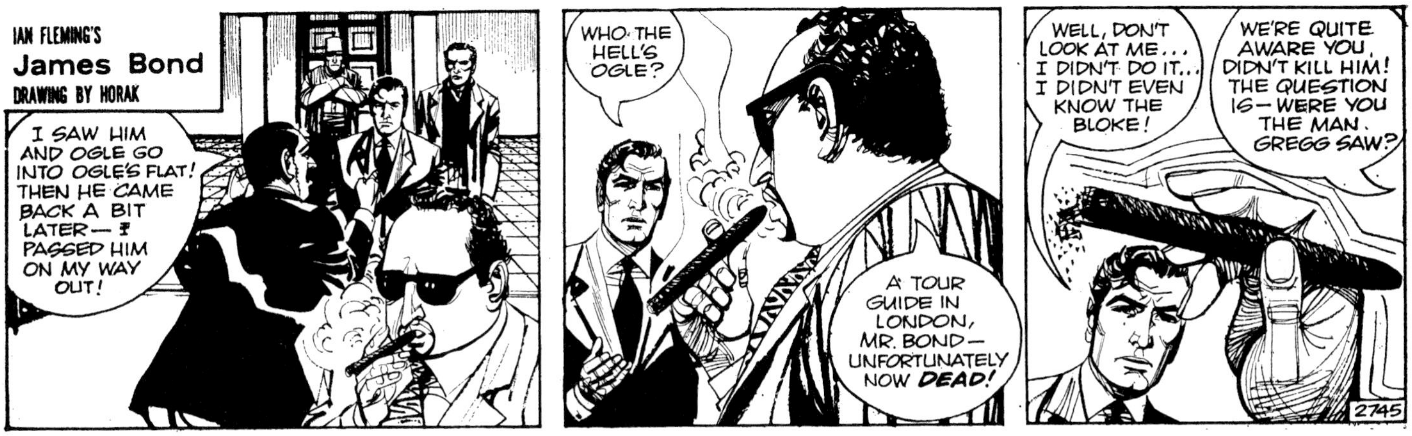
IAN FLEMING'S
James Bond
DRAWING BY HORAK
I SAW HIM AND OGLE GO INTO OGLE'S FLAT! THEN HE CAME BACK A BIT LATER— I PASSED HIM ON MY WAY OUT!
WHO THE HELL'S OGLE?
A TOUR GUIDE IN LONDON, MR. BOND— UNFORTUNATELY NOW DEAD!
WELL, DON'T LOOK AT ME... I DIDN'T DO IT... I DIDN'T EVEN KNOW THE BLOKE!
WE'RE QUITE AWARE YOU DIDN'T KILL HIM! THE QUESTION IS—WERE YOU THE MAN GREGG SAW?
2745

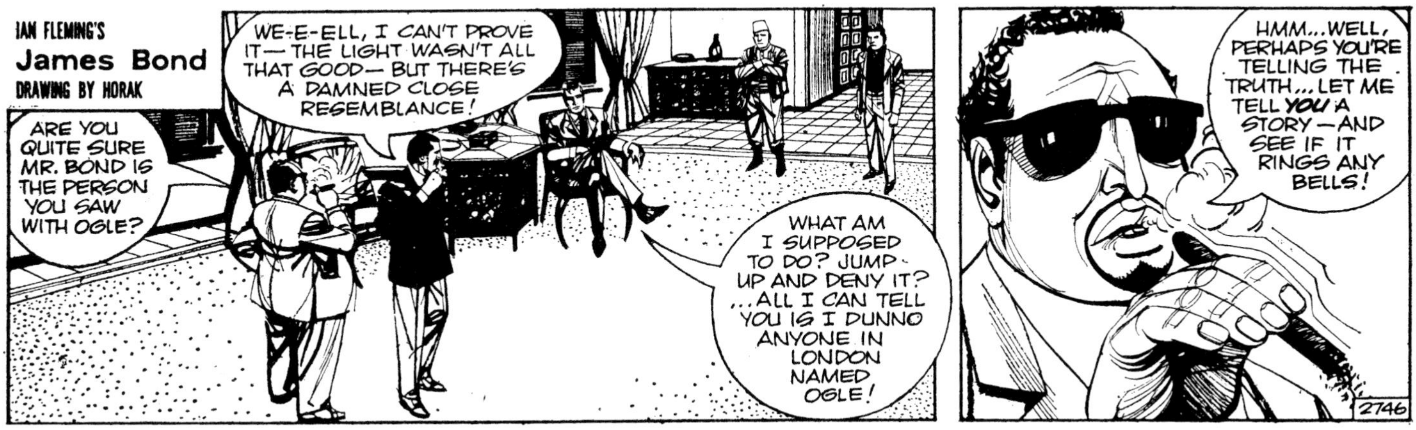
IAN FLEMING'S
James Bond
DRAWING BY HORAK
ARE YOU QUITE SURE MR. BOND IS THE PERSON YOU SAW WITH OGLE?
WE-E-ELL, I CAN'T PROVE IT— THE LIGHT WASN'T ALL THAT GOOD— BUT THERE'S A DAMNED CLOSE RESEMBLANCE!
WHAT AM I SUPPOSED TO DO? JUMP UP AND DENY IT? ...ALL I CAN TELL YOU IS I DUNNO ANYONE IN LONDON NAMED OGLE!
HMM...WELL, PERHAPS YOU'RE TELLING THE TRUTH... LET ME TELL YOU A STORY—AND SEE IF IT RINGS ANY BELLS!
2746

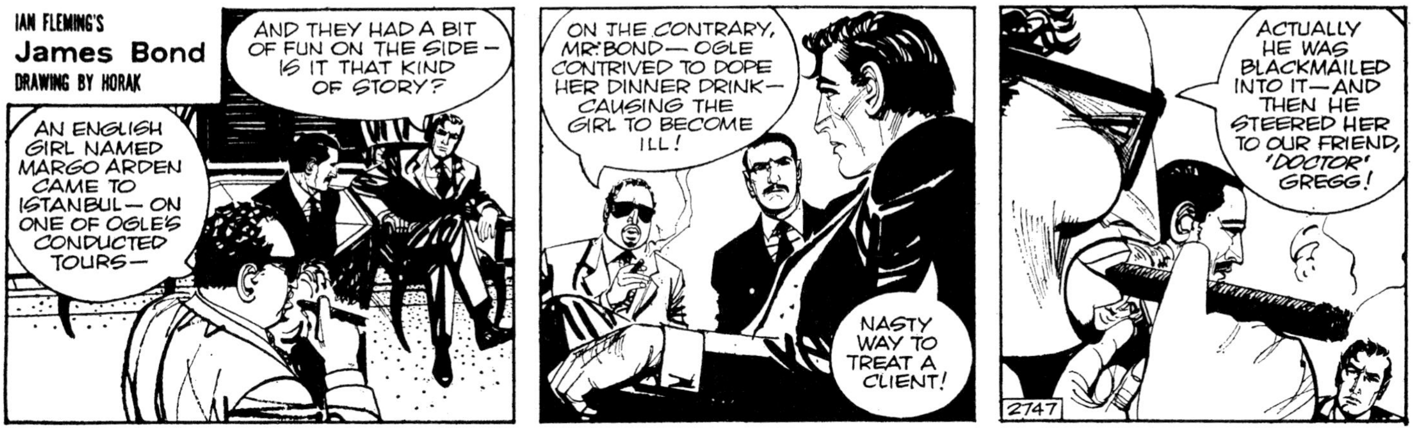
IAN FLEMING'S
James Bond
DRAWING BY HORAK
AN ENGLISH GIRL NAMED MARGO ARDEN CAME TO ISTANBUL— ON ONE OF OGLE'S CONDUCTED TOURS—
AND THEY HAD A BIT OF FUN ON THE SIDE— IS IT THAT KIND OF STORY?
ON THE CONTRARY, MR. BOND— OGLE CONTRIVED TO DOPE HER DINNER DRINK— CAUSING THE GIRL TO BECOME ILL!
NASTY WAY TO TREAT A CLIENT!
ACTUALLY HE WAS BLACKMAILED INTO IT—AND THEN HE STEERED HER TO OUR FRIEND, 'DOCTOR' GREGG!
2747

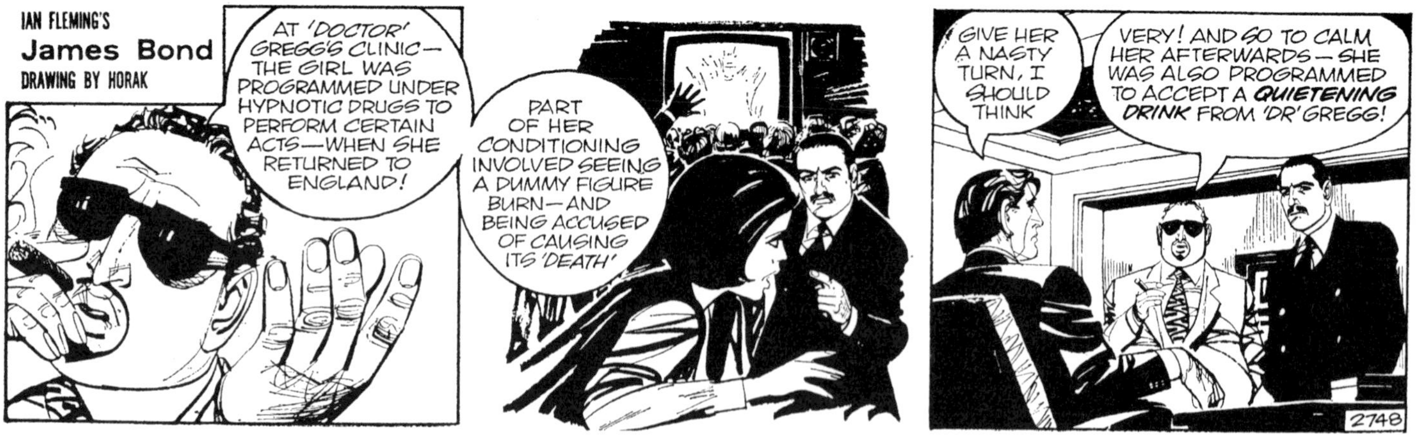
IAN FLEMING'S
James Bond
DRAWING BY HORAK
AT 'DOCTOR' GREGG'S CLINIC— THE GIRL WAS PROGRAMMED UNDER HYPNOTIC DRUGS TO PERFORM CERTAIN ACTS—WHEN SHE RETURNED TO ENGLAND!
PART OF HER CONDITIONING INVOLVED SEEING A DUMMY FIGURE BURN—AND BEING ACCUSED OF CAUSING ITS 'DEATH'
GIVE HER A NASTY TURN, I SHOULD THINK
VERY! AND SO TO CALM HER AFTERWARDS—SHE WAS ALSO PROGRAMMED TO ACCEPT A QUIETENING DRINK FROM 'DR' GREGG!
2748

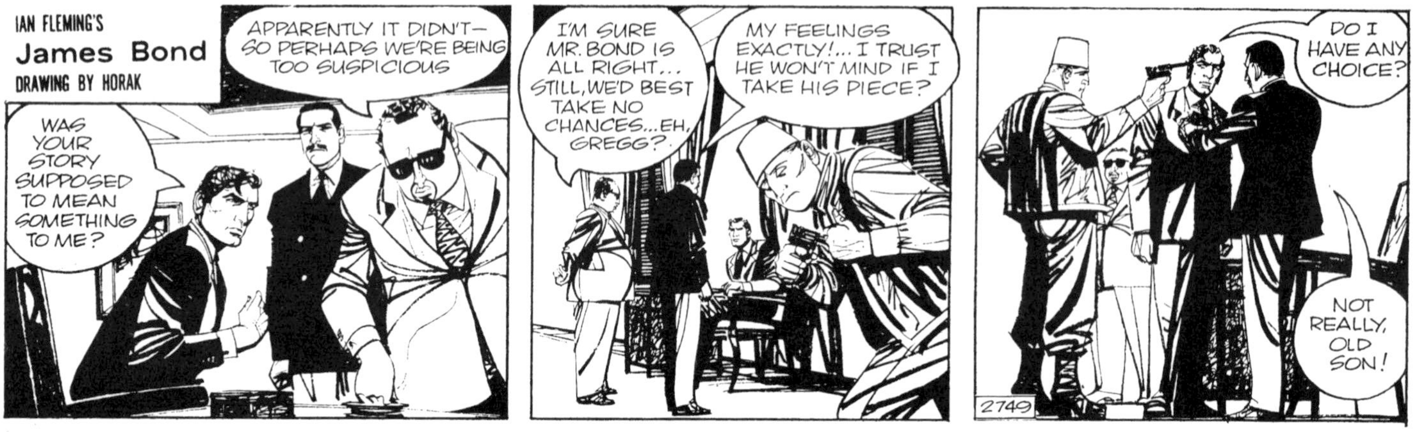
IAN FLEMING'S
James Bond
DRAWING BY HORAK
APPARENTLY IT DIDN'T— SO PERHAPS WE'RE BEING TOO SUSPICIOUS
WAS YOUR STORY SUPPOSED TO MEAN SOMETHING TO ME?
I'M SURE MR. BOND IS ALL RIGHT... STILL, WE'D BEST TAKE NO CHANCES...EH, GREGG?
MY FEELINGS EXACTLY!... I TRUST HE WON'T MIND IF I TAKE HIS PIECE?
DO I HAVE ANY CHOICE?
NOT REALLY, OLD SON!
2749

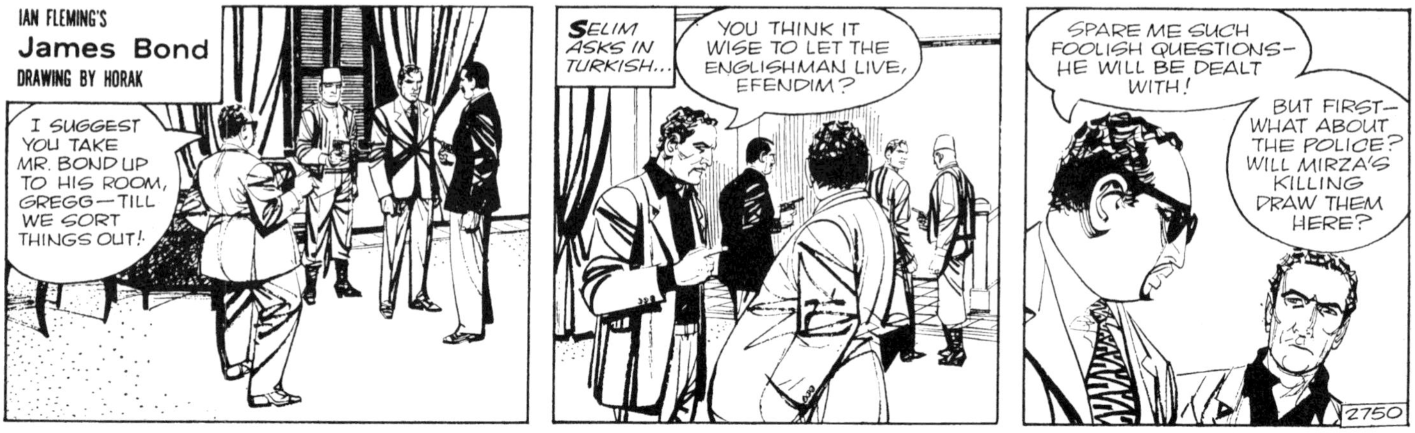
IAN FLEMING'S
James Bond
DRAWING BY HORAK
I SUGGEST YOU TAKE MR. BOND UP TO HIS ROOM, GREGG—TILL WE SORT THINGS OUT!
SELIM ASKS IN TURKISH...
YOU THINK IT WISE TO LET THE ENGLISHMAN LIVE, EFENDIM?
SPARE ME SUCH FOOLISH QUESTIONS— HE WILL BE DEALT WITH!
BUT FIRST— WHAT ABOUT THE POLICE? WILL MIRZA'S KILLING DRAW THEM HERE?
2750

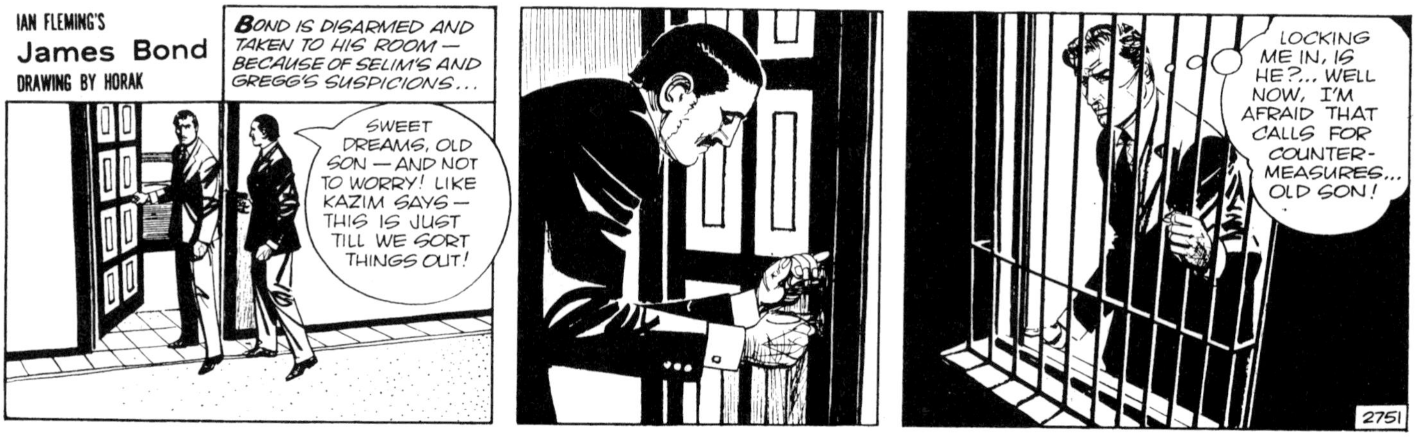
IAN FLEMING'S
James Bond
DRAWING BY HORAK
BOND IS DISARMED AND TAKEN TO HIS ROOM— BECAUSE OF SELIM'S AND GREGG'S SUSPICIONS...
SWEET DREAMS, OLD SON—AND NOT TO WORRY! LIKE KAZIM SAYS— THIS IS JUST TILL WE SORT THINGS OUT!
LOCKING ME IN, IS HE?... WELL NOW, I'M AFRAID THAT CALLS FOR COUNTER-MEASURES... OLD SON!
2751

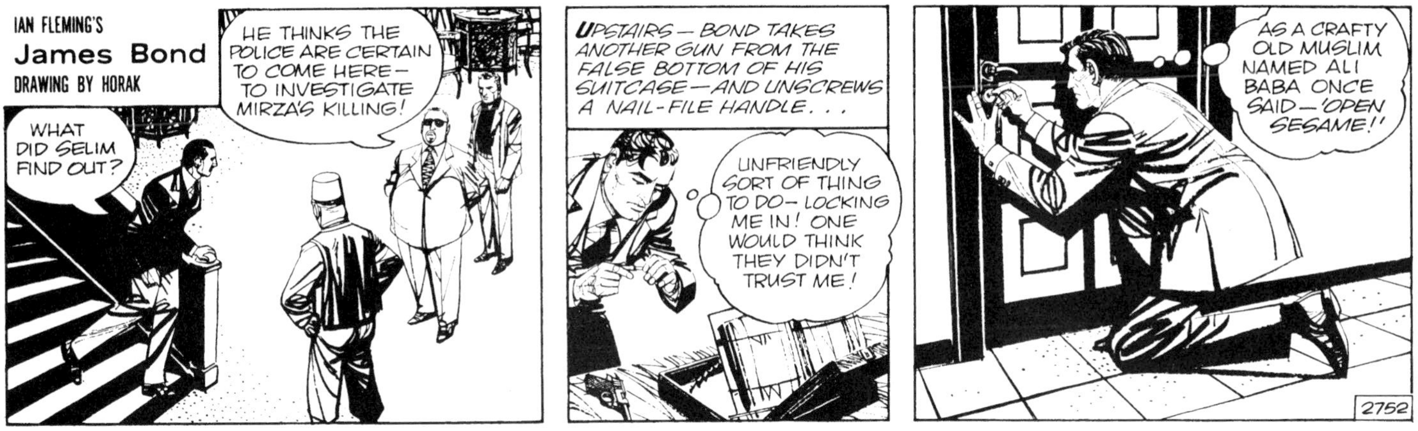
IAN FLEMING'S
James Bond
DRAWING BY HORAK
HE THINKS THE POLICE ARE CERTAIN TO COME HERE— TO INVESTIGATE MIRZA'S KILLING!
WHAT DID SELIM FIND OUT?
UPSTAIRS— BOND TAKES ANOTHER GUN FROM THE FALSE BOTTOM OF HIS SUITCASE—AND UNSCREWS A NAIL-FILE HANDLE . . .
UNFRIENDLY SORT OF THING TO DO- LOCKING ME IN! ONE WOULD THINK THEY DIDN'T TRUST ME!
AS A CRAFTY OLD MUSLIM NAMED ALI BABA ONCE SAID—'OPEN SESAME!'
2752

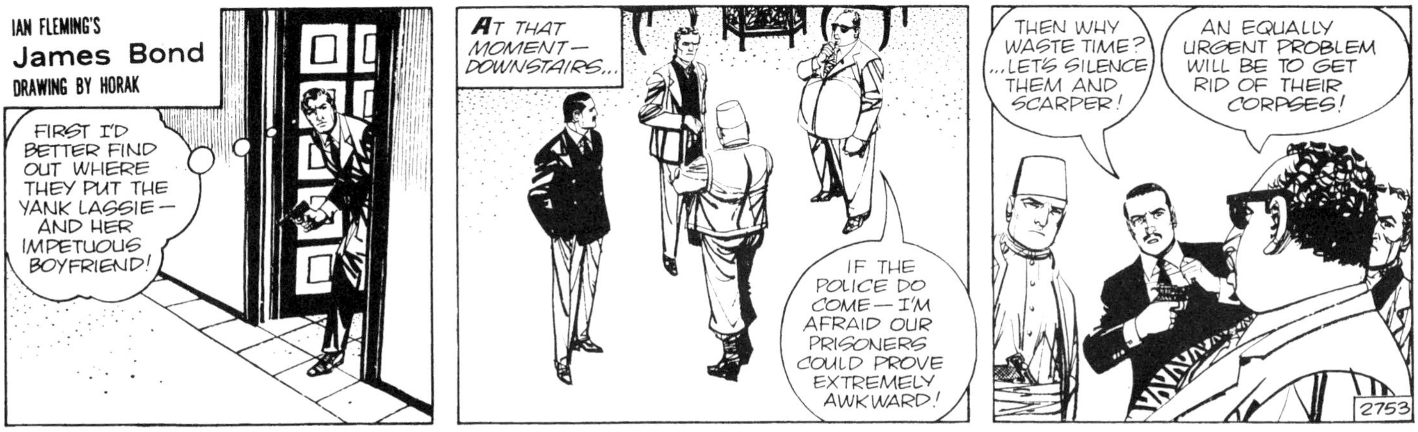
IAN FLEMING'S
James Bond
DRAWING BY HORAK
FIRST I'D BETTER FIND OUT WHERE THEY PUT THE YANK LASSIE— AND HER IMPETUOUS BOYFRIEND!
AT THAT MOMENT— DOWNSTAIRS...
IF THE POLICE DO COME— I'M AFRAID OUR PRISONERS COULD PROVE EXTREMELY AWKWARD!
THEN WHY WASTE TIME? ...LET'S SILENCE THEM AND SCARPER!
AN EQUALLY URGENT PROBLEM WILL BE TO GET RID OF THEIR CORPSES!
2753

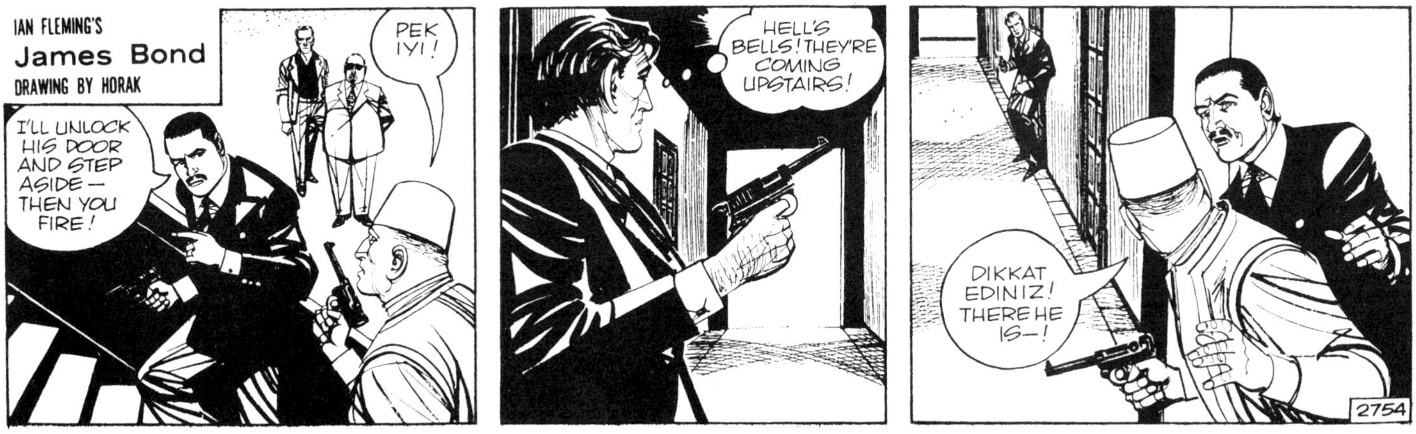
IAN FLEMING'S
James Bond
DRAWING BY HORAK
I'LL UNLOCK HIS DOOR AND STEP ASIDE— THEN YOU FIRE!
PEK IYI!
HELL'S BELLS! THEY'RE COMING UPSTAIRS!
DIKKAT EDINIZ! THERE HE IS—!
2754

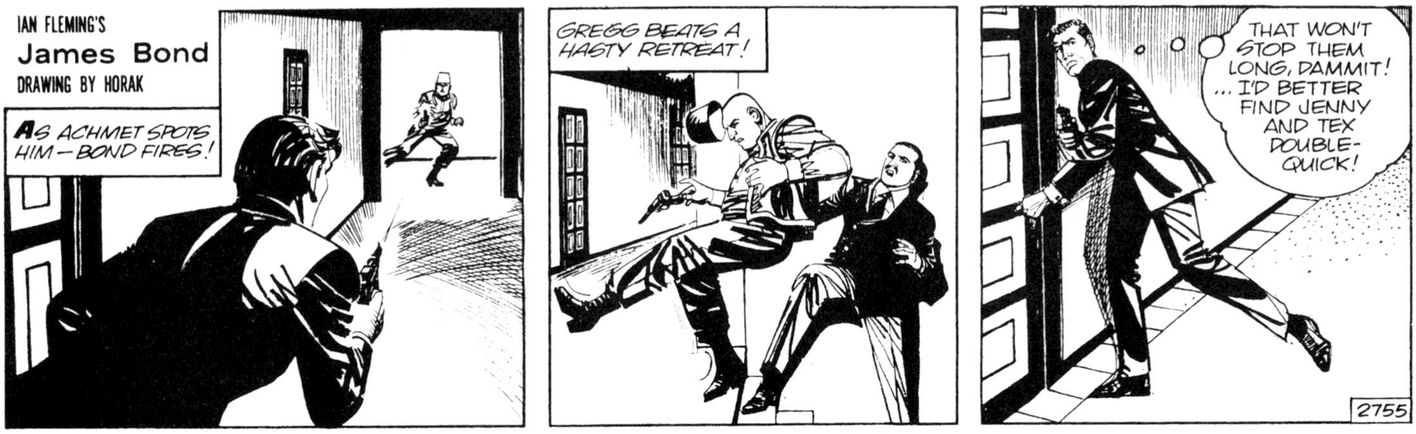
IAN FLEMING'S
James Bond
DRAWING BY HORAK
AS ACHMET SPOTS HIM— BOND FIRES!
GREGG BEATS A HASTY RETREAT!
THAT WON'T STOP THEM LONG, DAMMIT! ... I'D BETTER FIND JENNY AND TEX DOUBLE-QUICK!
2755

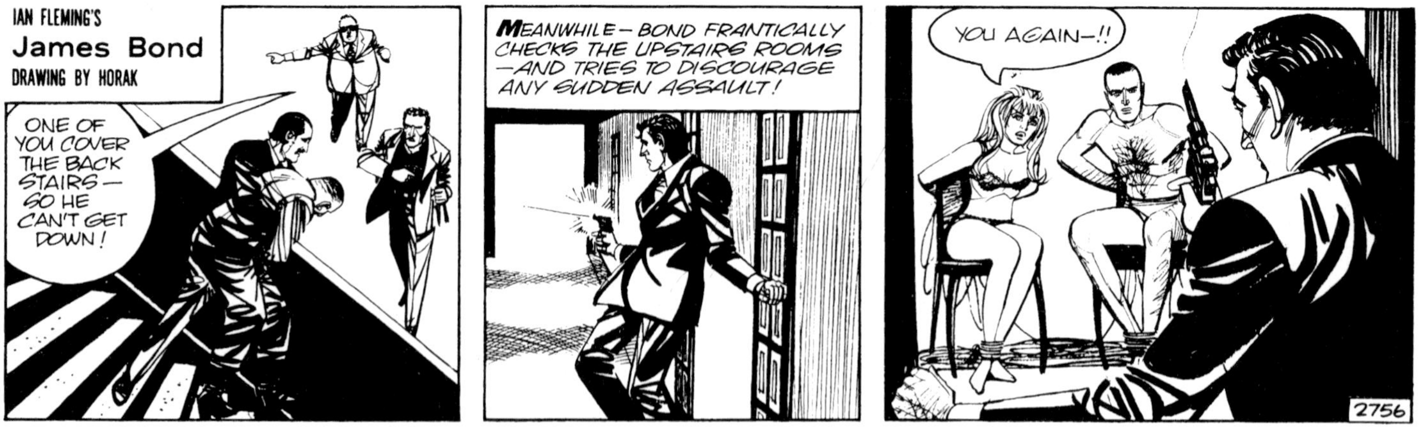
IAN FLEMING'S
James Bond
DRAWING BY HORAK
ONE OF YOU COVER THE BACK STAIRS — SO HE CAN'T GET DOWN!
MEANWHILE — BOND FRANTICALLY CHECKS THE UPSTAIRS ROOMS — AND TRIES TO DISCOURAGE ANY SUDDEN ASSAULT!
YOU AGAIN—!!
2756

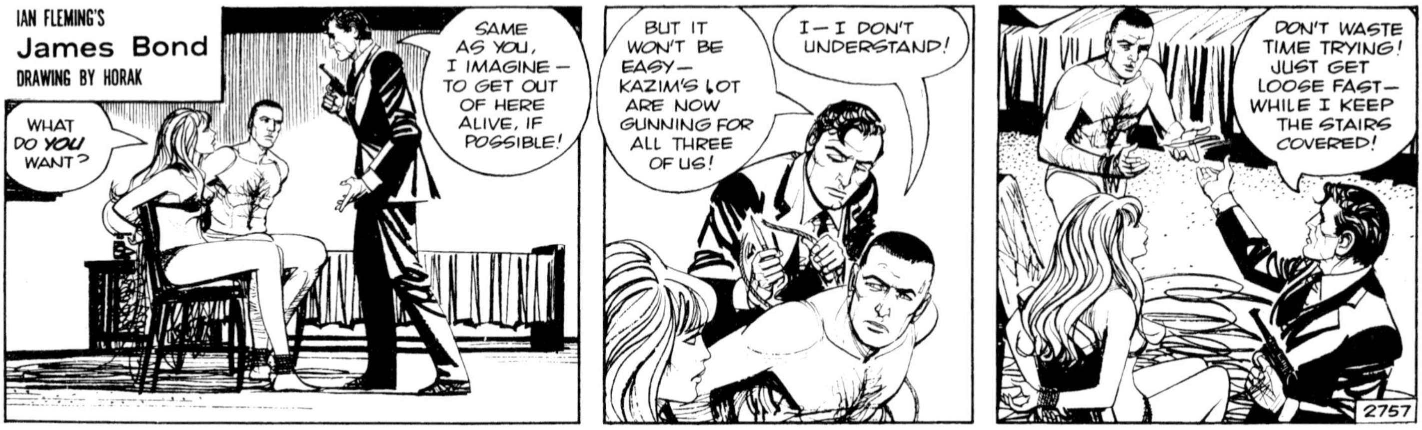
IAN FLEMING'S
James Bond
DRAWING BY HORAK
WHAT DO YOU WANT?
SAME AS YOU, I IMAGINE — TO GET OUT OF HERE ALIVE, IF POSSIBLE!
I — I DON'T UNDERSTAND!
BUT IT WON'T BE EASY — KAZIM'S LOT ARE NOW GUNNING FOR ALL THREE OF US!
DON'T WASTE TIME TRYING! JUST GET LOOSE FAST — WHILE I KEEP THE STAIRS COVERED!
2757

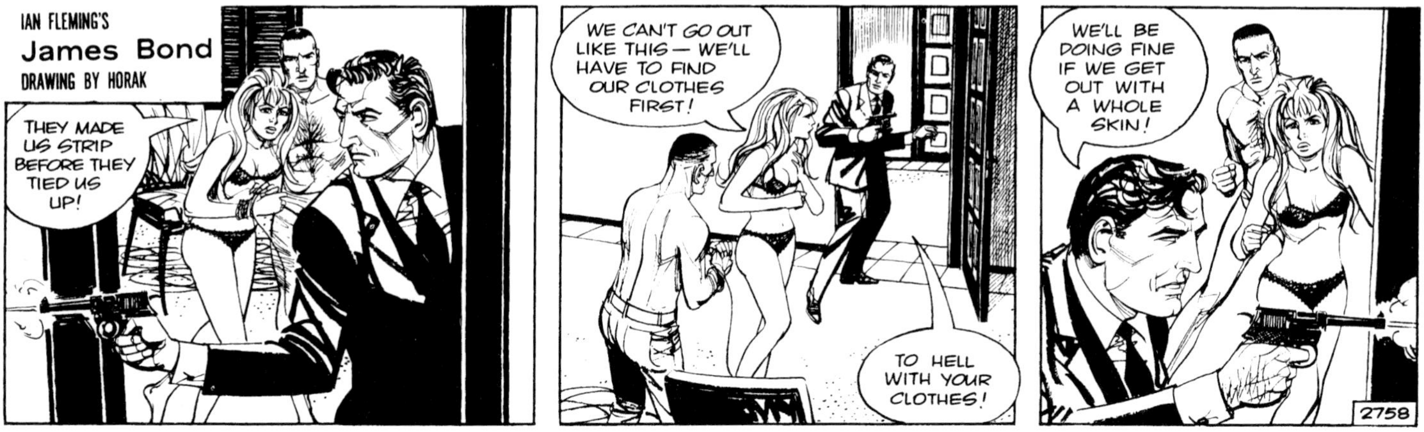
IAN FLEMING'S
James Bond
DRAWING BY HORAK
THEY MADE US STRIP BEFORE THEY TIED US UP!
WE CAN'T GO OUT LIKE THIS — WE'LL HAVE TO FIND OUR CLOTHES FIRST!
TO HELL WITH YOUR CLOTHES!
WE'LL BE DOING FINE IF WE GET OUT WITH A WHOLE SKIN!
2758

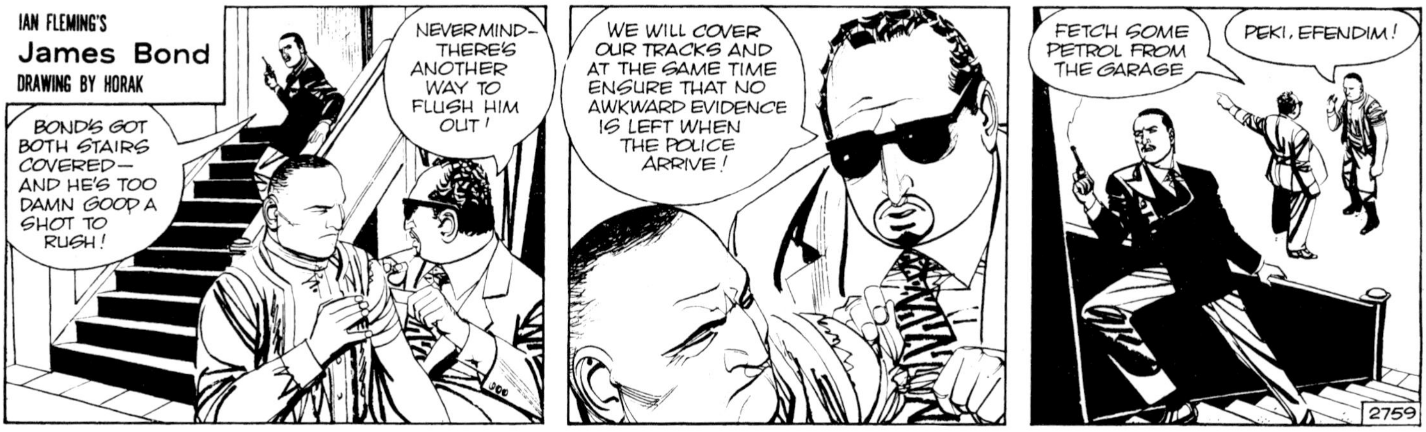
IAN FLEMING'S
James Bond
DRAWING BY HORAK
BOND'S GOT BOTH STAIRS COVERED — AND HE'S TOO DAMN GOOD A SHOT TO RUSH!
NEVERMIND — THERE'S ANOTHER WAY TO FLUSH HIM OUT!
WE WILL COVER OUR TRACKS AND AT THE SAME TIME ENSURE THAT NO AWKWARD EVIDENCE IS LEFT WHEN THE POLICE ARRIVE!
FETCH SOME PETROL FROM THE GARAGE
PEKI, EFENDIM!
2759

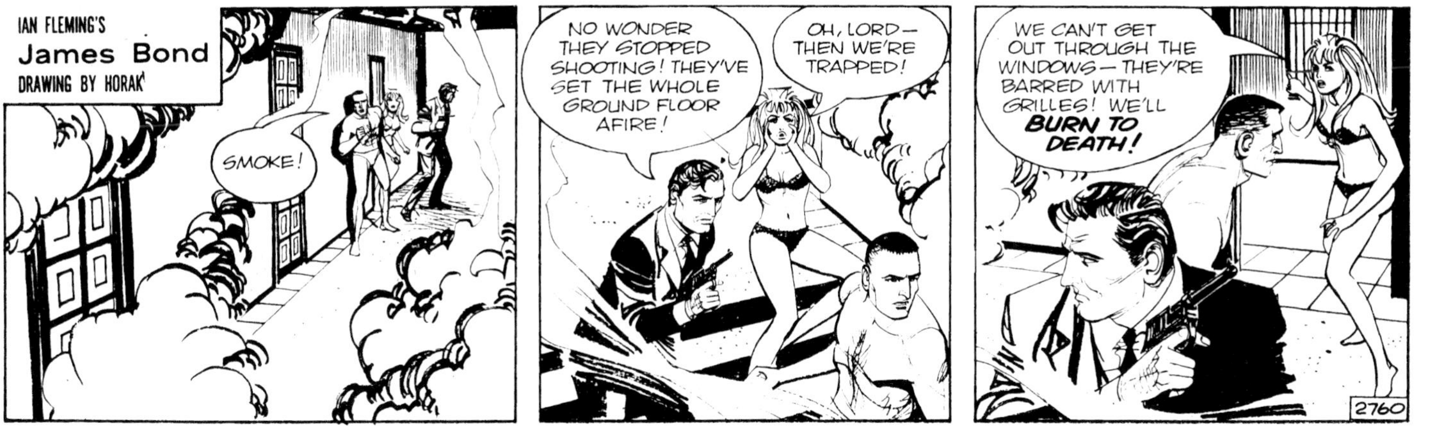
IAN FLEMING'S
James Bond
DRAWING BY HORAK
SMOKE!
NO WONDER THEY STOPPED SHOOTING! THEY'VE SET THE WHOLE GROUND FLOOR AFIRE!
OH, LORD— THEN WE'RE TRAPPED!
WE CAN'T GET OUT THROUGH THE WINDOWS—THEY'RE BARRED WITH GRILLES! WE'LL **BURN TO DEATH!**
2760

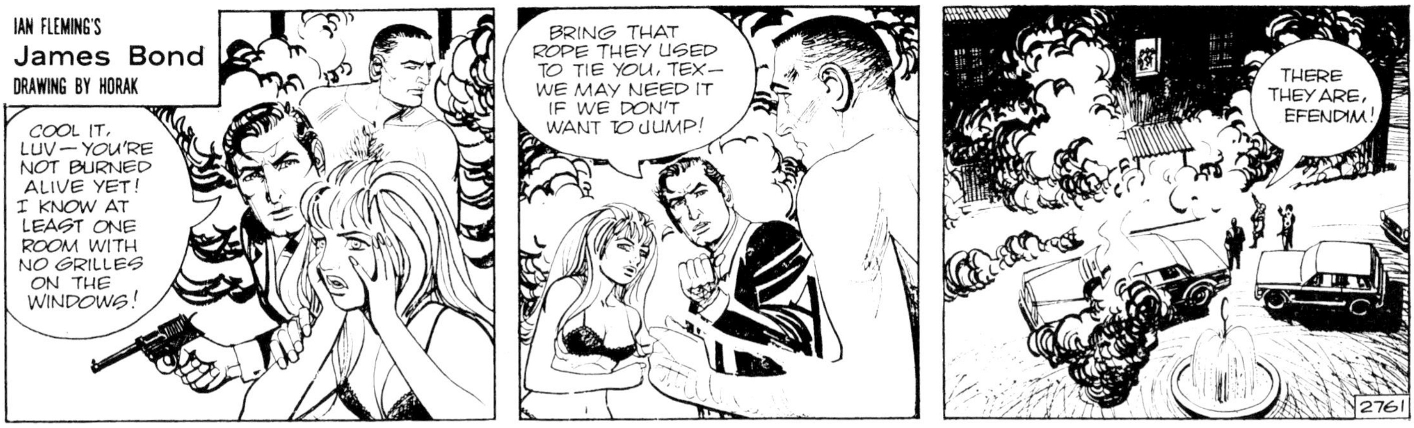
IAN FLEMING'S
James Bond
DRAWING BY HORAK
COOL IT, LUV—YOU'RE NOT BURNED ALIVE YET! I KNOW AT LEAST ONE ROOM WITH NO GRILLES ON THE WINDOWS!
BRING THAT ROPE THEY USED TO TIE YOU, TEX— WE MAY NEED IT IF WE DON'T WANT TO JUMP!
THERE THEY ARE, EFENDIM!
2761

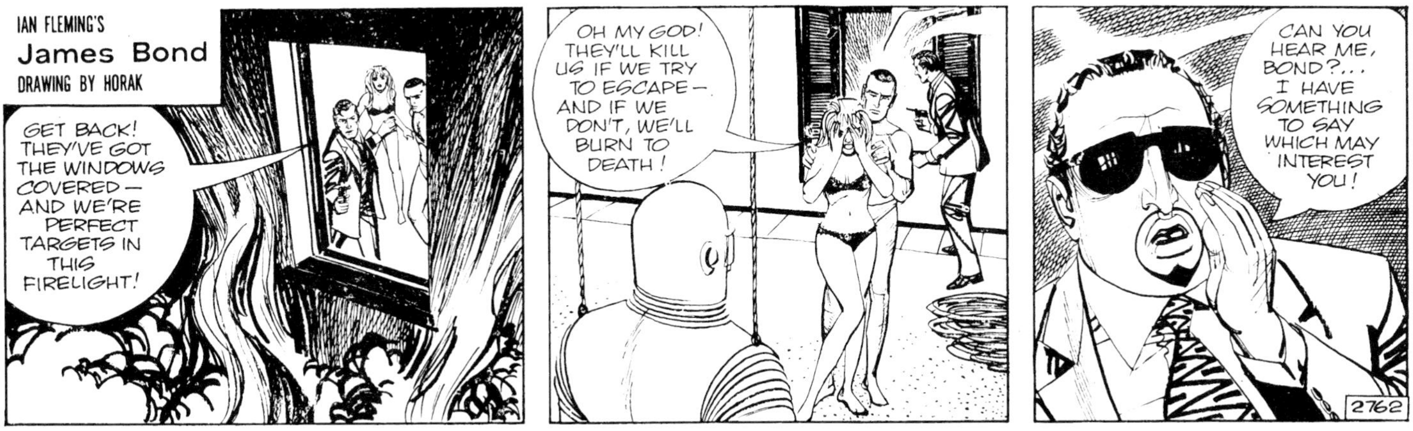
IAN FLEMING'S
James Bond
DRAWING BY HORAK
GET BACK! THEY'VE GOT THE WINDOWS COVERED— AND WE'RE PERFECT TARGETS IN THIS FIRELIGHT!
OH MY GOD! THEY'LL KILL US IF WE TRY TO ESCAPE— AND IF WE DON'T, WE'LL BURN TO DEATH!
CAN YOU HEAR ME, BOND?... I HAVE SOMETHING TO SAY WHICH MAY INTEREST YOU!
2762

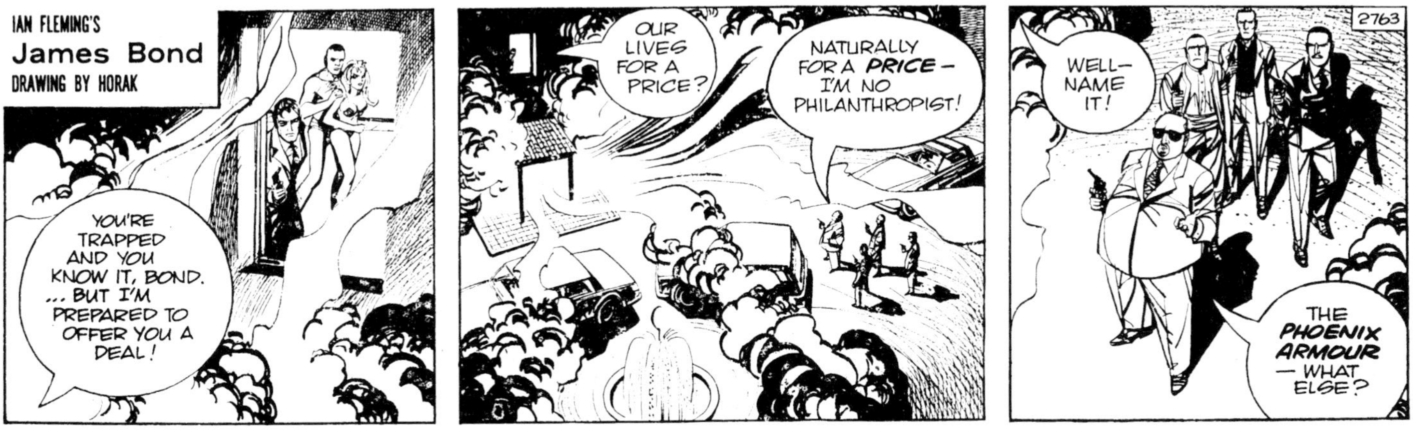
IAN FLEMING'S
James Bond
DRAWING BY HORAK
YOU'RE TRAPPED AND YOU KNOW IT, BOND. ... BUT I'M PREPARED TO OFFER YOU A DEAL!
OUR LIVES FOR A PRICE?
NATURALLY FOR A **PRICE**— I'M NO PHILANTHROPIST!
2763
WELL— NAME IT!
THE ***PHOENIX ARMOUR*** —WHAT ELSE?

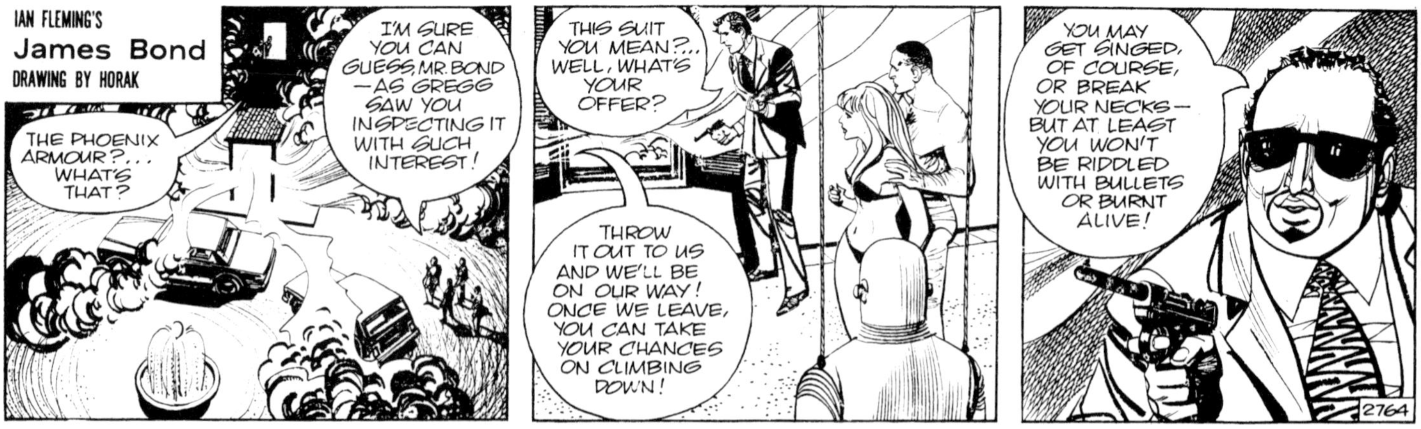
IAN FLEMING'S
James Bond
DRAWING BY HORAK
THE PHOENIX ARMOUR?... WHAT'S THAT?
I'M SURE YOU CAN GUESS, MR. BOND —AS GREGG SAW YOU INSPECTING IT WITH SUCH INTEREST!
THIS SUIT YOU MEAN?... WELL, WHAT'S YOUR OFFER?
THROW IT OUT TO US AND WE'LL BE ON OUR WAY! ONCE WE LEAVE, YOU CAN TAKE YOUR CHANCES ON CLIMBING DOWN!
YOU MAY GET SINGED, OF COURSE, OR BREAK YOUR NECKS— BUT AT LEAST YOU WON'T BE RIDDLED WITH BULLETS OR BURNT ALIVE!
2764

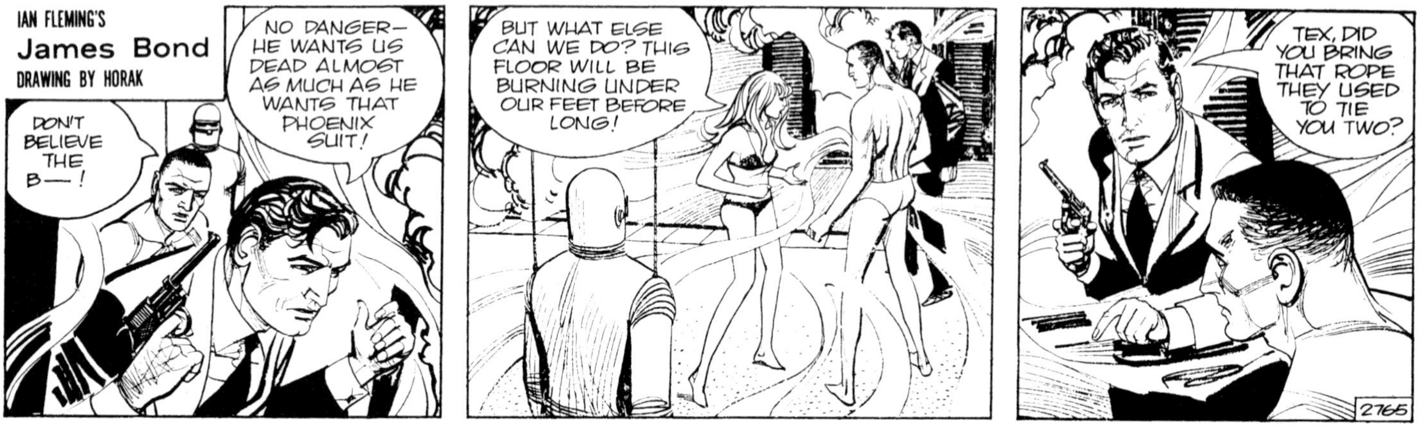
IAN FLEMING'S
James Bond
DRAWING BY HORAK
DON'T BELIEVE THE B—!
NO DANGER— HE WANTS US DEAD ALMOST AS MUCH AS HE WANTS THAT PHOENIX SUIT!
BUT WHAT ELSE CAN WE DO? THIS FLOOR WILL BE BURNING UNDER OUR FEET BEFORE LONG!
TEX, DID YOU BRING THAT ROPE THEY USED TO TIE YOU TWO?
2765

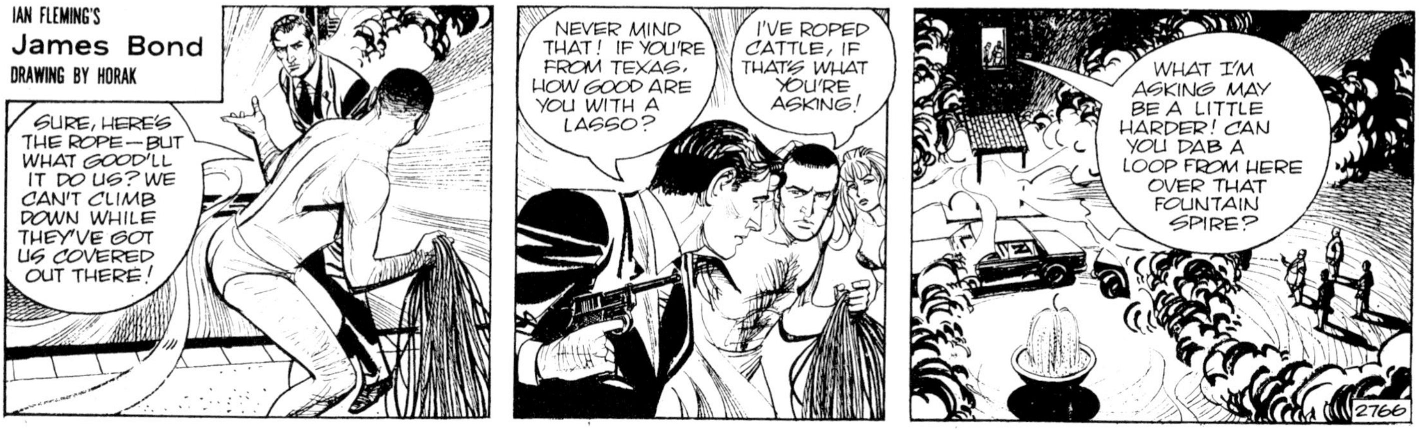
IAN FLEMING'S
James Bond
DRAWING BY HORAK
SURE, HERE'S THE ROPE—BUT WHAT GOOD'LL IT DO US? WE CAN'T CLIMB DOWN WHILE THEY'VE GOT US COVERED OUT THERE!
NEVER MIND THAT! IF YOU'RE FROM TEXAS, HOW GOOD ARE YOU WITH A LASSO?
I'VE ROPED CATTLE, IF THAT'S WHAT YOU'RE ASKING!
WHAT I'M ASKING MAY BE A LITTLE HARDER! CAN YOU DAB A LOOP FROM HERE OVER THAT FOUNTAIN SPIRE?
2766

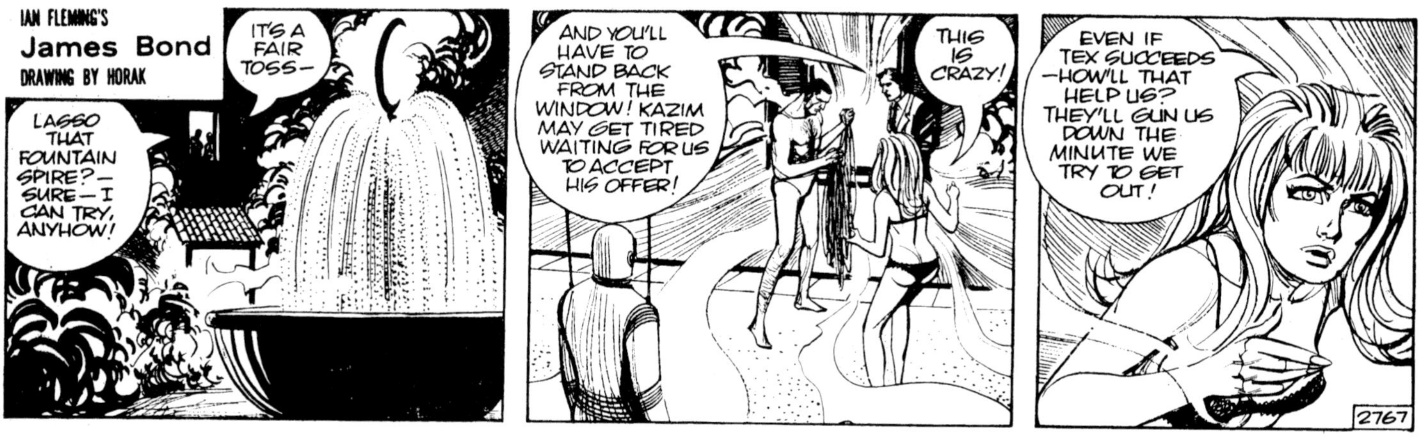
IAN FLEMING'S
James Bond
DRAWING BY HORAK
LASSO THAT FOUNTAIN SPIRE?— SURE—I CAN TRY, ANYHOW!
IT'S A FAIR TOSS—
AND YOU'LL HAVE TO STAND BACK FROM THE WINDOW! KAZIM MAY GET TIRED WAITING FOR US TO ACCEPT HIS OFFER!
THIS IS CRAZY!
EVEN IF TEX SUCCEEDS —HOW'LL THAT HELP US? THEY'LL GUN US DOWN THE MINUTE WE TRY TO GET OUT!
2767

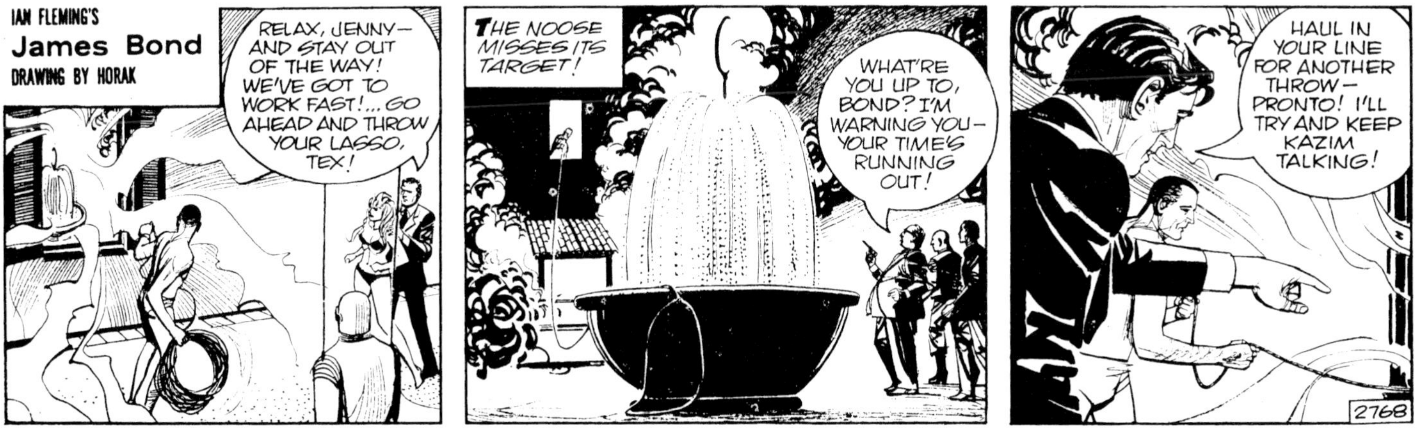
IAN FLEMING'S
James Bond
DRAWING BY HORAK
RELAX, JENNY— AND STAY OUT OF THE WAY! WE'VE GOT TO WORK FAST!... GO AHEAD AND THROW YOUR LASSO, TEX!
THE NOOSE MISSES ITS TARGET!
WHAT'RE YOU UP TO, BOND? I'M WARNING YOU— YOUR TIME'S RUNNING OUT!
HAUL IN YOUR LINE FOR ANOTHER THROW— PRONTO! I'LL TRY AND KEEP KAZIM TALKING!
2768

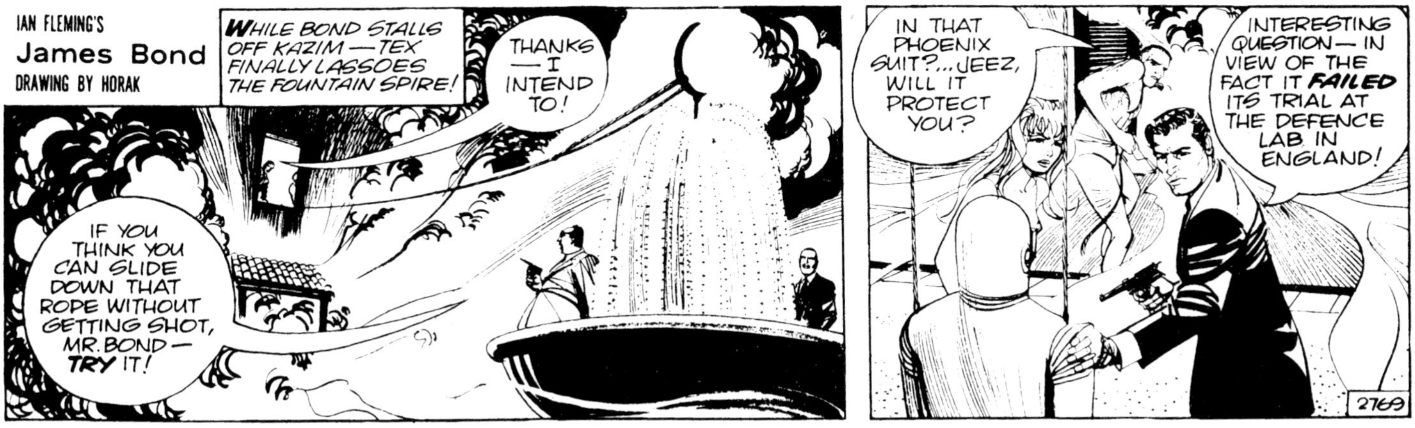
IAN FLEMING'S
James Bond
DRAWING BY HORAK
WHILE BOND STALLS OFF KAZIM —TEX FINALLY LASSOES THE FOUNTAIN SPIRE!
IF YOU THINK YOU CAN SLIDE DOWN THAT ROPE WITHOUT GETTING SHOT, MR. BOND— TRY IT!
THANKS —I INTEND TO!
IN THAT PHOENIX SUIT?... JEEZ, WILL IT PROTECT YOU?
INTERESTING QUESTION— IN VIEW OF THE FACT IT FAILED ITS TRIAL AT THE DEFENCE LAB IN ENGLAND!
2769

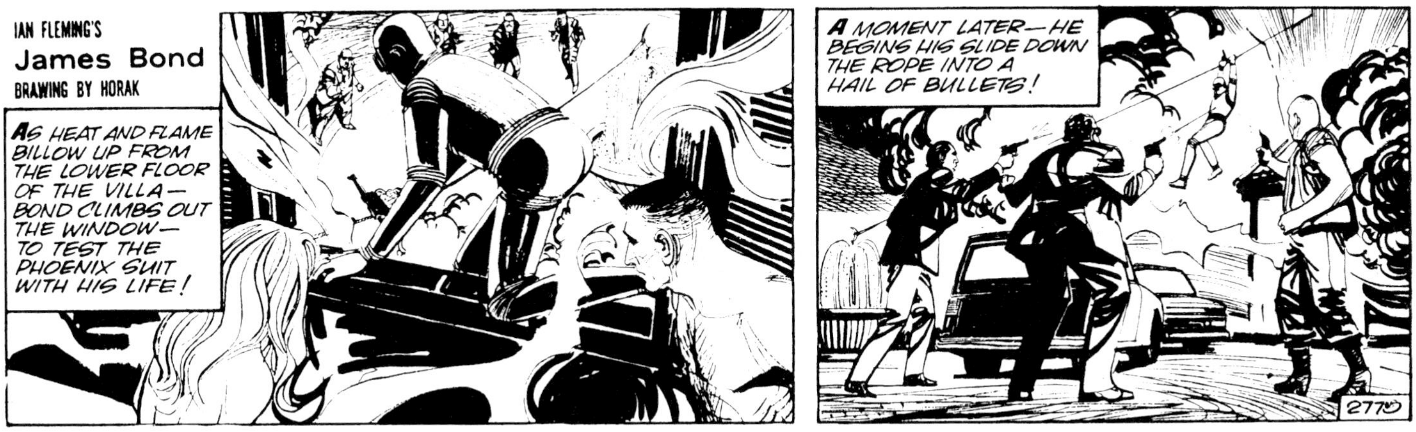
IAN FLEMING'S
James Bond
DRAWING BY HORAK
AS HEAT AND FLAME BILLOW UP FROM THE LOWER FLOOR OF THE VILLA— BOND CLIMBS OUT THE WINDOW— TO TEST THE PHOENIX SUIT WITH HIS LIFE!
A MOMENT LATER—HE BEGINS HIS SLIDE DOWN THE ROPE INTO A HAIL OF BULLETS!
2770

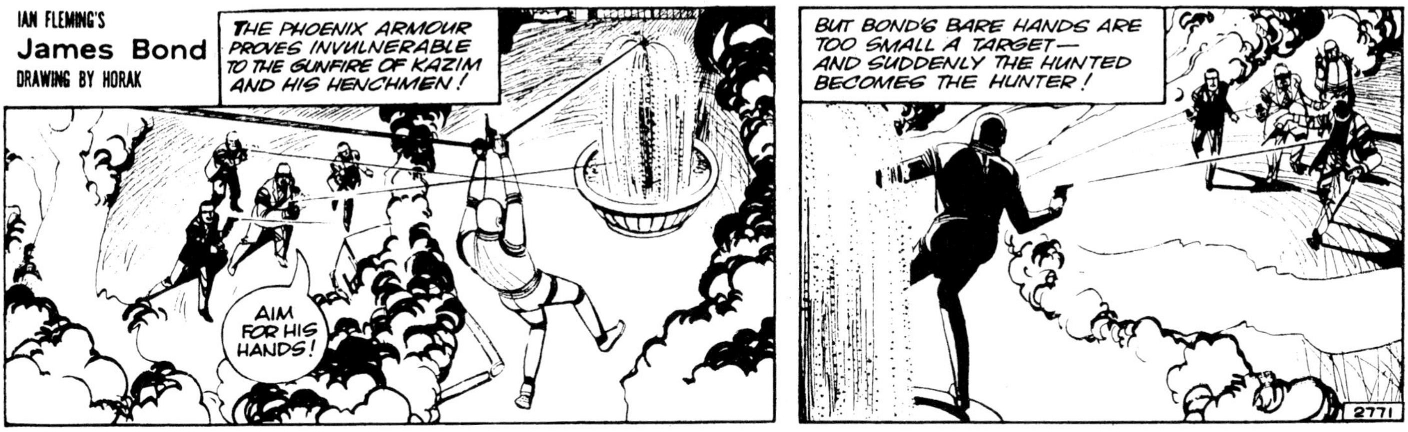
IAN FLEMING'S
James Bond
DRAWING BY HORAK
THE PHOENIX ARMOUR PROVES INVULNERABLE TO THE GUNFIRE OF KAZIM AND HIS HENCHMEN!
AIM FOR HIS HANDS!
BUT BOND'S BARE HANDS ARE TOO SMALL A TARGET— AND SUDDENLY THE HUNTED BECOMES THE HUNTER!
2771

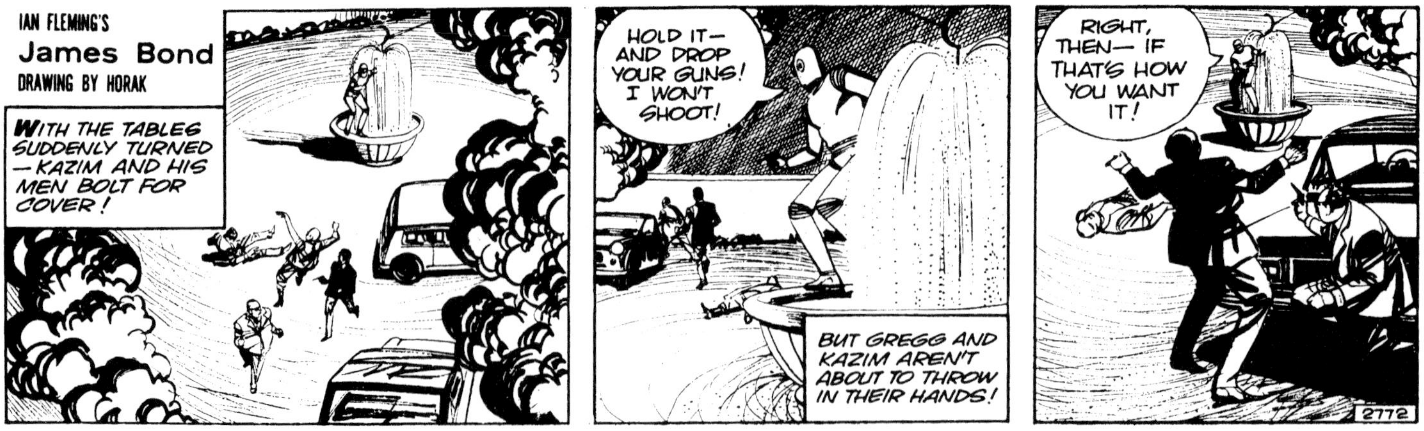
IAN FLEMING'S
James Bond
DRAWING BY HORAK
WITH THE TABLES SUDDENLY TURNED —KAZIM AND HIS MEN BOLT FOR COVER!
HOLD IT— AND DROP YOUR GUNS! I WON'T SHOOT!
BUT GREGG AND KAZIM AREN'T ABOUT TO THROW IN THEIR HANDS!
RIGHT, THEN— IF THAT'S HOW YOU WANT IT!
2772

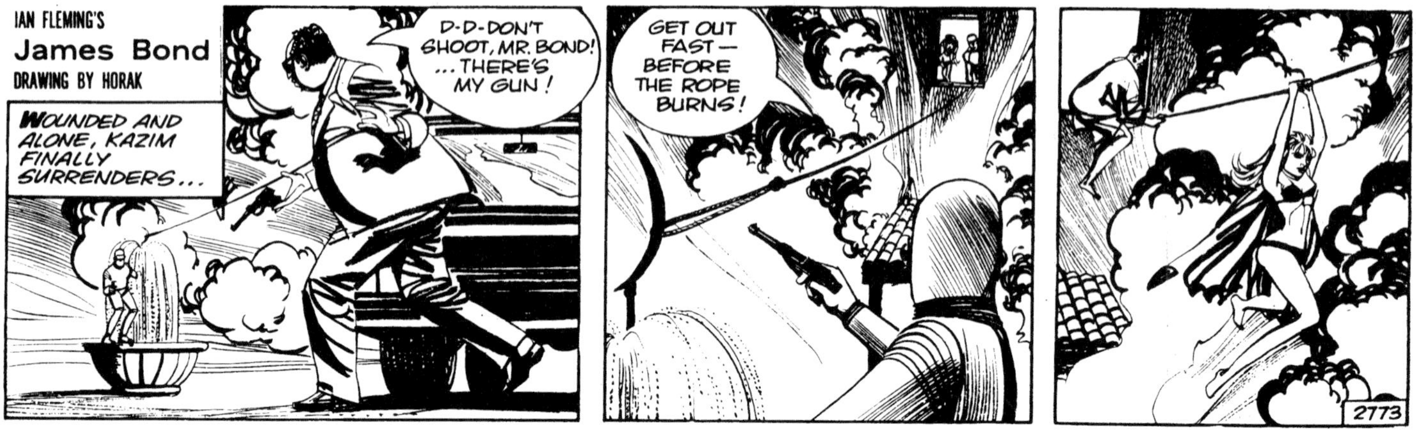
IAN FLEMING'S
James Bond
DRAWING BY HORAK
WOUNDED AND ALONE, KAZIM FINALLY SURRENDERS...
D-D-DON'T SHOOT, MR. BOND! ...THERE'S MY GUN!
GET OUT FAST— BEFORE THE ROPE BURNS!
2773

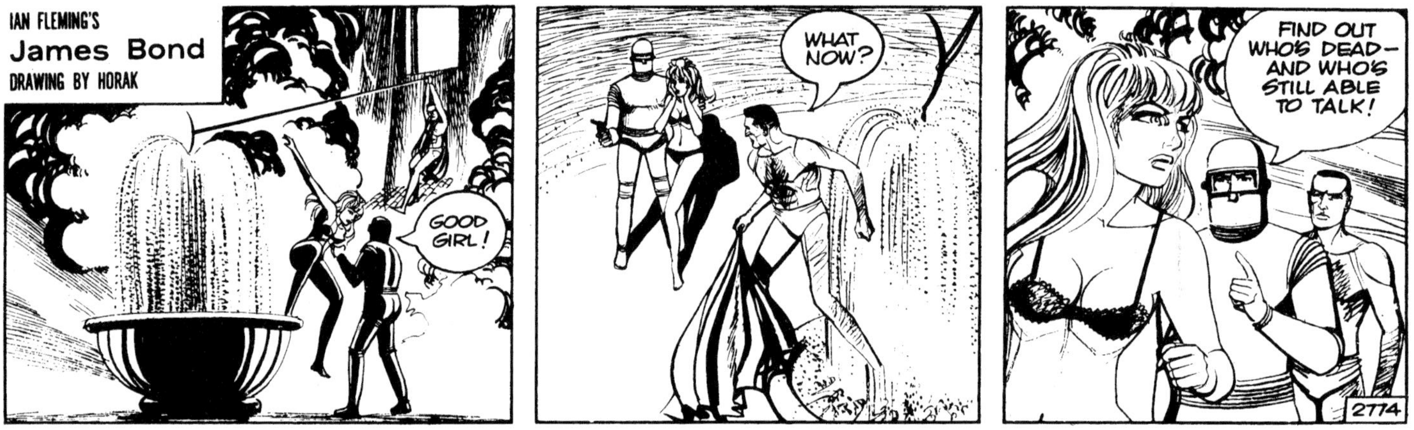
IAN FLEMING'S
James Bond
DRAWING BY HORAK
GOOD GIRL!
WHAT NOW?
FIND OUT WHO'S DEAD— AND WHO'S STILL ABLE TO TALK!
2774

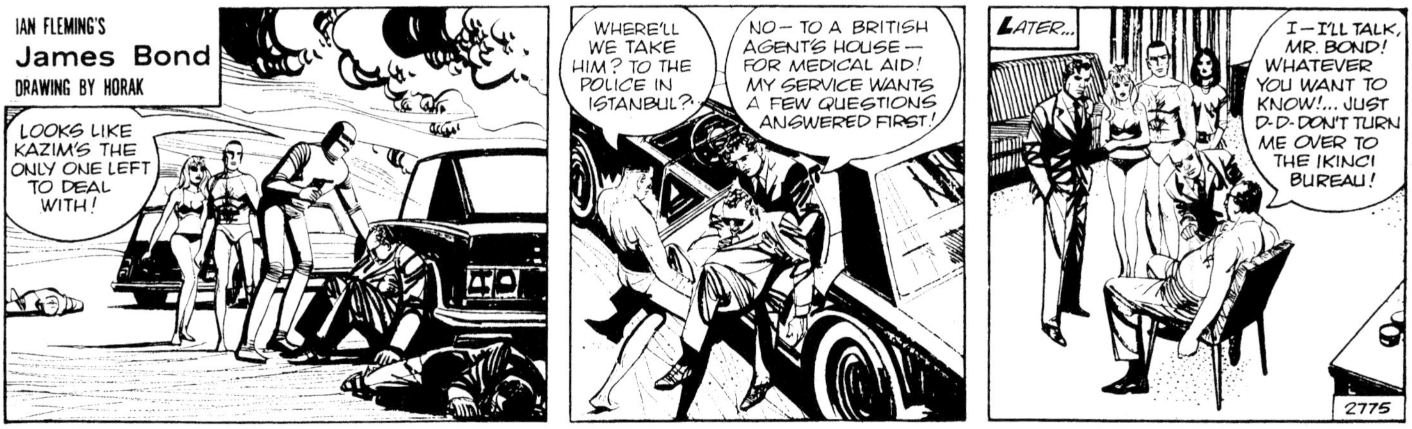
IAN FLEMING'S
James Bond
DRAWING BY HORAK
LOOKS LIKE KAZIM'S THE ONLY ONE LEFT TO DEAL WITH!
WHERE'LL WE TAKE HIM? TO THE POLICE IN ISTANBUL?
NO— TO A BRITISH AGENT'S HOUSE— FOR MEDICAL AID! MY SERVICE WANTS A FEW QUESTIONS ANSWERED FIRST!
LATER...
I—I'LL TALK, MR. BOND! WHATEVER YOU WANT TO KNOW!... JUST D-D-DON'T TURN ME OVER TO THE IKINCI BUREAU!
2775

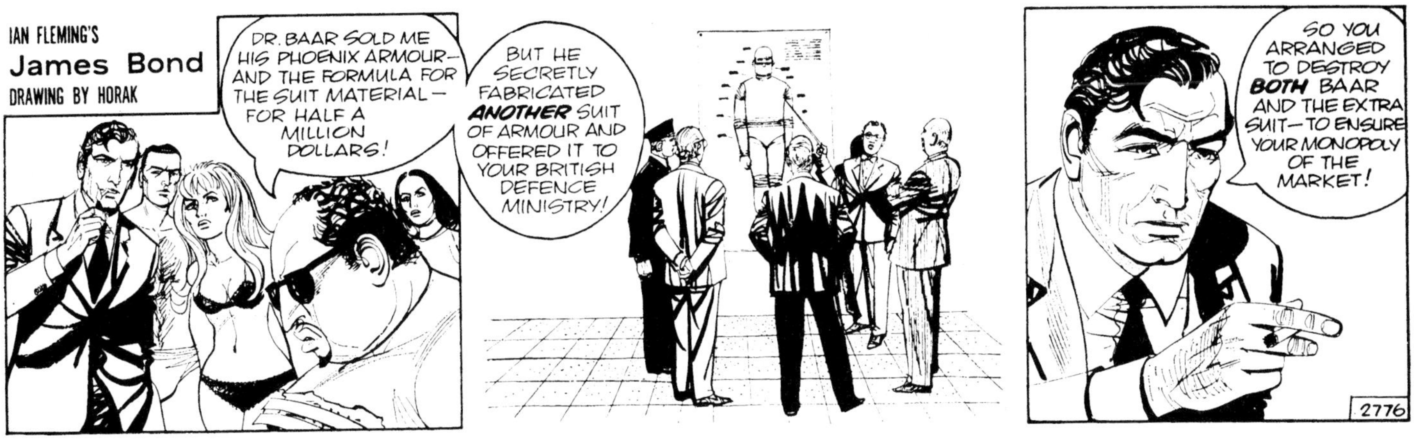
IAN FLEMING'S
James Bond
DRAWING BY HORAK
DR. BAAR SOLD ME HIS PHOENIX ARMOUR— AND THE FORMULA FOR THE SUIT MATERIAL— FOR HALF A MILLION DOLLARS!
BUT HE SECRETLY FABRICATED ANOTHER SUIT OF ARMOUR AND OFFERED IT TO YOUR BRITISH DEFENCE MINISTRY!
SO YOU ARRANGED TO DESTROY BOTH BAAR AND THE EXTRA SUIT—TO ENSURE YOUR MONOPOLY OF THE MARKET!
2776

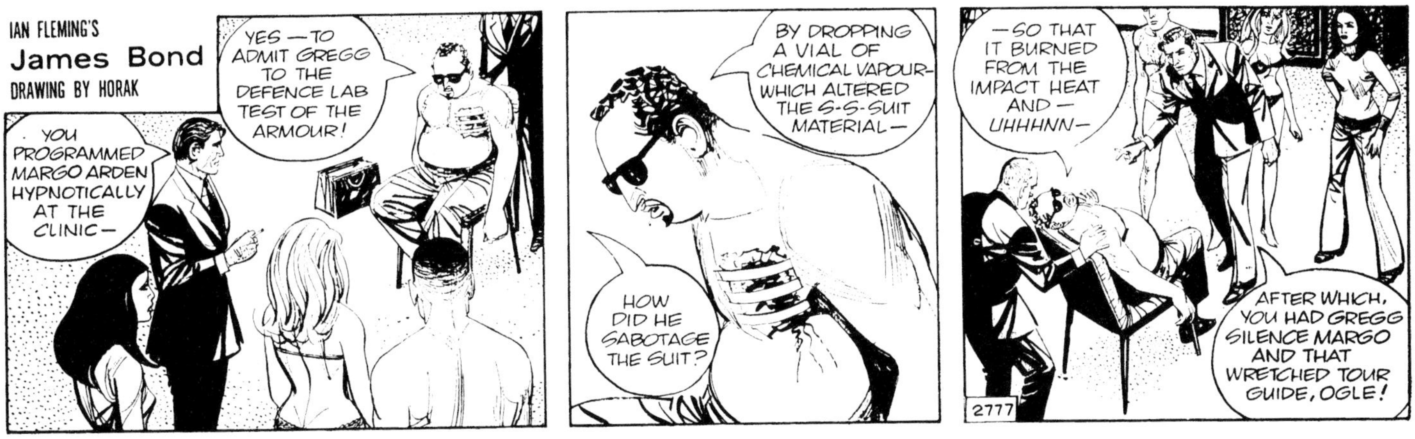
IAN FLEMING'S
James Bond
DRAWING BY HORAK
YOU PROGRAMMED MARGO ARDEN HYPNOTICALLY AT THE CLINIC—
YES—TO ADMIT GREGG TO THE DEFENCE LAB TEST OF THE ARMOUR!
HOW DID HE SABOTAGE THE SUIT?
BY DROPPING A VIAL OF CHEMICAL VAPOUR—WHICH ALTERED THE S-S-SUIT MATERIAL—
—SO THAT IT BURNED FROM THE IMPACT HEAT AND— UHHHNN—
AFTER WHICH, YOU HAD GREGG SILENCE MARGO AND THAT WRETCHED TOUR GUIDE, OGLE!
2777

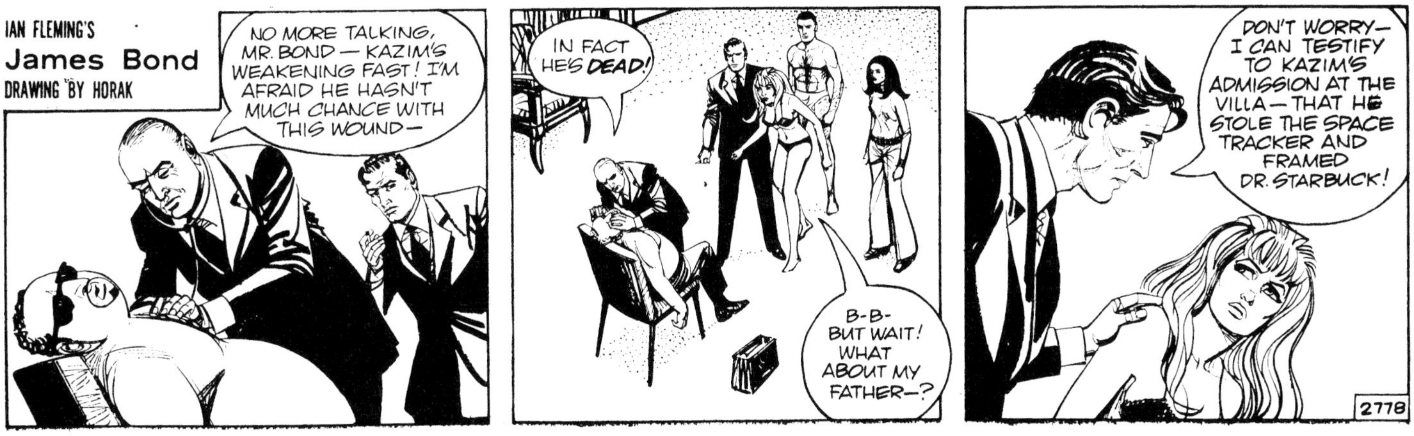
IAN FLEMING'S
James Bond
DRAWING BY HORAK
NO MORE TALKING, MR. BOND — KAZIM'S WEAKENING FAST! I'M AFRAID HE HASN'T MUCH CHANCE WITH THIS WOUND—
IN FACT HE'S DEAD!
B-B-BUT WAIT! WHAT ABOUT MY FATHER—?
DON'T WORRY— I CAN TESTIFY TO KAZIM'S ADMISSION AT THE VILLA—THAT HE STOLE THE SPACE TRACKER AND FRAMED DR. STARBUCK!
2778

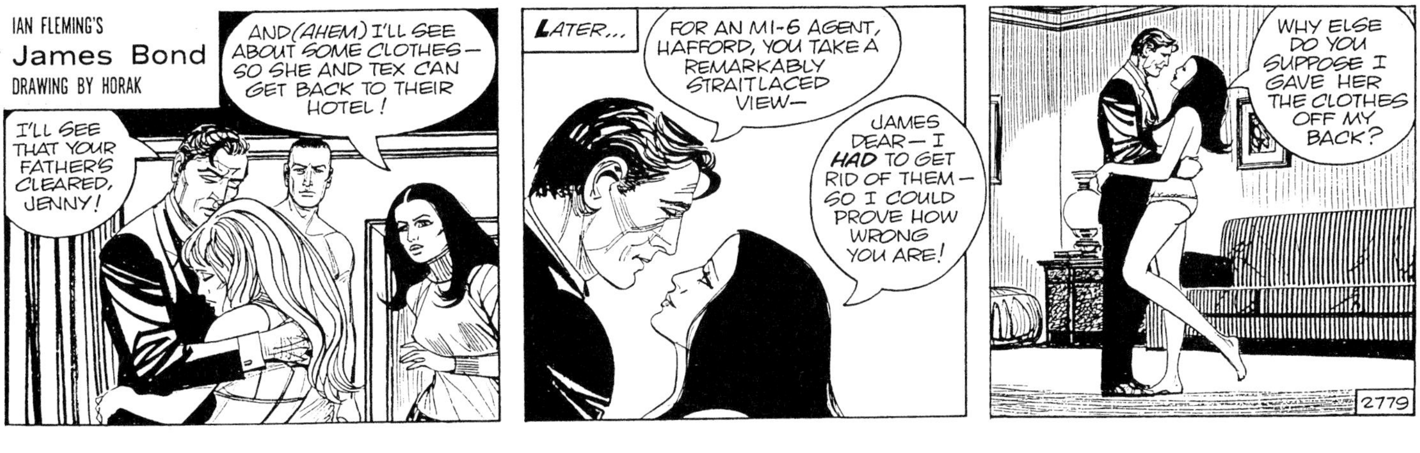
IAN FLEMING'S
James Bond
DRAWING BY HORAK
I'LL SEE THAT YOUR FATHER'S CLEARED, JENNY!
AND (AHEM) I'LL SEE ABOUT SOME CLOTHES— SO SHE AND TEX CAN GET BACK TO THEIR HOTEL!
LATER...
FOR AN MI-6 AGENT, HAFFORD, YOU TAKE A REMARKABLY STRAITLACED VIEW—
JAMES DEAR—I HAD TO GET RID OF THEM— SO I COULD PROVE HOW WRONG YOU ARE!
WHY ELSE DO YOU SUPPOSE I GAVE HER THE CLOTHES OFF MY BACK?
2779

IAN FLEMING'S
James Bond
DRAWING BY HORAK
TURK H
MI-6'S BEEN ON TO WASHINGTON— YOUR FATHER WILL BE FREE BY THE TIME YOU LAND BACK IN THE STATES!
HOW CAN I EVER THANK YOU?
THAT LOOKS LIKE A GOOD START!
LET'S NOT MAKE IT TOO GOOD— OR WE'LL MISS OUR TAKEOFF!
HE'S RIGHT, JAMES— I WOULDN'T WANT YOU TO MISS MY TAKEOFF!
2780
END OF STORY

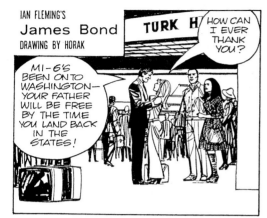

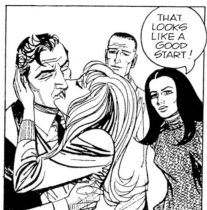

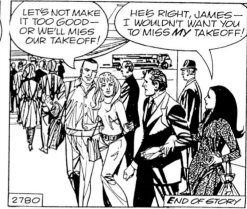

THE BLACK RUBY CAPER

One of the more complicated stories in the Lawrence canon, *The Black Ruby Caper* goes through an almost baffling series of twists and turns until 007's plan is revealed — only to pile on yet more twists as Bond desperately tries to figure out Ruby's intentions. Not to mention that the tale features not one, but two spy organisations — the 'Rubaiyat', presumably dissolved following the story's conclusion, and SMERSH.

Having evidently overcome his previous aversion to blackmail, 007 involves Ruby's girlfriend, Roanne Dreux, in his plans. But the weak-willed, subservient Dreux is no match for the real *Bond* girl in this caper, Damara Carver, who is portrayed throughout as uncompromising and smart, but, in the classic Fleming mode, just fragile enough to be scared by direct contact with the enemy. The contrast between the use of Dreux's and Carver's nudity is interesting; whereas Dreux is startled by Bond and made a victim by her nakedness at the beginning of the story, Carver uses it as leverage, intent on getting to her father.

A final note: the Lawrence-created Double-O agent, Suzi Kew, makes her second *Bond* appearance in this strip, after her debut in *Beware of Butterflies*.

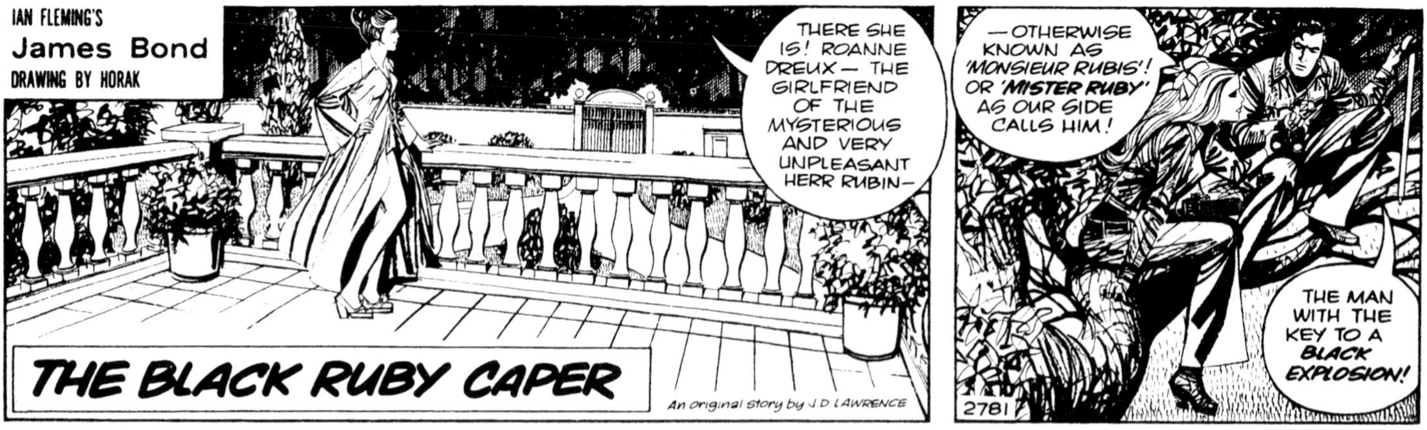
IAN FLEMING'S
James Bond
DRAWING BY HORAK
THERE SHE IS! ROANNE DREUX — THE GIRLFRIEND OF THE MYSTERIOUS AND VERY UNPLEASANT HERR RUBIN—
THE BLACK RUBY CAPER
An original story by J.D. LAWRENCE
—OTHERWISE KNOWN AS 'MONSIEUR RUBIS'! OR 'MISTER RUBY' AS OUR SIDE CALLS HIM!
THE MAN WITH THE KEY TO A BLACK EXPLOSION!
2781

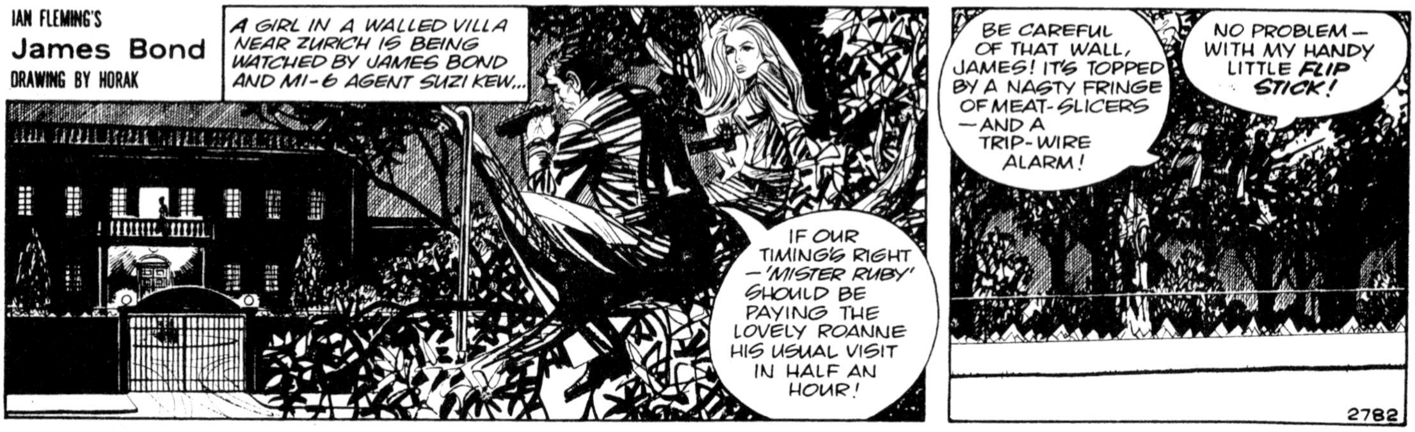
IAN FLEMING'S
James Bond
DRAWING BY HORAK
A GIRL IN A WALLED VILLA NEAR ZURICH IS BEING WATCHED BY JAMES BOND AND MI-6 AGENT SUZI KEW...
IF OUR TIMING'S RIGHT — 'MISTER RUBY' SHOULD BE PAYING THE LOVELY ROANNE HIS USUAL VISIT IN HALF AN HOUR!
BE CAREFUL OF THAT WALL, JAMES! IT'S TOPPED BY A NASTY FRINGE OF MEAT-SLICERS —AND A TRIP-WIRE ALARM!
NO PROBLEM — WITH MY HANDY LITTLE FLIP STICK!
2782

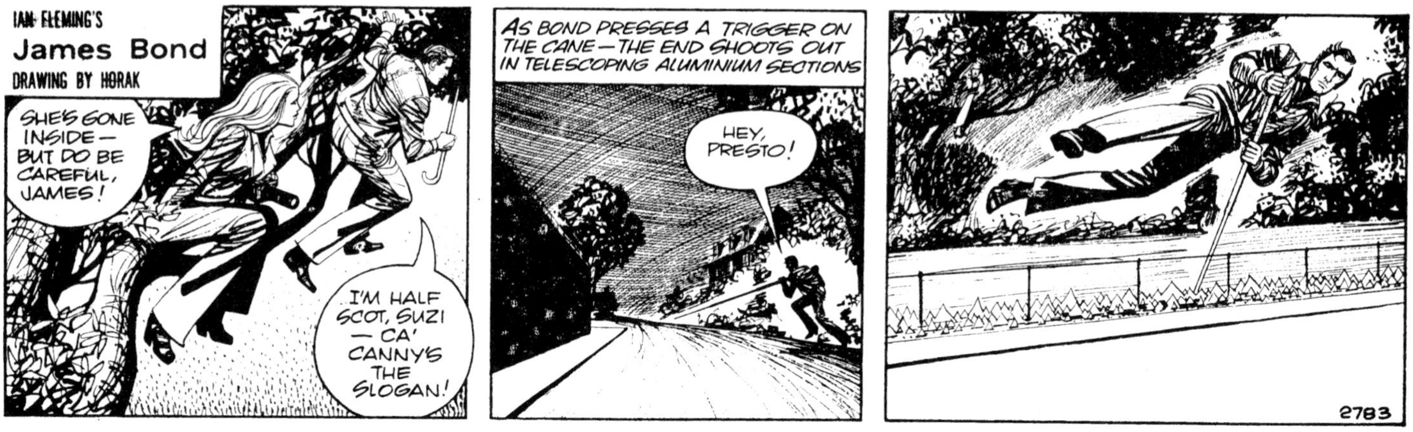
IAN FLEMING'S
James Bond
DRAWING BY HORAK
SHE'S GONE INSIDE— BUT DO BE CAREFUL, JAMES!
I'M HALF SCOT, SUZI — CA' CANNY'S THE SLOGAN!
AS BOND PRESSES A TRIGGER ON THE CANE — THE END SHOOTS OUT IN TELESCOPING ALUMINIUM SECTIONS
HEY, PRESTO!
2783

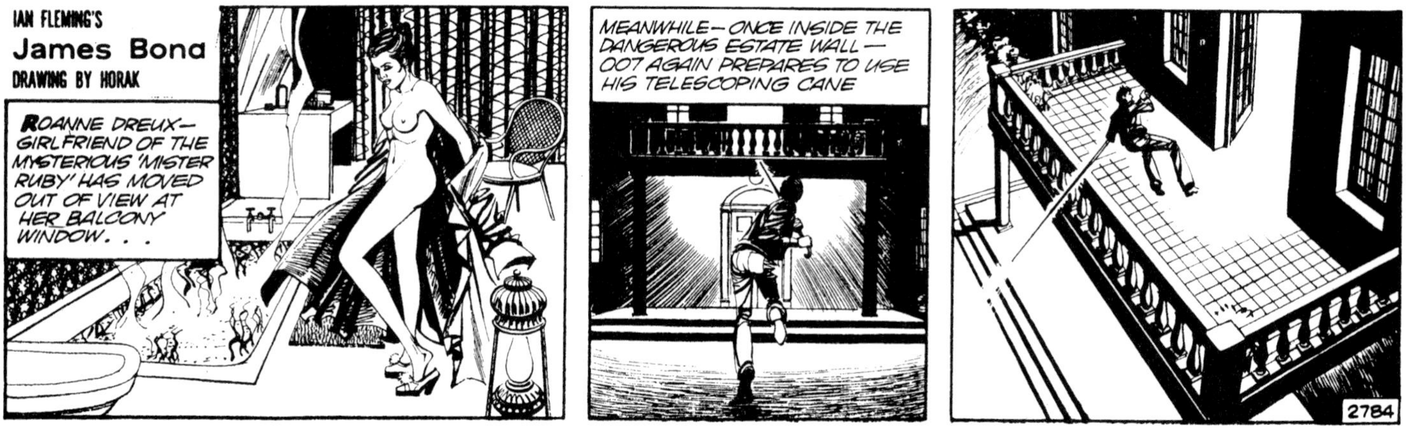
IAN FLEMING'S
James Bond
DRAWING BY HORAK
ROANNE DREUX— GIRLFRIEND OF THE MYSTERIOUS 'MISTER RUBY' HAS MOVED OUT OF VIEW AT HER BALCONY WINDOW . . .
MEANWHILE — ONCE INSIDE THE DANGEROUS ESTATE WALL — 007 AGAIN PREPARES TO USE HIS TELESCOPING CANE
2784

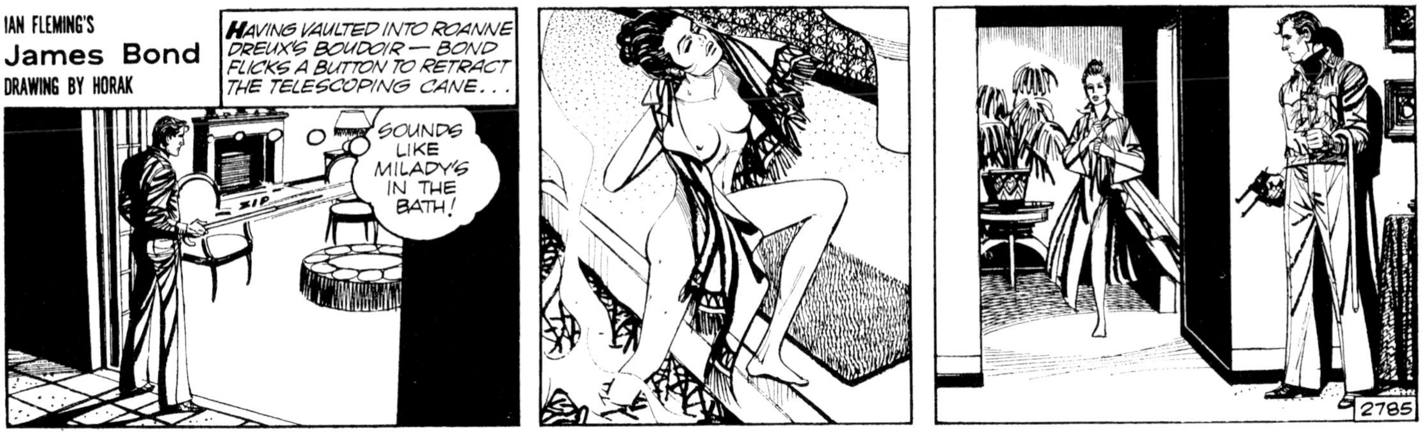
IAN FLEMING'S
James Bond
DRAWING BY HORAK
HAVING VAULTED INTO ROANNE DREUX'S BOUDOIR — BOND FLICKS A BUTTON TO RETRACT THE TELESCOPING CANE...
ZIP
SOUNDS LIKE MILADY'S IN THE BATH!
2785

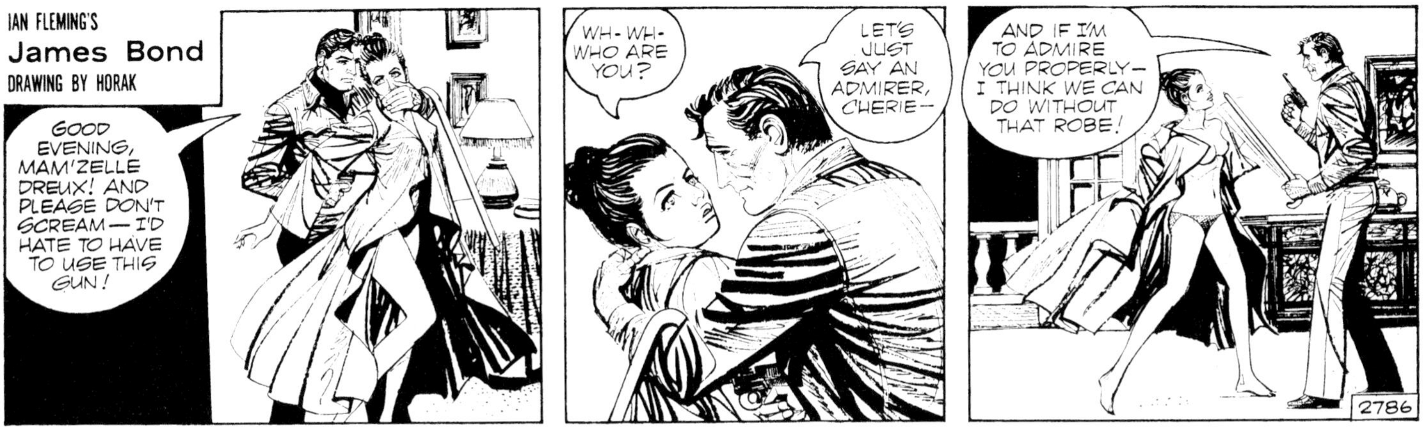
IAN FLEMING'S
James Bond
DRAWING BY HORAK
GOOD EVENING, MAM'ZELLE DREUX! AND PLEASE DON'T SCREAM — I'D HATE TO HAVE TO USE THIS GUN!
WH-WH-WHO ARE YOU?
LET'S JUST SAY AN ADMIRER, CHERIE—
AND IF I'M TO ADMIRE YOU PROPERLY— I THINK WE CAN DO WITHOUT THAT ROBE!
2786

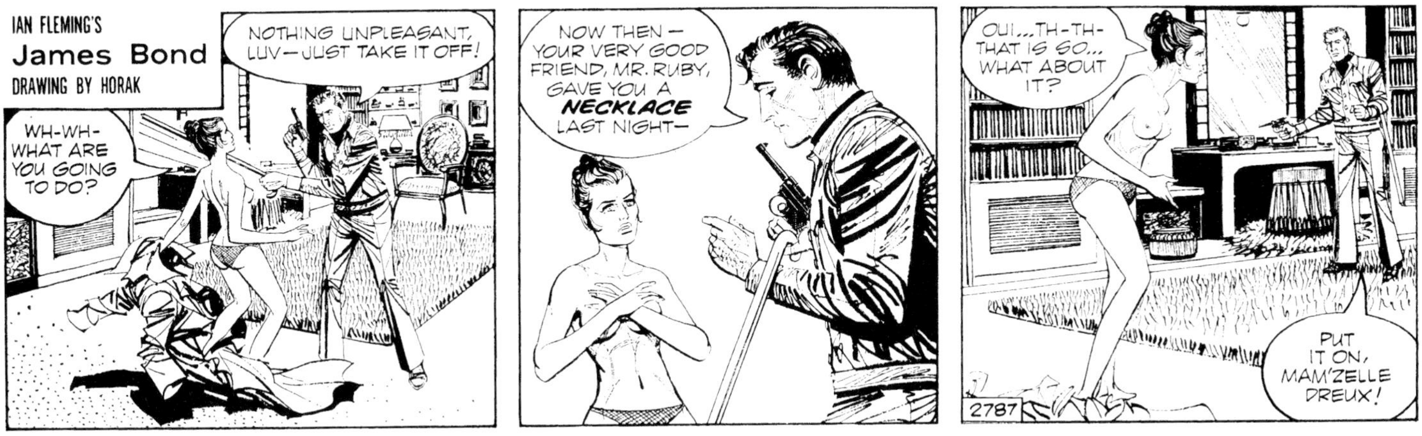
IAN FLEMING'S
James Bond
DRAWING BY HORAK
NOTHING UNPLEASANT, LUV—JUST TAKE IT OFF!
WH-WH-WHAT ARE YOU GOING TO DO?
NOW THEN — YOUR VERY GOOD FRIEND, MR. RUBY, GAVE YOU A NECKLACE LAST NIGHT—
OUI...TH-TH-THAT IS SO... WHAT ABOUT IT?
PUT IT ON, MAM'ZELLE DREUX!
2787

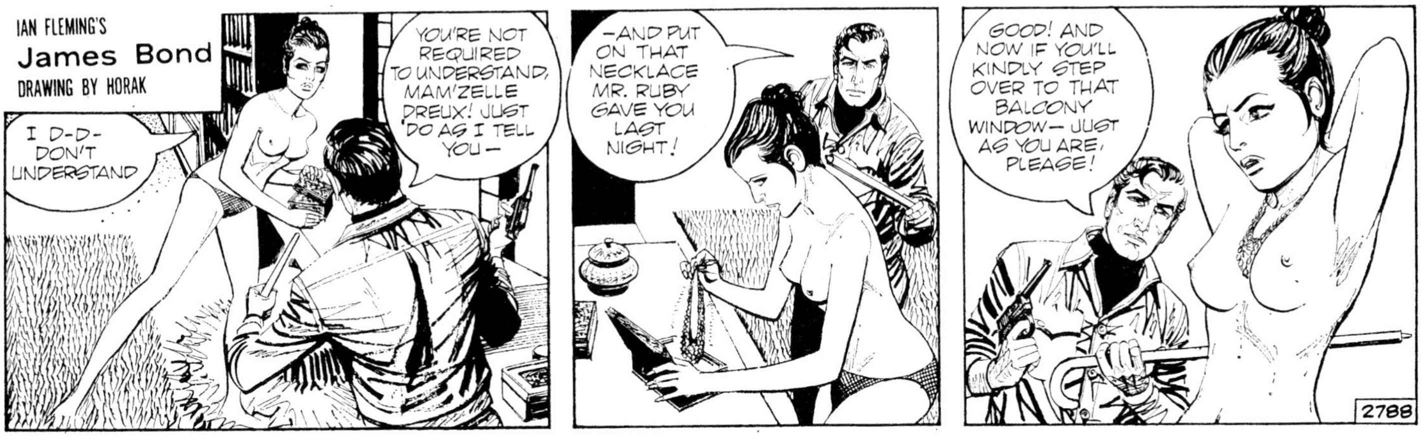
IAN FLEMING'S
James Bond
DRAWING BY HORAK
I D-D-DON'T UNDERSTAND
YOU'RE NOT REQUIRED TO UNDERSTAND, MAM'ZELLE DREUX! JUST DO AS I TELL YOU—
—AND PUT ON THAT NECKLACE MR. RUBY GAVE YOU LAST NIGHT!
GOOD! AND NOW IF YOU'LL KINDLY STEP OVER TO THAT BALCONY WINDOW— JUST AS YOU ARE, PLEASE!
2788

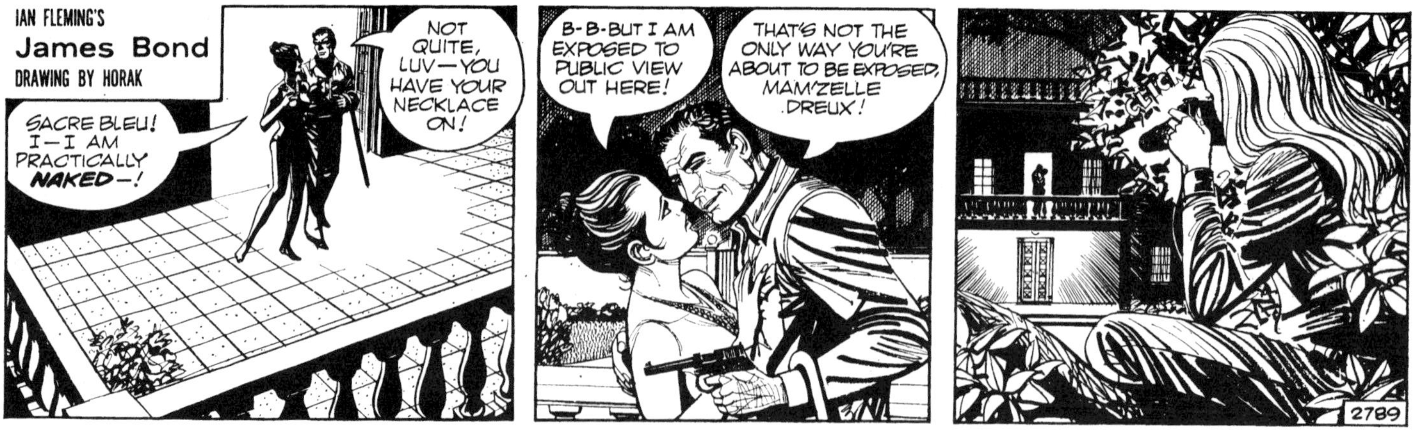
IAN FLEMING'S
James Bond
DRAWING BY HORAK
SACRE BLEU! I—I AM PRACTICALLY NAKED—!
NOT QUITE, LUV—YOU HAVE YOUR NECKLACE ON!
B-B-BUT I AM EXPOSED TO PUBLIC VIEW OUT HERE!
THAT'S NOT THE ONLY WAY YOU'RE ABOUT TO BE EXPOSED, MAM'ZELLE DREUX!
CLICK
2789

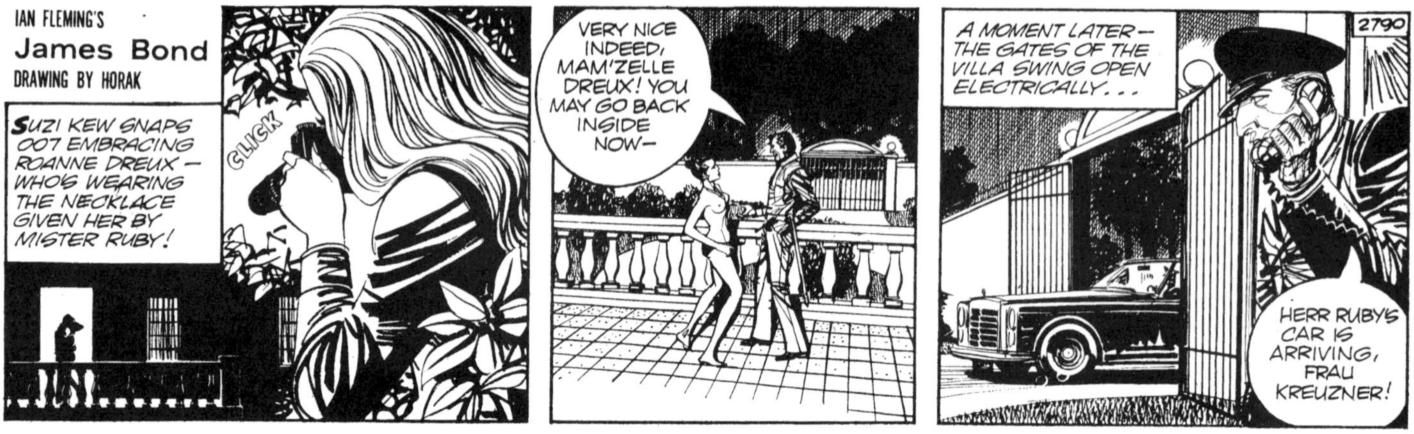
IAN FLEMING'S
James Bond
DRAWING BY HORAK
SUZI KEW SNAPS 007 EMBRACING ROANNE DREUX—WHO'S WEARING THE NECKLACE GIVEN HER BY MISTER RUBY!
CLICK
VERY NICE INDEED, MAM'ZELLE DREUX! YOU MAY GO BACK INSIDE NOW—
A MOMENT LATER—THE GATES OF THE VILLA SWING OPEN ELECTRICALLY . . .
2790
HERR RUBY'S CAR IS ARRIVING, FRAU KREUZNER!

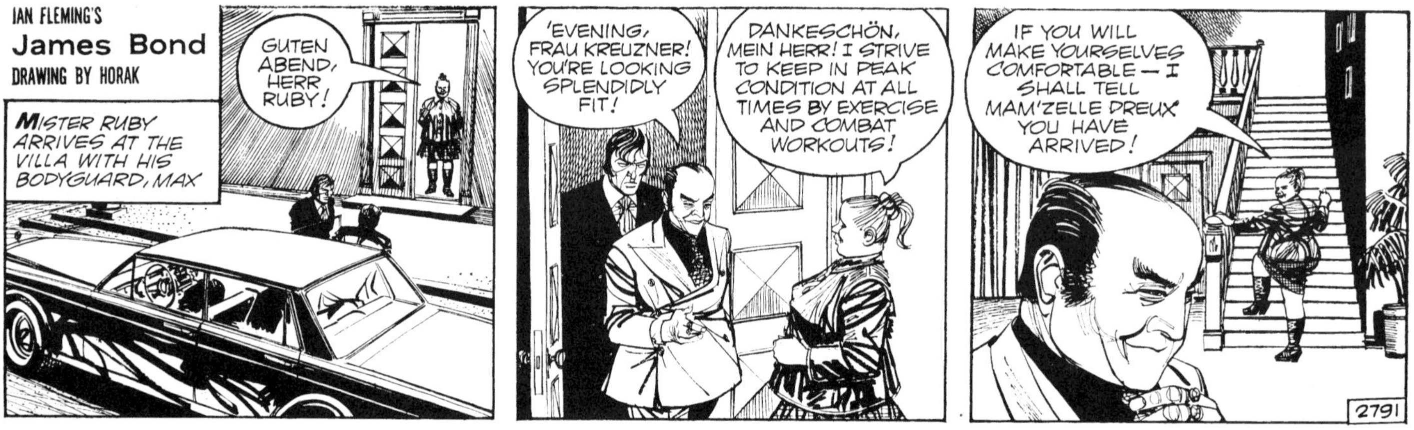
IAN FLEMING'S
James Bond
DRAWING BY HORAK
MISTER RUBY ARRIVES AT THE VILLA WITH HIS BODYGUARD, MAX
GUTEN ABEND, HERR RUBY!
'EVENING, FRAU KREUZNER! YOU'RE LOOKING SPLENDIDLY FIT!
DANKESCHÖN, MEIN HERR! I STRIVE TO KEEP IN PEAK CONDITION AT ALL TIMES BY EXERCISE AND COMBAT WORKOUTS!
IF YOU WILL MAKE YOURSELVES COMFORTABLE—I SHALL TELL MAM'ZELLE DREUX YOU HAVE ARRIVED!
2791

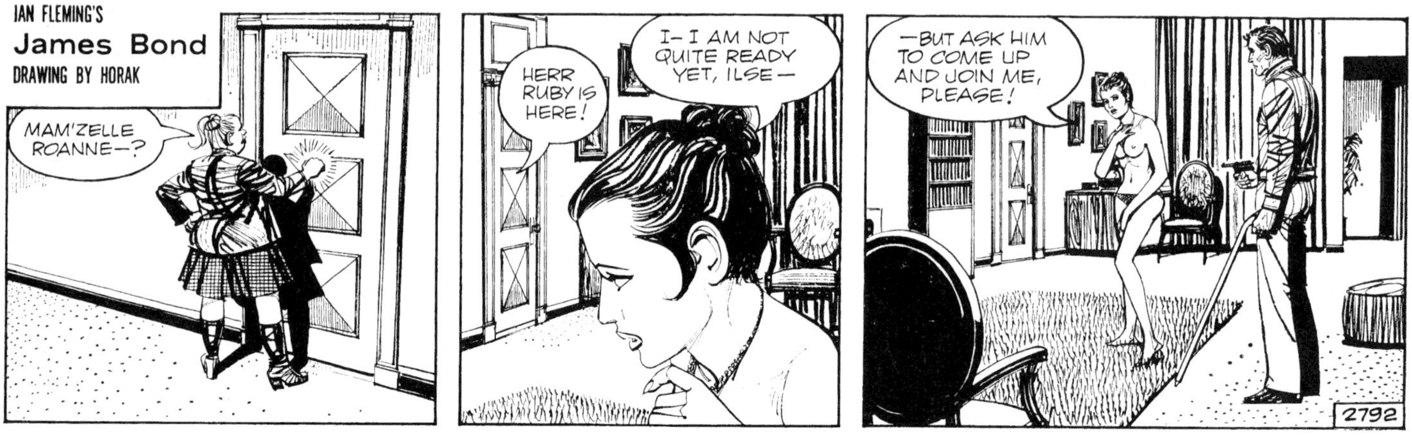
IAN FLEMING'S
James Bond
DRAWING BY HORAK
MAM'ZELLE ROANNE—?
HERR RUBY IS HERE!
I—I AM NOT QUITE READY YET, ILSE—
—BUT ASK HIM TO COME UP AND JOIN ME, PLEASE!
2792

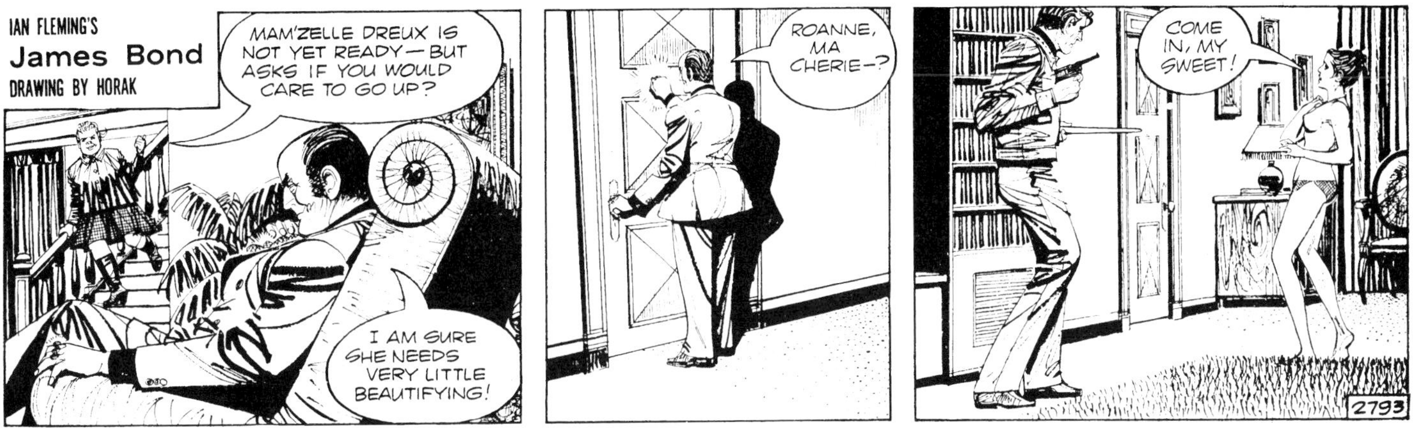
IAN FLEMING'S
James Bond
DRAWING BY HORAK
MAM'ZELLE DREUX IS NOT YET READY— BUT ASKS IF YOU WOULD CARE TO GO UP?
I AM SURE SHE NEEDS VERY LITTLE BEAUTIFYING!
ROANNE, MA CHERIE—?
COME IN, MY SWEET!
2793

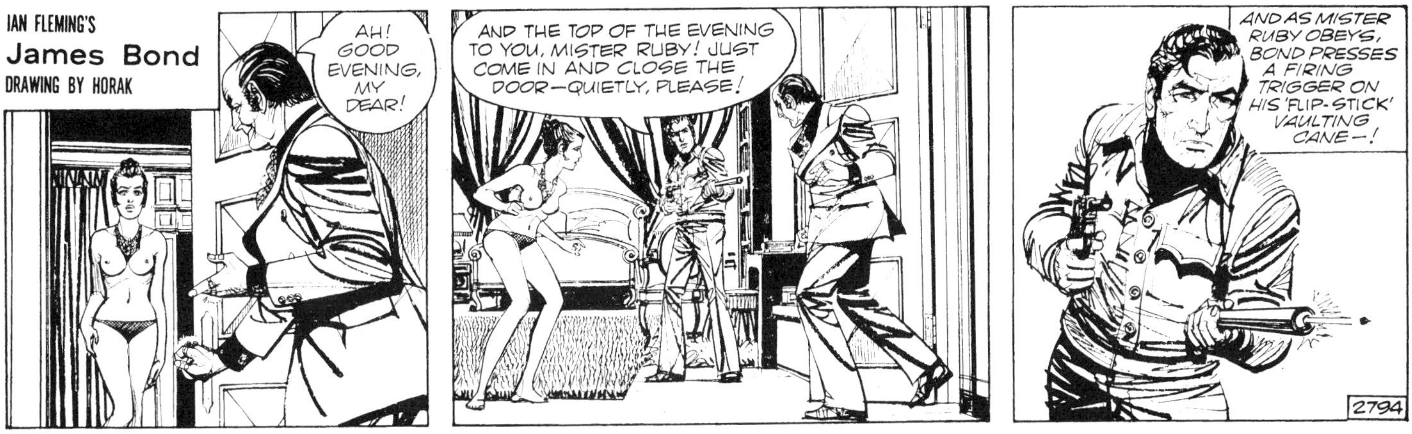
IAN FLEMING'S
James Bond
DRAWING BY HORAK
AH! GOOD EVENING, MY DEAR!
AND THE TOP OF THE EVENING TO YOU, MISTER RUBY! JUST COME IN AND CLOSE THE DOOR—QUIETLY, PLEASE!
AND AS MISTER RUBY OBEYS, BOND PRESSES A FIRING TRIGGER ON HIS 'FLIP-STICK' VAULTING CANE—!
2794

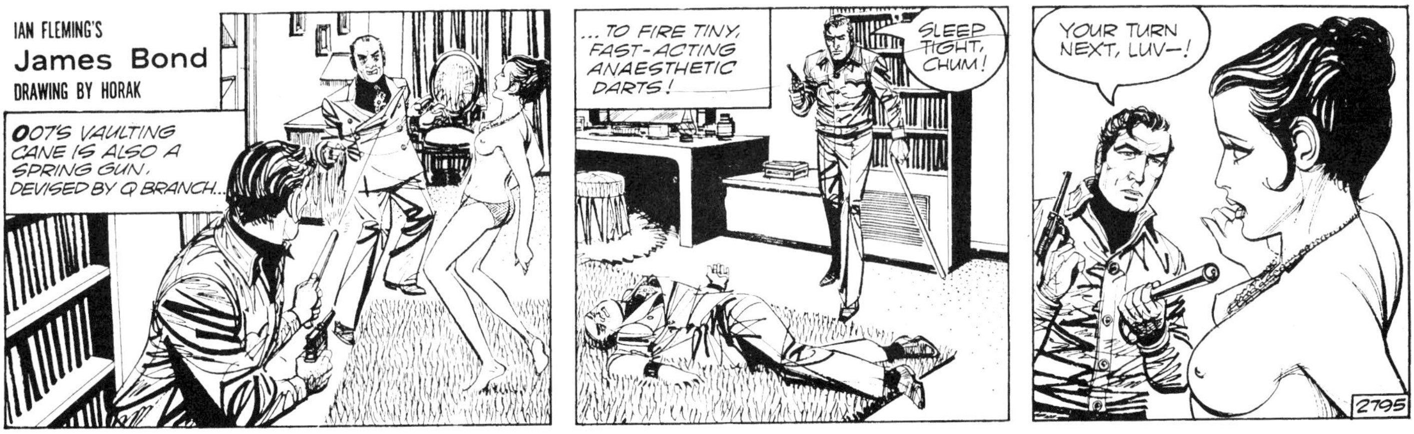
IAN FLEMING'S
James Bond
DRAWING BY HORAK
007'S VAULTING CANE IS ALSO A SPRING GUN, DEVISED BY Q BRANCH...
...TO FIRE TINY, FAST-ACTING ANAESTHETIC DARTS!
SLEEP TIGHT, CHUM!
YOUR TURN NEXT, LUV—!
2795

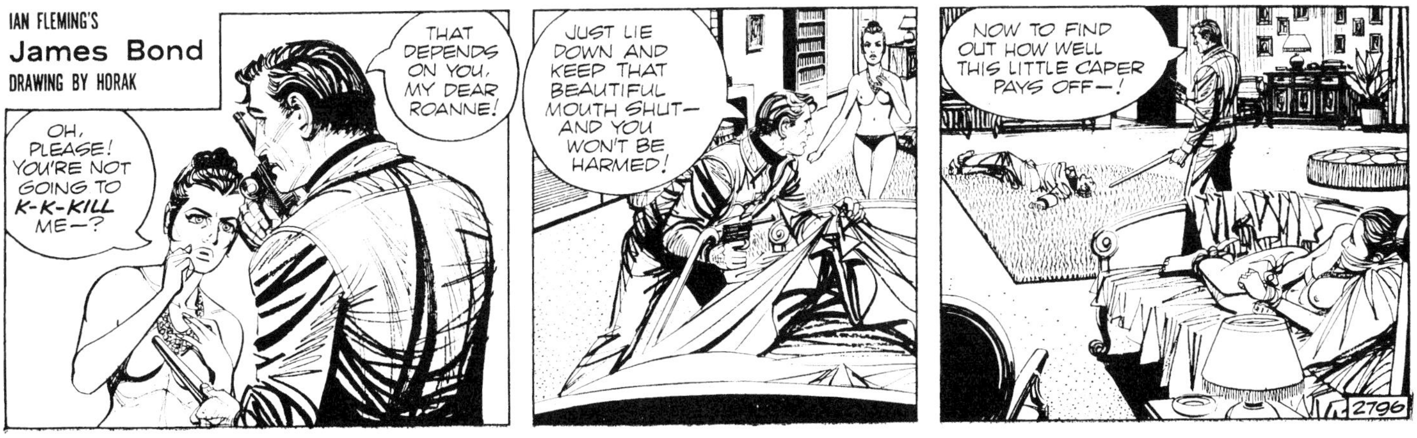
IAN FLEMING'S
James Bond
DRAWING BY HORAK
OH, PLEASE! YOU'RE NOT GOING TO K-K-KILL ME—?
THAT DEPENDS ON YOU, MY DEAR ROANNE!
JUST LIE DOWN AND KEEP THAT BEAUTIFUL MOUTH SHUT— AND YOU WON'T BE HARMED!
NOW TO FIND OUT HOW WELL THIS LITTLE CAPER PAYS OFF—!
2796

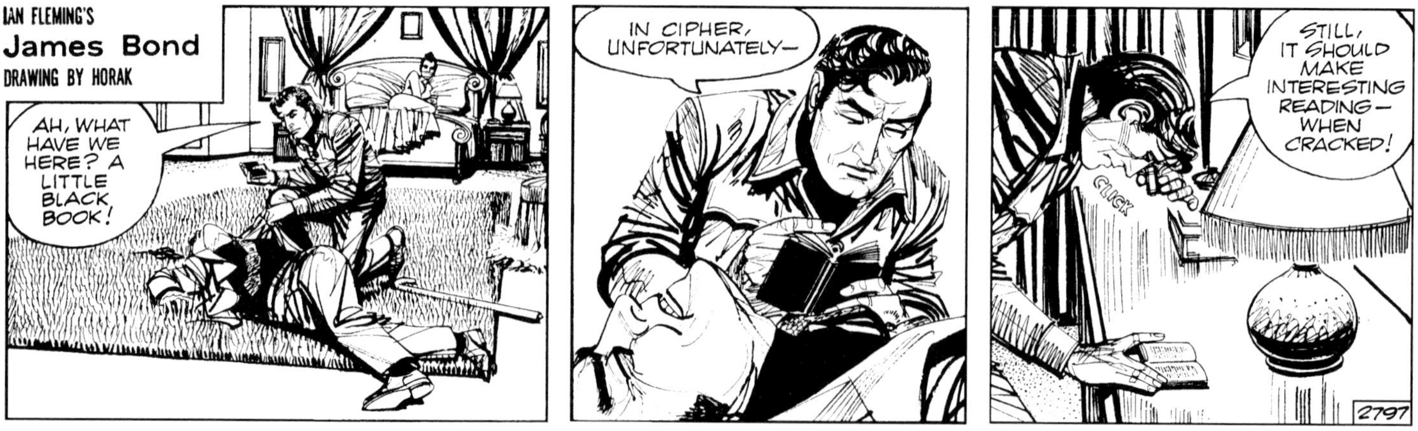
IAN FLEMING'S
James Bond
DRAWING BY HORAK
AH, WHAT HAVE WE HERE? A LITTLE BLACK BOOK!
IN CIPHER, UNFORTUNATELY—
STILL, IT SHOULD MAKE INTERESTING READING— WHEN CRACKED!
CLICK
2797

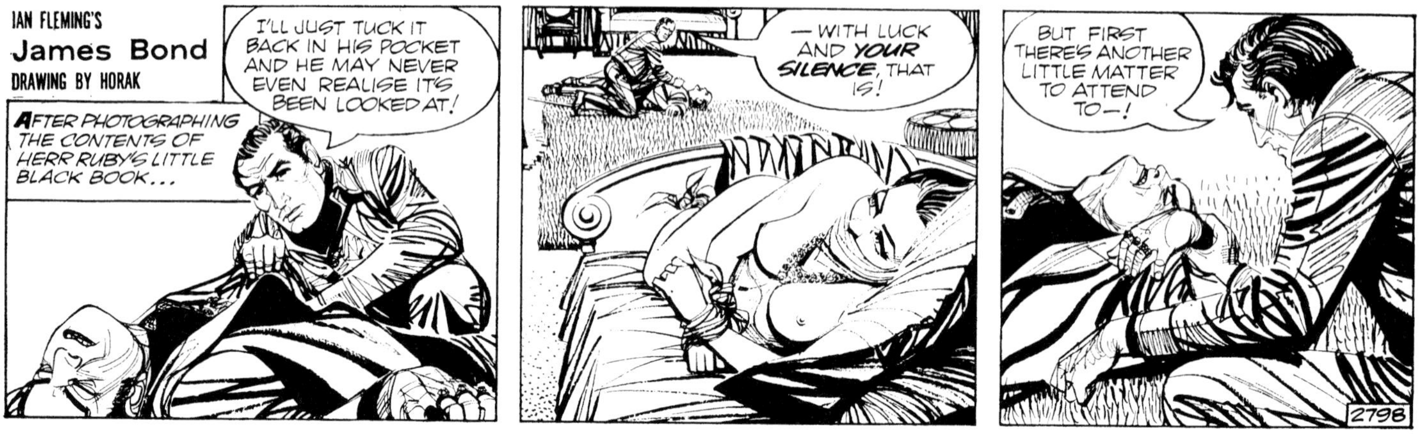
IAN FLEMING'S
James Bond
DRAWING BY HORAK
I'LL JUST TUCK IT BACK IN HIS POCKET AND HE MAY NEVER EVEN REALISE IT'S BEEN LOOKED AT!
AFTER PHOTOGRAPHING THE CONTENTS OF HERR RUBY'S LITTLE BLACK BOOK...
—WITH LUCK AND YOUR SILENCE, THAT IS!
BUT FIRST THERE'S ANOTHER LITTLE MATTER TO ATTEND TO—!
2798

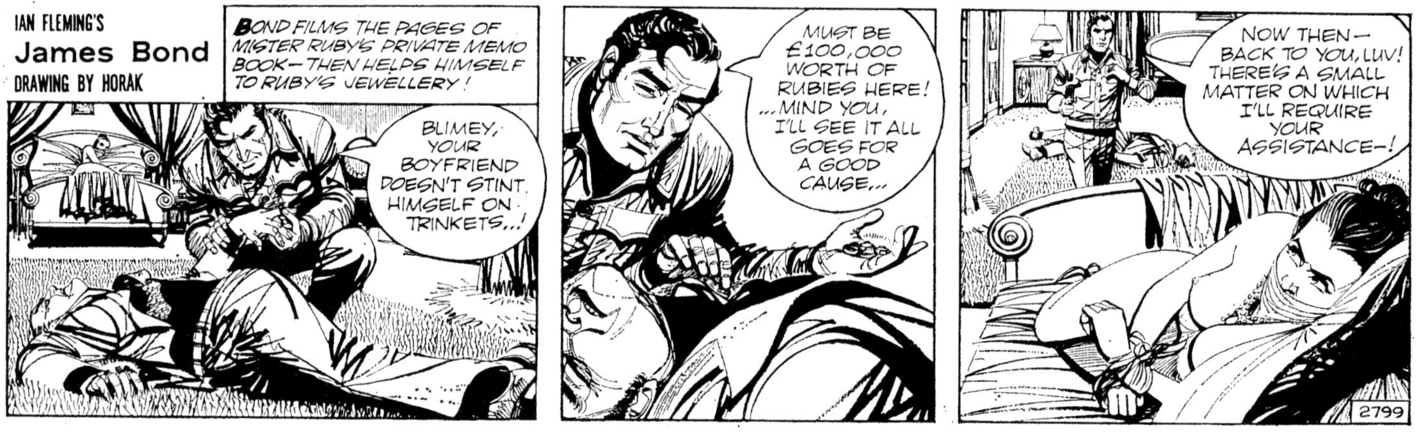
IAN FLEMING'S
James Bond
DRAWING BY HORAK
BOND FILMS THE PAGES OF MISTER RUBY'S PRIVATE MEMO BOOK—THEN HELPS HIMSELF TO RUBY'S JEWELLERY!
BLIMEY, YOUR BOYFRIEND DOESN'T STINT HIMSELF ON TRINKETS...!
MUST BE £100,000 WORTH OF RUBIES HERE! ...MIND YOU, I'LL SEE IT ALL GOES FOR A GOOD CAUSE...
NOW THEN— BACK TO YOU, LUV! THERE'S A SMALL MATTER ON WHICH I'LL REQUIRE YOUR ASSISTANCE—!
2799

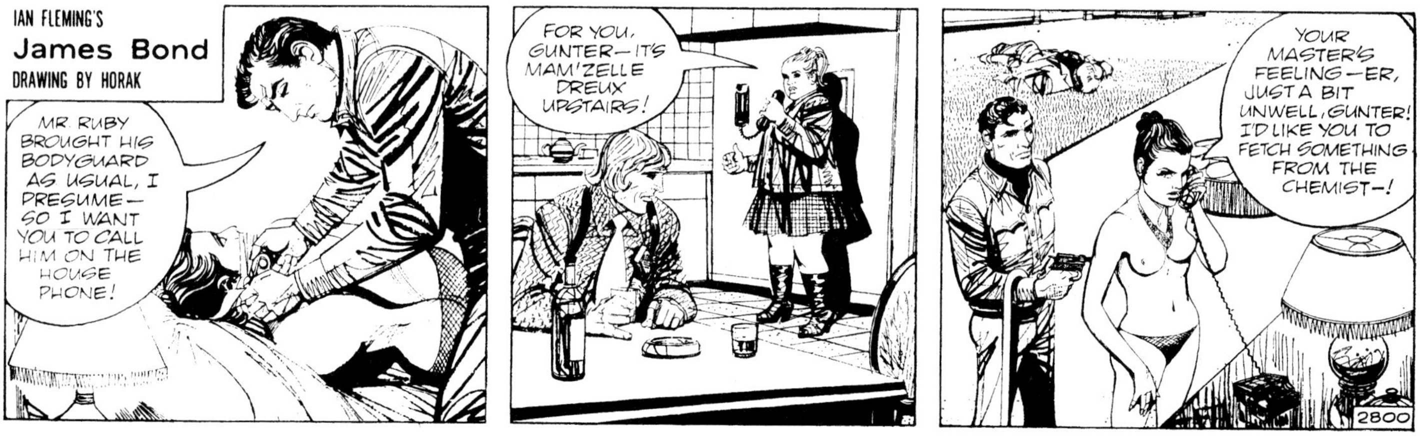
IAN FLEMING'S
James Bond
DRAWING BY HORAK
MR RUBY BROUGHT HIS BODYGUARD AS USUAL, I PRESUME— SO I WANT YOU TO CALL HIM ON THE HOUSE PHONE!
FOR YOU, GUNTER—IT'S MAM'ZELLE DREUX UPSTAIRS!
YOUR MASTER'S FEELING—ER, JUST A BIT UNWELL, GUNTER! I'D LIKE YOU TO FETCH SOMETHING FROM THE CHEMIST—!
2800

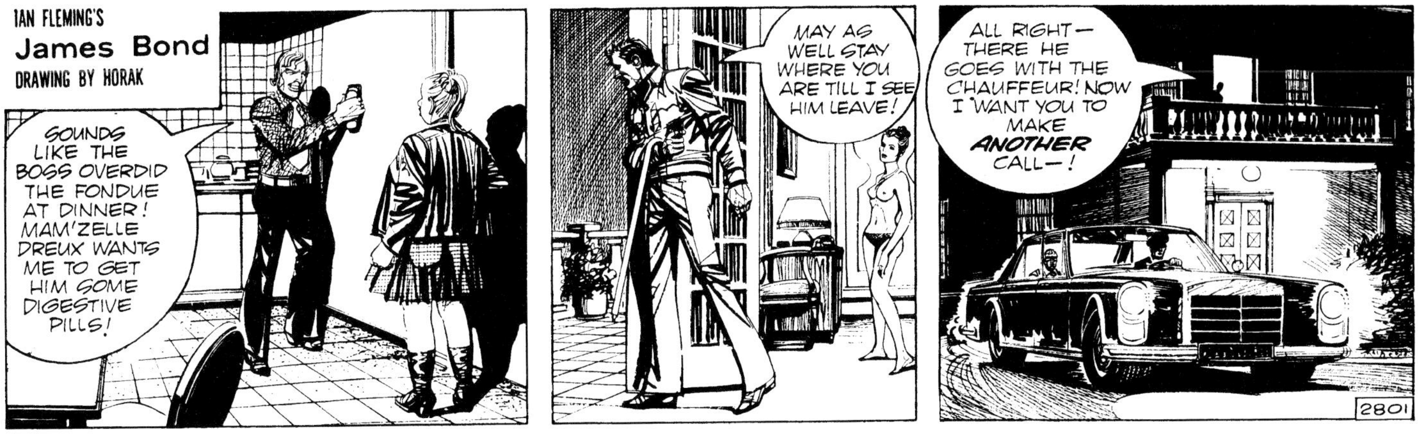
IAN FLEMING'S
James Bond
DRAWING BY HORAK
SOUNDS LIKE THE BOSS OVERDID THE FONDUE AT DINNER! MAM'ZELLE DREUX WANTS ME TO GET HIM SOME DIGESTIVE PILLS!
MAY AS WELL STAY WHERE YOU ARE TILL I SEE HIM LEAVE!
ALL RIGHT— THERE HE GOES WITH THE CHAUFFEUR! NOW I WANT YOU TO MAKE ANOTHER CALL—!
2801

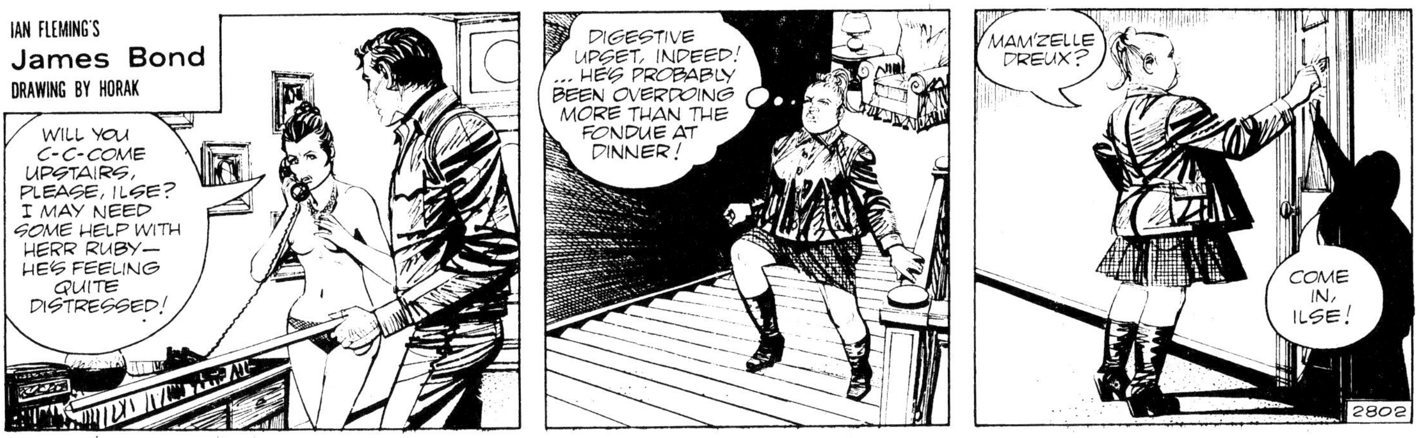
IAN FLEMING'S
James Bond
DRAWING BY HORAK
WILL YOU C-C-COME UPSTAIRS, PLEASE, ILSE? I MAY NEED SOME HELP WITH HERR RUBY— HE'S FEELING QUITE DISTRESSED!
DIGESTIVE UPSET, INDEED! ...HE'S PROBABLY BEEN OVERDOING MORE THAN THE FONDUE AT DINNER!
MAM'ZELLE DREUX?
COME IN, ILSE!
2802

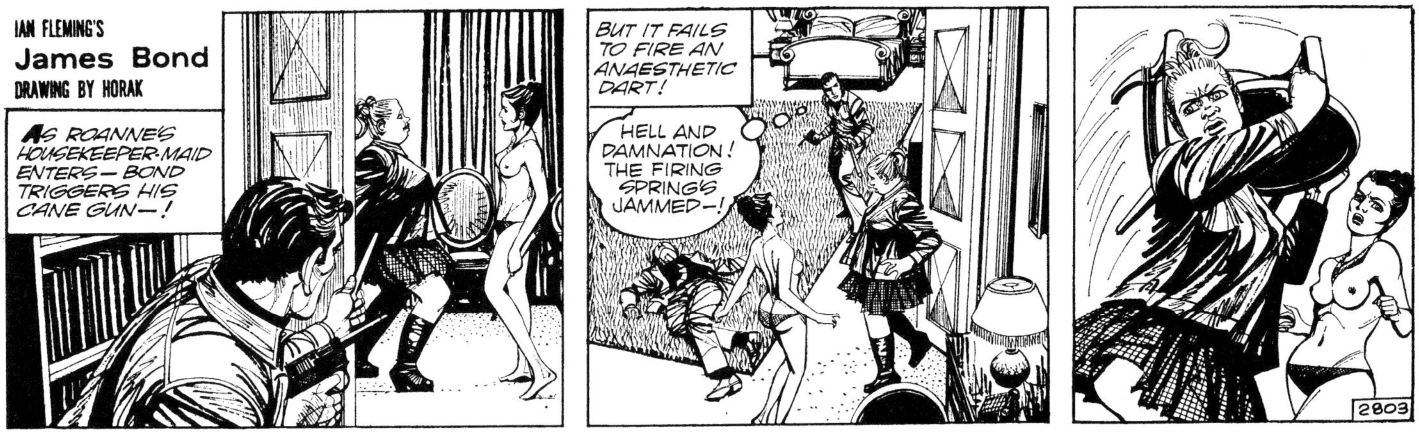
IAN FLEMING'S
James Bond
DRAWING BY HORAK
AS ROANNE'S HOUSEKEEPER-MAID ENTERS— BOND TRIGGERS HIS CANE GUN—!
BUT IT FAILS TO FIRE AN ANAESTHETIC DART!
HELL AND DAMNATION! THE FIRING SPRING'S JAMMED—!
2803

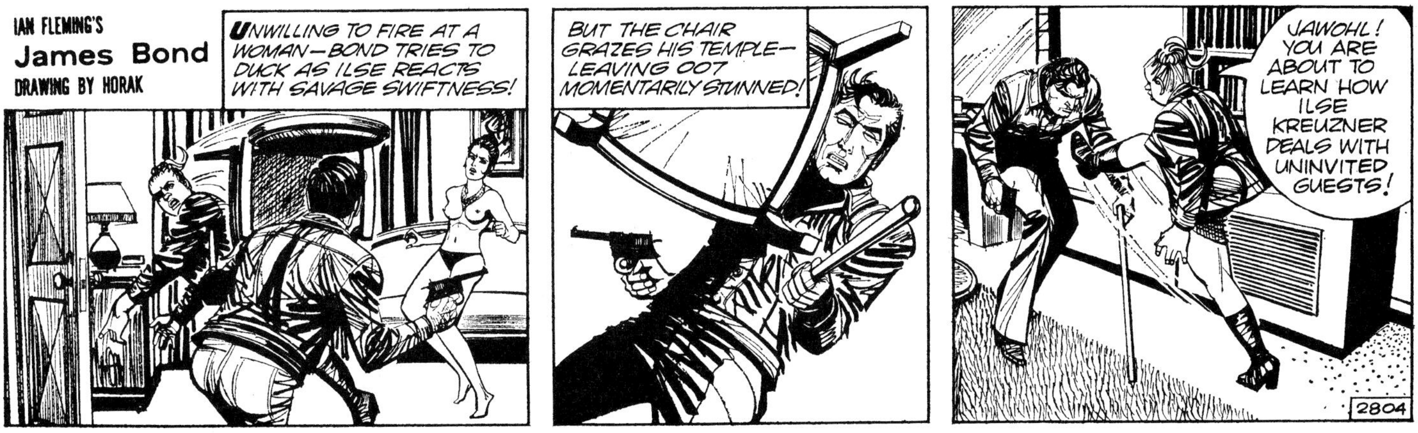
IAN FLEMING'S
James Bond
DRAWING BY HORAK
UNWILLING TO FIRE AT A WOMAN—BOND TRIES TO DUCK AS ILSE REACTS WITH SAVAGE SWIFTNESS!
BUT THE CHAIR GRAZES HIS TEMPLE— LEAVING 007 MOMENTARILY STUNNED!
JAWOHL! YOU ARE ABOUT TO LEARN HOW ILSE KREUZNER DEALS WITH UNINVITED GUESTS!
2804

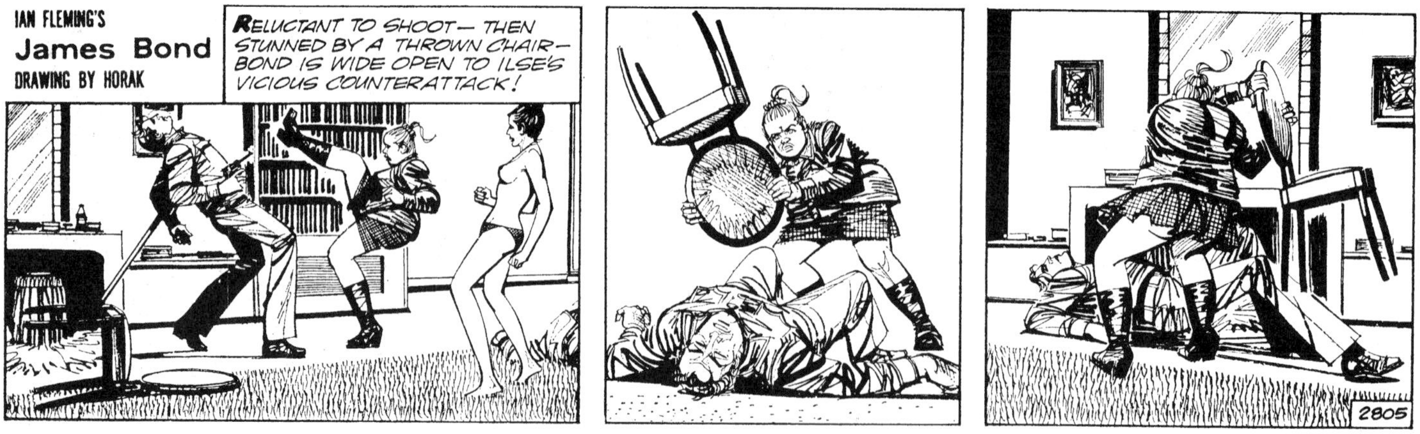
IAN FLEMING'S
James Bond
DRAWING BY HORAK
RELUCTANT TO SHOOT— THEN STUNNED BY A THROWN CHAIR-BOND IS WIDE OPEN TO ILSE'S VICIOUS COUNTERATTACK!
2805

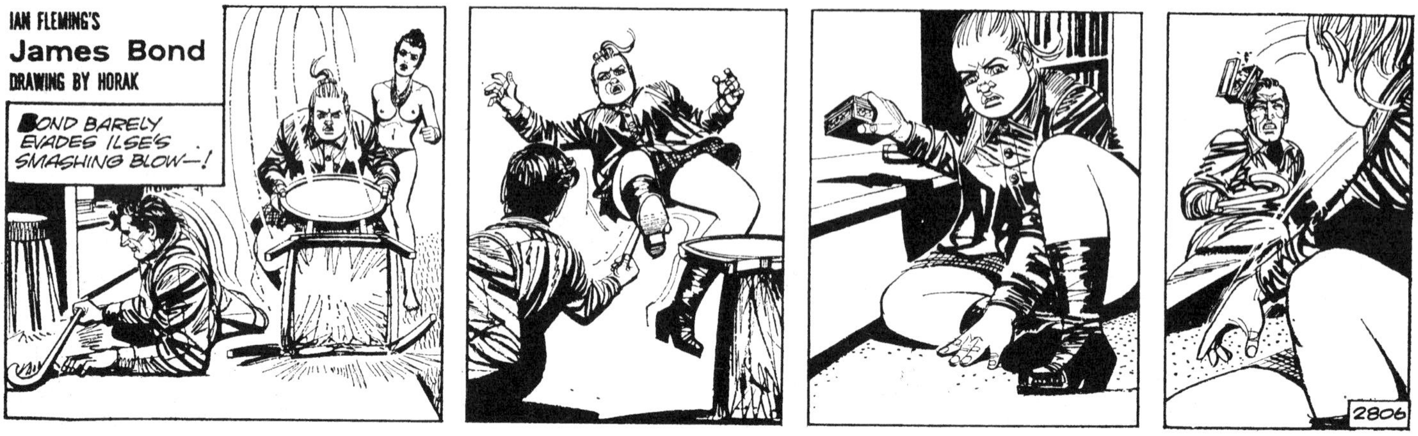
IAN FLEMING'S
James Bond
DRAWING BY HORAK
BOND BARELY EVADES ILSE'S SMASHING BLOW—!
2806

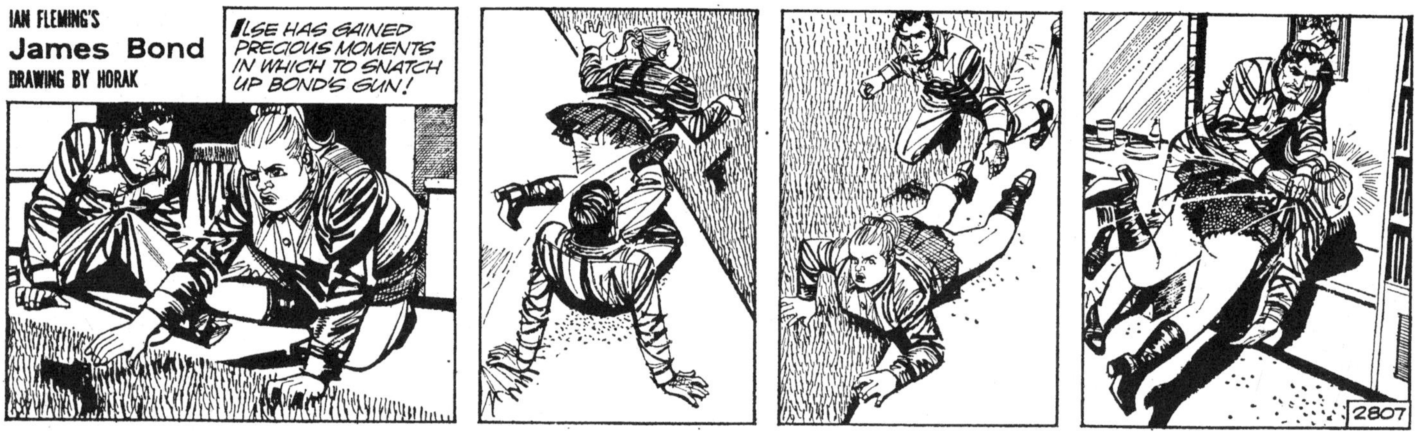
IAN FLEMING'S
James Bond
DRAWING BY HORAK
ILSE HAS GAINED PRECIOUS MOMENTS IN WHICH TO SNATCH UP BOND'S GUN!
2807

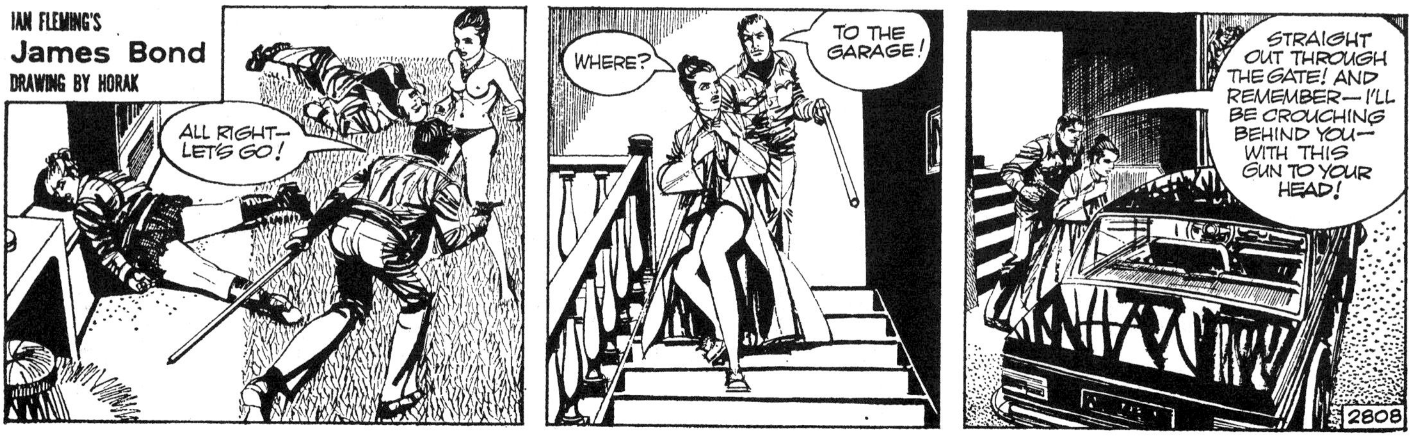
IAN FLEMING'S
James Bond
DRAWING BY HORAK
ALL RIGHT— LET'S GO!
WHERE?
TO THE GARAGE!
STRAIGHT OUT THROUGH THE GATE! AND REMEMBER— I'LL BE CROUCHING BEHIND YOU— WITH THIS GUN TO YOUR HEAD!
2808

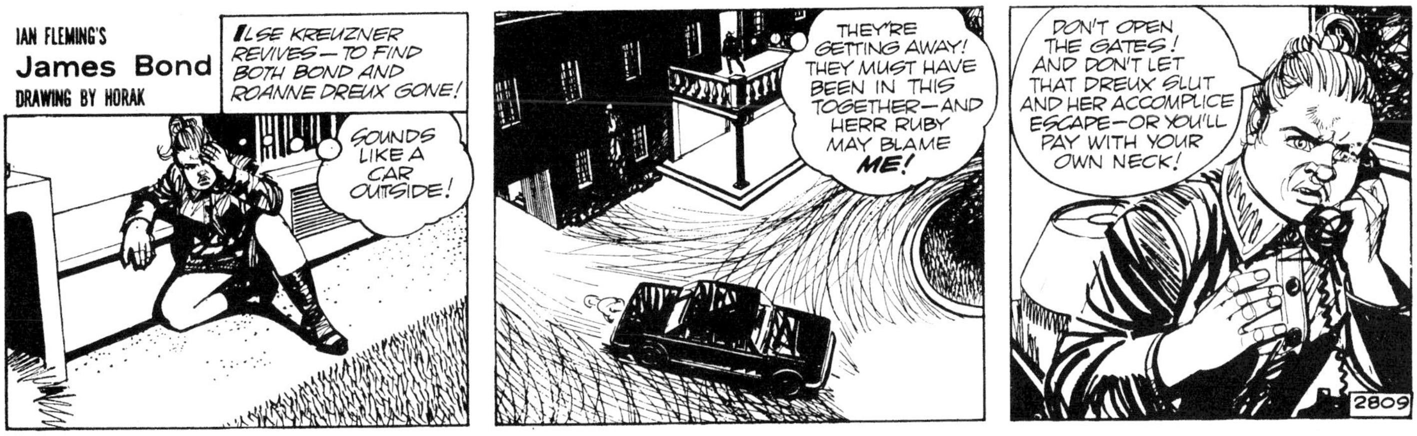
IAN FLEMING'S
James Bond
DRAWING BY HORAK
ILSE KREUZNER REVIVES—TO FIND BOTH BOND AND ROANNE DREUX GONE!
SOUNDS LIKE A CAR OUTSIDE!
THEY'RE GETTING AWAY! THEY MUST HAVE BEEN IN THIS TOGETHER—AND HERR RUBY MAY BLAME ME!
DON'T OPEN THE GATES! AND DON'T LET THAT DREUX SLUT AND HER ACCOMPLICE ESCAPE—OR YOU'LL PAY WITH YOUR OWN NECK!
2809

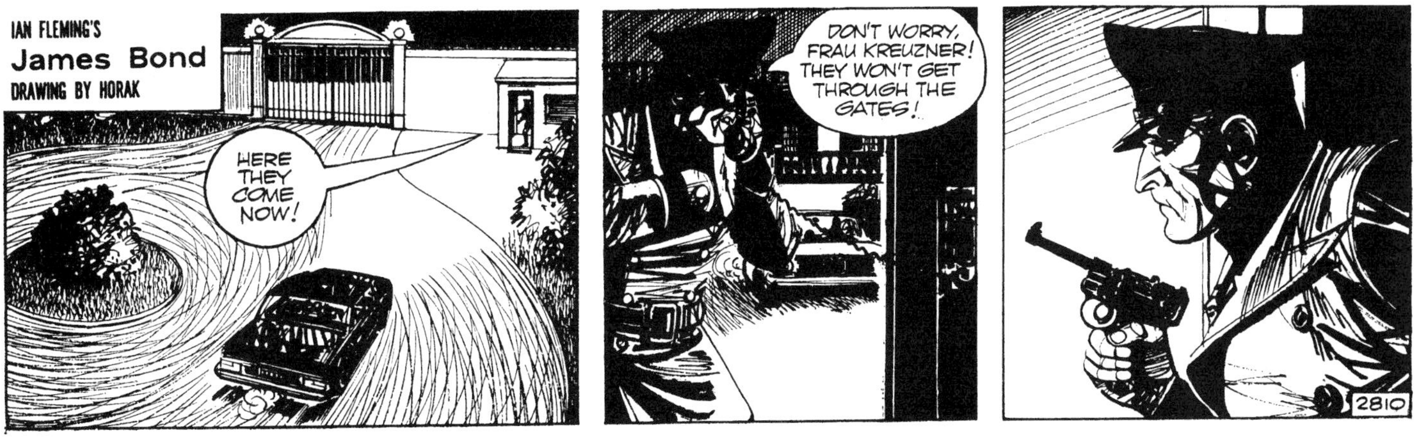
IAN FLEMING'S
James Bond
DRAWING BY HORAK
HERE THEY COME NOW!
DON'T WORRY, FRAU KREUZNER! THEY WON'T GET THROUGH THE GATES!
2810

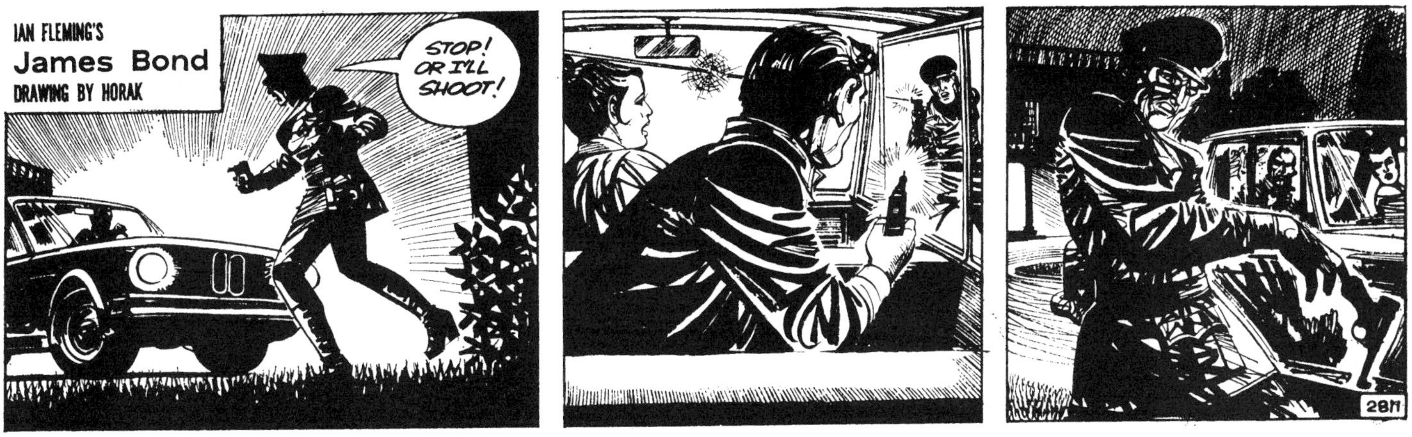
IAN FLEMING'S
James Bond
DRAWING BY HORAK
STOP! OR I'LL SHOOT!
2811

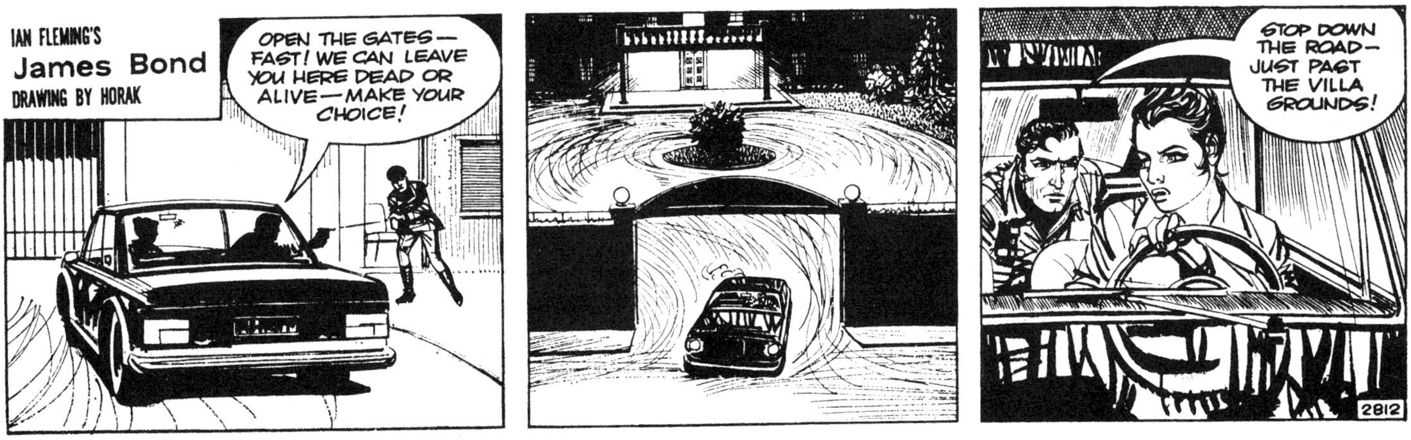
IAN FLEMING'S
James Bond
DRAWING BY HORAK
OPEN THE GATES—FAST! WE CAN LEAVE YOU HERE DEAD OR ALIVE—MAKE YOUR CHOICE!
STOP DOWN THE ROAD—JUST PAST THE VILLA GROUNDS!
2812

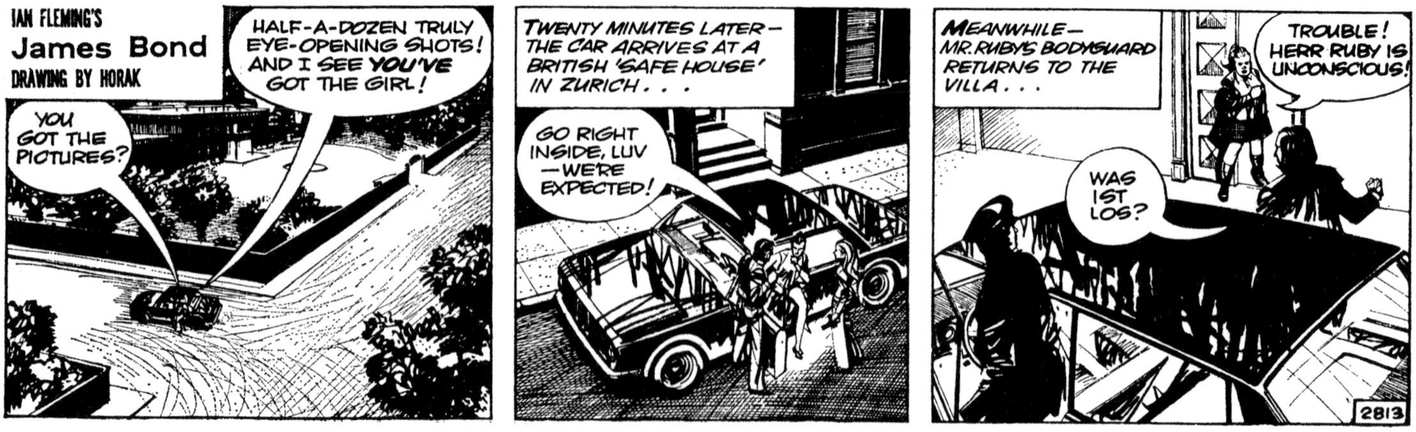
IAN FLEMING'S
James Bond
DRAWING BY HORAK
YOU GOT THE PICTURES?
HALF-A-DOZEN TRULY EYE-OPENING SHOTS! AND I SEE YOU'VE GOT THE GIRL!
TWENTY MINUTES LATER— THE CAR ARRIVES AT A BRITISH 'SAFE HOUSE' IN ZURICH . . .
GO RIGHT INSIDE, LUV —WE'RE EXPECTED!
MEANWHILE— MR. RUBY'S BODYGUARD RETURNS TO THE VILLA . . .
TROUBLE! HERR RUBY IS UNCONSCIOUS!
WAS IST LOS?
2813

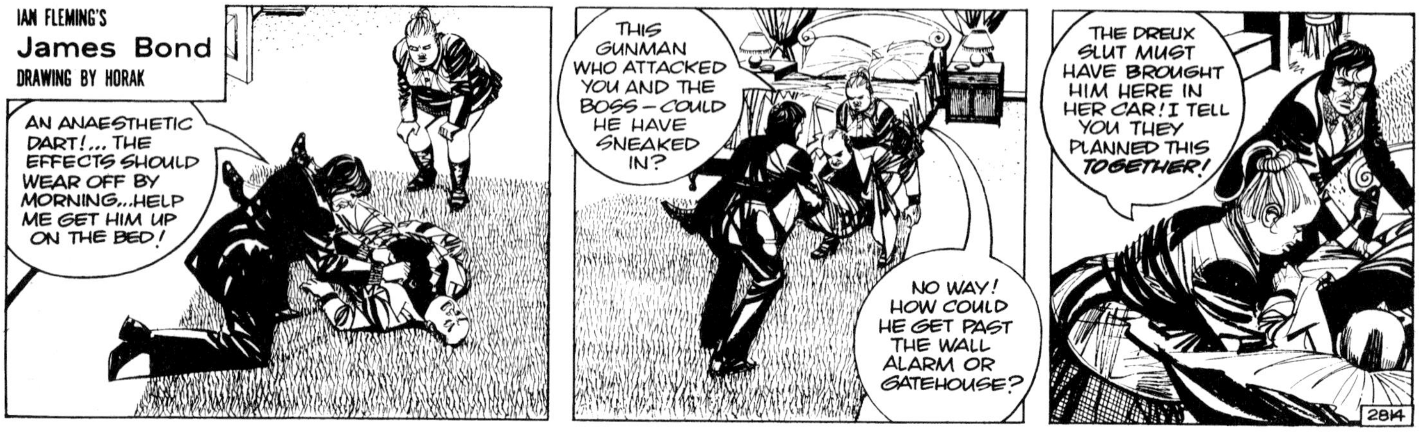
IAN FLEMING'S
James Bond
DRAWING BY HORAK
AN ANAESTHETIC DART!... THE EFFECTS SHOULD WEAR OFF BY MORNING...HELP ME GET HIM UP ON THE BED!
THIS GUNMAN WHO ATTACKED YOU AND THE BOSS—COULD HE HAVE SNEAKED IN?
NO WAY! HOW COULD HE GET PAST THE WALL ALARM OR GATEHOUSE?
THE DREUX SLUT MUST HAVE BROUGHT HIM HERE IN HER CAR! I TELL YOU THEY PLANNED THIS TOGETHER!
2814

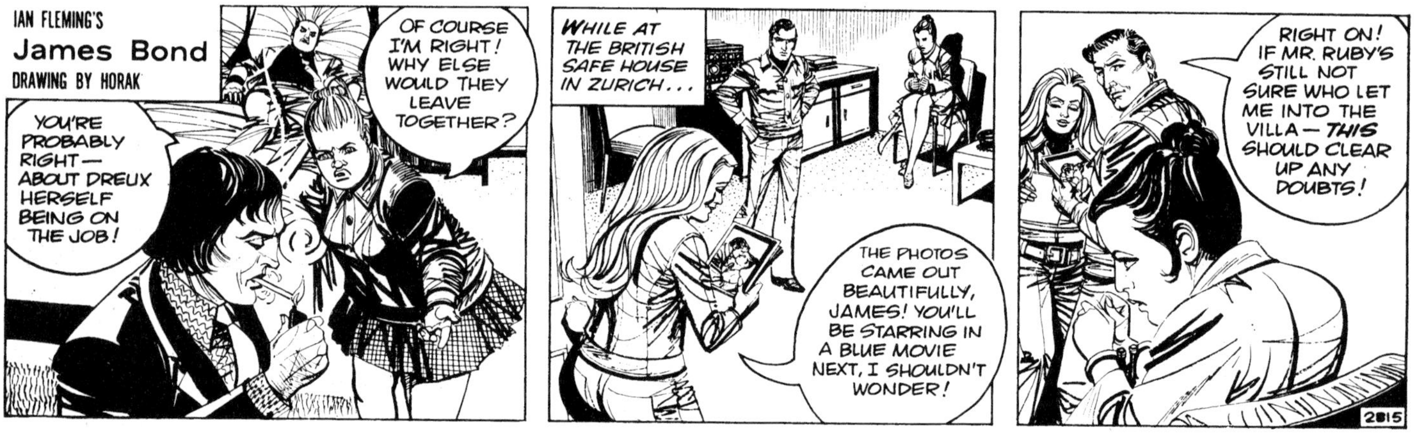
IAN FLEMING'S
James Bond
DRAWING BY HORAK
YOU'RE PROBABLY RIGHT— ABOUT DREUX HERSELF BEING ON THE JOB!
OF COURSE I'M RIGHT! WHY ELSE WOULD THEY LEAVE TOGETHER?
WHILE AT THE BRITISH SAFE HOUSE IN ZURICH . . .
THE PHOTOS CAME OUT BEAUTIFULLY, JAMES! YOU'LL BE STARRING IN A BLUE MOVIE NEXT, I SHOULDN'T WONDER!
RIGHT ON! IF MR. RUBY'S STILL NOT SURE WHO LET ME INTO THE VILLA—THIS SHOULD CLEAR UP ANY DOUBTS!
2815

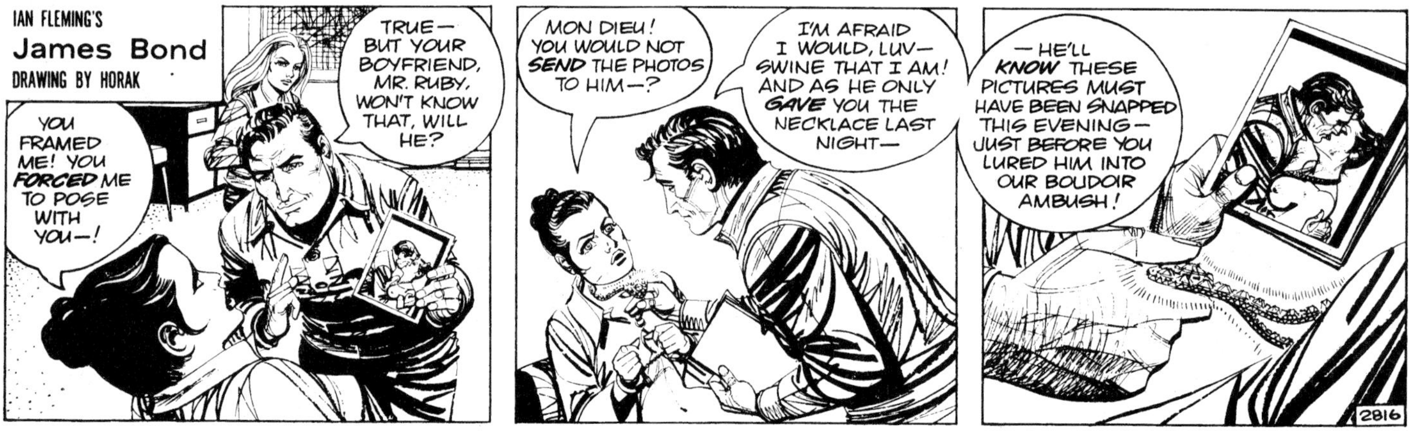
IAN FLEMING'S
James Bond
DRAWING BY HORAK
YOU FRAMED ME! YOU FORCED ME TO POSE WITH YOU—!
TRUE— BUT YOUR BOYFRIEND, MR. RUBY, WON'T KNOW THAT, WILL HE?
MON DIEU! YOU WOULD NOT SEND THE PHOTOS TO HIM—?
I'M AFRAID I WOULD, LUV— SWINE THAT I AM! AND AS HE ONLY GAVE YOU THE NECKLACE LAST NIGHT—
—HE'LL KNOW THESE PICTURES MUST HAVE BEEN SNAPPED THIS EVENING— JUST BEFORE YOU LURED HIM INTO OUR BOUDOIR AMBUSH!
2816

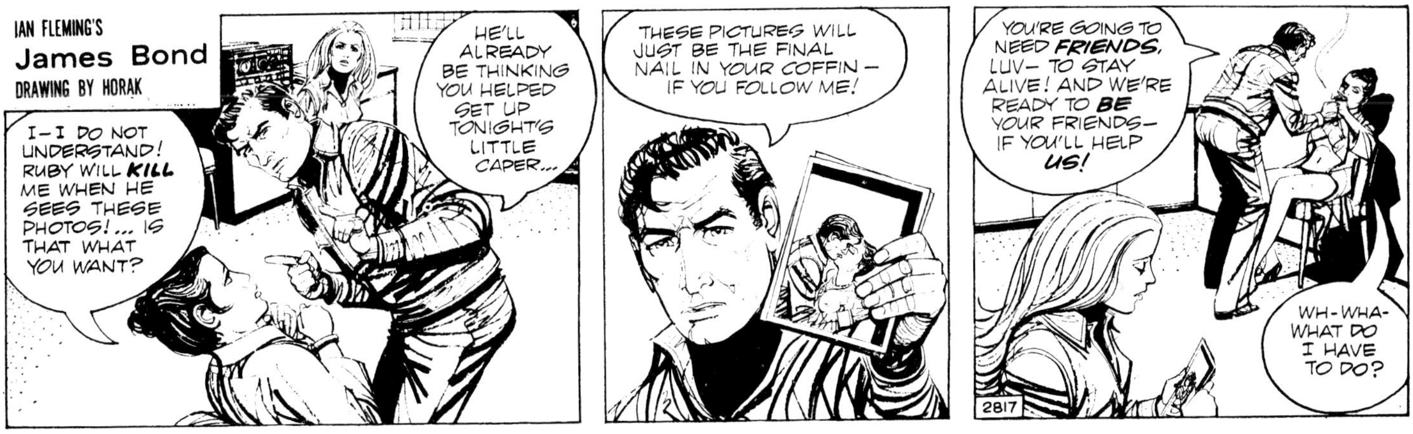
IAN FLEMING'S
James Bond
DRAWING BY HORAK
I–I DO NOT UNDERSTAND! RUBY WILL KILL ME WHEN HE SEES THESE PHOTOS!... IS THAT WHAT YOU WANT?
HE'LL ALREADY BE THINKING YOU HELPED SET UP TONIGHT'S LITTLE CAPER...
THESE PICTURES WILL JUST BE THE FINAL NAIL IN YOUR COFFIN – IF YOU FOLLOW ME!
YOU'RE GOING TO NEED FRIENDS, LUV– TO STAY ALIVE! AND WE'RE READY TO BE YOUR FRIENDS– IF YOU'LL HELP US!
WH-WHA-WHAT DO I HAVE TO DO?
2817

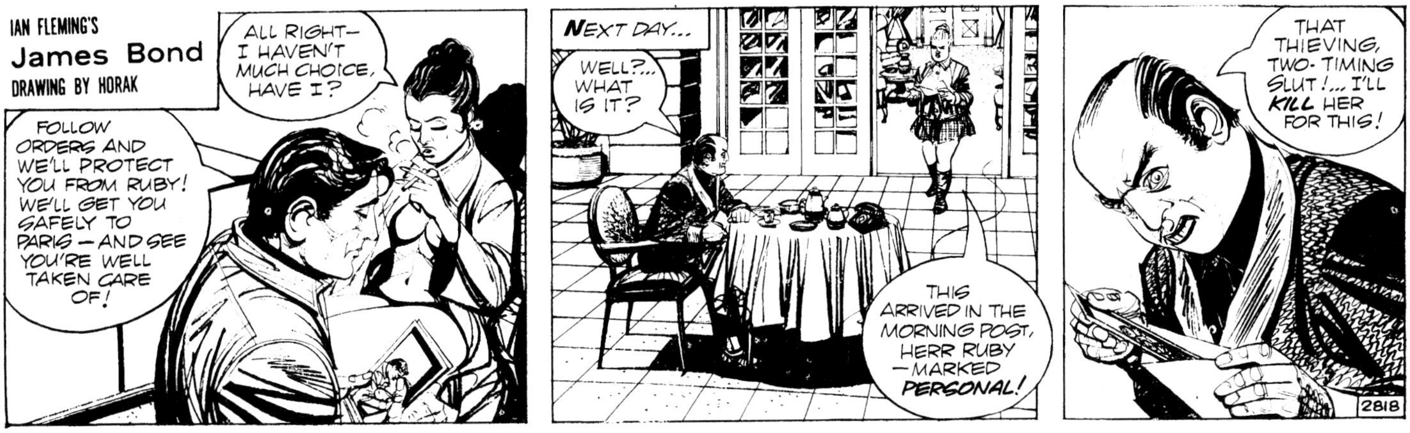
IAN FLEMING'S
James Bond
DRAWING BY HORAK
ALL RIGHT– I HAVEN'T MUCH CHOICE, HAVE I?
FOLLOW ORDERS AND WE'LL PROTECT YOU FROM RUBY! WE'LL GET YOU SAFELY TO PARIS – AND SEE YOU'RE WELL TAKEN CARE OF!
NEXT DAY...
WELL?... WHAT IS IT?
THIS ARRIVED IN THE MORNING POST, HERR RUBY –MARKED PERSONAL!
THAT THIEVING, TWO-TIMING SLUT!... I'LL KILL HER FOR THIS!
2818

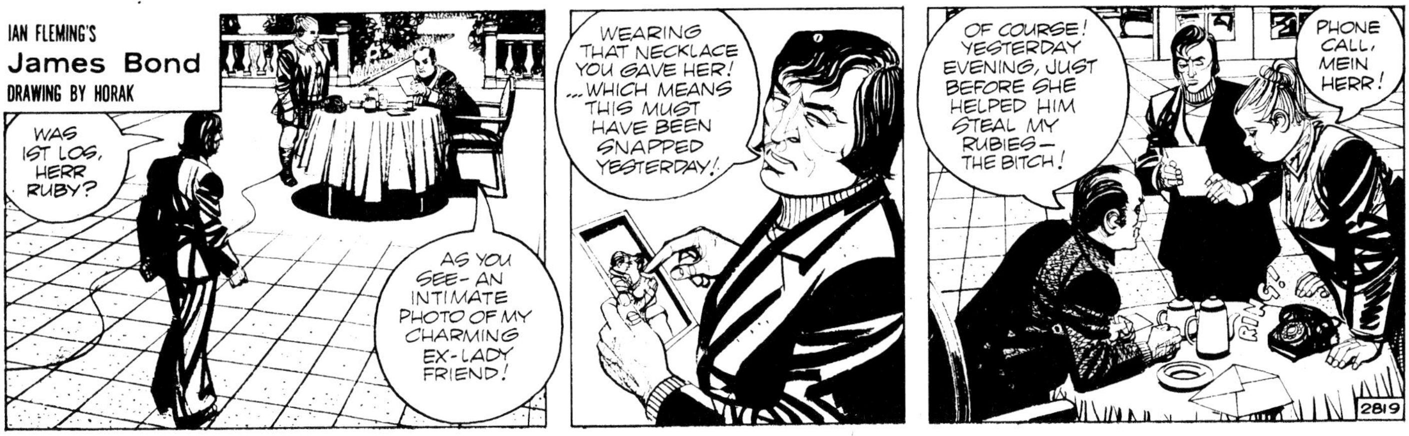
IAN FLEMING'S
James Bond
DRAWING BY HORAK
WAS IST LOS, HERR RUBY?
AS YOU SEE– AN INTIMATE PHOTO OF MY CHARMING EX-LADY FRIEND!
WEARING THAT NECKLACE YOU GAVE HER! ...WHICH MEANS THIS MUST HAVE BEEN SNAPPED YESTERDAY!
OF COURSE! YESTERDAY EVENING, JUST BEFORE SHE HELPED HIM STEAL MY RUBIES– THE BITCH!
PHONE CALL, MEIN HERR!
RING!
2819

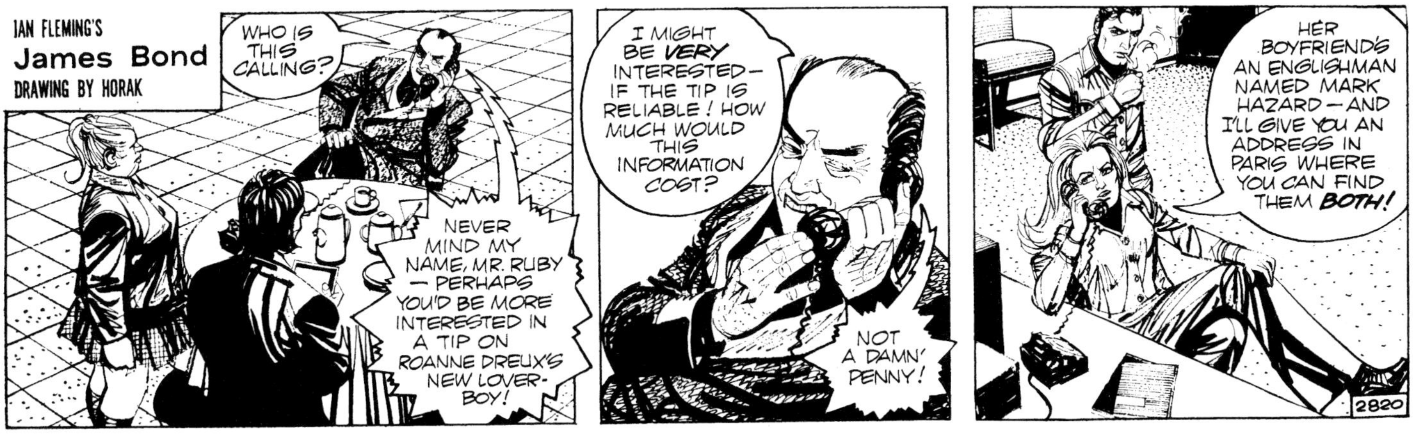
IAN FLEMING'S
James Bond
DRAWING BY HORAK
WHO IS THIS CALLING?
NEVER MIND MY NAME, MR. RUBY – PERHAPS YOU'D BE MORE INTERESTED IN A TIP ON ROANNE DREUX'S NEW LOVER-BOY!
I MIGHT BE VERY INTERESTED– IF THE TIP IS RELIABLE! HOW MUCH WOULD THIS INFORMATION COST?
NOT A DAMN' PENNY!
HER BOYFRIEND'S AN ENGLISHMAN NAMED MARK HAZARD – AND I'LL GIVE YOU AN ADDRESS IN PARIS WHERE YOU CAN FIND THEM BOTH!
2820

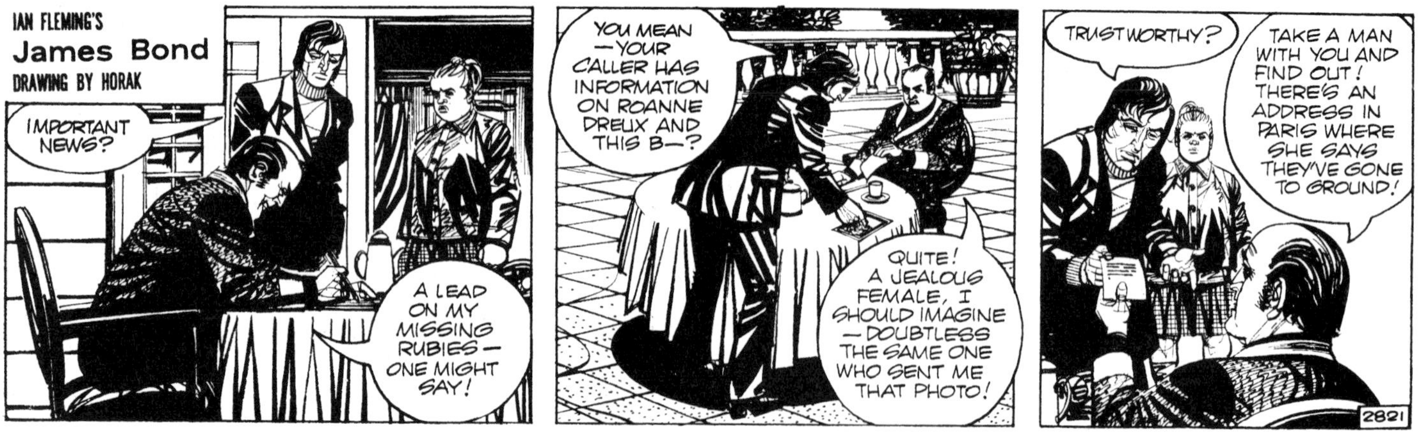
IAN FLEMING'S
James Bond
DRAWING BY HORAK
IMPORTANT NEWS?
A LEAD ON MY MISSING RUBIES— ONE MIGHT SAY!
YOU MEAN —YOUR CALLER HAS INFORMATION ON ROANNE DREUX AND THIS B—?
QUITE! A JEALOUS FEMALE, I SHOULD IMAGINE —DOUBTLESS THE SAME ONE WHO SENT ME THAT PHOTO!
TRUSTWORTHY?
TAKE A MAN WITH YOU AND FIND OUT! THERE'S AN ADDRESS IN PARIS WHERE SHE SAYS THEY'VE GONE TO GROUND!
2821

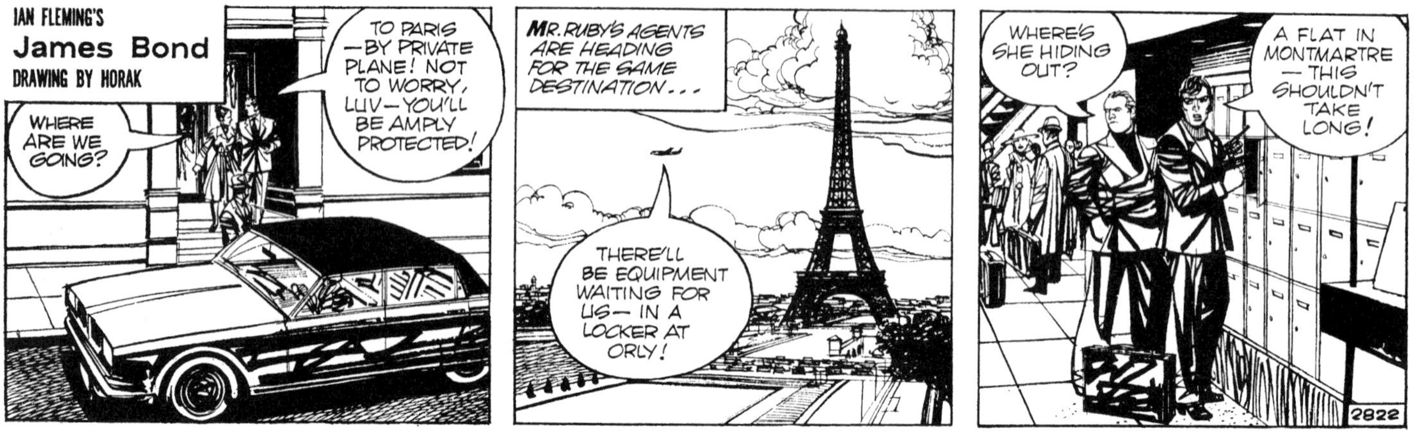
IAN FLEMING'S
James Bond
DRAWING BY HORAK
WHERE ARE WE GOING?
TO PARIS —BY PRIVATE PLANE! NOT TO WORRY, LUV—YOU'LL BE AMPLY PROTECTED!
MR. RUBY'S AGENTS ARE HEADING FOR THE SAME DESTINATION . . .
THERE'LL BE EQUIPMENT WAITING FOR US— IN A LOCKER AT ORLY!
WHERE'S SHE HIDING OUT?
A FLAT IN MONTMARTRE —THIS SHOULDN'T TAKE LONG!
2822

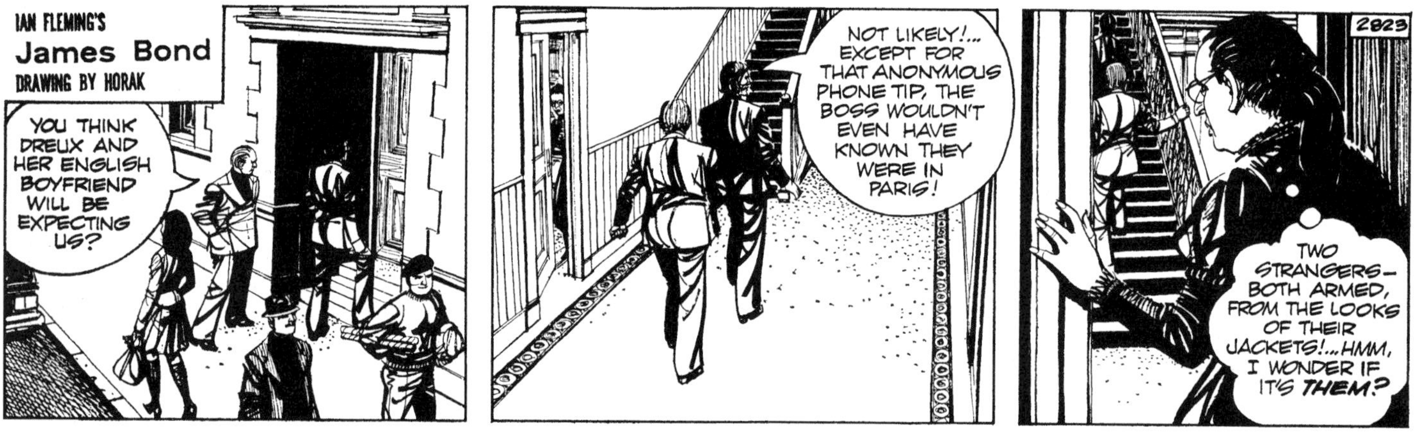
IAN FLEMING'S
James Bond
DRAWING BY HORAK
YOU THINK DREUX AND HER ENGLISH BOYFRIEND WILL BE EXPECTING US?
NOT LIKELY!... EXCEPT FOR THAT ANONYMOUS PHONE TIP, THE BOSS WOULDN'T EVEN HAVE KNOWN THEY WERE IN PARIS!
2823
TWO STRANGERS— BOTH ARMED, FROM THE LOOKS OF THEIR JACKETS!...HMM, I WONDER IF IT'S THEM?

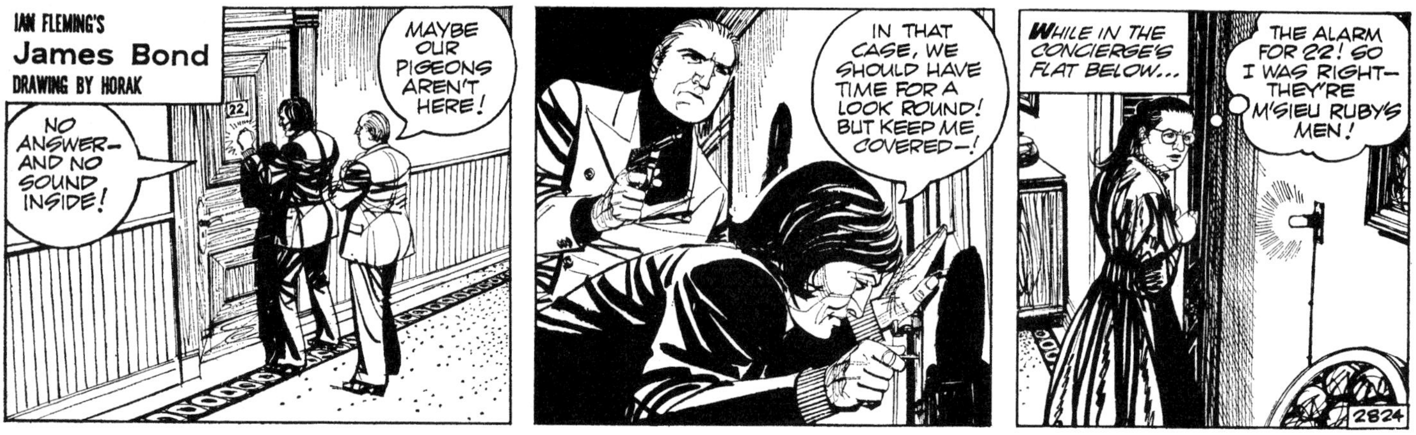
IAN FLEMING'S
James Bond
DRAWING BY HORAK
NO ANSWER— AND NO SOUND INSIDE!
MAYBE OUR PIGEONS AREN'T HERE!
IN THAT CASE, WE SHOULD HAVE TIME FOR A LOOK ROUND! BUT KEEP ME COVERED—!
WHILE IN THE CONCIERGE'S FLAT BELOW...
THE ALARM FOR 22! SO I WAS RIGHT— THEY'RE M'SIEU RUBY'S MEN!
2824

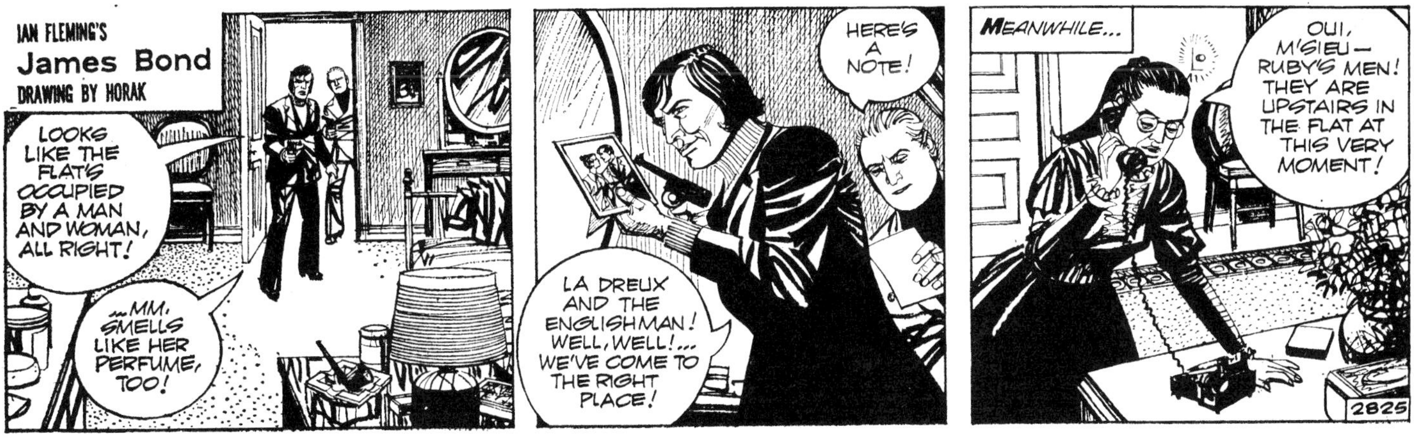
IAN FLEMING'S
James Bond
DRAWING BY HORAK
LOOKS LIKE THE FLAT'S OCCUPIED BY A MAN AND WOMAN, ALL RIGHT!
...MM. SMELLS LIKE HER PERFUME, TOO!
HERE'S A NOTE!
LA DREUX AND THE ENGLISHMAN! WELL, WELL!... WE'VE COME TO THE RIGHT PLACE!
MEANWHILE...
OUI, M'SIEU— RUBY'S MEN! THEY ARE UPSTAIRS IN THE FLAT AT THIS VERY MOMENT!
2825

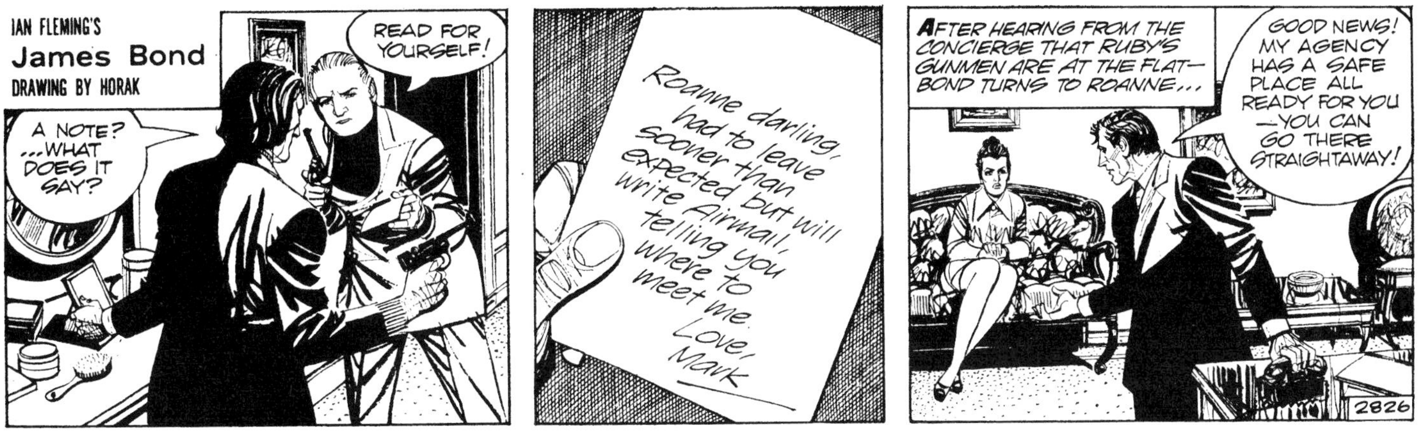
IAN FLEMING'S
James Bond
DRAWING BY HORAK
READ FOR YOURSELF!
A NOTE? ...WHAT DOES IT SAY?
Roanne darling, had to leave sooner than expected but will write Airmail, telling you where to meet me. Love, Mark
AFTER HEARING FROM THE CONCIERGE THAT RUBY'S GUNMEN ARE AT THE FLAT— BOND TURNS TO ROANNE...
GOOD NEWS! MY AGENCY HAS A SAFE PLACE ALL READY FOR YOU —YOU CAN GO THERE STRAIGHTAWAY!
2826

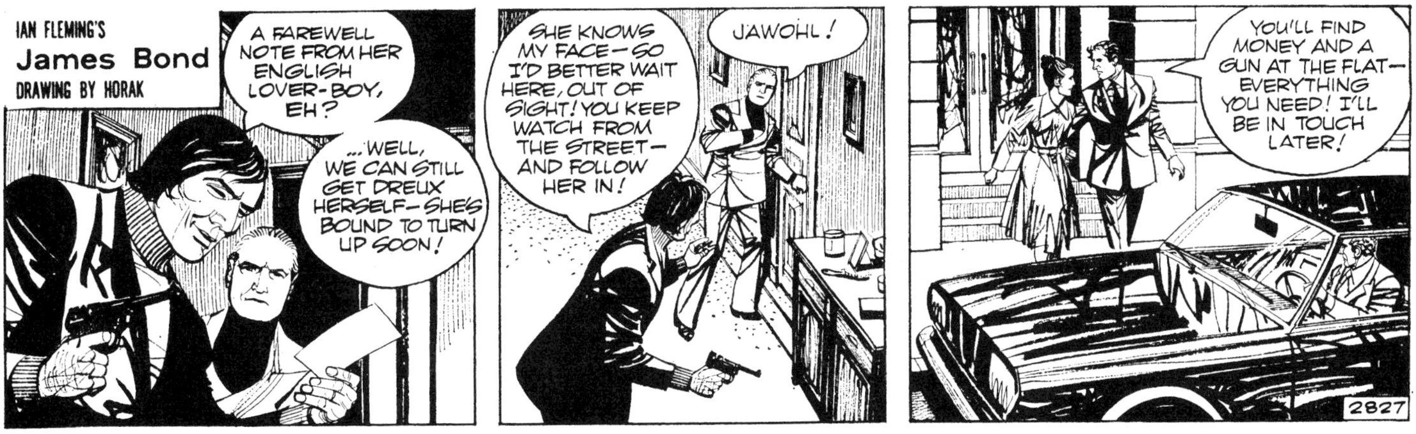
IAN FLEMING'S
James Bond
DRAWING BY HORAK
A FAREWELL NOTE FROM HER ENGLISH LOVER-BOY, EH?
...WELL, WE CAN STILL GET DREUX HERSELF—SHE'S BOUND TO TURN UP SOON!
SHE KNOWS MY FACE—SO I'D BETTER WAIT HERE, OUT OF SIGHT! YOU KEEP WATCH FROM THE STREET— AND FOLLOW HER IN!
JAWOHL!
YOU'LL FIND MONEY AND A GUN AT THE FLAT— EVERYTHING YOU NEED! I'LL BE IN TOUCH LATER!
2827

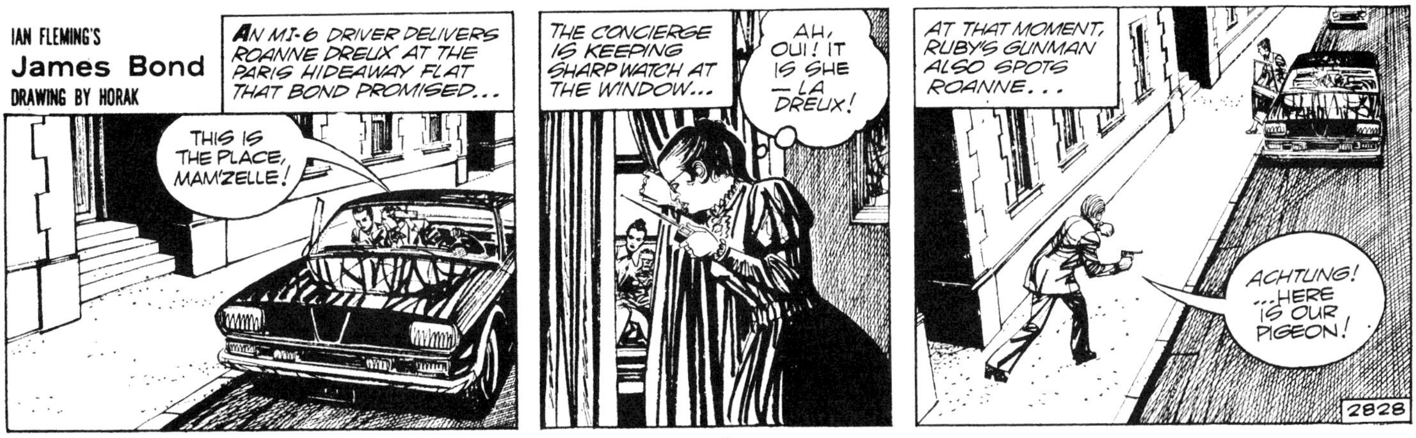
IAN FLEMING'S
James Bond
DRAWING BY HORAK
AN MI-6 DRIVER DELIVERS ROANNE DREUX AT THE PARIS HIDEAWAY FLAT THAT BOND PROMISED...
THIS IS THE PLACE, MAM'ZELLE!
THE CONCIERGE IS KEEPING SHARP WATCH AT THE WINDOW...
AH, OUI! IT IS SHE —LA DREUX!
AT THAT MOMENT, RUBY'S GUNMAN ALSO SPOTS ROANNE...
ACHTUNG! ...HERE IS OUR PIGEON!
2828

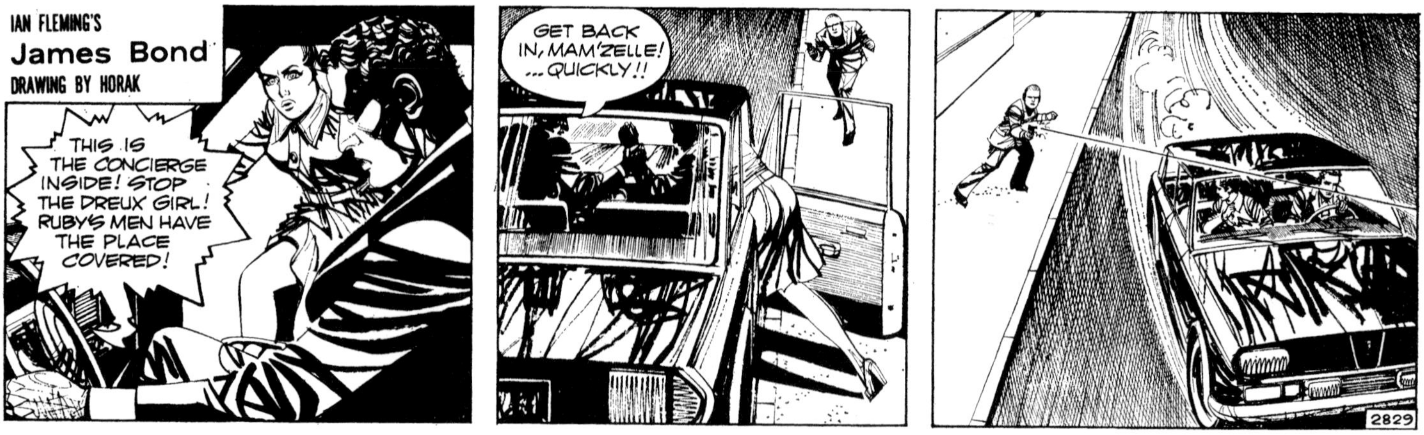
IAN FLEMING'S
James Bond
DRAWING BY HORAK
THIS IS THE CONCIERGE INSIDE! STOP THE DREUX GIRL! RUBY'S MEN HAVE THE PLACE COVERED!
GET BACK IN, MAM'ZELLE! ...QUICKLY!!
2829

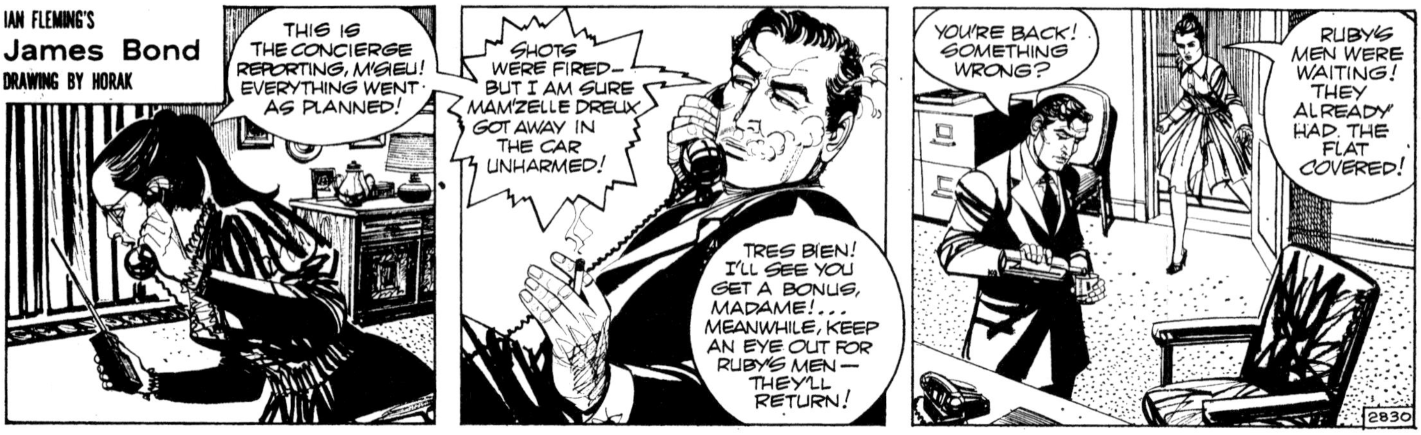
IAN FLEMING'S
James Bond
DRAWING BY HORAK
THIS IS THE CONCIERGE REPORTING, M'SIEU! EVERYTHING WENT AS PLANNED!
SHOTS WERE FIRED— BUT I AM SURE MAM'ZELLE DREUX GOT AWAY IN THE CAR UNHARMED!
TRES BIEN! I'LL SEE YOU GET A BONUS, MADAME!... MEANWHILE, KEEP AN EYE OUT FOR RUBY'S MEN— THEY'LL RETURN!
YOU'RE BACK! SOMETHING WRONG?
RUBY'S MEN WERE WAITING! THEY ALREADY HAD THE FLAT COVERED!
2830

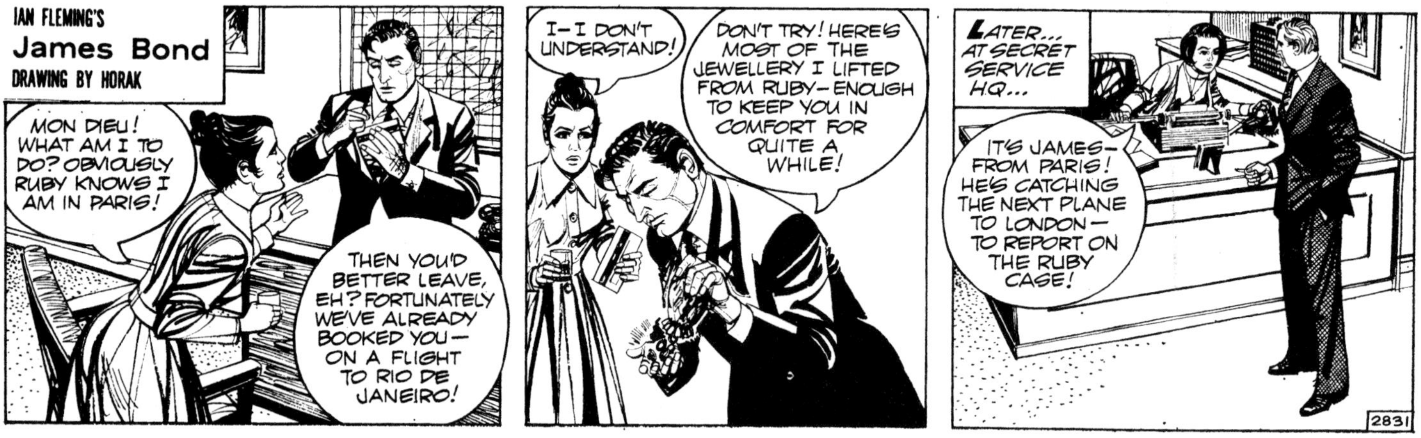
IAN FLEMING'S
James Bond
DRAWING BY HORAK
MON DIEU! WHAT AM I TO DO? OBVIOUSLY RUBY KNOWS I AM IN PARIS!
THEN YOU'D BETTER LEAVE, EH? FORTUNATELY WE'VE ALREADY BOOKED YOU— ON A FLIGHT TO RIO DE JANEIRO!
I-I DON'T UNDERSTAND!
DON'T TRY! HERE'S MOST OF THE JEWELLERY I LIFTED FROM RUBY—ENOUGH TO KEEP YOU IN COMFORT FOR QUITE A WHILE!
LATER... AT SECRET SERVICE HQ...
IT'S JAMES— FROM PARIS! HE'S CATCHING THE NEXT PLANE TO LONDON— TO REPORT ON THE RUBY CASE!
2831

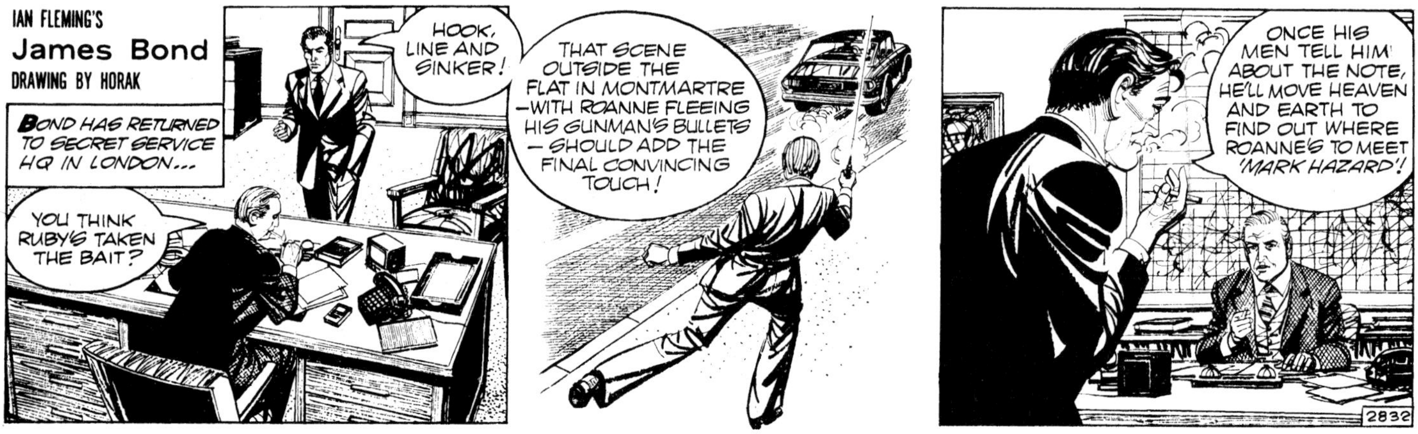
IAN FLEMING'S
James Bond
DRAWING BY HORAK
BOND HAS RETURNED TO SECRET SERVICE HQ IN LONDON...
YOU THINK RUBY'S TAKEN THE BAIT?
HOOK, LINE AND SINKER!
THAT SCENE OUTSIDE THE FLAT IN MONTMARTRE —WITH ROANNE FLEEING HIS GUNMAN'S BULLETS — SHOULD ADD THE FINAL CONVINCING TOUCH!
ONCE HIS MEN TELL HIM ABOUT THE NOTE, HE'LL MOVE HEAVEN AND EARTH TO FIND OUT WHERE ROANNE'S TO MEET 'MARK HAZARD'!
2832

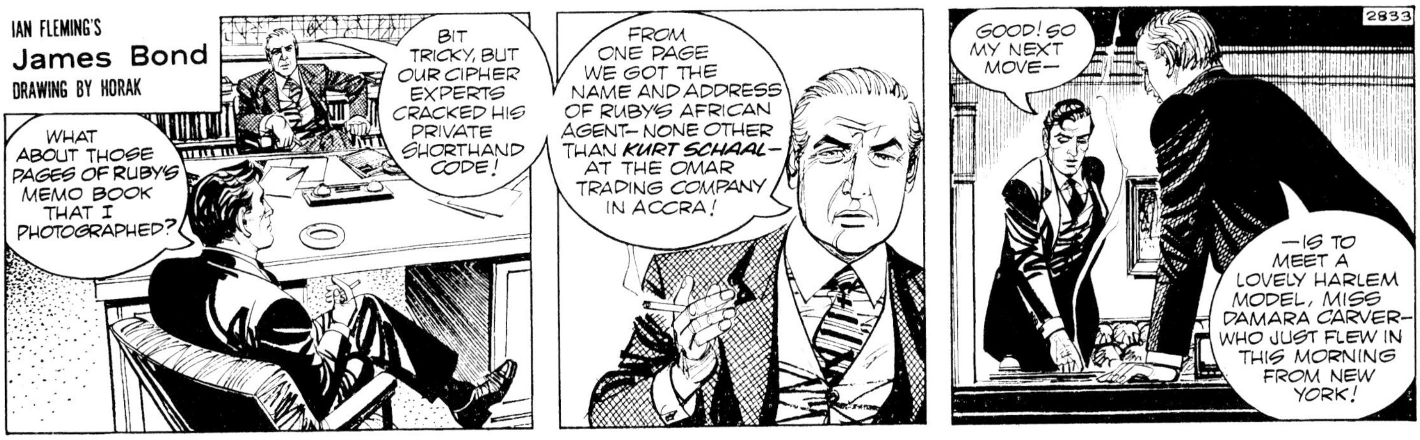
IAN FLEMING'S
James Bond
DRAWING BY HORAK
WHAT ABOUT THOSE PAGES OF RUBY'S MEMO BOOK THAT I PHOTOGRAPHED?
BIT TRICKY, BUT OUR CIPHER EXPERTS CRACKED HIS PRIVATE SHORTHAND CODE!
FROM ONE PAGE WE GOT THE NAME AND ADDRESS OF RUBY'S AFRICAN AGENT– NONE OTHER THAN KURT SCHAAL– AT THE OMAR TRADING COMPANY IN ACCRA!
2833
GOOD! SO MY NEXT MOVE—
—IS TO MEET A LOVELY HARLEM MODEL, MISS DAMARA CARVER– WHO JUST FLEW IN THIS MORNING FROM NEW YORK!

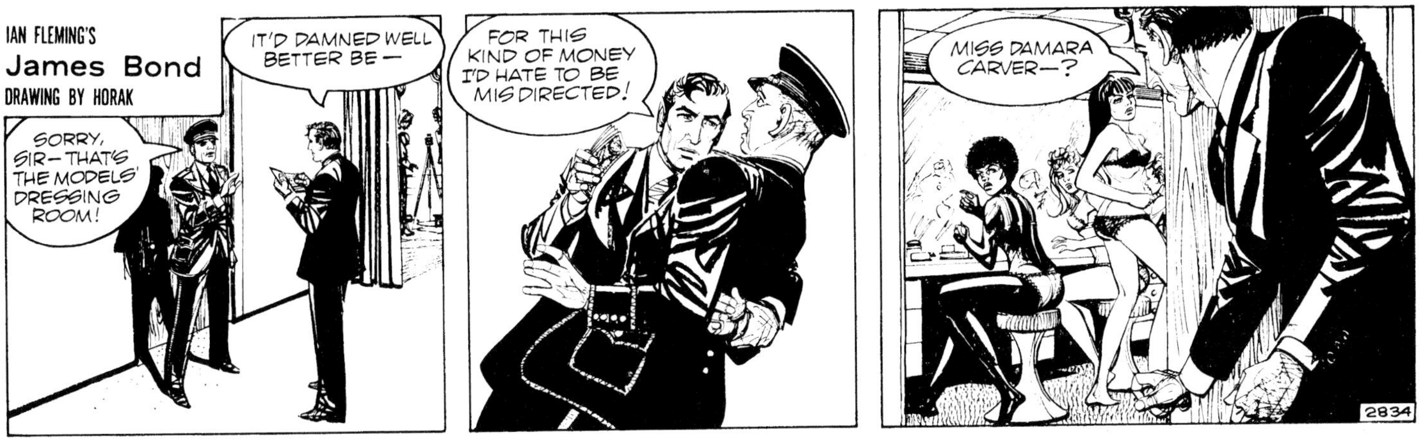
IAN FLEMING'S
James Bond
DRAWING BY HORAK
SORRY, SIR– THAT'S THE MODELS' DRESSING ROOM!
IT'D DAMNED WELL BETTER BE —
FOR THIS KIND OF MONEY I'D HATE TO BE MISDIRECTED!
MISS DAMARA CARVER—?
2834

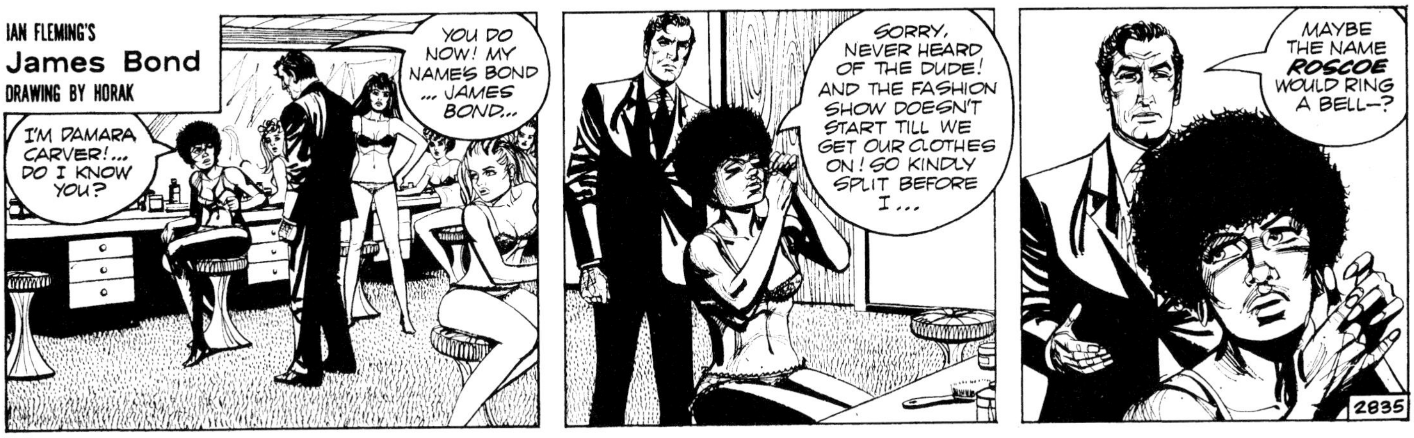
IAN FLEMING'S
James Bond
DRAWING BY HORAK
I'M DAMARA CARVER!... DO I KNOW YOU?
YOU DO NOW! MY NAME'S BOND ... JAMES BOND...
SORRY, NEVER HEARD OF THE DUDE! AND THE FASHION SHOW DOESN'T START TILL WE GET OUR CLOTHES ON! SO KINDLY SPLIT BEFORE I ...
MAYBE THE NAME ROSCOE WOULD RING A BELL–?
2835

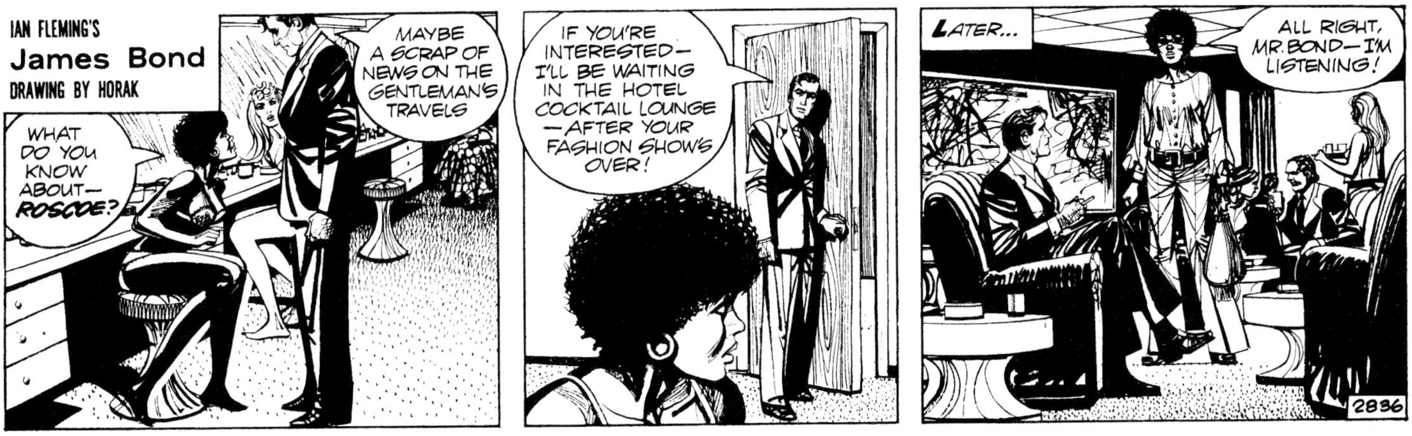
IAN FLEMING'S
James Bond
DRAWING BY HORAK
WHAT DO YOU KNOW ABOUT– ROSCOE?
MAYBE A SCRAP OF NEWS ON THE GENTLEMAN'S TRAVELS
IF YOU'RE INTERESTED– I'LL BE WAITING IN THE HOTEL COCKTAIL LOUNGE —AFTER YOUR FASHION SHOW'S OVER!
LATER...
ALL RIGHT, MR. BOND– I'M LISTENING!
2836

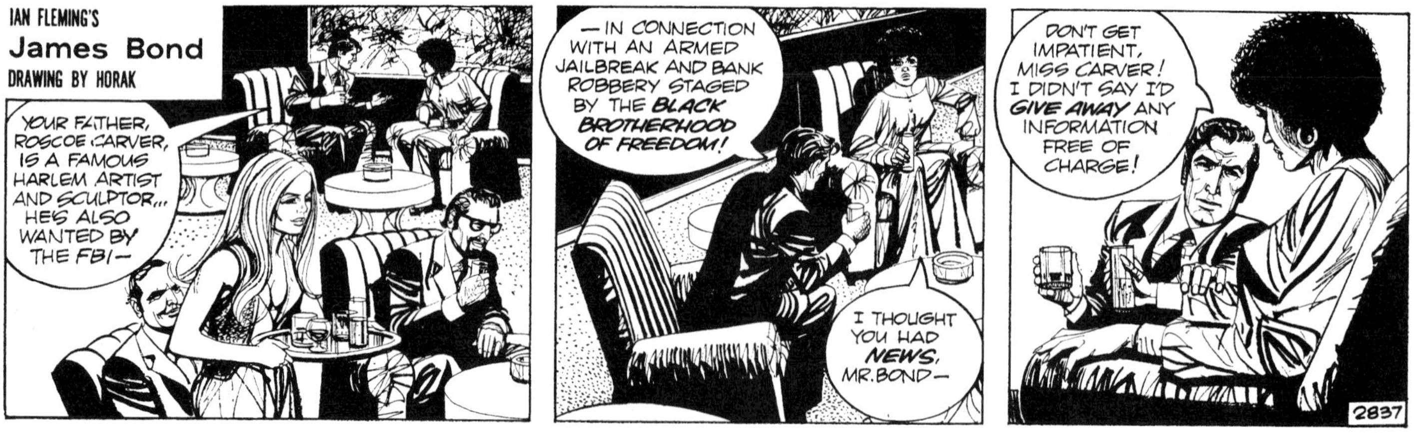
IAN FLEMING'S
James Bond
DRAWING BY HORAK
YOUR FATHER, ROSCOE CARVER, IS A FAMOUS HARLEM ARTIST AND SCULPTOR... HE'S ALSO WANTED BY THE FBI—
—IN CONNECTION WITH AN ARMED JAILBREAK AND BANK ROBBERY STAGED BY THE BLACK BROTHERHOOD OF FREEDOM!
I THOUGHT YOU HAD NEWS, MR. BOND—
DON'T GET IMPATIENT, MISS CARVER! I DIDN'T SAY I'D GIVE AWAY ANY INFORMATION FREE OF CHARGE!
2837

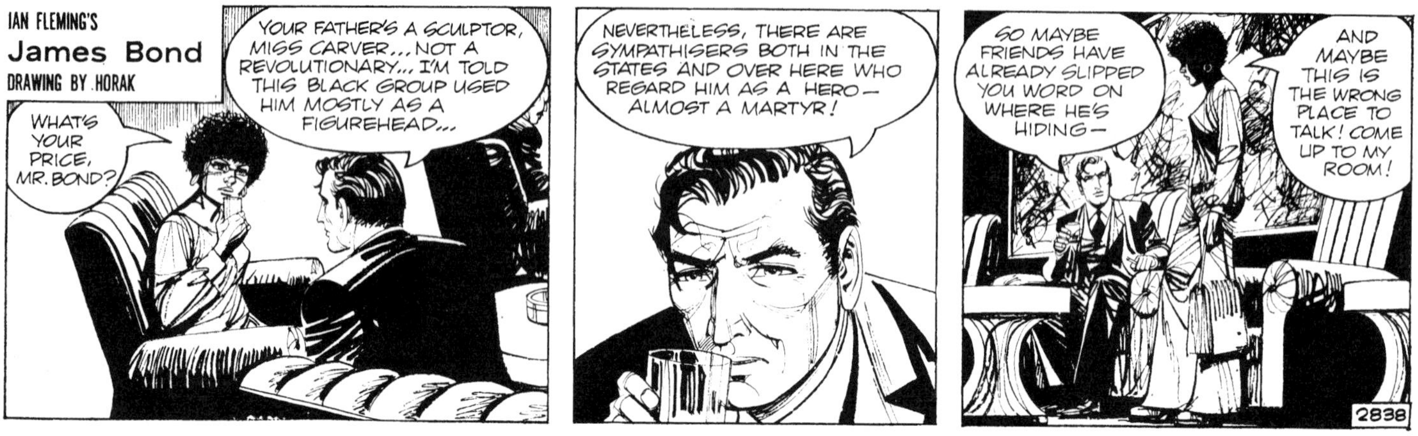
IAN FLEMING'S
James Bond
DRAWING BY HORAK
WHAT'S YOUR PRICE, MR. BOND?
YOUR FATHER'S A SCULPTOR, MISS CARVER... NOT A REVOLUTIONARY... I'M TOLD THIS BLACK GROUP USED HIM MOSTLY AS A FIGUREHEAD...
NEVERTHELESS, THERE ARE SYMPATHISERS BOTH IN THE STATES AND OVER HERE WHO REGARD HIM AS A HERO— ALMOST A MARTYR!
SO MAYBE FRIENDS HAVE ALREADY SLIPPED YOU WORD ON WHERE HE'S HIDING—
AND MAYBE THIS IS THE WRONG PLACE TO TALK! COME UP TO MY ROOM!
2838

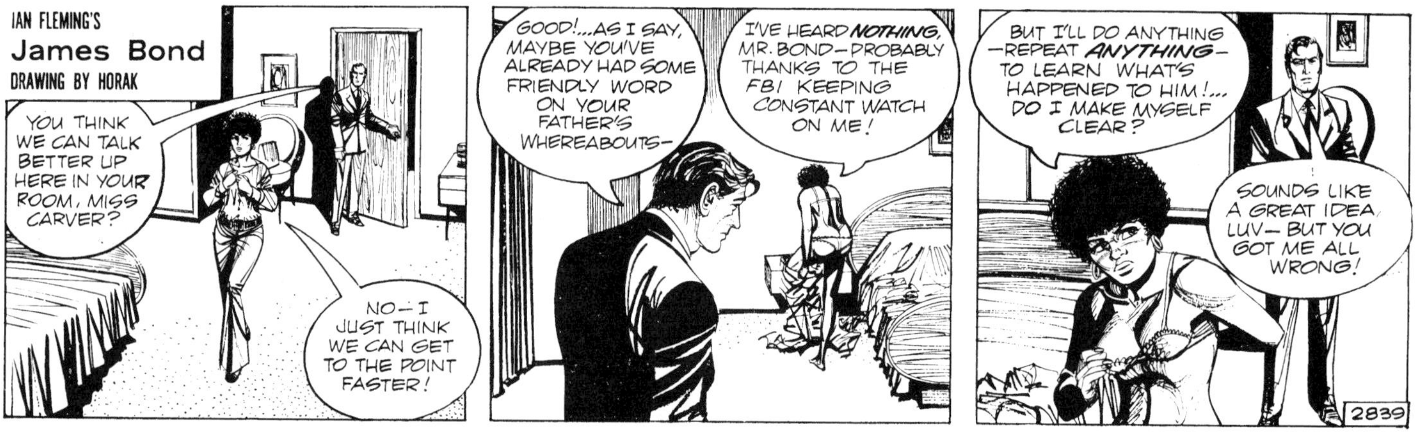
IAN FLEMING'S
James Bond
DRAWING BY HORAK
YOU THINK WE CAN TALK BETTER UP HERE IN YOUR ROOM, MISS CARVER?
NO—I JUST THINK WE CAN GET TO THE POINT FASTER!
GOOD!...AS I SAY, MAYBE YOU'VE ALREADY HAD SOME FRIENDLY WORD ON YOUR FATHER'S WHEREABOUTS—
I'VE HEARD NOTHING, MR. BOND—PROBABLY THANKS TO THE FBI KEEPING CONSTANT WATCH ON ME!
BUT I'LL DO ANYTHING —REPEAT ANYTHING— TO LEARN WHAT'S HAPPENED TO HIM!... DO I MAKE MYSELF CLEAR?
SOUNDS LIKE A GREAT IDEA LUV— BUT YOU GOT ME ALL WRONG!
2839

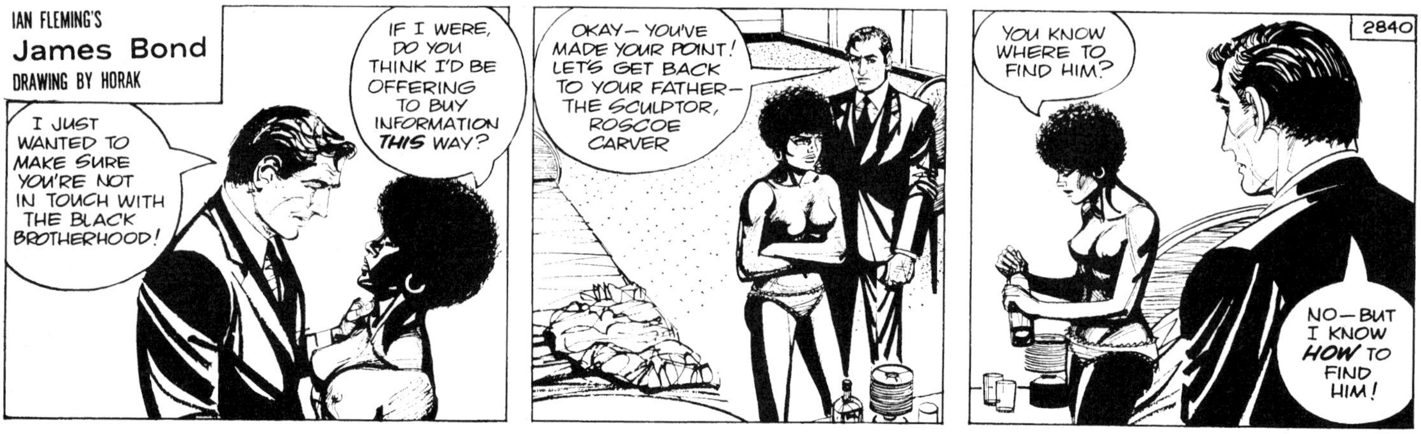
IAN FLEMING'S
James Bond
DRAWING BY HORAK
I JUST WANTED TO MAKE SURE YOU'RE NOT IN TOUCH WITH THE BLACK BROTHERHOOD!
IF I WERE, DO YOU THINK I'D BE OFFERING TO BUY INFORMATION THIS WAY?
OKAY— YOU'VE MADE YOUR POINT! LET'S GET BACK TO YOUR FATHER— THE SCULPTOR, ROSCOE CARVER
2840
YOU KNOW WHERE TO FIND HIM?
NO—BUT I KNOW HOW TO FIND HIM!

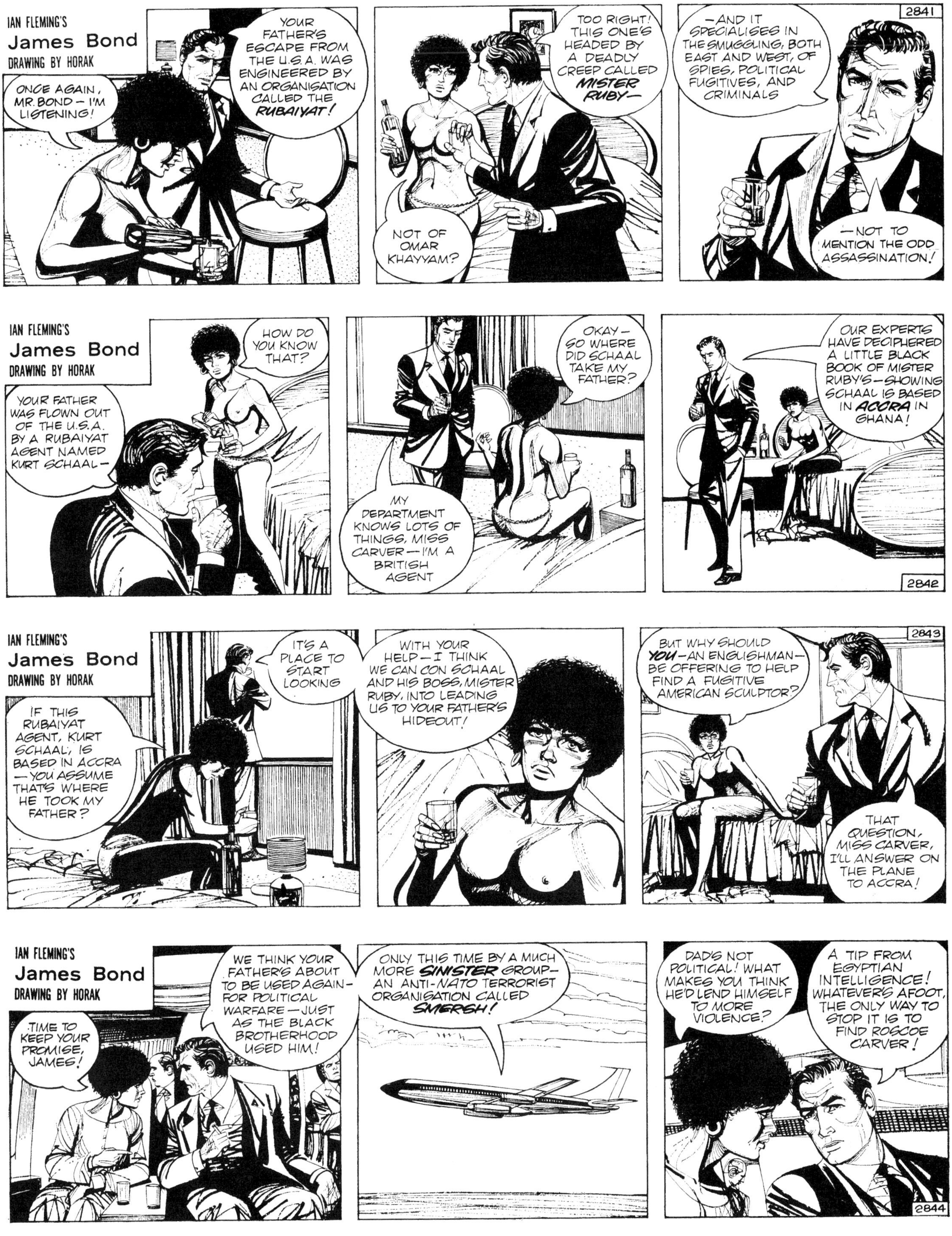

IAN FLEMING'S
James Bond
DRAWING BY HORAK
ONCE AGAIN, MR. BOND — I'M LISTENING!
YOUR FATHER'S ESCAPE FROM THE U.S.A. WAS ENGINEERED BY AN ORGANISATION CALLED THE RUBAIYAT!
NOT OF OMAR KHAYYAM?
TOO RIGHT! THIS ONE'S HEADED BY A DEADLY CREEP CALLED MISTER RUBY—
2841
—AND IT SPECIALISES IN THE SMUGGLING, BOTH EAST AND WEST, OF SPIES, POLITICAL FUGITIVES, AND CRIMINALS
—NOT TO MENTION THE ODD ASSASSINATION!
IAN FLEMING'S
James Bond
DRAWING BY HORAK
YOUR FATHER WAS FLOWN OUT OF THE U.S.A. BY A RUBAIYAT AGENT NAMED KURT SCHAAL—
HOW DO YOU KNOW THAT?
MY DEPARTMENT KNOWS LOTS OF THINGS, MISS CARVER — I'M A BRITISH AGENT
OKAY — SO WHERE DID SCHAAL TAKE MY FATHER?
OUR EXPERTS HAVE DECIPHERED A LITTLE BLACK BOOK OF MISTER RUBY'S — SHOWING SCHAAL IS BASED IN ACCRA IN GHANA!
2842
IAN FLEMING'S
James Bond
DRAWING BY HORAK
IF THIS RUBAIYAT AGENT, KURT SCHAAL, IS BASED IN ACCRA — YOU ASSUME THAT'S WHERE HE TOOK MY FATHER?
IT'S A PLACE TO START LOOKING
WITH YOUR HELP — I THINK WE CAN CON SCHAAL AND HIS BOSS, MISTER RUBY, INTO LEADING US TO YOUR FATHER'S HIDEOUT!
2843
BUT WHY SHOULD YOU — AN ENGLISHMAN — BE OFFERING TO HELP FIND A FUGITIVE AMERICAN SCULPTOR?
THAT QUESTION, MISS CARVER, I'LL ANSWER ON THE PLANE TO ACCRA!
IAN FLEMING'S
James Bond
DRAWING BY HORAK
TIME TO KEEP YOUR PROMISE, JAMES!
WE THINK YOUR FATHER'S ABOUT TO BE USED AGAIN — FOR POLITICAL WARFARE — JUST AS THE BLACK BROTHERHOOD USED HIM!
ONLY THIS TIME BY A MUCH MORE SINISTER GROUP — AN ANTI-NATO TERRORIST ORGANISATION CALLED SMERSH!
DAD'S NOT POLITICAL! WHAT MAKES YOU THINK HE'D LEND HIMSELF TO MORE VIOLENCE?
A TIP FROM EGYPTIAN INTELLIGENCE! WHATEVER'S AFOOT, THE ONLY WAY TO STOP IT IS TO FIND ROSCOE CARVER!
2844

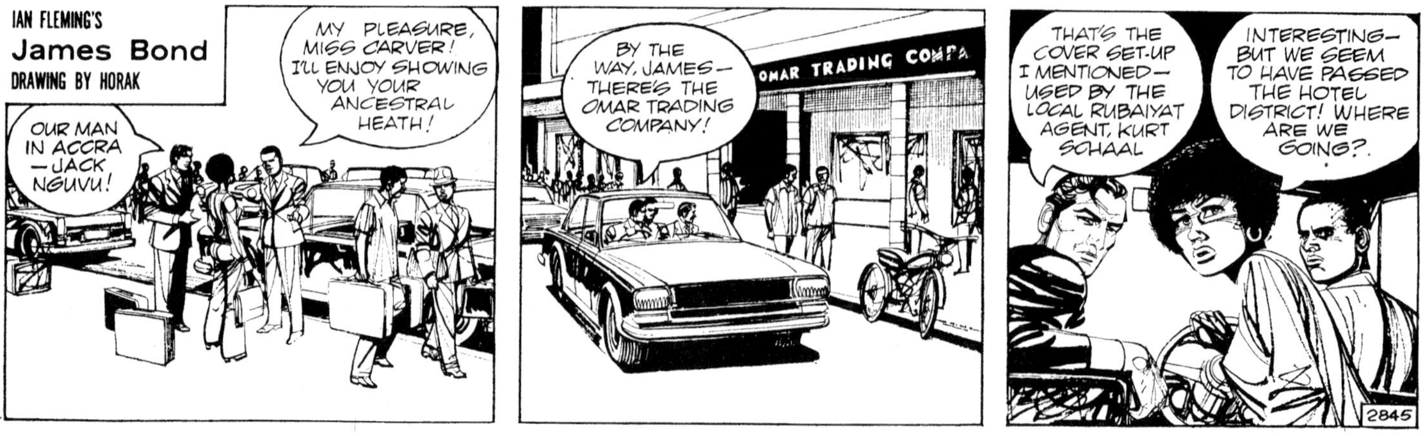
IAN FLEMING'S
James Bond
DRAWING BY HORAK
OUR MAN IN ACCRA —JACK NGUVU!
MY PLEASURE, MISS CARVER! I'LL ENJOY SHOWING YOU YOUR ANCESTRAL HEATH!
BY THE WAY, JAMES— THERE'S THE OMAR TRADING COMPANY!
OMAR TRADING COMPA
THAT'S THE COVER SET-UP I MENTIONED— USED BY THE LOCAL RUBAIYAT AGENT, KURT SCHAAL
INTERESTING— BUT WE SEEM TO HAVE PASSED THE HOTEL DISTRICT! WHERE ARE WE GOING?
2845

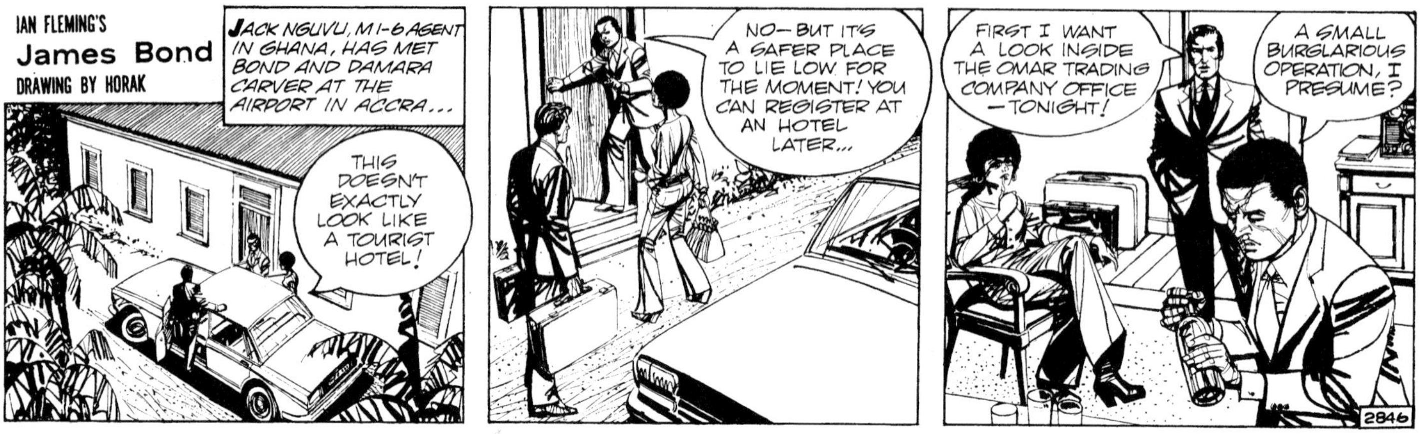
IAN FLEMING'S
James Bond
DRAWING BY HORAK
JACK NGUVU, M I-6 AGENT IN GHANA, HAS MET BOND AND DAMARA CARVER AT THE AIRPORT IN ACCRA...
THIS DOESN'T EXACTLY LOOK LIKE A TOURIST HOTEL!
NO— BUT IT'S A SAFER PLACE TO LIE LOW FOR THE MOMENT! YOU CAN REGISTER AT AN HOTEL LATER...
FIRST I WANT A LOOK INSIDE THE OMAR TRADING COMPANY OFFICE —TONIGHT!
A SMALL BURGLARIOUS OPERATION, I PRESUME?
2846

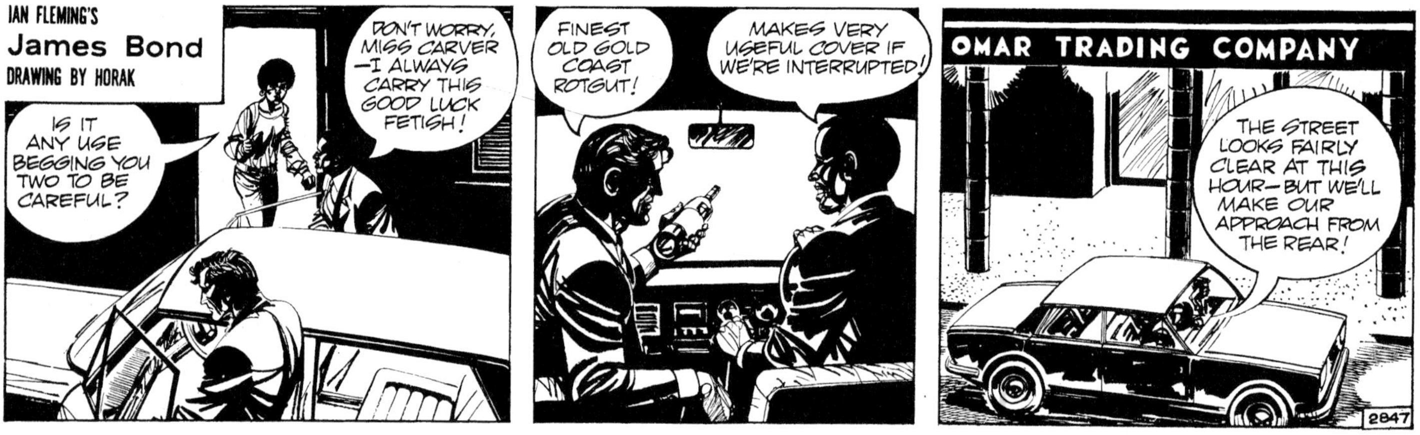
IAN FLEMING'S
James Bond
DRAWING BY HORAK
IS IT ANY USE BEGGING YOU TWO TO BE CAREFUL?
DON'T WORRY, MISS CARVER —I ALWAYS CARRY THIS GOOD LUCK FETISH!
FINEST OLD GOLD COAST ROTGUT!
MAKES VERY USEFUL COVER IF WE'RE INTERRUPTED!
OMAR TRADING COMPANY
THE STREET LOOKS FAIRLY CLEAR AT THIS HOUR— BUT WE'LL MAKE OUR APPROACH FROM THE REAR!
2847

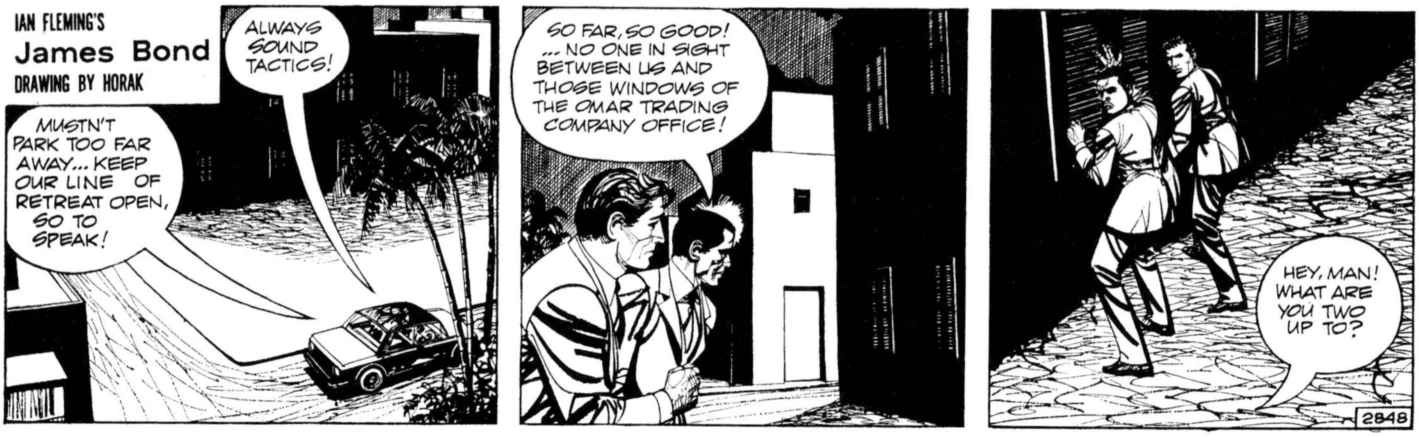
IAN FLEMING'S
James Bond
DRAWING BY HORAK
MUSTN'T PARK TOO FAR AWAY... KEEP OUR LINE OF RETREAT OPEN, SO TO SPEAK!
ALWAYS SOUND TACTICS!
SO FAR, SO GOOD! ... NO ONE IN SIGHT BETWEEN US AND THOSE WINDOWS OF THE OMAR TRADING COMPANY OFFICE!
HEY, MAN! WHAT ARE YOU TWO UP TO?
2848

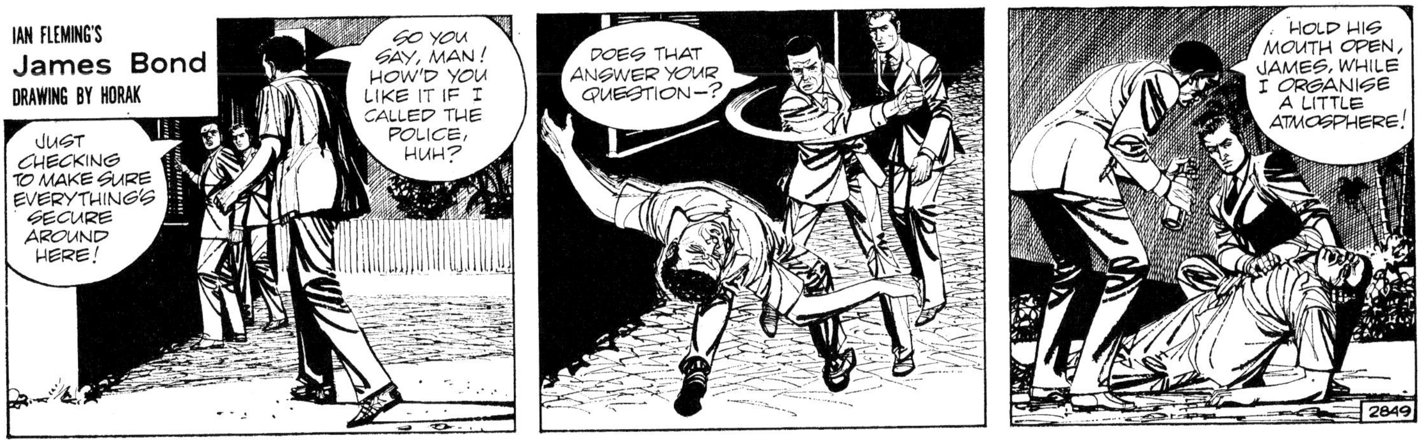
IAN FLEMING'S
James Bond
DRAWING BY HORAK
SO YOU SAY, MAN! HOW'D YOU LIKE IT IF I CALLED THE POLICE, HUH?
JUST CHECKING TO MAKE SURE EVERYTHING'S SECURE AROUND HERE!
DOES THAT ANSWER YOUR QUESTION—?
HOLD HIS MOUTH OPEN, JAMES, WHILE I ORGANISE A LITTLE ATMOSPHERE!
2849

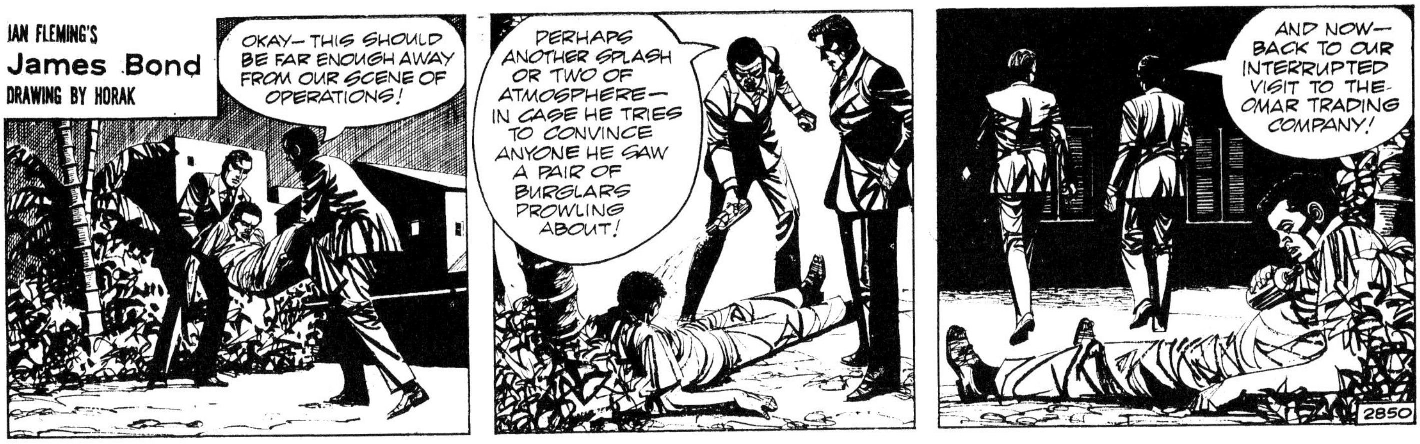
IAN FLEMING'S
James Bond
DRAWING BY HORAK
OKAY—THIS SHOULD BE FAR ENOUGH AWAY FROM OUR SCENE OF OPERATIONS!
PERHAPS ANOTHER SPLASH OR TWO OF ATMOSPHERE—IN CASE HE TRIES TO CONVINCE ANYONE HE SAW A PAIR OF BURGLARS PROWLING ABOUT!
AND NOW—BACK TO OUR INTERRUPTED VISIT TO THE OMAR TRADING COMPANY!
2850

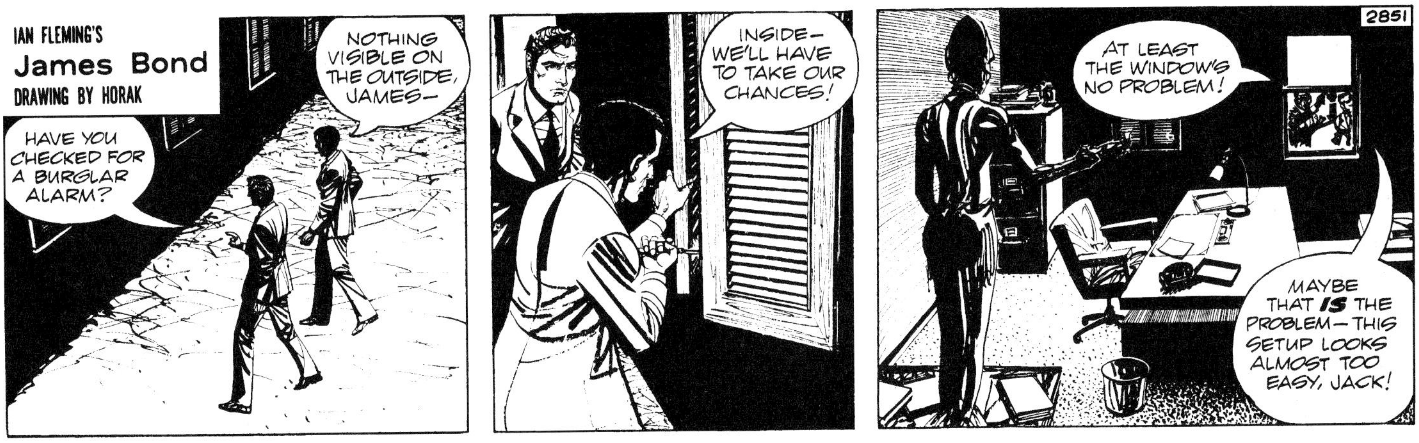
IAN FLEMING'S
James Bond
DRAWING BY HORAK
NOTHING VISIBLE ON THE OUTSIDE, JAMES—
HAVE YOU CHECKED FOR A BURGLAR ALARM?
INSIDE—WE'LL HAVE TO TAKE OUR CHANCES!
2851
AT LEAST THE WINDOW'S NO PROBLEM!
MAYBE THAT IS THE PROBLEM—THIS SETUP LOOKS ALMOST TOO EASY, JACK!

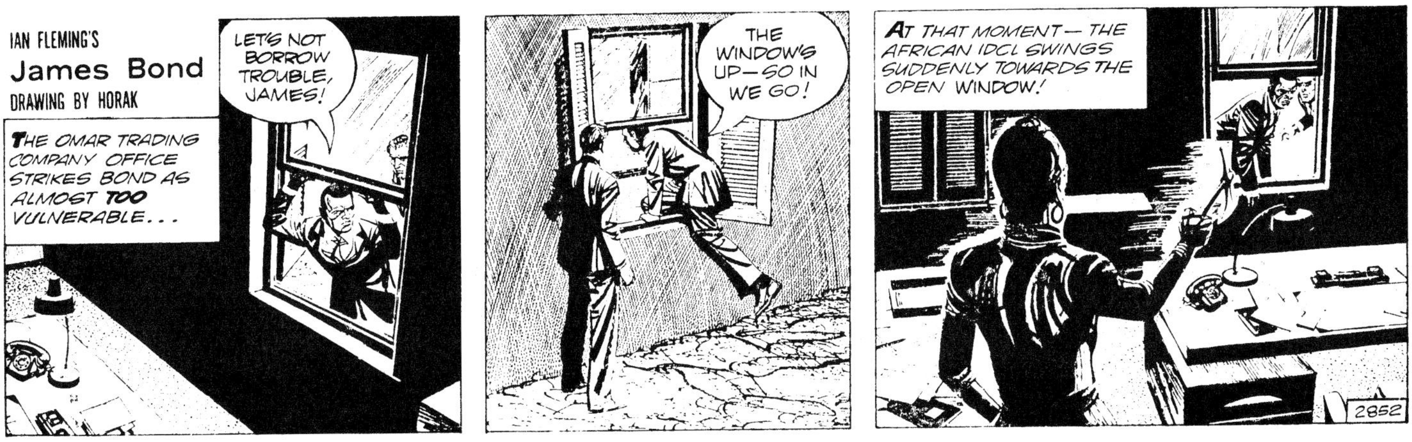
IAN FLEMING'S
James Bond
DRAWING BY HORAK
LET'S NOT BORROW TROUBLE, JAMES!
THE OMAR TRADING COMPANY OFFICE STRIKES BOND AS ALMOST TOO VULNERABLE...
THE WINDOW'S UP—SO IN WE GO!
AT THAT MOMENT—THE AFRICAN IDOL SWINGS SUDDENLY TOWARDS THE OPEN WINDOW!
2852

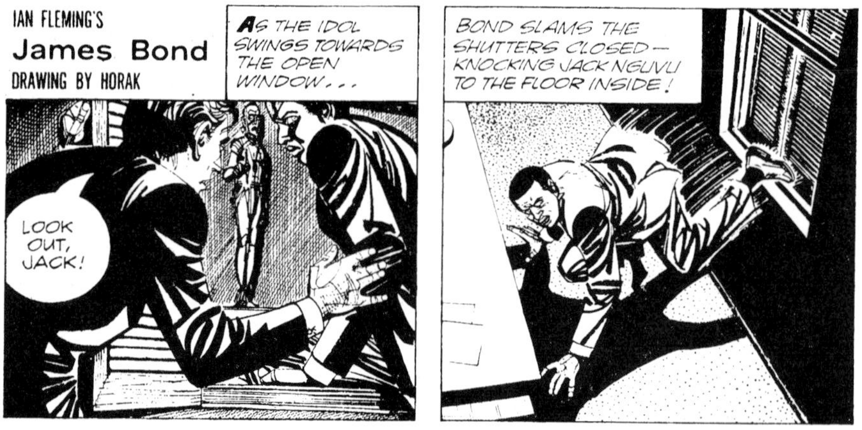
IAN FLEMING'S
James Bond
DRAWING BY HORAK
AS THE IDOL SWINGS TOWARDS THE OPEN WINDOW...
LOOK OUT, JACK!
BOND SLAMS THE SHUTTERS CLOSED— KNOCKING JACK NGUVU TO THE FLOOR INSIDE!
2853

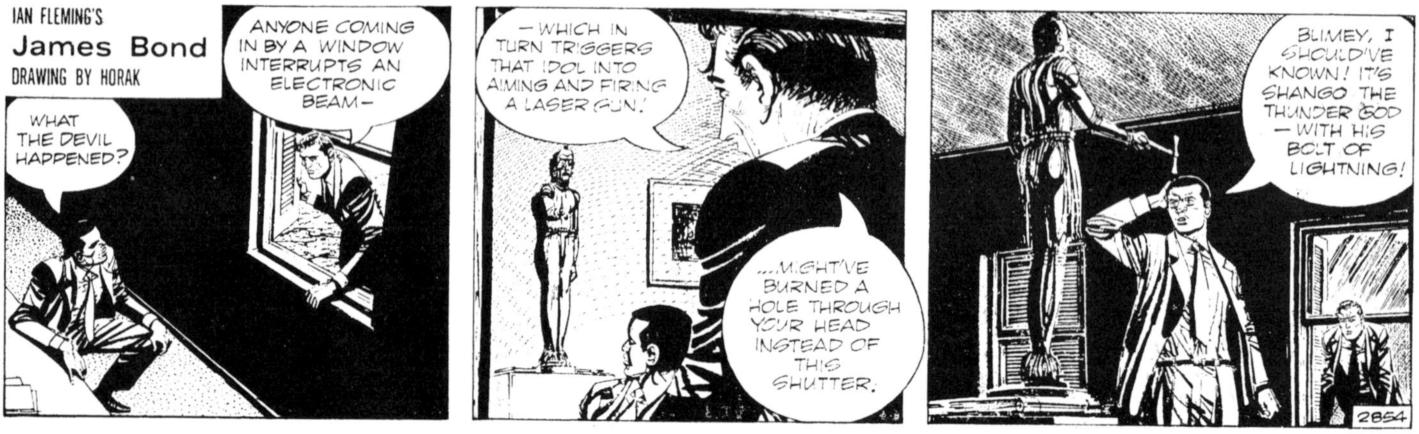
IAN FLEMING'S
James Bond
DRAWING BY HORAK
WHAT THE DEVIL HAPPENED?
ANYONE COMING IN BY A WINDOW INTERRUPTS AN ELECTRONIC BEAM—
—WHICH IN TURN TRIGGERS THAT IDOL INTO AIMING AND FIRING A LASER GUN!
...MIGHT'VE BURNED A HOLE THROUGH YOUR HEAD INSTEAD OF THIS SHUTTER!
BLIMEY, I SHOULD'VE KNOWN! IT'S SHANGO THE THUNDER GOD —WITH HIS BOLT OF LIGHTNING!
2854

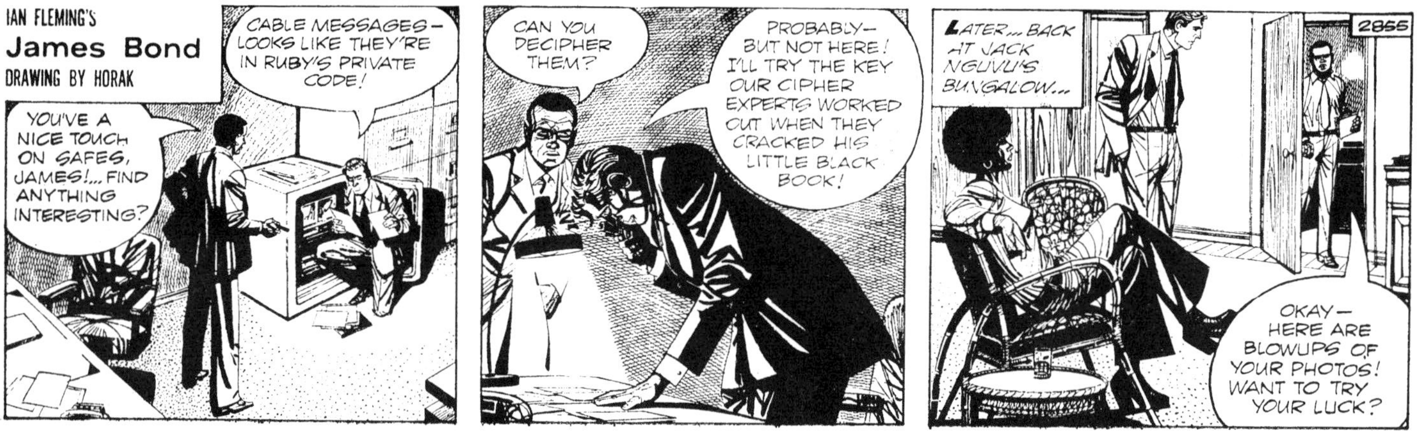
IAN FLEMING'S
James Bond
DRAWING BY HORAK
YOU'VE A NICE TOUCH ON SAFES, JAMES!... FIND ANYTHING INTERESTING?
CABLE MESSAGES— LOOKS LIKE THEY'RE IN RUBY'S PRIVATE CODE!
CAN YOU DECIPHER THEM?
PROBABLY— BUT NOT HERE! I'LL TRY THE KEY OUR CIPHER EXPERTS WORKED OUT WHEN THEY CRACKED HIS LITTLE BLACK BOOK!
LATER... BACK AT JACK NGUVU'S BUNGALOW...
OKAY— HERE ARE BLOWUPS OF YOUR PHOTOS! WANT TO TRY YOUR LUCK?
2855

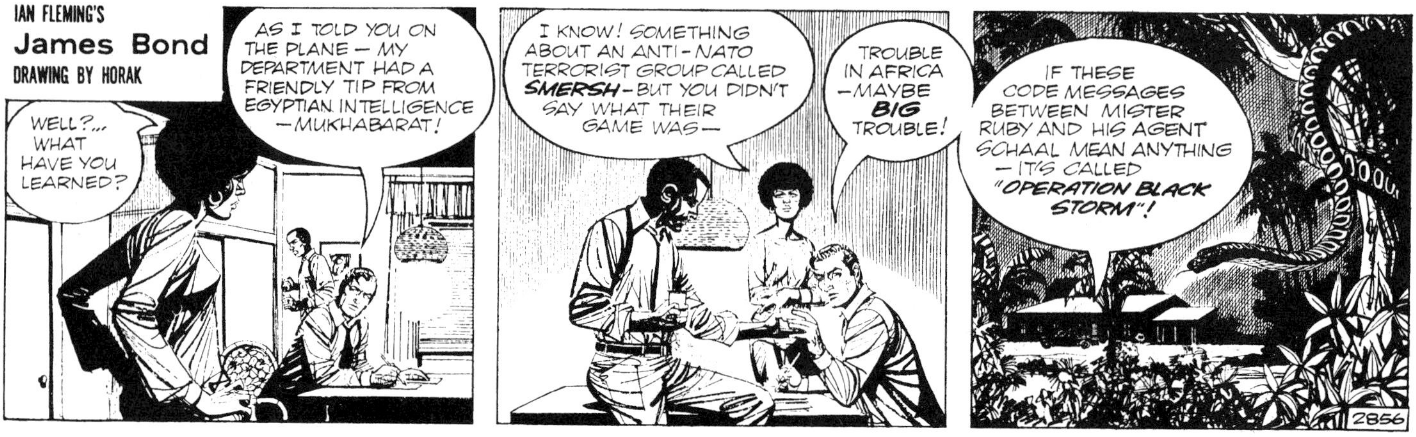
IAN FLEMING'S
James Bond
DRAWING BY HORAK
WELL?... WHAT HAVE YOU LEARNED?
AS I TOLD YOU ON THE PLANE — MY DEPARTMENT HAD A FRIENDLY TIP FROM EGYPTIAN INTELLIGENCE —MUKHABARAT!
I KNOW! SOMETHING ABOUT AN ANTI-NATO TERRORIST GROUP CALLED SMERSH— BUT YOU DIDN'T SAY WHAT THEIR GAME WAS—
TROUBLE IN AFRICA —MAYBE BIG TROUBLE!
IF THESE CODE MESSAGES BETWEEN MISTER RUBY AND HIS AGENT SCHAAL MEAN ANYTHING —IT'S CALLED "OPERATION BLACK STORM"!
2856

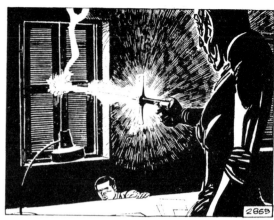

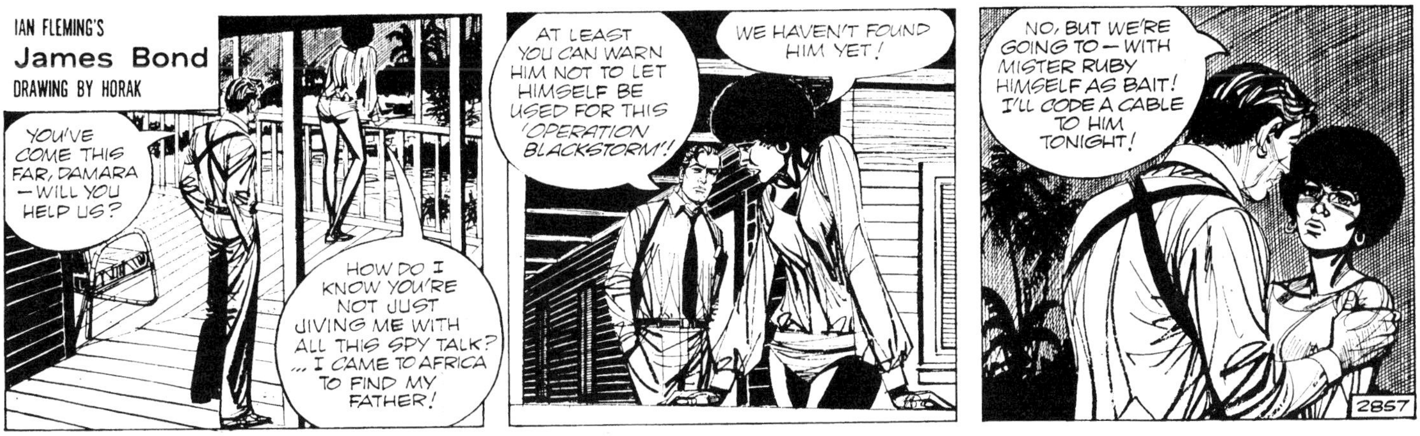
IAN FLEMING'S
James Bond
DRAWING BY HORAK
YOU'VE COME THIS FAR, DAMARA — WILL YOU HELP US?
HOW DO I KNOW YOU'RE NOT JUST JIVING ME WITH ALL THIS SPY TALK? ... I CAME TO AFRICA TO FIND MY FATHER!
AT LEAST YOU CAN WARN HIM NOT TO LET HIMSELF BE USED FOR THIS 'OPERATION BLACKSTORM'!
WE HAVEN'T FOUND HIM YET!
NO, BUT WE'RE GOING TO — WITH MISTER RUBY HIMSELF AS BAIT! I'LL CODE A CABLE TO HIM TONIGHT!
2857

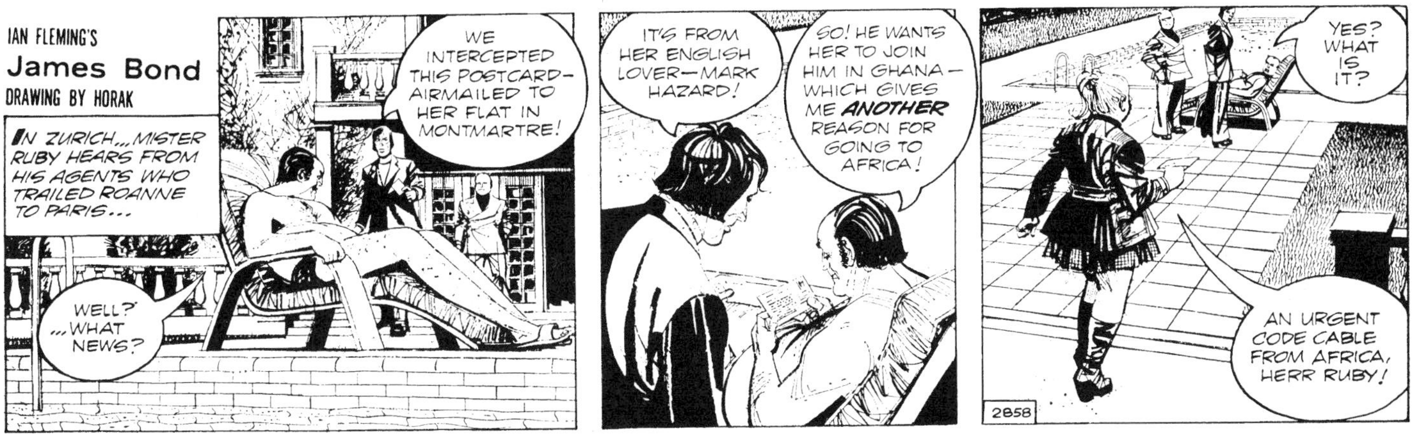
IAN FLEMING'S
James Bond
DRAWING BY HORAK
IN ZURICH... MISTER RUBY HEARS FROM HIS AGENTS WHO TRAILED ROANNE TO PARIS...
WELL? ...WHAT NEWS?
WE INTERCEPTED THIS POSTCARD — AIRMAILED TO HER FLAT IN MONTMARTRE!
IT'S FROM HER ENGLISH LOVER — MARK HAZARD!
SO! HE WANTS HER TO JOIN HIM IN GHANA — WHICH GIVES ME ANOTHER REASON FOR GOING TO AFRICA!
YES? WHAT IS IT?
AN URGENT CODE CABLE FROM AFRICA, HERR RUBY!
2858

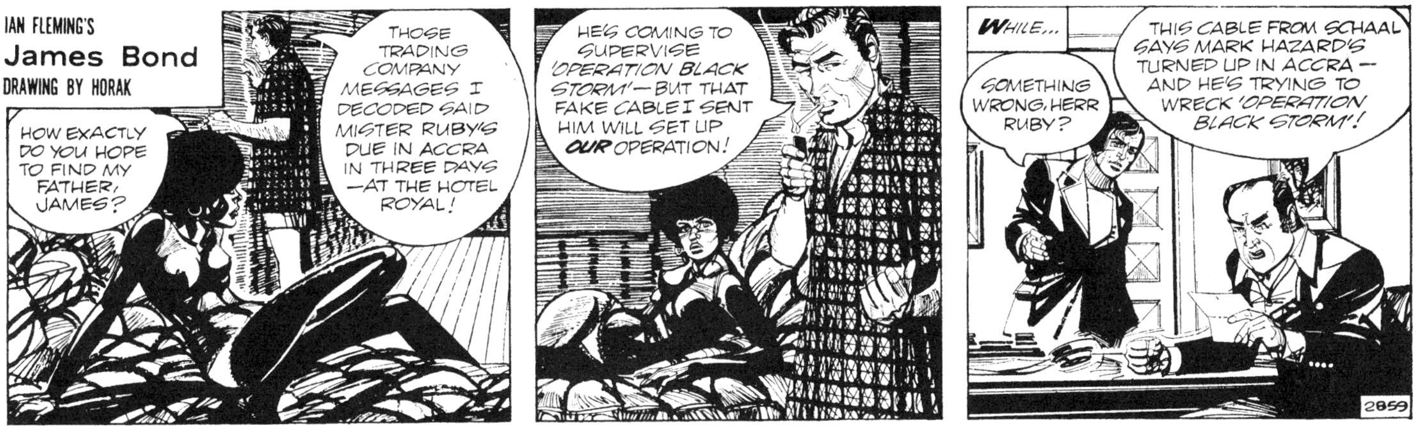
IAN FLEMING'S
James Bond
DRAWING BY HORAK
HOW EXACTLY DO YOU HOPE TO FIND MY FATHER, JAMES?
THOSE TRADING COMPANY MESSAGES I DECODED SAID MISTER RUBY'S DUE IN ACCRA IN THREE DAYS — AT THE HOTEL ROYAL!
HE'S COMING TO SUPERVISE 'OPERATION BLACK STORM' — BUT THAT FAKE CABLE I SENT HIM WILL SET UP OUR OPERATION!
WHILE...
SOMETHING WRONG, HERR RUBY?
THIS CABLE FROM SCHAAL SAYS MARK HAZARD'S TURNED UP IN ACCRA — AND HE'S TRYING TO WRECK 'OPERATION BLACK STORM'!
2859

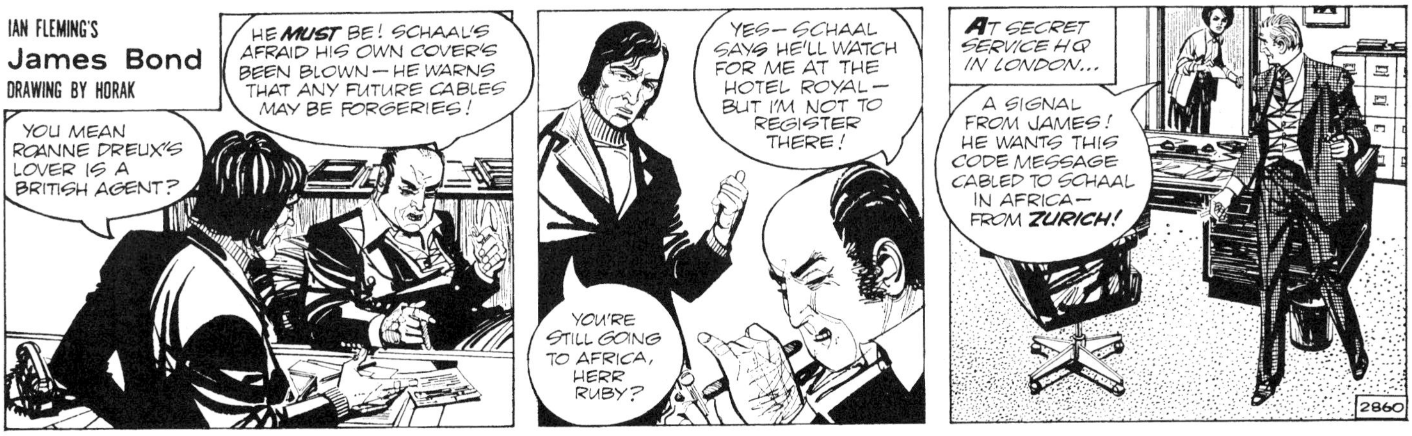
IAN FLEMING'S
James Bond
DRAWING BY HORAK
YOU MEAN ROANNE DREUX'S LOVER IS A BRITISH AGENT?
HE MUST BE! SCHAAL'S AFRAID HIS OWN COVER'S BEEN BLOWN — HE WARNS THAT ANY FUTURE CABLES MAY BE FORGERIES!
YOU'RE STILL GOING TO AFRICA, HERR RUBY?
YES — SCHAAL SAYS HE'LL WATCH FOR ME AT THE HOTEL ROYAL — BUT I'M NOT TO REGISTER THERE!
AT SECRET SERVICE HQ IN LONDON...
A SIGNAL FROM JAMES! HE WANTS THIS CODE MESSAGE CABLED TO SCHAAL IN AFRICA — FROM ZURICH!
2860

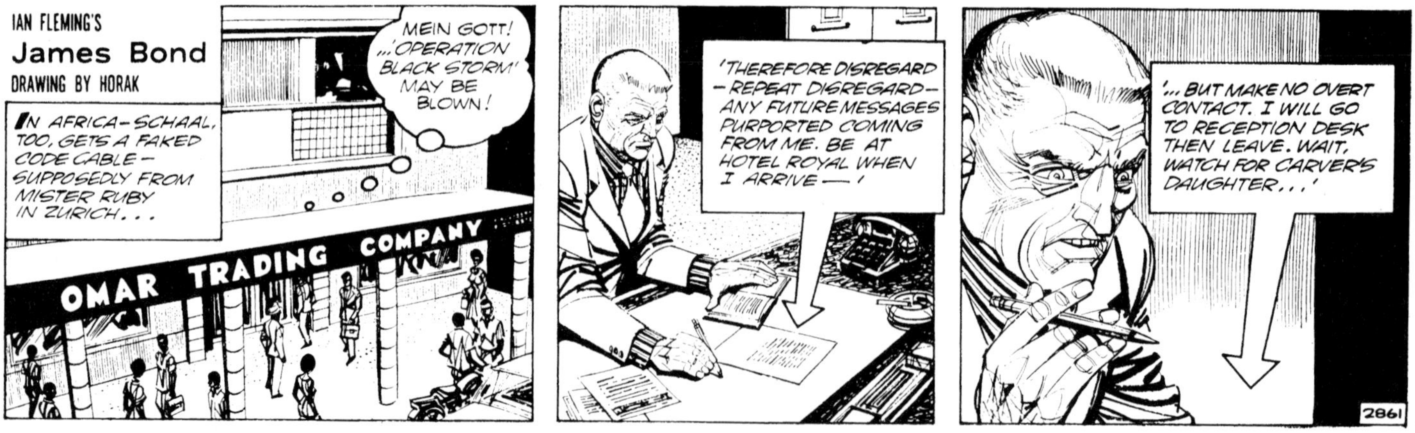
IAN FLEMING'S
James Bond
DRAWING BY HORAK
IN AFRICA—SCHAAL, TOO, GETS A FAKED CODE CABLE—SUPPOSEDLY FROM MISTER RUBY IN ZURICH . . .
MEIN GOTT! ...'OPERATION BLACK STORM' MAY BE BLOWN!
OMAR TRADING COMPANY
'THEREFORE DISREGARD—REPEAT DISREGARD—ANY FUTURE MESSAGES PURPORTED COMING FROM ME. BE AT HOTEL ROYAL WHEN I ARRIVE—'
'...BUT MAKE NO OVERT CONTACT. I WILL GO TO RECEPTION DESK THEN LEAVE. WAIT, WATCH FOR CARVER'S DAUGHTER...'
2861

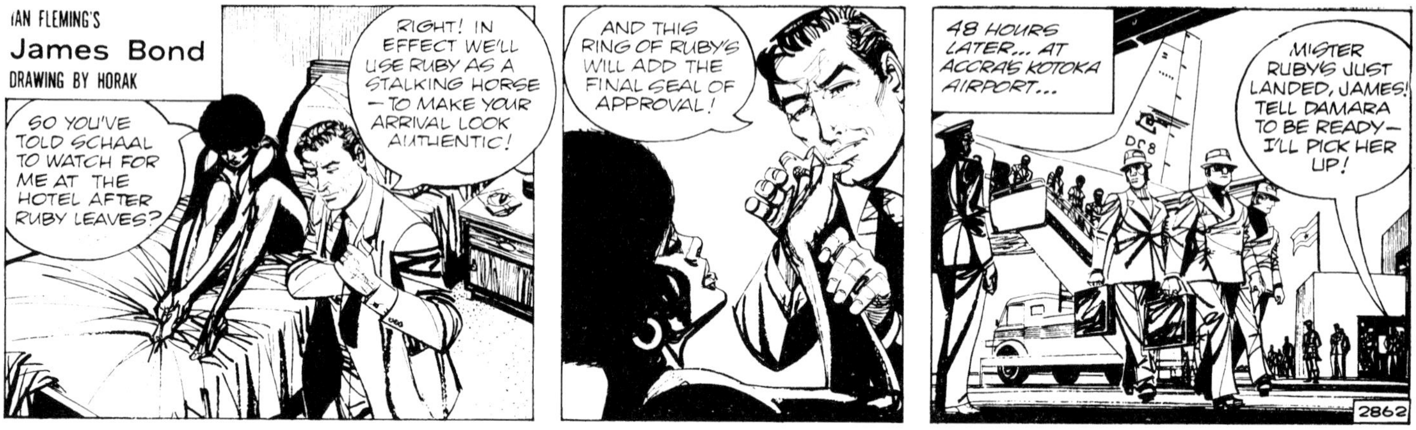
IAN FLEMING'S
James Bond
DRAWING BY HORAK
SO YOU'VE TOLD SCHAAL TO WATCH FOR ME AT THE HOTEL AFTER RUBY LEAVES?
RIGHT! IN EFFECT WE'LL USE RUBY AS A STALKING HORSE—TO MAKE YOUR ARRIVAL LOOK AUTHENTIC!
AND THIS RING OF RUBY'S WILL ADD THE FINAL SEAL OF APPROVAL!
48 HOURS LATER... AT ACCRA'S KOTOKA AIRPORT...
MISTER RUBY'S JUST LANDED, JAMES! TELL DAMARA TO BE READY—I'LL PICK HER UP!
2862

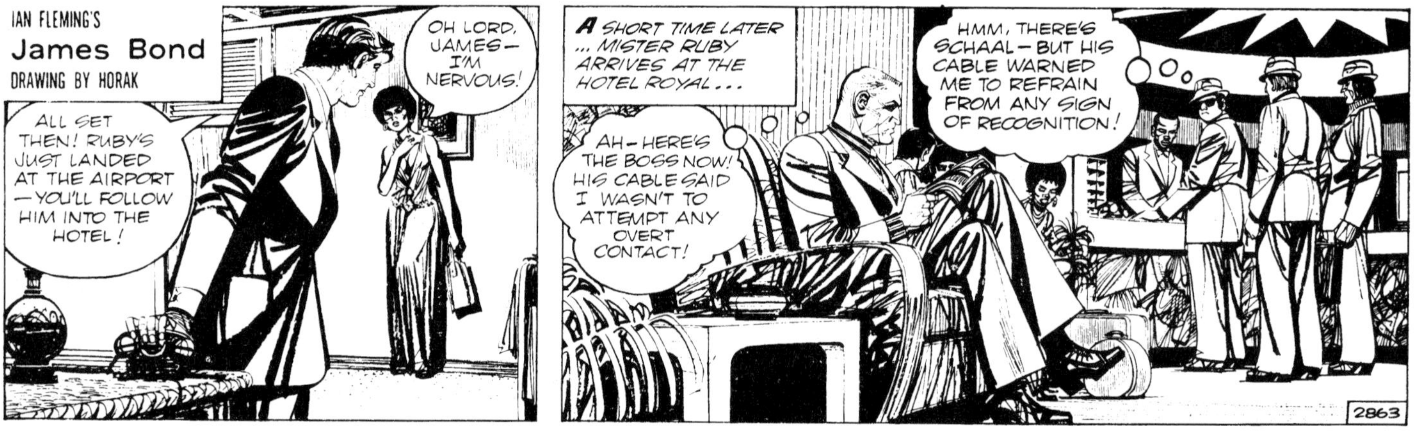
IAN FLEMING'S
James Bond
DRAWING BY HORAK
ALL SET THEN! RUBY'S JUST LANDED AT THE AIRPORT—YOU'LL FOLLOW HIM INTO THE HOTEL!
OH LORD, JAMES—I'M NERVOUS!
A SHORT TIME LATER ... MISTER RUBY ARRIVES AT THE HOTEL ROYAL...
AH—HERE'S THE BOSS NOW! HIS CABLE SAID I WASN'T TO ATTEMPT ANY OVERT CONTACT!
HMM, THERE'S SCHAAL—BUT HIS CABLE WARNED ME TO REFRAIN FROM ANY SIGN OF RECOGNITION!
2863

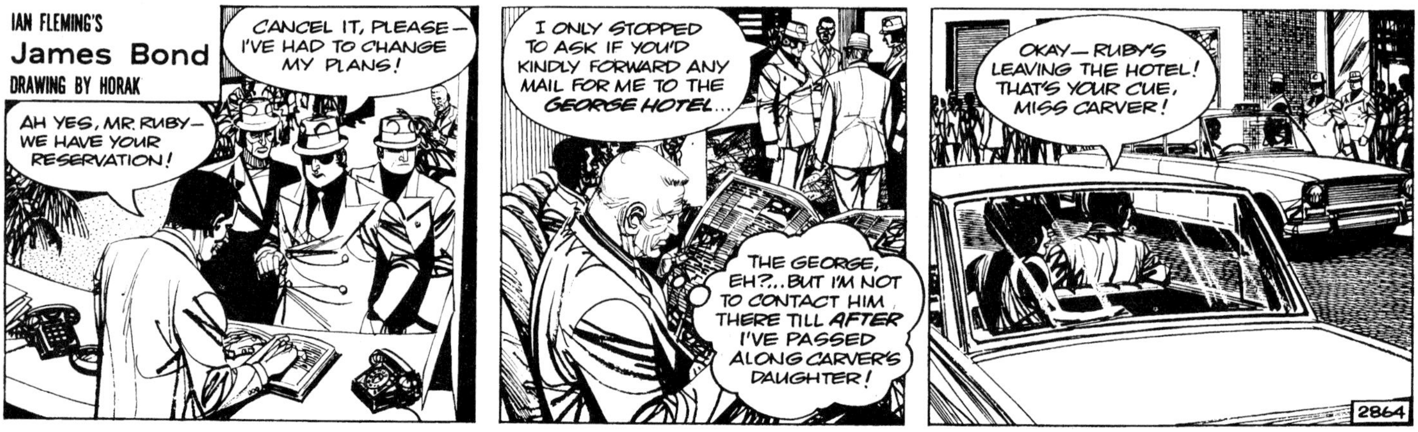
IAN FLEMING'S
James Bond
DRAWING BY HORAK
AH YES, MR. RUBY—WE HAVE YOUR RESERVATION!
CANCEL IT, PLEASE—I'VE HAD TO CHANGE MY PLANS!
I ONLY STOPPED TO ASK IF YOU'D KINDLY FORWARD ANY MAIL FOR ME TO THE GEORGE HOTEL...
THE GEORGE, EH?...BUT I'M NOT TO CONTACT HIM THERE TILL AFTER I'VE PASSED ALONG CARVER'S DAUGHTER!
OKAY—RUBY'S LEAVING THE HOTEL! THAT'S YOUR CUE, MISS CARVER!
2864

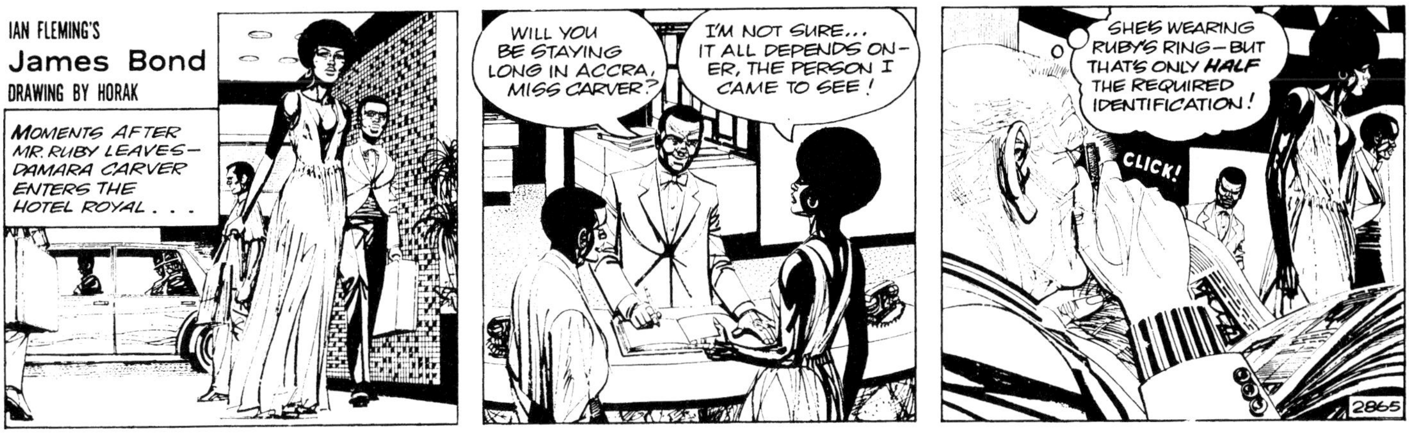
IAN FLEMING'S
James Bond
DRAWING BY HORAK
MOMENTS AFTER MR. RUBY LEAVES— DAMARA CARVER ENTERS THE HOTEL ROYAL . . .
WILL YOU BE STAYING LONG IN ACCRA, MISS CARVER?
I'M NOT SURE... IT ALL DEPENDS ON— ER, THE PERSON I CAME TO SEE!
SHE'S WEARING RUBY'S RING—BUT THAT'S ONLY HALF THE REQUIRED IDENTIFICATION!
CLICK!
2865

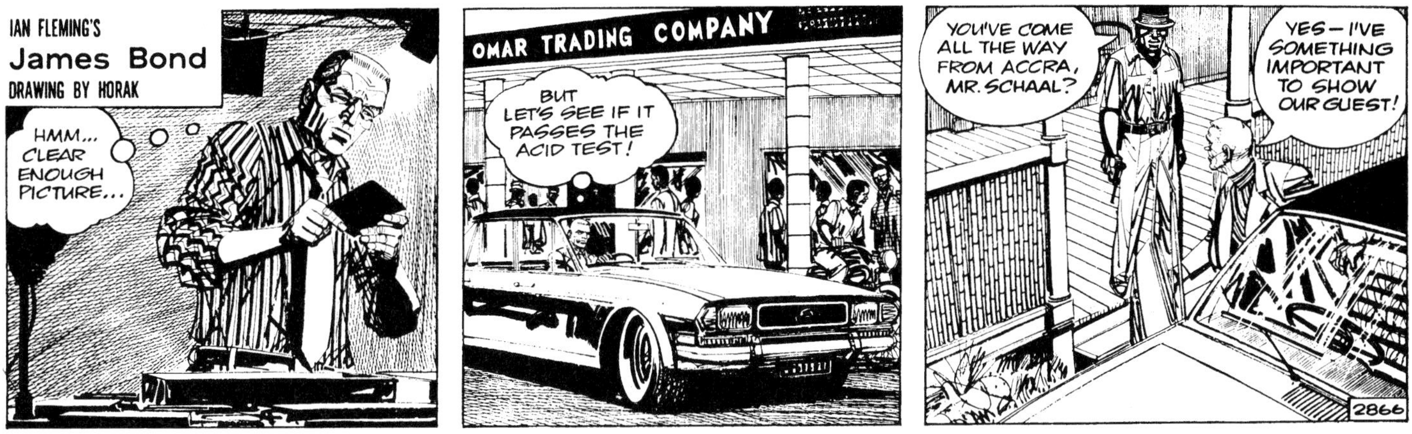
IAN FLEMING'S
James Bond
DRAWING BY HORAK
HMM... CLEAR ENOUGH PICTURE...
OMAR TRADING COMPANY
BUT LET'S SEE IF IT PASSES THE ACID TEST!
YOU'VE COME ALL THE WAY FROM ACCRA, MR. SCHAAL?
YES—I'VE SOMETHING IMPORTANT TO SHOW OUR GUEST!
2866

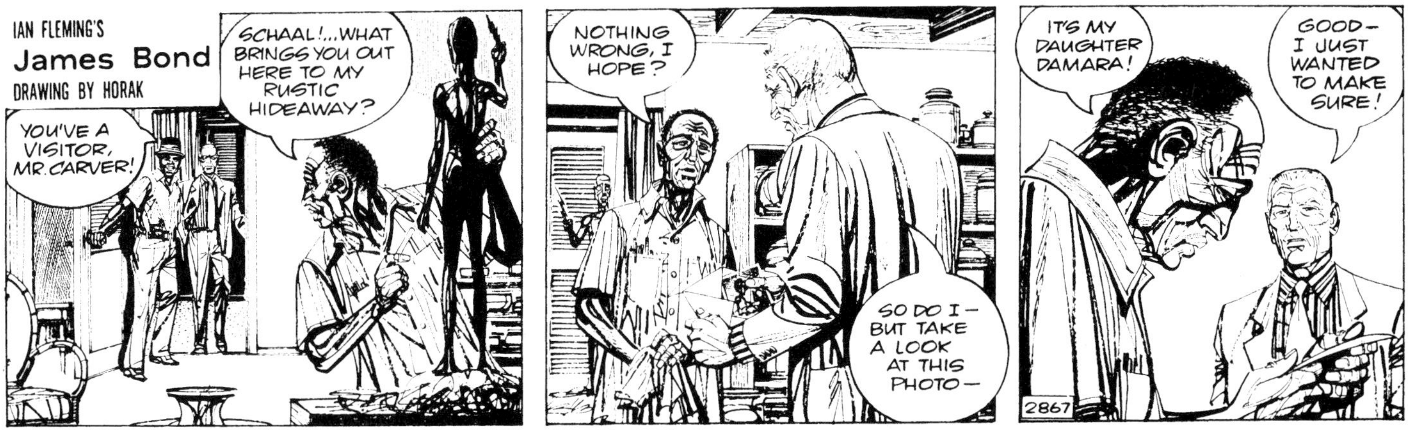
IAN FLEMING'S
James Bond
DRAWING BY HORAK
YOU'VE A VISITOR, MR. CARVER!
SCHAAL!...WHAT BRINGS YOU OUT HERE TO MY RUSTIC HIDEAWAY?
NOTHING WRONG, I HOPE?
SO DO I— BUT TAKE A LOOK AT THIS PHOTO—
IT'S MY DAUGHTER DAMARA!
GOOD— I JUST WANTED TO MAKE SURE!
2867

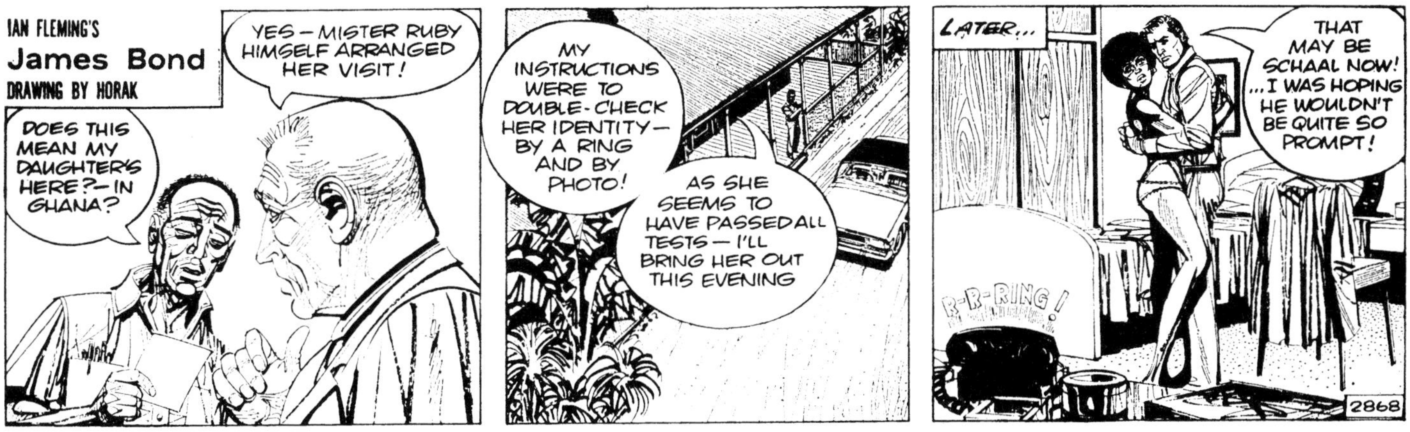
IAN FLEMING'S
James Bond
DRAWING BY HORAK
DOES THIS MEAN MY DAUGHTER'S HERE?—IN GHANA?
YES—MISTER RUBY HIMSELF ARRANGED HER VISIT!
MY INSTRUCTIONS WERE TO DOUBLE-CHECK HER IDENTITY— BY A RING AND BY PHOTO!
AS SHE SEEMS TO HAVE PASSED ALL TESTS—I'LL BRING HER OUT THIS EVENING
LATER...
THAT MAY BE SCHAAL NOW! ...I WAS HOPING HE WOULDN'T BE QUITE SO PROMPT!
R-R-RING!
2868

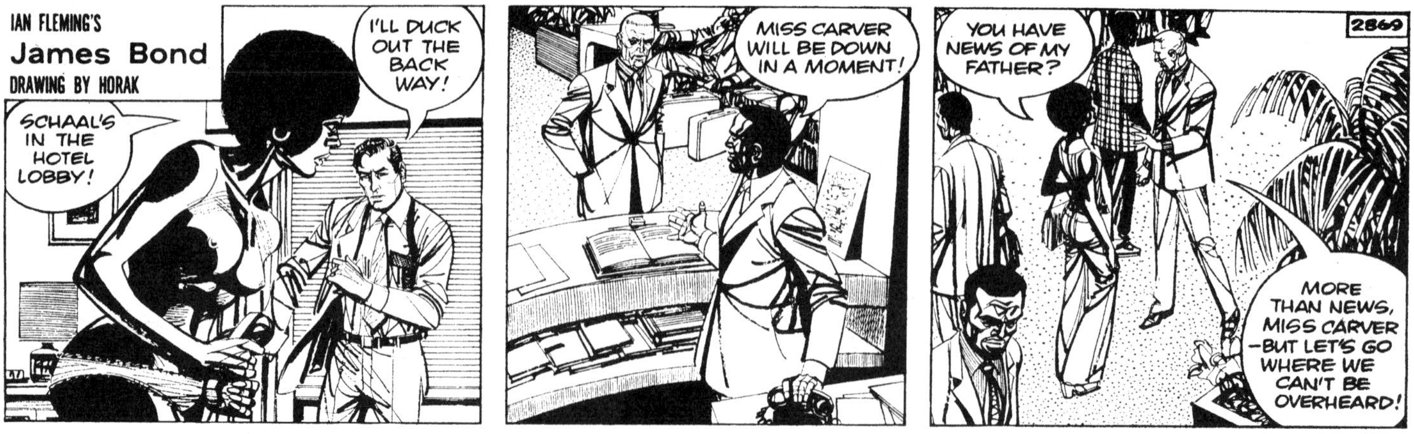
IAN FLEMING'S
James Bond
DRAWING BY HORAK
SCHAAL'S IN THE HOTEL LOBBY!
I'LL DUCK OUT THE BACK WAY!
MISS CARVER WILL BE DOWN IN A MOMENT!
YOU HAVE NEWS OF MY FATHER?
MORE THAN NEWS, MISS CARVER —BUT LET'S GO WHERE WE CAN'T BE OVERHEARD!
2869

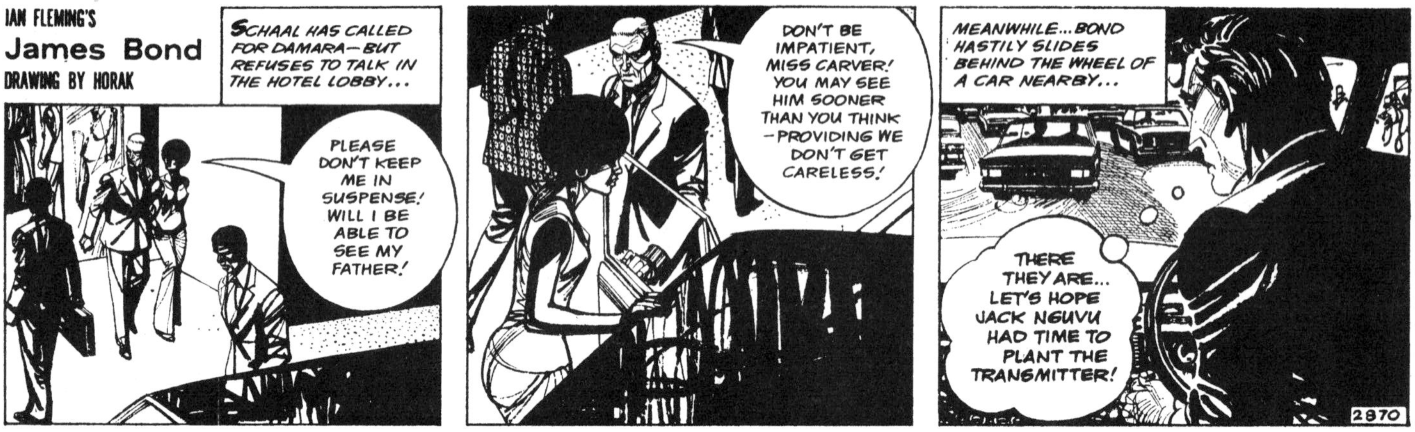
IAN FLEMING'S
James Bond
DRAWING BY HORAK
SCHAAL HAS CALLED FOR DAMARA—BUT REFUSES TO TALK IN THE HOTEL LOBBY...
PLEASE DON'T KEEP ME IN SUSPENSE! WILL I BE ABLE TO SEE MY FATHER!
DON'T BE IMPATIENT, MISS CARVER! YOU MAY SEE HIM SOONER THAN YOU THINK —PROVIDING WE DON'T GET CARELESS!
MEANWHILE...BOND HASTILY SLIDES BEHIND THE WHEEL OF A CAR NEARBY...
THERE THEY ARE... LET'S HOPE JACK NGUVU HAD TIME TO PLANT THE TRANSMITTER!
2870

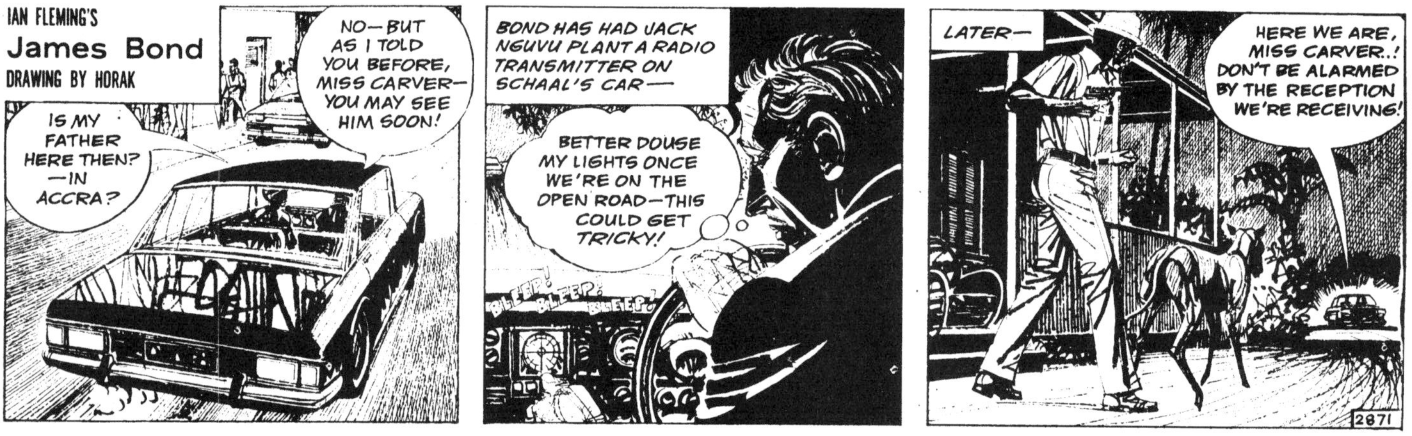
IAN FLEMING'S
James Bond
DRAWING BY HORAK
IS MY FATHER HERE THEN? —IN ACCRA?
NO—BUT AS I TOLD YOU BEFORE, MISS CARVER— YOU MAY SEE HIM SOON!
BOND HAS HAD JACK NGUVU PLANT A RADIO TRANSMITTER ON SCHAAL'S CAR—
BETTER DOUSE MY LIGHTS ONCE WE'RE ON THE OPEN ROAD—THIS COULD GET TRICKY!
LATER—
HERE WE ARE, MISS CARVER..! DON'T BE ALARMED BY THE RECEPTION WE'RE RECEIVING!
2871

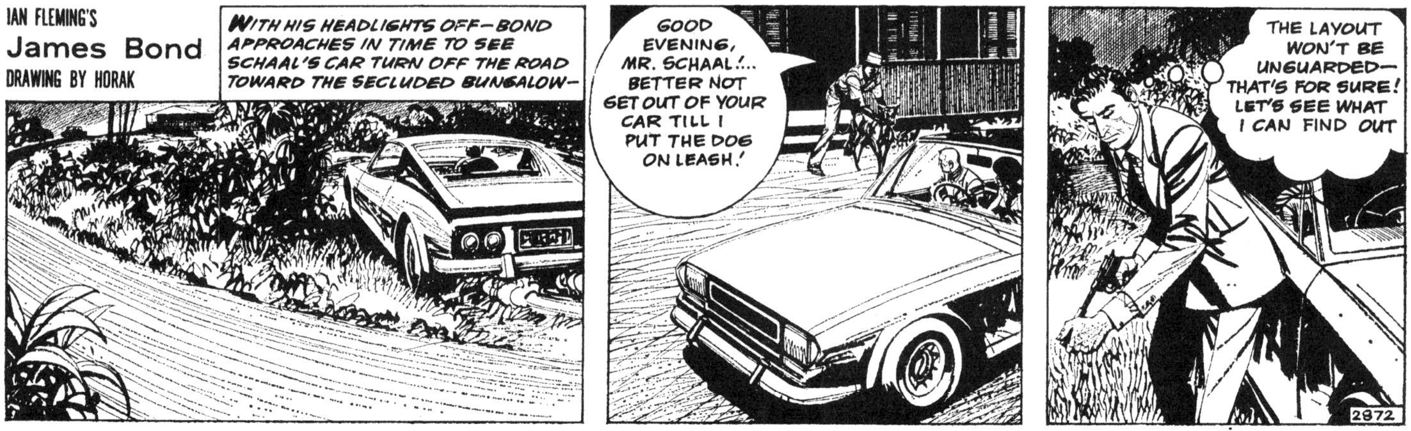
IAN FLEMING'S
James Bond
DRAWING BY HORAK
WITH HIS HEADLIGHTS OFF—BOND APPROACHES IN TIME TO SEE SCHAAL'S CAR TURN OFF THE ROAD TOWARD THE SECLUDED BUNGALOW—
GOOD EVENING, MR. SCHAAL!... BETTER NOT GET OUT OF YOUR CAR TILL I PUT THE DOG ON LEASH!
THE LAYOUT WON'T BE UNGUARDED— THAT'S FOR SURE! LET'S SEE WHAT I CAN FIND OUT
2872

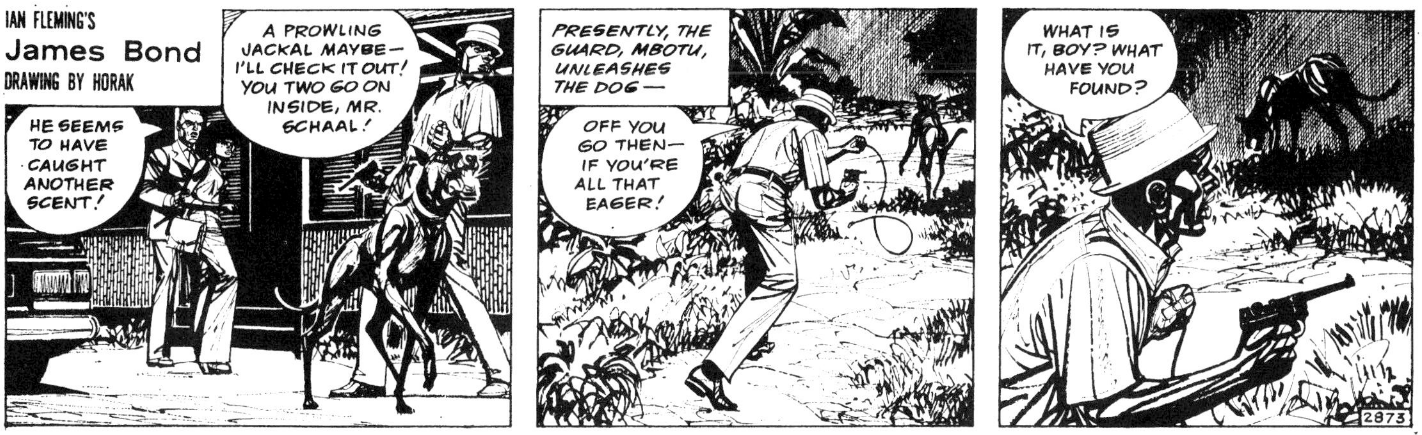
IAN FLEMING'S
James Bond
DRAWING BY HORAK
HE SEEMS TO HAVE CAUGHT ANOTHER SCENT!
A PROWLING JACKAL MAYBE— I'LL CHECK IT OUT! YOU TWO GO ON INSIDE, MR. SCHAAL!
PRESENTLY, THE GUARD, MBOTU, UNLEASHES THE DOG—
OFF YOU GO THEN— IF YOU'RE ALL THAT EAGER!
WHAT IS IT, BOY? WHAT HAVE YOU FOUND?
2873

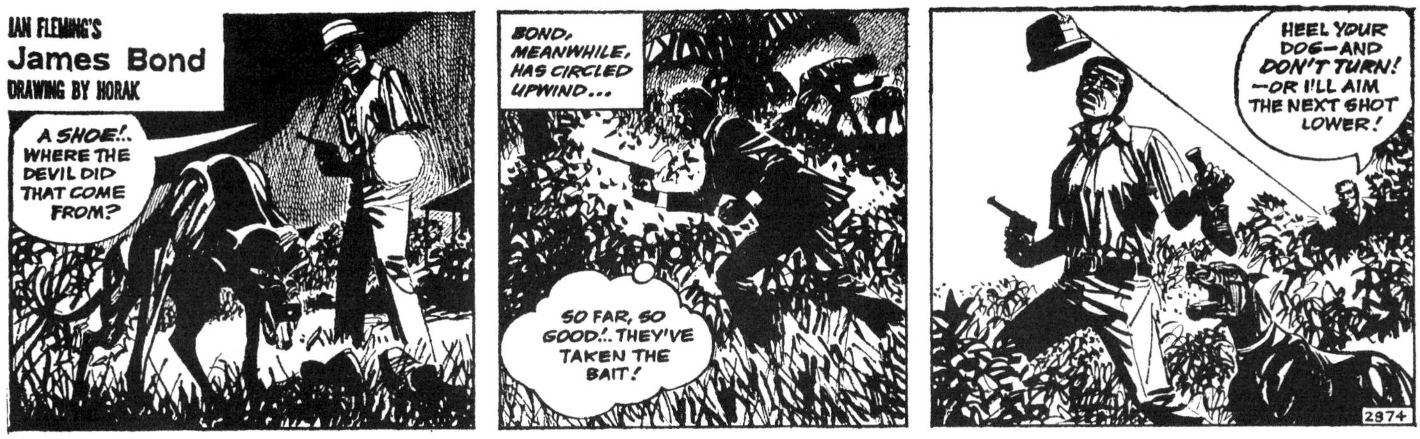
IAN FLEMING'S
James Bond
DRAWING BY HORAK
A SHOE!.. WHERE THE DEVIL DID THAT COME FROM?
BOND, MEANWHILE, HAS CIRCLED UPWIND...
SO FAR, SO GOOD!.. THEY'VE TAKEN THE BAIT!
HEEL YOUR DOG—AND DON'T TURN! —OR I'LL AIM THE NEXT SHOT LOWER!
2874

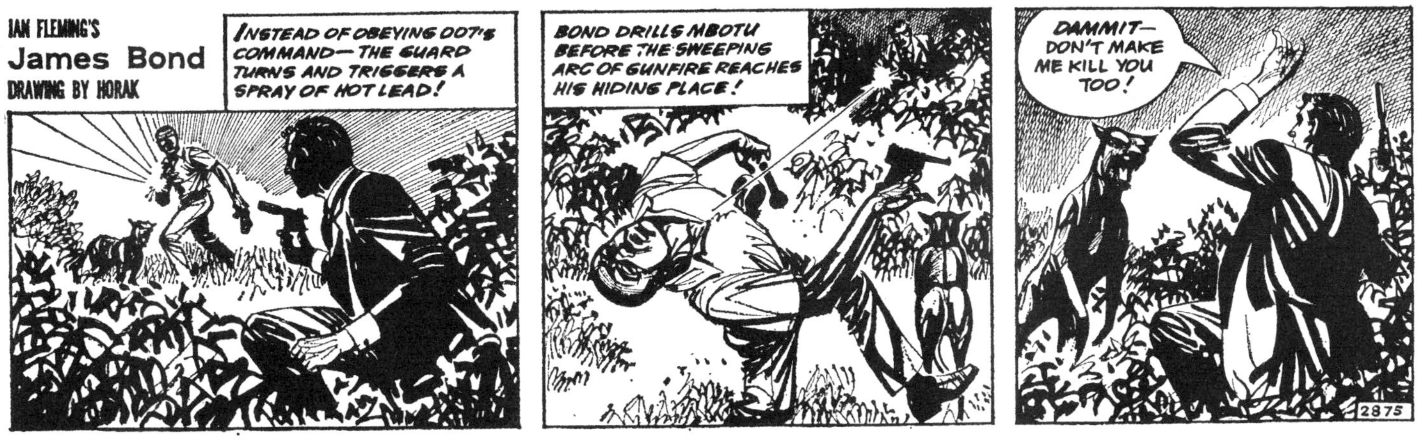
IAN FLEMING'S
James Bond
DRAWING BY HORAK
INSTEAD OF OBEYING 007's COMMAND— THE GUARD TURNS AND TRIGGERS A SPRAY OF HOT LEAD!
BOND DRILLS MBOTU BEFORE THE SWEEPING ARC OF GUNFIRE REACHES HIS HIDING PLACE!
DAMMIT— DON'T MAKE ME KILL YOU TOO!
2875

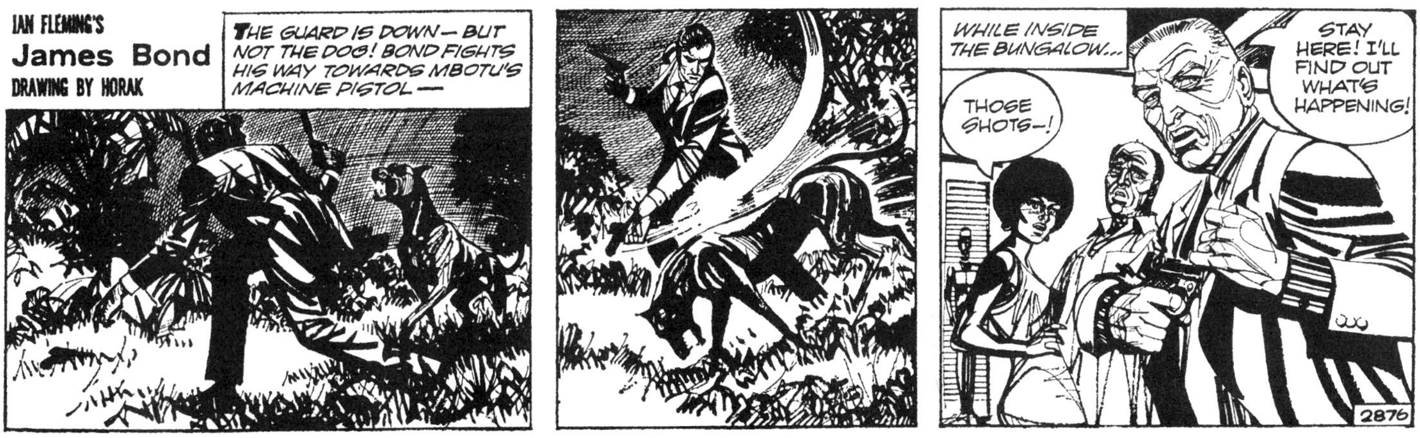
IAN FLEMING'S
James Bond
DRAWING BY HORAK
THE GUARD IS DOWN— BUT NOT THE DOG! BOND FIGHTS HIS WAY TOWARDS MBOTU'S MACHINE PISTOL—
WHILE INSIDE THE BUNGALOW...
THOSE SHOTS—!
STAY HERE! I'LL FIND OUT WHAT'S HAPPENING!
2876

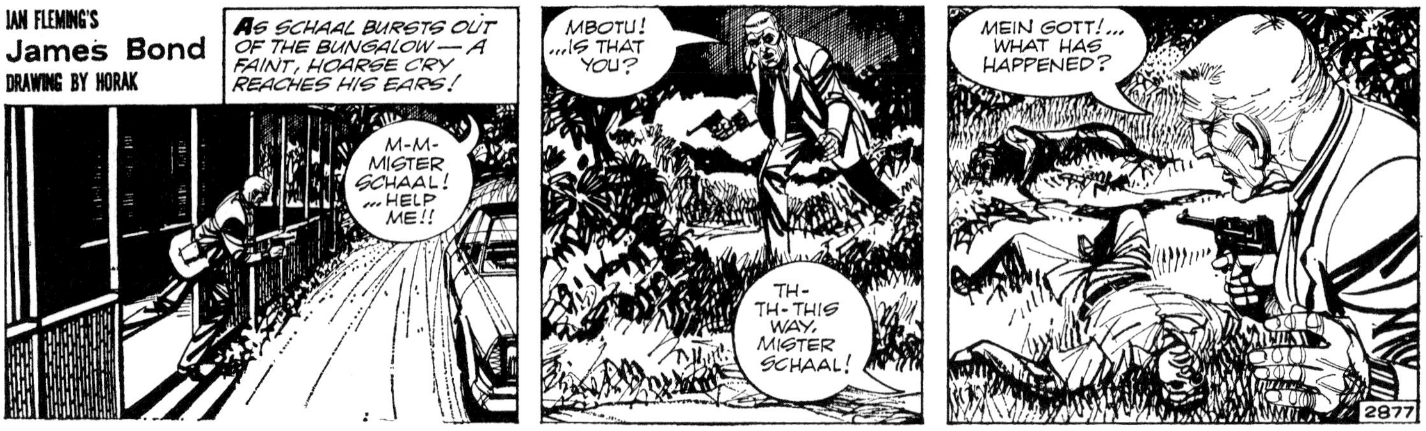
IAN FLEMING'S
James Bond
DRAWING BY HORAK
AS SCHAAL BURSTS OUT OF THE BUNGALOW — A FAINT, HOARSE CRY REACHES HIS EARS!
M-M-MISTER SCHAAL! ...HELP ME!!
MBOTU! ...IS THAT YOU?
TH-TH-THIS WAY, MISTER SCHAAL!
MEIN GOTT!... WHAT HAS HAPPENED?
2877

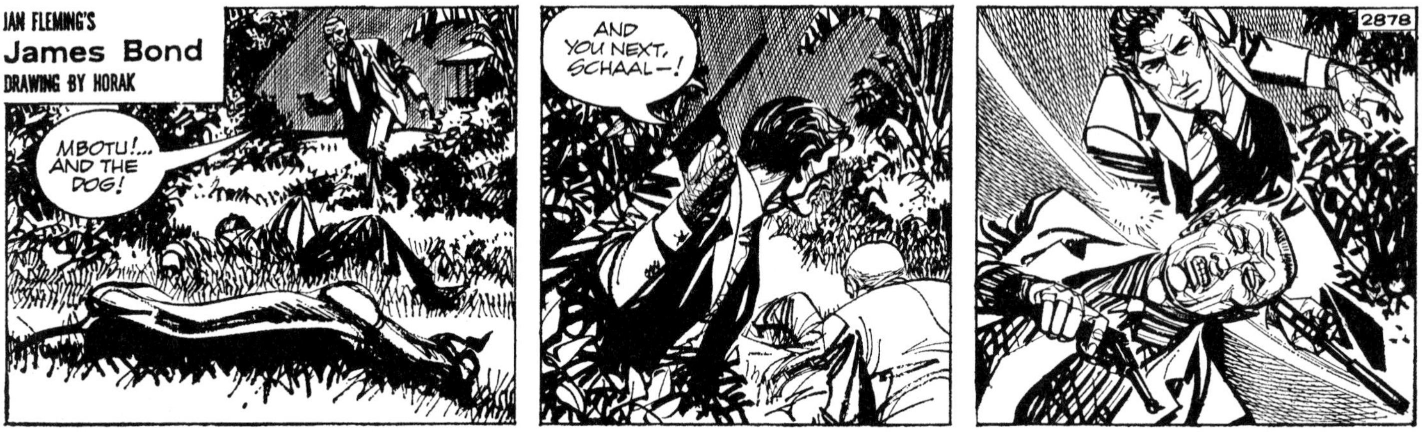
IAN FLEMING'S
James Bond
DRAWING BY HORAK
MBOTU!... AND THE DOG!
AND YOU NEXT, SCHAAL—!
2878

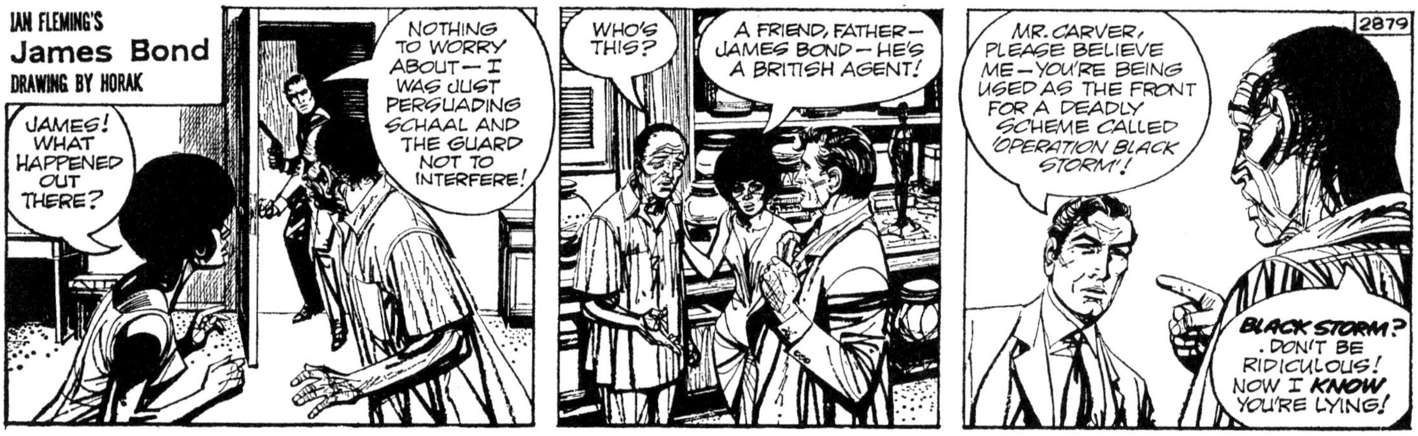
IAN FLEMING'S
James Bond
DRAWING BY HORAK
JAMES! WHAT HAPPENED OUT THERE?
NOTHING TO WORRY ABOUT — I WAS JUST PERSUADING SCHAAL AND THE GUARD NOT TO INTERFERE!
WHO'S THIS?
A FRIEND, FATHER — JAMES BOND — HE'S A BRITISH AGENT!
2879
MR. CARVER, PLEASE BELIEVE ME — YOU'RE BEING USED AS THE FRONT FOR A DEADLY SCHEME CALLED 'OPERATION BLACK STORM'!
BLACK STORM? DON'T BE RIDICULOUS! NOW I KNOW YOU'RE LYING!

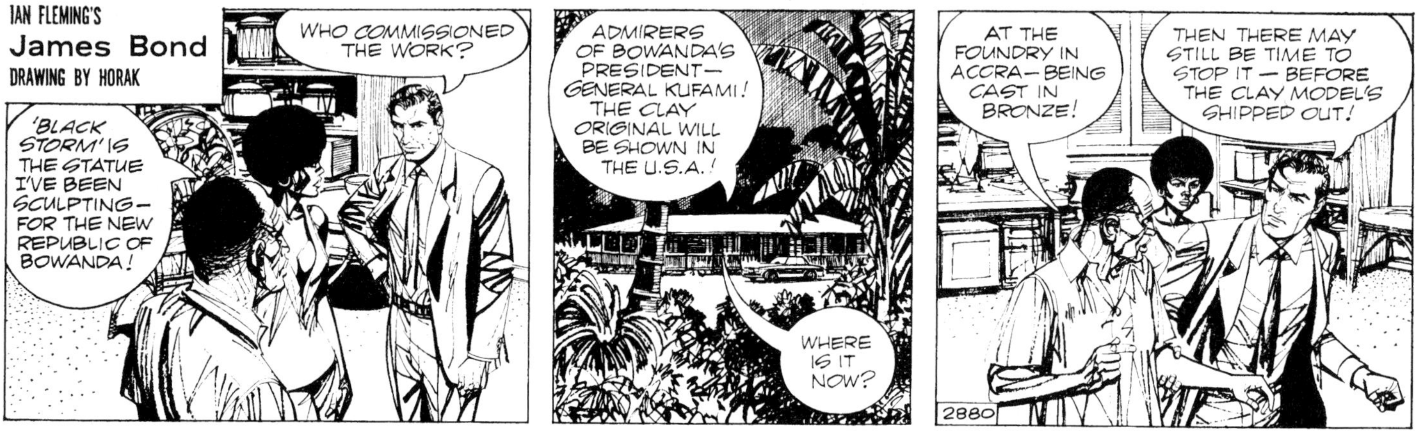
IAN FLEMING'S
James Bond
DRAWING BY HORAK
WHO COMMISSIONED THE WORK?
'BLACK STORM' IS THE STATUE I'VE BEEN SCULPTING — FOR THE NEW REPUBLIC OF BOWANDA!
ADMIRERS OF BOWANDA'S PRESIDENT — GENERAL KUFAMI! THE CLAY ORIGINAL WILL BE SHOWN IN THE U.S.A.!
WHERE IS IT NOW?
AT THE FOUNDRY IN ACCRA — BEING CAST IN BRONZE!
THEN THERE MAY STILL BE TIME TO STOP IT — BEFORE THE CLAY MODEL'S SHIPPED OUT!
2880

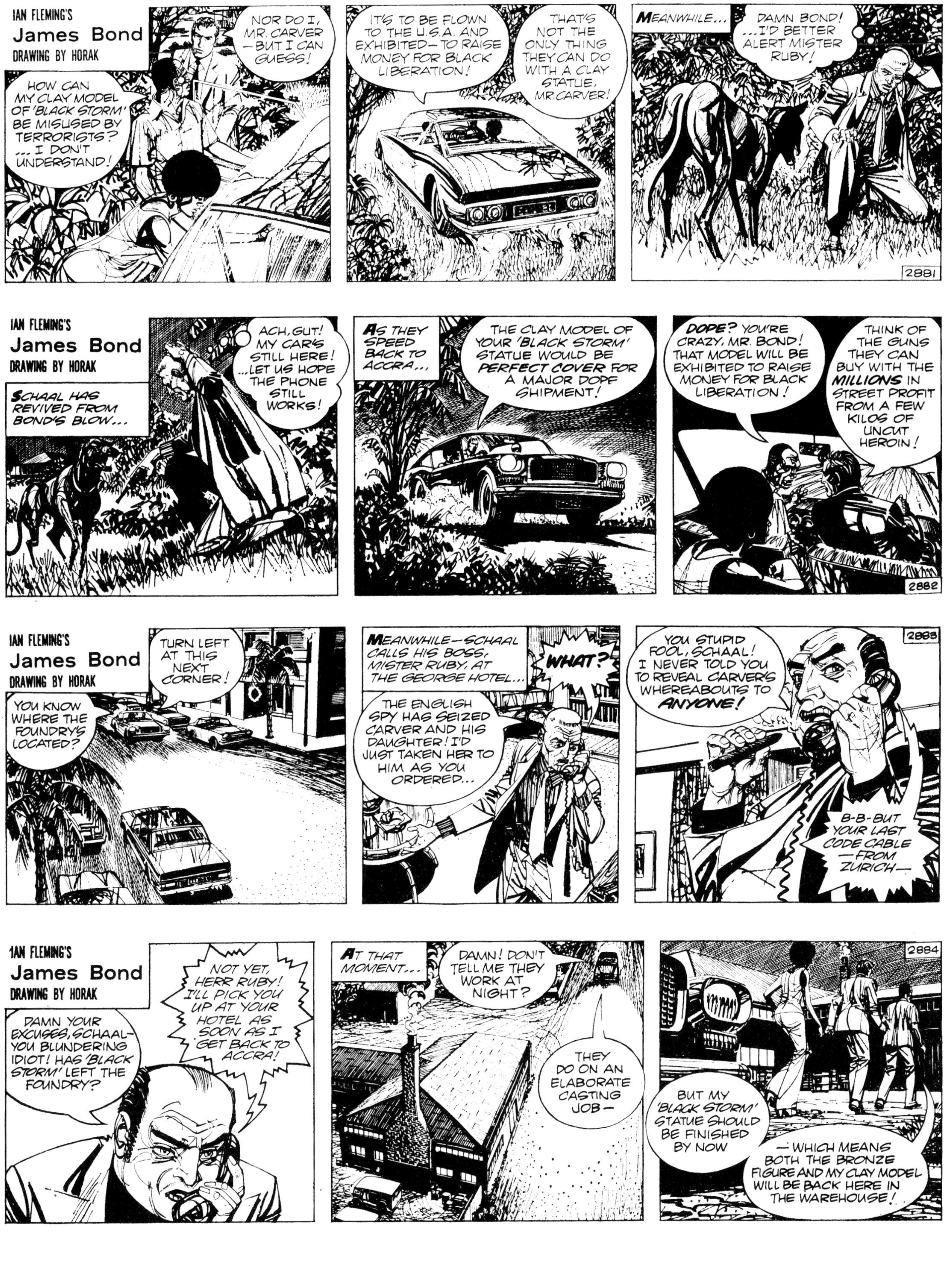
IAN FLEMING'S
James Bond
DRAWING BY HORAK
HOW CAN MY CLAY MODEL OF 'BLACK STORM' BE MISUSED BY TERRORISTS? ... I DON'T UNDERSTAND!
NOR DO I, MR. CARVER — BUT I CAN GUESS!
IT'S TO BE FLOWN TO THE U.S.A. AND EXHIBITED — TO RAISE MONEY FOR BLACK LIBERATION!
THAT'S NOT THE ONLY THING THEY CAN DO WITH A CLAY STATUE, MR. CARVER!
MEANWHILE...
DAMN BOND! ...I'D BETTER ALERT MISTER RUBY!
2881
IAN FLEMING'S
James Bond
DRAWING BY HORAK
SCHAAL HAS REVIVED FROM BOND'S BLOW...
ACH, GUT! MY CAR'S STILL HERE! ...LET US HOPE THE PHONE STILL WORKS!
AS THEY SPEED BACK TO ACCRA...
THE CLAY MODEL OF YOUR 'BLACK STORM' STATUE WOULD BE PERFECT COVER FOR A MAJOR DOPE SHIPMENT!
DOPE? YOU'RE CRAZY, MR. BOND! THAT MODEL WILL BE EXHIBITED TO RAISE MONEY FOR BLACK LIBERATION!
THINK OF THE GUNS THEY CAN BUY WITH THE MILLIONS IN STREET PROFIT FROM A FEW KILOS OF UNCUT HEROIN!
2882
IAN FLEMING'S
James Bond
DRAWING BY HORAK
YOU KNOW WHERE THE FOUNDRY'S LOCATED?
TURN LEFT AT THIS NEXT CORNER!
MEANWHILE — SCHAAL CALLS HIS BOSS, MISTER RUBY, AT THE GEORGE HOTEL...
THE ENGLISH SPY HAS SEIZED CARVER AND HIS DAUGHTER! I'D JUST TAKEN HER TO HIM AS YOU ORDERED...
WHAT?
2883
YOU STUPID FOOL, SCHAAL! I NEVER TOLD YOU TO REVEAL CARVER'S WHEREABOUTS TO ANYONE!
B-B-BUT YOUR LAST CODE CABLE — FROM ZURICH —
IAN FLEMING'S
James Bond
DRAWING BY HORAK
DAMN YOUR EXCUSES, SCHAAL — YOU BLUNDERING IDIOT! HAS 'BLACK STORM' LEFT THE FOUNDRY?
NOT YET, HERR RUBY! I'LL PICK YOU UP AT YOUR HOTEL AS SOON AS I GET BACK TO ACCRA!
AT THAT MOMENT...
DAMN! DON'T TELL ME THEY WORK AT NIGHT?
THEY DO ON AN ELABORATE CASTING JOB —
2884
BUT MY 'BLACK STORM' STATUE SHOULD BE FINISHED BY NOW
— WHICH MEANS BOTH THE BRONZE FIGURE AND MY CLAY MODEL WILL BE BACK HERE IN THE WAREHOUSE!

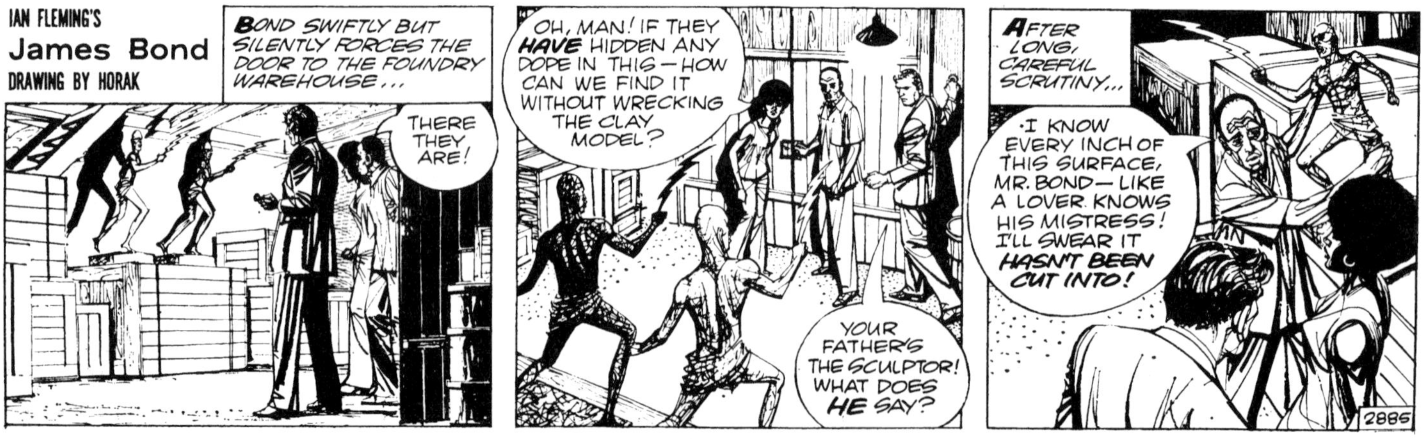
IAN FLEMING'S
James Bond
DRAWING BY HORAK
BOND SWIFTLY BUT SILENTLY FORCES THE DOOR TO THE FOUNDRY WAREHOUSE...
THERE THEY ARE!
OH, MAN! IF THEY HAVE HIDDEN ANY DOPE IN THIS – HOW CAN WE FIND IT WITHOUT WRECKING THE CLAY MODEL?
YOUR FATHER'S THE SCULPTOR! WHAT DOES HE SAY?
AFTER LONG, CAREFUL SCRUTINY...
- I KNOW EVERY INCH OF THIS SURFACE, MR. BOND – LIKE A LOVER KNOWS HIS MISTRESS! I'LL SWEAR IT HASN'T BEEN CUT INTO!
2885

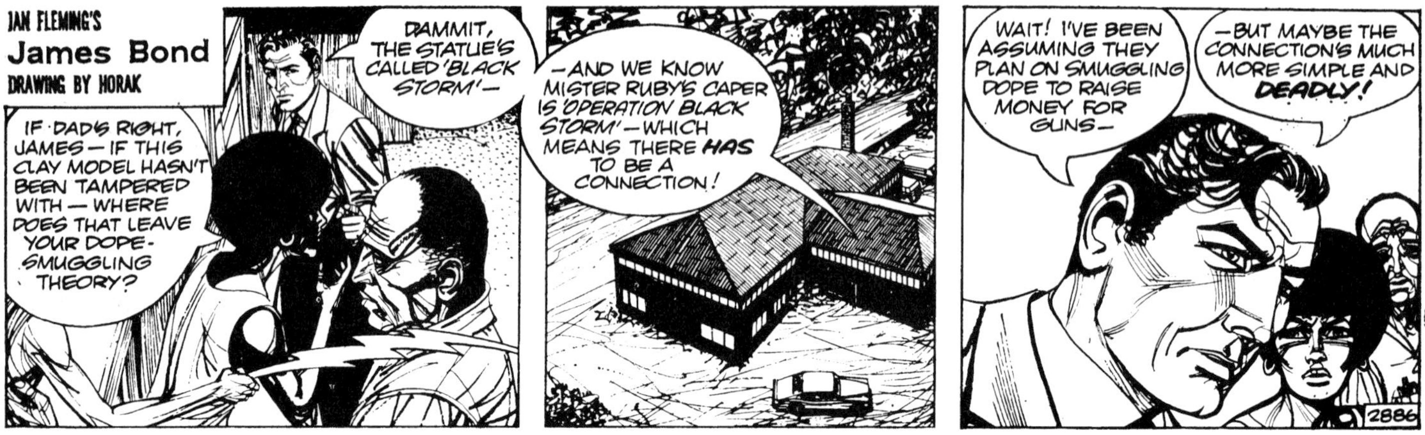
IAN FLEMING'S
James Bond
DRAWING BY HORAK
IF DAD'S RIGHT, JAMES – IF THIS CLAY MODEL HASN'T BEEN TAMPERED WITH – WHERE DOES THAT LEAVE YOUR DOPE-SMUGGLING THEORY?
DAMMIT, THE STATUE'S CALLED 'BLACK STORM' –
– AND WE KNOW MISTER RUBY'S CAPER IS 'OPERATION BLACK STORM' – WHICH MEANS THERE HAS TO BE A CONNECTION!
WAIT! I'VE BEEN ASSUMING THEY PLAN ON SMUGGLING DOPE TO RAISE MONEY FOR GUNS –
– BUT MAYBE THE CONNECTION'S MUCH MORE SIMPLE AND DEADLY!
2886

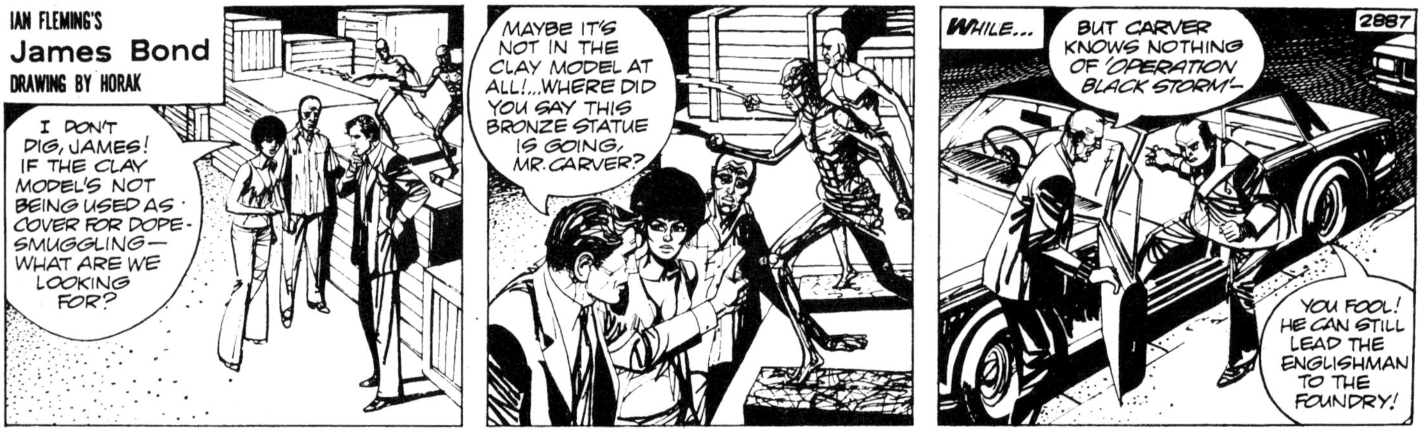
IAN FLEMING'S
James Bond
DRAWING BY HORAK
I DON'T DIG, JAMES! IF THE CLAY MODEL'S NOT BEING USED AS COVER FOR DOPE-SMUGGLING – WHAT ARE WE LOOKING FOR?
MAYBE IT'S NOT IN THE CLAY MODEL AT ALL!... WHERE DID YOU SAY THIS BRONZE STATUE IS GOING, MR. CARVER?
WHILE...
BUT CARVER KNOWS NOTHING OF 'OPERATION BLACK STORM' –
YOU FOOL! HE CAN STILL LEAD THE ENGLISHMAN TO THE FOUNDRY!
2887

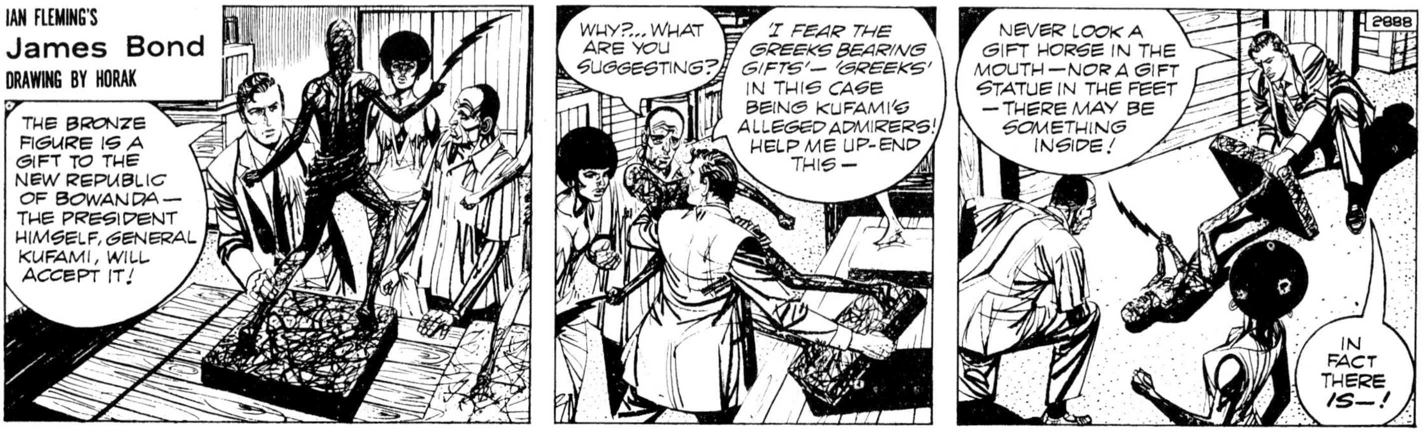
IAN FLEMING'S
James Bond
DRAWING BY HORAK
THE BRONZE FIGURE IS A GIFT TO THE NEW REPUBLIC OF BOWANDA – THE PRESIDENT HIMSELF, GENERAL KUFAMI, WILL ACCEPT IT!
WHY?... WHAT ARE YOU SUGGESTING?
'I FEAR THE GREEKS BEARING GIFTS' – 'GREEKS' IN THIS CASE BEING KUFAMI'S ALLEGED ADMIRERS! HELP ME UP-END THIS –
NEVER LOOK A GIFT HORSE IN THE MOUTH – NOR A GIFT STATUE IN THE FEET – THERE MAY BE SOMETHING INSIDE!
IN FACT THERE IS –!
2888

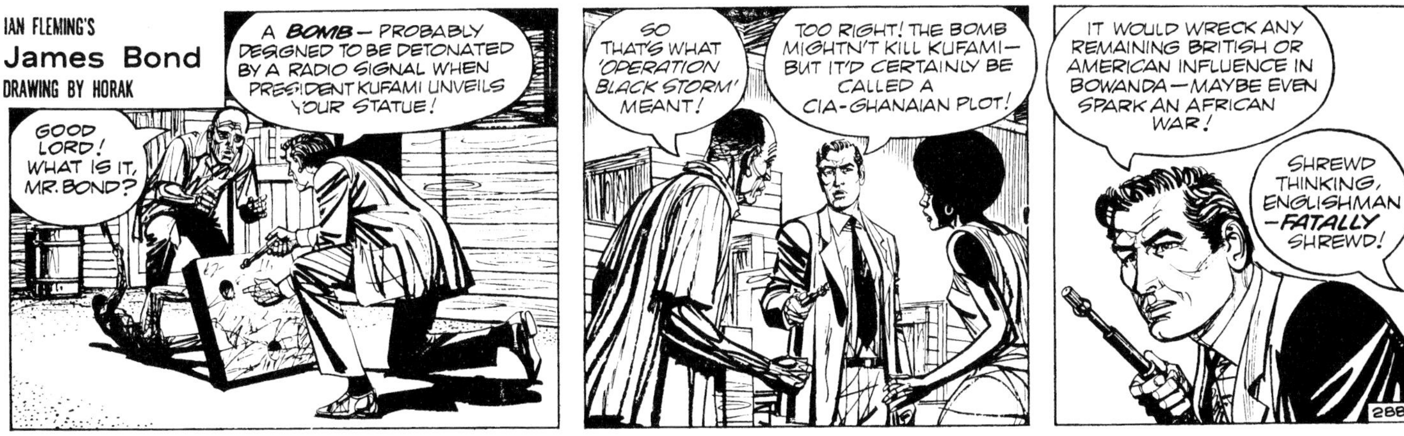
IAN FLEMING'S
James Bond
DRAWING BY HORAK
A BOMB — PROBABLY DESIGNED TO BE DETONATED BY A RADIO SIGNAL WHEN PRESIDENT KUFAMI UNVEILS YOUR STATUE!
GOOD LORD! WHAT IS IT, MR. BOND?
SO THAT'S WHAT 'OPERATION BLACK STORM' MEANT!
TOO RIGHT! THE BOMB MIGHTN'T KILL KUFAMI — BUT IT'D CERTAINLY BE CALLED A CIA-GHANAIAN PLOT!
IT WOULD WRECK ANY REMAINING BRITISH OR AMERICAN INFLUENCE IN BOWANDA — MAYBE EVEN SPARK AN AFRICAN WAR!
SHREWD THINKING, ENGLISHMAN — FATALLY SHREWD!
2889

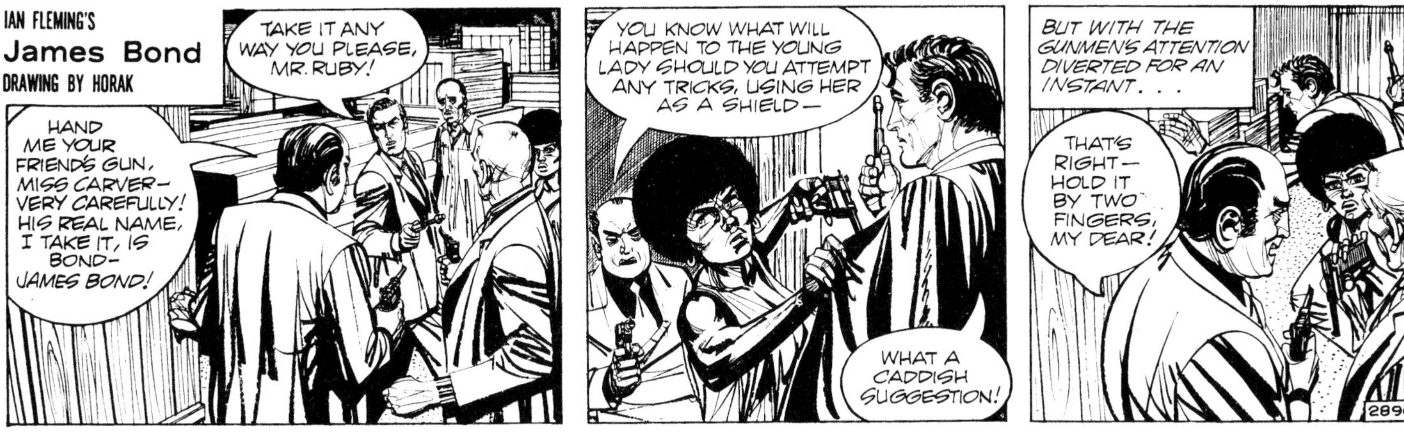
IAN FLEMING'S
James Bond
DRAWING BY HORAK
TAKE IT ANY WAY YOU PLEASE, MR. RUBY!
HAND ME YOUR FRIEND'S GUN, MISS CARVER — VERY CAREFULLY! HIS REAL NAME, I TAKE IT, IS BOND — JAMES BOND!
YOU KNOW WHAT WILL HAPPEN TO THE YOUNG LADY SHOULD YOU ATTEMPT ANY TRICKS, USING HER AS A SHIELD —
WHAT A CADDISH SUGGESTION!
BUT WITH THE GUNMEN'S ATTENTION DIVERTED FOR AN INSTANT . . .
THAT'S RIGHT — HOLD IT BY TWO FINGERS, MY DEAR!
2890

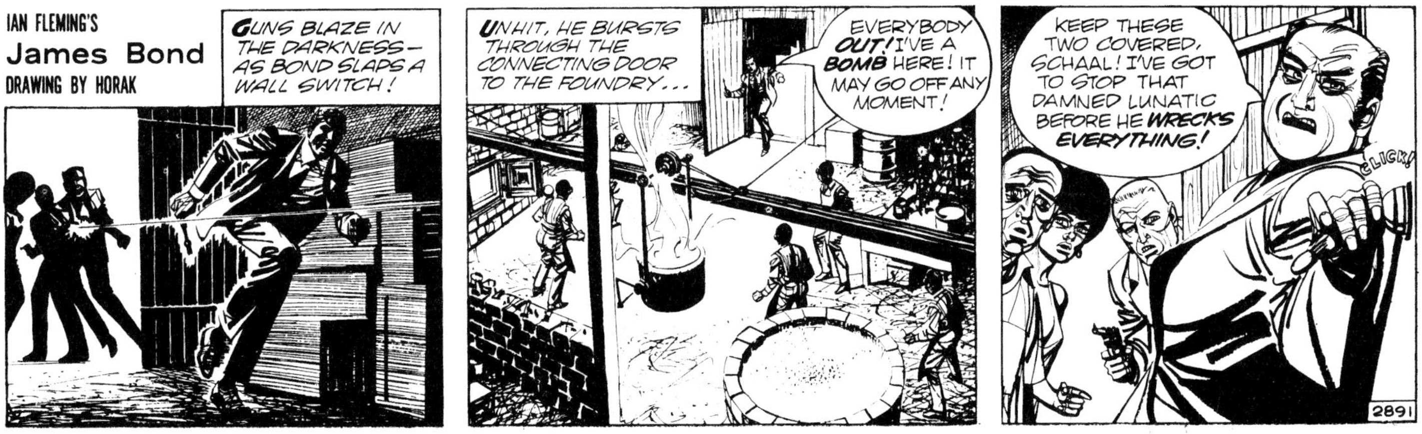
IAN FLEMING'S
James Bond
DRAWING BY HORAK
GUNS BLAZE IN THE DARKNESS — AS BOND SLAPS A WALL SWITCH!
UNHIT, HE BURSTS THROUGH THE CONNECTING DOOR TO THE FOUNDRY...
EVERYBODY OUT! I'VE A BOMB HERE! IT MAY GO OFF ANY MOMENT!
KEEP THESE TWO COVERED, SCHAAL! I'VE GOT TO STOP THAT DAMNED LUNATIC BEFORE HE WRECKS EVERYTHING!
CLICK!
2891

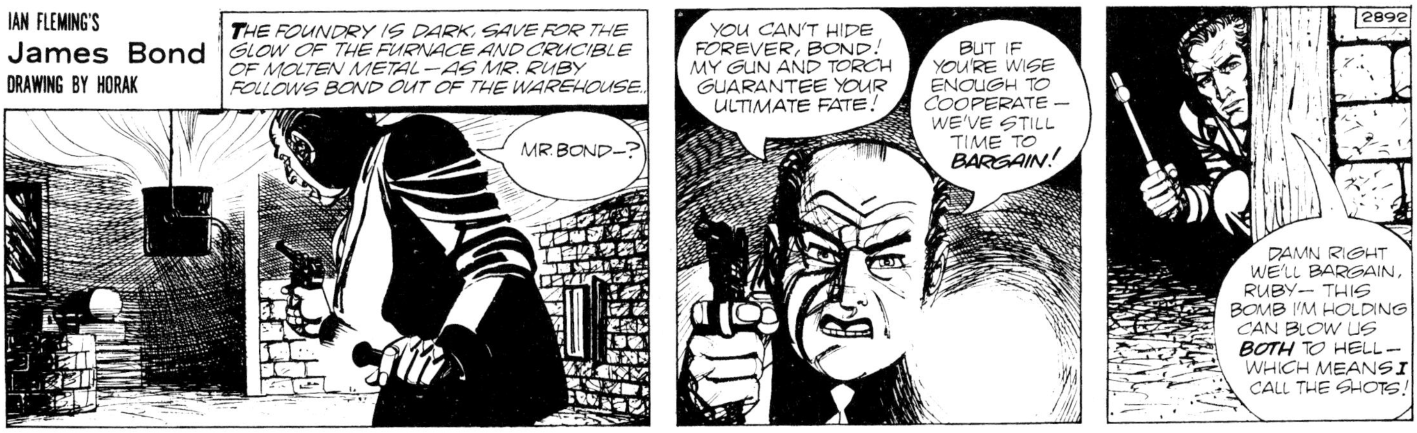
IAN FLEMING'S
James Bond
DRAWING BY HORAK
THE FOUNDRY IS DARK, SAVE FOR THE GLOW OF THE FURNACE AND CRUCIBLE OF MOLTEN METAL — AS MR. RUBY FOLLOWS BOND OUT OF THE WAREHOUSE..
MR. BOND —?
YOU CAN'T HIDE FOREVER, BOND! MY GUN AND TORCH GUARANTEE YOUR ULTIMATE FATE!
BUT IF YOU'RE WISE ENOUGH TO COOPERATE — WE'VE STILL TIME TO BARGAIN!
2892
DAMN RIGHT WE'LL BARGAIN, RUBY — THIS BOMB I'M HOLDING CAN BLOW US BOTH TO HELL — WHICH MEANS I CALL THE SHOTS!

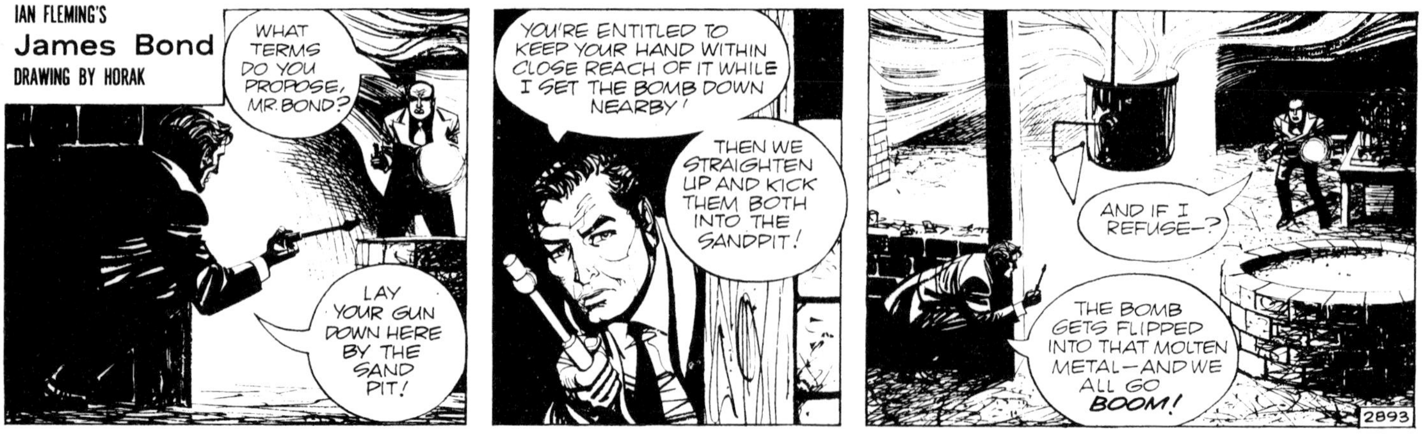
IAN FLEMING'S
James Bond
DRAWING BY HORAK
WHAT TERMS DO YOU PROPOSE, MR. BOND?
LAY YOUR GUN DOWN HERE BY THE SAND PIT!
YOU'RE ENTITLED TO KEEP YOUR HAND WITHIN CLOSE REACH OF IT WHILE I SET THE BOMB DOWN NEARBY!
THEN WE STRAIGHTEN UP AND KICK THEM BOTH INTO THE SANDPIT!
AND IF I REFUSE–?
THE BOMB GETS FLIPPED INTO THAT MOLTEN METAL—AND WE ALL GO BOOM!
2893

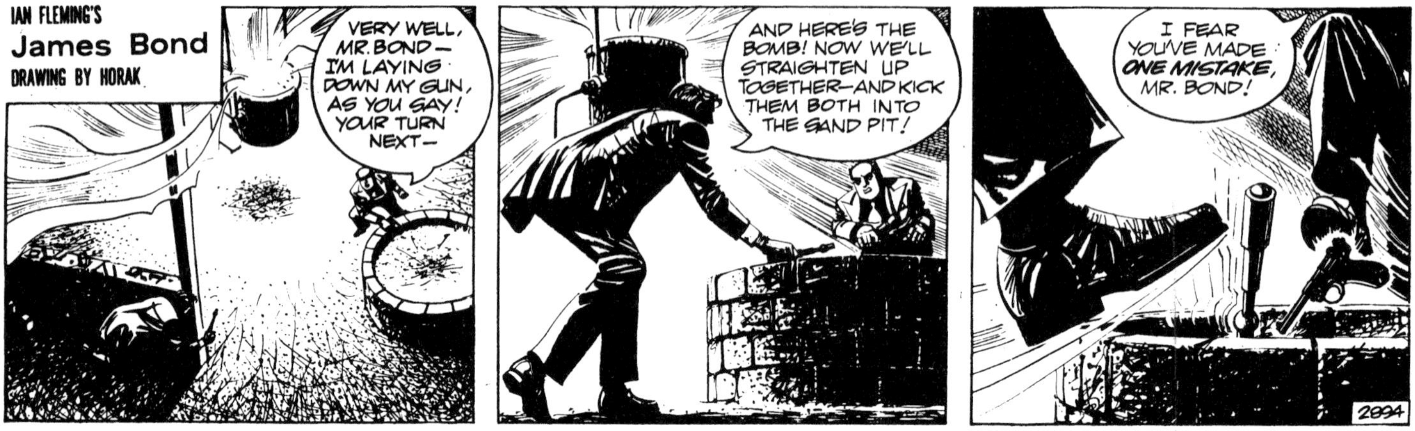
IAN FLEMING'S
James Bond
DRAWING BY HORAK
VERY WELL, MR. BOND— I'M LAYING DOWN MY GUN, AS YOU SAY! YOUR TURN NEXT—
AND HERE'S THE BOMB! NOW WE'LL STRAIGHTEN UP TOGETHER—AND KICK THEM BOTH INTO THE SAND PIT!
I FEAR YOU'VE MADE ONE MISTAKE, MR. BOND!
2894

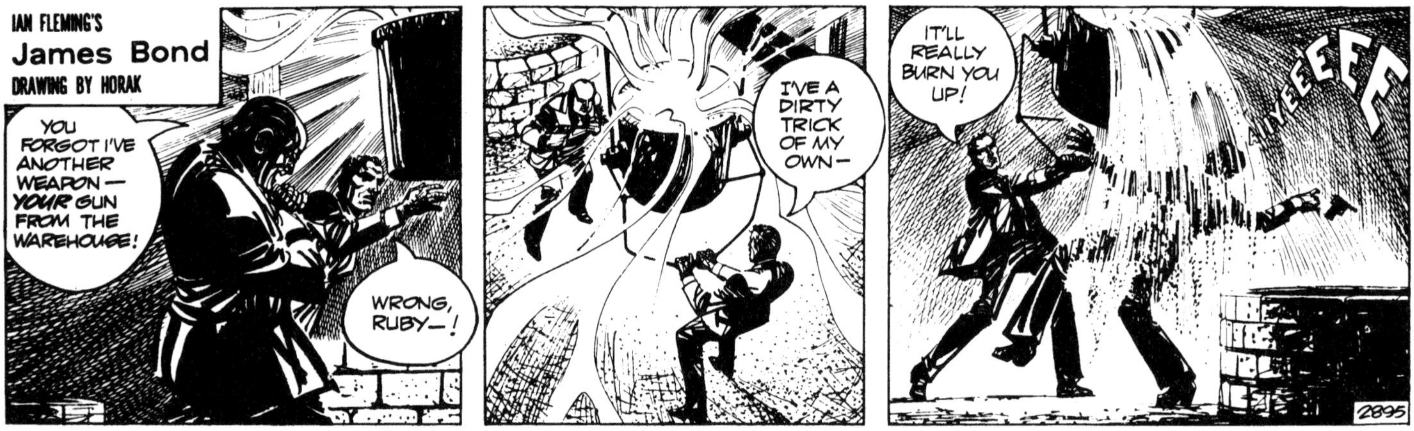
IAN FLEMING'S
James Bond
DRAWING BY HORAK
YOU FORGOT I'VE ANOTHER WEAPON— YOUR GUN FROM THE WAREHOUSE!
WRONG, RUBY—!
I'VE A DIRTY TRICK OF MY OWN—
IT'LL REALLY BURN YOU UP!
AIYEEEEE
2895

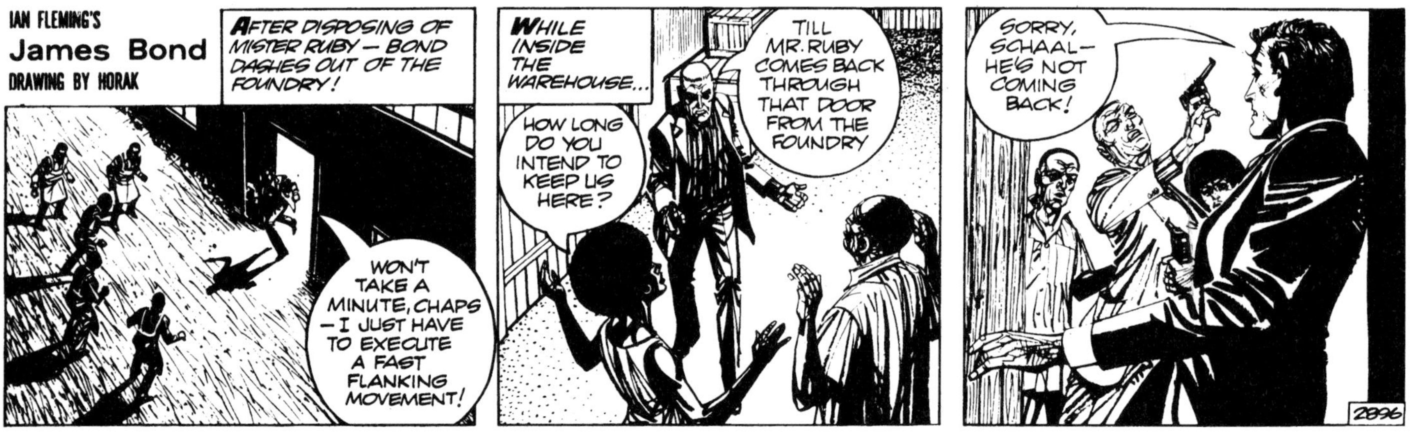
IAN FLEMING'S
James Bond
DRAWING BY HORAK
AFTER DISPOSING OF MISTER RUBY — BOND DASHES OUT OF THE FOUNDRY!
WON'T TAKE A MINUTE, CHAPS —I JUST HAVE TO EXECUTE A FAST FLANKING MOVEMENT!
WHILE INSIDE THE WAREHOUSE...
HOW LONG DO YOU INTEND TO KEEP US HERE?
TILL MR. RUBY COMES BACK THROUGH THAT DOOR FROM THE FOUNDRY
SORRY, SCHAAL— HE'S NOT COMING BACK!
2896

IAN FLEMING'S
James Bond
DRAWING BY HORAK
YOUR FATHER'S QUITE THE LION OF THE HOUR, DAMARA–EVEN IN THE EYES OF THE CIA!
FOR HELPING TO STOP 'OPERATION BLACK STORM' YOU TWO'LL PROBABLY RATE A HEROES' WELCOME IN THE STATES!
NOT ME! I'M STAYING ON HERE A WHILE— THAT IS, IF YOU'LL STICK AROUND TOO, JAMES!
JUST WHAT DID YOU HAVE IN MIND?
CALL IT A CULTURAL EXCHANGE PROGRAMME! LATER ON AT THE HOTEL, WE CAN LAY OUT ALL THE SPECIFICS IN BLACK AND WHITE!
2897

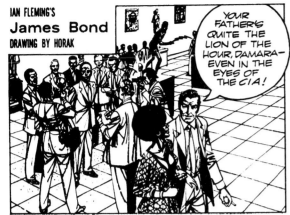

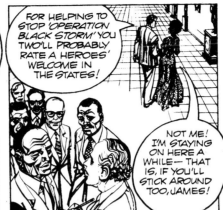

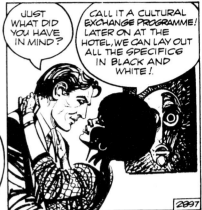

TILL DEATH DO US PART

*T*ill *Death Do Us Part* makes for a fascinating companion-piece to *The Black Ruby Caper*, inasmuch as it presents an inversion of the story dynamic of the latter; whereas previously, Bond has resorted to the callous blackmail and manipulation of a villain's girlfriend, in this case, he plays it (more or less) straight — as he has to, in order to win Arda Petrich's trust. Interesting, too, is that the female protagonist again spends much of the action semi-nude, which as with *The Black Ruby Caper*'s Mme. Dreux, seems to serve to emphasise Arda's vulnerability.

Horak's brilliant use of series of concentric circles to imply sound, especially during the car chase, should be noted in this story. Instead of initially picturing the police cars after 007, Horak instead uses the circles — similar to sound waves — to suggest their presence, as seen in panels 2911 and 2912. Particularly clever is Horak's switch in 'camera angle' between the two panels to suggest that the police are gaining; 2911's front shot of the vehicle, with sound-circles behind it, become's 2912's high angle on the back of the car, as the circles begin to overlap...

The presence of the typically bizarre 'Q'-branch vehicle is perhaps a sign of the influence of the more gadget-heavy film series on the strips. Indeed, the chase involving this car echoes the action/comedy elements of the extended chases during *Live and Let Die*, in cinemas two years previous to this story's publication.

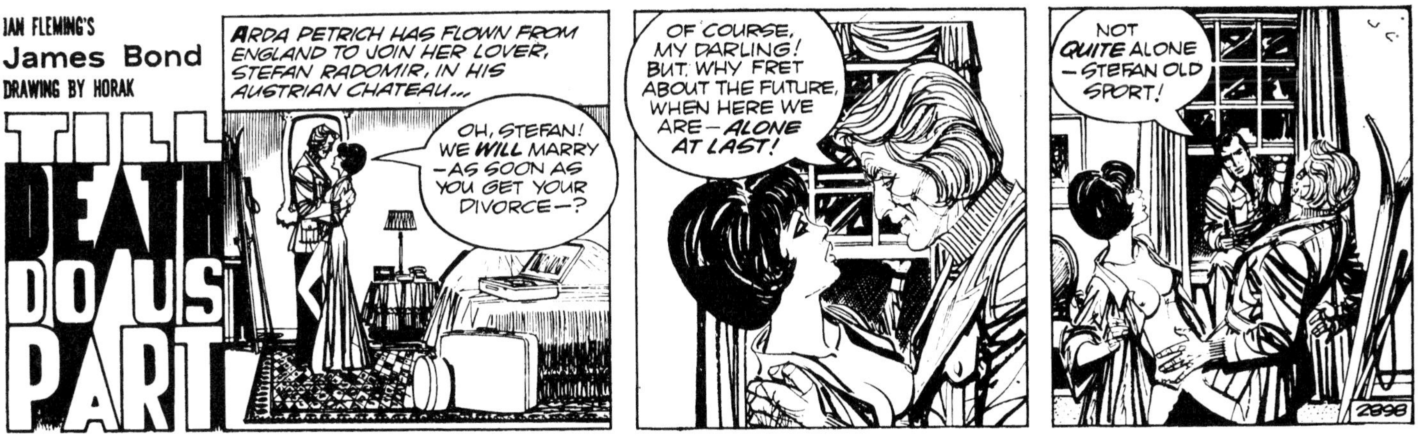
IAN FLEMING'S
James Bond
DRAWING BY HORAK
TILL DEATH DO US PART
ARDA PETRICH HAS FLOWN FROM ENGLAND TO JOIN HER LOVER, STEFAN RADOMIR, IN HIS AUSTRIAN CHATEAU...
OH, STEFAN! WE WILL MARRY —AS SOON AS YOU GET YOUR DIVORCE—?
OF COURSE, MY DARLING! BUT, WHY FRET ABOUT THE FUTURE, WHEN HERE WE ARE—ALONE AT LAST!
NOT QUITE ALONE —STEFAN OLD SPORT!
2898

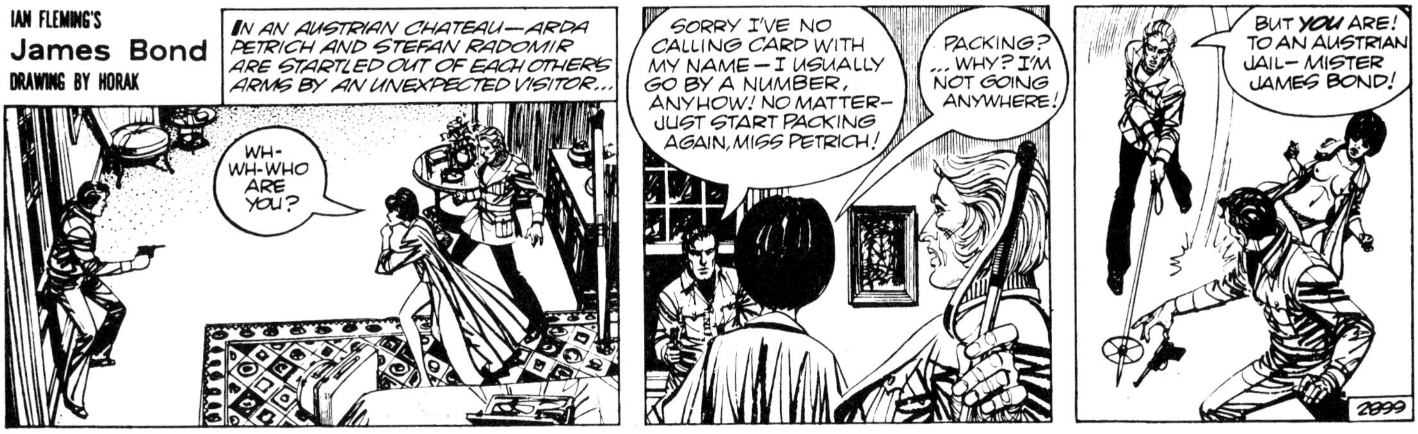
IAN FLEMING'S
James Bond
DRAWING BY HORAK
IN AN AUSTRIAN CHATEAU—ARDA PETRICH AND STEFAN RADOMIR ARE STARTLED OUT OF EACH OTHER'S ARMS BY AN UNEXPECTED VISITOR...
WH-WH-WHO ARE YOU?
SORRY I'VE NO CALLING CARD WITH MY NAME—I USUALLY GO BY A NUMBER, ANYHOW! NO MATTER—JUST START PACKING AGAIN, MISS PETRICH!
PACKING? ...WHY? I'M NOT GOING ANYWHERE!
BUT YOU ARE! TO AN AUSTRIAN JAIL—MISTER JAMES BOND!
2899

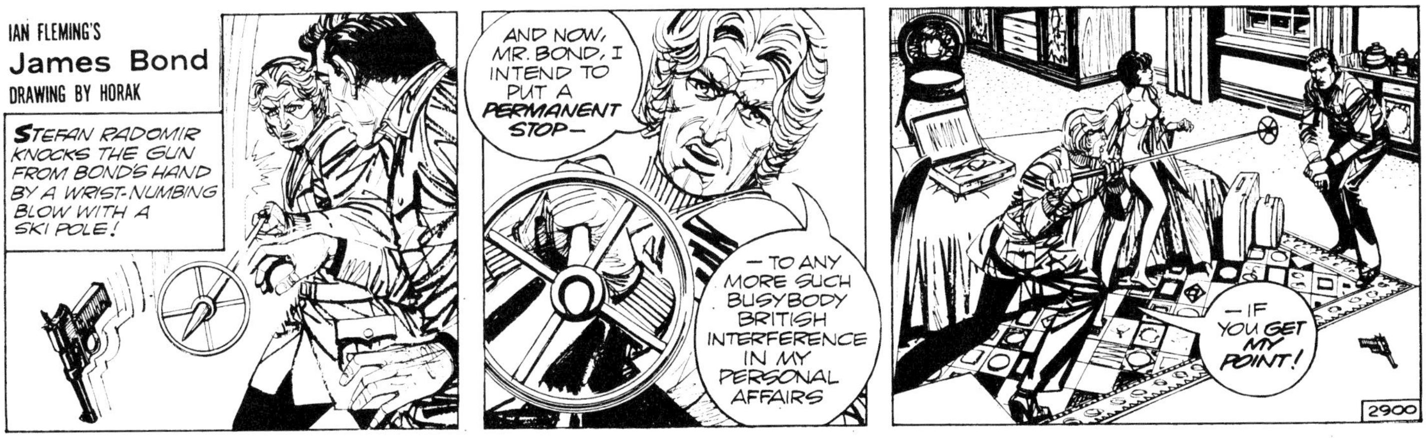
IAN FLEMING'S
James Bond
DRAWING BY HORAK
STEFAN RADOMIR KNOCKS THE GUN FROM BOND'S HAND BY A WRIST-NUMBING BLOW WITH A SKI POLE!
AND NOW, MR. BOND, I INTEND TO PUT A PERMANENT STOP—
—TO ANY MORE SUCH BUSYBODY BRITISH INTERFERENCE IN MY PERSONAL AFFAIRS
—IF YOU GET MY POINT!
2900

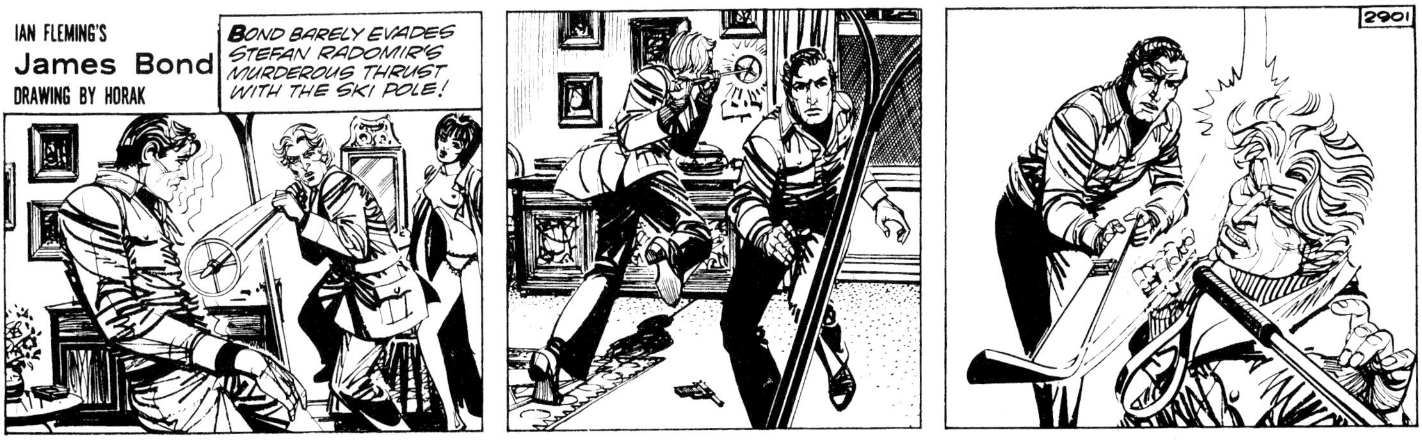
IAN FLEMING'S
James Bond
DRAWING BY HORAK
BOND BARELY EVADES STEFAN RADOMIR'S MURDEROUS THRUST WITH THE SKI POLE!
2901

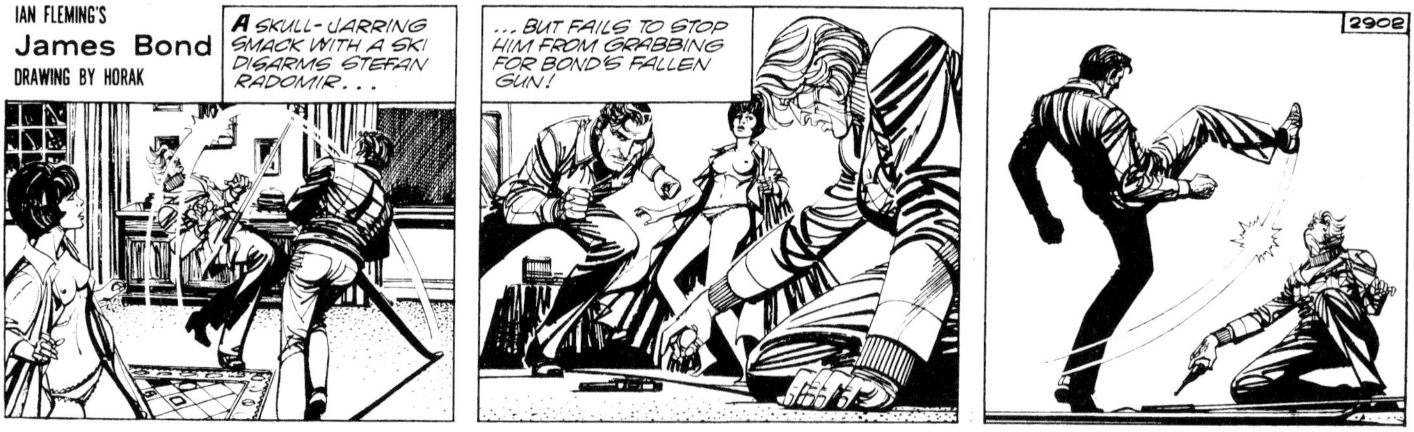
IAN FLEMING'S
James Bond
DRAWING BY HORAK
A SKULL-JARRING SMACK WITH A SKI DISARMS STEFAN RADOMIR...
...BUT FAILS TO STOP HIM FROM GRABBING FOR BOND'S FALLEN GUN!
2902

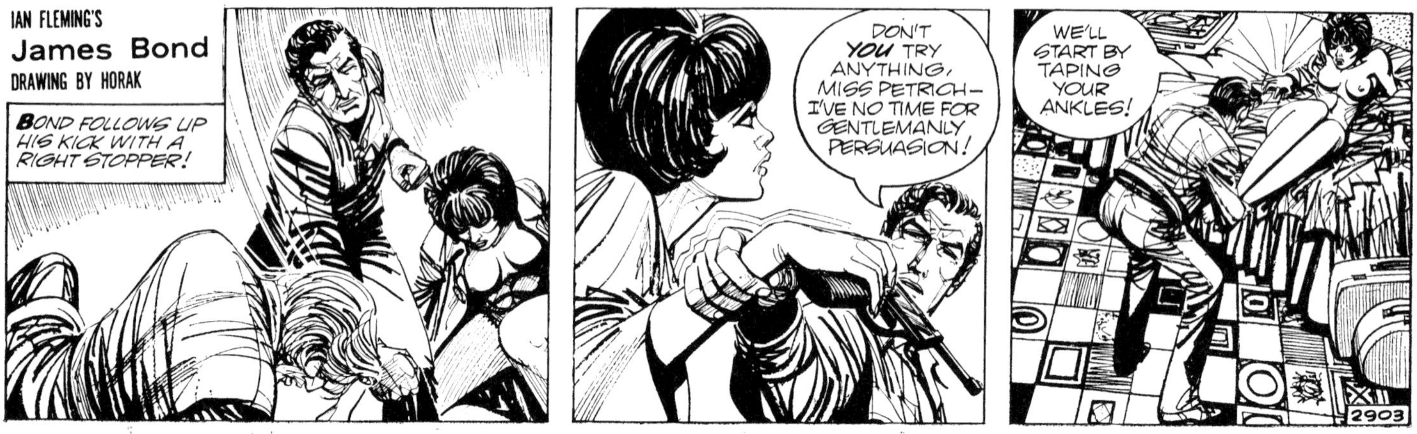
IAN FLEMING'S
James Bond
DRAWING BY HORAK
BOND FOLLOWS UP HIS KICK WITH A RIGHT STOPPER!
DON'T YOU TRY ANYTHING, MISS PETRICH—I'VE NO TIME FOR GENTLEMANLY PERSUASION!
WE'LL START BY TAPING YOUR ANKLES!
2903

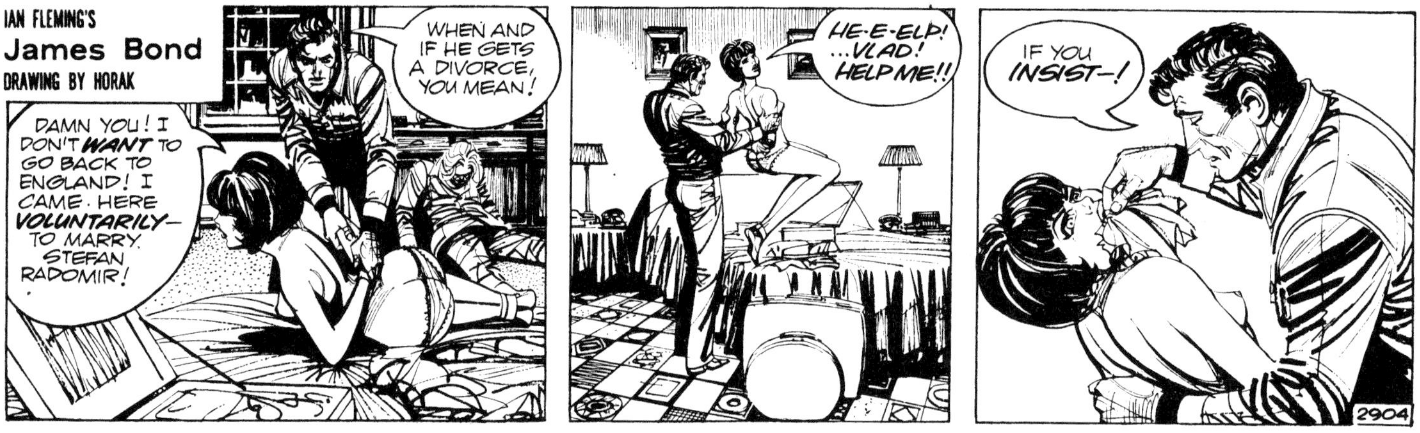
IAN FLEMING'S
James Bond
DRAWING BY HORAK
DAMN YOU! I DON'T WANT TO GO BACK TO ENGLAND! I CAME HERE VOLUNTARILY—TO MARRY STEFAN RADOMIR!
WHEN AND IF HE GETS A DIVORCE, YOU MEAN!
HE-E-ELP! ...VLAD! HELP ME!!
IF YOU INSIST—!
2904

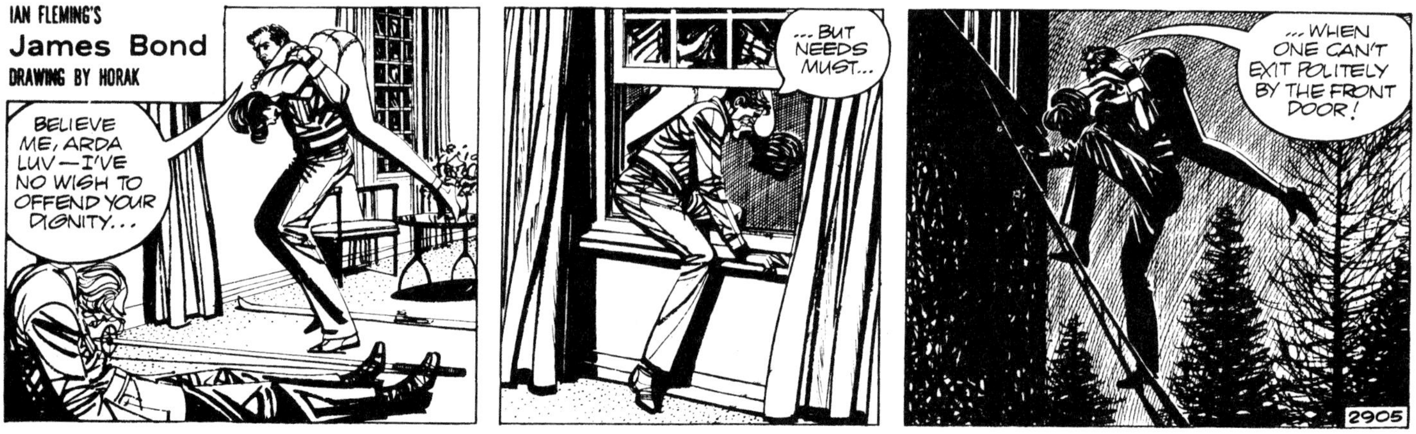
IAN FLEMING'S
James Bond
DRAWING BY HORAK
BELIEVE ME, ARDA LUV—I'VE NO WISH TO OFFEND YOUR DIGNITY...
...BUT NEEDS MUST...
...WHEN ONE CAN'T EXIT POLITELY BY THE FRONT DOOR!
2905

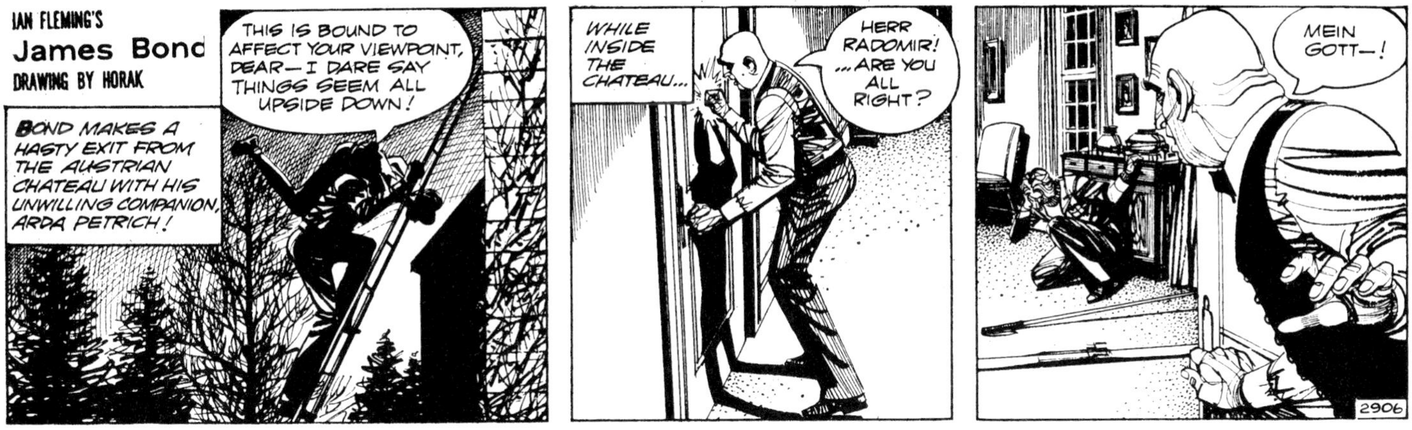
IAN FLEMING'S
James Bond
DRAWING BY HORAK
BOND MAKES A HASTY EXIT FROM THE AUSTRIAN CHATEAU WITH HIS UNWILLING COMPANION, ARDA PETRICH!
THIS IS BOUND TO AFFECT YOUR VIEWPOINT, DEAR — I DARE SAY THINGS SEEM ALL UPSIDE DOWN!
WHILE INSIDE THE CHATEAU...
HERR RADOMIR! ...ARE YOU ALL RIGHT?
MEIN GOTT—!
2906

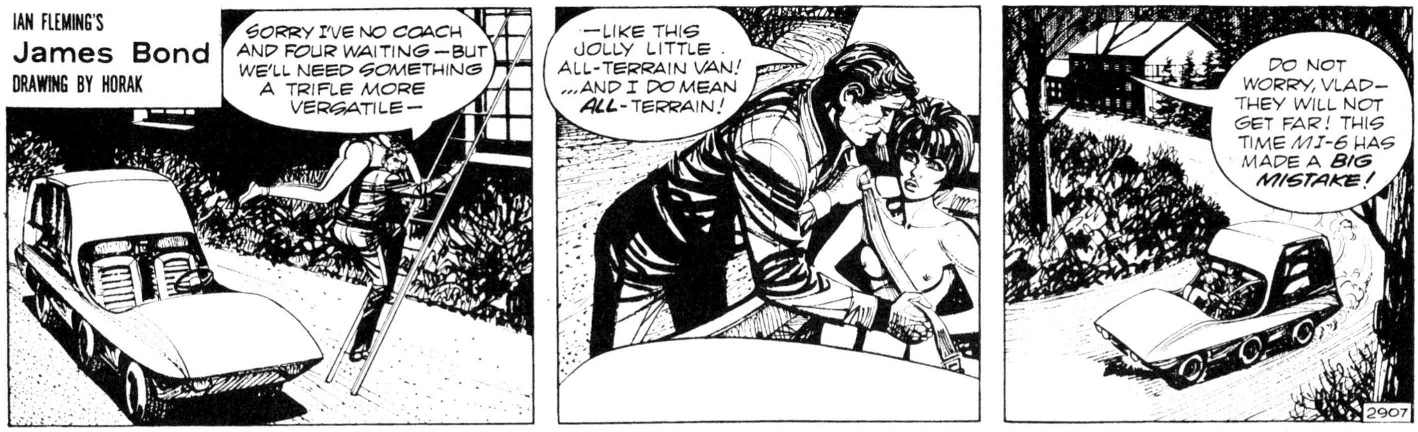
IAN FLEMING'S
James Bond
DRAWING BY HORAK
SORRY I'VE NO COACH AND FOUR WAITING — BUT WE'LL NEED SOMETHING A TRIFLE MORE VERSATILE —
— LIKE THIS JOLLY LITTLE ALL-TERRAIN VAN! ...AND I DO MEAN ALL-TERRAIN!
DO NOT WORRY, VLAD — THEY WILL NOT GET FAR! THIS TIME MI-6 HAS MADE A BIG MISTAKE!
2907

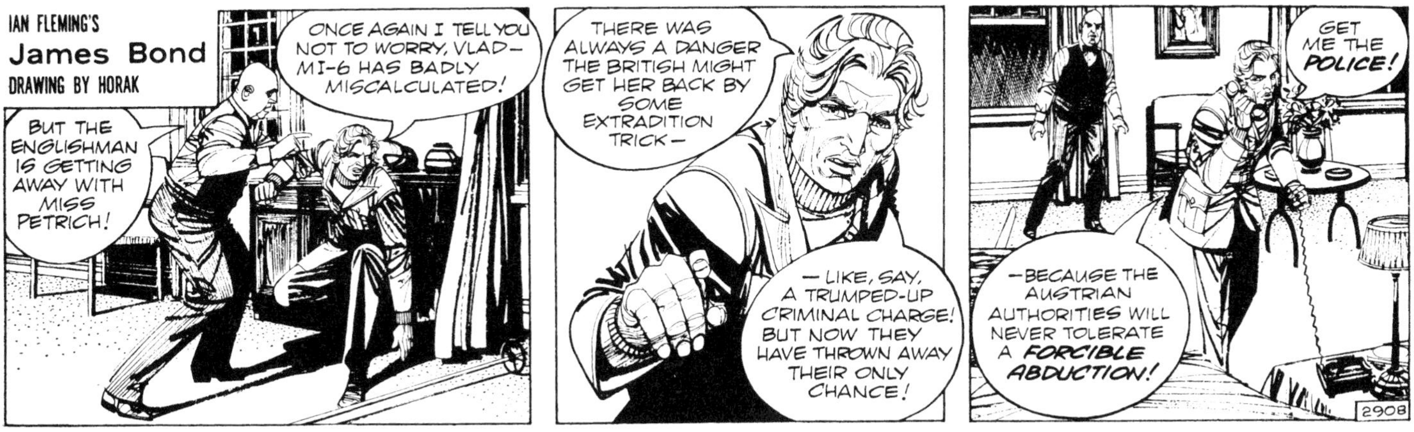
IAN FLEMING'S
James Bond
DRAWING BY HORAK
BUT THE ENGLISHMAN IS GETTING AWAY WITH MISS PETRICH!
ONCE AGAIN I TELL YOU NOT TO WORRY, VLAD — MI-6 HAS BADLY MISCALCULATED!
THERE WAS ALWAYS A DANGER THE BRITISH MIGHT GET HER BACK BY SOME EXTRADITION TRICK —
— LIKE, SAY, A TRUMPED-UP CRIMINAL CHARGE! BUT NOW THEY HAVE THROWN AWAY THEIR ONLY CHANCE!
GET ME THE POLICE!
— BECAUSE THE AUSTRIAN AUTHORITIES WILL NEVER TOLERATE A FORCIBLE ABDUCTION!
2908

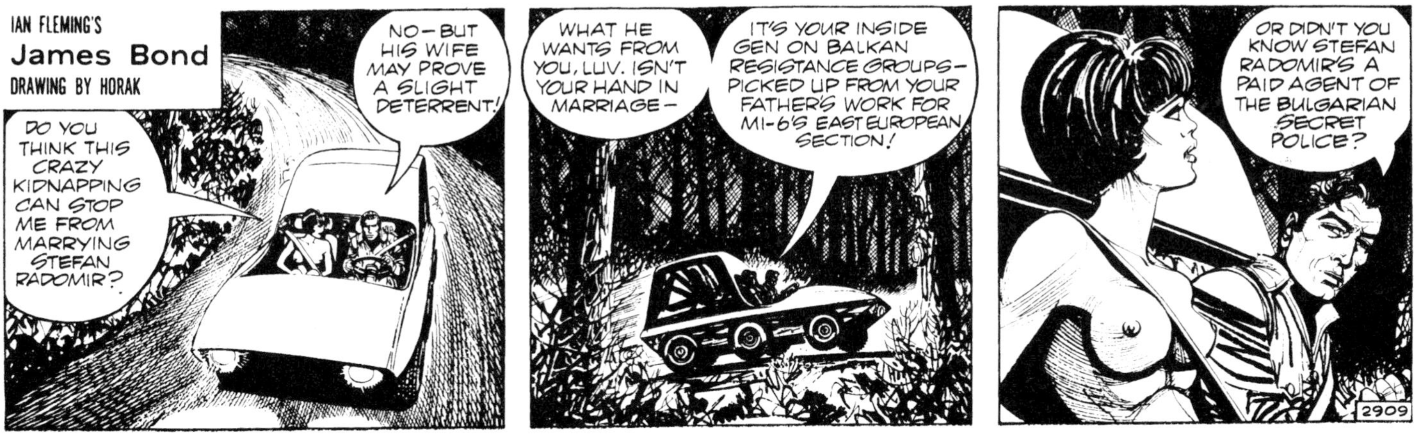
IAN FLEMING'S
James Bond
DRAWING BY HORAK
DO YOU THINK THIS CRAZY KIDNAPPING CAN STOP ME FROM MARRYING STEFAN RADOMIR?
NO — BUT HIS WIFE MAY PROVE A SLIGHT DETERRENT!
WHAT HE WANTS FROM YOU, LUV, ISN'T YOUR HAND IN MARRIAGE —
IT'S YOUR INSIDE GEN ON BALKAN RESISTANCE GROUPS — PICKED UP FROM YOUR FATHER'S WORK FOR MI-6'S EAST EUROPEAN SECTION!
OR DIDN'T YOU KNOW STEFAN RADOMIR'S A PAID AGENT OF THE BULGARIAN SECRET POLICE?
2909

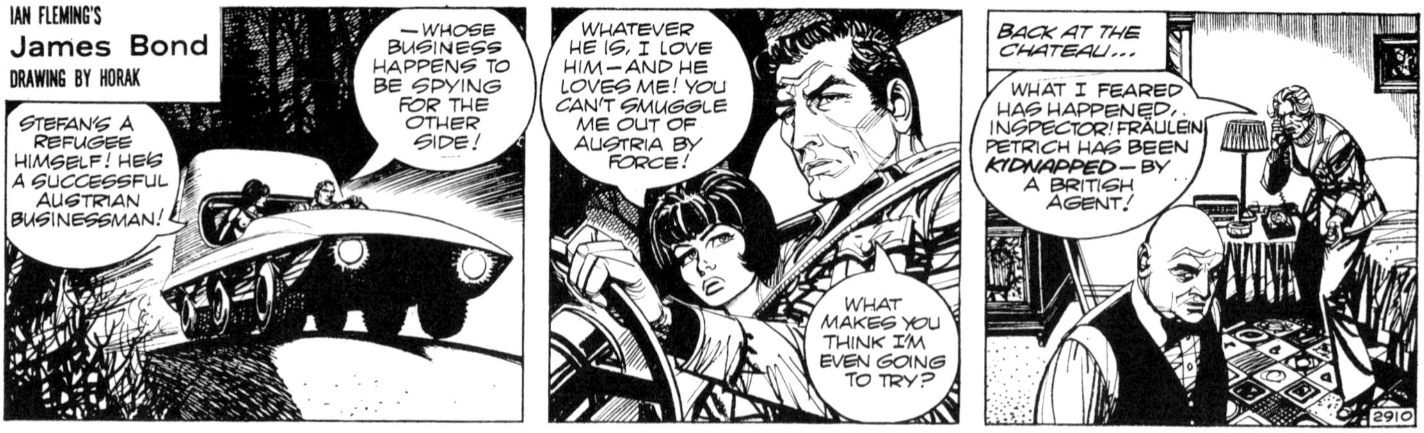
IAN FLEMING'S
James Bond
DRAWING BY HORAK
STEFAN'S A REFUGEE HIMSELF! HE'S A SUCCESSFUL AUSTRIAN BUSINESSMAN!
—WHOSE BUSINESS HAPPENS TO BE SPYING FOR THE OTHER SIDE!
WHATEVER HE IS, I LOVE HIM—AND HE LOVES ME! YOU CAN'T SMUGGLE ME OUT OF AUSTRIA BY FORCE!
WHAT MAKES YOU THINK I'M EVEN GOING TO TRY?
BACK AT THE CHATEAU...
WHAT I FEARED HAS HAPPENED, INSPECTOR! FRÄULEIN PETRICH HAS BEEN KIDNAPPED—BY A BRITISH AGENT!
2910

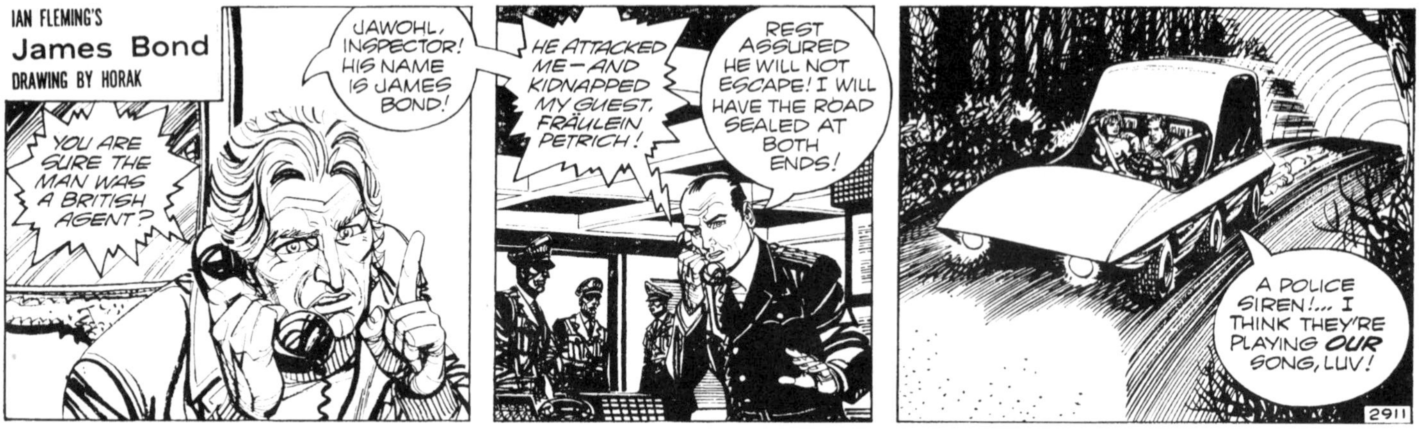
IAN FLEMING'S
James Bond
DRAWING BY HORAK
YOU ARE SURE THE MAN WAS A BRITISH AGENT?
JAWOHL, INSPECTOR! HIS NAME IS JAMES BOND!
HE ATTACKED ME—AND KIDNAPPED MY GUEST, FRÄULEIN PETRICH!
REST ASSURED HE WILL NOT ESCAPE! I WILL HAVE THE ROAD SEALED AT BOTH ENDS!
A POLICE SIREN!... I THINK THEY'RE PLAYING OUR SONG, LUV!
2911

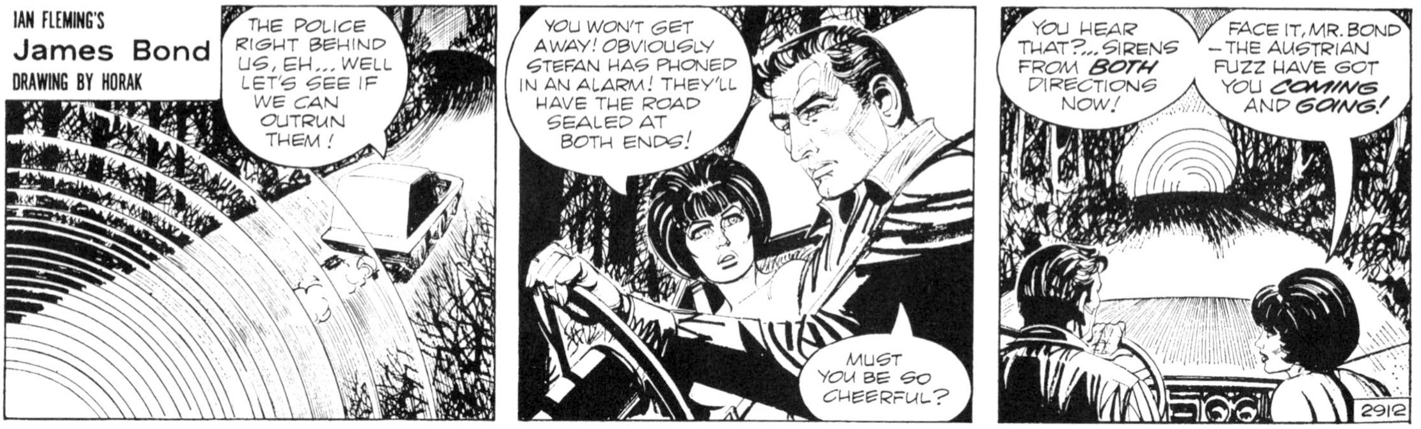
IAN FLEMING'S
James Bond
DRAWING BY HORAK
THE POLICE RIGHT BEHIND US, EH... WELL LET'S SEE IF WE CAN OUTRUN THEM!
YOU WON'T GET AWAY! OBVIOUSLY STEFAN HAS PHONED IN AN ALARM! THEY'LL HAVE THE ROAD SEALED AT BOTH ENDS!
MUST YOU BE SO CHEERFUL?
YOU HEAR THAT?... SIRENS FROM BOTH DIRECTIONS NOW!
FACE IT, MR. BOND—THE AUSTRIAN FUZZ HAVE GOT YOU COMING AND GOING!
2912

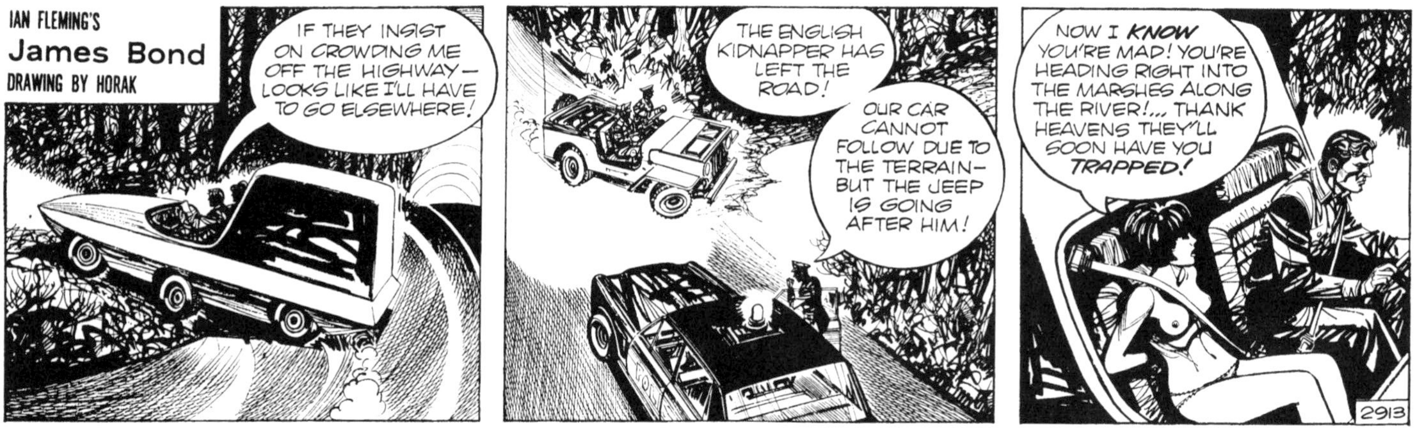
IAN FLEMING'S
James Bond
DRAWING BY HORAK
IF THEY INSIST ON CROWDING ME OFF THE HIGHWAY—LOOKS LIKE I'LL HAVE TO GO ELSEWHERE!
THE ENGLISH KIDNAPPER HAS LEFT THE ROAD!
OUR CAR CANNOT FOLLOW DUE TO THE TERRAIN—BUT THE JEEP IS GOING AFTER HIM!
NOW I KNOW YOU'RE MAD! YOU'RE HEADING RIGHT INTO THE MARSHES ALONG THE RIVER!... THANK HEAVENS THEY'LL SOON HAVE YOU TRAPPED!
2913

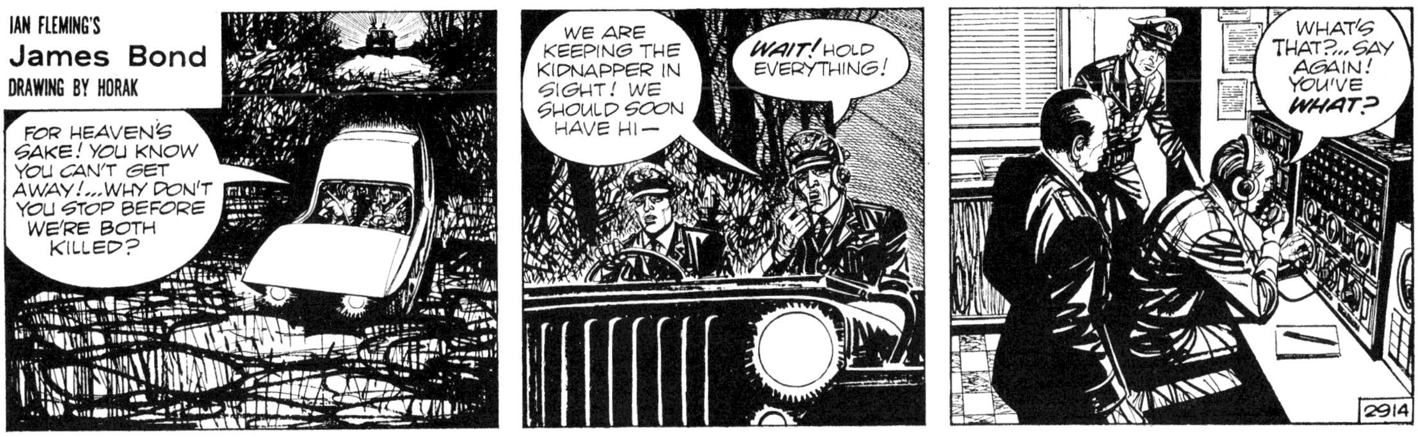
IAN FLEMING'S
James Bond
DRAWING BY HORAK
FOR HEAVEN'S SAKE! YOU KNOW YOU CAN'T GET AWAY!... WHY DON'T YOU STOP BEFORE WE'RE BOTH KILLED?
WE ARE KEEPING THE KIDNAPPER IN SIGHT! WE SHOULD SOON HAVE HI—
WAIT! HOLD EVERYTHING!
WHAT'S THAT?... SAY AGAIN! YOU'VE WHAT?
2914

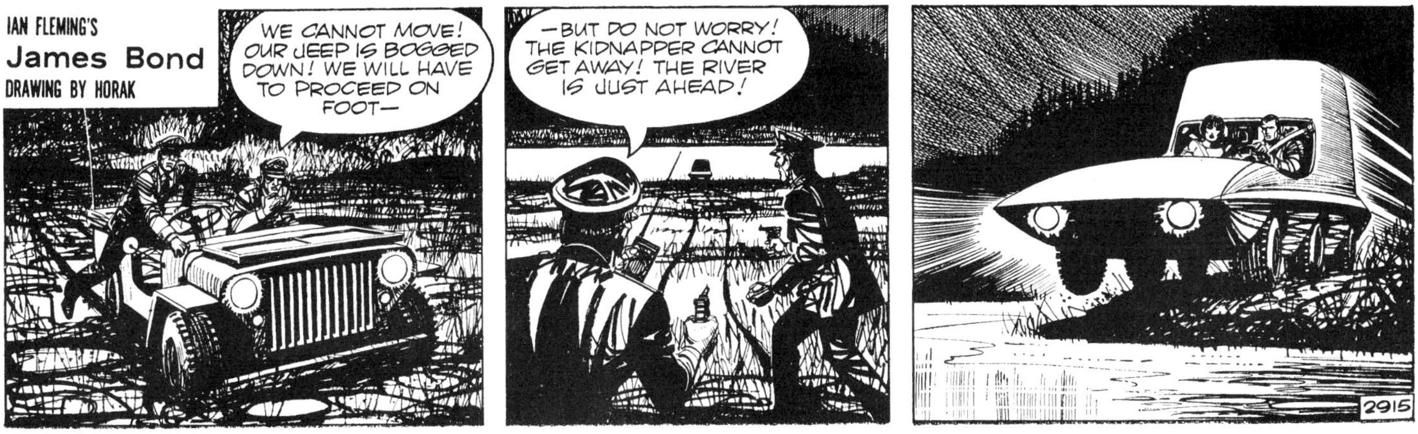
IAN FLEMING'S
James Bond
DRAWING BY HORAK
WE CANNOT MOVE! OUR JEEP IS BOGGED DOWN! WE WILL HAVE TO PROCEED ON FOOT—
—BUT DO NOT WORRY! THE KIDNAPPER CANNOT GET AWAY! THE RIVER IS JUST AHEAD!
2915

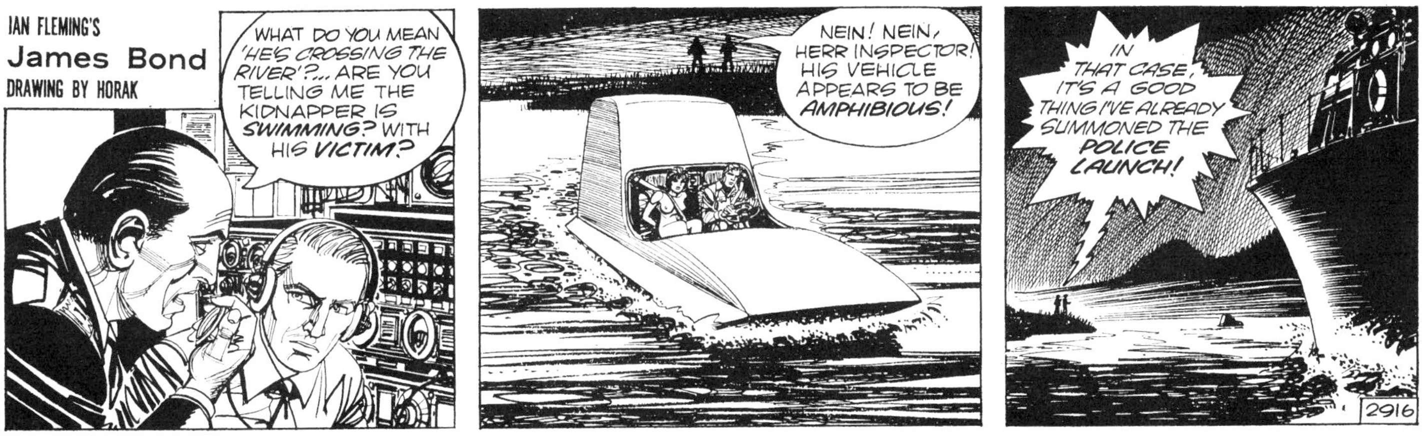
IAN FLEMING'S
James Bond
DRAWING BY HORAK
WHAT DO YOU MEAN 'HE'S CROSSING THE RIVER'?... ARE YOU TELLING ME THE KIDNAPPER IS SWIMMING? WITH HIS VICTIM?
NEIN! NEIN, HERR INSPECTOR! HIS VEHICLE APPEARS TO BE AMPHIBIOUS!
IN THAT CASE, IT'S A GOOD THING I'VE ALREADY SUMMONED THE POLICE LAUNCH!
2916

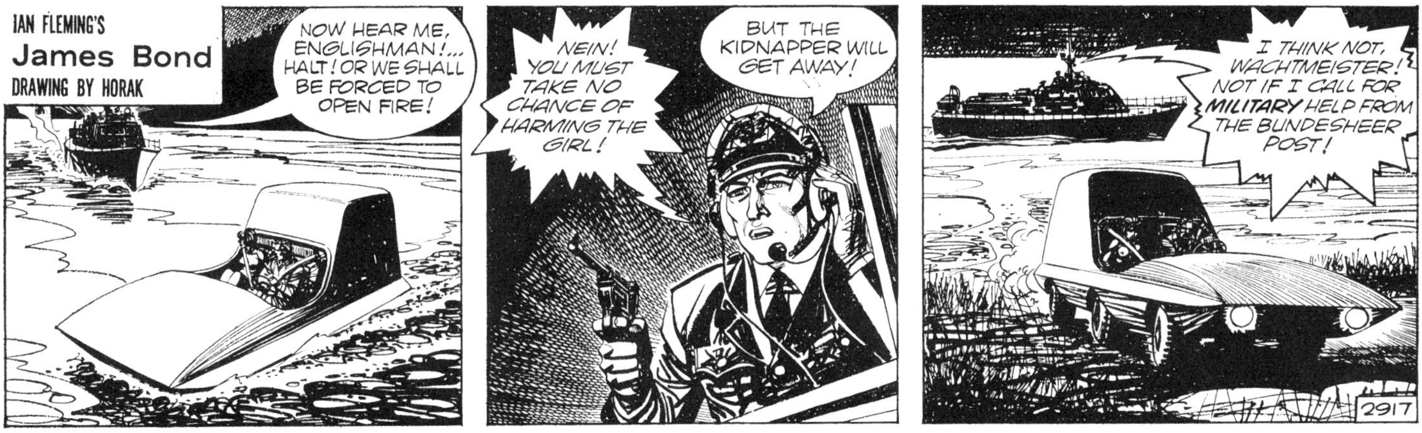
IAN FLEMING'S
James Bond
DRAWING BY HORAK
NOW HEAR ME, ENGLISHMAN!... HALT! OR WE SHALL BE FORCED TO OPEN FIRE!
NEIN! YOU MUST TAKE NO CHANCE OF HARMING THE GIRL!
BUT THE KIDNAPPER WILL GET AWAY!
I THINK NOT, WACHTMEISTER! NOT IF I CALL FOR MILITARY HELP FROM THE BUNDESHEER POST!
2917

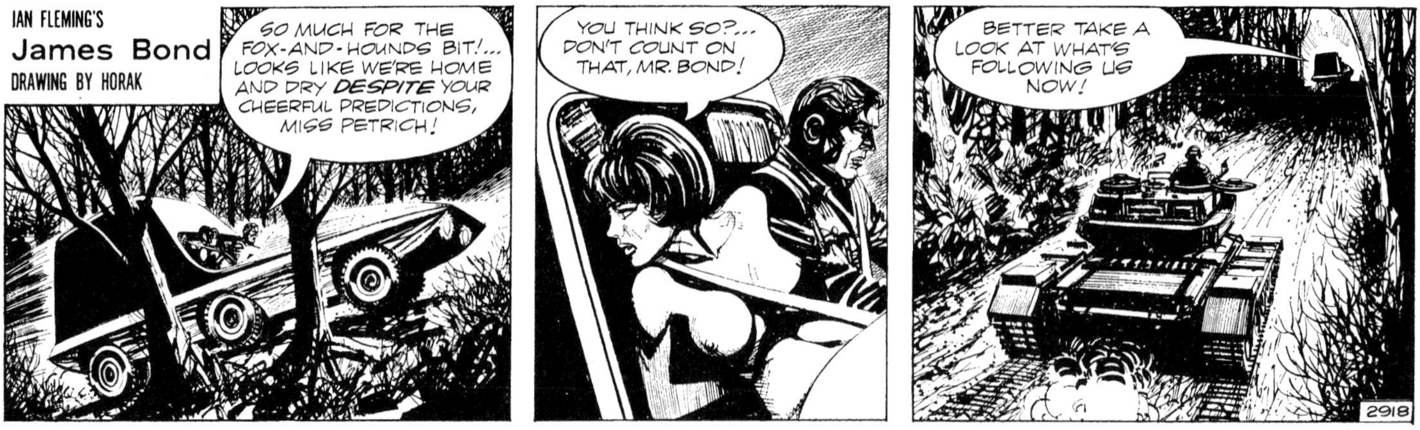
IAN FLEMING'S
James Bond
DRAWING BY HORAK
SO MUCH FOR THE FOX-AND-HOUNDS BIT!... LOOKS LIKE WE'RE HOME AND DRY DESPITE YOUR CHEERFUL PREDICTIONS, MISS PETRICH!
YOU THINK SO?... DON'T COUNT ON THAT, MR. BOND!
BETTER TAKE A LOOK AT WHAT'S FOLLOWING US NOW!
2918

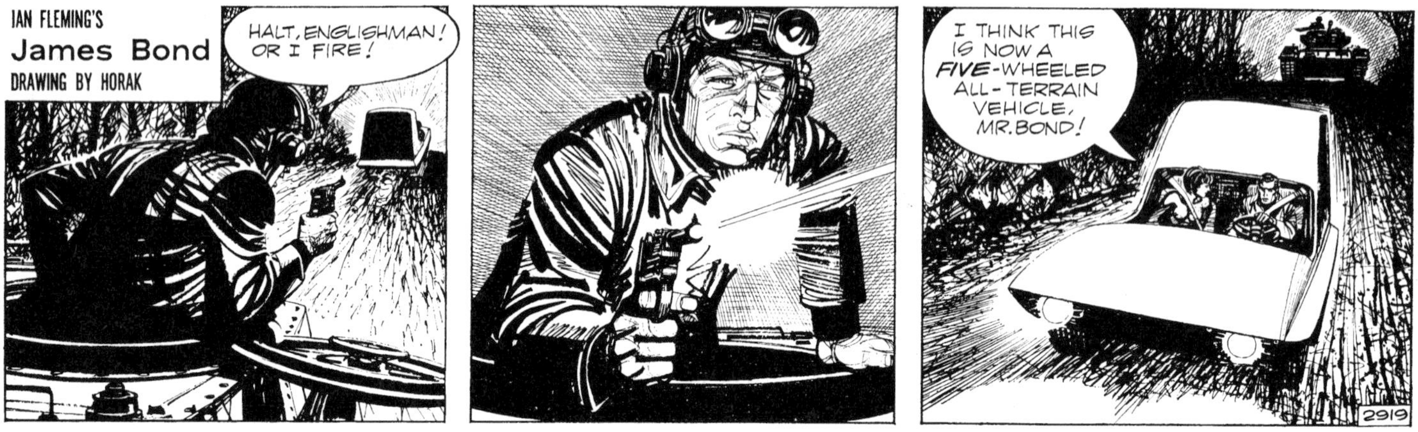
IAN FLEMING'S
James Bond
DRAWING BY HORAK
HALT, ENGLISHMAN! OR I FIRE!
I THINK THIS IS NOW A FIVE-WHEELED ALL-TERRAIN VEHICLE, MR. BOND!
2919

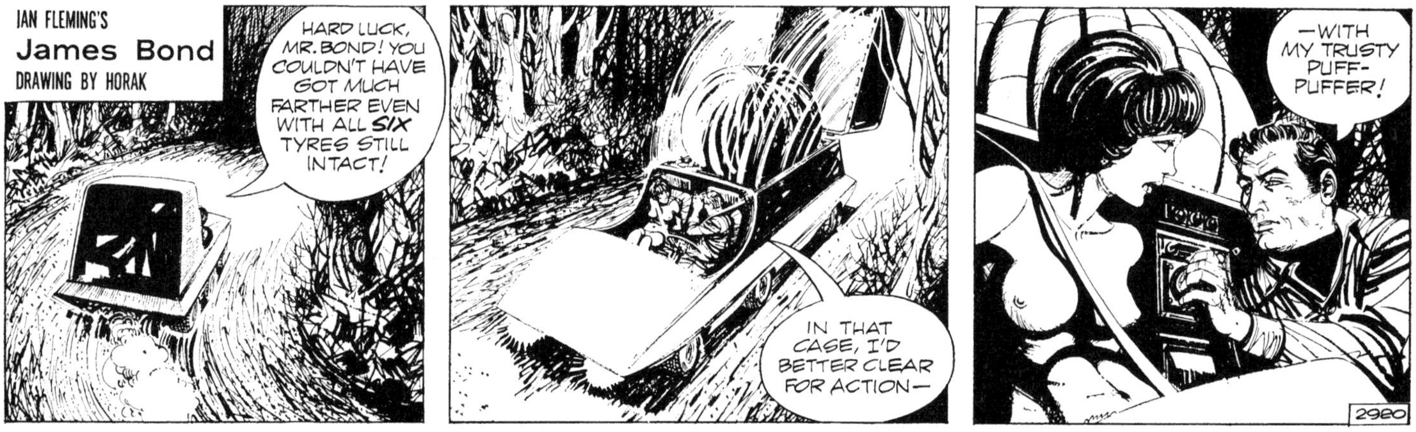
IAN FLEMING'S
James Bond
DRAWING BY HORAK
HARD LUCK, MR. BOND! YOU COULDN'T HAVE GOT MUCH FARTHER EVEN WITH ALL SIX TYRES STILL INTACT!
IN THAT CASE, I'D BETTER CLEAR FOR ACTION—
—WITH MY TRUSTY PUFF-PUFFER!
2920

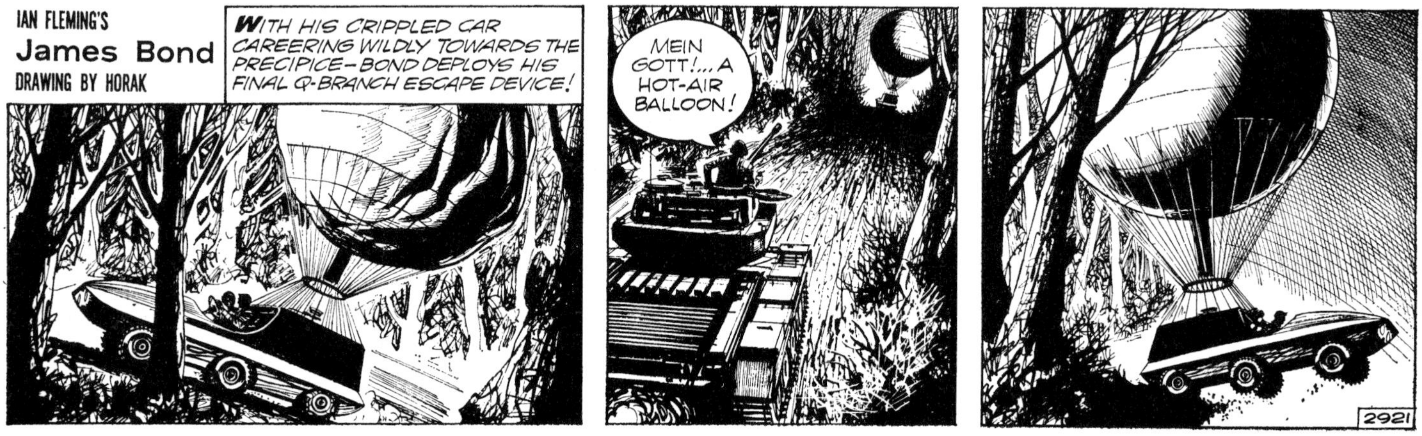
IAN FLEMING'S
James Bond
DRAWING BY HORAK
WITH HIS CRIPPLED CAR CAREERING WILDLY TOWARDS THE PRECIPICE—BOND DEPLOYS HIS FINAL Q-BRANCH ESCAPE DEVICE!
MEIN GOTT!... A HOT-AIR BALLOON!
2921

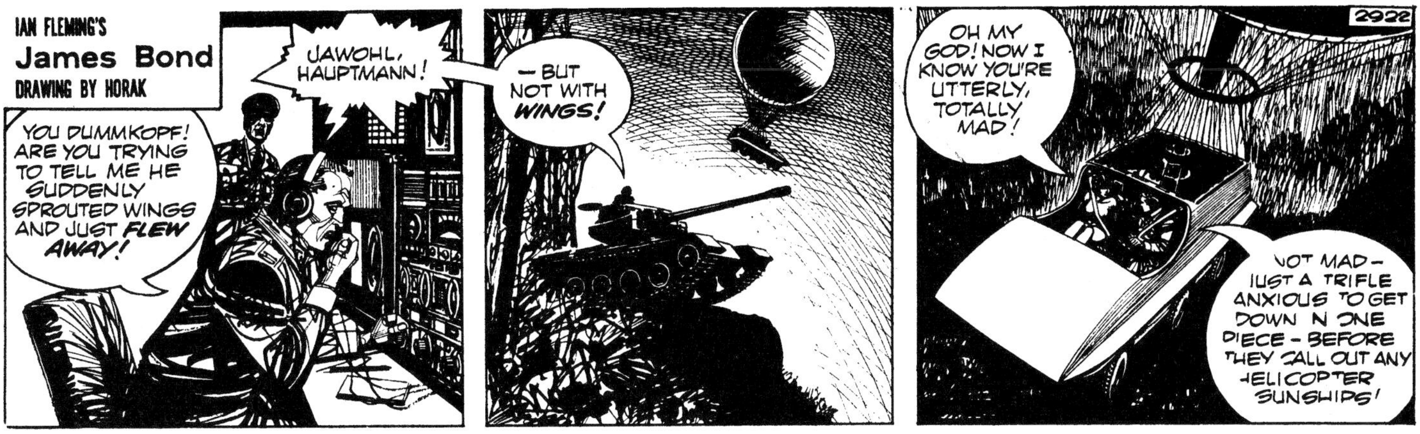
IAN FLEMING'S
James Bond
DRAWING BY HORAK
YOU DUMMKOPF! ARE YOU TRYING TO TELL ME HE SUDDENLY SPROUTED WINGS AND JUST FLEW AWAY!
JAWOHL, HAUPTMANN!
—BUT NOT WITH WINGS!
2922
OH MY GOD! NOW I KNOW YOU'RE UTTERLY, TOTALLY MAD!
NOT MAD—JUST A TRIFLE ANXIOUS TO GET DOWN IN ONE PIECE—BEFORE THEY CALL OUT ANY HELICOPTER GUNSHIPS!

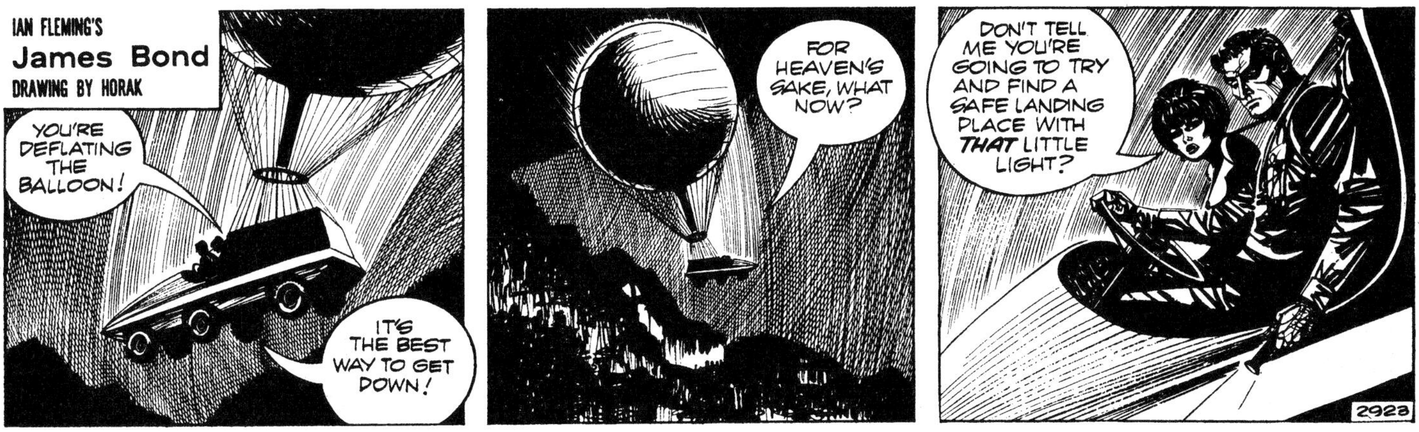
IAN FLEMING'S
James Bond
DRAWING BY HORAK
YOU'RE DEFLATING THE BALLOON!
IT'S THE BEST WAY TO GET DOWN!
FOR HEAVEN'S SAKE, WHAT NOW?
DON'T TELL ME YOU'RE GOING TO TRY AND FIND A SAFE LANDING PLACE WITH THAT LITTLE LIGHT?
2923

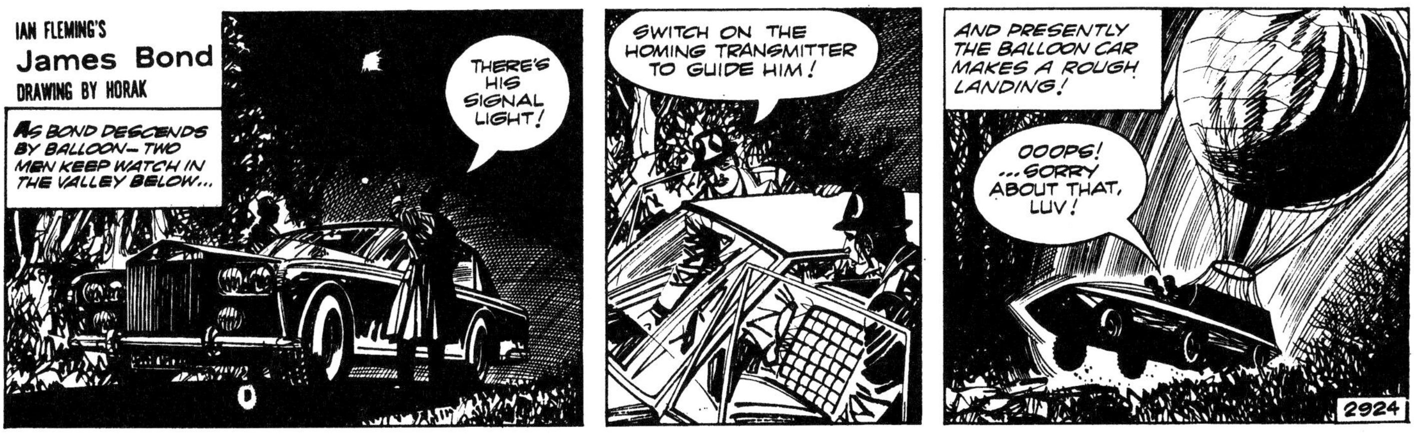
IAN FLEMING'S
James Bond
DRAWING BY HORAK
AS BOND DESCENDS BY BALLOON—TWO MEN KEEP WATCH IN THE VALLEY BELOW...
THERE'S HIS SIGNAL LIGHT!
SWITCH ON THE HOMING TRANSMITTER TO GUIDE HIM!
AND PRESENTLY THE BALLOON CAR MAKES A ROUGH LANDING!
OOOPS! ...SORRY ABOUT THAT, LUV!
2924

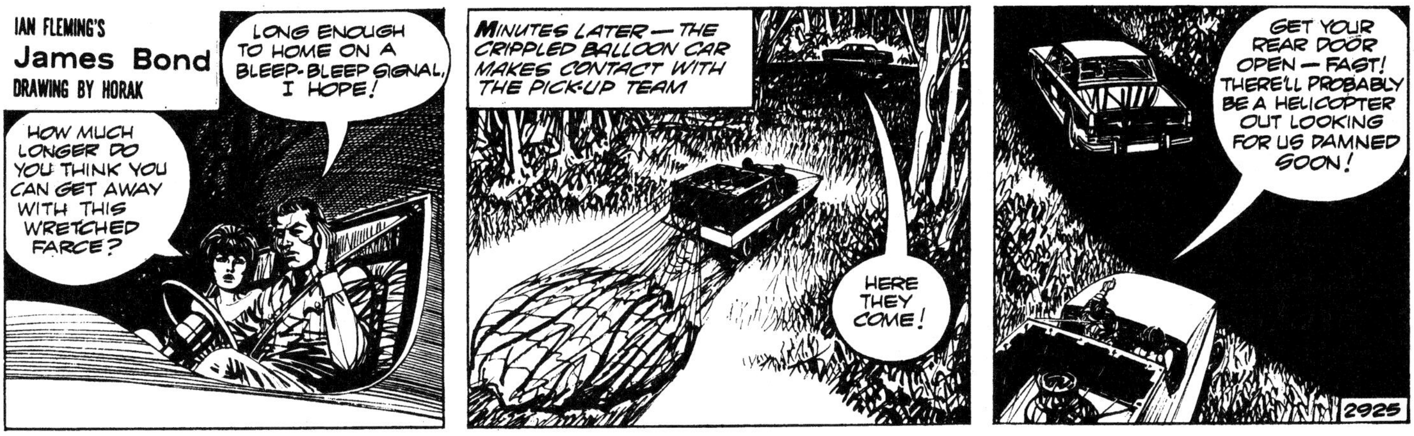
IAN FLEMING'S
James Bond
DRAWING BY HORAK
HOW MUCH LONGER DO YOU THINK YOU CAN GET AWAY WITH THIS WRETCHED FARCE?
LONG ENOUGH TO HOME ON A BLEEP-BLEEP SIGNAL, I HOPE!
MINUTES LATER—THE CRIPPLED BALLOON CAR MAKES CONTACT WITH THE PICK-UP TEAM
HERE THEY COME!
GET YOUR REAR DOOR OPEN—FAST! THERE'LL PROBABLY BE A HELICOPTER OUT LOOKING FOR US DAMNED SOON!
2925

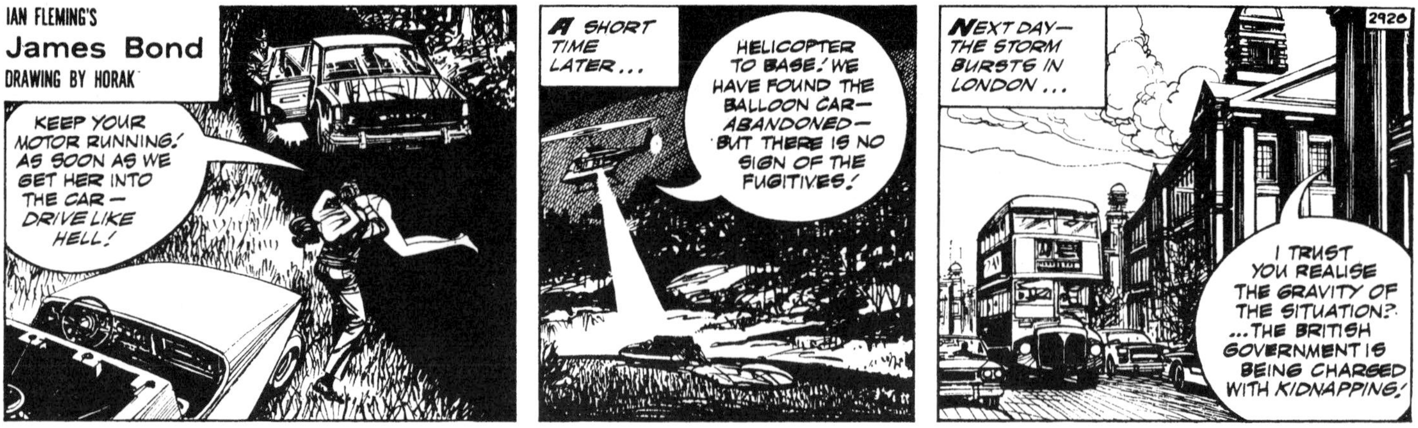
IAN FLEMING'S
James Bond
DRAWING BY HORAK
KEEP YOUR MOTOR RUNNING! AS SOON AS WE GET HER INTO THE CAR — DRIVE LIKE HELL!
A SHORT TIME LATER...
HELICOPTER TO BASE! WE HAVE FOUND THE BALLOON CAR— ABANDONED— BUT THERE IS NO SIGN OF THE FUGITIVES!
NEXT DAY— THE STORM BURSTS IN LONDON...
I TRUST YOU REALISE THE GRAVITY OF THE SITUATION? ...THE BRITISH GOVERNMENT IS BEING CHARGED WITH KIDNAPPING!
2926

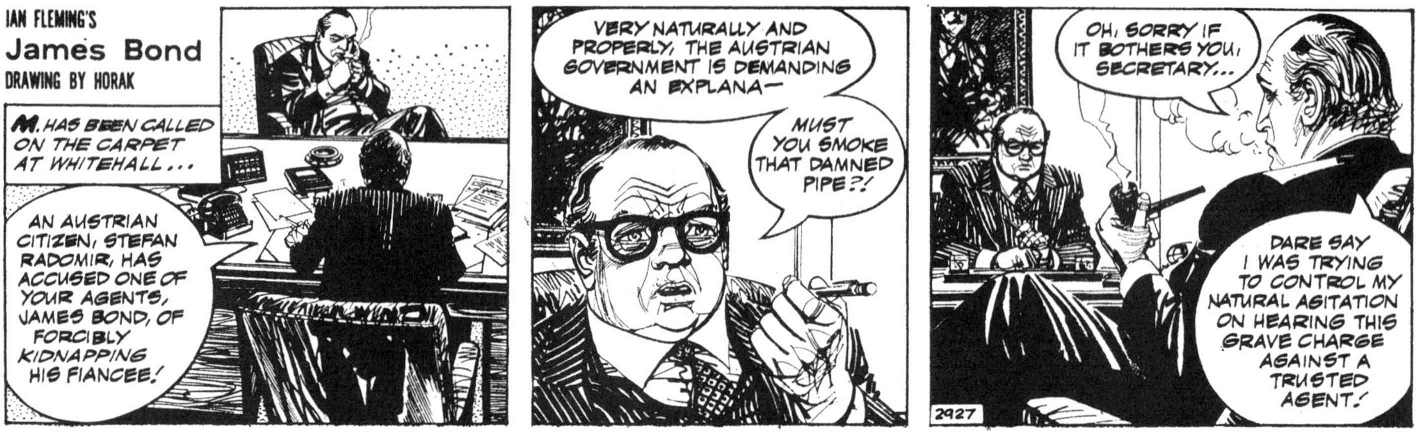
IAN FLEMING'S
James Bond
DRAWING BY HORAK
M. HAS BEEN CALLED ON THE CARPET AT WHITEHALL...
AN AUSTRIAN CITIZEN, STEFAN RADOMIR, HAS ACCUSED ONE OF YOUR AGENTS, JAMES BOND, OF FORCIBLY KIDNAPPING HIS FIANCEE!
VERY NATURALLY AND PROPERLY, THE AUSTRIAN GOVERNMENT IS DEMANDING AN EXPLANA—
MUST YOU SMOKE THAT DAMNED PIPE?!
OH, SORRY IF IT BOTHERS YOU, SECRETARY...
DARE SAY I WAS TRYING TO CONTROL MY NATURAL AGITATION ON HEARING THIS GRAVE CHARGE AGAINST A TRUSTED AGENT!
2927

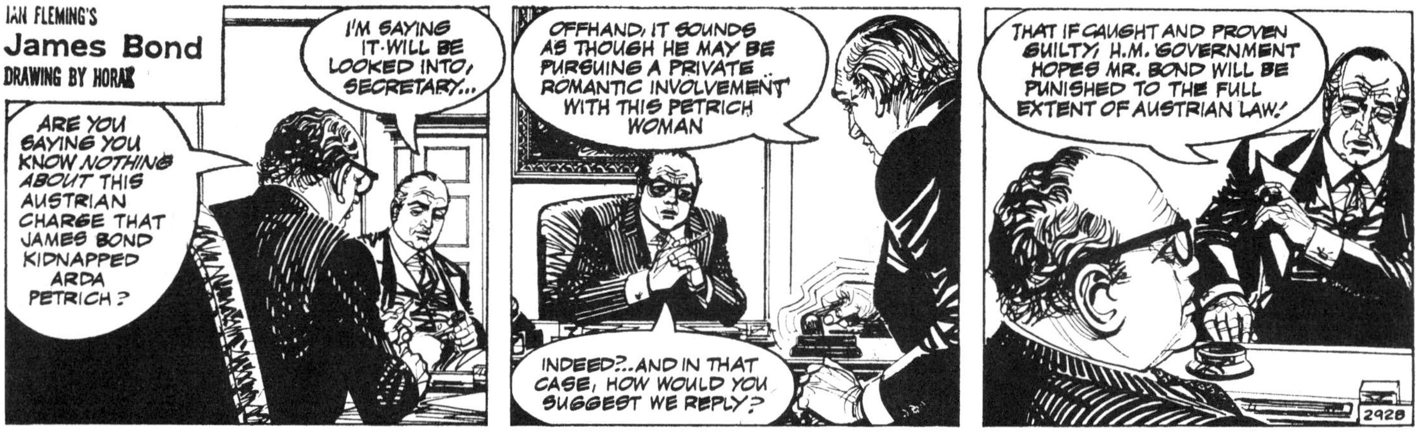
IAN FLEMING'S
James Bond
DRAWING BY HORAK
ARE YOU SAYING YOU KNOW NOTHING ABOUT THIS AUSTRIAN CHARGE THAT JAMES BOND KIDNAPPED ARDA PETRICH?
I'M SAYING IT WILL BE LOOKED INTO, SECRETARY...
OFFHAND, IT SOUNDS AS THOUGH HE MAY BE PURSUING A PRIVATE 'ROMANTIC INVOLVEMENT' WITH THIS PETRICH WOMAN
INDEED?..AND IN THAT CASE, HOW WOULD YOU SUGGEST WE REPLY?
THAT IF CAUGHT AND PROVEN GUILTY, H.M. GOVERNMENT HOPES MR. BOND WILL BE PUNISHED TO THE FULL EXTENT OF AUSTRIAN LAW!
2928

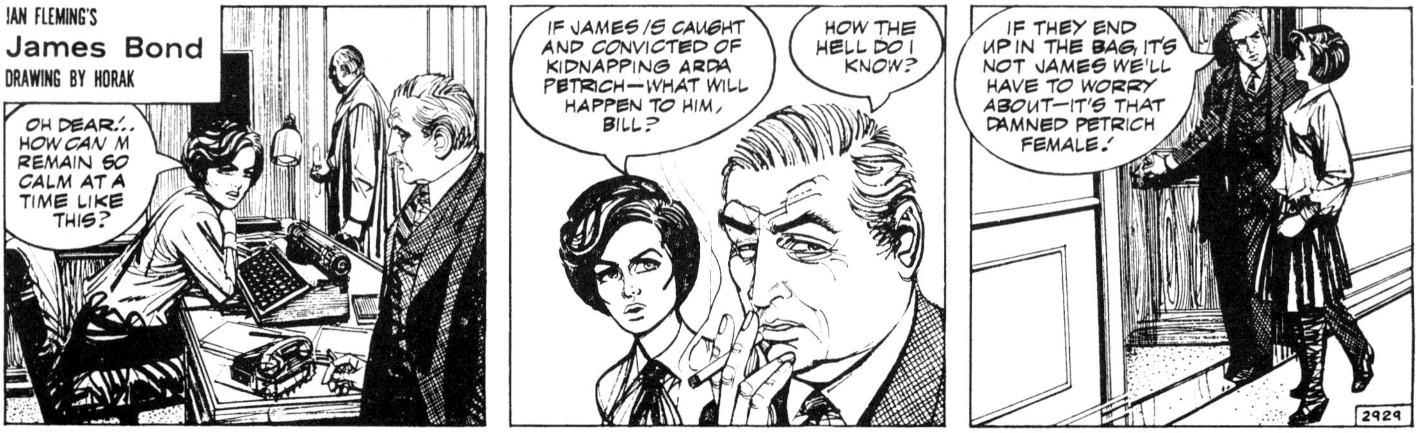
IAN FLEMING'S
James Bond
DRAWING BY HORAK
OH DEAR!.. HOW CAN M REMAIN SO CALM AT A TIME LIKE THIS?
IF JAMES IS CAUGHT AND CONVICTED OF KIDNAPPING ARDA PETRICH—WHAT WILL HAPPEN TO HIM, BILL?
HOW THE HELL DO I KNOW?
IF THEY END UP IN THE BAG, IT'S NOT JAMES WE'LL HAVE TO WORRY ABOUT—IT'S THAT DAMNED PETRICH FEMALE!
2929

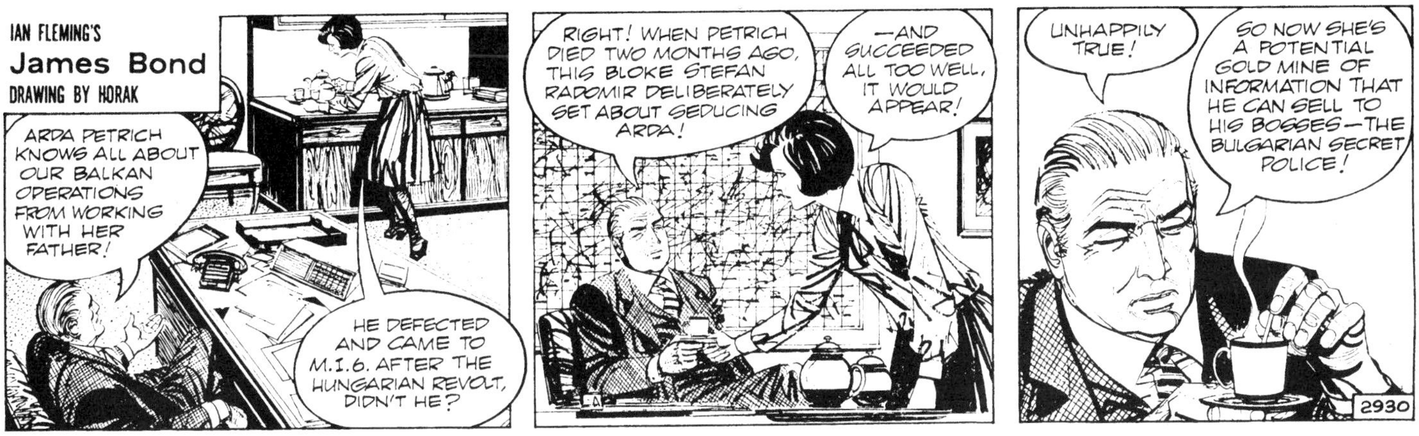
IAN FLEMING'S
James Bond
DRAWING BY HORAK
ARDA PETRICH KNOWS ALL ABOUT OUR BALKAN OPERATIONS FROM WORKING WITH HER FATHER!
HE DEFECTED AND CAME TO M.I.6. AFTER THE HUNGARIAN REVOLT, DIDN'T HE?
RIGHT! WHEN PETRICH DIED TWO MONTHS AGO, THIS BLOKE STEFAN RADOMIR DELIBERATELY SET ABOUT SEDUCING ARDA!
—AND SUCCEEDED ALL TOO WELL, IT WOULD APPEAR!
UNHAPPILY TRUE!
SO NOW SHE'S A POTENTIAL GOLD MINE OF INFORMATION THAT HE CAN SELL TO HIS BOSSES—THE BULGARIAN SECRET POLICE!
2930

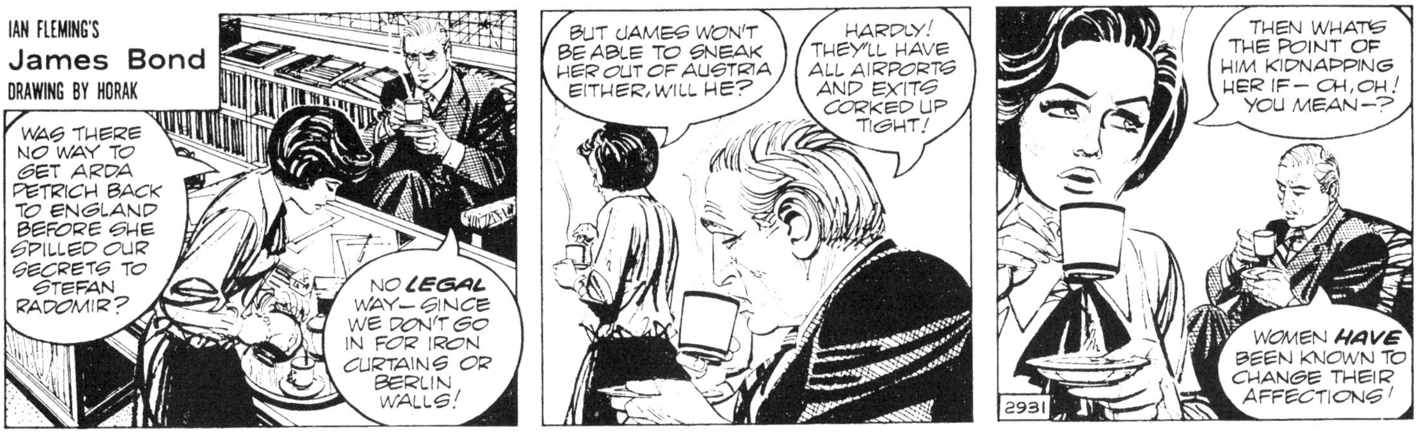
IAN FLEMING'S
James Bond
DRAWING BY HORAK
WAS THERE NO WAY TO GET ARDA PETRICH BACK TO ENGLAND BEFORE SHE SPILLED OUR SECRETS TO STEFAN RADOMIR?
NO LEGAL WAY—SINCE WE DON'T GO IN FOR IRON CURTAINS OR BERLIN WALLS!
BUT JAMES WON'T BE ABLE TO SNEAK HER OUT OF AUSTRIA EITHER, WILL HE?
HARDLY! THEY'LL HAVE ALL AIRPORTS AND EXITS CORKED UP TIGHT!
THEN WHAT'S THE POINT OF HIM KIDNAPPING HER IF—OH, OH! YOU MEAN—?
WOMEN HAVE BEEN KNOWN TO CHANGE THEIR AFFECTIONS!
2931

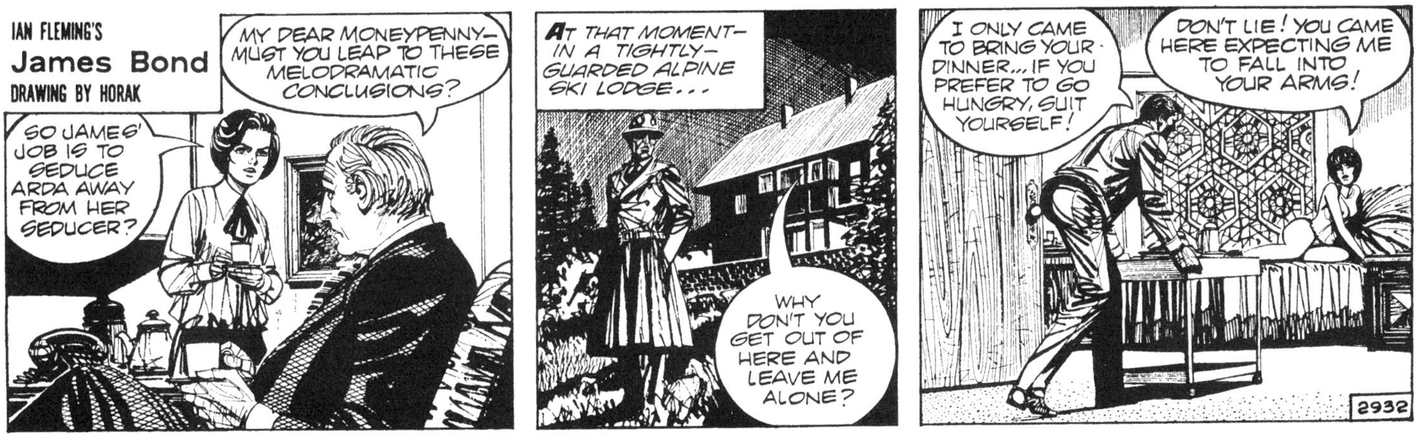
IAN FLEMING'S
James Bond
DRAWING BY HORAK
MY DEAR MONEYPENNY—MUST YOU LEAP TO THESE MELODRAMATIC CONCLUSIONS?
SO JAMES' JOB IS TO SEDUCE ARDA AWAY FROM HER SEDUCER?
AT THAT MOMENT—IN A TIGHTLY-GUARDED ALPINE SKI LODGE...
WHY DON'T YOU GET OUT OF HERE AND LEAVE ME ALONE?
I ONLY CAME TO BRING YOUR DINNER... IF YOU PREFER TO GO HUNGRY, SUIT YOURSELF!
DON'T LIE! YOU CAME HERE EXPECTING ME TO FALL INTO YOUR ARMS!
2932

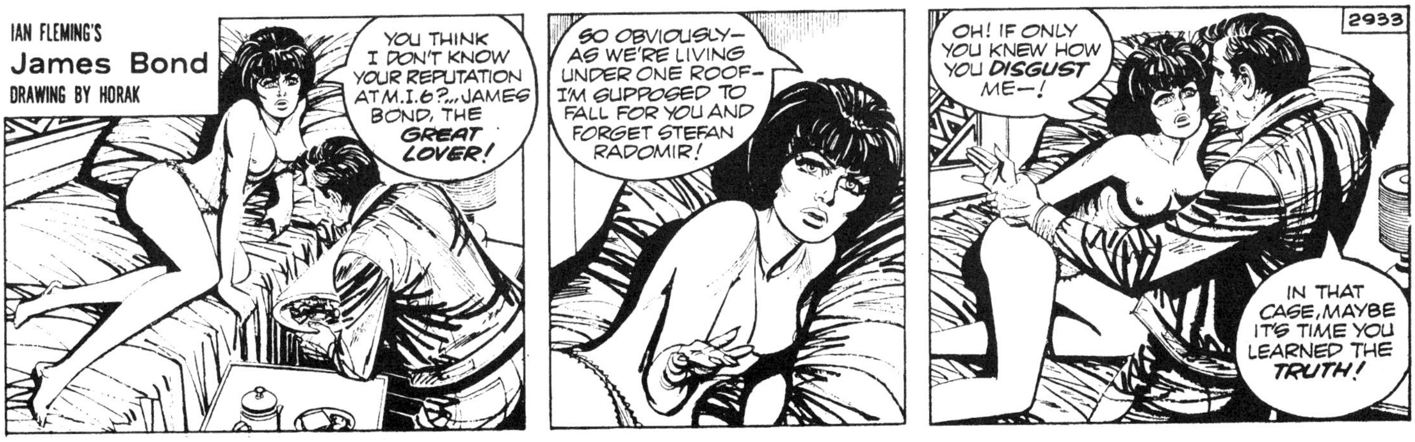
IAN FLEMING'S
James Bond
DRAWING BY HORAK
YOU THINK I DON'T KNOW YOUR REPUTATION AT M.I.6?... JAMES BOND, THE GREAT LOVER!
SO OBVIOUSLY—AS WE'RE LIVING UNDER ONE ROOF—I'M SUPPOSED TO FALL FOR YOU AND FORGET STEFAN RADOMIR!
2933
OH! IF ONLY YOU KNEW HOW YOU DISGUST ME—!
IN THAT CASE, MAYBE IT'S TIME YOU LEARNED THE TRUTH!

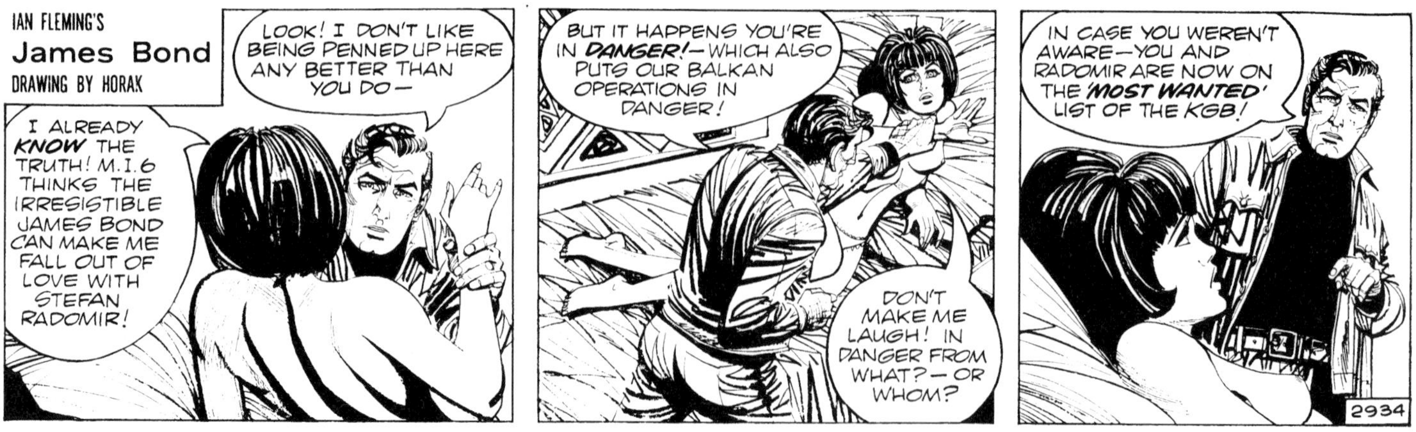
IAN FLEMING'S
James Bond
DRAWING BY HORAK
LOOK! I DON'T LIKE BEING PENNED UP HERE ANY BETTER THAN YOU DO—
I ALREADY KNOW THE TRUTH! M.I.6 THINKS THE IRRESISTIBLE JAMES BOND CAN MAKE ME FALL OUT OF LOVE WITH STEFAN RADOMIR!
BUT IT HAPPENS YOU'RE IN DANGER!—WHICH ALSO PUTS OUR BALKAN OPERATIONS IN DANGER!
DON'T MAKE ME LAUGH! IN DANGER FROM WHAT?—OR WHOM?
IN CASE YOU WEREN'T AWARE—YOU AND RADOMIR ARE NOW ON THE 'MOST WANTED' LIST OF THE KGB!
2934

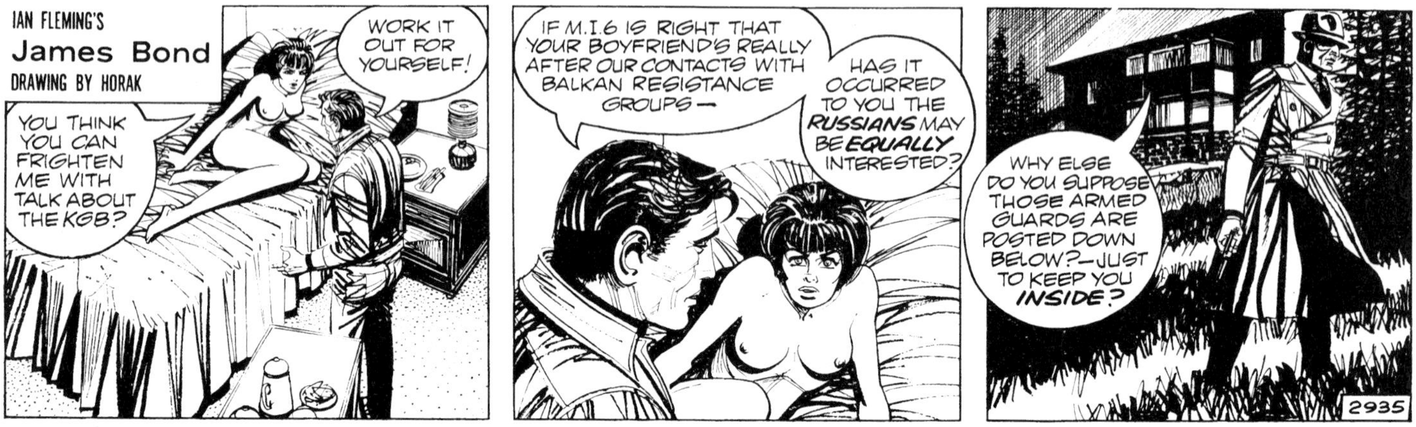
IAN FLEMING'S
James Bond
DRAWING BY HORAK
WORK IT OUT FOR YOURSELF!
YOU THINK YOU CAN FRIGHTEN ME WITH TALK ABOUT THE KGB?
IF M.I.6 IS RIGHT THAT YOUR BOYFRIEND'S REALLY AFTER OUR CONTACTS WITH BALKAN RESISTANCE GROUPS—
HAS IT OCCURRED TO YOU THE RUSSIANS MAY BE EQUALLY INTERESTED?
WHY ELSE DO YOU SUPPOSE THOSE ARMED GUARDS ARE POSTED DOWN BELOW?—JUST TO KEEP YOU INSIDE?
2935

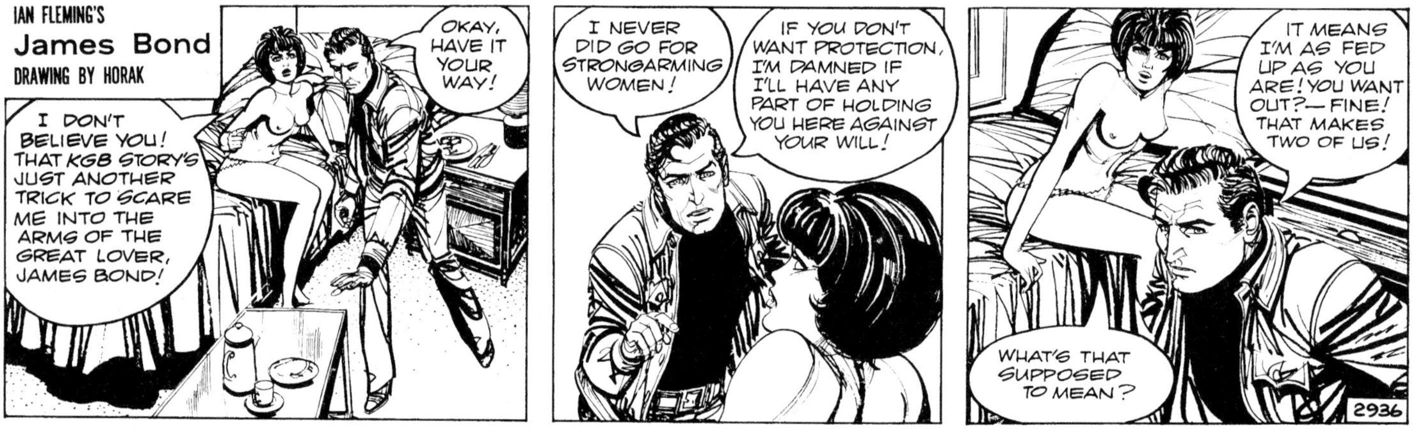
IAN FLEMING'S
James Bond
DRAWING BY HORAK
OKAY, HAVE IT YOUR WAY!
I DON'T BELIEVE YOU! THAT KGB STORY'S JUST ANOTHER TRICK TO SCARE ME INTO THE ARMS OF THE GREAT LOVER, JAMES BOND!
I NEVER DID GO FOR STRONGARMING WOMEN!
IF YOU DON'T WANT PROTECTION, I'M DAMNED IF I'LL HAVE ANY PART OF HOLDING YOU HERE AGAINST YOUR WILL!
IT MEANS I'M AS FED UP AS YOU ARE! YOU WANT OUT?—FINE! THAT MAKES TWO OF US!
WHAT'S THAT SUPPOSED TO MEAN?
2936

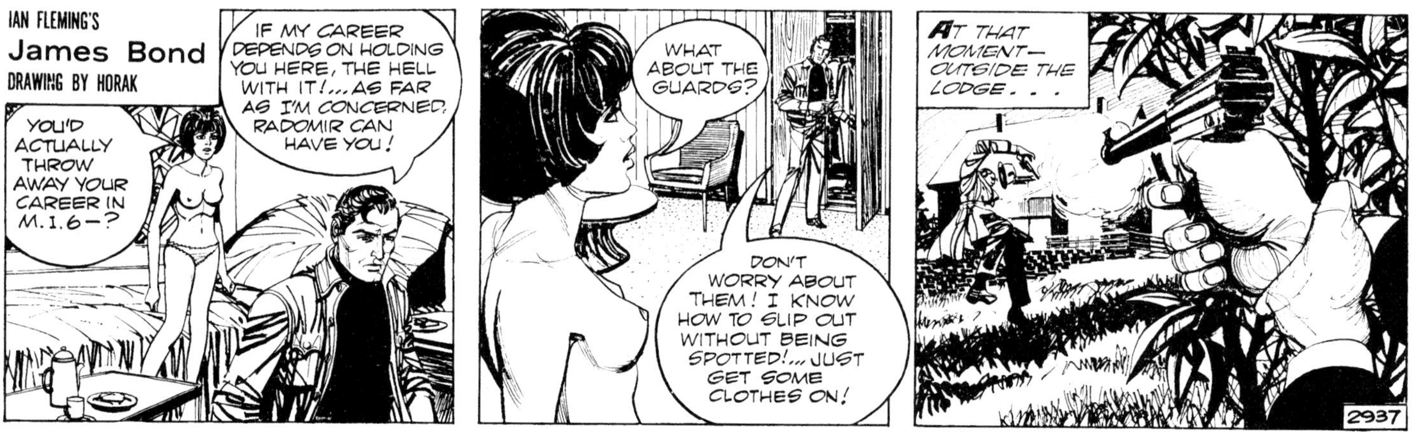
IAN FLEMING'S
James Bond
DRAWING BY HORAK
IF MY CAREER DEPENDS ON HOLDING YOU HERE, THE HELL WITH IT!... AS FAR AS I'M CONCERNED, RADOMIR CAN HAVE YOU!
YOU'D ACTUALLY THROW AWAY YOUR CAREER IN M.I.6—?
WHAT ABOUT THE GUARDS?
DON'T WORRY ABOUT THEM! I KNOW HOW TO SLIP OUT WITHOUT BEING SPOTTED!... JUST GET SOME CLOTHES ON!
AT THAT MOMENT—OUTSIDE THE LODGE...
2937

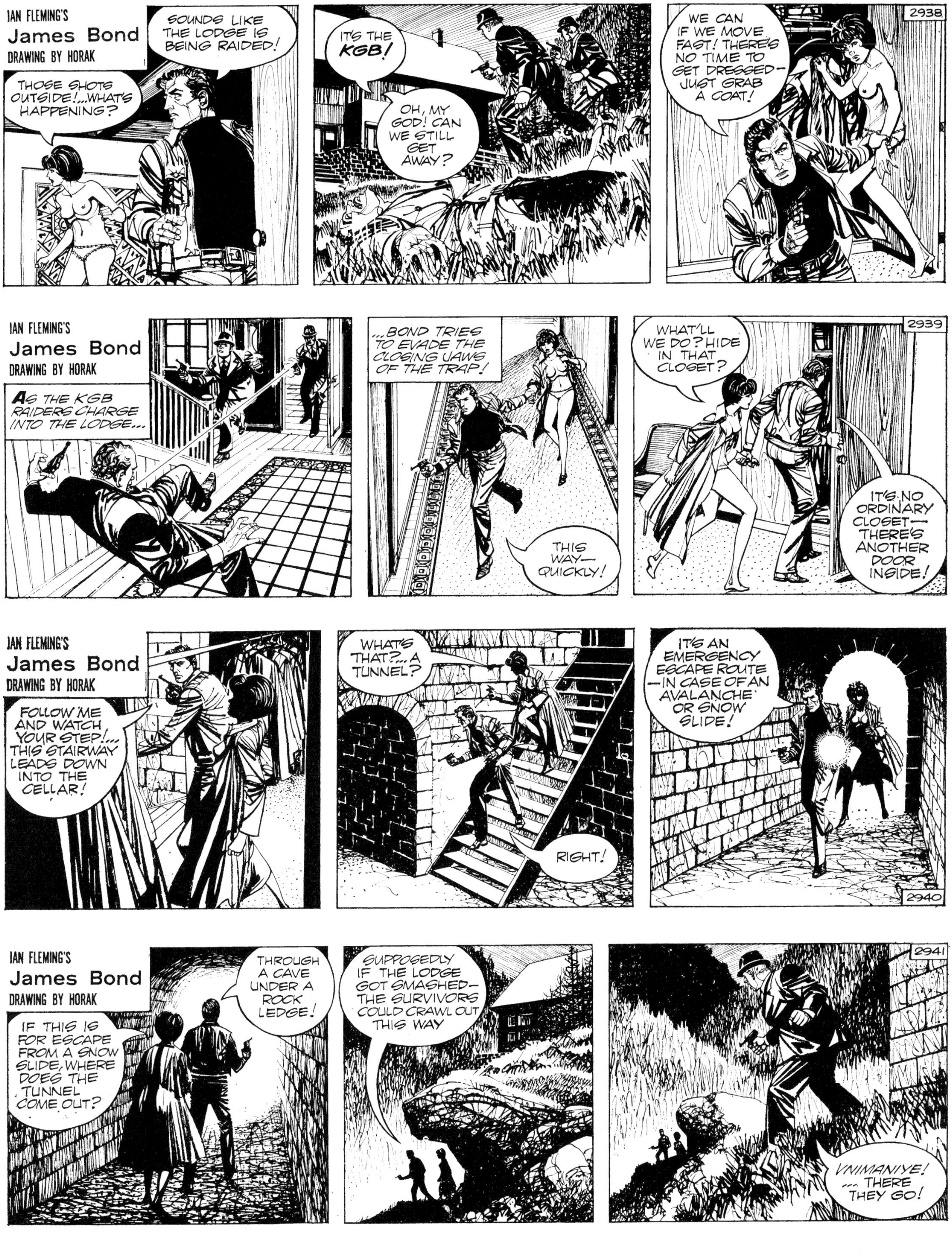
IAN FLEMING'S
James Bond
DRAWING BY HORAK
THOSE SHOTS OUTSIDE!... WHAT'S HAPPENING?
SOUNDS LIKE THE LODGE IS BEING RAIDED!
IT'S THE KGB!
OH, MY GOD! CAN WE STILL GET AWAY?
2938
WE CAN IF WE MOVE FAST! THERE'S NO TIME TO GET DRESSED— JUST GRAB A COAT!
IAN FLEMING'S
James Bond
DRAWING BY HORAK
AS THE KGB RAIDERS CHARGE INTO THE LODGE...
...BOND TRIES TO EVADE THE CLOSING JAWS OF THE TRAP!
THIS WAY— QUICKLY!
2939
WHAT'LL WE DO? HIDE IN THAT CLOSET?
IT'S NO ORDINARY CLOSET— THERE'S ANOTHER DOOR INSIDE!
IAN FLEMING'S
James Bond
DRAWING BY HORAK
FOLLOW ME AND WATCH YOUR STEP!... THIS STAIRWAY LEADS DOWN INTO THE CELLAR!
WHAT'S THAT?... A TUNNEL?
RIGHT!
IT'S AN EMERGENCY ESCAPE ROUTE —IN CASE OF AN AVALANCHE OR SNOW SLIDE!
2940
IAN FLEMING'S
James Bond
DRAWING BY HORAK
IF THIS IS FOR ESCAPE FROM A SNOW SLIDE, WHERE DOES THE TUNNEL COME OUT?
THROUGH A CAVE UNDER A ROCK LEDGE!
SUPPOSEDLY IF THE LODGE GOT SMASHED— THE SURVIVORS COULD CRAWL OUT THIS WAY
2941
VNIMANIYE! ... THERE THEY GO!

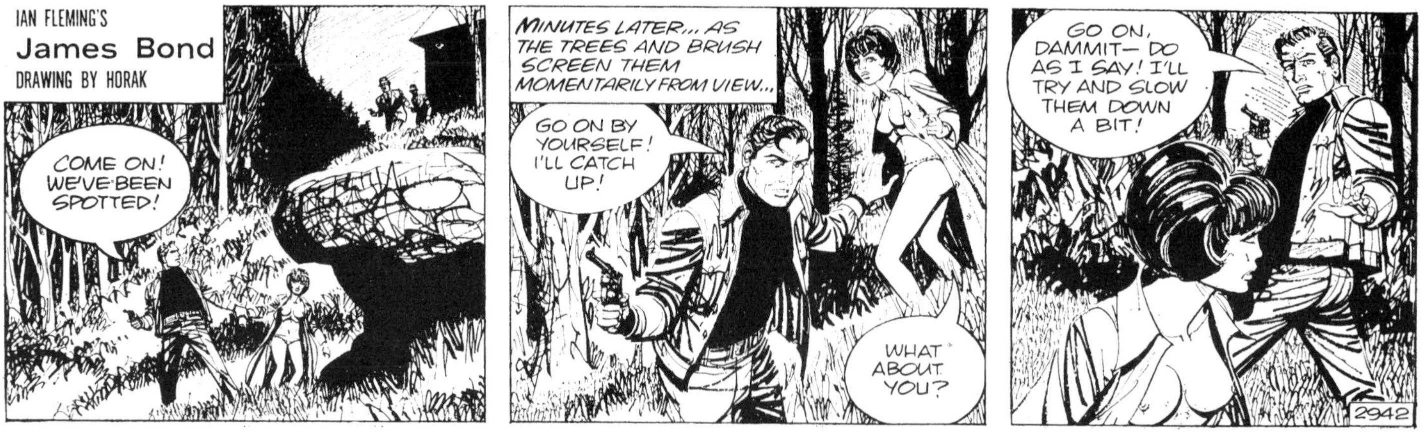
IAN FLEMING'S
James Bond
DRAWING BY HORAK
COME ON! WE'VE BEEN SPOTTED!
MINUTES LATER... AS THE TREES AND BRUSH SCREEN THEM MOMENTARILY FROM VIEW...
GO ON BY YOURSELF! I'LL CATCH UP!
WHAT ABOUT YOU?
GO ON, DAMMIT— DO AS I SAY! I'LL TRY AND SLOW THEM DOWN A BIT!
2942

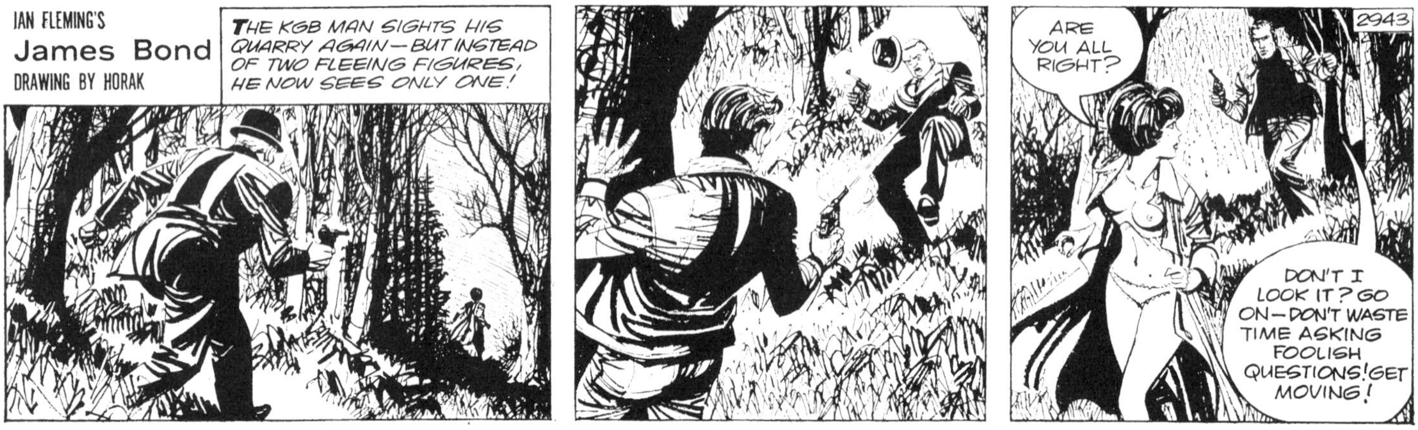
IAN FLEMING'S
James Bond
DRAWING BY HORAK
THE KGB MAN SIGHTS HIS QUARRY AGAIN—BUT INSTEAD OF TWO FLEEING FIGURES, HE NOW SEES ONLY ONE!
2943
ARE YOU ALL RIGHT?
DON'T I LOOK IT? GO ON—DON'T WASTE TIME ASKING FOOLISH QUESTIONS! GET MOVING!

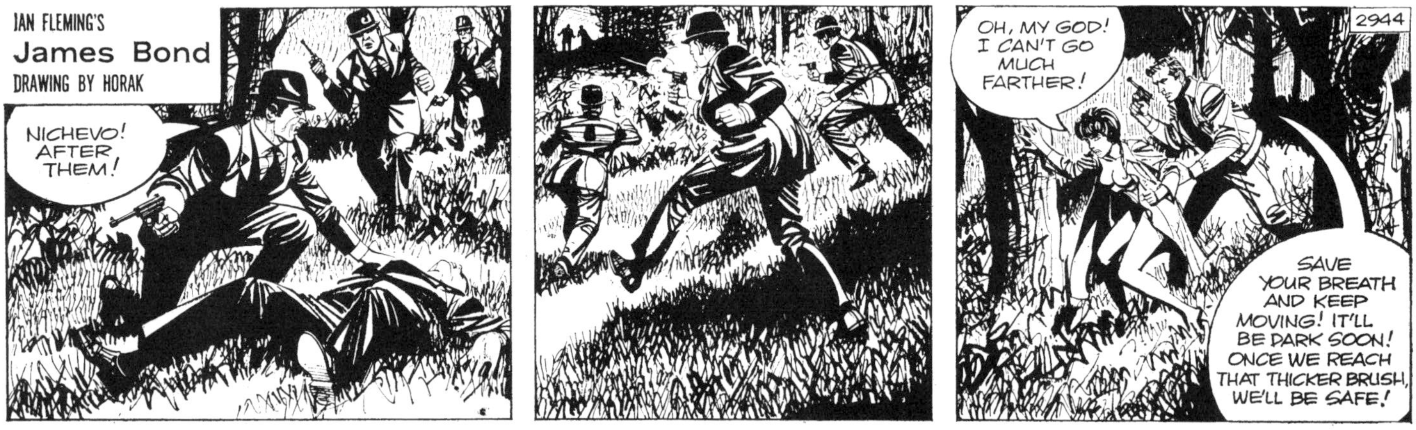
IAN FLEMING'S
James Bond
DRAWING BY HORAK
NICHEVO! AFTER THEM!
2944
OH, MY GOD! I CAN'T GO MUCH FARTHER!
SAVE YOUR BREATH AND KEEP MOVING! IT'LL BE DARK SOON! ONCE WE REACH THAT THICKER BRUSH, WE'LL BE SAFE!

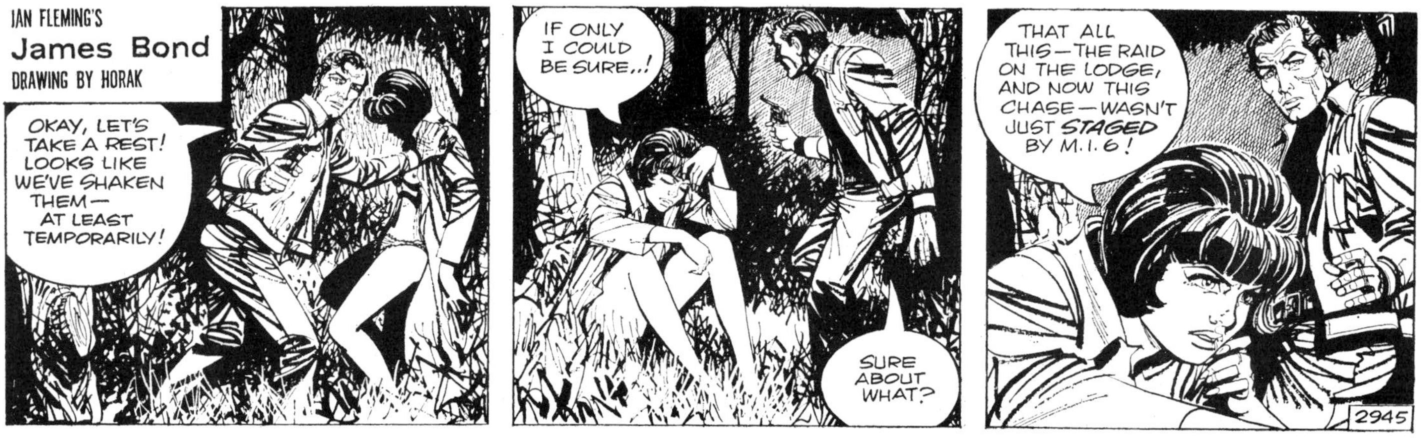
IAN FLEMING'S
James Bond
DRAWING BY HORAK
OKAY, LET'S TAKE A REST! LOOKS LIKE WE'VE SHAKEN THEM— AT LEAST TEMPORARILY!
IF ONLY I COULD BE SURE...!
SURE ABOUT WHAT?
THAT ALL THIS—THE RAID ON THE LODGE, AND NOW THIS CHASE—WASN'T JUST STAGED BY M.I.6!
2945

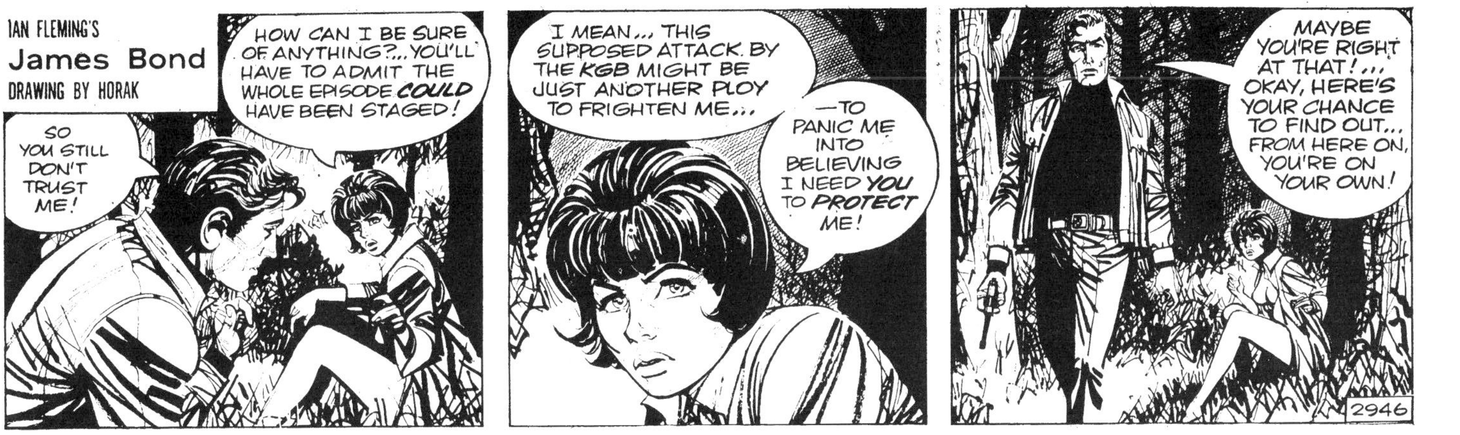
IAN FLEMING'S
James Bond
DRAWING BY HORAK
SO YOU STILL DON'T TRUST ME!
HOW CAN I BE SURE OF ANYTHING?... YOU'LL HAVE TO ADMIT THE WHOLE EPISODE COULD HAVE BEEN STAGED!
I MEAN... THIS SUPPOSED ATTACK BY THE KGB MIGHT BE JUST ANOTHER PLOY TO FRIGHTEN ME...
—TO PANIC ME INTO BELIEVING I NEED YOU TO PROTECT ME!
MAYBE YOU'RE RIGHT AT THAT!... OKAY, HERE'S YOUR CHANCE TO FIND OUT... FROM HERE ON, YOU'RE ON YOUR OWN!
2946

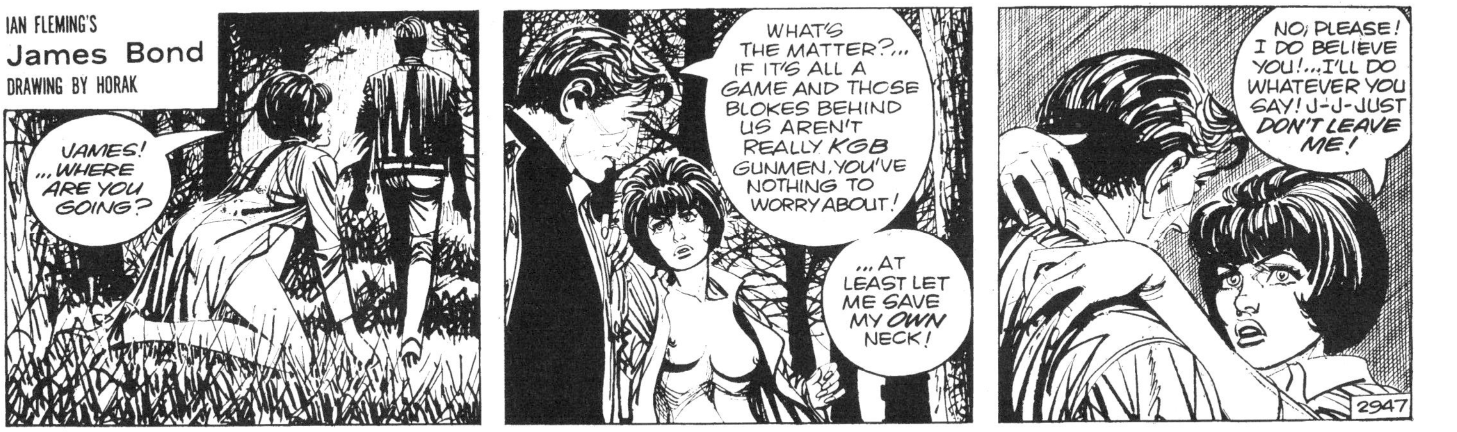
IAN FLEMING'S
James Bond
DRAWING BY HORAK
JAMES! ...WHERE ARE YOU GOING?
WHAT'S THE MATTER?... IF IT'S ALL A GAME AND THOSE BLOKES BEHIND US AREN'T REALLY KGB GUNMEN, YOU'VE NOTHING TO WORRY ABOUT!
...AT LEAST LET ME SAVE MY OWN NECK!
NO, PLEASE! I DO BELIEVE YOU!...I'LL DO WHATEVER YOU SAY! J-J-JUST DON'T LEAVE ME!
2947

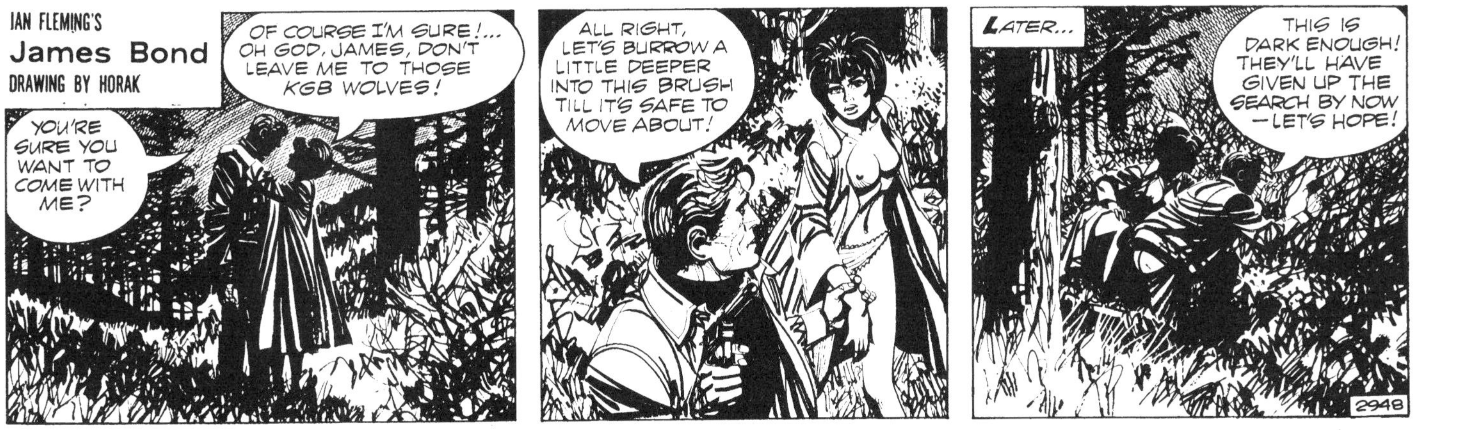
IAN FLEMING'S
James Bond
DRAWING BY HORAK
YOU'RE SURE YOU WANT TO COME WITH ME?
OF COURSE I'M SURE!... OH GOD, JAMES, DON'T LEAVE ME TO THOSE KGB WOLVES!
ALL RIGHT, LET'S BURROW A LITTLE DEEPER INTO THIS BRUSH TILL IT'S SAFE TO MOVE ABOUT!
LATER...
THIS IS DARK ENOUGH! THEY'LL HAVE GIVEN UP THE SEARCH BY NOW —LET'S HOPE!
2948

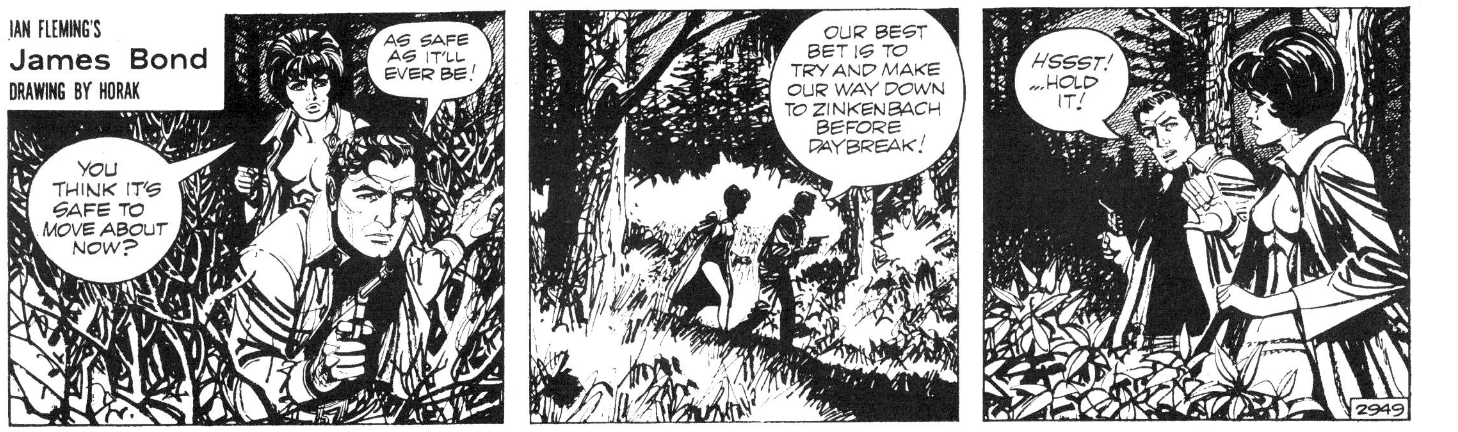
IAN FLEMING'S
James Bond
DRAWING BY HORAK
YOU THINK IT'S SAFE TO MOVE ABOUT NOW?
AS SAFE AS IT'LL EVER BE!
OUR BEST BET IS TO TRY AND MAKE OUR WAY DOWN TO ZINKENBACH BEFORE DAYBREAK!
HSSST! ...HOLD IT!
2949

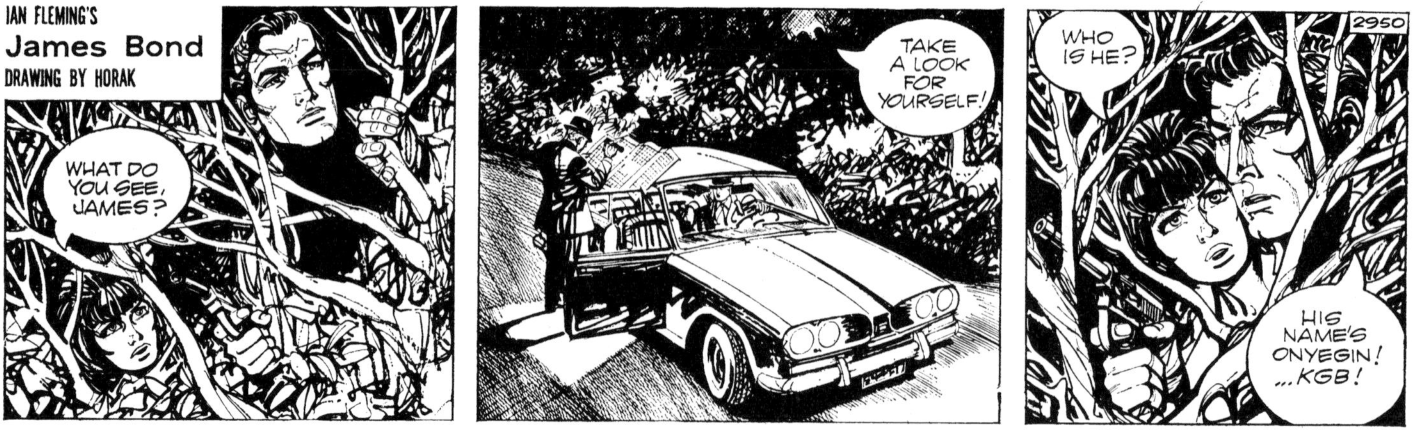
IAN FLEMING'S
James Bond
DRAWING BY HORAK
WHAT DO YOU SEE, JAMES?
TAKE A LOOK FOR YOURSELF!
2950
WHO IS HE?
HIS NAME'S ONYEGIN! ...KGB!

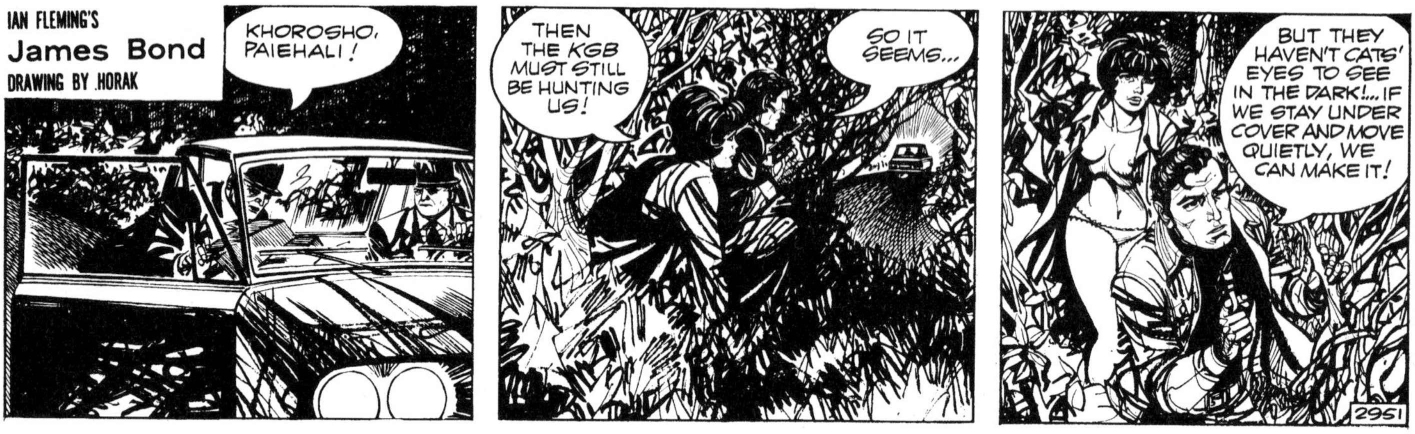
IAN FLEMING'S
James Bond
DRAWING BY HORAK
KHOROSHO, PAIEHALI!
THEN THE KGB MUST STILL BE HUNTING US!
SO IT SEEMS...
BUT THEY HAVEN'T CATS' EYES TO SEE IN THE DARK!...IF WE STAY UNDER COVER AND MOVE QUIETLY, WE CAN MAKE IT!
2951

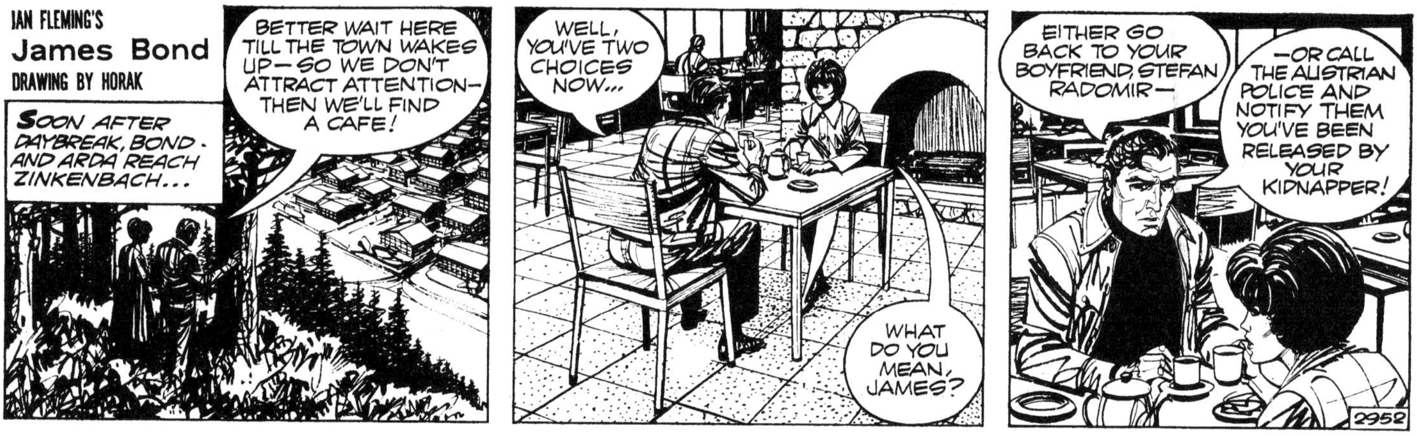
IAN FLEMING'S
James Bond
DRAWING BY HORAK
SOON AFTER DAYBREAK, BOND AND ARDA REACH ZINKENBACH...
BETTER WAIT HERE TILL THE TOWN WAKES UP—SO WE DON'T ATTRACT ATTENTION—THEN WE'LL FIND A CAFE!
WELL, YOU'VE TWO CHOICES NOW...
WHAT DO YOU MEAN, JAMES?
EITHER GO BACK TO YOUR BOYFRIEND, STEFAN RADOMIR—
—OR CALL THE AUSTRIAN POLICE AND NOTIFY THEM YOU'VE BEEN RELEASED BY YOUR KIDNAPPER!
2952

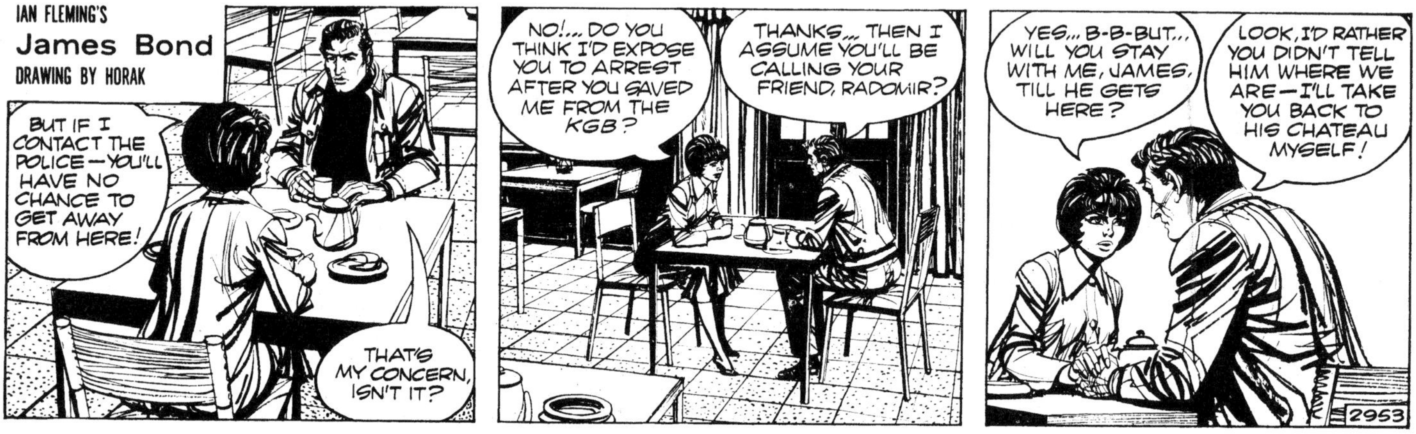
IAN FLEMING'S
James Bond
DRAWING BY HORAK
BUT IF I CONTACT THE POLICE—YOU'LL HAVE NO CHANCE TO GET AWAY FROM HERE!
THAT'S MY CONCERN, ISN'T IT?
NO!... DO YOU THINK I'D EXPOSE YOU TO ARREST AFTER YOU SAVED ME FROM THE KGB?
THANKS... THEN I ASSUME YOU'LL BE CALLING YOUR FRIEND, RADOMIR?
YES... B-B-BUT... WILL YOU STAY WITH ME, JAMES, TILL HE GETS HERE?
LOOK, I'D RATHER YOU DIDN'T TELL HIM WHERE WE ARE—I'LL TAKE YOU BACK TO HIS CHATEAU MYSELF!
2953

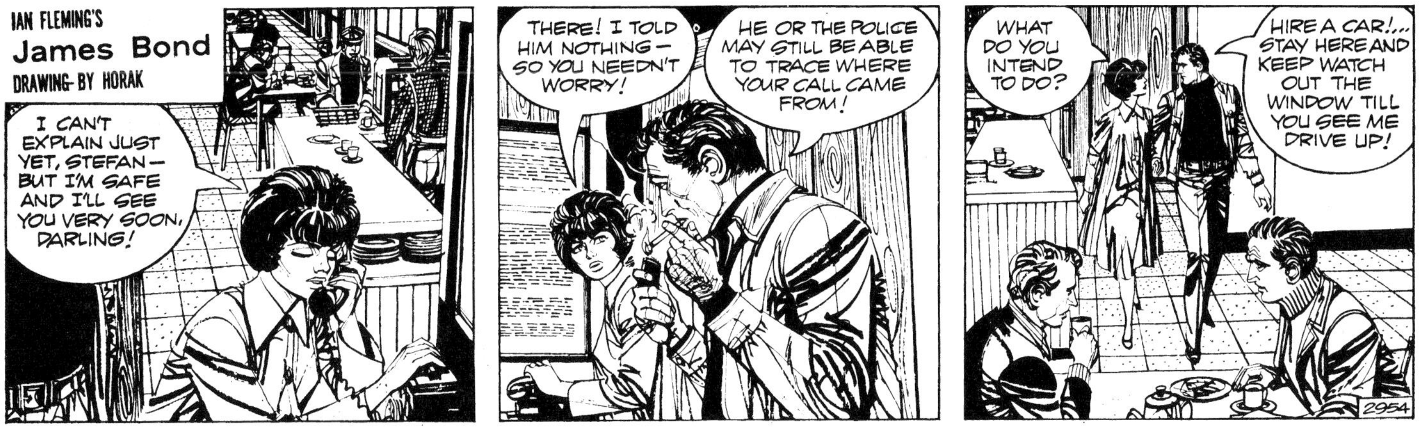
IAN FLEMING'S
James Bond
DRAWING BY HORAK
I CAN'T EXPLAIN JUST YET, STEFAN— BUT I'M SAFE AND I'LL SEE YOU VERY SOON, DARLING!
THERE! I TOLD HIM NOTHING— SO YOU NEEDN'T WORRY!
HE OR THE POLICE MAY STILL BE ABLE TO TRACE WHERE YOUR CALL CAME FROM!
WHAT DO YOU INTEND TO DO?
HIRE A CAR!... STAY HERE AND KEEP WATCH OUT THE WINDOW TILL YOU SEE ME DRIVE UP!
2954

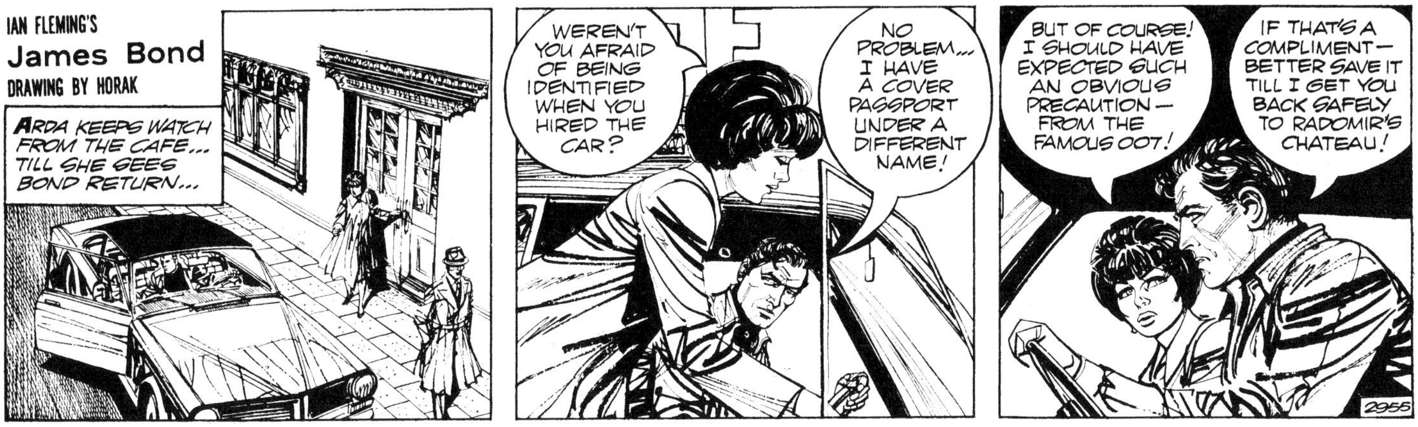
IAN FLEMING'S
James Bond
DRAWING BY HORAK
ARDA KEEPS WATCH FROM THE CAFE... TILL SHE SEES BOND RETURN...
WEREN'T YOU AFRAID OF BEING IDENTIFIED WHEN YOU HIRED THE CAR?
NO PROBLEM... I HAVE A COVER PASSPORT UNDER A DIFFERENT NAME!
BUT OF COURSE! I SHOULD HAVE EXPECTED SUCH AN OBVIOUS PRECAUTION— FROM THE FAMOUS 007!
IF THAT'S A COMPLIMENT— BETTER SAVE IT TILL I GET YOU BACK SAFELY TO RADOMIR'S CHATEAU!
2955

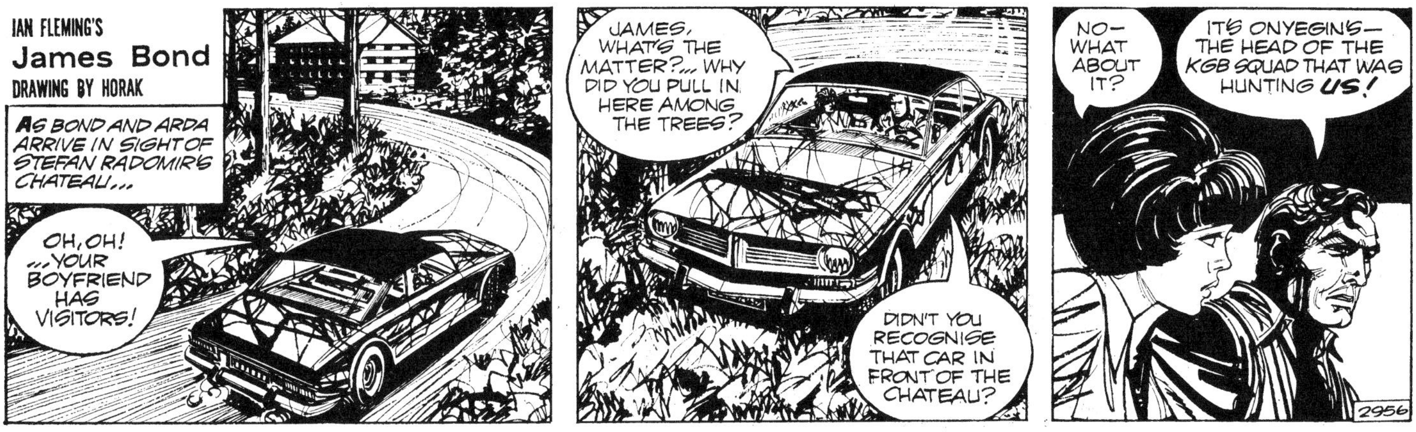
IAN FLEMING'S
James Bond
DRAWING BY HORAK
AS BOND AND ARDA ARRIVE IN SIGHT OF STEFAN RADOMIR'S CHATEAU...
OH, OH! ...YOUR BOYFRIEND HAS VISITORS!
JAMES, WHAT'S THE MATTER?... WHY DID YOU PULL IN HERE AMONG THE TREES?
DIDN'T YOU RECOGNISE THAT CAR IN FRONT OF THE CHATEAU?
NO— WHAT ABOUT IT?
IT'S ONYEGIN'S— THE HEAD OF THE KGB SQUAD THAT WAS HUNTING US!
2956

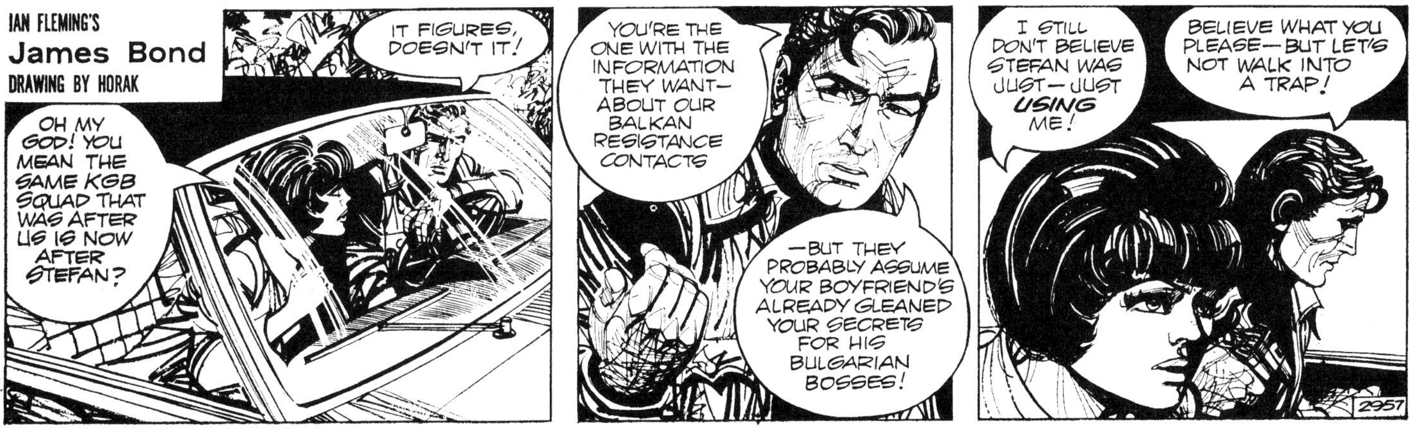
IAN FLEMING'S
James Bond
DRAWING BY HORAK
OH MY GOD! YOU MEAN THE SAME KGB SQUAD THAT WAS AFTER US IS NOW AFTER STEFAN?
IT FIGURES, DOESN'T IT!
YOU'RE THE ONE WITH THE INFORMATION THEY WANT— ABOUT OUR BALKAN RESISTANCE CONTACTS
—BUT THEY PROBABLY ASSUME YOUR BOYFRIEND'S ALREADY GLEANED YOUR SECRETS FOR HIS BULGARIAN BOSSES!
I STILL DON'T BELIEVE STEFAN WAS JUST— JUST USING ME!
BELIEVE WHAT YOU PLEASE— BUT LET'S NOT WALK INTO A TRAP!
2957

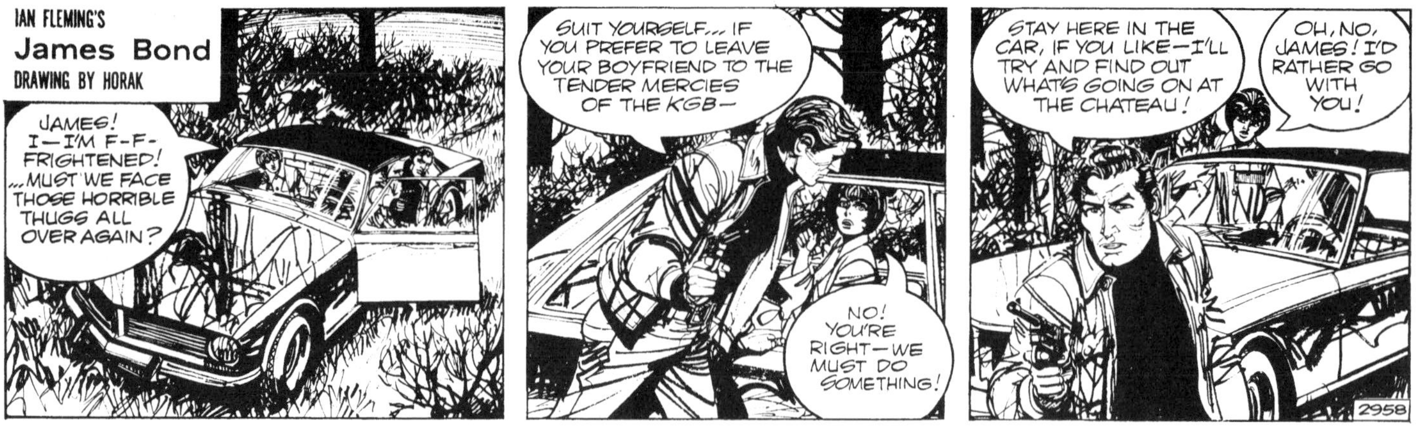
IAN FLEMING'S
James Bond
DRAWING BY HORAK
JAMES! I—I'M F-F-FRIGHTENED! ...MUST WE FACE THOSE HORRIBLE THUGS ALL OVER AGAIN?
SUIT YOURSELF... IF YOU PREFER TO LEAVE YOUR BOYFRIEND TO THE TENDER MERCIES OF THE KGB—
NO! YOU'RE RIGHT—WE MUST DO SOMETHING!
STAY HERE IN THE CAR, IF YOU LIKE—I'LL TRY AND FIND OUT WHAT'S GOING ON AT THE CHATEAU!
OH, NO, JAMES! I'D RATHER GO WITH YOU!
2958

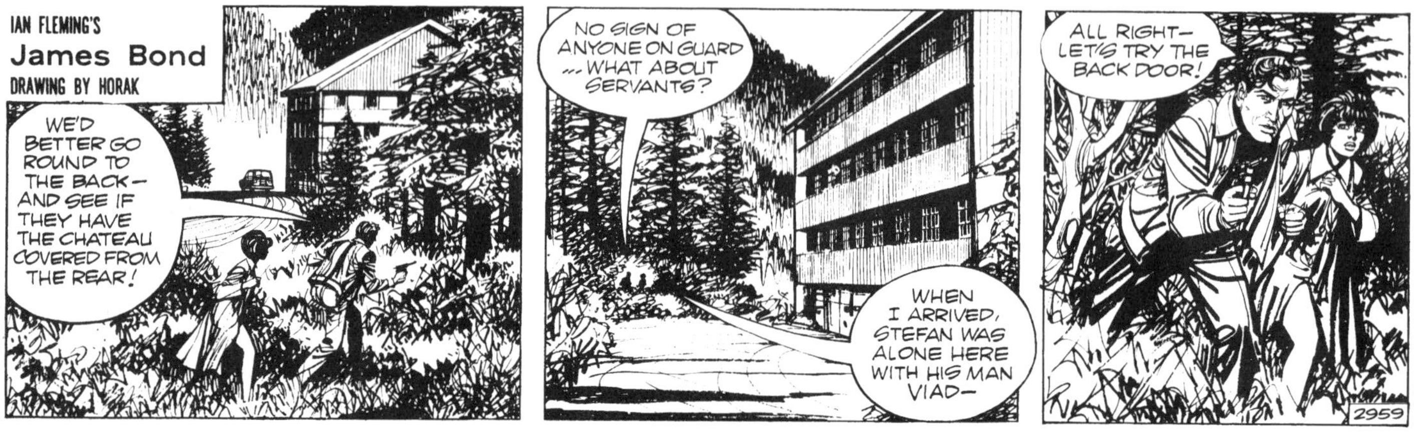
IAN FLEMING'S
James Bond
DRAWING BY HORAK
WE'D BETTER GO ROUND TO THE BACK—AND SEE IF THEY HAVE THE CHATEAU COVERED FROM THE REAR!
NO SIGN OF ANYONE ON GUARD ...WHAT ABOUT SERVANTS?
WHEN I ARRIVED, STEFAN WAS ALONE HERE WITH HIS MAN VIAD—
ALL RIGHT—LET'S TRY THE BACK DOOR!
2959

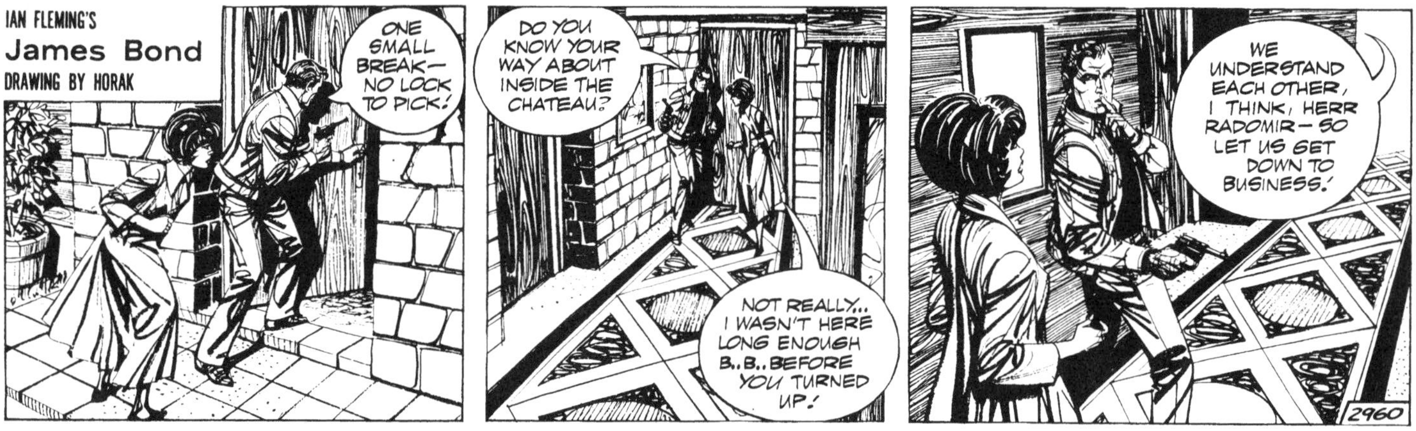
IAN FLEMING'S
James Bond
DRAWING BY HORAK
ONE SMALL BREAK—NO LOCK TO PICK!
DO YOU KNOW YOUR WAY ABOUT INSIDE THE CHATEAU?
NOT REALLY... I WASN'T HERE LONG ENOUGH B..B..BEFORE YOU TURNED UP!
WE UNDERSTAND EACH OTHER, I THINK, HERR RADOMIR—SO LET US GET DOWN TO BUSINESS!
2960

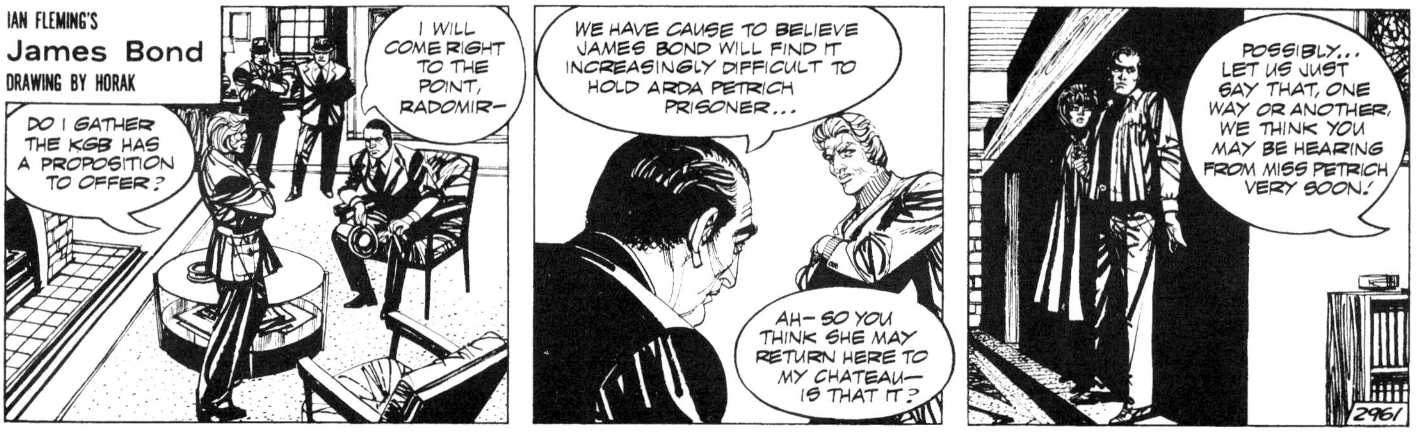
IAN FLEMING'S
James Bond
DRAWING BY HORAK
I WILL COME RIGHT TO THE POINT, RADOMIR—
DO I GATHER THE KGB HAS A PROPOSITION TO OFFER?
WE HAVE CAUSE TO BELIEVE JAMES BOND WILL FIND IT INCREASINGLY DIFFICULT TO HOLD ARDA PETRICH PRISONER...
AH—SO YOU THINK SHE MAY RETURN HERE TO MY CHATEAU—IS THAT IT?
POSSIBLY... LET US JUST SAY THAT, ONE WAY OR ANOTHER, WE THINK YOU MAY BE HEARING FROM MISS PETRICH VERY SOON!
2961

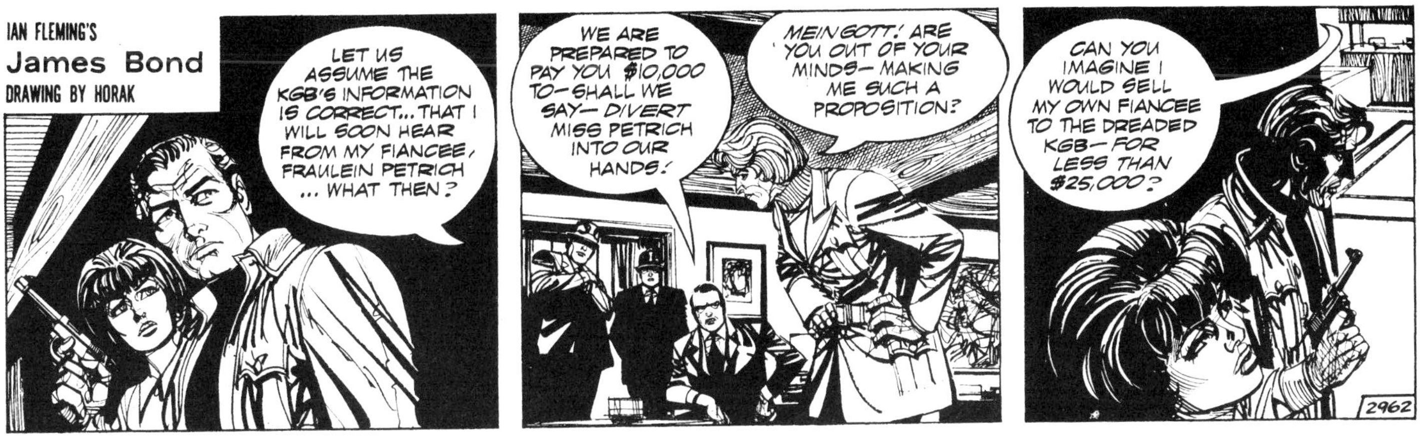
IAN FLEMING'S
James Bond
DRAWING BY HORAK
LET US ASSUME THE KGB'S INFORMATION IS CORRECT... THAT I WILL SOON HEAR FROM MY FIANCEE, FRAULEIN PETRICH ... WHAT THEN?
WE ARE PREPARED TO PAY YOU $10,000 TO—SHALL WE SAY—DIVERT MISS PETRICH INTO OUR HANDS!
MEIN GOTT! ARE YOU OUT OF YOUR MINDS—MAKING ME SUCH A PROPOSITION?
CAN YOU IMAGINE I WOULD SELL MY OWN FIANCEE TO THE DREADED KGB—FOR LESS THAN $25,000?
2962

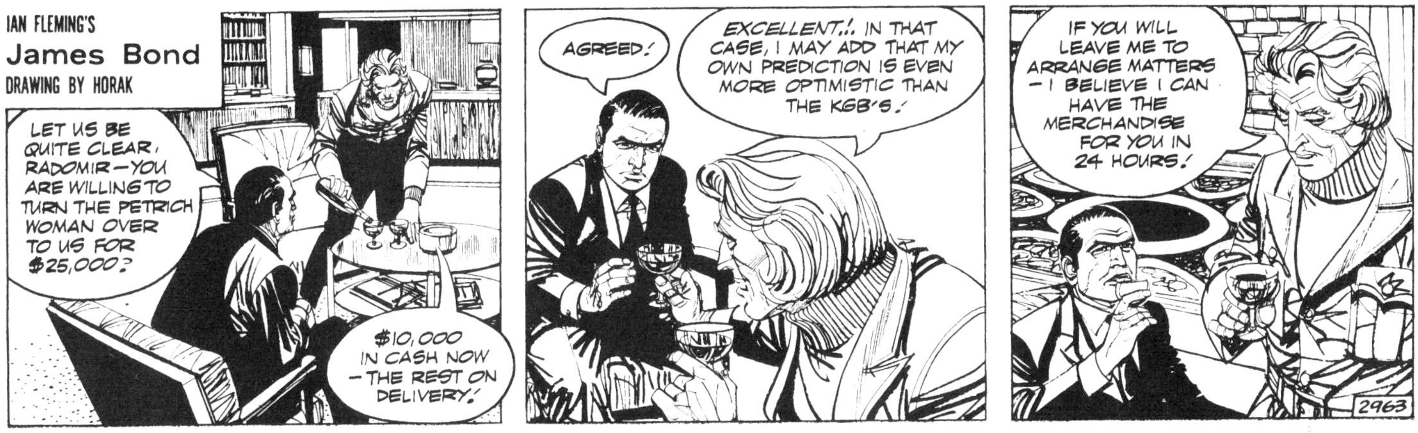
IAN FLEMING'S
James Bond
DRAWING BY HORAK
LET US BE QUITE CLEAR, RADOMIR—YOU ARE WILLING TO TURN THE PETRICH WOMAN OVER TO US FOR $25,000?
$10,000 IN CASH NOW —THE REST ON DELIVERY!
AGREED!
EXCELLENT!. IN THAT CASE, I MAY ADD THAT MY OWN PREDICTION IS EVEN MORE OPTIMISTIC THAN THE KGB'S!
IF YOU WILL LEAVE ME TO ARRANGE MATTERS —I BELIEVE I CAN HAVE THE MERCHANDISE FOR YOU IN 24 HOURS!
2963

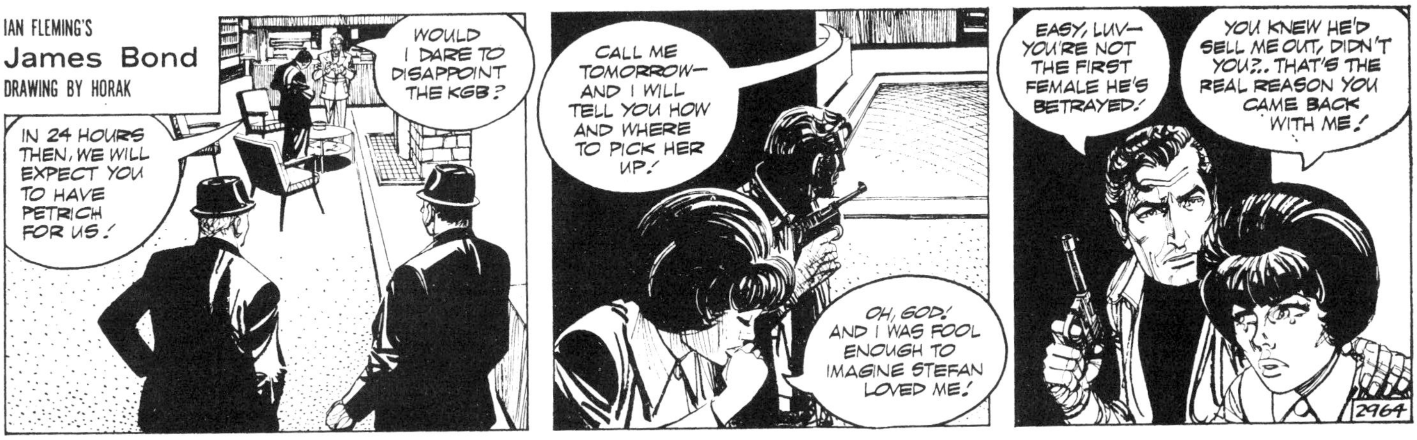
IAN FLEMING'S
James Bond
DRAWING BY HORAK
IN 24 HOURS THEN, WE WILL EXPECT YOU TO HAVE PETRICH FOR US!
WOULD I DARE TO DISAPPOINT THE KGB?
CALL ME TOMORROW— AND I WILL TELL YOU HOW AND WHERE TO PICK HER UP!
OH, GOD! AND I WAS FOOL ENOUGH TO IMAGINE STEFAN LOVED ME!
EASY, LUV— YOU'RE NOT THE FIRST FEMALE HE'S BETRAYED!
YOU KNEW HE'D SELL ME OUT, DIDN'T YOU?.. THAT'S THE REAL REASON YOU CAME BACK WITH ME!
2964

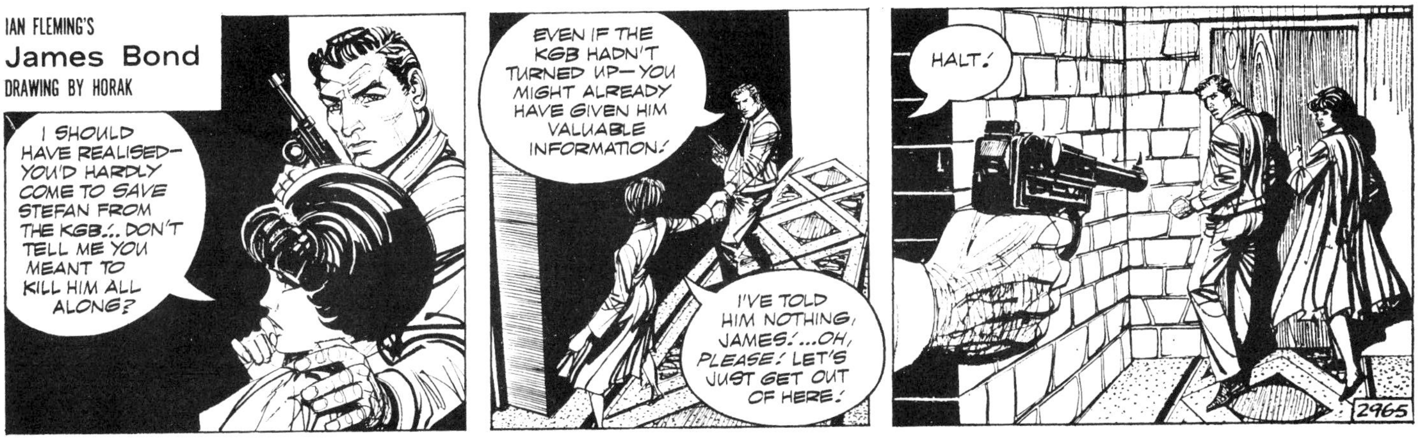
IAN FLEMING'S
James Bond
DRAWING BY HORAK
I SHOULD HAVE REALISED— YOU'D HARDLY COME TO SAVE STEFAN FROM THE KGB!.. DON'T TELL ME YOU MEANT TO KILL HIM ALL ALONG?
EVEN IF THE KGB HADN'T TURNED UP—YOU MIGHT ALREADY HAVE GIVEN HIM VALUABLE INFORMATION!
I'VE TOLD HIM NOTHING, JAMES!...OH, PLEASE! LET'S JUST GET OUT OF HERE!
HALT!
2965

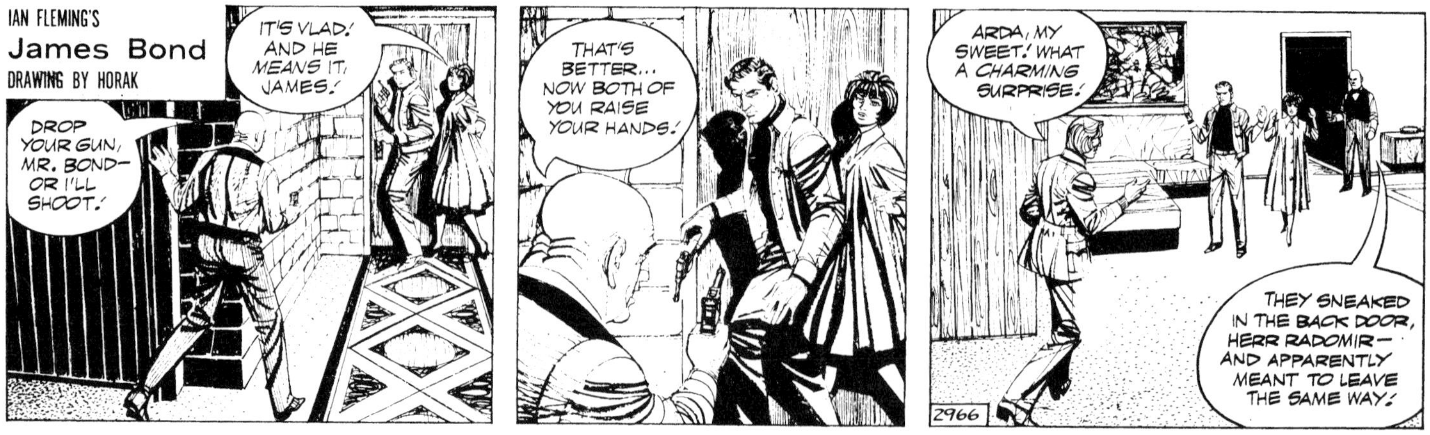
IAN FLEMING'S
James Bond
DRAWING BY HORAK
DROP YOUR GUN, MR. BOND—OR I'LL SHOOT.!
IT'S VLAD.! AND HE MEANS IT, JAMES.!
THAT'S BETTER... NOW BOTH OF YOU RAISE YOUR HANDS.!
ARDA, MY SWEET.! WHAT A CHARMING SURPRISE.!
THEY SNEAKED IN THE BACK DOOR, HERR RADOMIR—AND APPARENTLY MEANT TO LEAVE THE SAME WAY.!
2966

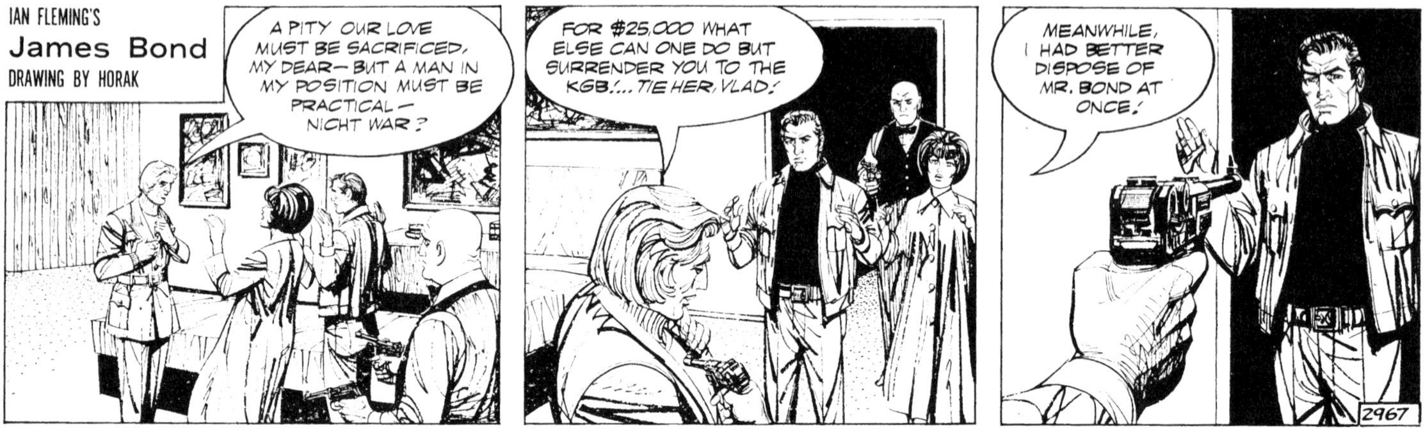
IAN FLEMING'S
James Bond
DRAWING BY HORAK
A PITY OUR LOVE MUST BE SACRIFICED, MY DEAR—BUT A MAN IN MY POSITION MUST BE PRACTICAL—NICHT WAR?
FOR $25,000 WHAT ELSE CAN ONE DO BUT SURRENDER YOU TO THE KGB.!... TIE HER, VLAD.!
MEANWHILE, I HAD BETTER DISPOSE OF MR. BOND AT ONCE.!
2967

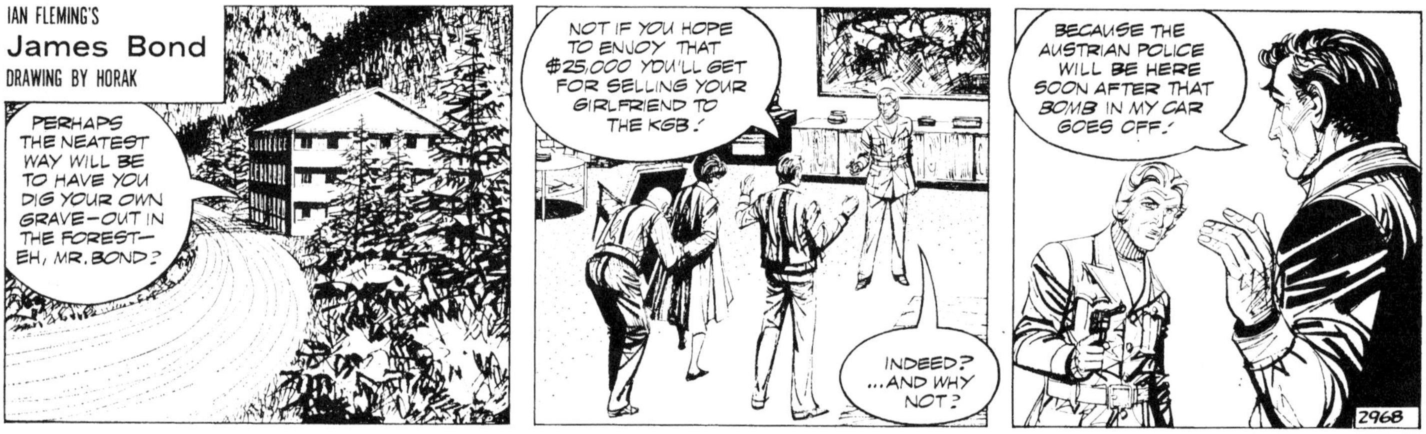
IAN FLEMING'S
James Bond
DRAWING BY HORAK
PERHAPS THE NEATEST WAY WILL BE TO HAVE YOU DIG YOUR OWN GRAVE—OUT IN THE FOREST—EH, MR. BOND?
NOT IF YOU HOPE TO ENJOY THAT $25,000 YOU'LL GET FOR SELLING YOUR GIRLFRIEND TO THE KGB.!
INDEED? ...AND WHY NOT?
BECAUSE THE AUSTRIAN POLICE WILL BE HERE SOON AFTER THAT BOMB IN MY CAR GOES OFF.!
2968

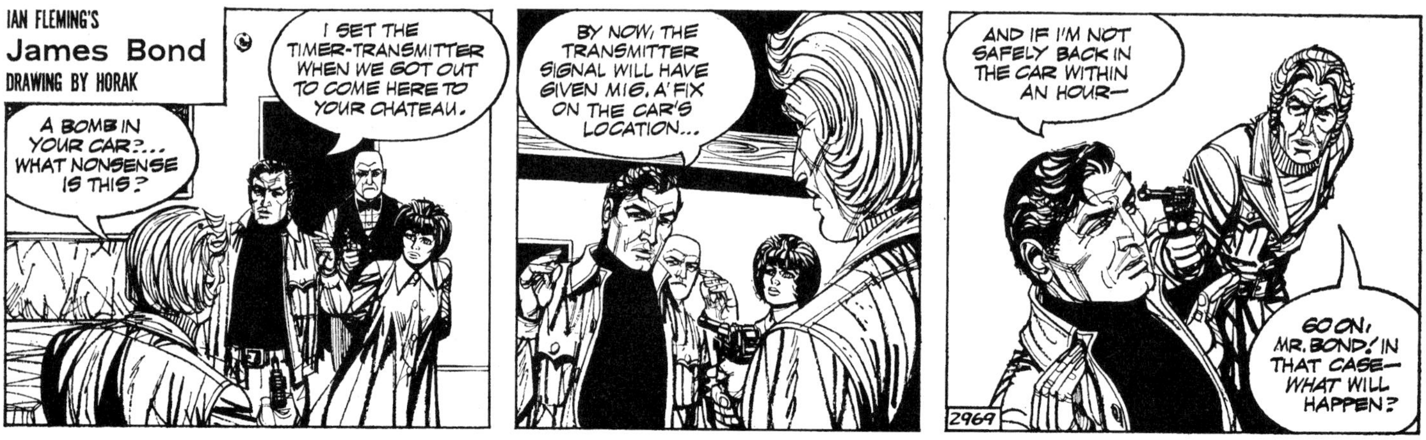
IAN FLEMING'S
James Bond
DRAWING BY HORAK
A BOMB IN YOUR CAR?... WHAT NONSENSE IS THIS?
I SET THE TIMER-TRANSMITTER WHEN WE GOT OUT TO COME HERE TO YOUR CHATEAU.
BY NOW, THE TRANSMITTER SIGNAL WILL HAVE GIVEN MI6 A FIX ON THE CAR'S LOCATION...
AND IF I'M NOT SAFELY BACK IN THE CAR WITHIN AN HOUR—
GO ON, MR. BOND.! IN THAT CASE—WHAT WILL HAPPEN?
2969

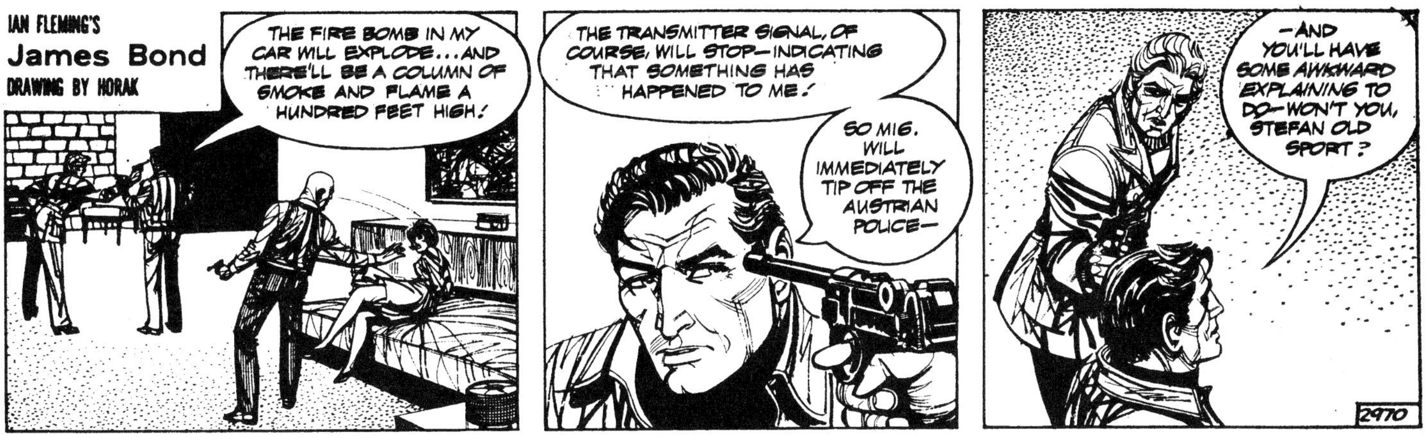
IAN FLEMING'S
James Bond
DRAWING BY HORAK
THE FIRE BOMB IN MY CAR WILL EXPLODE... AND THERE'LL BE A COLUMN OF SMOKE AND FLAME A HUNDRED FEET HIGH!
THE TRANSMITTER SIGNAL, OF COURSE, WILL STOP—INDICATING THAT SOMETHING HAS HAPPENED TO ME!
SO MI6. WILL IMMEDIATELY TIP OFF THE AUSTRIAN POLICE—
—AND YOU'LL HAVE SOME AWKWARD EXPLAINING TO DO—WON'T YOU, STEFAN OLD SPORT?
2970

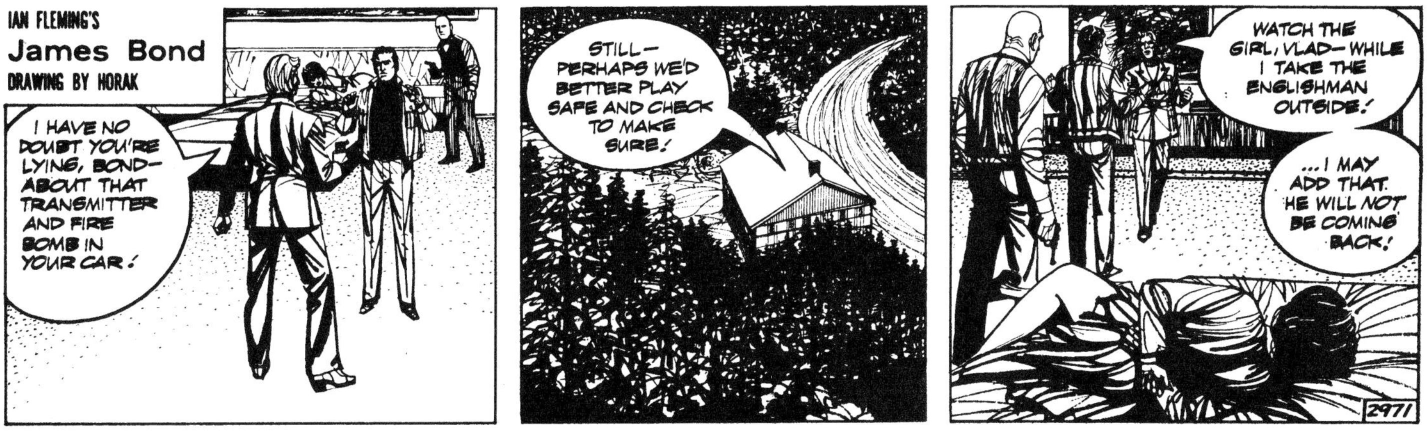
IAN FLEMING'S
James Bond
DRAWING BY HORAK
I HAVE NO DOUBT YOU'RE LYING, BOND—ABOUT THAT TRANSMITTER AND FIRE BOMB IN YOUR CAR!
STILL—PERHAPS WE'D BETTER PLAY SAFE AND CHECK TO MAKE SURE!
WATCH THE GIRL, VLAD—WHILE I TAKE THE ENGLISHMAN OUTSIDE!
...I MAY ADD THAT. HE WILL NOT BE COMING BACK!
2971

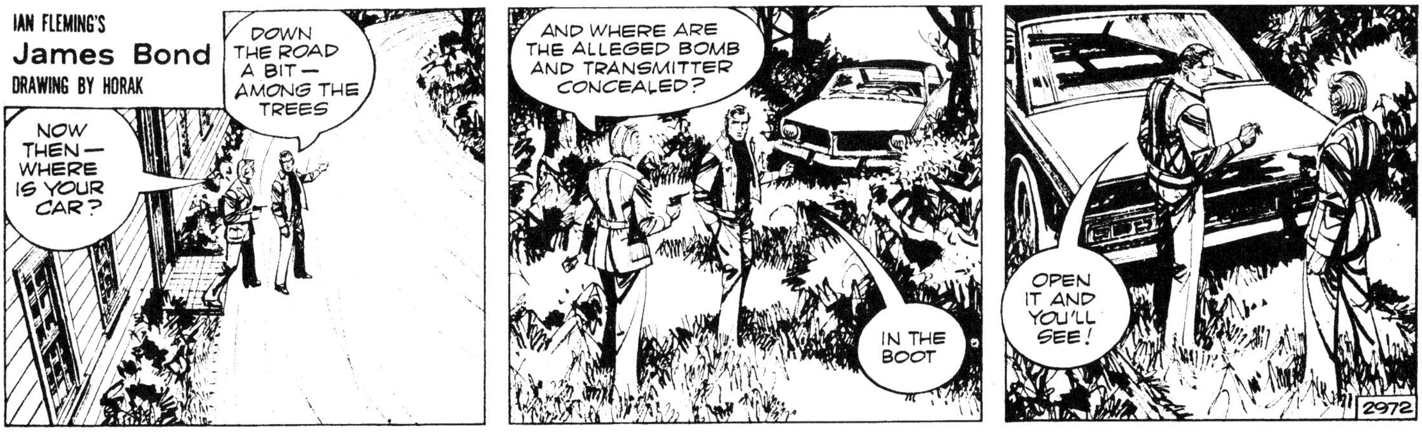
IAN FLEMING'S
James Bond
DRAWING BY HORAK
NOW THEN—WHERE IS YOUR CAR?
DOWN THE ROAD A BIT—AMONG THE TREES
AND WHERE ARE THE ALLEGED BOMB AND TRANSMITTER CONCEALED?
IN THE BOOT
OPEN IT AND YOU'LL SEE!
2972

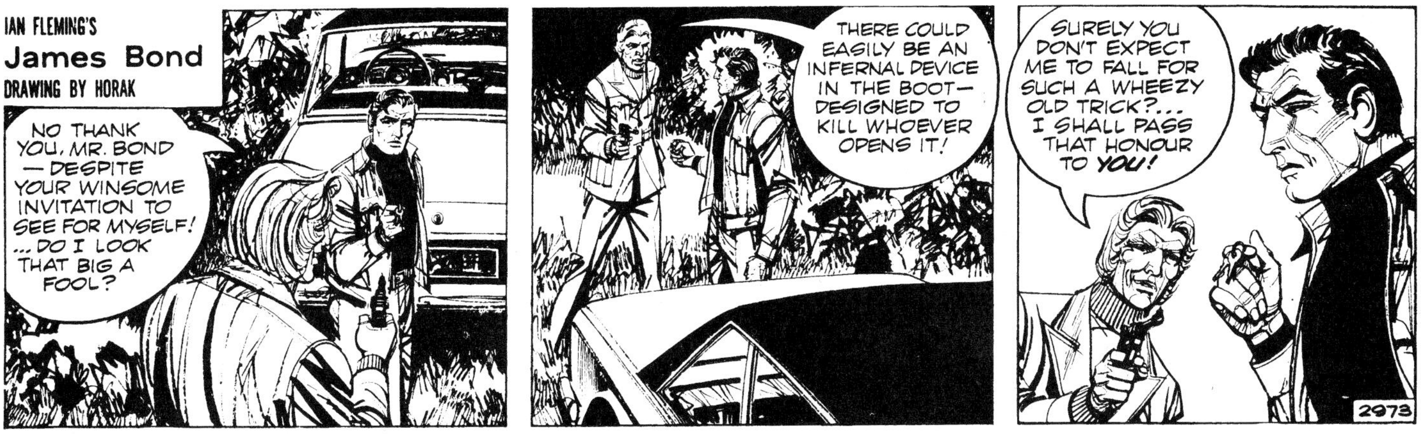
IAN FLEMING'S
James Bond
DRAWING BY HORAK
NO THANK YOU, MR. BOND—DESPITE YOUR WINSOME INVITATION TO SEE FOR MYSELF! ...DO I LOOK THAT BIG A FOOL?
THERE COULD EASILY BE AN INFERNAL DEVICE IN THE BOOT—DESIGNED TO KILL WHOEVER OPENS IT!
SURELY YOU DON'T EXPECT ME TO FALL FOR SUCH A WHEEZY OLD TRICK?... I SHALL PASS THAT HONOUR TO YOU!
2973

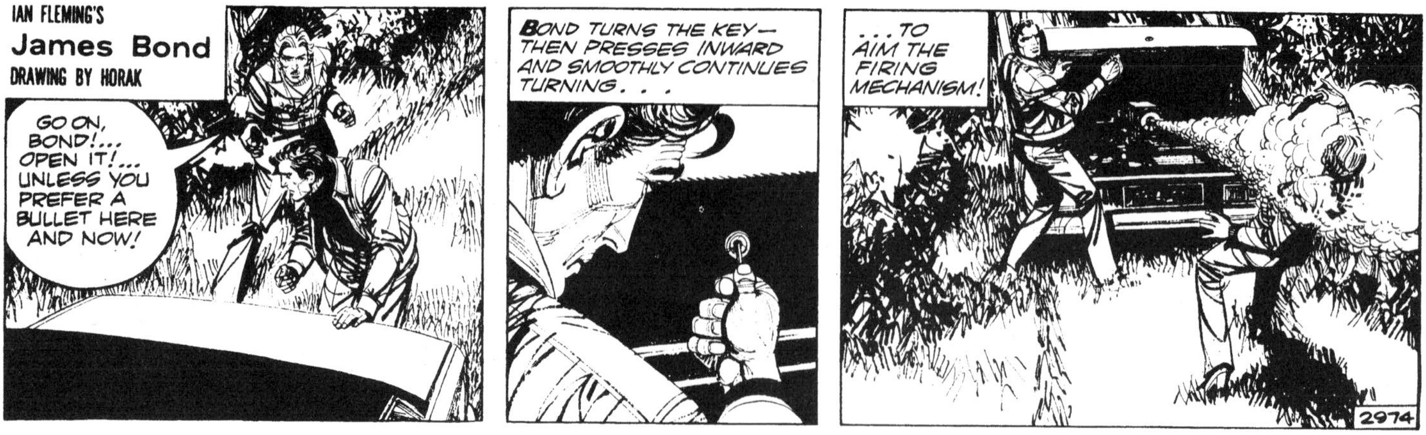
IAN FLEMING'S James Bond DRAWING BY HORAK
GO ON, BOND!... OPEN IT!... UNLESS YOU PREFER A BULLET HERE AND NOW!
BOND TURNS THE KEY— THEN PRESSES INWARD AND SMOOTHLY CONTINUES TURNING . . .
. . . TO AIM THE FIRING MECHANISM!
2974

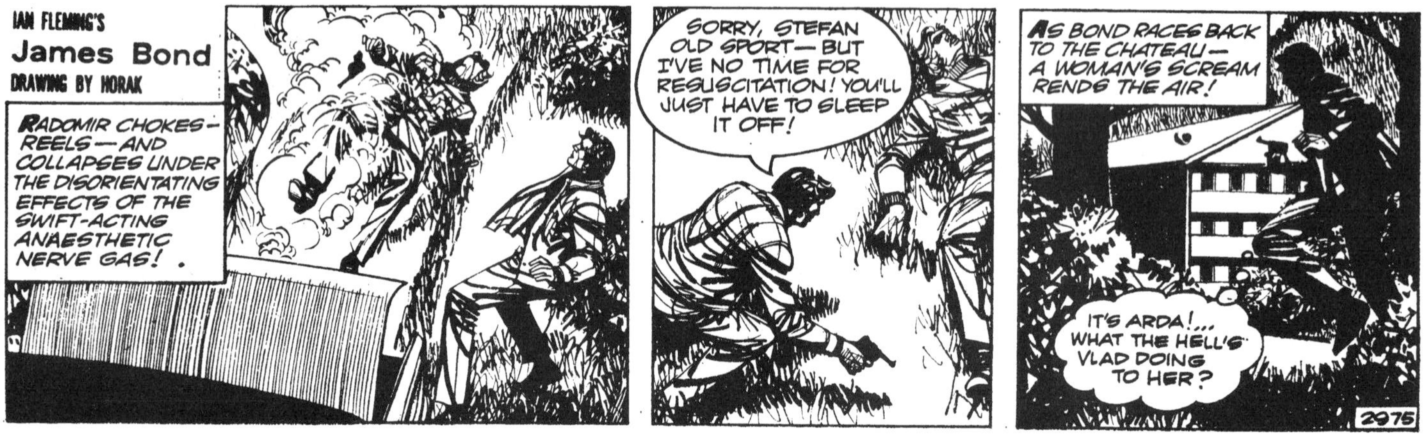
IAN FLEMING'S James Bond DRAWING BY HORAK
RADOMIR CHOKES- REELS—AND COLLAPSES UNDER THE DISORIENTATING EFFECTS OF THE SWIFT-ACTING ANAESTHETIC NERVE GAS!
SORRY, STEFAN OLD SPORT—BUT I'VE NO TIME FOR RESUSCITATION! YOU'LL JUST HAVE TO SLEEP IT OFF!
AS BOND RACES BACK TO THE CHATEAU— A WOMAN'S SCREAM RENDS THE AIR!
IT'S ARDA!... WHAT THE HELL'S VLAD DOING TO HER?
2975

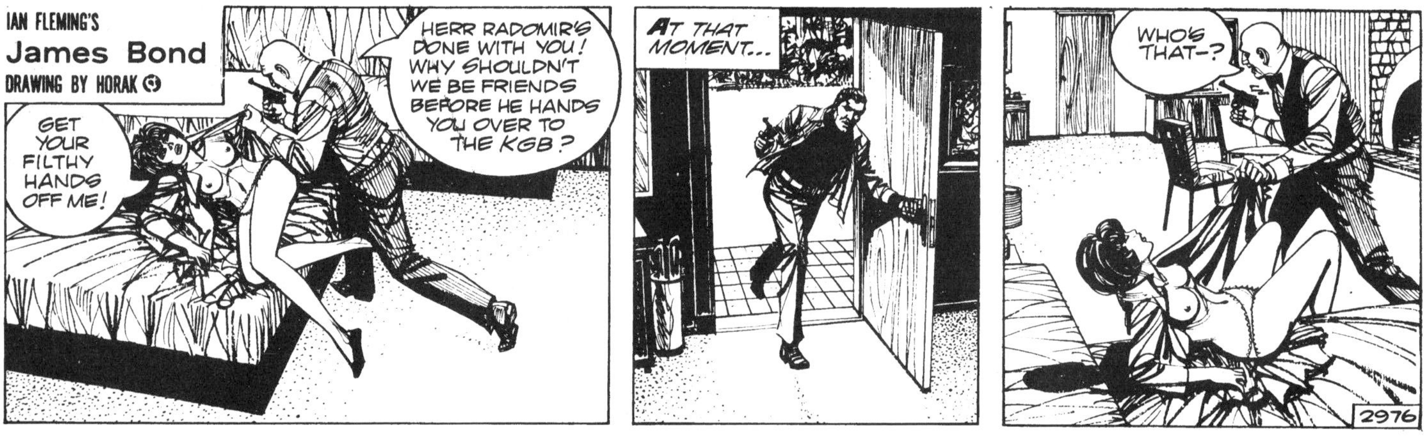
IAN FLEMING'S James Bond DRAWING BY HORAK ©
GET YOUR FILTHY HANDS OFF ME!
HERR RADOMIR'S DONE WITH YOU! WHY SHOULDN'T WE BE FRIENDS BEFORE HE HANDS YOU OVER TO THE KGB?
AT THAT MOMENT...
WHO'S THAT—?
2976

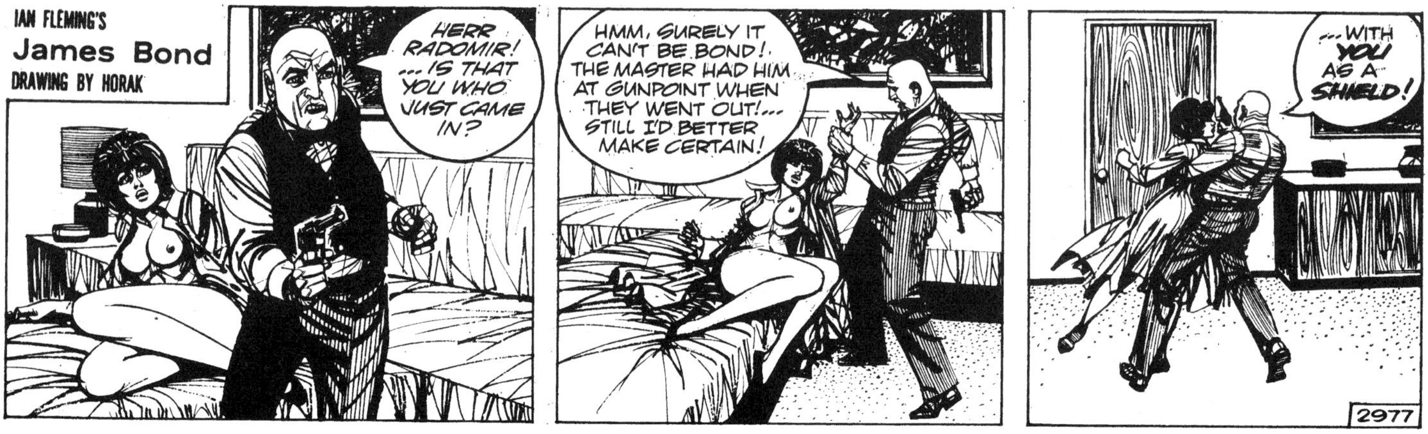
IAN FLEMING'S James Bond DRAWING BY HORAK
HERR RADOMIR! ...IS THAT YOU WHO JUST CAME IN?
HMM, SURELY IT CAN'T BE BOND! THE MASTER HAD HIM AT GUNPOINT WHEN THEY WENT OUT!... STILL I'D BETTER MAKE CERTAIN!
...WITH YOU AS A SHIELD!
2977

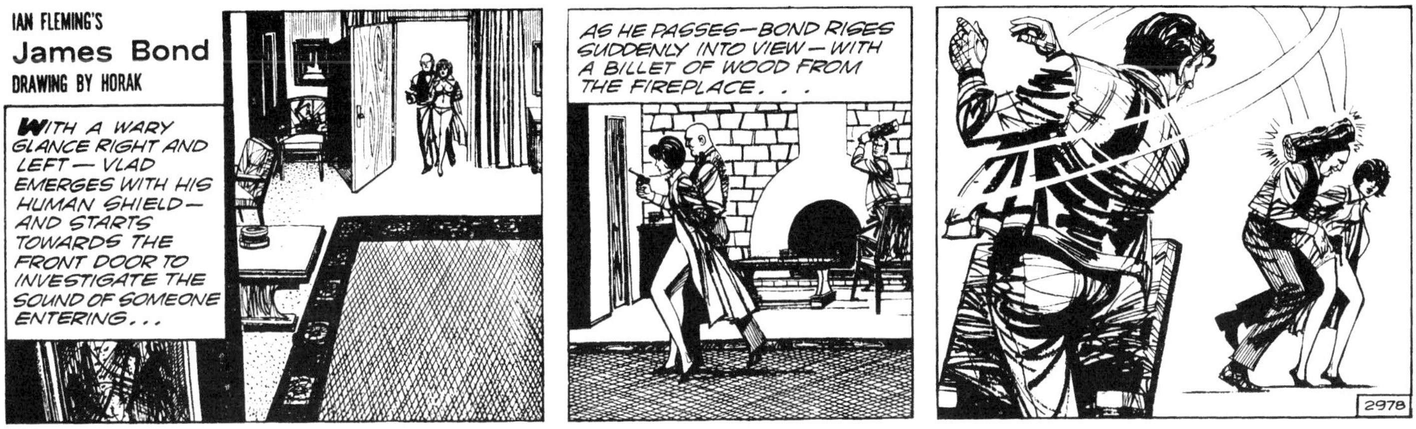
IAN FLEMING'S
James Bond
DRAWING BY HORAK
WITH A WARY GLANCE RIGHT AND LEFT — VLAD EMERGES WITH HIS HUMAN SHIELD — AND STARTS TOWARDS THE FRONT DOOR TO INVESTIGATE THE SOUND OF SOMEONE ENTERING . . .
AS HE PASSES—BOND RISES SUDDENLY INTO VIEW—WITH A BILLET OF WOOD FROM THE FIREPLACE . . .
2978

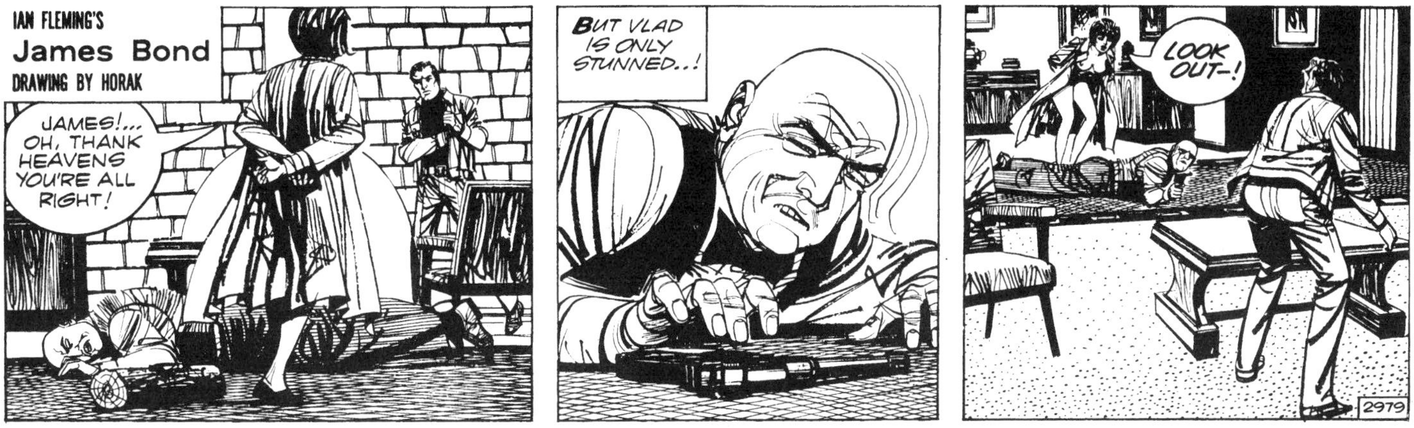
IAN FLEMING'S
James Bond
DRAWING BY HORAK
JAMES!... OH, THANK HEAVENS YOU'RE ALL RIGHT!
BUT VLAD IS ONLY STUNNED..!
LOOK OUT-!
2979

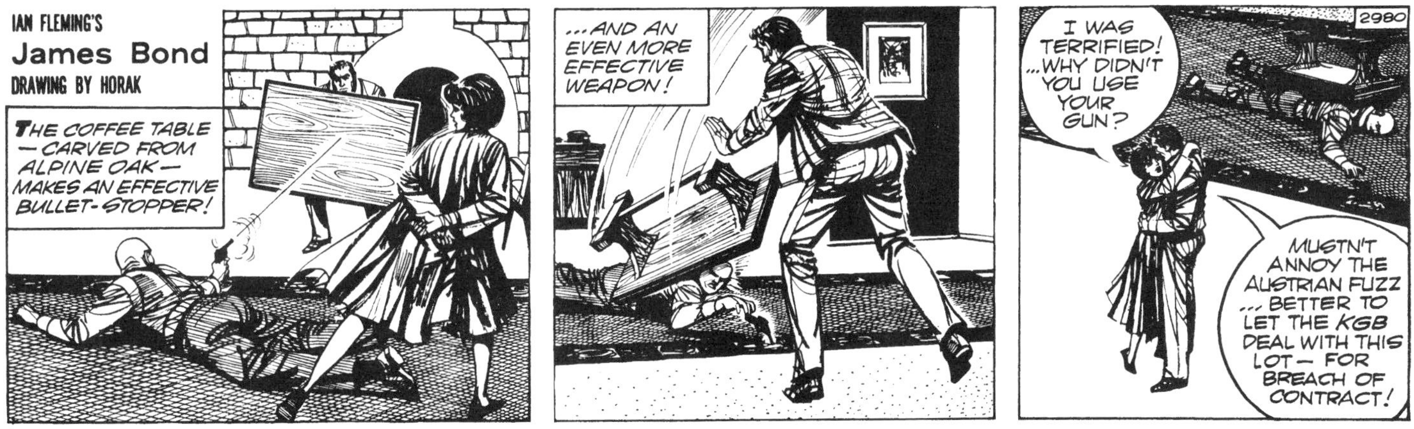
IAN FLEMING'S
James Bond
DRAWING BY HORAK
THE COFFEE TABLE — CARVED FROM ALPINE OAK — MAKES AN EFFECTIVE BULLET-STOPPER!
...AND AN EVEN MORE EFFECTIVE WEAPON!
2980
I WAS TERRIFIED! ...WHY DIDN'T YOU USE YOUR GUN?
MUSTN'T ANNOY THE AUSTRIAN FUZZ ... BETTER TO LET THE KGB DEAL WITH THIS LOT— FOR BREACH OF CONTRACT!

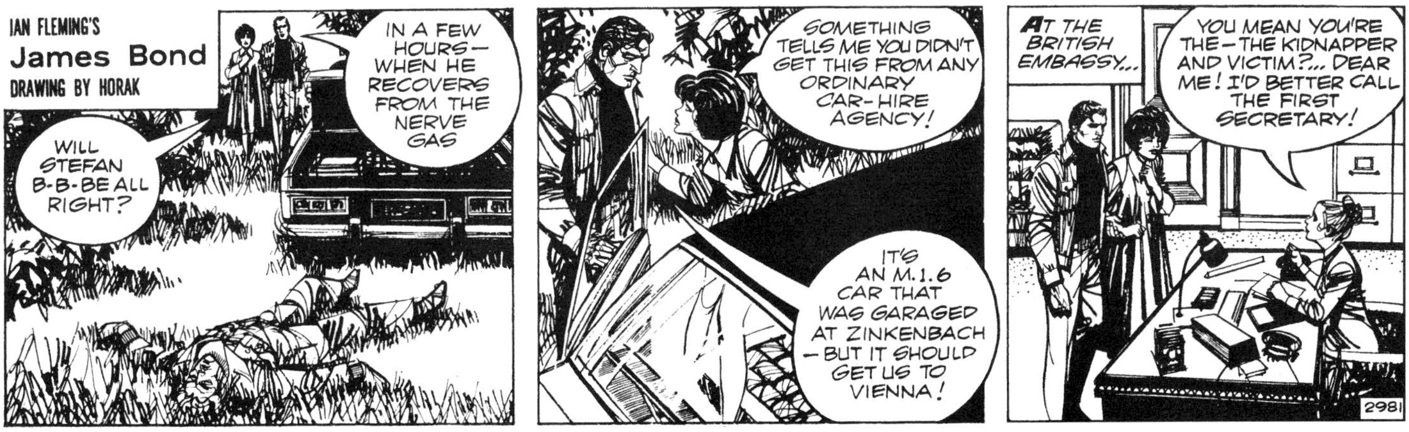
IAN FLEMING'S
James Bond
DRAWING BY HORAK
WILL STEFAN B-B-BE ALL RIGHT?
IN A FEW HOURS— WHEN HE RECOVERS FROM THE NERVE GAS
SOMETHING TELLS ME YOU DIDN'T GET THIS FROM ANY ORDINARY CAR-HIRE AGENCY!
IT'S AN M.1.6 CAR THAT WAS GARAGED AT ZINKENBACH — BUT IT SHOULD GET US TO VIENNA!
AT THE BRITISH EMBASSY...
YOU MEAN YOU'RE THE — THE KIDNAPPER AND VICTIM?... DEAR ME! I'D BETTER CALL THE FIRST SECRETARY!
2981

IAN FLEMING'S
James Bond
DRAWING BY HORAK
NOT ONLY DID JAMES NOT KIDNAP ME—HE WAS HELPING ME ESCAPE FROM HERR RADOMIR'S DISTASTEFUL AND UNWELCOME ATTENTIONS!
WELL—IS THE AUSTRIAN GOVERNMENT SATISFIED, GENTLEMEN? —OR DO YOU WISH TO INTERVIEW MISS PETRICH ALONE?
ON THE CONTRARY, HERR SECRETARY—IT WOULD APPEAR THOSE TWO WISH TO BE ALONE!
2982

IAN FLEMING'S
James Bond
DRAWING BY HORAK
OH, JAMES! I WAS HOPING FOR MORE TIME TO OURSELVES ONCE WE'RE BACK IN LONDON!
DON'T WORRY! AFTER WE MEET OUR RECEPTION COMMITTEE-
—I PROMISE YOU I'LL ARRANGE FOR SOME COSY PRIVACY!
I WONDER IF ARDA EVER THOUGHT THOSE KGB MEN MIGHT'VE BEEN FAKES?
MY DEAR MONEYPENNY! WHATEVER PUT THAT CYNICAL NOTION IN YOUR HEAD?
2983

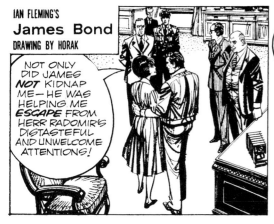

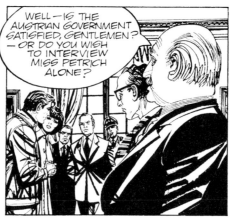

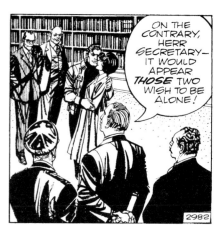

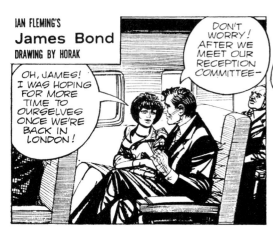

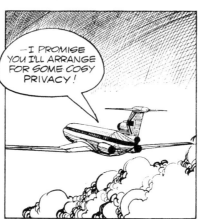

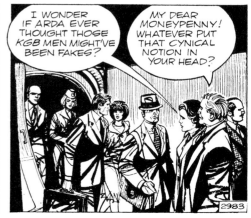

THE TORCH-TIME AFFAIR

A twist-filled tale with a healthy dose of sexual frisson, *The Torch-Time Affair* is less film-influenced than some of Lawrence's other tales, and provides Bond with another classic femme fatale antagonist in the form of Carmen Perez, as well as another appearance for Double-O agent Suzi Kew.

The story, in fact, almost works as a 'fair play' mystery — one which allows the reader to puzzle out the clues him- or her-self, based on visual clues in the story. Unfortunately, however, Bond doesn't reveal the significance of the fiery sword on Perez's key-ring until the mystery has been solved.

Horak's design for Carmen Perez is well-handled; the heavy black he puts into her eyebrows and around her eyes gives her face a rather cruel look, in keeping with her role in the plot.

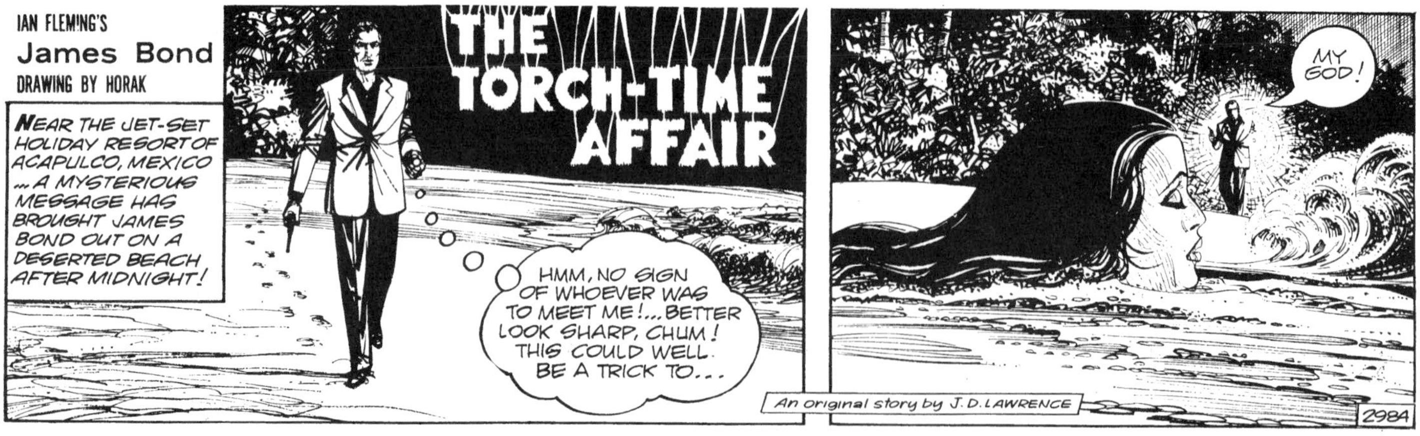
IAN FLEMING'S
James Bond
DRAWING BY HORAK
THE TORCH-TIME AFFAIR
NEAR THE JET-SET HOLIDAY RESORT OF ACAPULCO, MEXICO ... A MYSTERIOUS MESSAGE HAS BROUGHT JAMES BOND OUT ON A DESERTED BEACH AFTER MIDNIGHT!
HMM, NO SIGN OF WHOEVER WAS TO MEET ME!... BETTER LOOK SHARP, CHUM! THIS COULD WELL BE A TRICK TO...
MY GOD!
An original story by J.D.LAWRENCE
2984

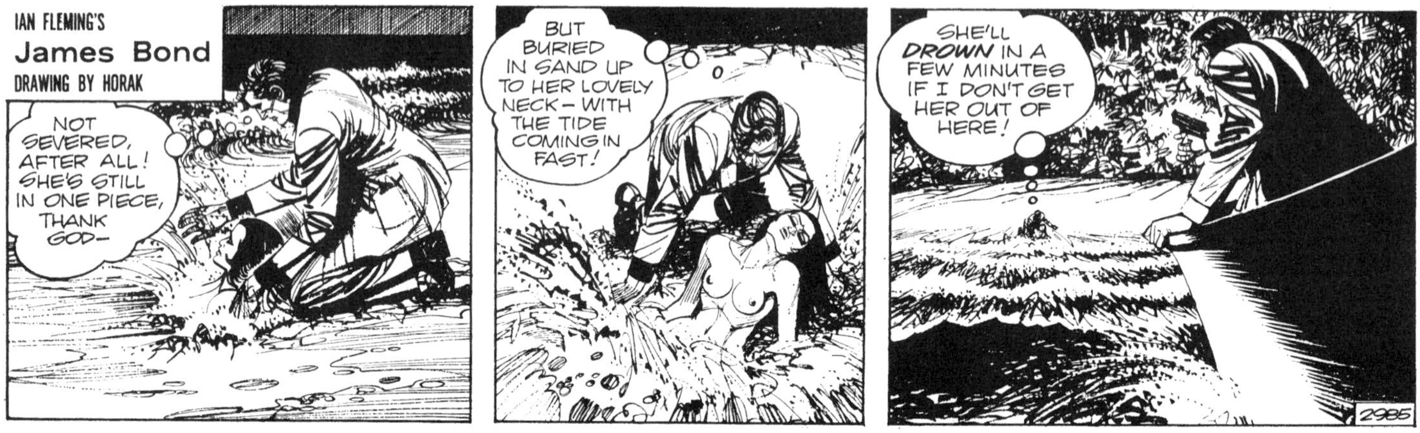
IAN FLEMING'S
James Bond
DRAWING BY HORAK
NOT SEVERED, AFTER ALL! SHE'S STILL IN ONE PIECE, THANK GOD–
BUT BURIED IN SAND UP TO HER LOVELY NECK – WITH THE TIDE COMING IN FAST!
SHE'LL DROWN IN A FEW MINUTES IF I DON'T GET HER OUT OF HERE!
2985

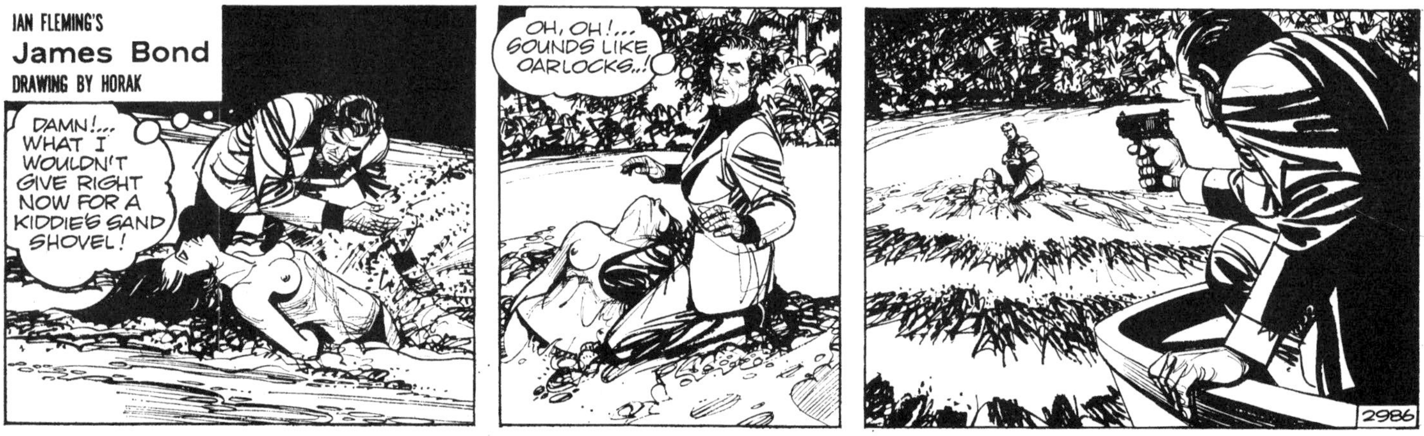
IAN FLEMING'S
James Bond
DRAWING BY HORAK
DAMN!... WHAT I WOULDN'T GIVE RIGHT NOW FOR A KIDDIE'S SAND SHOVEL!
OH, OH!... SOUNDS LIKE OARLOCKS..!
2986

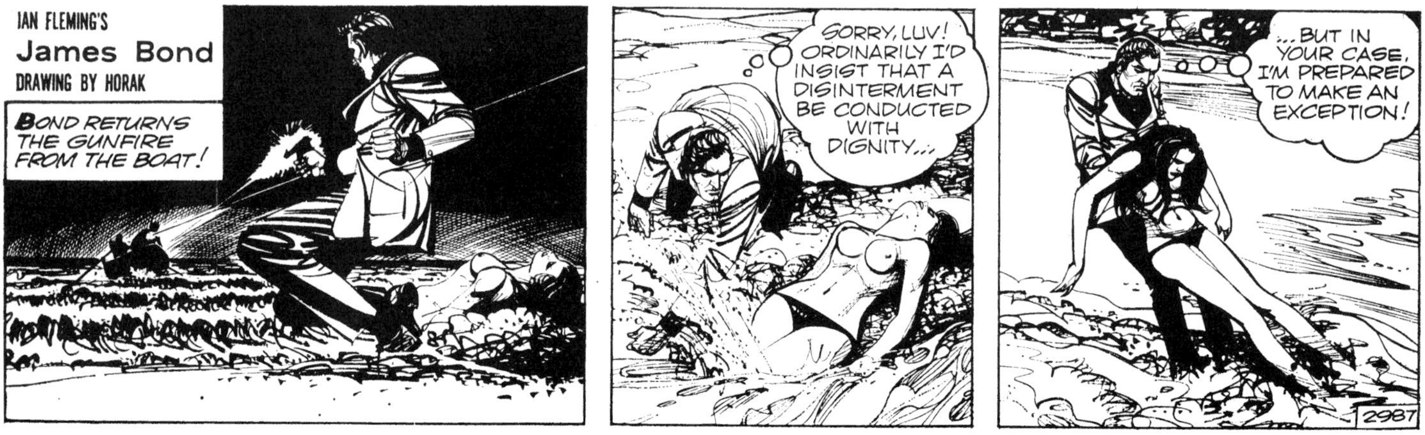
IAN FLEMING'S
James Bond
DRAWING BY HORAK
BOND RETURNS THE GUNFIRE FROM THE BOAT!
SORRY, LUV! ORDINARILY I'D INSIST THAT A DISINTERMENT BE CONDUCTED WITH DIGNITY...
...BUT IN YOUR CASE, I'M PREPARED TO MAKE AN EXCEPTION!
2987

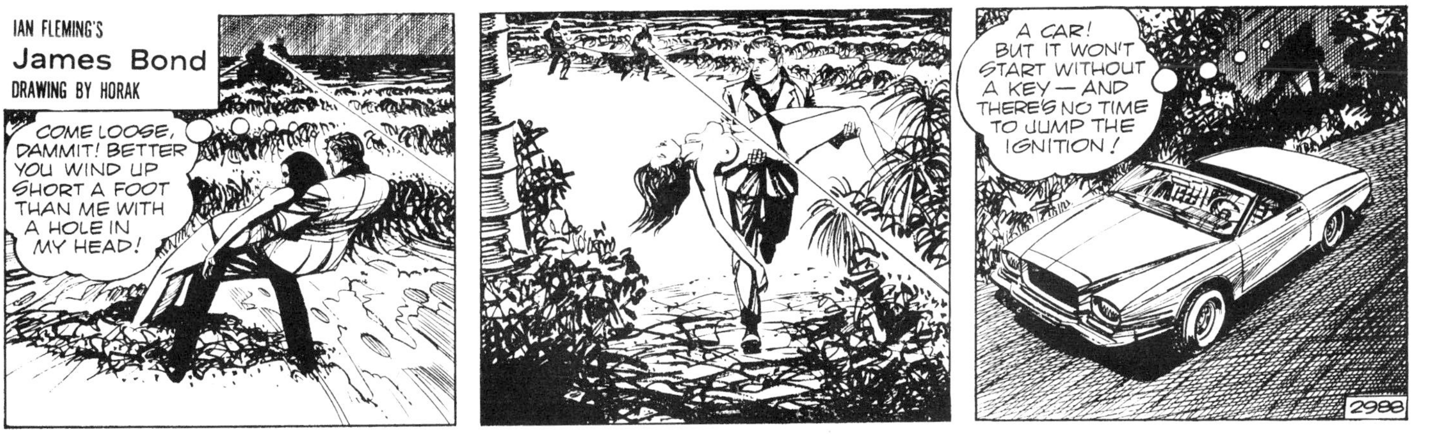
IAN FLEMING'S
James Bond
DRAWING BY HORAK
COME LOOSE, DAMMIT! BETTER YOU WIND UP SHORT A FOOT THAN ME WITH A HOLE IN MY HEAD!
A CAR! BUT IT WON'T START WITHOUT A KEY — AND THERE'S NO TIME TO JUMP THE IGNITION!
2988

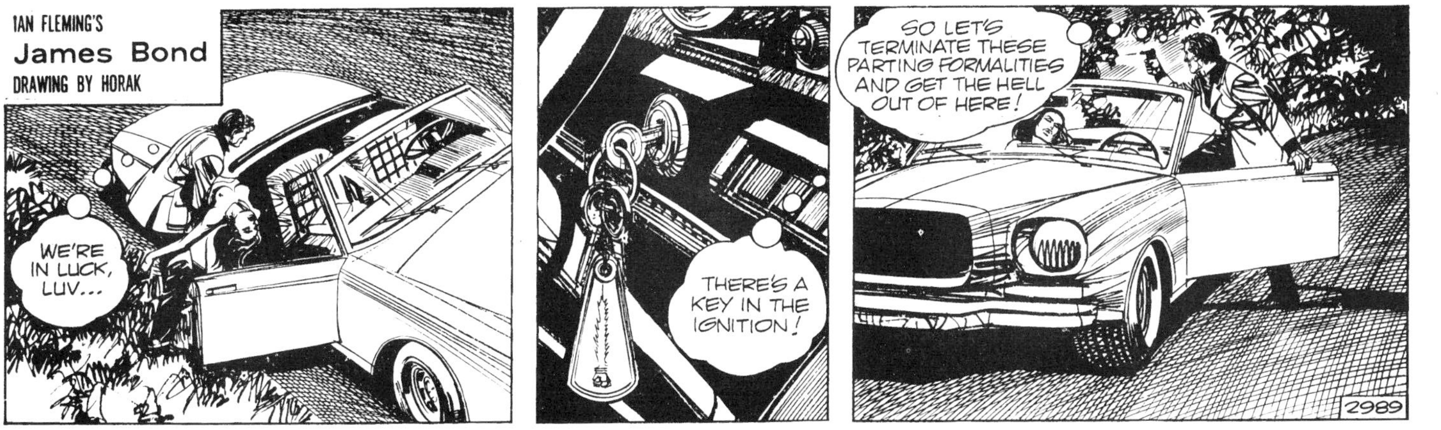
IAN FLEMING'S
James Bond
DRAWING BY HORAK
WE'RE IN LUCK, LUV...
THERE'S A KEY IN THE IGNITION!
SO LET'S TERMINATE THESE PARTING FORMALITIES AND GET THE HELL OUT OF HERE!
2989

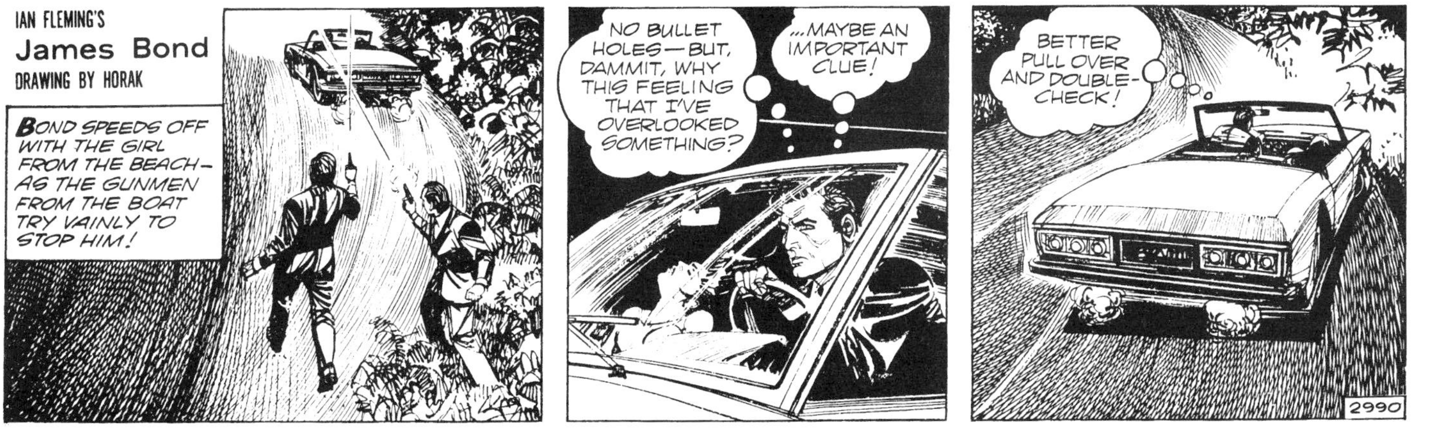
IAN FLEMING'S
James Bond
DRAWING BY HORAK
BOND SPEEDS OFF WITH THE GIRL FROM THE BEACH – AS THE GUNMEN FROM THE BOAT TRY VAINLY TO STOP HIM!
NO BULLET HOLES — BUT, DAMMIT, WHY THIS FEELING THAT I'VE OVERLOOKED SOMETHING?
...MAYBE AN IMPORTANT CLUE!
BETTER PULL OVER AND DOUBLE-CHECK!
2990

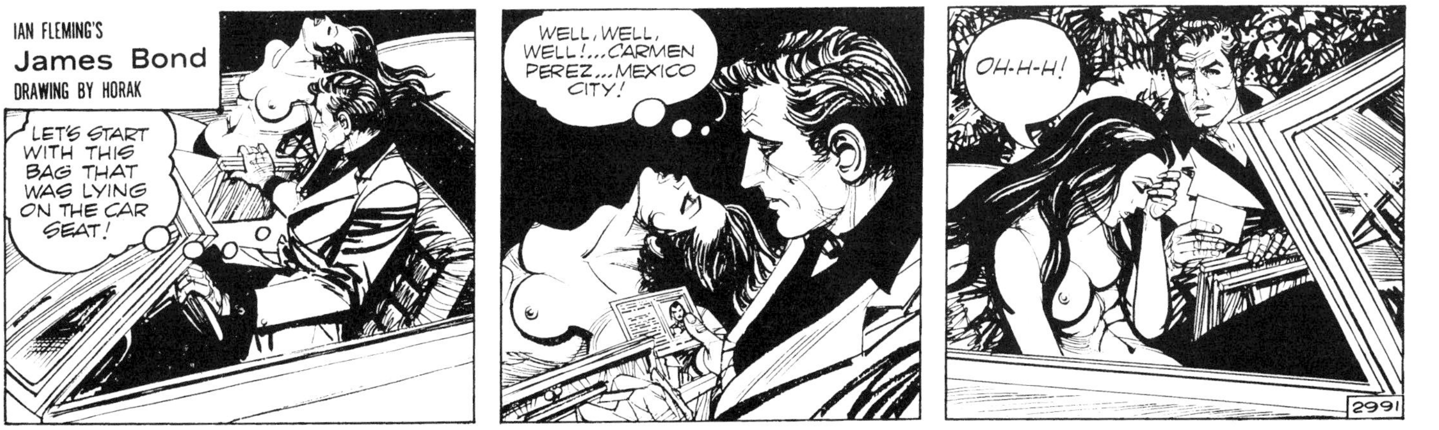
IAN FLEMING'S
James Bond
DRAWING BY HORAK
LET'S START WITH THIS BAG THAT WAS LYING ON THE CAR SEAT!
WELL, WELL, WELL!...CARMEN PEREZ...MEXICO CITY!
OH-H-H!
2991

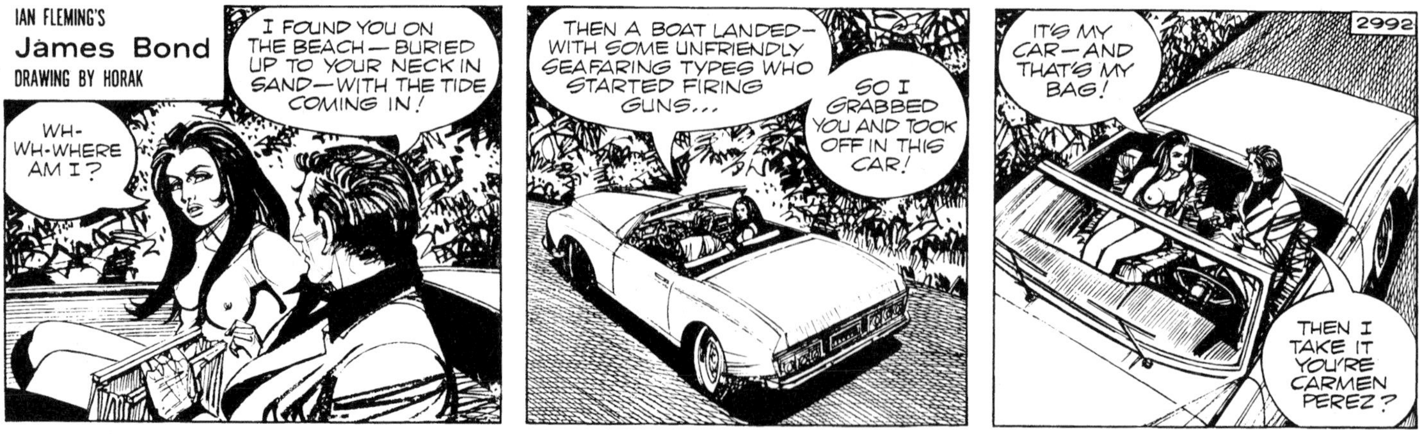
IAN FLEMING'S
James Bond
DRAWING BY HORAK
I FOUND YOU ON THE BEACH—BURIED UP TO YOUR NECK IN SAND—WITH THE TIDE COMING IN!
WH-WH-WHERE AM I?
THEN A BOAT LANDED—WITH SOME UNFRIENDLY SEAFARING TYPES WHO STARTED FIRING GUNS...
SO I GRABBED YOU AND TOOK OFF IN THIS CAR!
2992
IT'S MY CAR—AND THAT'S MY BAG!
THEN I TAKE IT YOU'RE CARMEN PEREZ?

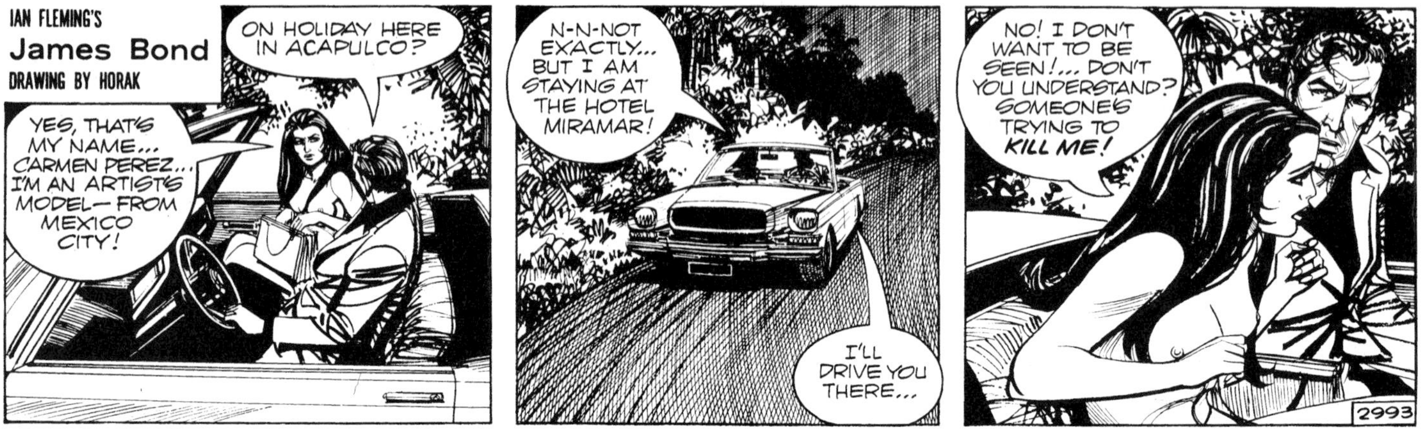
IAN FLEMING'S
James Bond
DRAWING BY HORAK
ON HOLIDAY HERE IN ACAPULCO?
YES, THAT'S MY NAME... CARMEN PEREZ... I'M AN ARTIST'S MODEL—FROM MEXICO CITY!
N-N-NOT EXACTLY... BUT I AM STAYING AT THE HOTEL MIRAMAR!
I'LL DRIVE YOU THERE...
NO! I DON'T WANT TO BE SEEN!... DON'T YOU UNDERSTAND? SOMEONE'S TRYING TO KILL ME!
2993

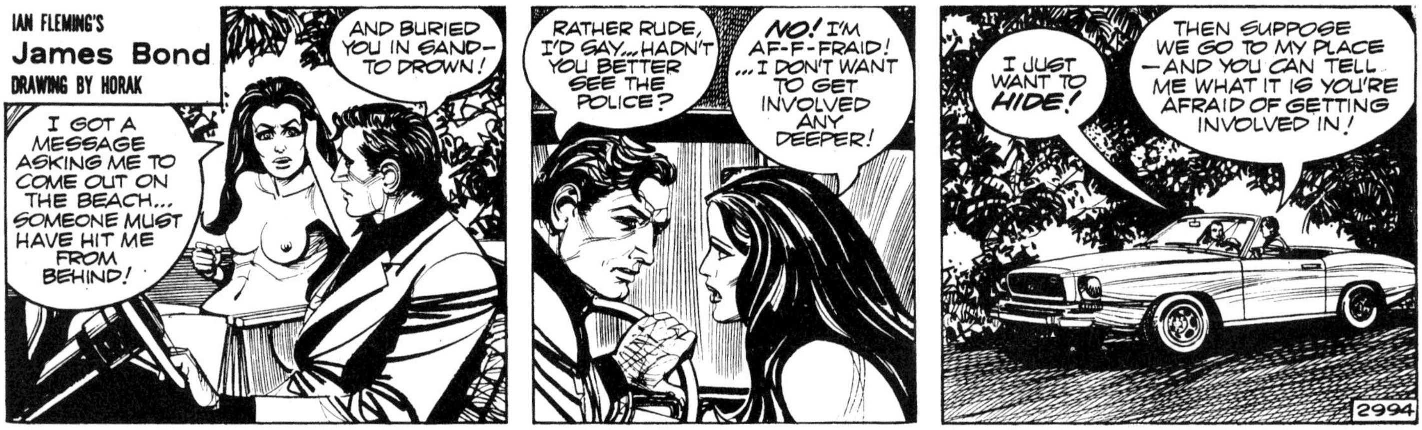
IAN FLEMING'S
James Bond
DRAWING BY HORAK
AND BURIED YOU IN SAND—TO DROWN!
I GOT A MESSAGE ASKING ME TO COME OUT ON THE BEACH... SOMEONE MUST HAVE HIT ME FROM BEHIND!
RATHER RUDE, I'D SAY... HADN'T YOU BETTER SEE THE POLICE?
NO! I'M AF-F-FRAID! ...I DON'T WANT TO GET INVOLVED ANY DEEPER!
I JUST WANT TO HIDE!
THEN SUPPOSE WE GO TO MY PLACE—AND YOU CAN TELL ME WHAT IT IS YOU'RE AFRAID OF GETTING INVOLVED IN!
2994

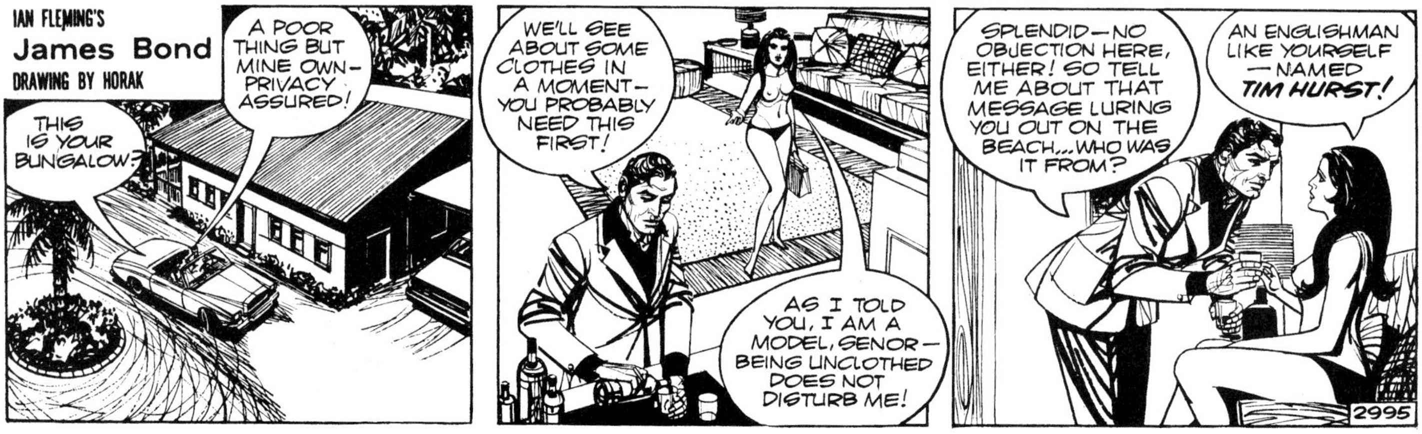
IAN FLEMING'S
James Bond
DRAWING BY HORAK
A POOR THING BUT MINE OWN—PRIVACY ASSURED!
THIS IS YOUR BUNGALOW?
WE'LL SEE ABOUT SOME CLOTHES IN A MOMENT—YOU PROBABLY NEED THIS FIRST!
AS I TOLD YOU, I AM A MODEL, SENOR—BEING UNCLOTHED DOES NOT DISTURB ME!
SPLENDID—NO OBJECTION HERE, EITHER! SO TELL ME ABOUT THAT MESSAGE LURING YOU OUT ON THE BEACH... WHO WAS IT FROM?
AN ENGLISHMAN LIKE YOURSELF—NAMED TIM HURST!
2995

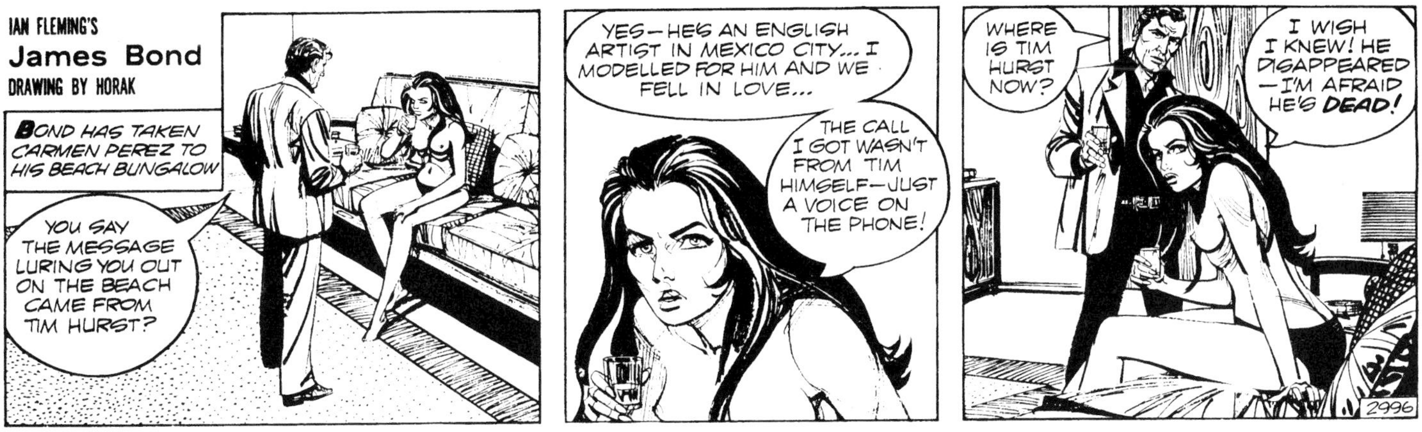
IAN FLEMING'S
James Bond
DRAWING BY HORAK
BOND HAS TAKEN CARMEN PEREZ TO HIS BEACH BUNGALOW
YOU SAY THE MESSAGE LURING YOU OUT ON THE BEACH CAME FROM TIM HURST?
YES—HE'S AN ENGLISH ARTIST IN MEXICO CITY... I MODELLED FOR HIM AND WE FELL IN LOVE...
THE CALL I GOT WASN'T FROM TIM HIMSELF—JUST A VOICE ON THE PHONE!
WHERE IS TIM HURST NOW?
I WISH I KNEW! HE DISAPPEARED —I'M AFRAID HE'S DEAD!
2996

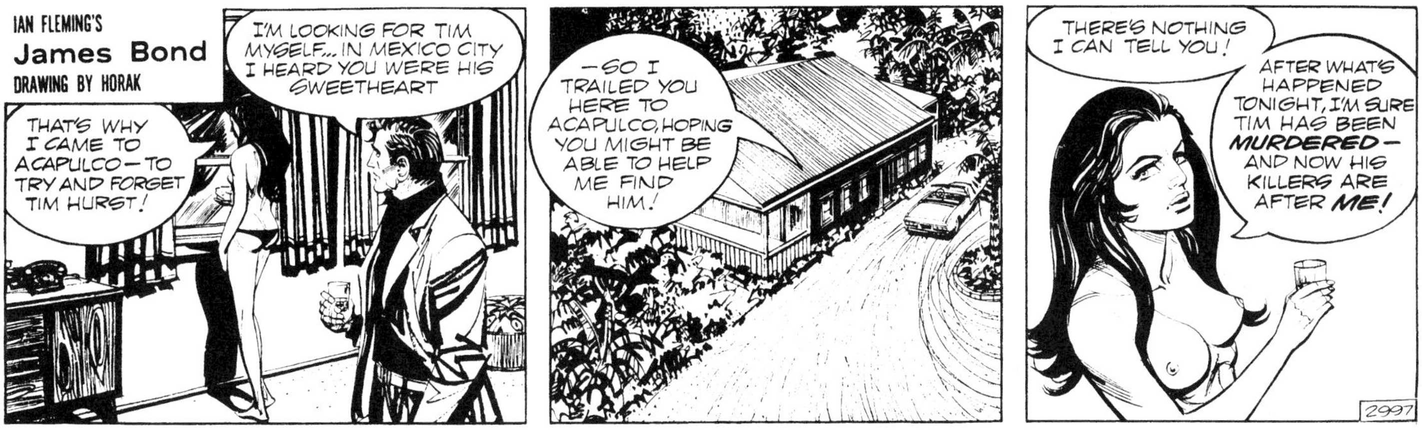
IAN FLEMING'S
James Bond
DRAWING BY HORAK
I'M LOOKING FOR TIM MYSELF... IN MEXICO CITY I HEARD YOU WERE HIS SWEETHEART
THAT'S WHY I CAME TO ACAPULCO—TO TRY AND FORGET TIM HURST!
—SO I TRAILED YOU HERE TO ACAPULCO, HOPING YOU MIGHT BE ABLE TO HELP ME FIND HIM!
THERE'S NOTHING I CAN TELL YOU!
AFTER WHAT'S HAPPENED TONIGHT, I'M SURE TIM HAS BEEN MURDERED—AND NOW HIS KILLERS ARE AFTER ME!
2997

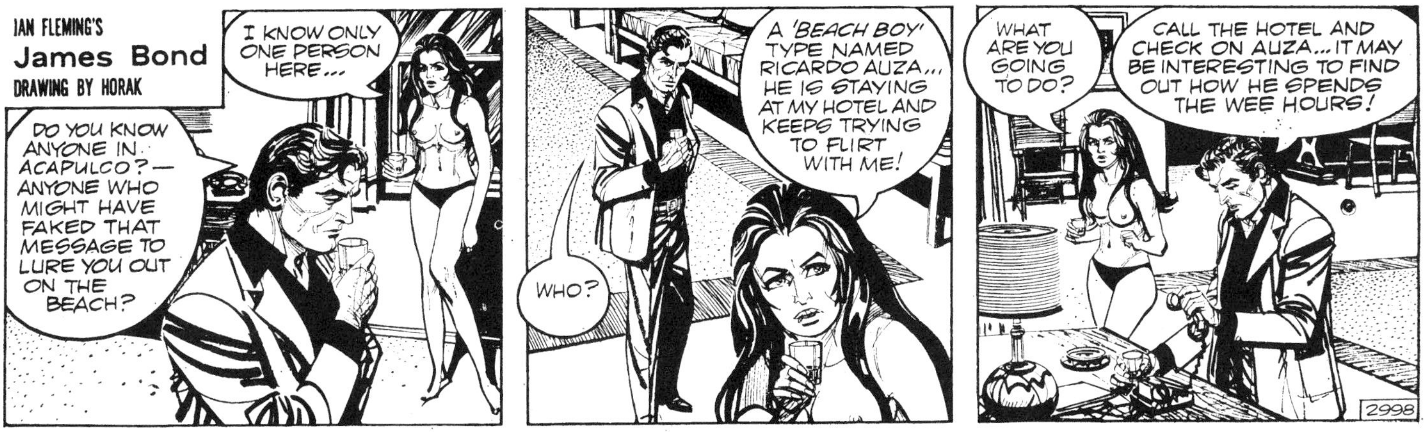
IAN FLEMING'S
James Bond
DRAWING BY HORAK
DO YOU KNOW ANYONE IN ACAPULCO?—ANYONE WHO MIGHT HAVE FAKED THAT MESSAGE TO LURE YOU OUT ON THE BEACH?
I KNOW ONLY ONE PERSON HERE...
WHO?
A 'BEACH BOY' TYPE NAMED RICARDO AUZA... HE IS STAYING AT MY HOTEL AND KEEPS TRYING TO FLIRT WITH ME!
WHAT ARE YOU GOING TO DO?
CALL THE HOTEL AND CHECK ON AUZA... IT MAY BE INTERESTING TO FIND OUT HOW HE SPENDS THE WEE HOURS!
2998

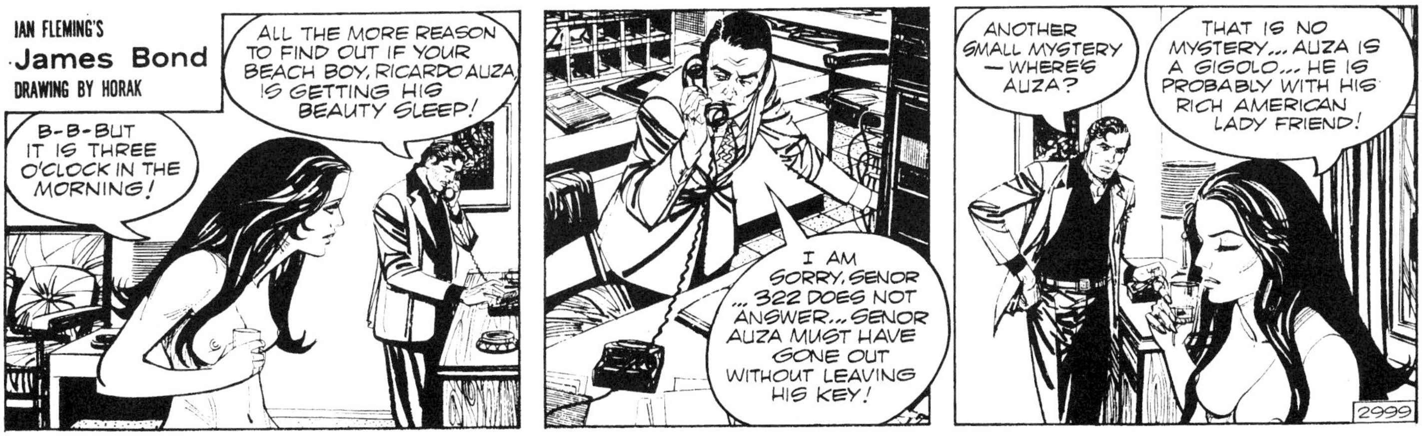
IAN FLEMING'S
James Bond
DRAWING BY HORAK
ALL THE MORE REASON TO FIND OUT IF YOUR BEACH BOY, RICARDO AUZA IS GETTING HIS BEAUTY SLEEP!
B-B-BUT IT IS THREE O'CLOCK IN THE MORNING!
I AM SORRY, SENOR ... 322 DOES NOT ANSWER... SENOR AUZA MUST HAVE GONE OUT WITHOUT LEAVING HIS KEY!
ANOTHER SMALL MYSTERY —WHERE'S AUZA?
THAT IS NO MYSTERY... AUZA IS A GIGOLO... HE IS PROBABLY WITH HIS RICH AMERICAN LADY FRIEND!
2999

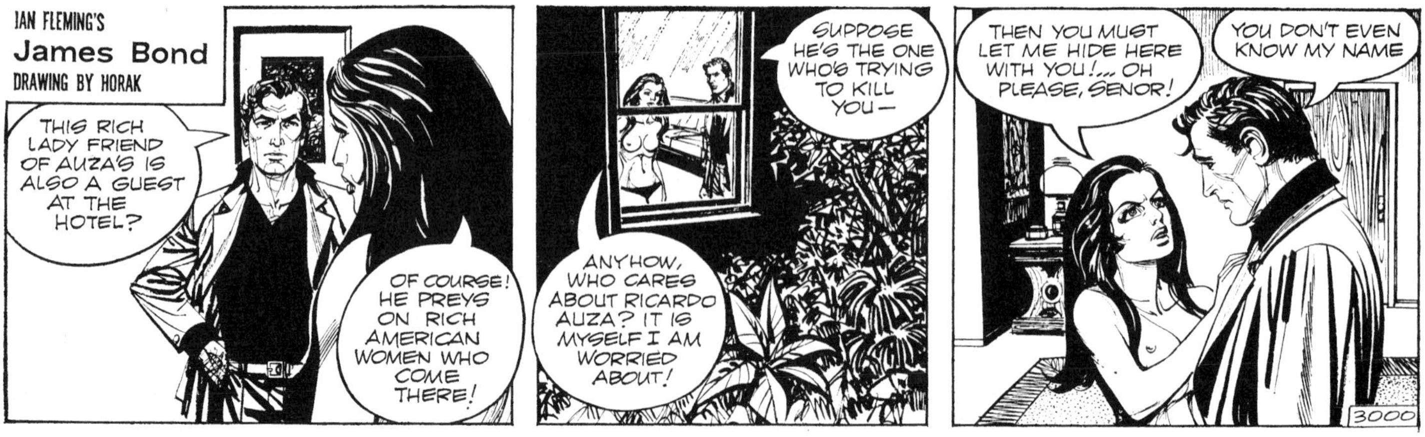
IAN FLEMING'S
James Bond
DRAWING BY HORAK
THIS RICH LADY FRIEND OF AUZA'S IS ALSO A GUEST AT THE HOTEL?
OF COURSE! HE PREYS ON RICH AMERICAN WOMEN WHO COME THERE!
SUPPOSE HE'S THE ONE WHO'S TRYING TO KILL YOU—
ANYHOW, WHO CARES ABOUT RICARDO AUZA? IT IS MYSELF I AM WORRIED ABOUT!
THEN YOU MUST LET ME HIDE HERE WITH YOU!... OH PLEASE, SENOR!
YOU DON'T EVEN KNOW MY NAME
3000

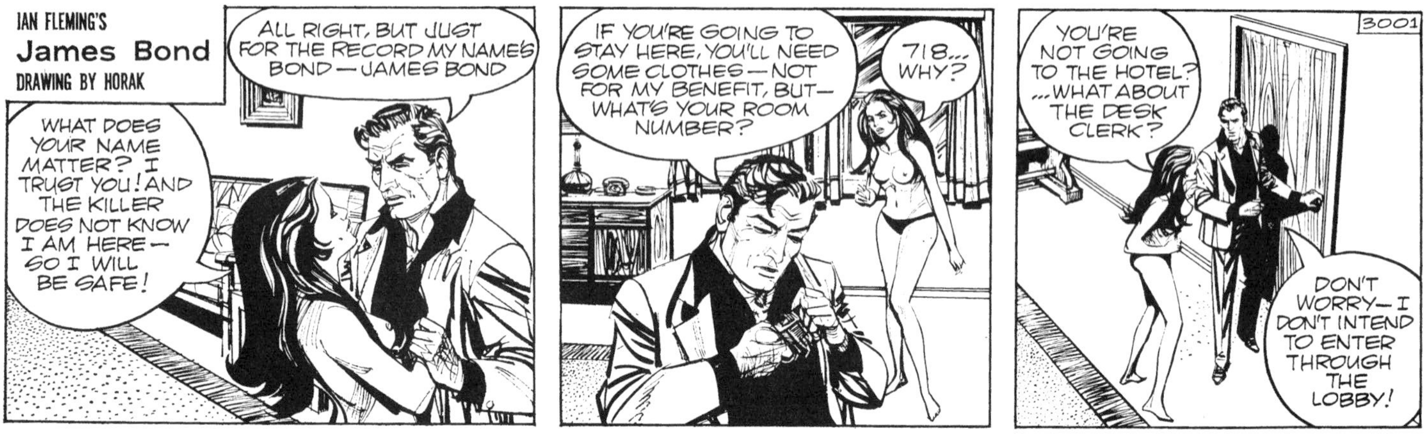
IAN FLEMING'S
James Bond
DRAWING BY HORAK
ALL RIGHT, BUT JUST FOR THE RECORD MY NAME'S BOND — JAMES BOND
WHAT DOES YOUR NAME MATTER? I TRUST YOU! AND THE KILLER DOES NOT KNOW I AM HERE— SO I WILL BE SAFE!
IF YOU'RE GOING TO STAY HERE, YOU'LL NEED SOME CLOTHES — NOT FOR MY BENEFIT, BUT— WHAT'S YOUR ROOM NUMBER?
718... WHY?
3001
YOU'RE NOT GOING TO THE HOTEL? ...WHAT ABOUT THE DESK CLERK?
DON'T WORRY—I DON'T INTEND TO ENTER THROUGH THE LOBBY!

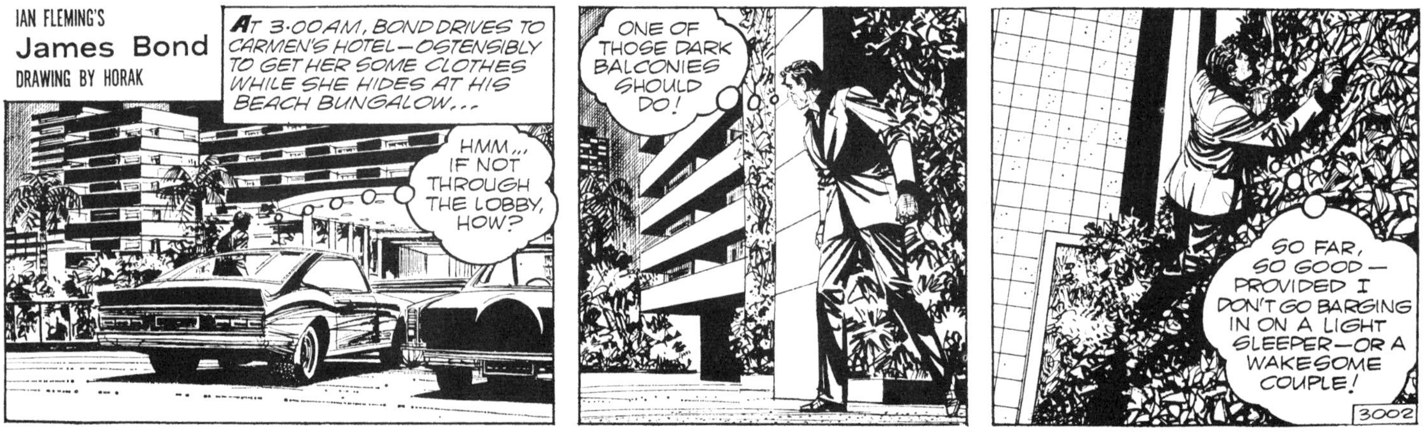
IAN FLEMING'S
James Bond
DRAWING BY HORAK
AT 3.00 AM, BOND DRIVES TO CARMEN'S HOTEL — OSTENSIBLY TO GET HER SOME CLOTHES WHILE SHE HIDES AT HIS BEACH BUNGALOW...
HMM... IF NOT THROUGH THE LOBBY, HOW?
ONE OF THOSE DARK BALCONIES SHOULD DO!
SO FAR, SO GOOD — PROVIDED I DON'T GO BARGING IN ON A LIGHT SLEEPER—OR A WAKESOME COUPLE!
3002

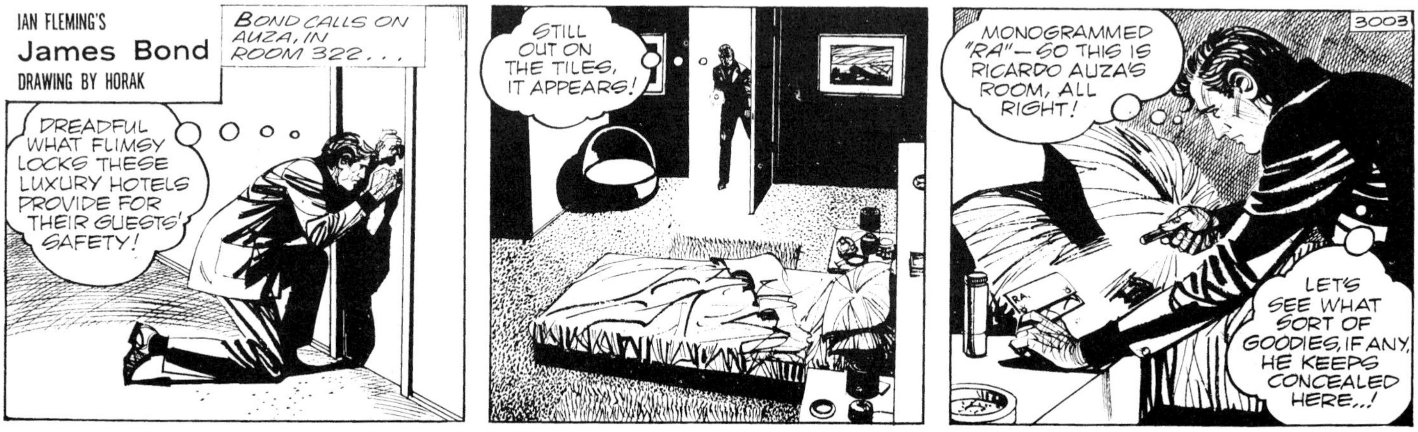
IAN FLEMING'S
James Bond
DRAWING BY HORAK
BOND CALLS ON AUZA, IN ROOM 322...
DREADFUL WHAT FLIMSY LOCKS THESE LUXURY HOTELS PROVIDE FOR THEIR GUESTS' SAFETY!
STILL OUT ON THE TILES, IT APPEARS!
3003
MONOGRAMMED "RA"— SO THIS IS RICARDO AUZA'S ROOM, ALL RIGHT!
LET'S SEE WHAT SORT OF GOODIES, IF ANY, HE KEEPS CONCEALED HERE...!

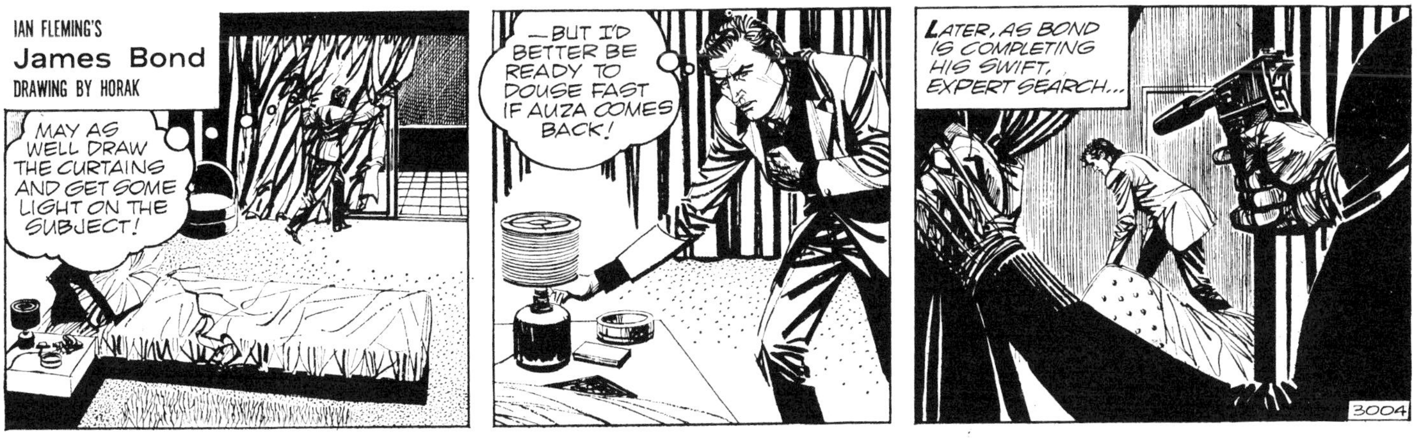
IAN FLEMING'S
James Bond
DRAWING BY HORAK
MAY AS WELL DRAW THE CURTAINS AND GET SOME LIGHT ON THE SUBJECT!
—BUT I'D BETTER BE READY TO DOUSE FAST IF AUZA COMES BACK!
LATER, AS BOND IS COMPLETING HIS SWIFT, EXPERT SEARCH...
3004

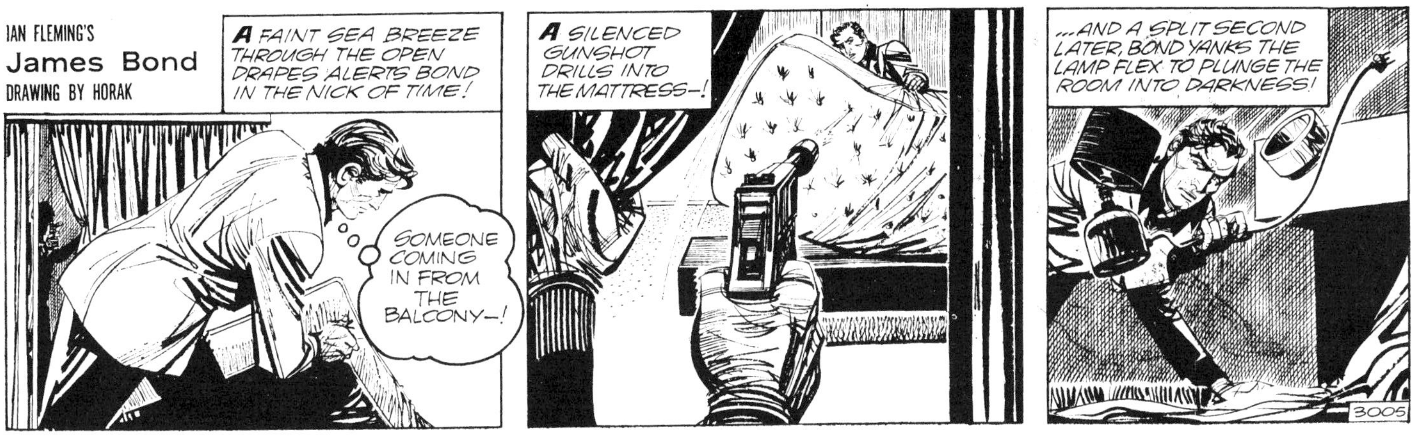
IAN FLEMING'S
James Bond
DRAWING BY HORAK
A FAINT SEA BREEZE THROUGH THE OPEN DRAPES ALERTS BOND IN THE NICK OF TIME!
SOMEONE COMING IN FROM THE BALCONY—!
A SILENCED GUNSHOT DRILLS INTO THE MATTRESS—!
...AND A SPLIT SECOND LATER, BOND YANKS THE LAMP FLEX TO PLUNGE THE ROOM INTO DARKNESS!
3005

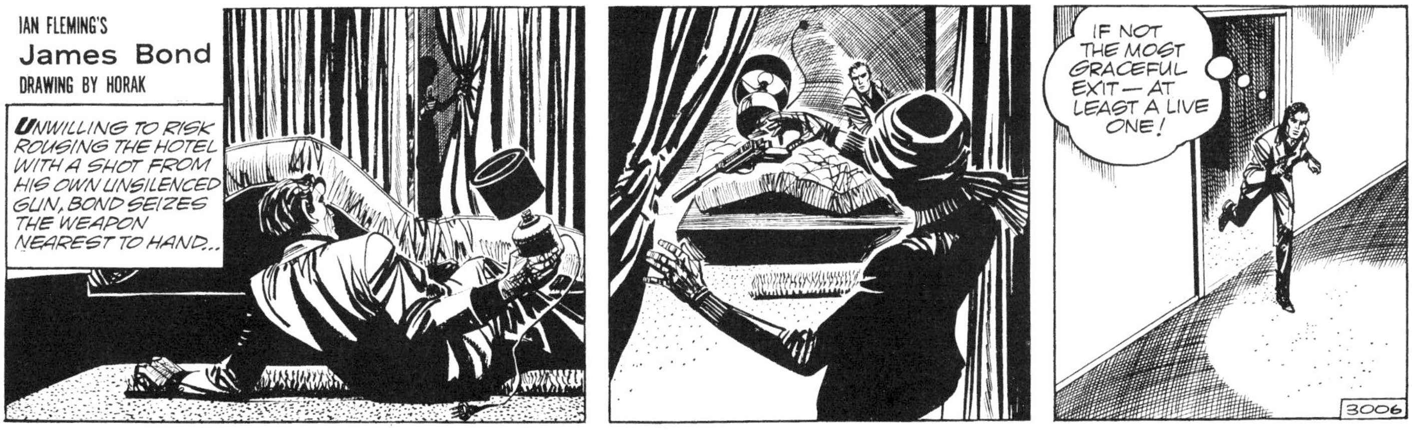
IAN FLEMING'S
James Bond
DRAWING BY HORAK
UNWILLING TO RISK ROUSING THE HOTEL WITH A SHOT FROM HIS OWN UNSILENCED GUN, BOND SEIZES THE WEAPON NEAREST TO HAND...
IF NOT THE MOST GRACEFUL EXIT — AT LEAST A LIVE ONE!
3006

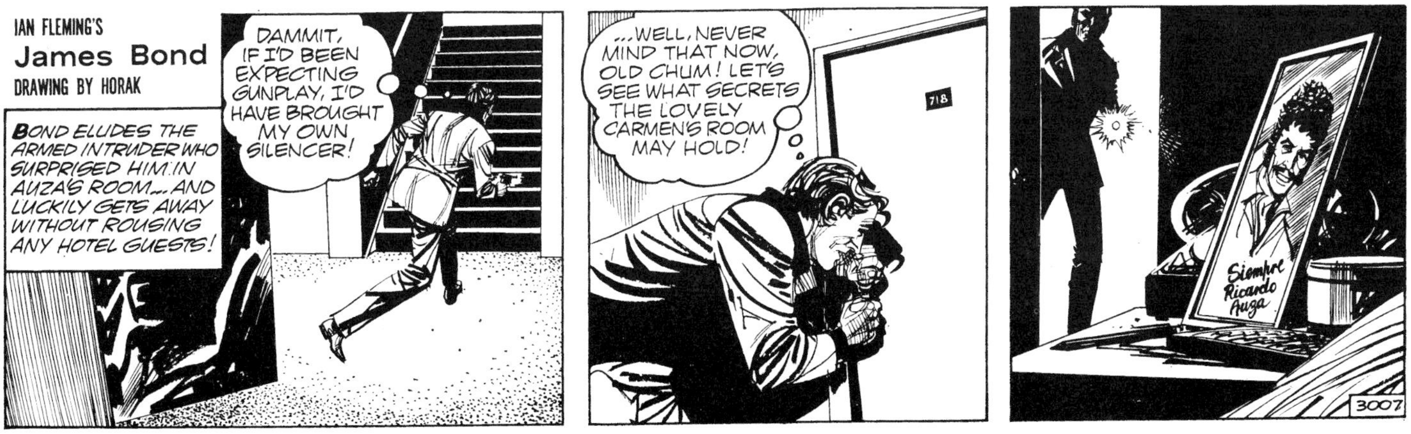
IAN FLEMING'S
James Bond
DRAWING BY HORAK
BOND ELUDES THE ARMED INTRUDER WHO SURPRISED HIM IN AUZA'S ROOM... AND LUCKILY GETS AWAY WITHOUT ROUSING ANY HOTEL GUESTS!
DAMMIT, IF I'D BEEN EXPECTING GUNPLAY, I'D HAVE BROUGHT MY OWN SILENCER!
...WELL, NEVER MIND THAT NOW, OLD CHUM! LET'S SEE WHAT SECRETS THE LOVELY CARMEN'S ROOM MAY HOLD!
718
Siempre Ricardo Auga
3007

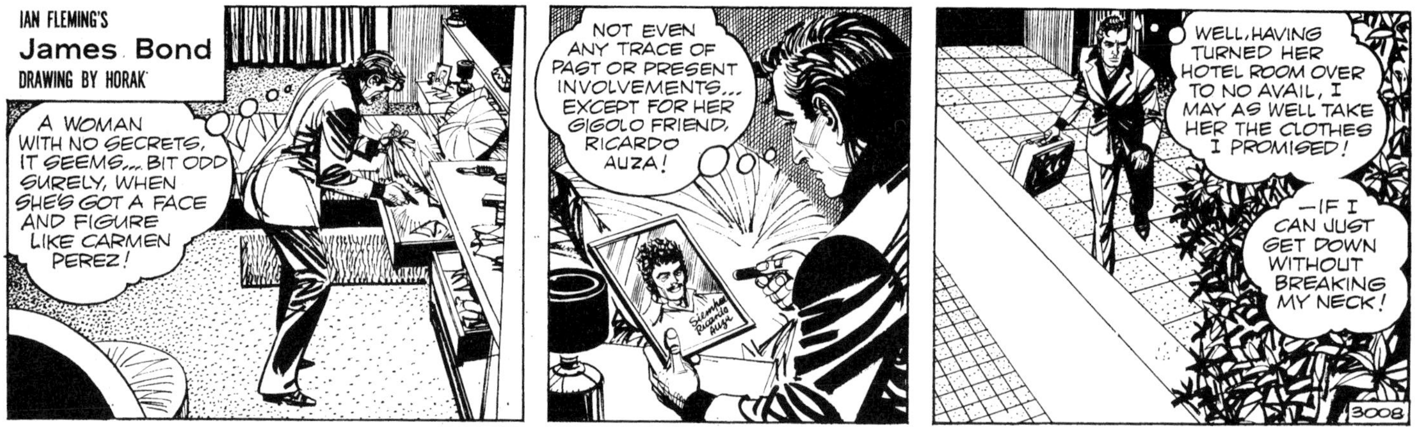
IAN FLEMING'S
James Bond
DRAWING BY HORAK
A WOMAN WITH NO SECRETS, IT SEEMS... BIT ODD SURELY, WHEN SHE'S GOT A FACE AND FIGURE LIKE CARMEN PEREZ!
NOT EVEN ANY TRACE OF PAST OR PRESENT INVOLVEMENTS... EXCEPT FOR HER GIGOLO FRIEND, RICARDO AUZA!
WELL, HAVING TURNED HER HOTEL ROOM OVER TO NO AVAIL, I MAY AS WELL TAKE HER THE CLOTHES I PROMISED!
—IF I CAN JUST GET DOWN WITHOUT BREAKING MY NECK!
3008

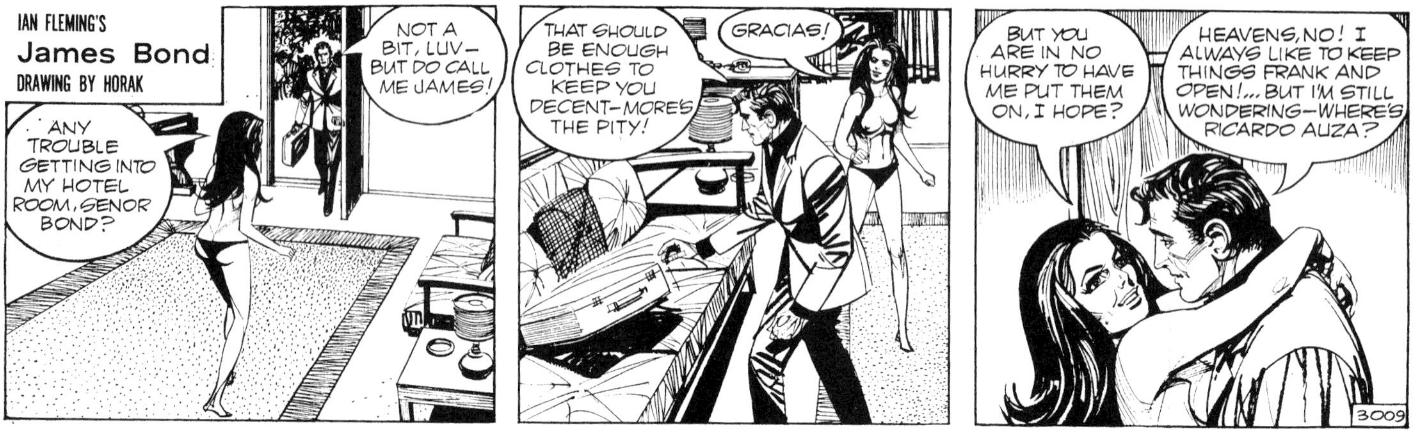
IAN FLEMING'S
James Bond
DRAWING BY HORAK
ANY TROUBLE GETTING INTO MY HOTEL ROOM, SENOR BOND?
NOT A BIT, LUV— BUT DO CALL ME JAMES!
THAT SHOULD BE ENOUGH CLOTHES TO KEEP YOU DECENT—MORE'S THE PITY!
GRACIAS!
BUT YOU ARE IN NO HURRY TO HAVE ME PUT THEM ON, I HOPE?
HEAVENS, NO! I ALWAYS LIKE TO KEEP THINGS FRANK AND OPEN!... BUT I'M STILL WONDERING—WHERE'S RICARDO AUZA?
3009

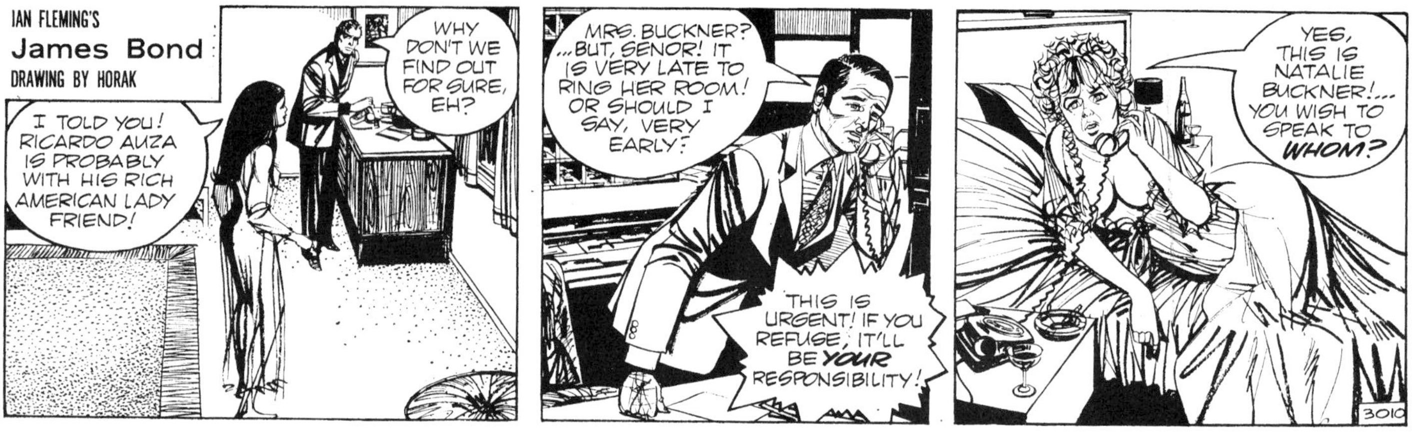
IAN FLEMING'S
James Bond
DRAWING BY HORAK
I TOLD YOU! RICARDO AUZA IS PROBABLY WITH HIS RICH AMERICAN LADY FRIEND!
WHY DON'T WE FIND OUT FOR SURE, EH?
MRS. BUCKNER? ...BUT, SENOR! IT IS VERY LATE TO RING HER ROOM! OR SHOULD I SAY, VERY EARLY?
THIS IS URGENT! IF YOU REFUSE, IT'LL BE YOUR RESPONSIBILITY!
YES, THIS IS NATALIE BUCKNER!... YOU WISH TO SPEAK TO WHOM?
3010

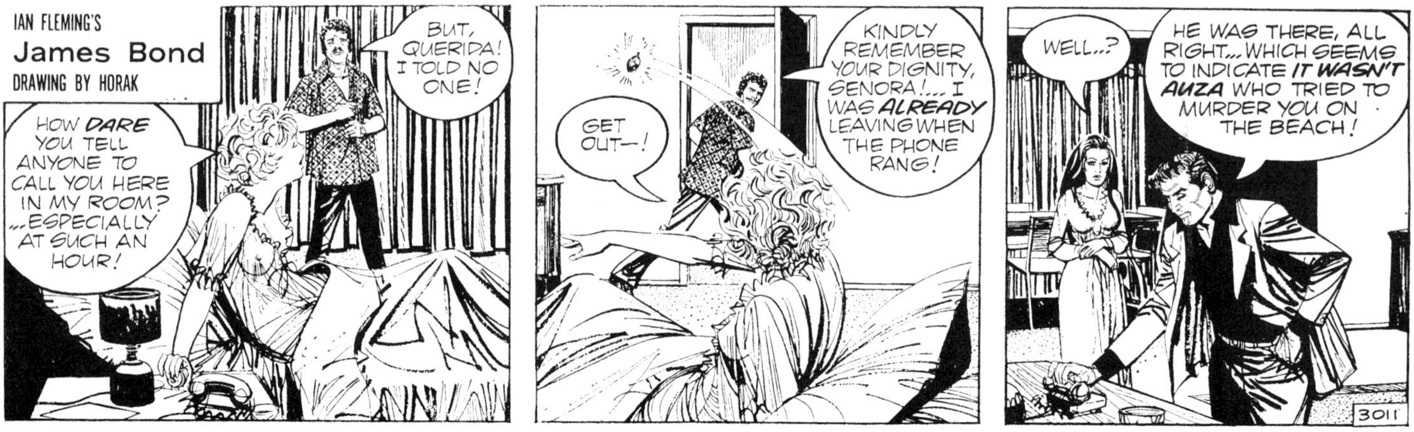
IAN FLEMING'S
James Bond
DRAWING BY HORAK
HOW DARE YOU TELL ANYONE TO CALL YOU HERE IN MY ROOM? ...ESPECIALLY AT SUCH AN HOUR!
BUT, QUERIDA! I TOLD NO ONE!
GET OUT—!
KINDLY REMEMBER YOUR DIGNITY, SENORA!... I WAS ALREADY LEAVING WHEN THE PHONE RANG!
WELL...?
HE WAS THERE, ALL RIGHT... WHICH SEEMS TO INDICATE IT WASN'T AUZA WHO TRIED TO MURDER YOU ON THE BEACH!
3011

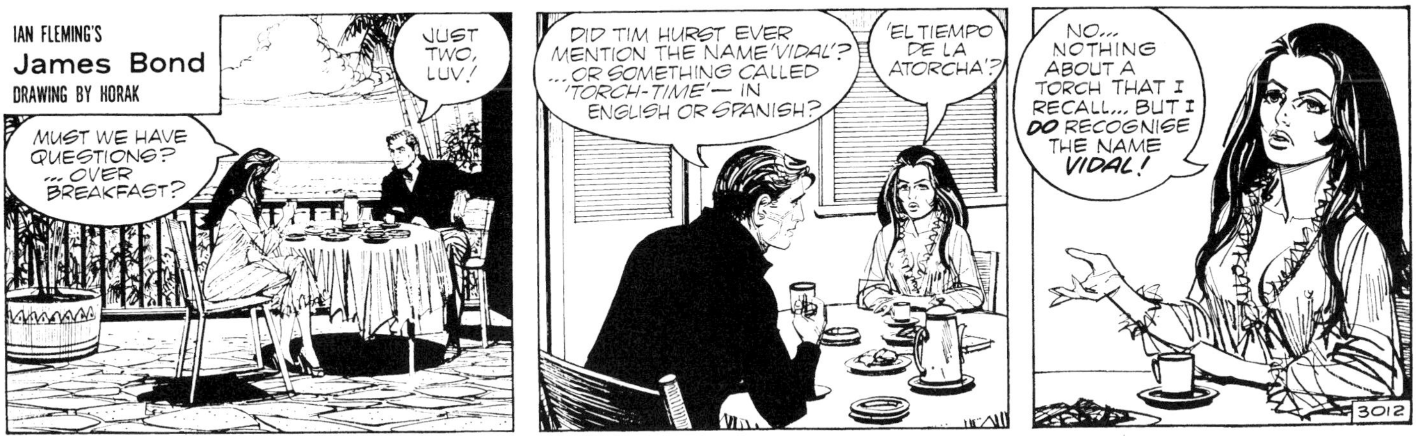
IAN FLEMING'S
James Bond
DRAWING BY HORAK
JUST TWO, LUV!
MUST WE HAVE QUESTIONS? ...OVER BREAKFAST?
DID TIM HURST EVER MENTION THE NAME 'VIDAL'? ...OR SOMETHING CALLED 'TORCH-TIME'— IN ENGLISH OR SPANISH?
'EL TIEMPO DE LA ATORCHA'?
NO... NOTHING ABOUT A TORCH THAT I RECALL... BUT I DO RECOGNISE THE NAME VIDAL!
3012

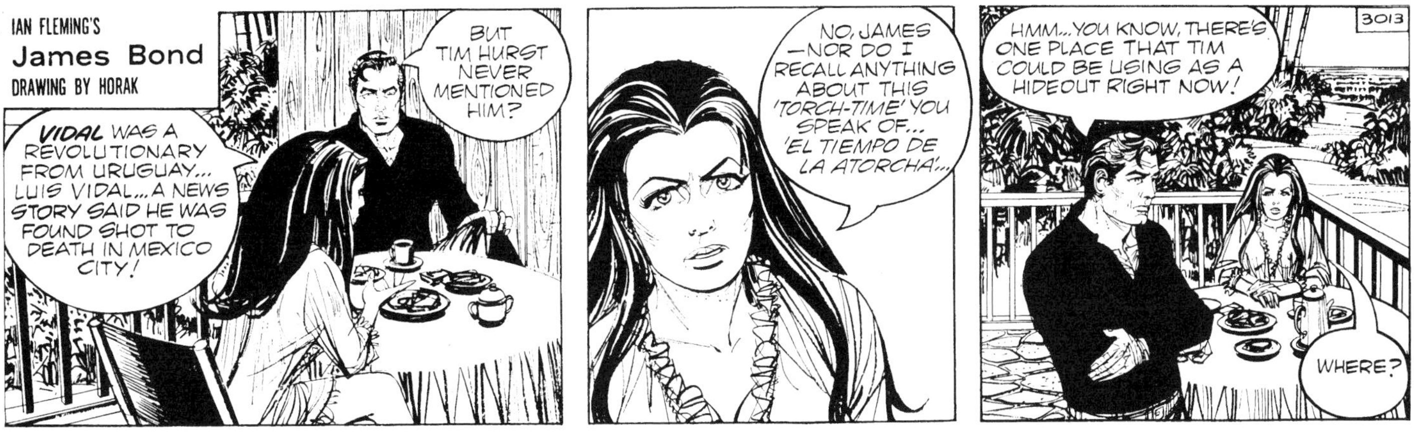
IAN FLEMING'S
James Bond
DRAWING BY HORAK
BUT TIM HURST NEVER MENTIONED HIM?
VIDAL WAS A REVOLUTIONARY FROM URUGUAY... LUIS VIDAL... A NEWS STORY SAID HE WAS FOUND SHOT TO DEATH IN MEXICO CITY!
NO, JAMES —NOR DO I RECALL ANYTHING ABOUT THIS 'TORCH-TIME' YOU SPEAK OF... 'EL TIEMPO DE LA ATORCHA'...
3013
HMM... YOU KNOW, THERE'S ONE PLACE THAT TIM COULD BE USING AS A HIDEOUT RIGHT NOW!
WHERE?

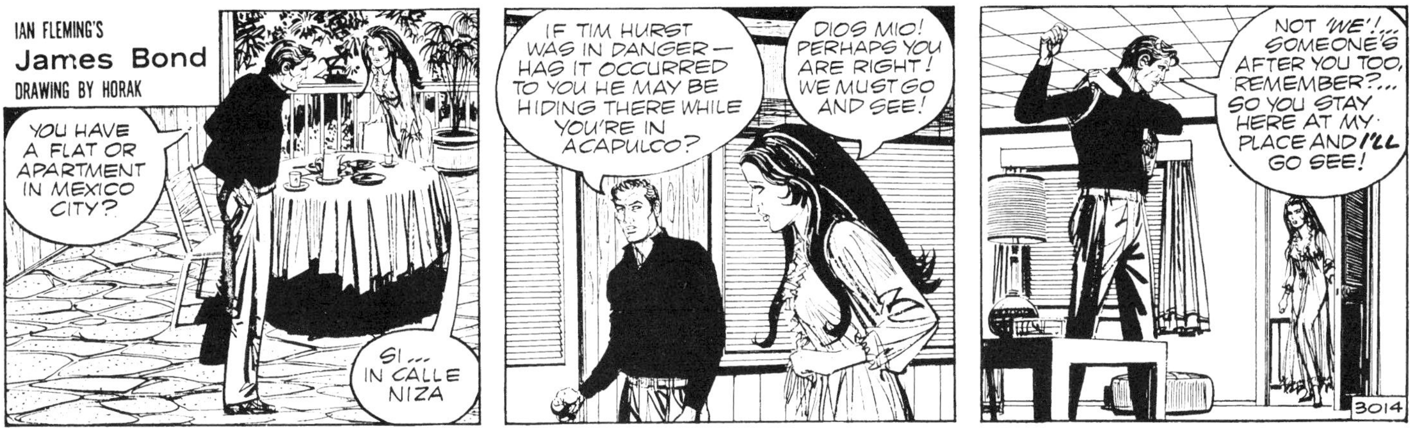
IAN FLEMING'S
James Bond
DRAWING BY HORAK
YOU HAVE A FLAT OR APARTMENT IN MEXICO CITY?
SI... IN CALLE NIZA
IF TIM HURST WAS IN DANGER— HAS IT OCCURRED TO YOU HE MAY BE HIDING THERE WHILE YOU'RE IN ACAPULCO?
DIOS MIO! PERHAPS YOU ARE RIGHT! WE MUST GO AND SEE!
NOT 'WE'!... SOMEONE'S AFTER YOU TOO, REMEMBER?... SO YOU STAY HERE AT MY PLACE AND I'LL GO SEE!
3014

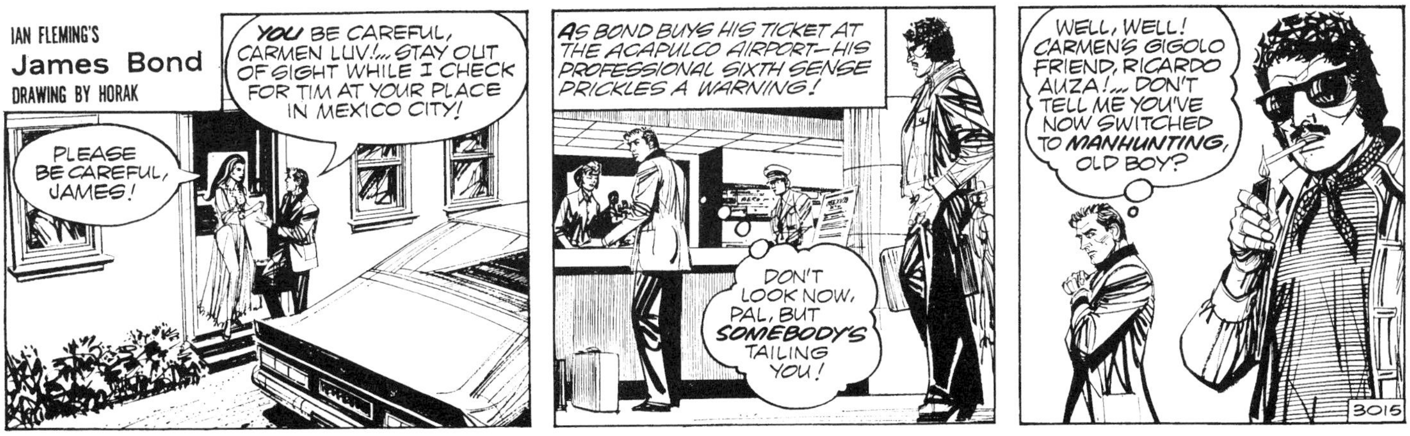
IAN FLEMING'S
James Bond
DRAWING BY HORAK
YOU BE CAREFUL, CARMEN LUV!... STAY OUT OF SIGHT WHILE I CHECK FOR TIM AT YOUR PLACE IN MEXICO CITY!
PLEASE BE CAREFUL, JAMES!
AS BOND BUYS HIS TICKET AT THE ACAPULCO AIRPORT—HIS PROFESSIONAL SIXTH SENSE PRICKLES A WARNING!
DON'T LOOK NOW, PAL, BUT SOMEBODY'S TAILING YOU!
WELL, WELL! CARMEN'S GIGOLO FRIEND, RICARDO AUZA!... DON'T TELL ME YOU'VE NOW SWITCHED TO MANHUNTING, OLD BOY?
3015

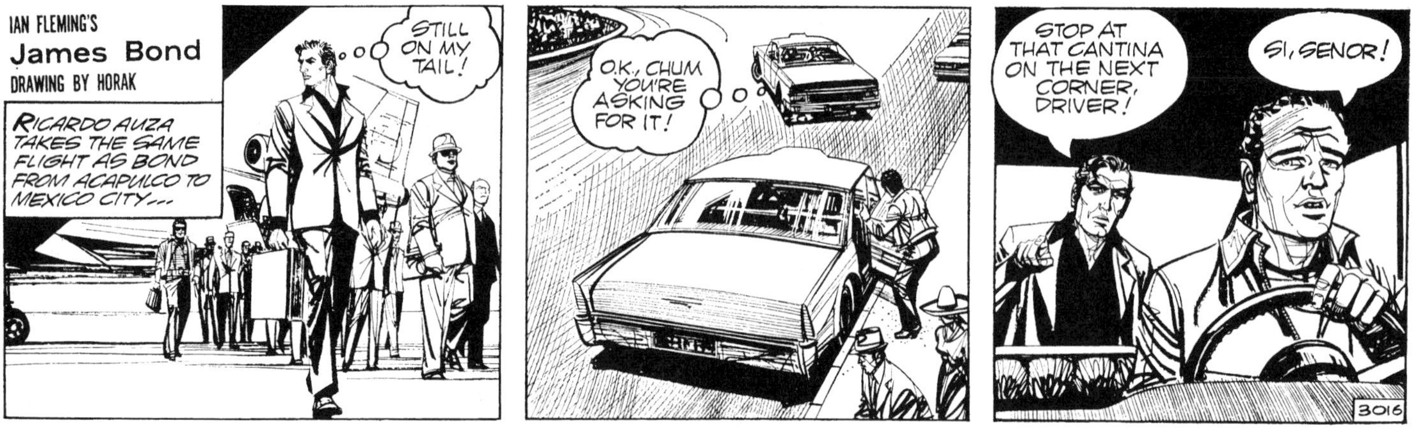
IAN FLEMING'S
James Bond
DRAWING BY HORAK
RICARDO AUZA TAKES THE SAME FLIGHT AS BOND FROM ACAPULCO TO MEXICO CITY---
STILL ON MY TAIL!
O.K., CHUM YOU'RE ASKING FOR IT!
STOP AT THAT CANTINA ON THE NEXT CORNER, DRIVER!
SI, SENOR!
3016

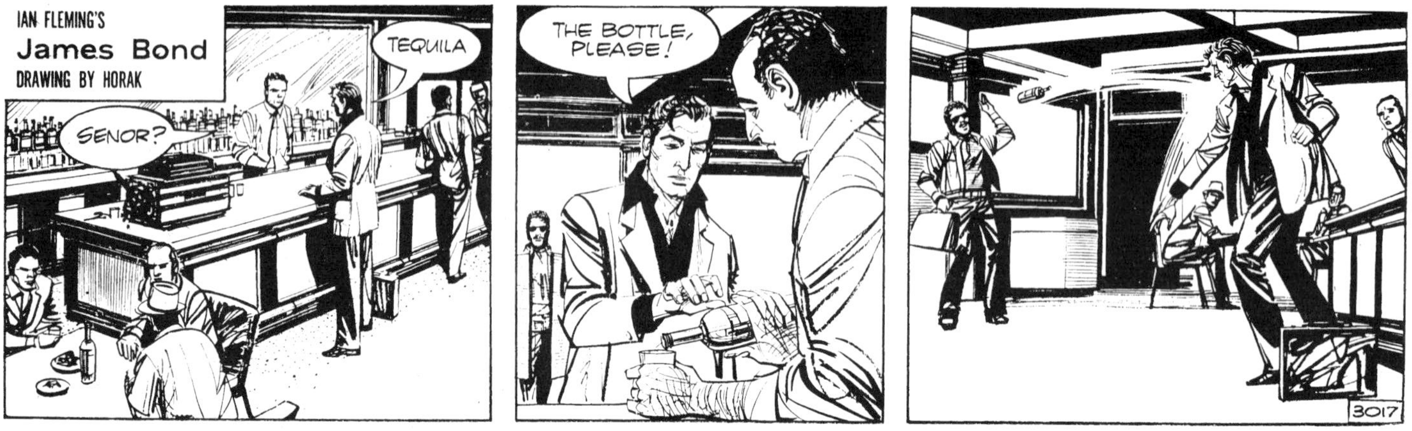
IAN FLEMING'S
James Bond
DRAWING BY HORAK
SENOR?
TEQUILA
THE BOTTLE, PLEASE!
3017

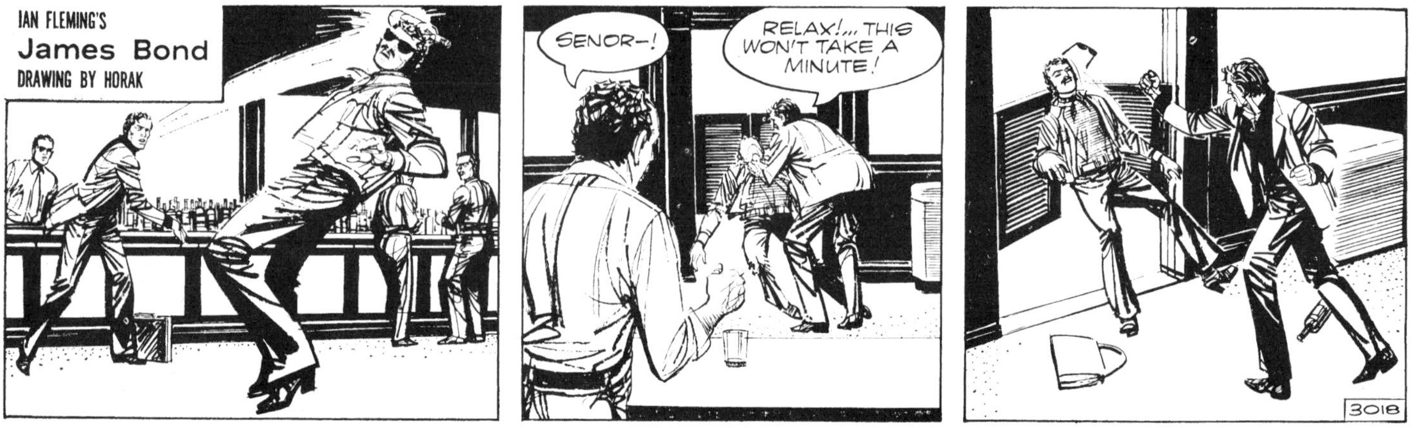
IAN FLEMING'S
James Bond
DRAWING BY HORAK
SENOR-!
RELAX!... THIS WON'T TAKE A MINUTE!
3018

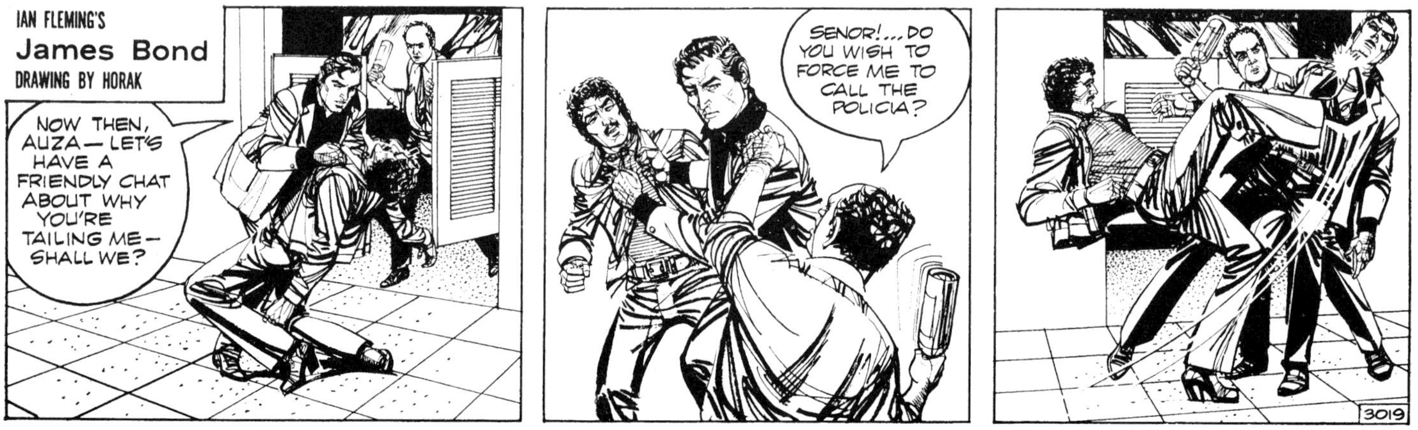
IAN FLEMING'S
James Bond
DRAWING BY HORAK
NOW THEN, AUZA— LET'S HAVE A FRIENDLY CHAT ABOUT WHY YOU'RE TAILING ME— SHALL WE?
SENOR!... DO YOU WISH TO FORCE ME TO CALL THE POLICIA?
3019

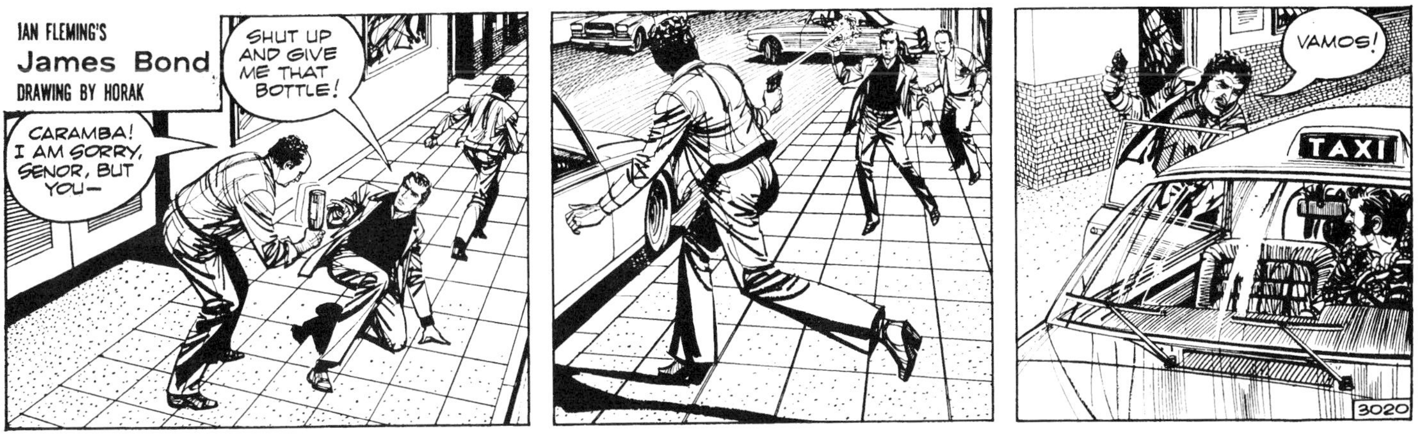
IAN FLEMING'S
James Bond
DRAWING BY HORAK
SHUT UP AND GIVE ME THAT BOTTLE!
CARAMBA! I AM SORRY, SENOR, BUT YOU—
VAMOS!
TAXI
3020

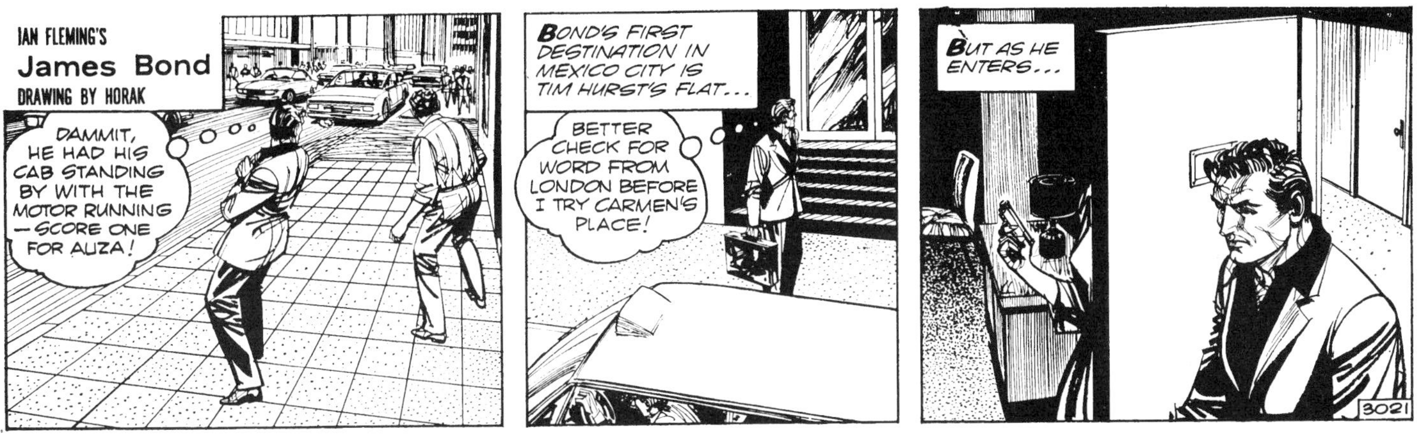
IAN FLEMING'S
James Bond
DRAWING BY HORAK
DAMMIT, HE HAD HIS CAB STANDING BY WITH THE MOTOR RUNNING —SCORE ONE FOR AUZA!
BOND'S FIRST DESTINATION IN MEXICO CITY IS TIM HURST'S FLAT...
BETTER CHECK FOR WORD FROM LONDON BEFORE I TRY CARMEN'S PLACE!
BUT AS HE ENTERS...
3021

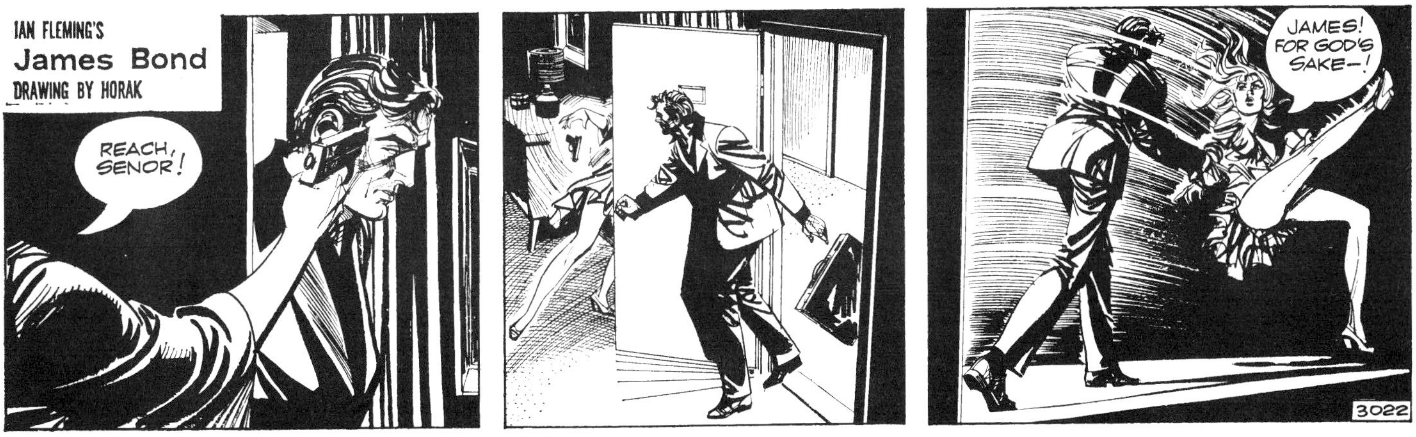
IAN FLEMING'S
James Bond
DRAWING BY HORAK
REACH, SENOR!
JAMES! FOR GOD'S SAKE—!
3022

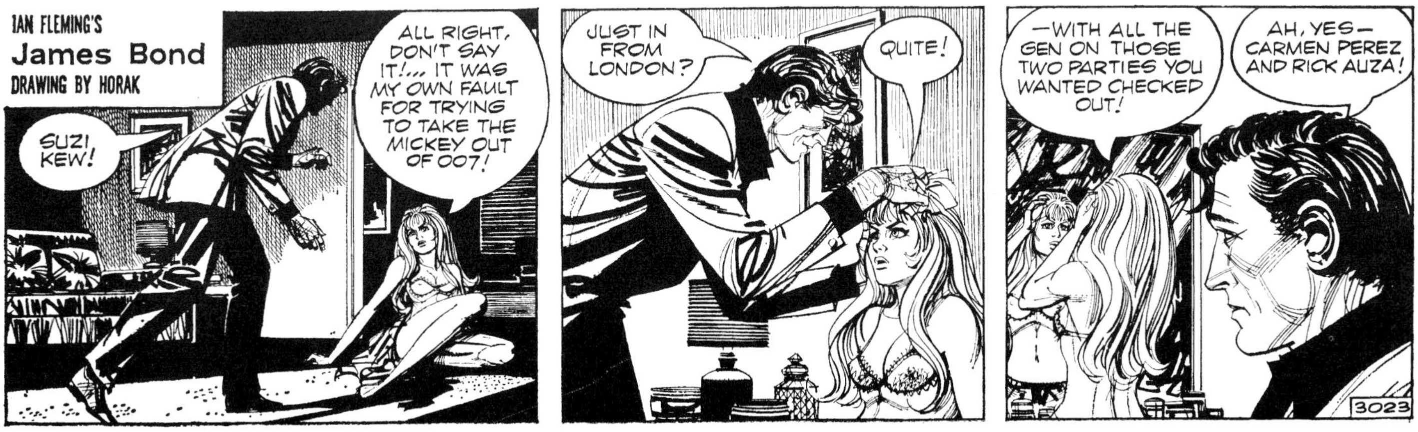
IAN FLEMING'S
James Bond
DRAWING BY HORAK
SUZI KEW!
ALL RIGHT, DON'T SAY IT!... IT WAS MY OWN FAULT FOR TRYING TO TAKE THE MICKEY OUT OF 007!
JUST IN FROM LONDON?
QUITE!
—WITH ALL THE GEN ON THOSE TWO PARTIES YOU WANTED CHECKED OUT!
AH, YES— CARMEN PEREZ AND RICK AUZA!
3023

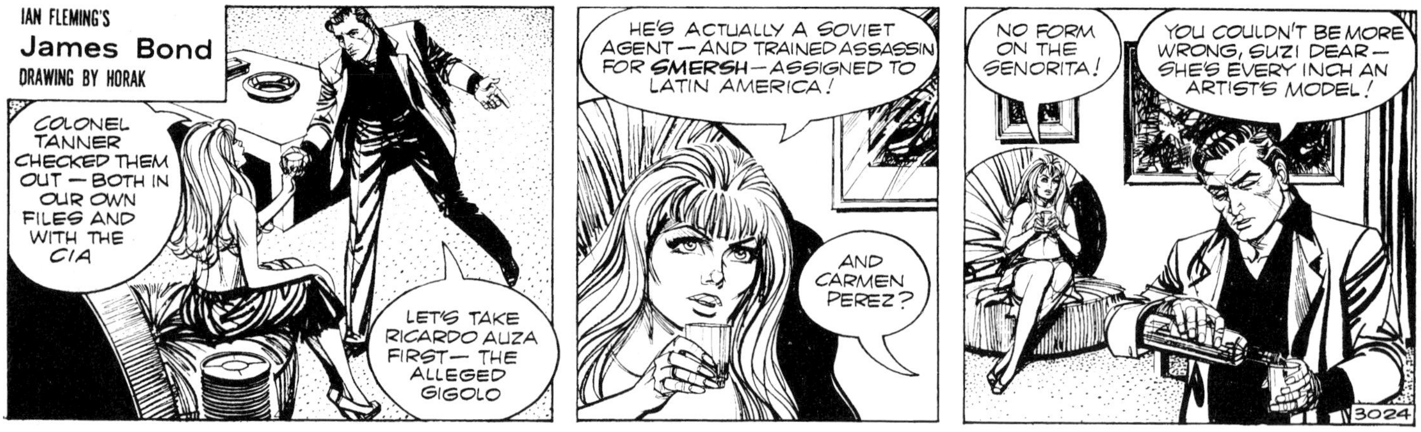
IAN FLEMING'S
James Bond
DRAWING BY HORAK
COLONEL TANNER CHECKED THEM OUT — BOTH IN OUR OWN FILES AND WITH THE CIA
LET'S TAKE RICARDO AUZA FIRST— THE ALLEGED GIGOLO
HE'S ACTUALLY A SOVIET AGENT — AND TRAINED ASSASSIN FOR SMERSH — ASSIGNED TO LATIN AMERICA!
AND CARMEN PEREZ?
NO FORM ON THE SENORITA!
YOU COULDN'T BE MORE WRONG, SUZI DEAR — SHE'S EVERY INCH AN ARTIST'S MODEL!
3024

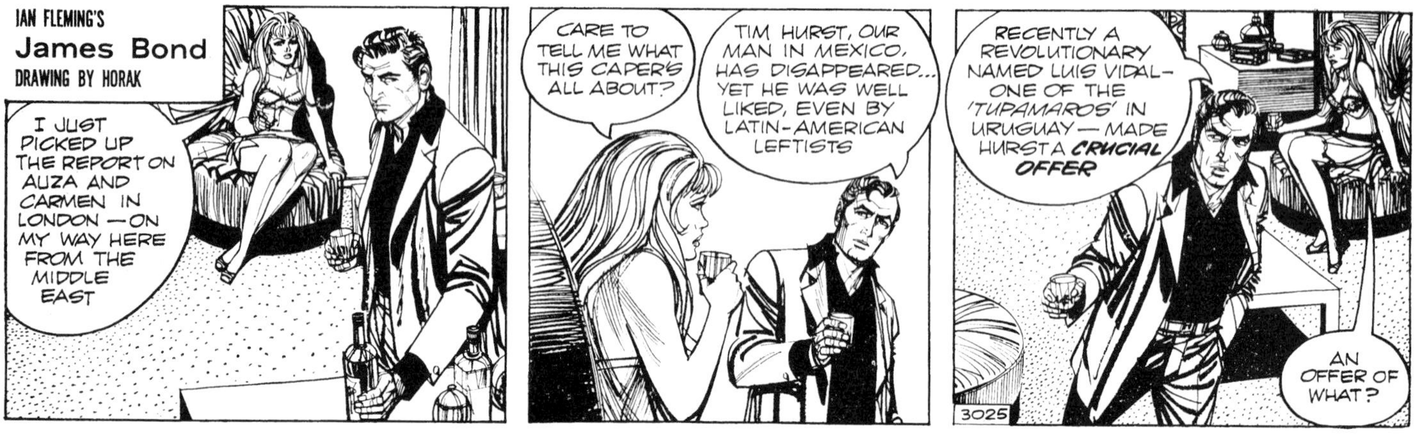
IAN FLEMING'S
James Bond
DRAWING BY HORAK
I JUST PICKED UP THE REPORT ON AUZA AND CARMEN IN LONDON — ON MY WAY HERE FROM THE MIDDLE EAST
CARE TO TELL ME WHAT THIS CAPER'S ALL ABOUT?
TIM HURST, OUR MAN IN MEXICO, HAS DISAPPEARED... YET HE WAS WELL LIKED, EVEN BY LATIN-AMERICAN LEFTISTS
3025
RECENTLY A REVOLUTIONARY NAMED LUIS VIDAL — ONE OF THE 'TUPAMAROS' IN URUGUAY — MADE HURST A CRUCIAL OFFER
AN OFFER OF WHAT?

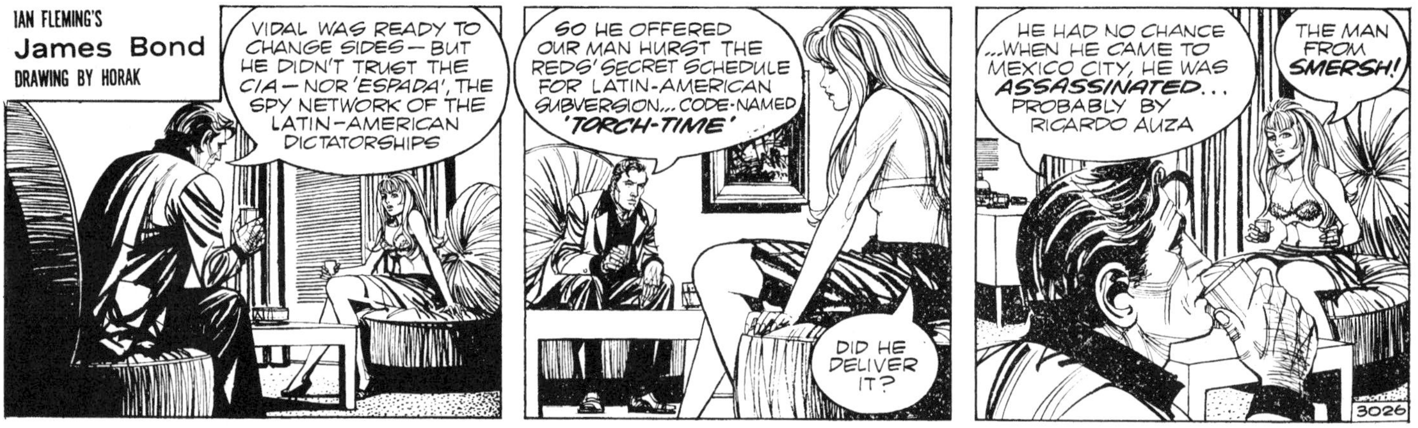
IAN FLEMING'S
James Bond
DRAWING BY HORAK
VIDAL WAS READY TO CHANGE SIDES — BUT HE DIDN'T TRUST THE CIA — NOR 'ESPADA', THE SPY NETWORK OF THE LATIN-AMERICAN DICTATORSHIPS
SO HE OFFERED OUR MAN HURST THE REDS' SECRET SCHEDULE FOR LATIN-AMERICAN SUBVERSION... CODE-NAMED 'TORCH-TIME'
DID HE DELIVER IT?
...HE HAD NO CHANCE ...WHEN HE CAME TO MEXICO CITY, HE WAS ASSASSINATED... PROBABLY BY RICARDO AUZA
THE MAN FROM SMERSH!
3026

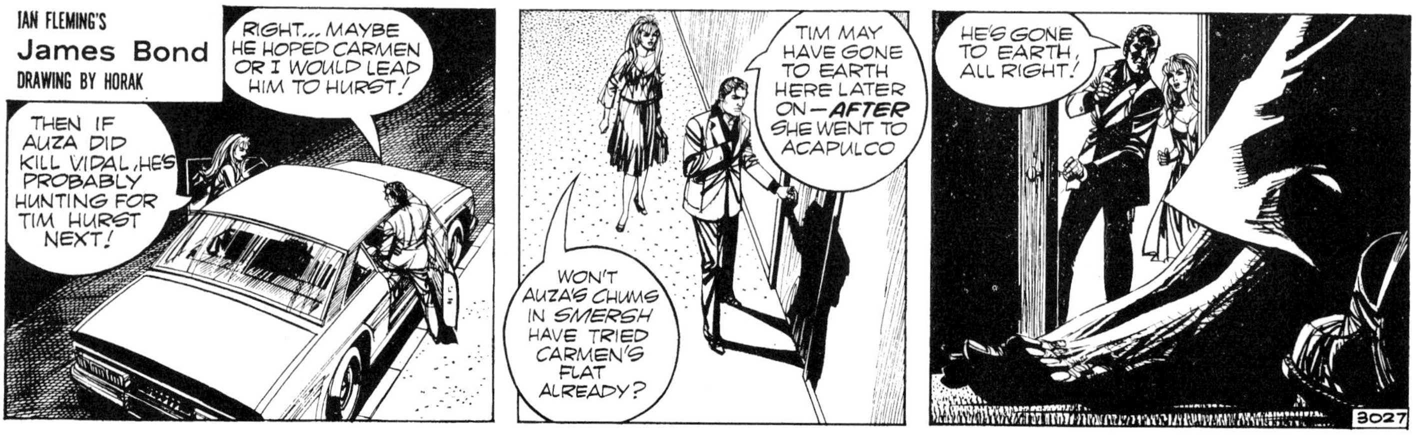
IAN FLEMING'S
James Bond
DRAWING BY HORAK
THEN IF AUZA DID KILL VIDAL, HE'S PROBABLY HUNTING FOR TIM HURST NEXT!
RIGHT... MAYBE HE HOPED CARMEN OR I WOULD LEAD HIM TO HURST!
WON'T AUZA'S CHUMS IN SMERSH HAVE TRIED CARMEN'S FLAT ALREADY?
TIM MAY HAVE GONE TO EARTH HERE LATER ON — AFTER SHE WENT TO ACAPULCO
HE'S GONE TO EARTH, ALL RIGHT!
3027

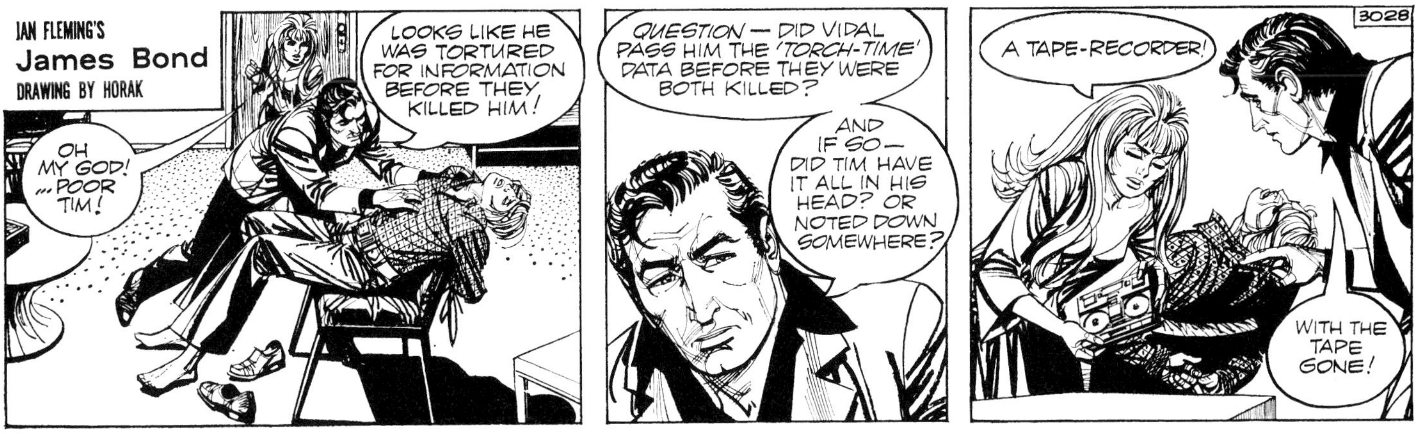
IAN FLEMING'S
James Bond
DRAWING BY HORAK
OH MY GOD! ...POOR TIM!
LOOKS LIKE HE WAS TORTURED FOR INFORMATION BEFORE THEY KILLED HIM!
QUESTION — DID VIDAL PASS HIM THE 'TORCH-TIME' DATA BEFORE THEY WERE BOTH KILLED?
AND IF SO — DID TIM HAVE IT ALL IN HIS HEAD? OR NOTED DOWN SOMEWHERE?
3028
A TAPE-RECORDER!
WITH THE TAPE GONE!

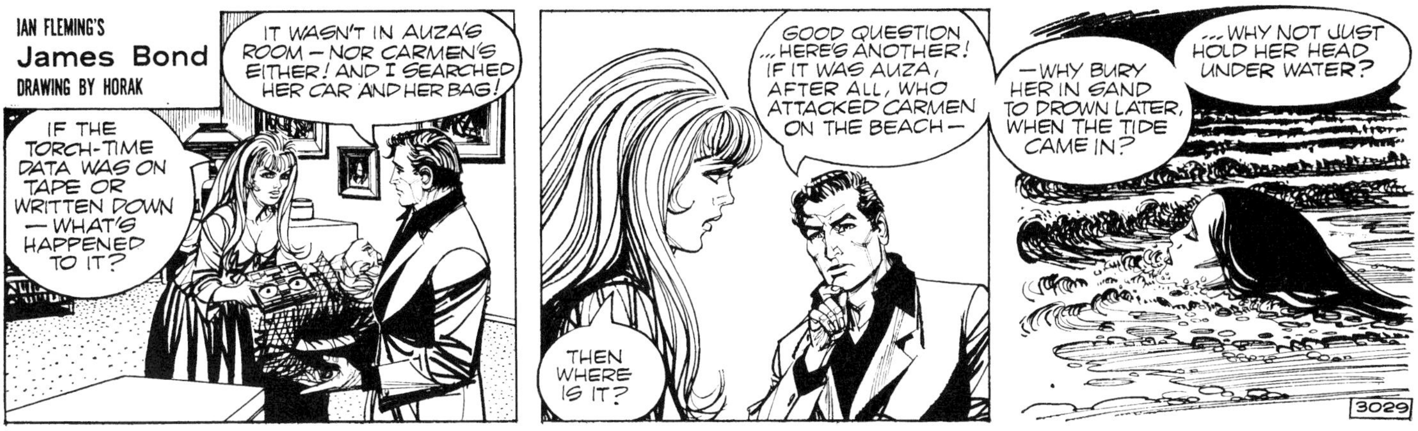
IAN FLEMING'S
James Bond
DRAWING BY HORAK
IT WASN'T IN AUZA'S ROOM — NOR CARMEN'S EITHER! AND I SEARCHED HER CAR AND HER BAG!
IF THE TORCH-TIME DATA WAS ON TAPE OR WRITTEN DOWN — WHAT'S HAPPENED TO IT?
THEN WHERE IS IT?
GOOD QUESTION ...HERE'S ANOTHER! IF IT WAS AUZA, AFTER ALL, WHO ATTACKED CARMEN ON THE BEACH —
— WHY BURY HER IN SAND TO DROWN LATER, WHEN THE TIDE CAME IN?
...WHY NOT JUST HOLD HER HEAD UNDER WATER?
3029

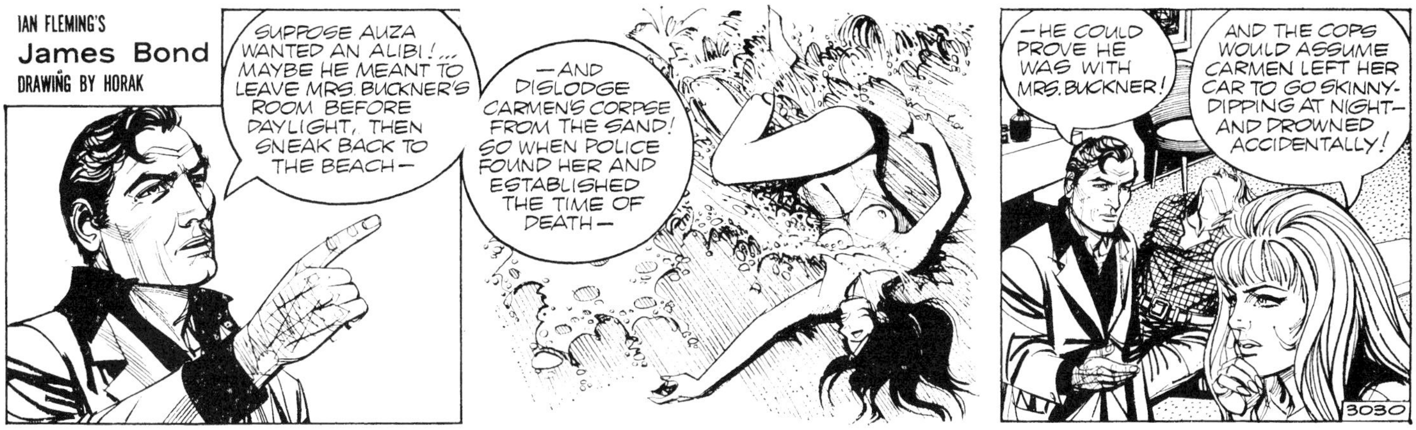
IAN FLEMING'S
James Bond
DRAWING BY HORAK
SUPPOSE AUZA WANTED AN ALIBI!... MAYBE HE MEANT TO LEAVE MRS. BUCKNER'S ROOM BEFORE DAYLIGHT, THEN SNEAK BACK TO THE BEACH —
— AND DISLODGE CARMEN'S CORPSE FROM THE SAND! SO WHEN POLICE FOUND HER AND ESTABLISHED THE TIME OF DEATH —
— HE COULD PROVE HE WAS WITH MRS. BUCKNER!
AND THE COPS WOULD ASSUME CARMEN LEFT HER CAR TO GO SKINNY-DIPPING AT NIGHT — AND DROWNED ACCIDENTALLY!
3030

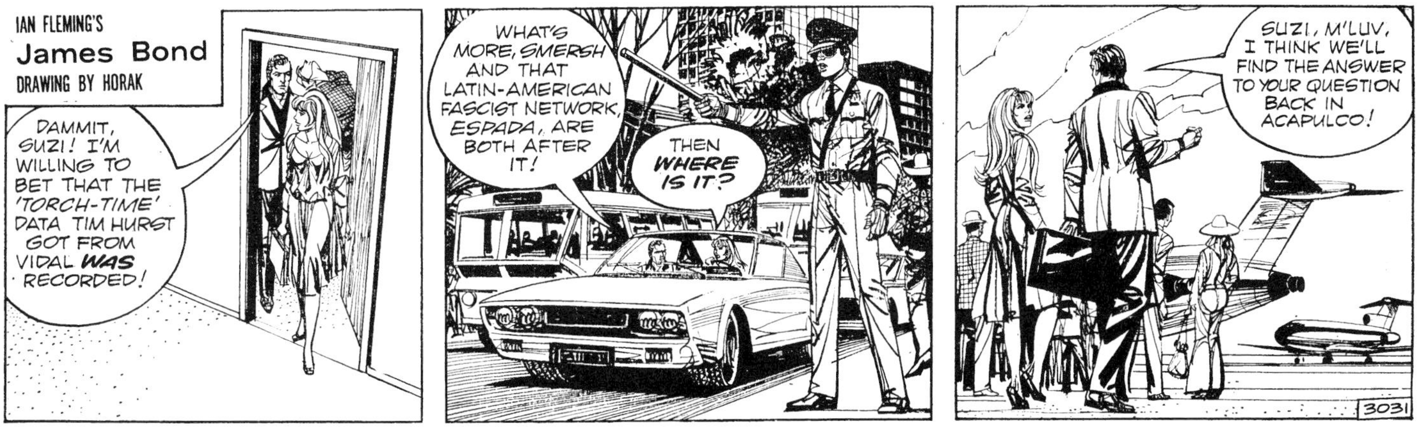
IAN FLEMING'S
James Bond
DRAWING BY HORAK
DAMMIT, SUZI! I'M WILLING TO BET THAT THE 'TORCH-TIME' DATA TIM HURST GOT FROM VIDAL WAS RECORDED!
WHAT'S MORE, SMERSH AND THAT LATIN-AMERICAN FASCIST NETWORK, ESPADA, ARE BOTH AFTER IT!
THEN WHERE IS IT?
SUZI, M'LUV, I THINK WE'LL FIND THE ANSWER TO YOUR QUESTION BACK IN ACAPULCO!
3031

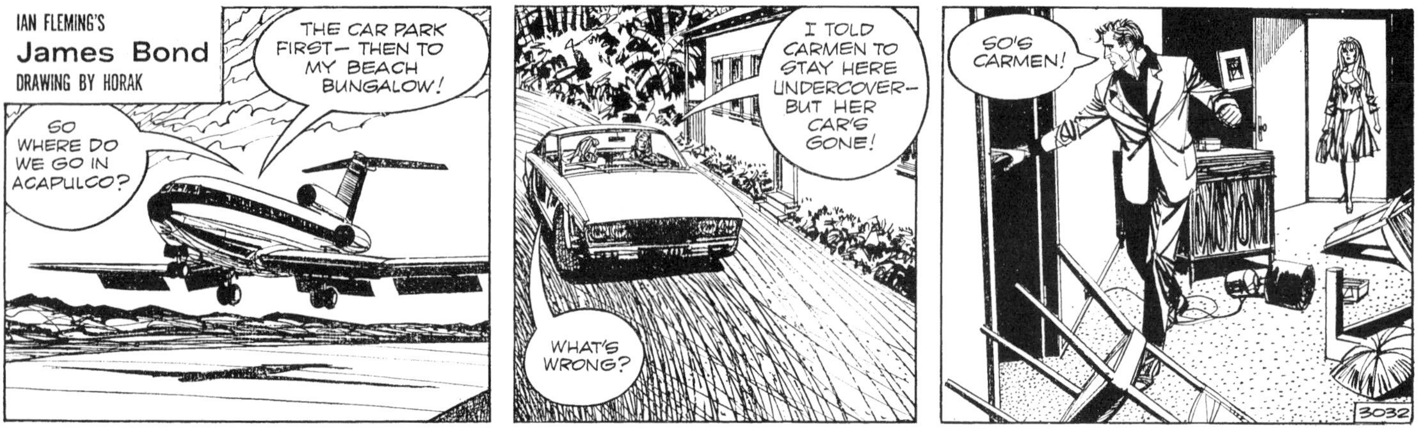
IAN FLEMING'S
James Bond
DRAWING BY HORAK
SO WHERE DO WE GO IN ACAPULCO?
THE CAR PARK FIRST— THEN TO MY BEACH BUNGALOW!
I TOLD CARMEN TO STAY HERE UNDERCOVER— BUT HER CAR'S GONE!
WHAT'S WRONG?
SO'S CARMEN!
3032

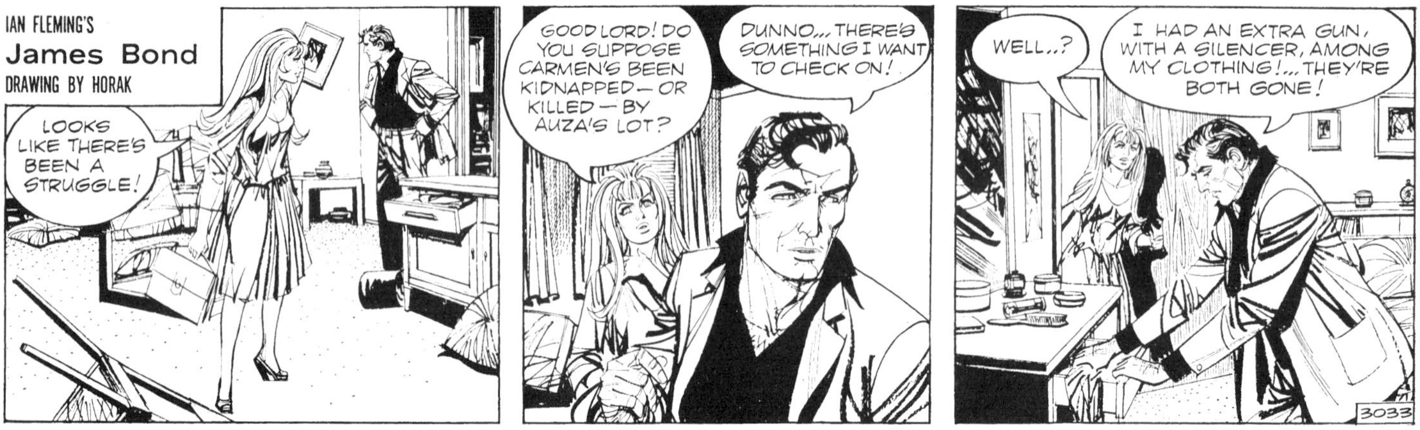
IAN FLEMING'S
James Bond
DRAWING BY HORAK
LOOKS LIKE THERE'S BEEN A STRUGGLE!
GOOD LORD! DO YOU SUPPOSE CARMEN'S BEEN KIDNAPPED— OR KILLED— BY AUZA'S LOT?
DUNNO,,, THERE'S SOMETHING I WANT TO CHECK ON!
WELL,,?
I HAD AN EXTRA GUN, WITH A SILENCER, AMONG MY CLOTHING!,,, THEY'RE BOTH GONE!
3033

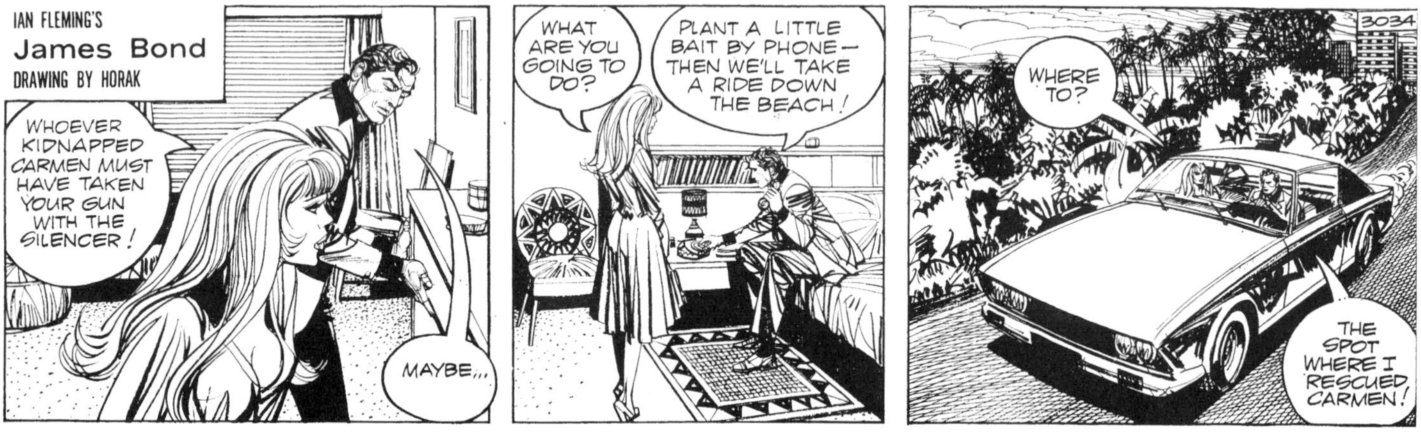
IAN FLEMING'S
James Bond
DRAWING BY HORAK
WHOEVER KIDNAPPED CARMEN MUST HAVE TAKEN YOUR GUN WITH THE SILENCER!
MAYBE,,,
WHAT ARE YOU GOING TO DO?
PLANT A LITTLE BAIT BY PHONE— THEN WE'LL TAKE A RIDE DOWN THE BEACH!
3034
WHERE TO?
THE SPOT WHERE I RESCUED CARMEN!

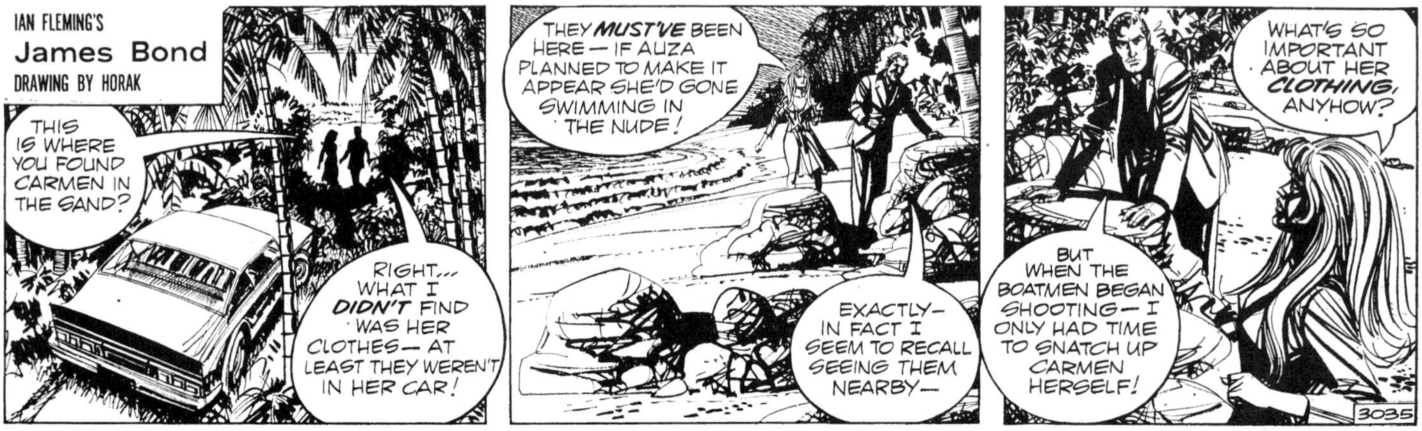
IAN FLEMING'S
James Bond
DRAWING BY HORAK
THIS IS WHERE YOU FOUND CARMEN IN THE SAND?
RIGHT,,, WHAT I DIDN'T FIND WAS HER CLOTHES— AT LEAST THEY WEREN'T IN HER CAR!
THEY MUST'VE BEEN HERE— IF AUZA PLANNED TO MAKE IT APPEAR SHE'D GONE SWIMMING IN THE NUDE!
EXACTLY— IN FACT I SEEM TO RECALL SEEING THEM NEARBY—
WHAT'S SO IMPORTANT ABOUT HER CLOTHING, ANYHOW?
BUT WHEN THE BOATMEN BEGAN SHOOTING— I ONLY HAD TIME TO SNATCH UP CARMEN HERSELF!
3035

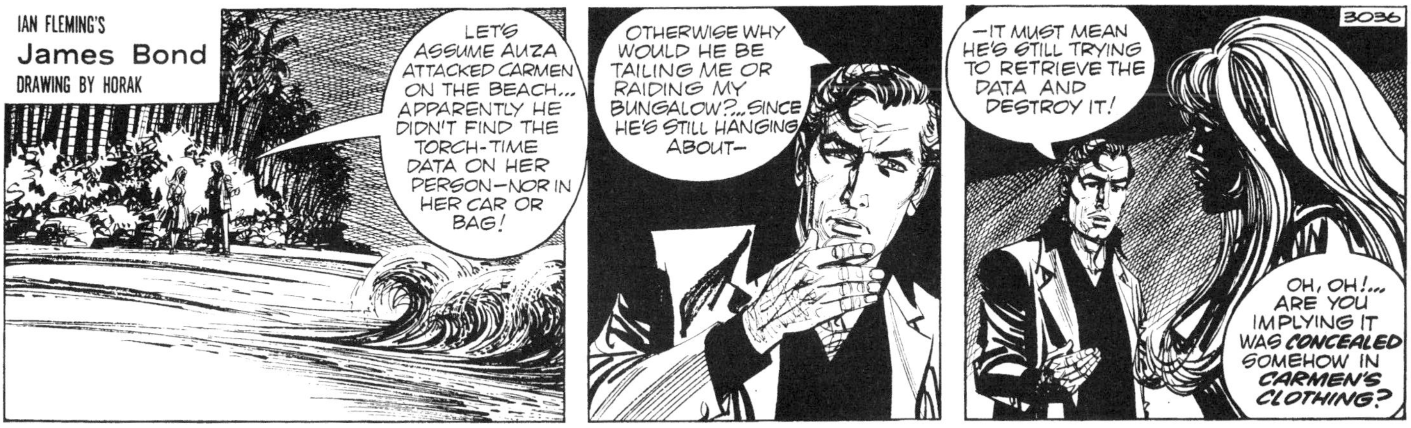
IAN FLEMING'S
James Bond
DRAWING BY HORAK
LET'S ASSUME AUZA ATTACKED CARMEN ON THE BEACH... APPARENTLY HE DIDN'T FIND THE TORCH-TIME DATA ON HER PERSON—NOR IN HER CAR OR BAG!
OTHERWISE WHY WOULD HE BE TAILING ME OR RAIDING MY BUNGALOW?... SINCE HE'S STILL HANGING ABOUT—
—IT MUST MEAN HE'S STILL TRYING TO RETRIEVE THE DATA AND DESTROY IT!
OH, OH!... ARE YOU IMPLYING IT WAS **CONCEALED** SOMEHOW IN **CARMEN'S CLOTHING?**
3036

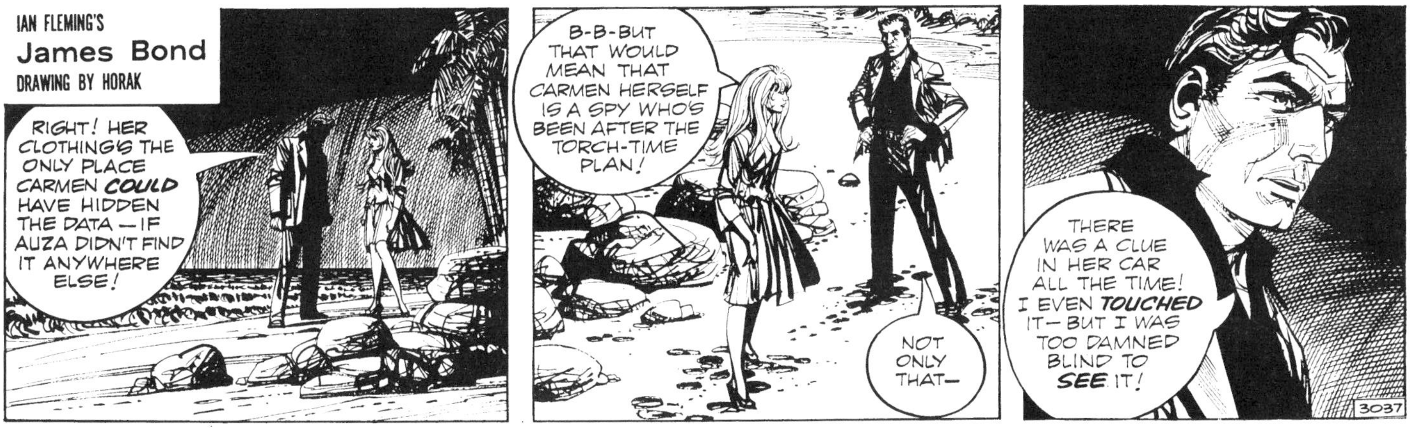
IAN FLEMING'S
James Bond
DRAWING BY HORAK
RIGHT! HER CLOTHING'S THE ONLY PLACE CARMEN **COULD** HAVE HIDDEN THE DATA — IF AUZA DIDN'T FIND IT ANYWHERE ELSE!
B-B-BUT THAT WOULD MEAN THAT CARMEN HERSELF IS A SPY WHO'S BEEN AFTER THE TORCH-TIME PLAN!
NOT ONLY THAT—
THERE WAS A CLUE IN HER CAR ALL THE TIME! I EVEN **TOUCHED** IT— BUT I WAS TOO DAMNED BLIND TO **SEE** IT!
3037

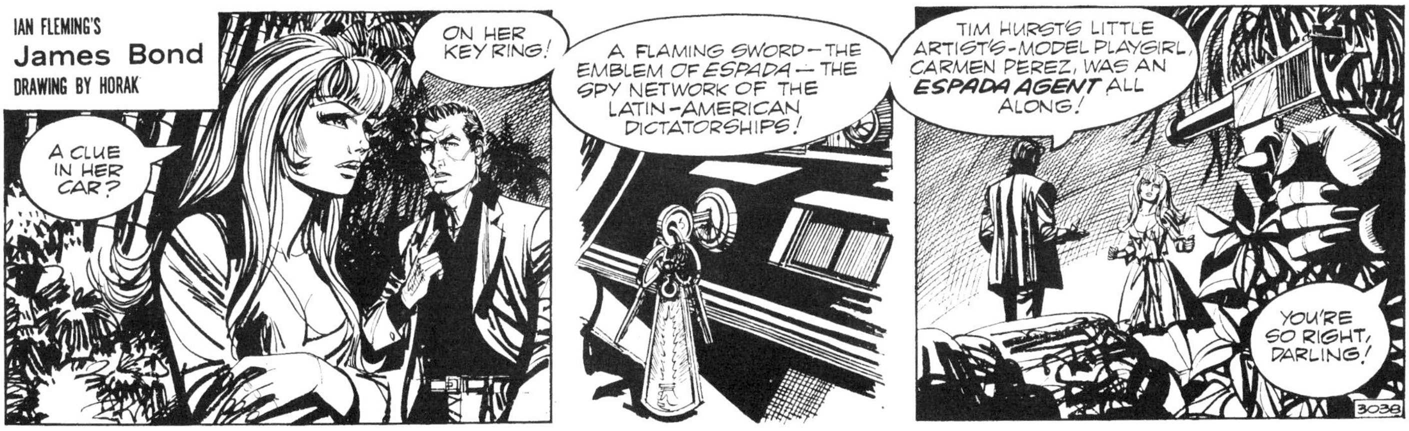
IAN FLEMING'S
James Bond
DRAWING BY HORAK
A CLUE IN HER CAR?
ON HER KEY RING!
A FLAMING SWORD—THE EMBLEM OF *ESPADA*—THE SPY NETWORK OF THE LATIN-AMERICAN DICTATORSHIPS!
TIM HURST'S LITTLE ARTIST'S-MODEL PLAYGIRL, CARMEN PEREZ, WAS AN **ESPADA AGENT** ALL ALONG!
YOU'RE SO RIGHT, DARLING!
3038

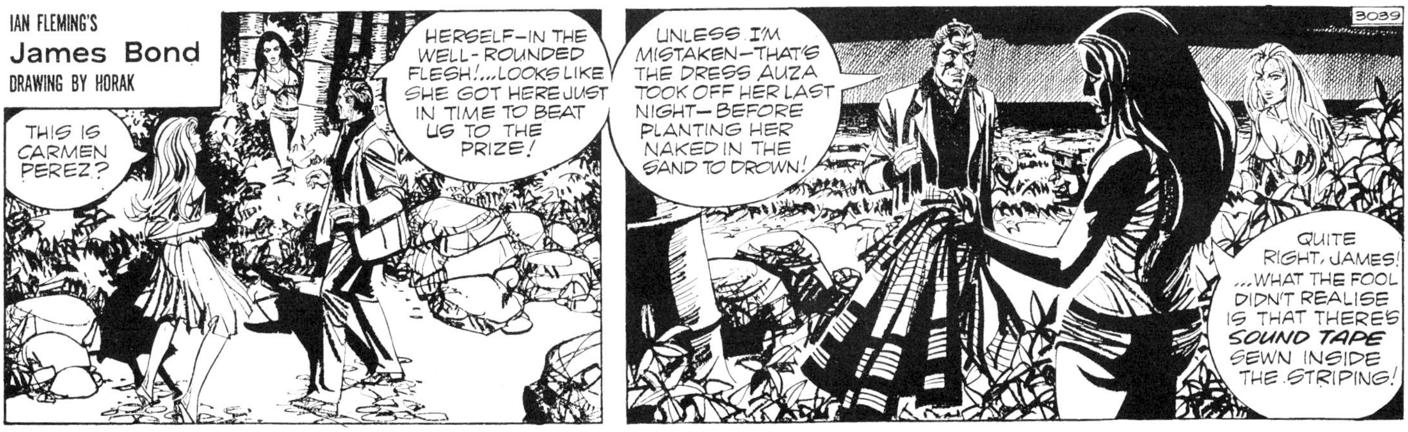
IAN FLEMING'S
James Bond
DRAWING BY HORAK
THIS IS CARMEN PEREZ?
HERSELF—IN THE WELL-ROUNDED FLESH!... LOOKS LIKE SHE GOT HERE JUST IN TIME TO BEAT US TO THE PRIZE!
UNLESS I'M MISTAKEN—THAT'S THE DRESS AUZA TOOK OFF HER LAST NIGHT—BEFORE PLANTING HER NAKED IN THE SAND TO DROWN!
QUITE RIGHT, JAMES! ...WHAT THE FOOL DIDN'T REALISE IS THAT THERE'S **SOUND TAPE** SEWN INSIDE THE STRIPING!
3039

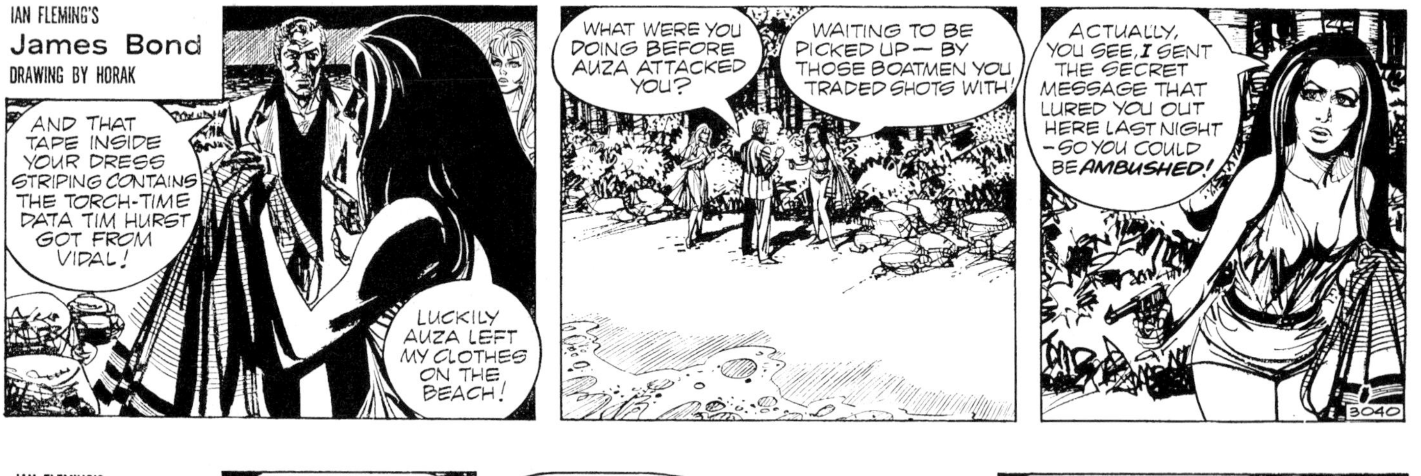
IAN FLEMING'S
James Bond
DRAWING BY HORAK
AND THAT TAPE INSIDE YOUR DRESS STRIPING CONTAINS THE TORCH-TIME DATA TIM HURST GOT FROM VIDAL!
LUCKILY AUZA LEFT MY CLOTHES ON THE BEACH!
WHAT WERE YOU DOING BEFORE AUZA ATTACKED YOU?
WAITING TO BE PICKED UP — BY THOSE BOATMEN YOU TRADED SHOTS WITH!
ACTUALLY, YOU SEE, I SENT THE SECRET MESSAGE THAT LURED YOU OUT HERE LAST NIGHT — SO YOU COULD BE AMBUSHED!
3040

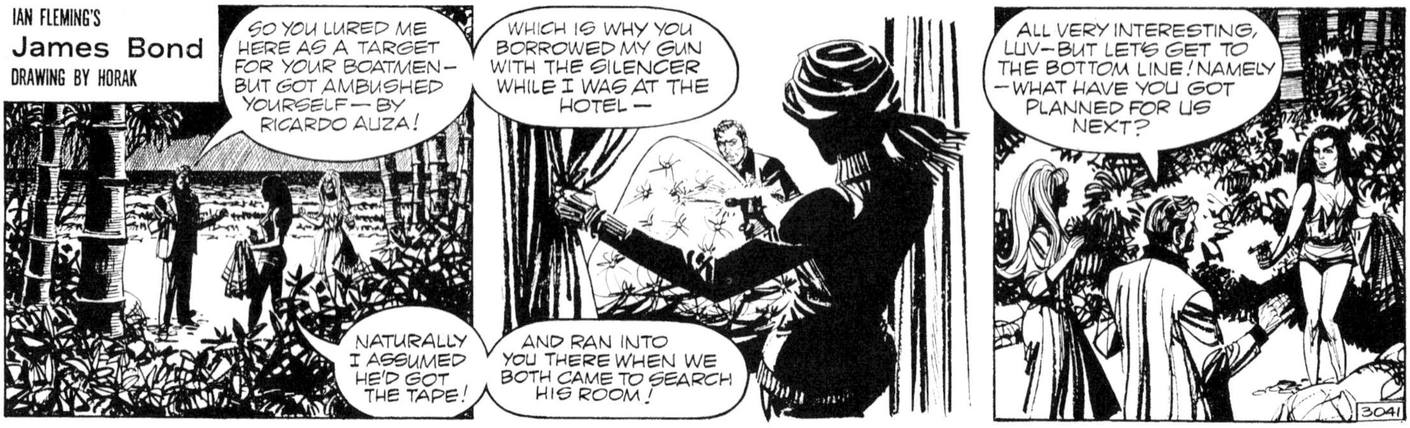
IAN FLEMING'S
James Bond
DRAWING BY HORAK
SO YOU LURED ME HERE AS A TARGET FOR YOUR BOATMEN — BUT GOT AMBUSHED YOURSELF — BY RICARDO AUZA!
NATURALLY I ASSUMED HE'D GOT THE TAPE!
WHICH IS WHY YOU BORROWED MY GUN WITH THE SILENCER WHILE I WAS AT THE HOTEL —
AND RAN INTO YOU THERE WHEN WE BOTH CAME TO SEARCH HIS ROOM!
ALL VERY INTERESTING, LUV — BUT LET'S GET TO THE BOTTOM LINE! NAMELY — WHAT HAVE YOU GOT PLANNED FOR US NEXT?
3041

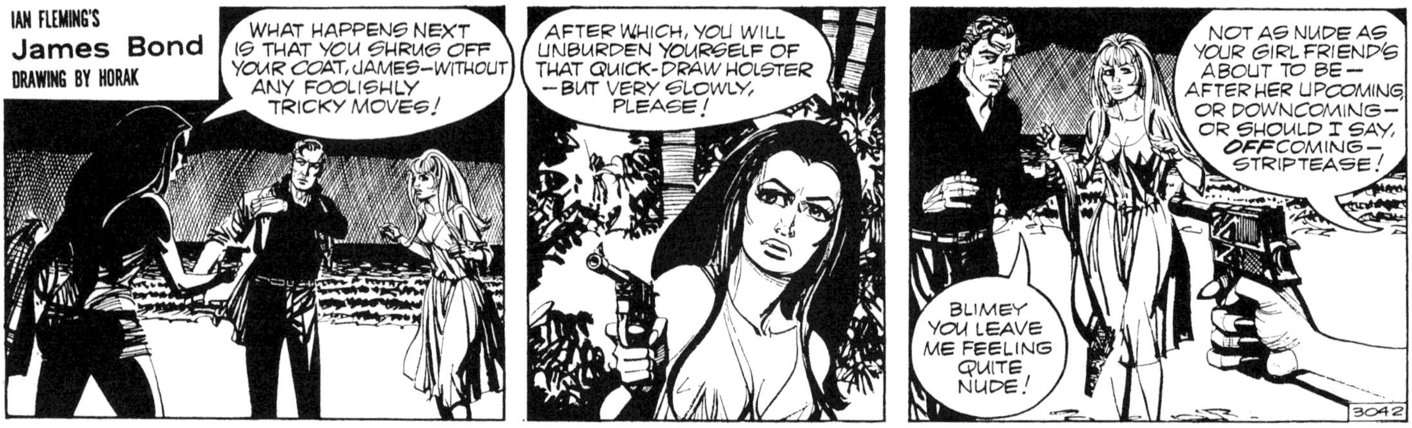
IAN FLEMING'S
James Bond
DRAWING BY HORAK
WHAT HAPPENS NEXT IS THAT YOU SHRUG OFF YOUR COAT, JAMES — WITHOUT ANY FOOLISHLY TRICKY MOVES!
AFTER WHICH, YOU WILL UNBURDEN YOURSELF OF THAT QUICK-DRAW HOLSTER — BUT VERY SLOWLY, PLEASE!
BLIMEY YOU LEAVE ME FEELING QUITE NUDE!
NOT AS NUDE AS YOUR GIRL FRIEND'S ABOUT TO BE — AFTER HER UPCOMING, OR DOWNCOMING — OR SHOULD I SAY, OFFCOMING — STRIPTEASE!
3042

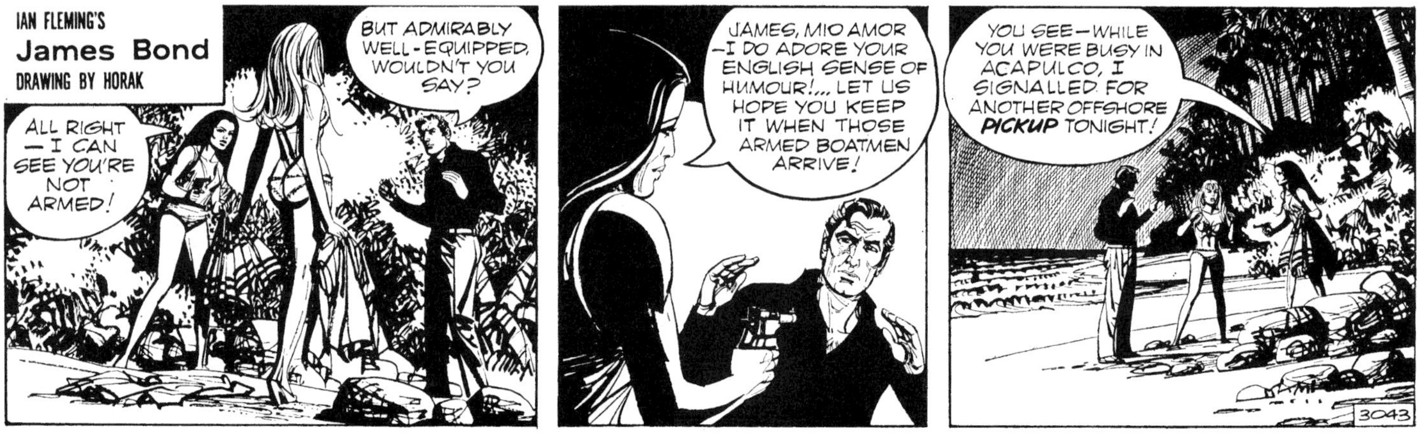
IAN FLEMING'S
James Bond
DRAWING BY HORAK
ALL RIGHT — I CAN SEE YOU'RE NOT ARMED!
BUT ADMIRABLY WELL-EQUIPPED, WOULDN'T YOU SAY?
JAMES, MIO AMOR — I DO ADORE YOUR ENGLISH SENSE OF HUMOUR!... LET US HOPE YOU KEEP IT WHEN THOSE ARMED BOATMEN ARRIVE!
YOU SEE — WHILE YOU WERE BUSY IN ACAPULCO, I SIGNALLED FOR ANOTHER OFFSHORE PICKUP TONIGHT!
3043

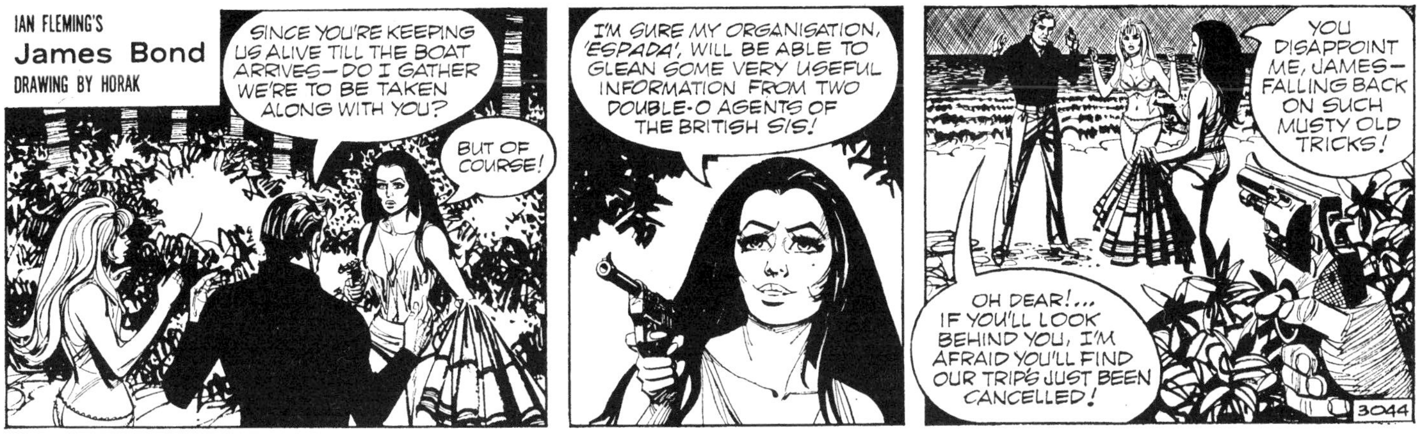
IAN FLEMING'S
James Bond
DRAWING BY HORAK
SINCE YOU'RE KEEPING US ALIVE TILL THE BOAT ARRIVES—DO I GATHER WE'RE TO BE TAKEN ALONG WITH YOU?
BUT OF COURSE!
I'M SURE MY ORGANISATION, 'ESPADA', WILL BE ABLE TO GLEAN SOME VERY USEFUL INFORMATION FROM TWO DOUBLE-O AGENTS OF THE BRITISH S/S!
YOU DISAPPOINT ME, JAMES—FALLING BACK ON SUCH MUSTY OLD TRICKS!
OH DEAR!... IF YOU'LL LOOK BEHIND YOU, I'M AFRAID YOU'LL FIND OUR TRIP'S JUST BEEN CANCELLED!
3044

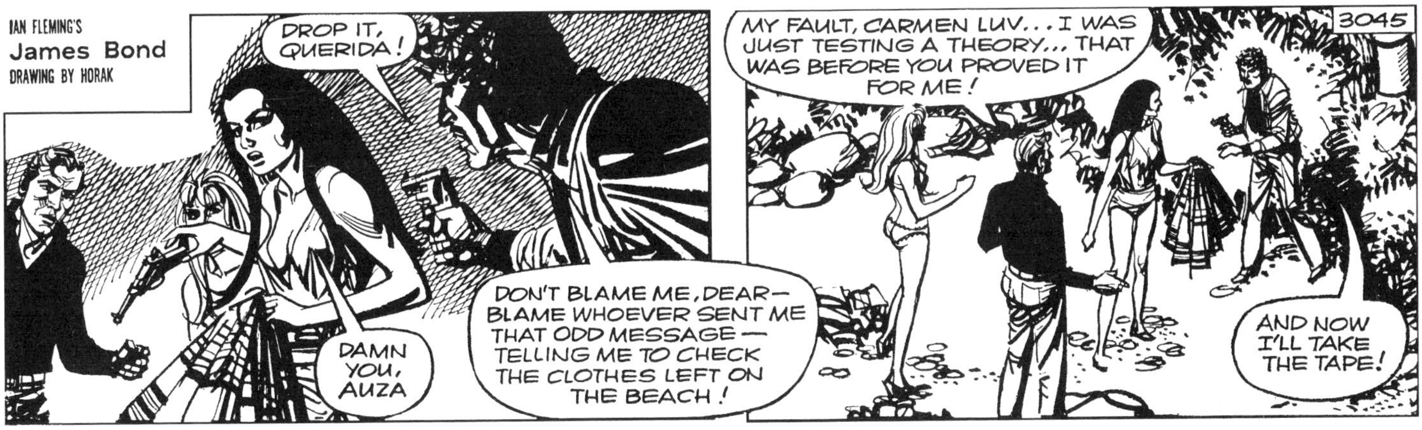
IAN FLEMING'S
James Bond
DRAWING BY HORAK
DROP IT, QUERIDA!
DAMN YOU, AUZA
DON'T BLAME ME, DEAR—BLAME WHOEVER SENT ME THAT ODD MESSAGE—TELLING ME TO CHECK THE CLOTHES LEFT ON THE BEACH!
3045
MY FAULT, CARMEN LUV... I WAS JUST TESTING A THEORY... THAT WAS BEFORE YOU PROVED IT FOR ME!
AND NOW I'LL TAKE THE TAPE!

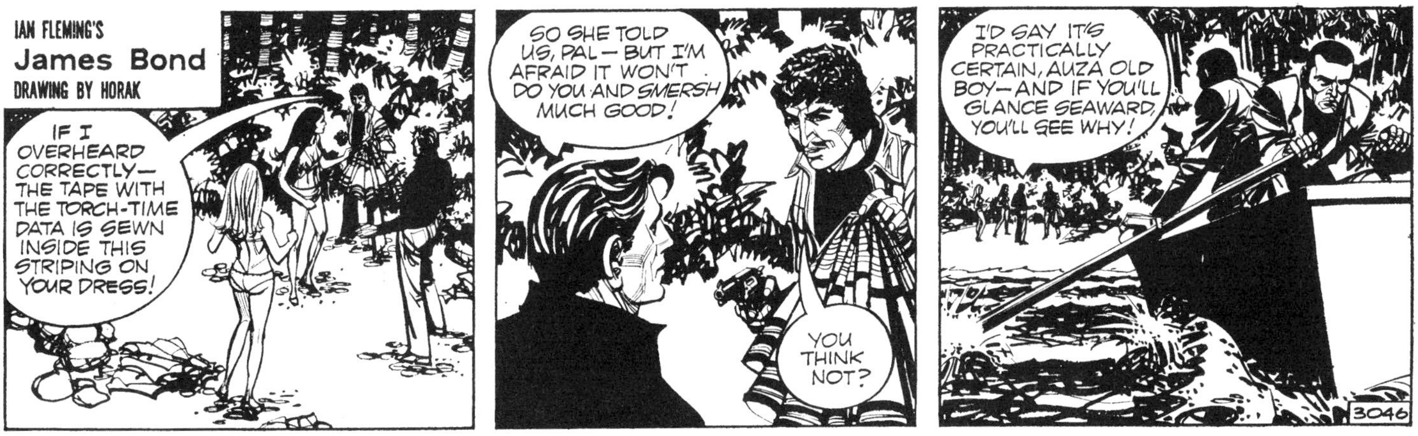
IAN FLEMING'S
James Bond
DRAWING BY HORAK
IF I OVERHEARD CORRECTLY—THE TAPE WITH THE TORCH-TIME DATA IS SEWN INSIDE THIS STRIPING ON YOUR DRESS!
SO SHE TOLD US, PAL—BUT I'M AFRAID IT WON'T DO YOU AND SMERSH MUCH GOOD!
YOU THINK NOT?
I'D SAY IT'S PRACTICALLY CERTAIN, AUZA OLD BOY—AND IF YOU'LL GLANCE SEAWARD, YOU'LL SEE WHY!
3046

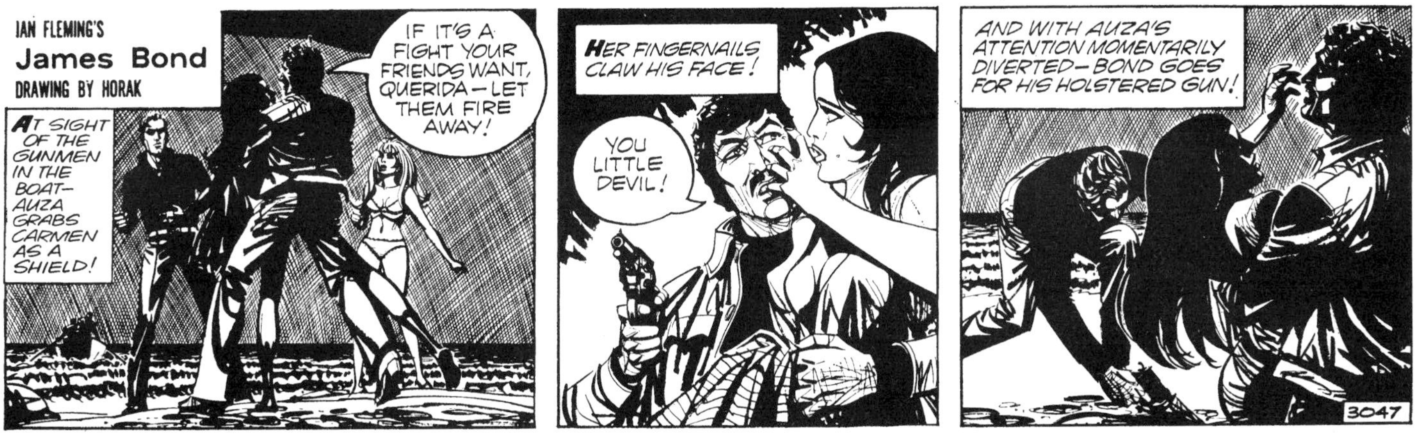
IAN FLEMING'S
James Bond
DRAWING BY HORAK
AT SIGHT OF THE GUNMEN IN THE BOAT—AUZA GRABS CARMEN AS A SHIELD!
IF IT'S A FIGHT YOUR FRIENDS WANT, QUERIDA—LET THEM FIRE AWAY!
HER FINGERNAILS CLAW HIS FACE!
YOU LITTLE DEVIL!
AND WITH AUZA'S ATTENTION MOMENTARILY DIVERTED—BOND GOES FOR HIS HOLSTERED GUN!
3047

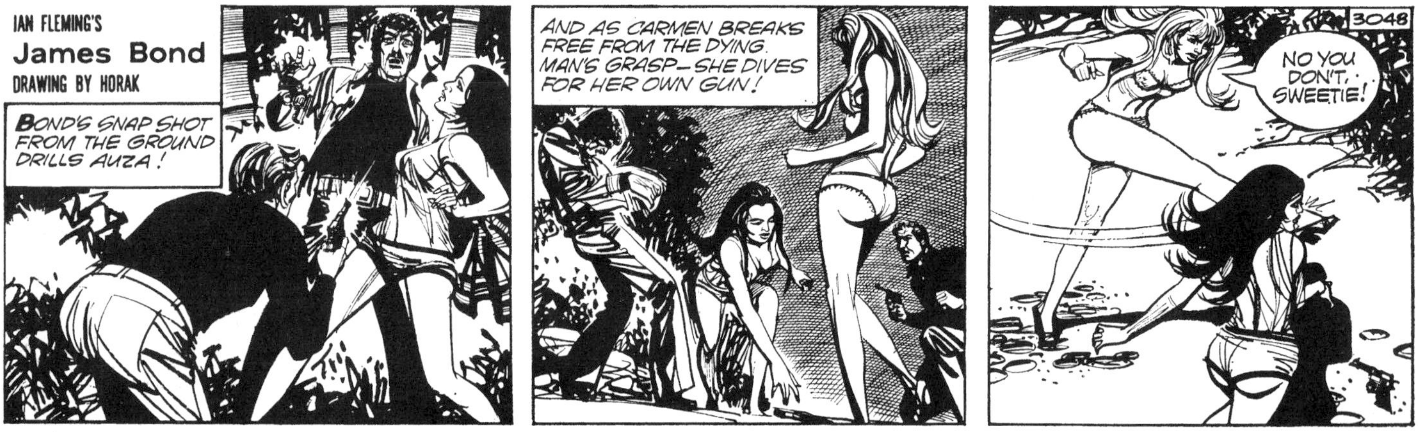
IAN FLEMING'S
James Bond
DRAWING BY HORAK
BOND'S SNAP SHOT FROM THE GROUND DRILLS AUZA!
AND AS CARMEN BREAKS FREE FROM THE DYING MAN'S GRASP–SHE DIVES FOR HER OWN GUN!
3048
NO YOU DON'T, SWEETIE!

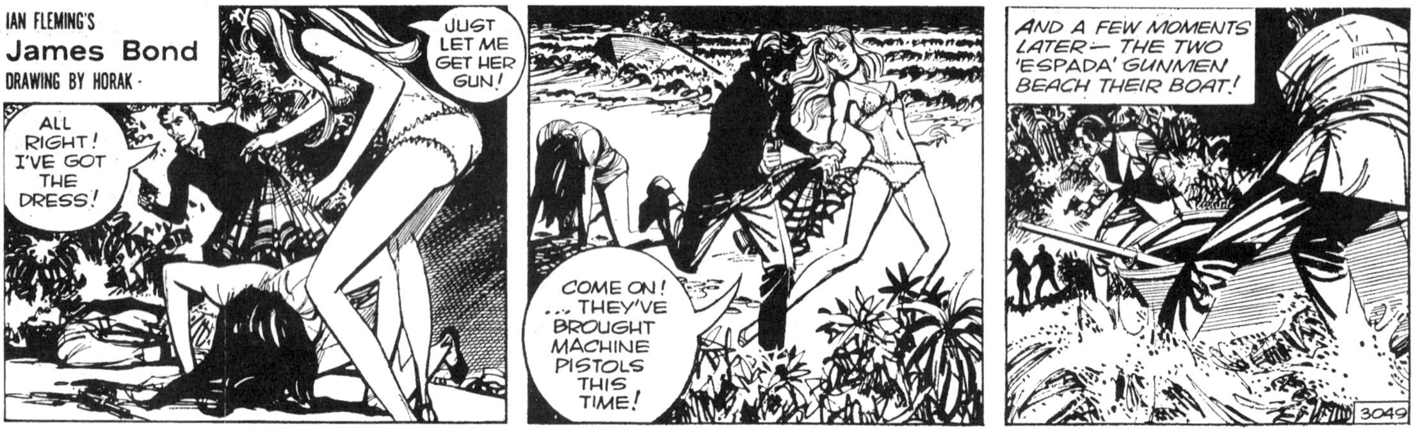
IAN FLEMING'S
James Bond
DRAWING BY HORAK
JUST LET ME GET HER GUN!
ALL RIGHT! I'VE GOT THE DRESS!
COME ON! ...THEY'VE BROUGHT MACHINE PISTOLS THIS TIME!
AND A FEW MOMENTS LATER– THE TWO 'ESPADA' GUNMEN BEACH THEIR BOAT!
3049

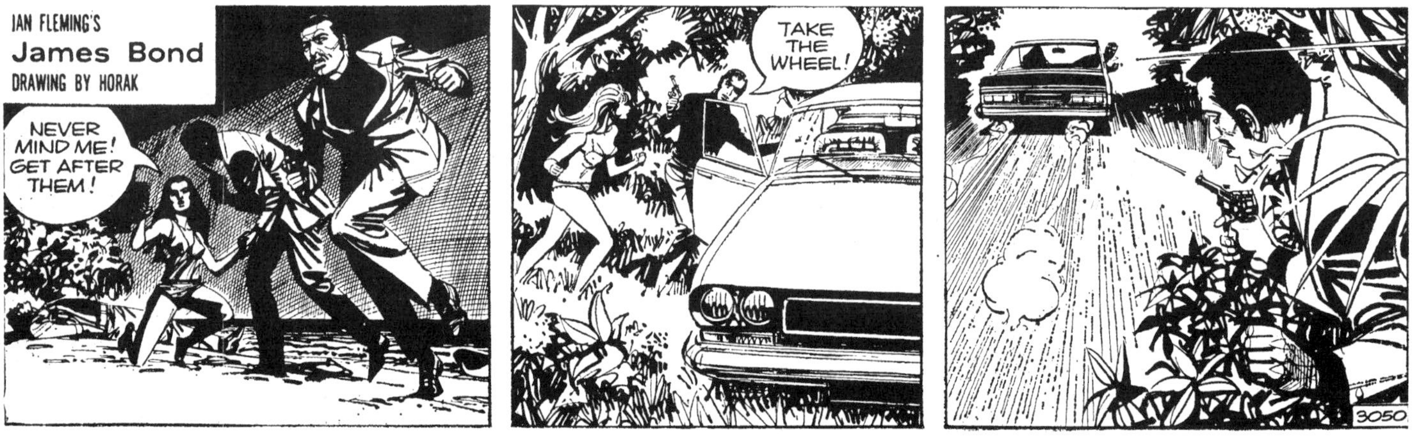
IAN FLEMING'S
James Bond
DRAWING BY HORAK
NEVER MIND ME! GET AFTER THEM!
TAKE THE WHEEL!
3050

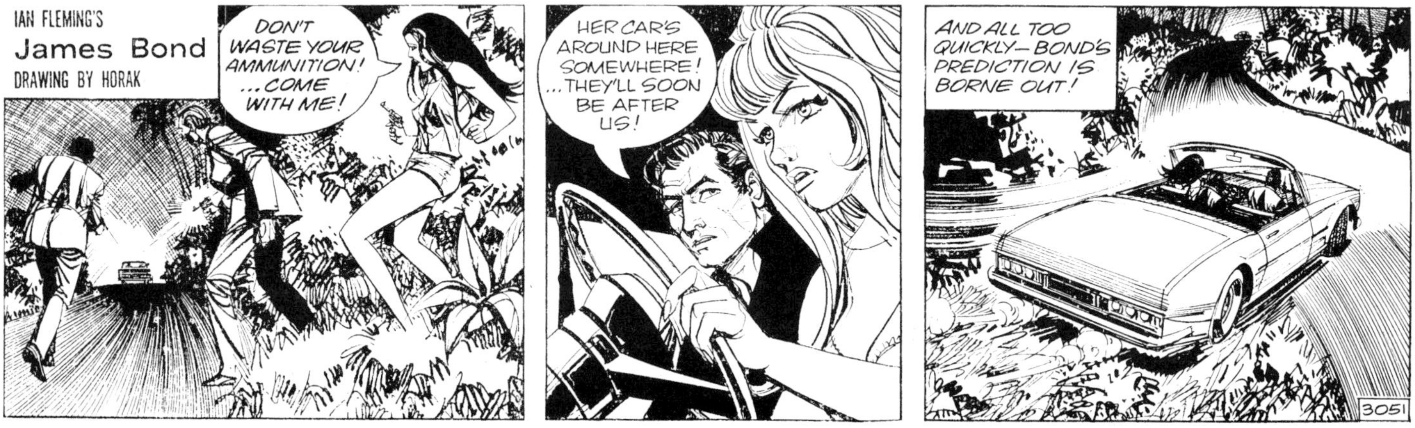
IAN FLEMING'S
James Bond
DRAWING BY HORAK
DON'T WASTE YOUR AMMUNITION! ...COME WITH ME!
HER CAR'S AROUND HERE SOMEWHERE! ...THEY'LL SOON BE AFTER US!
AND ALL TOO QUICKLY–BOND'S PREDICTION IS BORNE OUT!
3051

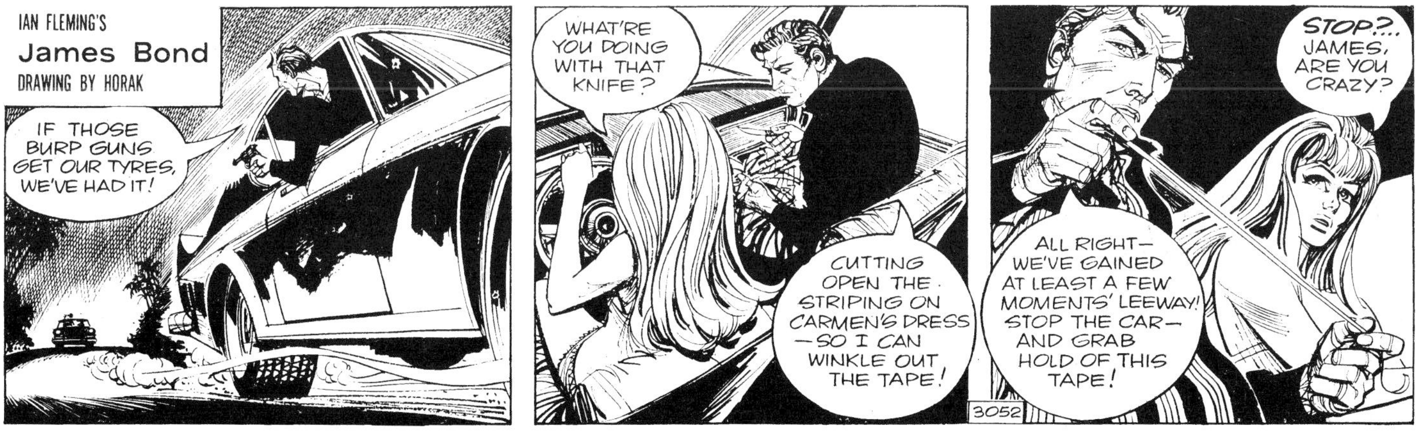
IAN FLEMING'S
James Bond
DRAWING BY HORAK
IF THOSE BURP GUNS GET OUR TYRES, WE'VE HAD IT!
WHAT'RE YOU DOING WITH THAT KNIFE?
CUTTING OPEN THE STRIPING ON CARMEN'S DRESS —SO I CAN WINKLE OUT THE TAPE!
3052
STOP?... JAMES, ARE YOU CRAZY?
ALL RIGHT— WE'VE GAINED AT LEAST A FEW MOMENTS' LEEWAY! STOP THE CAR— AND GRAB HOLD OF THIS TAPE!

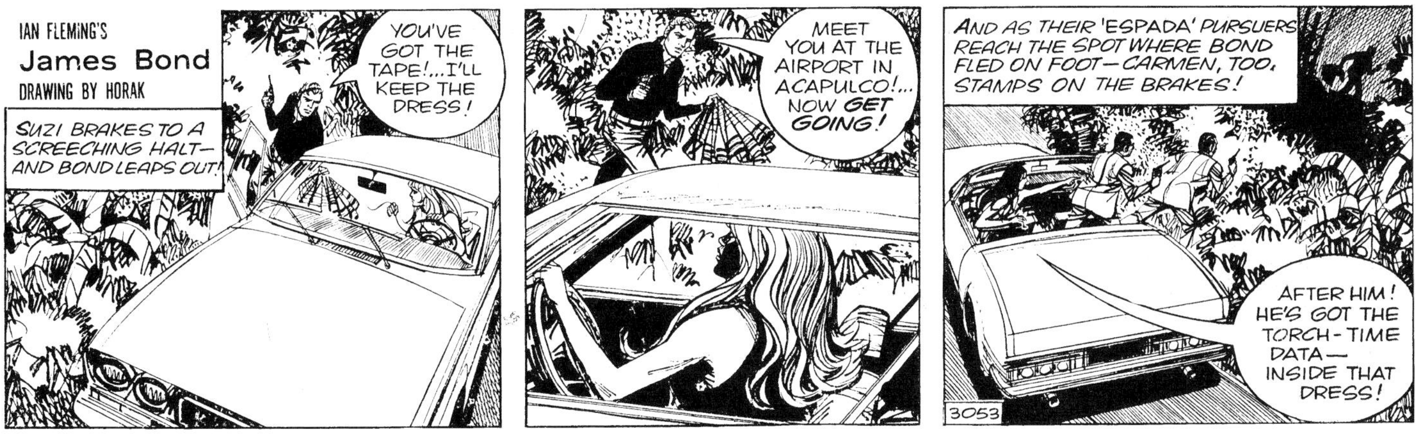
IAN FLEMING'S
James Bond
DRAWING BY HORAK
SUZI BRAKES TO A SCREECHING HALT— AND BOND LEAPS OUT!
YOU'VE GOT THE TAPE!...I'LL KEEP THE DRESS!
MEET YOU AT THE AIRPORT IN ACAPULCO!... NOW GET GOING!
AND AS THEIR 'ESPADA' PURSUERS REACH THE SPOT WHERE BOND FLED ON FOOT—CARMEN, TOO, STAMPS ON THE BRAKES!
AFTER HIM! HE'S GOT THE TORCH-TIME DATA— INSIDE THAT DRESS!
3053

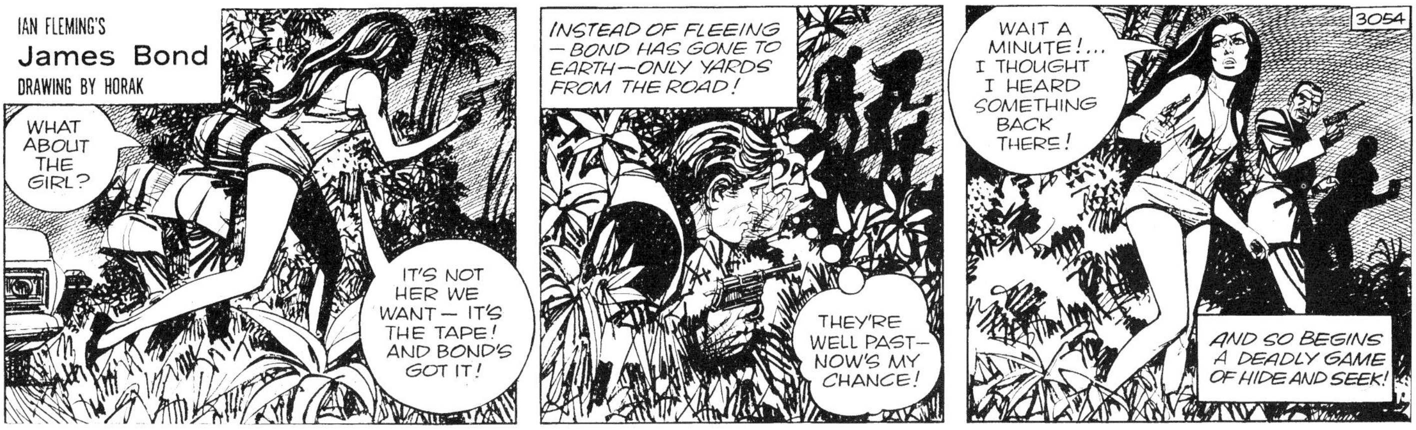
IAN FLEMING'S
James Bond
DRAWING BY HORAK
WHAT ABOUT THE GIRL?
IT'S NOT HER WE WANT— IT'S THE TAPE! AND BOND'S GOT IT!
INSTEAD OF FLEEING —BOND HAS GONE TO EARTH—ONLY YARDS FROM THE ROAD!
THEY'RE WELL PAST— NOW'S MY CHANCE!
3054
WAIT A MINUTE!... I THOUGHT I HEARD SOMETHING BACK THERE!
AND SO BEGINS A DEADLY GAME OF HIDE AND SEEK!

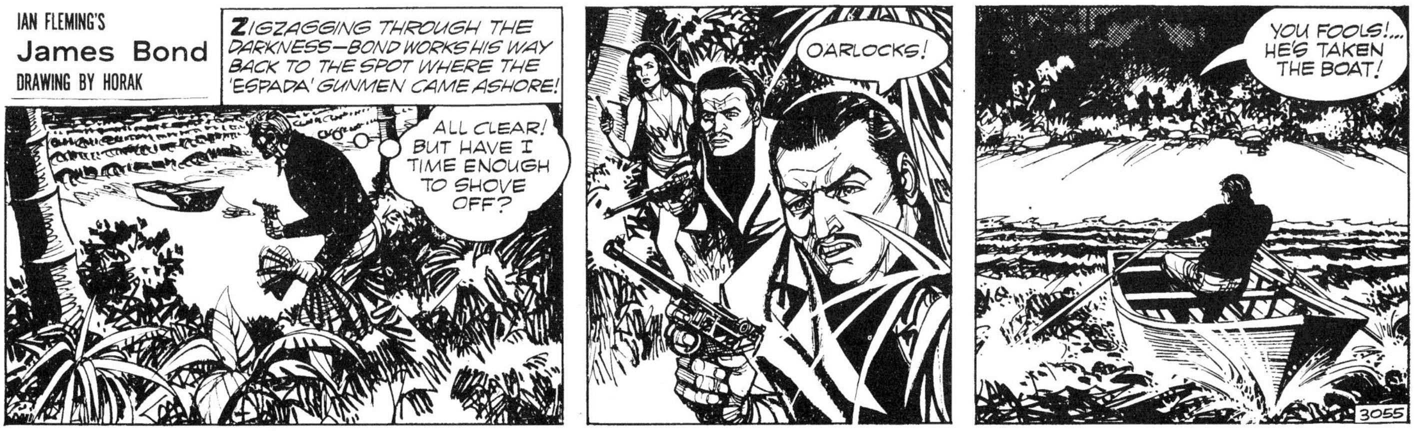
IAN FLEMING'S
James Bond
DRAWING BY HORAK
ZIGZAGGING THROUGH THE DARKNESS—BOND WORKS HIS WAY BACK TO THE SPOT WHERE THE 'ESPADA' GUNMEN CAME ASHORE!
ALL CLEAR! BUT HAVE I TIME ENOUGH TO SHOVE OFF?
OARLOCKS!
YOU FOOLS!... HE'S TAKEN THE BOAT!
3055

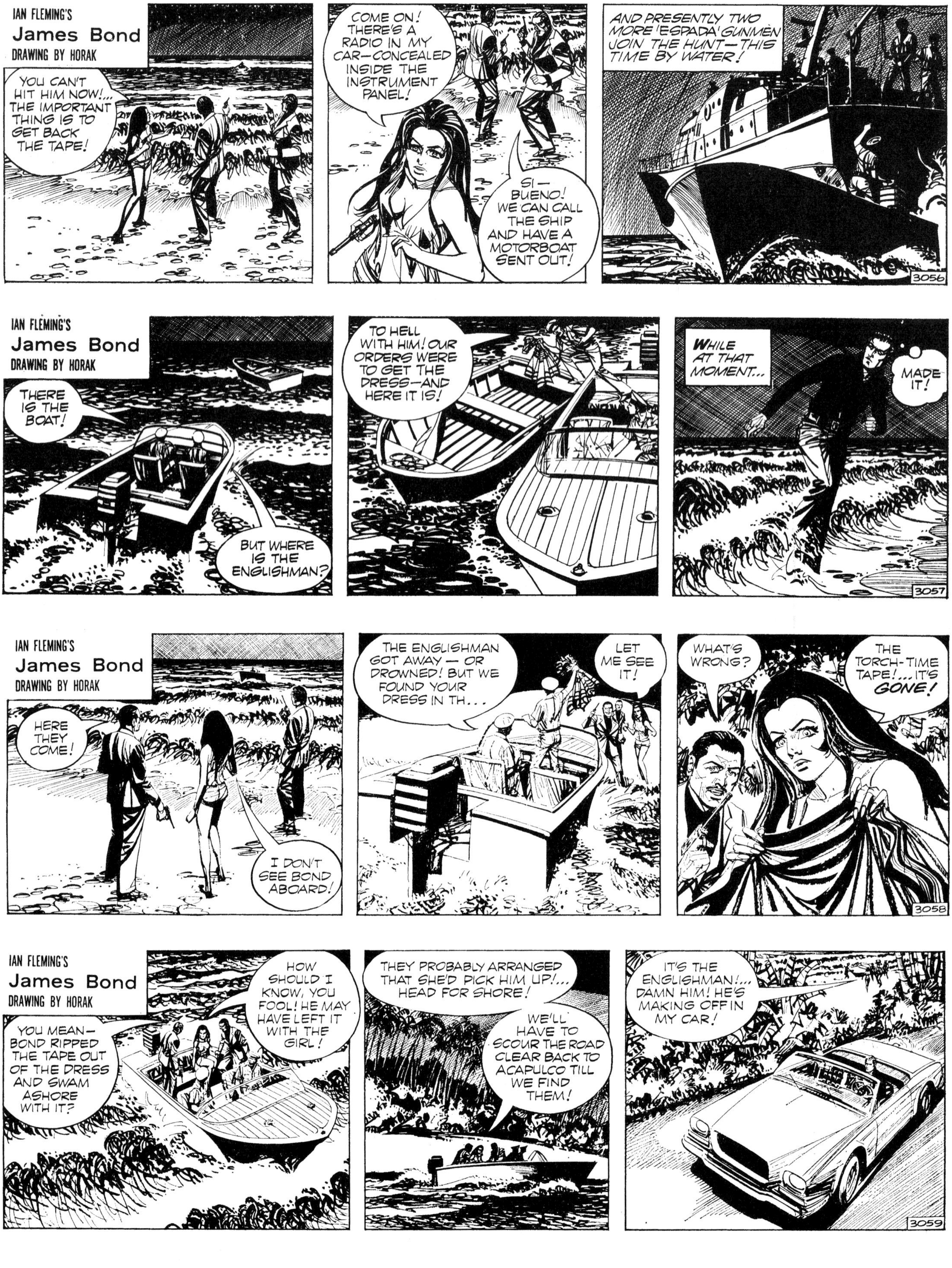
IAN FLEMING'S
James Bond
DRAWING BY HORAK
YOU CAN'T HIT HIM NOW!... THE IMPORTANT THING IS TO GET BACK THE TAPE!
COME ON! THERE'S A RADIO IN MY CAR—CONCEALED INSIDE THE INSTRUMENT PANEL!
SI—BUENO! WE CAN CALL THE SHIP AND HAVE A MOTORBOAT SENT OUT!
AND PRESENTLY TWO MORE 'ESPADA' GUNMEN JOIN THE HUNT—THIS TIME BY WATER!
3056
IAN FLEMING'S
James Bond
DRAWING BY HORAK
THERE IS THE BOAT!
BUT WHERE IS THE ENGLISHMAN?
TO HELL WITH HIM! OUR ORDERS WERE TO GET THE DRESS—AND HERE IT IS!
WHILE AT THAT MOMENT...
MADE IT!
3057
IAN FLEMING'S
James Bond
DRAWING BY HORAK
HERE THEY COME!
I DON'T SEE BOND ABOARD!
THE ENGLISHMAN GOT AWAY— OR DROWNED! BUT WE FOUND YOUR DRESS IN TH...
LET ME SEE IT!
WHAT'S WRONG?
THE TORCH-TIME TAPE!... IT'S GONE!
3058
IAN FLEMING'S
James Bond
DRAWING BY HORAK
YOU MEAN—BOND RIPPED THE TAPE OUT OF THE DRESS AND SWAM ASHORE WITH IT?
HOW SHOULD I KNOW, YOU FOOL! HE MAY HAVE LEFT IT WITH THE GIRL!
THEY PROBABLY ARRANGED THAT SHE'D PICK HIM UP!... HEAD FOR SHORE!
WE'LL HAVE TO SCOUR THE ROAD CLEAR BACK TO ACAPULCO TILL WE FIND THEM!
IT'S THE ENGLISHMAN!... DAMN HIM! HE'S MAKING OFF IN MY CAR!
3059

IAN FLEMING'S
James Bond
DRAWING BY HORAK
JAMES! THANK GOD YOU'RE SAFE!
SO'S THE TAPE, I TRUST?
OF COURSE!
GOOD GIRL! AND YOU'VE GOT YOURSELF CLOTHED AGAIN, I SEE...
3060
OH WELL, NO MATTER—WE'LL SOON REMEDY THAT WHEN WE GET TO LONDON!
End of story

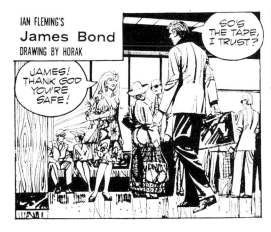

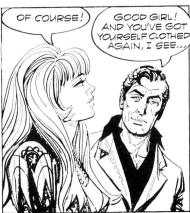

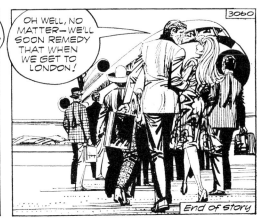

THE COMPLETE
JAMES BOND
SYNDICATED NEWSPAPER CHECKLIST

The following is a complete checklist of *James Bond* strips to have appeared in the *Express* newspapers and been syndicated in non-UK newspapers.

STORY	WRITER	ARTISTS	DATE	SERIAL No.
Serialised in the *Daily Express*				
Casino Royale	IF/AH	JM	7.7.58–13.12.58	1–138
Live and Let Die	IF/HG	JM	15.12.58–28.3.59	139-225
Moonraker	IF/HG	JM	30.3.59–8.8.59	226-339
Diamonds Are Forever	IF/HG	JM	10.8.59–30.1.60	340-487
From Russia With Love	IF/HG	JM	3.2.60–21.5.60	488-583
Dr. No	IF/PO	JM	23.5.60–1.10.60	584-697
Goldfinger	IF/HG	JM	3.10.60–1.4.61	698-849
Risico	IF/HG	JM	3.4.61–24.6.61	850-921
From A View To A Kill	IF/HG	JM	25.6.61–9.9.61	922-987
For Your Eyes Only	IF/HG	JM	11.9.61–9.12.61	988-1065
Thunderball	IF/HG	JM	11.12.61–10.2.62	1066-1128*
Series aborted prematurely				
(Series Two)				
On Her Majesty's Secret Service	IF/HG	JM	29.6.64–17.5.65	1–274
You Only Live Twice	IF/HG	JM	18.5.65–8.1.66	275–475
(Series Three)				
The Man With the Golden Gun	IF/JL	YH	10.1.66–10.9.66	1–209
The Living Daylights	IF/JL	YH	12.9.66–12.11.66	210–263
Octopussy	IF/JL	YH	14.11.66–27.5.67	264–428
The Hildebrand Rarity	IF/JL	YH	29.5.67–16.12.67	429–602
The Spy Who Loved Me	IF/JL	YH	18.12.67–3.10.68	603–815
The Harpies	JL	YH	4.10.68–23.6.69	816–1037
River of Death	JL	YH	24.6.69–29.11.69	1038–1174
Colonel Sun	KA/JL	YH	1.12.69–20.8.70	1175–1393
The Golden Ghost	JL	YH	21.8.70–16.1.71	1394–1519
Fear Face	JL	YH	18.1.71–20.4.71	1520–1596
Double Jeopardy	JL	YH	21.4.71–28.8.71	1597–1708
Starfire	JL	YH	30.8.71–24.12.71	1709–1809
Trouble Spot	JL	YH	28.12.71–10.6.72	1810–1951
Isle of Condors	JL	YH	12.6.72–21.10.72	1952–2065
The League of Vampires	JL	YH	25.10.72–28.2.73	2066–2172
Die With My Boots On	JL	YH	1.3.73–18.6.73	2173–2256
The Girl Machine	JL	YH	19.6.73–3.12.73	2257–2407
Beware of Butterflies	JL	YH	4.12.73–11.5.74	2408–2541
The Nevsky Nude	JL	YH	13.5.74–21.9.74	2542–2655
The Phoenix Project	JL	YH	23.9.74–18.2.75	2656–2780
The Black Ruby Caper	JL	YH	19.2.75–15.7.75	2781–2897
Till Death Do Us Part	JL	YH	7.7.75–14.10.75	2898–2983
The Torch–Time Affair	JL	YH	15.10.75–15.1.76	2984–3060
Hot-Shot	JL	YH	16.1.76–1.6.76	3061–3178
Nightbird	JL	YH	2.6.76–4.11.76	3179–3312
Ape of Diamonds	JL	YH	5.11.76–22.1.77	3313–3437

STORY	WRITER	ARTISTS	DATE	SERIAL No.
Serialised in the *Sunday Express*				
(Series Four)				
When the Wizard Awakes	JL	YH	30.1.77–22.5.77	1–54
Syndicated strips not featured in newspapers in the UK				
Sea Dragon	JL	YH	not applicable	55–192
Death Wing	JL	YH	not applicable	193–354
The Xanadu Connection	JL	YH	not applicable	355–468
Shark Bait	JL	YH	not applicable	469–636
Serialised in the *Daily Star*				
(Series Five)				
Doomcrack	JL	HN	2.2.81–19.8.81	1–174
The Paradise Plot	JL	JM	20.8.81–4.6.82	175–378
Deathmask	JL	JM	7.6.82–8.2.83	379–552
Flittermouse	JL	JM	9.2.83–20.5.83	553–624
Polestar	JL	JM	23.5.83–15.7.83	625–719*
Series stopped publishing in the Daily Star at 673				
Syndicated strips not featured in UK newspapers				
The Scent of Danger	JL	JM	not applicable	720–821
Snake Goddess	JL	YH	not applicable	822–893
Double Eagle	JL	YH	not applicable	894–965

GLOSSARY

KEY TO CREATORS

IF: IAN FLEMING
AH: ANTHONY HERN
HG: HENRY GAMMIDGE
PO: PETER O'DONNELL
JL: JIM LAWRENCE
KA: KINGSLEY AMIS
(under pseudonym Robert Markham)
JM: JOHN MCLUSKY
YH: YAROSLAV HORAK
HN: HARRY NORTH

SERIAL NUMBERS

Each serial number represents a day. However, in Scotland, some strips were published in the *Daily Express* on days when there were Bank Holidays in England and Wales; these were designated by the suffix 'a' after the serial number on the strips.

NOBODY DOES IT BETTER...

ISBN: 1 84023 690 6

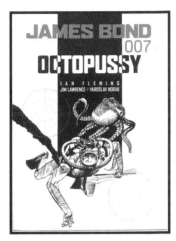

ISBN: 1 84023 743 0

ISBN: 1 84023 674 4

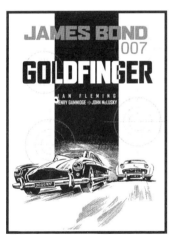

ISBN: 1 84023 908 5

ISBN: 1 84023 843 7

ISBN: 1 84576 089 1

ISBN: 1 84756 174 X

ISBN: 1 84576 175 8

ISBN: 1 84576 261 4

ISBN: 1 84756 269 X

AVAILABLE NOW!

JAMES BOND 007 WILL RETURN....

JAMES BOND
007
NIGHTBIRD
IAN FLEMING
JIM LAWRENCE
YAROSLAV HORAK

COMING SOON FROM TITAN BOOKS!

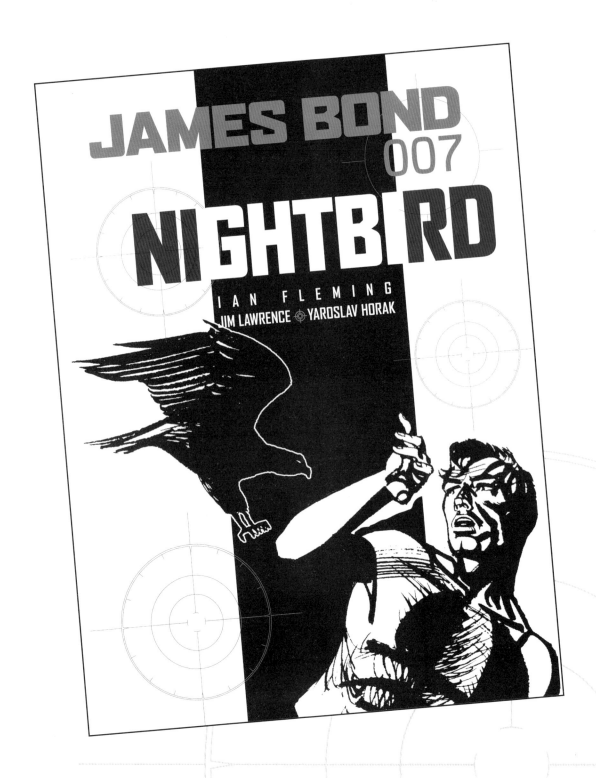